Finland

Sweden

Norway

E. Germany

enmark

Neth.

Czechoslovakia

Hungary

Romania

Poland

Yugoslavia

tria

Bulgaria

France

Greece

land

USSR

Italy

Turkey Leb.

Albania

Syria

Israel

Iraq

Tunisia

Iran

Algeria

Libya

Egypt

Jordan

Bahrain

Saudi

Arabia

U.A.E.

Yemen

Qatar

Mali

Niger

Oman

Chad

Sudan

South Yemen

Nigeria

Djibouti

Benin

Ethiopia

Somalia

Togo

Uganda

roon

Kenya

Rep.

Rwanda

torial

Burundi

uinea

Zaire

Tanzania

Gabon

. Congo

Zambia

Namibia

Mauritius

Zimbabwe

Madagascar

South Africa

Malawi

Mozambique

Botswana

Lesotho

Swaziland

Afghanistan

Mongolia

N. Korea

China

Japan

S. Korea

Pakistan

Taiwan

Nepal

Bhutan

Burma

Vietnam

India

Bangladesh

Laos

Philippines

Sri Lanka

Malaysia

Kampuchea

Thailand

Singapore

Papua-
New Guinea

Indonesia

Australia

WORLD POLITICS

WORLD POLITICS
THE MENU FOR CHOICE

Second Edition

Bruce Russett
Yale University

Harvey Starr
Indiana University

W. H. Freeman and Company
New York   Oxford

Library of Congress Cataloging in Publication Data

Russett, Bruce M.
  World politics.

  Includes index.
  1. International relations.   I. Starr, Harvey.
II. Title.
JX1391.R88   1985   327   84-24673
ISBN 0-7167-1701-8

Printed in the United States of America

1 2 3 4 5 6 7 8 9   MP   3 2 1 0 8 9 8 7 6 5

CONTENTS

PREFACE

Many of us who study and teach world politics have witnessed a revolution in the discipline. We have changed the ways we think about the subject: standards of concept formation, of logic, and of evidence are markedly different from what they were. Our progress in research, however, has not been matched by equal progress in communicating new knowledge, either to students or to laypeople in general. We wrote this book to convey to beginning and intermediate students of world politics some common core of the theory, method, and substance of our field.

If there has been a revolution in the study of world politics, that revolution can be consolidated only when we have the pedagogical skill and tools to educate the next generation. Otherwise the revolution will experience a well-deserved Thermidor reaction. The consolidation we have tried for in *World Politics* is inclusive rather than exclusive. That is, we have sought to synthesize the best of the older tradition with newer approaches.

In the first place, we have provided a substantial component of theory, from older and newer sources. Students must learn something about how theory is constructed and tested, and we therefore deal in some degree with scientific method, providing some "how to do it" material to give the student standards for recognizing well-executed research. Students need to learn a respect for evidence and learn to recognize a statement for which no evidence could be relevant. Perhaps more important is "how to think about it." To survive in a rapidly changing world, as active citizens rather than passive objects of historic forces, people must develop a good set of basic concepts and questions, a taste for analysis, a certain degree of skepticism for the "revealed wisdom" of authority, and some tolerance for ambiguity on a subject— the behavior of large human organizations coping with very complex problems—where the extent of our understanding is, at best, barely adequate.

Second, we have provided a substantial amount of historical and contemporary facts about the world. One kind of "fact" is the evidence needed to support or disconfirm major theoretical statements. We have tried to give the student some sense of the volume and quality of evidence relevant to various statements. When we know the evidence to be reasonably solid, we have tried to document that. When we consider the evidence sparse or ambiguous, we have tried to indicate that. This means that we have given some references to empirical research, so students—or instructors—will not have to take our statements on faith. On the other hand, we have tried not to overburden readers with scientific detail or pedantry.

Another kind of essential fact is, simply, information on what it is, and has been, like "out there." History and information on the contemporary systems are essential. We have also therefore provided material on the characteristics of the major national and nonnational participants in world politics, and on the scope and function of major institutions. We have frequently introduced or punctuated our theoretical discussions with detail on how the world works, or has worked. The reader will see examples of this not only in the text, but in endpaper maps and the two (quite different) appendixes: a chronology and a set of comparative data on states' characteristics. In this we have tried to walk a path that will have some appeal to traditionalists as well as to "hard-nosed" scientists.

Any consolidation demands a concern with questions of value: what the world "should" be like as well as what it is like. Sometimes all of us can gain; sometimes one's security is another's insecurity. Sometimes we must choose between equity and security, or between peace and justice. Students need guidance on how choices can be made, or perhaps avoided—guidance that attends to both the ethical and the empirical dimensions of choice.

Finally, the substance of what is taught today is very different from the substance of courses a decade or two ago. In *World Politics* we have tried to combine discussion of security issues with international political economy and to suggest how the two are in fact related. For example, they come together in the causes and consequences of arms races and in world environmental problems. At the end of the book we show how needs for growth, equity, political liberty, and peace are inextricably linked.

We have organized the book in two major parts. Part I introduces the student to the modern study of world politics and sets out the six levels of analysis we find useful: the global system, relations between states, the societal level, the governmental level, roles, and the individual actor. The book's subtitle (*The Menu for Choice*) illustrates our perspective that decision makers are in fact limited in their selections by the rather constrained menu presented by global conditions. (The menu analogy appropriately evokes images both of restaurants and computers.) We discuss and illustrate how influences at various levels affect the process or act of choice. In Part II we apply these analytical perspectives to particular issues. Topics we consider include arms races, deterrence and arms control, theories about poor countries' dependence on rich ones and possible alternatives to dependence, the implications of interdependence among industrialized countries (we try to understand why these countries are, almost without precedent or parallel, at peace among themselves), problems of achieving collective goods in the context of global environmental problems, and finally an evaluation of demands for continued economic growth in a world of scarce resources and population pressures. We try to communicate a sense that rigorous theory is essential to any comprehension of these very real contemporary problems.

We owe thanks to innumerable colleagues and students over the years we have been working toward the production of this book. Rather than single out some for expressions of gratitude here, we will pass over those who in the past contributed to the formation of our thinking. Many, but not all of them, will find themselves footnoted. Here we shall merely thank those who read and commented on parts or all of the manuscript for the first or second edition: Steven Chan, Claudio Cioffi-Revilla, Robert Dorff, Jeffrey Hart, Darril Hudson,

Robert Jervis, Brian Job, Robert Keohane, Douglas Nelson, James Ray, J. David Singer, and Dina Zinnes. Parts of the manuscript report research done with the assistance of grants from the John Simon Guggenheim Foundation, the National Science Foundation, and the German Marshall Fund. Our home universities, Yale and Indiana, really did provide fine environments for research and reflection. Visiting appointments—for Bruce Russett at the Institute for Research in Social Science of the University of North Carolina at Chapel Hill (special thanks to Director Frank Munger) and the Netherlands Institute for Advanced Study, and for Harvey Starr at the University of Aberdeen (special thanks to Professor Frank Bealey)—provided stimulating as well as pleasurable environments. We hope that all of these people will in some degree be pleased with the outcome; any embarrassment with it must be ours alone.

January 1985

Bruce Russett
Harvey Starr

PART I

ANALYTICAL DIMENSIONS

*I would rather understand a single
cause than be king of Persia.*

—DEMOCRITUS OF ABDERA

ANALYZING WORLD POLITICS: LEVELS OF ANALYSIS AND CONSTRAINT

THREE FOREIGN POLICY DECISIONS

Dropping the Atomic Bomb

On August 6, 1945, the U.S. bomber *Enola Gay* dropped an atomic bomb on the Japanese city of Hiroshima. Coupled with the explosion of another bomb over Nagasaki three days later, this act precipitated the Japanese surrender and the end of World War II. Nearly 200,000 people, most of them noncombatant civilians, ultimately died from the explosions. These two bombings represented the first—and so far the last—time nuclear weapons were used against enemy targets. Exploding a bomb of this magnitude (about 4,000 times larger than the biggest "conventional" World War II explosive) marked an enormous leap in killing ability. At the same time it brought forth the age of nuclear deterrence, when peace among the great powers is kept, at least in part, by the awesome threat of mutual annihilation. At the time of these bombings both scientists and statesmen realized that they were doing something that would fundamentally change the future; the nuclear physicist J. Robert Oppenheimer, on watching the first test explosion a month before Hiroshima, quoted to himself the phrase from the Hindu scriptures, the *Bhagavad Gita,* "I am become death, destroyer of worlds."

Despite the magnitude of this act and the precedents it set, there was remarkably little discussion within the American government as to whether the bomb should be used in war. Questions of morality either were ignored or quickly stilled with the argument that, overall, use of the bomb would save lives. The only alternative to using the bomb to force Japan's surrender seemed to be an American invasion of the Japanese home islands, in which 30,000 American casualties and hundreds of thousands of Japanese could be expected in the first month. As American Secretary of War Henry L. Stimson later put it, "At no time did I ever hear it suggested by the President, or by other responsible members of the government, that atomic energy should not be used in war." British Prime Minister Winston Churchill reported that "the decision whether or not to use the atomic bomb to compel the surrender of Japan was never even an issue. There was unanimous, automatic, unquestioned agreement."[1] How can we explain this?

Particular characteristics of President Harry Truman may have made some difference. Before President Franklin Roosevelt's death in April 1945, it was assumed that the atomic bomb would be used in combat, although Roosevelt had not entirely ruled out the possibility of first warning the enemy and demonstrating the bomb's power in a test. But Truman was inexperienced and uninformed about foreign affairs; when he became president he was not even aware that the atomic bomb project existed. He was therefore in no position to challenge the existing basic assumption about the bomb's intended use, nor to dissent sharply from the military and foreign policy plans that had been put into effect by the advisers he inherited from Roosevelt. Only one adviser (Admiral William Leahy, whose opinion had already been devalued by his prediction that the bomb would not work at all) disagreed with the general consensus. There was some disagreement among the nuclear scientists who had produced the bomb, but even among them the prevailing opinion was that they could "propose no technical demonstration likely to bring an end to the war; we can see no acceptable alternative to direct military use."

---

1. Winston S. Churchill, *Triumph and Tragedy* (Boston: Houghton Mifflin, 1953), p. 639.

Truman was caught up in the near unanimity around him; Roosevelt, although more experienced and politically stronger, probably would not have behaved much differently. Bureaucratic momentum carried matters along, and it would have required either a very unusual president or an exceptionally open structure of decision making even to slow that momentum. Furthermore, the only alternative looked dangerous, technically and politically. If the Japanese were first warned and the bomb tested publicly in some deserted spot, there was the risk that it would not go off or not look very impressive. Not only might the Japanese then be left unimpressed, but some advisers also feared that Congress would then be in a political uproar over the fizzled demonstration and consequent American casualties to be suffered in an invasion. Nowhere—in the executive branch, in Congress, or in the public at large—was there much disagreement over the belief that the war should be ended as soon as possible, principally to spare American lives. Consequently, there were few moral restraints on the use of weapons in war. Certainly there had been little objection to earlier conventional bombing of civilian targets in Germany and Japan.

The basic constraints, therefore, stemmed from the international situation—war against a determined opponent in an era when the moral and legal restrictions on warfare were few. Moreover, the international balance of forces likely to emerge after the war reinforced this perspective. The wartime Soviet-American alliance was deteriorating rapidly, especially in the face of severe disagreements about who should control Eastern Europe. Most American decision makers welcomed the atomic bomb as a so-called "master card" for "atomic diplomacy" to impress the Russians with American power and to encourage them to make concessions to the American view about how the postwar world should be organized. Additionally, the Soviet Union had not yet entered the war with Japan. If the atomic bomb could force Japanese surrender before the Russians were to attack Japan (in fact, the surrender came after such an attack), it would help to limit Russian intrusion into Japanese-controlled portions of the Far East. Most American foreign policy decision makers largely agreed on these perceptions, as did most members of Congress and most opinion leaders in the American public.[2]

---

2. Two valuable studies we have drawn on here are Barton J. Bernstein, "Roosevelt, Truman, and the Atomic Bomb: A Reinterpretation," *Political Science Quarterly* 90, 1 (Spring 1977), 23–69; and Herbert Feis, *The Atomic Bomb and the End of World War II* (Princeton, N.J.: Princeton University Press, 1961).

Invading an Ally: Czechoslovakia

The wartime decision to drop the atomic bomb seems, in hindsight, to be one that would have been reached by almost any American leader who was president at that time—however much anyone might now regret that decision. Other foreign policy decisions do not seem so constrained. For example, since the Soviet-created coup in 1948, Czechoslovakia has had a Communist government. But in August 1968 the Soviet leaders were forced to decide what to do about the political developments in Czechoslovakia following events of the "Prague spring" that year. A new liberal government under Alexander Dubcek had taken power from the former hardline regime and had pledged to carry out democratization and economic reforms. The change in policies became very dramatic, and it began to look as though some form of Western democracy and even independence from the Soviet Union might emerge. In July the USSR demanded an end to liberalization, but the process continued. Then on August 20, Soviet and other Eastern European troops invaded Czechoslovakia. Dubcek was ousted, and a much more restrictive regime imposed. The Soviet government had taken drastic military action in peacetime at the cost of substantial international ill will and an interruption of the then-emerging détente with the United States.

We cannot to this day explain the decision, nor do we have the kind of detailed information about Soviet decision making that we have for the United States atomic bomb decision. Nevertheless, we can offer a range of hypotheses that at least illustrate the kind of analysis that could in principle explain the Soviet decision. Indeed, some or even all of the hypotheses might be correct, since none are contradicted by available evidence, and each could have made a contribution to explaining the decision that was reached.

First, we might focus on the particular Soviet leaders at the time, Leonid Brezhnev and Aleksei Kosygin. Possibly they were more fearful, more bellicose, or simply less imaginative than other contemporary Russian leaders or even past leaders such as Khrushchev and Stalin. Or we might look less at personal characteristics of the leaders than at their political situations. Ever since the death of Stalin, Soviet leaders have had somewhat weaker positions of authority. They lack the Stalinist instruments of very tight control (extreme terror instilled by the secret police and a thoroughly dominated party bureaucracy) that might enable them to carry through policies—such as tolerating the new Czech government—that would be unpopular with major interest groups. And we should consider characteristics of the Soviet political system that would make accommodation difficult for any leader. The Red Army is very important in Soviet internal politics; because of its concerns with military security, it would strenuously resist any move that might weaken the Soviet Union's system of military alliances or given an opening to external enemies.

Additionally, the Soviet Union's current and historic positions in the international system are relevant. The repeated invasions and occupations of Russia over the centuries has made all of Moscow's rulers fearful of attack and anxious to build a secure alliance system of subservient states on Russia's borders. The new regime in Czechoslovakia revived this concern. Communist ideology and the continuing conflict with capitalist powers since 1918 provide another reason why Soviet leaders might fear having a non-Communist or even an anti-Communist state on their border. All these sensitivities are intensified in a world of bipolar conflict with the United States and also of hostility with China, their major neighbor to the east. These aspects of the international system interact with characteristics of the Soviet internal system. Finally, in addition to military threats from outside, one should remember the possible vulnerability of the Soviet internal regime to the demonstration that a liberal democratic government in a former satellite country could work. It would have provided an example to other nations of Eastern Europe, and ultimately to the Russian people themselves, that might lead to major changes in the goals, constitutional forms, or personnel of the Moscow government.[3]

Managing a Penetrated Economy

From 1945 until 1964, Brazil had a democratic government. In 1964, a variety of political and economic problems became overwhelming. The economy had stagnated, inflation was rampant, and President João Goulart adopted policies that angered the middle class, large landowners, foreign investors, the U.S. government, and the military. As a result, the army seized power and changed government policies. They instituted a tough dictatorship, repressing workers and peasants. They adopted a set of policies intended to spur economic growth by keeping

---

3. See Jiri Valenta, *Soviet Intervention in Czechoslovakia, 1968* (Baltimore, Md.: Johns Hopkins University Press, 1979).

wages low, attracting foreign investors, and building state-owned and privately owned domestic industries. For a time these policies succeeded handsomely on their terms. The economy grew by almost 10 percent a year, and many people became very prosperous. Others did not, however; their standards of living improved little if at all and in some cases actually fell, thanks to the government policies that held down wages and forbade strikes. After a while the boom of the "Brazilian miracle" went bust.

Trouble first appeared in 1973, when world oil prices began to rise sharply because OPEC succeeded in restricting petroleum output and in agreeing on the prices member countries would charge for petroleum products. Brazil produces very little oil, and its economic development largely depended on automobile transportation and expensive consumer appliances. The new oil bill put a tremendous burden on Brazil's balance of international payments, a burden made worse by the world economic recession that sharply reduced markets for many of Brazil's new manufactured goods. For a while the Brazilian government coped with the problem by obtaining large loans from foreign banks and international lending organizations. By 1979 Brazil's foreign debts amounted to almost a third of its gross national product (GNP). That might have been tolerable if the world economy had recovered sharply, which would have enabled Brazil to increase its exports and meet the payments on its loans. But that did not happen in any sustained way, and from 1980 to well into 1983 the world remained in a serious economic recession. Brazil continued to accumulate new debts just to meet the interest due on its old loans. By the end of 1982, Brazil's foreign debt amounted to $86 billion, about four times the value of its annual export earnings. Worse, the interest payments alone amounted to about half of all its export earnings. At the same time, the economy declined sharply. Brazil's GNP per capita fell 12 percent between 1980 and 1983, and employment in manufacturing dropped to the 1973 level despite a growth of 25 million in the nation's population.

Because the tough military dictatorship violated the democratic political traditions of Brazil, and especially because the government's economic policies failed so evidently, political discontent rose markedly. The government began to relax restrictions on the press and to restore other civil liberties, and it held elections to the Brazilian Congress (under electoral rules rigged somewhat in favor of the government-backed party). The political relaxation under President João Baptista Figueiredo was known as the *abertura*, or opening. Elections for Congress and state legislatures were held in 1982, and a presidential election was scheduled for January 1985. (Though that election was to be indirect, with only the electoral college chosen by popular vote, and again the system was rigged to insure a majority for the government party.) Many people demanded more freedoms; others feared that democracy would result in strikes, increased demands by the masses, and political and economic chaos.

In the midst of this uncertain situation, economic conditions continued to worsen. The inflation rate reached 175 percent, and it became clear that the country could not meet even the interest payments on its huge foreign debt, let alone repay any of the principal. Faced with the risk of a Brazilian default on the loans, its lenders began to work out a scheme for postponing and rescheduling the debt payments. About 20 percent of the debt was owed to foreign governments and international agencies like the International Monetary Fund. The rest was owed to private banks: about 25 percent to U.S. banks and 55 percent to banks in Europe, Japan, and elsewhere. The foreign banks were desperately afraid of a Brazilian default, which would have caused many big American and European commercial banks to be unable to pay *their* creditors and thus to fail, possibly setting off a worldwide financial crisis. They had little choice but to permit rescheduling, even though that meant delays in receipts and lower interest payments. But they set a stiff price for the rescheduling. They forced the Brazilian government to accept a package of austerity measures that, although they would make the country more creditworthy, also exacted terrible costs from ordinary Brazilians.

President Figueriedo had to go before the Brazilian Congress for legislation to cut government spending and to limit the increase in all salaries to about half the rate of increase in inflation. (Food prices had risen even faster, at the rate of 250 percent in the major cities.) There were days of rioting in São Paulo, Brazil's biggest and most industrialized state; the liberal governor finally had to call in the army to restore order. The Brazilian Congress—still controlled by the government party and until then basically compliant with the government's wishes—voted down the austerity package. The president imposed emergency police powers, banned public gatherings, and issued his own decree to replace the rejected legislation. At this price the Brazilian government received a bailout of new loans and a rescheduling of old loans, which amounted to $11 billion, with no confidence that the situation would be a great deal better in the following year. Political liberalization was endangered by the fears that it would get out of hand and magnify the economic crisis still more and by demands for new political freedoms (including a completely unrestricted presidential election) as the people's price for accepting the austerity measures. Brazil's political future, including the brave *abertura,* which was still very incomplete even twenty years after the initial military seizure of power, looked highly dubious.

Brazil's experience in the early 1980s was not too different from that of many other underdeveloped countries. Argentina and Mexico had similar problems with foreign debt. So did Nigeria, which formerly rode the crest of the oil price boom. Nigeria's democratic government proved too fragile to handle the economic crisis and was overthrown by the army. All of these countries shared similar vulnerabilities. Their economies were in grave trouble because of the global recession, and their problems compounded by mismanagement, corruption, and over-ambitious development plans. Their export markets contracted, and they could not pay their ever-mounting debts. Yet these were countries with immense natural resources, often with a large class of technicians, managers, and skilled entrepreneurs, and with large internal markets that seemed to promise some prospect of self-sufficiency. But these countries simply could not achieve self-sufficiency. They were tied too closely to the ups and downs of the world market, and their economies were too greatly under the influence of foreign investors and lenders. Those foreign interests were obliged to protect themselves and to impose political demands on the debtor governments, which had little choice but to accept the demands. Neither the personality of any particular leader nor the form of government made much difference. (The terms were essentially the same for the dictator General Reynaldo Bignone in Argentina as for his newly elected successor in a free election, President Raúl Alfonsín.) These big and potentially prosperous countries were deeply penetrated by global financial and political interests and were caught up in events they could not control.

We see here a merging of foreign and domestic policy. Nationalization and regulation of foreign industry, borrowing from abroad, and devaluing the currency cut across any neat foreign-domestic dividing line. The conduct of elections or the repression of dissent would seem to be domestic policies—except in this case when their execution had such clear implications for foreign approval or the ability to meet foreign commitments. Such a merging of foreign and domestic policy may happen in *any* country, but it is especially widespread in poor and especially small countries that are extensively penetrated from abroad.

LEVELS OF ANALYSIS

The preceding three sketches—America in 1945, Russia in 1968, and Brazil in recent years—illustrate very different times, rich and poor countries, and both military and economic concerns. The quality of evidence for explaining a decision maker's policy choice varies from one case to another, as does the plausibility of the speculations we offer. Nevertheless, it is obvious that different classes of explanations can be offered for each policy choice and that the plausibility of these classes also varies. Personal characteristics of the leaders seem more relevant to the Soviet case and even the U.S. case than to the case of Brazil. International influences matter much more for Brazil than for either of the others. Regime characteristics appear least important for the U.S. example. We could go on in this vein without firm conclusions about a complete ranking of relative influences in all cases.

Remember that as political scientists we usually find it difficult to predict a single event, such as the American decision to drop the atomic bomb or the Soviet decision to invade Czechoslovakia. More often we try to understand why certain classes of events occur—for example, why states engage in acts of violence generally. Most political scientists see their job as one of trying to detect comparable preceding events that seem to produce similar types of behavior. In our attempts to uncover causes, or the preceding events, we have found it useful to distinguish between *levels of analysis*—points on an ascending scale of size and complexity. These levels include units whose behavior we attempt to describe, predict, or explain, as well as units whose impact on individual decision makers we examine. That is, a level may refer to "actors," such as states or individuals whose behavior we are trying to explain, or (as we have been using here) to different kinds of influences on those actors.[4] In our earlier examples, we used influences from various levels of analysis to explain decisions made by national leaders.

The International System and the Nation-State

In a well-known article written in 1961, J. David Singer introduced the idea of levels of analysis, discussing two broad levels: the international

---

4. In social science, *dependent* (to be explained) variables and *independent* (part of the explanation) variables are usually distinguished.

system and the nation-state. By so doing, he highlighted a major distinction used when looking for influences on foreign policy: (1) those that are internal or domestic, coming from within the boundaries of the nation-state, and (2) those that are external, originating outside the state's boundaries.

Singer argued that the international system level is the most comprehensive level of analysis, permitting the observer to study international relations as a whole. The nation-state level of analysis allows us to use a decision-making approach as well as a far more detailed description of foreign policy behavior. Thus, although the international system level provides a more comprehensive picture of patterns and generalizations, the nation-state level provides a picture of greater depth, detail, and intensity. Singer summarizes the level of analysis question with the following set of analogies:

> In any area of scholarly inquiry, there are always several ways in which the phenomena under study may be sorted and arranged for purposes of systematic analysis. Whether in the physical or social sciences, the observer may choose to focus upon the parts or upon the whole, upon the components or upon the system. He may, for example, choose between the flowers or the garden, the rocks or the quarry, the trees or the forest, the houses or the neighborhood, the cars or the traffic jam, the delinquents or the gang, the legislators or the legislature, and so on.[5]

In international relations it is possible to study the flowers/rocks/trees/houses/cars/delinquents/legislators, or to shift the level of analysis and study the garden/quarry/forest/neighborhood/traffic jam/gang/legislature. In the first case we might study the internal politics of the nation-state as it affects the decision makers who choose among alternatives to create the foreign policy of that state. In the second case we might study the international system as it forms part of the larger environment, helping to determine which alternatives are even available to the decision makers. Decision makers in turn constantly try, insofar as possible, to shape and control that environment.

Thus, distinguishing among various levels of analysis helps to clarify what kinds of questions might be answered most profitably from

---

5. J. David Singer, "The Level-of-Analysis Problem in International Relations," in Klaus Knorr and Sidney Verba (Eds.), *The International System: Theoretical Essays* (Princeton, N.J.: Princeton University Press, 1961), pp. 77–92. However, see William B. Moul's critique, "The Level of Analysis Problem Revisited," *Canadian Journal of Political Science* 6(1973), 494–513. Other critiques may be found in Kenneth Waltz, *Theory of International Politics* (Reading, Mass.: Addison-Wesley, 1979).

which perspective. But this approach also allows us to see how questions are linked across levels. The various sets of factors involved in the Brazilian case illustrate how different domestic and international levels blend into one another and link together.

Six Levels of Analysis

Singer's distinction is a valuable one, but in later work analysts have found a scheme that identifies six levels more useful.[6] They are: (1) *individual decision makers* and their characteristics, (2) the *roles* occupied by the decision makers, (3) the structure of the *government* within which the decision makers operate, (4) the *society* within which the decision makers live and which they govern, (5) the sets of *relations* that exist between the decision makers' nation-state and the other international actors, and (6) the *world system* (see Figure 1.1).

Individual Decision Makers   At the lowest or most disaggregated level of analysis, we have individual decision makers. In what ways—early education and socialization, personality characteristics, or even biological makeup and physical health—does the particular occupant of a major foreign policymaking role differ from other individuals who have held or might have held the position in the past? Explanations at this level must relate differences in the characteristics of decision makers to differences in the decisions they make.

Roles of Decision Makers   A decision maker, however, does not act only because of his or her particular individual personality. When acting on behalf of an organization, he or she is the focal point of innumerable pressures and constraints. Thus, at the second level of analysis, the decision maker acts in a particular way because of his or her role in the society and political system. That is, we would expect any Air Force chief of staff, regardless of differences in personality or ideology from other top military officers, to be concerned with protecting the Air Force as an institution—to see that it receives a fair share of budgets, equipment, and talented personnel and to see that the Air Force is

---

6. This analytical scheme is adapted from the one presented in James N. Rosenau, *The Scientific Study of Foreign Policy*, rev. ed. (London: Frances Pinter, 1980), chap. 6. The six levels presented in this book, their added complexity, and our use of them also address a number of points in Moul's critique.

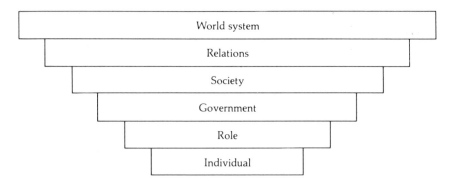

Figure 1.1
Levels of analysis in world politics.

assigned missions that will improve its operating capabilities but not overtax them in hopeless causes.

Any individual—military or civilian—placed in charge of an institution has a responsibility to look out for the interests of that institution. He or she must also consider the interests of other people and institutions and not pursue the organization's interests completely to the exclusion of all others. At heart, however, the person in charge knows that if he or she doesn't protect his or her own institution, no one else will. Other institutions are protected through the pursuit of their own "enlightened self-interest," and by the existence of institutions at higher levels that include them. Thus, the secretary of defense must arbitrate among the interests of the three services (and the civilian defense bureaucracy), and the president must somehow reconcile the interests of all competing military and civilian groups. As part of any look at the individual's role, we must consider the small-group environment within which he or she acts and ask how group interaction affects both perceptions and actions.

In addition to the more narrowly defined institutional interests, we must also assume that people tend to acquire other interests and perspectives from their roles in society. For example, military education (at one of the service academies or in an ROTC program) is designed to produce a set of attitudes and perspectives that is different from what might be fostered at an Ivy League institution or the civilian programs at a state university. Similarly, corporate executives typically acquire a set of attitudes and perspectives that are not necessarily specific to the particular companies they run yet are broadly shared with other executives and distinct from those of labor union officials.

Governmental Structure Another set of influences on the decisions that will be made by organization leaders—and for our concern here, by government officials—is determined by the structure of the government in which they operate. Most obviously, a democratic system of government with frequent and truly competitive elections will pose a different set of opportunities and constraints for decision makers than will an authoritarian government. In the former, it is probably necessary for a leader to build a wider base of approval for his or her actions; yet he or she is likely to be held accountable for those actions at elections held at regular, specified intervals. In an authoritarian system, a leader can build a more narrow political base, repressing those who oppose him or her. Yet there is always the fear of a coup or revolt by opponents. Subtler differences in government types are also important. For example, an American president typically has more control over the cabinet and less over the legislature than does a British prime minister.

Characteristics of the Society Expanding our set of influences still further, we come to nongovernmental characteristics of the society as a whole that affect or condition choices. Governments of rich countries have far more material resources at their disposal than do those of poor countries; they can afford large quantities of modern weapons and can offer economic assistance to other states. At the same time, their citizens expect á high and ever-rising standard of living. The government must therefore see that economic prosperity and access to vital raw materials are maintained.

On another dimension, big countries have more resources at their disposal than do small countries. China and India can afford nuclear weapons far more readily than can Laos or Ireland. Small and poor countries like Peru are especially likely to be deeply penetrated by other countries or by nonstate actors like multinational corporations. What a leader can do and wants to do is substantially determined by the kind of country he or she represents.

On still another dimension are various theories about the requirements or results of capitalism—theories about capitalist economies being driven by military-industrial complexes or in the direction of imperialism. For evidence, we might ask whether most capitalist countries are significantly more war prone than most socialist countries, and if so, why.

International Relations Moreover, states' actions toward each other are influenced by the relationship between them, that is, by the characteristics of the two states. Thus, a small, weak country will act far differently toward a neighboring small, weak country than it will toward a neighboring superpower. Finland must keep a much more wary eye on the Soviet Union than on Norway. Democracies may maintain peaceful relations with each other, but the differences between a democracy and a neighboring dictatorship may bring them into conflict. Rich and poor countries are likely to develop a relationship of dominance or dependence vis-à-vis each other that looks very different (asymmetrical) depending on the country in which you sit.

The World System   Finally, it is essential to consider the wider international, regional, or global system in which a decision maker must operate. A world of two great superpowers differs in very important ways from a world of four or five powers of essentially equal strength. A world of two superpowers tends to focus world fears and antagonisms between those two countries; a world of several equal powers produces at least the possibility of shifting alliances or coalitions to balance power without creating permanent antipathies. Thus, the number of powers—or in some analyses the number of poles in the system—makes a difference.

Another aspect of the large system that makes a difference is the level of wealth and especially of technological development. As an environment for political decision makers, the contemporary world is a far different place from the world of the eighteenth century. Technologies of rapid communication, transportation, and mass destruction have revolutionized the character of warfare and the means whereby national security must be sought. These technologies—and the enormous structure of industry and commerce supported by the wealth of the modern world—also have created a far more interdependent system than was true decades or centuries ago. A cutback in Middle East oil production, the collapse of a major stock market, or an increase in atmospheric pollution from nuclear tests can produce virtually instant and often drastic worldwide repercussions. Thus, as part of the world system, we shall also have to discuss some nonstate actors, or transnational organizations, like intergovernmental organizations (for instance, the International Monetary Fund), as well as nongovernmental organizations such as religious groups, terrorist bands, and multinational corporations.

It is also essential to bear in mind the degree to which any system is hierarchical. The view from the top is very different from the view from the bottom. For powers at the top, it is necessary to keep a sharp watch on the allegiances of small allies and neutrals. Maintaining a balance of power between the top powers may seem to require intervention in the affairs of small states to keep them in line or to maintain access to bases or resources. States at the bottom of the heap, however, expect to have interventions imposed upon them. The quality of relations between the big powers also matters to those elsewhere in the hierarchy—would détente mean less incentive for superpowers to intervene in the affairs of small states or, on the contrary, would it merely mean that each superpower would feel it had a safer and freer hand to control its own sphere of influence?

Other Actors in World Politics

These basic levels of analysis will serve as organizing principles for most of this book. In Part I we shall proceed systematically through these various levels, identifying some of the most important ideas or theories about how these levels affect national decision making by providing constraints and opportunities. We will focus primarily on the policies adopted by the governments of nation-states as influenced by various entities at different levels of analysis within each state's total environment. This focus is typical of the field of study known as international relations or international politics. In many ways the state remains the most significant single type of actor in determining conditions of war and peace as well as the distribution of income and resources.

There are good reasons, nevertheless, to refer now to our field of study as *world politics* to emphasize the importance of actors other than nation-states. This distinction is observed in the title of this book, and we shall refer many times to nonstate actors. A decision maker typically acts not merely on his or her own behalf but also on behalf of some group or organization. One is the nation-state itself, for whom a president or prime minister may act, but other organizations relevant to world politics include: (1) private organizations operating within a nation-state, such as interest groups and banks; (2) parts of national governments, such as the ministry of defense or the Republican leadership of the House of Representatives; and (3) transnational organizations.

All these groups are important agents (or actors) in world politics. Although we shall give special attention to the state as actor, we must always remember that it acts within an environment that consists of individuals and a wide variety of other group actors. A careful use of a levels-of-analysis perspective will identify other major actors who are also important and who are also affected by various elements in the environment. Multinational corporations, for instance, need stable and predictable (if not necessarily completely peaceful) relations between the superpowers if they are to pursue global profits safely. In turn, multinational corporations may create an economic interdependence among states that very seriously inhibits these states from making war, which would sever the bonds of trade and prosperity. Multinational corporations change the relative size and power of social groups and classes where they invest; for example, they increase the labor force in some industries and expand the middle class of technicians and managers. In turn, the political demands of these people, such as attracting more foreign corporations or nationalizing those already in the country, are strengthened. In any case, actors interact across separate levels of analysis.

When we say actors interact, it is not just a matter of one affecting the other in a one-way chain of causation. This is a large part of what we mean by another term that will be used frequently in this book: system. *A system is a set of interacting elements.* When we speak of a global or regional system, we imply that the major elements or influences at different levels of analysis affect each other. Nation-states affect multinational corporations and vice versa; nation-states develop new military technologies and in turn are constrained by the destructive capabilities of those technologies. We must be sensitive to effects in both directions.

In an extreme sense, the interactions of a system mean that everything affects everything else. If you kill a single butterfly, you reduce the stock of genetic material in the next generation of butterflies and therefore change the pattern of evolution for future butterflies—and the predators who feed on butterflies. Over millions of years of evolution, you will have an unknowable effect on life and even on the physical environment that life modifies. Probably those effects will be trivial, but they could be very large. One mark of a good analyst is the ability to simplify a complex reality in a way that concentrates on the most important relationships and at least temporarily ignores the others. According to Jacob Bronowski,

> I believe that there are no events anywhere in the universe which are not tied to every other event in the universe.... But you cannot carry on science on the supposition that you are going to be able to connect every event with every other event.... It is, therefore, an essential part of the methodology of science to divide the world for any experiment into what

we regard as relevant and what we regard, for purposes of that experiment, as irrelevant.[7]

Any simplification leaves something out. Any level of analysis ignores something important, and another simplification—another level of analysis—will tell us something a little different. But we have to start somewhere. Certain types of questions about national decision makers' behavior are more readily answered from one level than from another. Questions that can be answered from various levels allow one to get different perspectives on the same question and require different kinds of evidence. Information on individual leaders' perceptions and true preferences may, for instance, be very hard to obtain. One may contend that nearly all leaders of poor and weak countries have the same preferences in a given situation; thus, detailed information on preferences is not needed so long as one has adequate information at the societal level of analysis. The choice of level of analysis is therefore determined by data availability and by one's theory, but the choice cannot be capricious: Several different classes of influence (levels of analysis) must be identified and looked for in every analytical instance. Explanations from different levels need not exclude each other. They may be complementary, each making a contribution to our understanding. To some degree, estimates of the relative weight of each contribution can be compiled through the techniques of data gathering and analysis typical of modern social science. But in other degrees we remain more in the realm of speculation, intuition, and informed wisdom.

THE "MENU" OF WORLD POLITICIANS AND CONSTRAINTS ON DECISION MAKERS

The linkages across the various levels of analysis have been studied by a number of international relations scholars. One very useful starting place is the work of Harold and Margaret Sprout,[8] where they discuss the *ecological triad*. This triad is composed of three elements: (1) an actor

---

7. Jacob Bronowski, *The Origins of Knowledge and Imagination* (New Haven, Conn.: Yale University Press, 1978), p. 58.

8. See especially their article, "Environmental Factors in the Study of International Politics," in James N. Rosenau (Ed.), *International Politics and Foreign Policy*, 2nd ed. (New York: Free Press, 1969), pp. 41–56. The discussion of the Sprouts' ideas in the following pages is taken chiefly from this article.

of some sort, (2) an environment that surrounds the actor, and (3) the actor-environment relationship. We think of the foreign policy maker as the most basic entity in our study, a person who must behave within the very complex environment that surrounds him or her.

We may also think of each level of analysis as describing one of the environments within which the decision maker must operate. Each of these environments surrounds, affects, and especially *constrains* the foreign policy decision maker. These environments fit over one another like a set of Chinese boxes. For example, at the individual level we are interested in the specific decision maker and the specific psychological and physical environment he or she possesses. This is why we study the health of people such as Franklin Roosevelt at the Yalta conference in 1945 or of Yuri Andropov during the cooling of U.S.-Soviet relations, or the psychological makeup of dictators such as Hitler or Stalin. We study all the things that made Harry S Truman the person he was in order to understand why he permitted the United States to drop the atomic bomb. We study Brezhnev to see if paranoid tendencies or deeply rooted insecurities influenced his decision to invade Czechoslovakia. The levels of analysis allow us to start here. But they also make it clear that the individual decision maker works within the environment created by his or her role within a governmental organization, the environment created by that government or by the society in which the decision maker lives, and the international system.

The Entity-Environment Relationship

The usefulness of these ideas comes when we *link* the entity and the environment—when we see how and why the different environments constrain or limit what the entities are able to do and what they are likely to do. The entity-environment relationships can be thought of in a number of ways. The Sprouts provide three types of entity-environment relationships that are particularly useful.

The first of these is called *environmental possibilism*. Here the environment is seen as a set of constraints on what it is actually possible for the entity to do in the environment. In certain periods of history, international actors (entities) could not interact with other entities due to spatial and geographic conditions; interactions were later made possible by technological innovations. Thus, Napoleon could not threaten Moscow with nuclear destruction (nor could the Germans in 1914, although the Germans could get to Moscow more quickly than Napoleon through the existence of railroads); the Romans couldn't move their legions from Italy to Britain within a matter of hours (or even days); Teddy Roosevelt in 1905 couldn't raise American prestige by sending a man to the moon (he had to settle for sending the U.S. Navy on a round-the-world cruise); Darius of Persia could not pick up a telephone to reason out his differences with Alexander the Great before Alexander crossed into Asia; and the Spanish in the Middle Ages could not draw upon the resources of the New World to defeat the initial Islamic invasion of Iberia (since the New World was not yet known to exist). The list could go on and on. The basic idea is that decision makers are constrained in their behavior by the actual possibilities in their "objective" environment.

The Sprouts call another relationship *environmental probabilism*. They refer to the environmental constraints in any situation that make certain behavior more or less likely—that there is some normally expected behavior in the situation under consideration. Given that states can interact, that it is possible, what is the *probability* they will act in certain ways? (For example, what is the probability that the United States and the USSR will become rivals, as the only two superpowers after World War II? Or the probability that Egypt and Israel, being regional powers with a history of enmity and bloodshed, will go to war? Or the probability of interaction between Burma and Bolivia, small powers in different regions of the world that are separated by thousands of miles? Or that a bloc leader would use force to maintain control over that bloc and its sphere of influence?) Or, given the characteristics of the domestic environment (its size, wealth, form of government, and ethnic diversity), what is the probability of certain behavior? (For example, the probability of the British or Japanese or Americans becoming naval powers? Of the Swiss following a policy of neutrality? Of the probability of external intervention in civil wars during the post-World War II era?)

Finally, the Sprouts also discuss *cognitive behaviorism*, which is the familiar principle that a person reacts to his or her milieu as he or she perceives it. A decision maker is linked to the environment through *images* of that environment. Decision makers behave only on the basis of how they perceive the world. This perception may be very different from what the world is actually like. Such differences may be brought home in many ways when the decision maker attempts to implement a policy in the real world: If someone perceives a glass patio door to be open when it is not, the consequences of operating on such beliefs can be shattering. For example, when Neville Chamberlain, the British prime minister, perceived that Hitler could be appeased and gave in to him at Munich, the result was more Nazi expansion. History also provides us with the picture of Hitler years later, isolated in his Berlin bunker, moving imaginary divisions around on a map—divisions that were real only to him and that had no impact on the Red Army as it moved inexorably toward the German capital.

When we study different environments or levels of analysis, we are thus also interested in how they affect the image of the world that decision makers hold—how they affect the perceptions of decision makers and how they affect the amount, type, and nature of incoming information upon which these images are modified, changed, or reinforced. Put another way, how do different environments or levels affect what decision makers see as possible and probable? In sum, the various environments to which the decision-making entity must adapt can limit what is possible and can affect decision makers' perceptions of what is possible and probable.

Bruce Russett has tied these perceptions together with his analogy to the "menu."[9] The person (actor) who enters a restaurant is confronted by a gastronomical environment (the menu). The menu provides a number of behavioral opportunities, not determining the diner's choice but constraining what is possible (e.g., pizza, lasagna, and linguini are possible in an Italian restaurant, but not chicken chow mein or matzo ball soup). The menu also affects the probability of behavior through price, portion size, side dishes, specials, and the restaurant's reputation for certain foods. Thus, the diner at the Italian restaurant, which its menu proclaims has served pizza since 1910 and which serves over fifty varieties of pizza at low prices, is most probably going to order a pizza. Yet other choices exist, and the probabilities are affected by how the diner sees those choices—cognitive behaviorism. Though the restaurant is not known for its lasagna, which is also extraordinarily expensive, lasagna is still a possibility. A patron who is Russian and unable to read English (and even is unfamiliar with the Roman alphabet), may order the lasagna believing he or she is ordering pizza. A patron who is rich and who is obsessed with lasagna of any quality may also order this dish. Thus, knowledge of a patron's individual decision-making process in conjunction with the menu (the possibility of lasagna), as well as how he or she views the menu, permits us to analyze this particular diner's behavior.

9. Bruce M. Russett, "A Macroscopic View of International Politics," in James N. Rosenau, Vincent Davis, and M. A. East (Eds.), *The Analysis of International Politics* (New York: Free Press, 1972), pp. 109–124.

Opportunity and Willingness

We can look at the relationship between entities and environments from yet another perspective, using two concepts developed by Harvey Starr: opportunity and willingness.[10] Each of the environments can be seen as providing decision makers with a set of opportunities. *Opportunity* means that conditions exist that permit sufficient interaction between states, that adequate capabilities and resources exist to allow certain kinds of actions to take place, and that decision makers perceive both the range of possible interactions and the extent of capabilities.

Opportunity may best be illustrated with a reference to Lewis Fry Richardson, one of the pioneers of peace research. Richardson, concerned with "deadly quarrels," drew a parallel between war and murder. He asked why people in one country tended to murder each other more often than they murder foreigners. He drew the simple conclusion that there is much less opportunity to murder foreigners, since there are far fewer contacts with them.[11] In fact, police records indicate that a person is most likely to be murdered by close relatives and friends, because constant contact and high levels of interactions provide the opportunity for murder.

Similarly, Bolivia and Burma are unlikely to fight one another because their range of interaction is too limited to allow a conflict to develop; Cuba will not declare war on the United States because its capabilities are too limited; and we found Panama challenging the United States over the Panama Canal in the 1970s because it accurately perceived that international and domestic conditions permitted a challenge that could not have taken place before World War II (or perhaps before Vietnam). Thus, opportunity is a concept that draws together various aspects of the Sprouts' environmental triad and overlaps probabilism and cognitive behaviorism.

Willingness is concerned with the motivations that lead people to avail themselves of opportunities. Willingness deals with the goals and motivations of decision makers and focuses on why decision makers choose one alternative over another. Willingness is therefore based on perceptions of threat and emotions like fear, insecurity, and revenge. Thus, there has been ample opportunity for Canada to declare war on

---

10. Harvey Starr, " 'Opportunity' and 'Willingness' as Ordering Concepts in the Study of War," *International Interactions* 4 (1978), 363–387.

11. Lewis F. Richardson, *Statistics of Deadly Quarrels* (Chicago: Quadrangle Books, 1961), p. 288.

the United States; Canada has had adequate interactions with the United States to make conflict plausible. It had, in its alliance with Britain, a reasonable capability base from which to wage such a war, and its decision makers undoubtedly recognized these factors. Yet Canada did not declare war: It did not feel threatened by the United States or desire revenge, and thus it was unwilling to choose this course of action.

We have attempted in this section to show how the levels of analysis can be linked. The Sprouts provide a link through the concepts of probabilism, possibilism, and cognitive behaviorism. The various environments, together with the images held by the decision makers, delimit the range of actions that are possible and probable. Russett's example of a menu highlights how these factors go together to influence choice. And, finally, Starr demonstrates a linkage from a somewhat different perspective, using the concepts of opportunity and willingness. The systemic, relational, and societal levels provide most of the opportunities; the societal, governmental, and role levels affect motivations for individual willingness to pursue certain acts.

For two decades the academic writings of former Secretary of State Henry Kissinger stressed the domestic and international constraints on the foreign policy decision maker. The true statesman, Kissinger stressed, understood these constraints and learned to work within them to achieve the desired aims. In trying to understand the behavior of states, then, we are interested in seeing how and what foreign policy makers choose to do. These choices run the full range of behavior from the most violent international conflict to the most harmonious international cooperation. Although people often think of the international arena as a realm of conflict, there has been a remarkable amount of neutral or cooperative behavior. Although in theory states are independent or sovereign and thus may do whatever they please, states have always limited their behavior in important ways.

PLAN OF THE BOOK

The rest of Part I will follow the levels-of-analysis presentation from the preceding pages. First, however, we shall give a brief overview in Chapter 2 of how world politics can be studied; we shall stress the scientific approach. Then, before moving on to discussions about the levels of analysis, we shall discuss the various actors on the world stage in Chapter 3. Because we shall be concentrating on the nation-state in this book, much attention will be given to the nation, nationalism, and the state and to how the nation-state compares with other international actors.

Part I will include the most comprehensive context or environment and work its way down to the most specific. Chapters 4 and 5 will deal with the world system and how the global environment affects the behavior of international actors. Chapters 6 and 7 will look at relations among states and how states interact. The following three chapters will cover the domestic environment of states and how societal and governmental factors affect foreign policy and world politics. Finally, Chapters 11 and 12 will investigate the behavior of decision makers: people who are constrained by their roles and by their own individual characteristics that affect the way they perceive the world. Part I offers the reader a better understanding of the complex set of environments within which foreign policy decision makers work.

2

ANALYZING WORLD POLITICS: HOW TO DO IT

A "NEW" STUDY OF WORLD POLITICS

World War I left leaders and ordinary people aghast. The balance of power between the major states, a system that had provided a very substantial degree of peace in Europe since the end of the Napoleonic Wars in 1815, had been violently upset. The war lasted four years and left about nine million soldiers dead. Many people, perhaps foremost among them the American president, Woodrow Wilson, concluded that the balance-of-power system was fatally flawed and a new world order had to be constructed. These people, known as idealists, supported formation of the League of Nations and other institutions of international law, hoping to build a system of collective security in which democratic nations would be especially peace loving and in which all nations would band together to defeat unjust aggression. World War II, however, disillusioned many of these idealists. Democracy was overthrown in Germany, Italy, Spain, and elsewhere, and the members of the League did not band together against the fascists and Nazis until it was almost too late.

After World War II, people once again vowed that global wars must be prevented. The idealists supported creation of a new organization—the United Nations—to replace the League of Nations, once again putting their faith in the benefits of collective security, the rule of law, and spreading democracy. Others, however, were very skeptical. They insisted that what was needed was a realistic rather than idealistic view of international politics. According to *realism*—the central approach to the study of international politics for several decades and perhaps even now—people are self-interested and selfish, seeking to dominate others. In addition, realists consider nation-states as by far the most important actors in world politics, and most states are assumed to be rational, united actors pursuing essentially the same goals, regardless of their form of government or type of economic organization.

According to realists a system of competing nation-states is basically an *anarchic* system, literally a system without a government or ruling authority. States compete with one another, must look out for their own interests, and cannot appeal to some higher authority to enforce international law. This is in many ways an accurate description of the world in which we live. But anarchic does not necessarily mean disorderly. On the contrary, there is a great deal of order and predictability in the behavior of nation-states. Usually states do obey international law, not particularly because they are "good," but because it is in their interest to seem law abiding and to encourage others to obey the law. Nation-states cooperate in thousands of ways: in the peaceful conduct of trade and finance, the movement of people across national borders, communication and information exchange, medical cooperation against disease, and many others. Without this cooperation the substantial peace and prosperity we know would be completely impossible. Realism as an approach to international relations helps to explain why states fight or threaten each other but is less effective in explaining much of the cooperative behavior we see—the order within the anarchy. More important, it does not suggest how more order can be created without imposing some world empire. It is that need to explain order and to seek greater order in a dangerously armed world that compels us to pay attention to actors other than nation-states (especially international and transnational organizations) and to issues other than the pursuit of power (like trade, development, or pollution control).

In this way, *idealism* remains a powerful antidote to excessive attention to power politics. According to idealism, ideals and moral principles are goals to strive for and criteria for evaluating our behavior. As realism was a reaction to the idealist failure to control Nazi Germany, idealism is a reaction to the dangers of too much power politics and the maximization of power. Idealism has reemerged in recent years as realist power politics, with its incessant threats and counterthreats, risks bringing on a new and even more terrible war.

Just as there have always been different philosophical views about the current or desired nature of world politics, there have also been different views about how world politics should be studied. Some people, especially the realists with their insistence on the overwhelming importance of nation-states as actors, have stressed the study of diplomatic history—the study of actions by national governments. Others, especially idealists, have attended especially to the study and development of international law.

Another approach—one not primarily associated with either of the philosophical perspectives—has been to use relevant results and methods from the behavioral sciences, such as anthropology, economics, psychology, and sociology. This has been reinforced by the rise of analytic and quantitative research concepts, models, and methods. This approach makes greater use of the comparative study of quantitative data and, in using systematic evidence about what *is*, remedies the excesses of both the diplomatic-historical (realist) approach and the international law approach (idealist) that had dominated earlier studies.[1] The historical approach was highly descriptive, based on persuasive and presumably plausible arguments. Much of the earlier writing was also prescriptive, describing the ills of the international system and then advising what ought to be done about them. International law was both a legalistic and moral/ethical approach to international relations, concerned with describing and evaluating the behavior of states and then prescribing ways in which they should behave.

Given the crucial international problems that appeared after 1945, many scholars and analysts felt that only a more systematic understanding of these problems would lead to their solution. Problems of war and peace took on new meanings with the advent of nuclear weap-

---

1. On realism and idealism, see Richard W. Mansbach and John A. Vasquez, *In Search of Theory: A New Paradigm for Global Politics* (New York: Columbia University Press, 1981). On the rise of the social scientific study of world politics, see Karl W. Deutsch, "The Coming Crisis of Cross-National and International Research in the United States," *American Council of Learned Societies Newsletter* 19 (1968), no. 1, pp. 1–7. For an overview of the scientific study of international politics, see Dina A. Zinnes, *Contemporary Research in International Relations* (New York: Free Press, 1976).

ons. The interdependence and complexity of the world became greater as the Western colonial empires broke up, scores of new states were created, and political and economic hierarchies around the world were reordered.

The Scientific Approach

Faced with such problems, major intellectual objections arose to earlier approaches to the study of international relations. Historical and legal approaches stressed the description of unique events and sought to explain them. The intellectual reaction sought instead to attempt the study of international relations in a scientific manner, using the procedures and methods of science (as other social sciences, such as economics and psychology, had done previously). Thus, the preference was to stress *comparability* and not uniqueness—to look for patterns of behavior and probabilities that certain behavior would occur. In approaching the study of international relations in this way, stress was placed on finding and developing tools for organizing the intellectual complexity of the field—the development of concepts, frameworks, and theories. The scientific approach stresses a probabilistic explanation of human affairs. This is what Jacob Bronowski called the "revolution" of thought in modern science, "replacing the concept of the inevitable effect with that of the probable trend. . . . History is neither determined nor random. At any moment it moves forward into an area whose general shape is known, but whose boundaries are uncertain in a calculable way."[2]

The scientific approach thus assumes that knowledge is possible by investigating patterns of behavior, regularities of actions, and recurring responses in political behavior. Social science is concerned with generalizations about classes or types of phenomena. It assumes that over the long run, most historic parallels will transcend the specific times, places, and personalities involved. The comparative method assumes that similarities and patterns exist that will be of use in explaining what has happened and why. Much of the work done in the comparative study of foreign policy has attempted to discover patterns among national characteristics of various kinds and the foreign-policy behavior of states. The comparative approach may attempt to provide

---

2. Jacob Bronowski, *The Common Sense of Science* (London: Heinemann, 1951), pp. 86–87.

interpretations of foreign policy behaviors that are applicable cross-nationally (i.e., comparisons of several nations at a particular time) or longitudinally (i.e., comparisons of conditions in one or more nations over several points in time). Foreign policy can thus be seen as a mixture of random (chance) factors and regularities that can be discovered. Regularities have systematic effects on foreign policy. As such, they can be discerned and their influence on foreign-policy behavior can be explained.

One point that should be stressed is that comparison is a research technique common to many disciplines. Its application to foreign policy is relatively recent, beginning only in the mid-1960s. By that time comparison had established itself as an important approach in other social sciences and other areas of political science. The existence of ever-growing numbers of nation-states and other international actors made it possible (and to some scholars absolutely necessary) to study foreign policy from a large-scale comparative perspective. When one asks any comparative question about two objects (e.g., which is larger, stronger, or richer?) the answer will depend on developing measures by which the objects can be compared, categorized, and ranked. By so doing, objects—in our case, nation-states—can be measured along a number of dimensions. Besides measurement, we now have some important descriptive data on what a nation-state and/or a set of nation-states (and the global system at some point in time) look like (e.g., see Chapter 8 and Appendix B). By finding patterns in measurement we understand not only a group of units or nation-states; we also have a better idea of what *each* nation-state is like because we can compare or measure that nation-state against others or against summary measures such as averages, medians, and so forth. In doing so not only do we guard against assumptions that specific states are unique in certain ways (when they are not), but we can also spot the truly exceptional (or *deviant*) case. Finally, comparison is essential to the scientific method of inquiry. The aim of social science is to develop generalized statements that lead to tested theories of international behavior. Thus, if we have a theory that suggests large countries are likelier to go to war, we need measures of size and of "war proneness" to investigate it, and we need to include big and small countries as well as countries that are peaceful and countries that are war-prone.

In a very basic way this comparative approach distinguishes the study of international relations or politics from the study of international history. Some traditionalists and historians believe that humanity—and international relations especially—is the least promising area for scientific study because events are too complex and too singular. Traditional techniques would all but exclude comparability, generalization, and cumulativeness, which result from the assumption that patterns exist. Denying these regularities leaves one to study only singular cases or to produce detailed descriptions. If the counterassumption that every historical event is truly unique and thus noncomparable is firmly believed, then the gulf between the traditionalist and the scientist is indeed unbridgeable. Some scholars appear to hold this position; however, we don't believe it (and probably neither do they). But everyone has compared two events at some time. By comparing things, we admit the possibility of certain similarities across events. Using a case study to illustrate some concept or phenomenon reveals the same agreement with the principle of comparison and the possibility of patterns. The most basic rationale for the study of society—that the past can be used as some sort of guide to the future—must also rest on the similarities of events and the existence of regularities.

Exactly what *science* is has been a subject of complex discussion and argument by philosophers of science and epistemologists. However, we feel that the first major step into the realm of scientific inquiry is to assume the comparability of events. The "scientificness" of inquiry is a continuum or range. It starts with acceptance of some basic assumptions and continues with the use and application of more steps in the scientific method and more rigorous analytic tools and methodologies. The end point is *sciences*. Biology, astronomy, physics, and chemistry are all equally scientific, but the conclusions and theories in each of these fields have taken different forms and been determined by using different methodologies. Because the study of international relations does not or may never look like physics with its "universal laws," it does not mean that international relations cannot be scientific.

We see a great variety of approaches. There is a popularly labeled "traditional-scientific" division. On the more traditional end are people studying diverse time periods and historical regimes. Their work ranges from highly specific case studies and historical descriptions to broad discussions of nature of international relations. The methods used range from the analysis of ethical and moral philosophy, through description, to complex analytic accounts of events. Among those who are self-consciously scientific are those who stress data gathering and those who stress theoretical development—the "counters" and the "poets." There are middle-range theorists and grand theorists, those in pursuit of policy relevance and those concerned with theoretical elegance. There are hypothesis testers and mathematical modelers, inductive theorists and deductive theorists. There are those who engage in creating theories of the international system and those who stress decision making, those who use game theory and laboratory experiments and those who use quantitative history and aggregate data from large numbers of states or lengthy time periods. But underlying *all* these approaches is some agreement that events can be compared.

The new study of international relations arose with the help of new research opportunities. The desire to study large numbers of cases and large numbers of variables and to provide statistical description and analysis would have been frustrated if the necessary technology had not become available after World War II. Electronic computers made possible the quick and accurate processing of large amounts of data even for complex statistical and mathematical analyses. At the same time, funds from private foundations and various agencies of the federal government made more research opportunities available.[3]

The best way to indicate the results of these influences on the study of international relations is to follow Davis Bobrow's lead and take two imaginary trips to the library. In 1946 we would find a world politics library composed mainly of books and articles describing the historical relationships and experience of states (e.g., French foreign policy from Napoleon to the Crimean war or U.S.-Russian relations during the nineteenth century), current events, diplomatic practice, and international law and organization (with a heavy emphasis on the League of Nations). If we walked into the same library today all of the above materials would still be there. But in addition there would be analyses using the concepts and methods of the philosophy of science, logic, statistics, and mathematics. There would be many works drawing on the concepts, methods, and findings of economics, sociology, anthropology, psychology and social psychology, organizational behavior, cybernetics (the study of information and communication), systems analysis, biology and ethology, geography, and others. The number and diversity of concepts, methods, and findings being used to study international relations have expanded enormously. Today's library reflects the change in emphasis from historical description to a more general, comparative, and systematic scientific approach.

---

3. The identification and discussion of these three factors—new international concerns, intellectual objections, and new research opportunities—is based on the work of Davis Bobrow, *International Relations, New Approaches* (New York: Free Press, 1972), chap. 2.

THEORY AND EVIDENCE

A key element in science is the painstaking development of *theory.* Theory provides us with a way to organize and order facts into data:

> More specifically, a theory is a set of interconnected statements. This set of statements comprises (1) sentences introducing terms that refer to the basic concepts of the theory (theoretical terms); (2) sentences that relate the basic concepts to each other; and (3) sentences that relate some theoretical statements to a set of possible observations.[4]

Theory thus helps to separate the important from the trivial by pointing out what we really wish to look at and what is unimportant enough to ignore. Theories are used to define, label, and classify the phenomena of world politics carefully and, in so doing, provide the basis for *systematic* evidence for our explanations of the world. Because we can argue an opposite and plausible reason or hypothesis for almost every aspect of human interaction (e.g., "absence makes the heart grow fonder" or "out of sight, out of mind"), we need systematic evidence to test theory. A good theory is one that can be supported or rejected through explicit analysis and systematic use of data. A theory that cannot be tested—and which cannot be disproven in any conceivable way—cannot get us very far. Think, for example, of the proposition "people always act to advance their own self-interest, no matter how much they delude themselves or others into thinking they are acting in someone else's interest." Since the proponent of such an argument can always support the argument ("the person in question is deluding himself about his motives"), and since that statement cannot be checked with evidence (we cannot get inside the person's mind to look), the self-interest proposition cannot be disproven. It is not a scientific statement, because any evidence can be interpreted to agree. It also is a useless statement, because it doesn't tell us what the person's specific behavior will be.

Hypotheses, Laws, and Probability Statements

Theoretical statements that relate to possible observations are called *hypotheses.* The testing of hypotheses—checking their predictions against

---

4. Garvin McCain and Erwin M. Segal, *The Game of Science,* 2nd ed. (Monterey, Calif.: Brooks/Cole, 1973), p. 99. This book is a clear and helpful introduction to scientific method. Another helpful book is Charles A. Lave and James G. March, *An Introduction to Models in the Social Sciences* (New York: Harper & Row, 1975).

observation—is a central activity of science. Hypotheses that are confirmed in virtually all of the classes of phenomena to which they are applied are often known as *laws*. In the social sciences, interesting laws are quite rare. The phenomena of social science are so complex, with many different influences or causes acting on a particular event, and our knowledge of these complex phenomena is still so imperfect that few laws have been established. Even with much more theory and research, we are likely to have only *probability statements*—statements that most phenomena of a given class will behave in a certain way most of the time. This is why social scientists find it hard to predict how particular events will develop, for example, whether a particular foreign policy crisis will be resolved or escalate into war. At best, the social scientist can give no more than a probability that a particular action (a threat, a promise, or a concession) will be followed by the desired result. Policymakers, understandably, would like more certainty.

When we say we are hoping to make general statements about phenomena in international relations, we do not necessarily mean timeless generalizations that apply to all countries at all times. Such timeless generalizations may be possible in physics, but they are difficult to derive in political science. All states, for instance, may have to react in some way to a shift in the international balance of power against them. But how they will react depends on other circumstances. They may react by making war, forming new alliances, building up their national power bases, or making concessions to their opponents. Which choice states make depends on the opportunities they have (whether powerful allies are available and whether they can conceivably win a war) and on their disposition or willingness to act on various possibilities (whether their domestic ideology permits them to ally with a potential partner state and whether the government is strong enough at home to survive making concessions to a foreign enemy).

In different contexts, therefore, the same cause will have different effects. Context thus adds new variables that affect the relationship under study, and these variables often operate at different levels of analysis. In our discussion above, what had been a generalization about the international system is modified by societal or governmental characteristics. The complex and changing nature of relationships in world politics thus makes them difficult to analyze.[5]

---

5. See Benjamin A. Most and Harvey Starr, "Conceptualizing 'War': Consequences for Theory and Research," *Journal of Conflict Resolution* 27 (March 1983), 137–159.

To understand world politics, we need to have a high tolerance for ambiguity, uncertainty, the imperfect state of human knowledge, and the whys of human society and politics. The phenomena are extraordinarily complex, and we know far less than we would like. You will doubtless yearn at times for more certainty, more conviction, than the authors of this book can give about the causes and possible solutions of various problems. If we seemed to give you certainty, we would be dishonest. Knowing what it is that you don't know, why you don't know it, and what you might do to remedy your ignorance is a part of wisdom and maturity. A child wants and needs answers; too much ignorance by those on whom the child is dependent can be intolerably threatening. An adult, by contrast, has learned to cope with such threats. No mature adult can be satisfied with ignorance, but intellectually and emotionally an adult learns to distinguish relative ignorance from relative knowledge and to chart a course of inquiry and action from that distinction.

Empirical Reality

In reviewing ideas or theories about world politics, we shall be considering propositions whose degree of truth varies greatly. Some statements of fact about *empirical reality* will be made with confidence, sometimes because they have been systematically and thoroughly tested by the standard procedures of social science—they represent, in other words, hypotheses that have been widely confirmed. In other cases statements may be made with confidence simply because they are a part of accepted "wisdom"—even though they may not rest on an elaborate basis of scientific examination, they are thought to be more or less self-evident by most observers. Perhaps they can be logically deduced from other statements that are widely accepted or that rest on solid scientific procedure. Fully useful and reliable statements combine elements of logic and of empirical study.

If statements have been supported by empirical study, it is also important that they be derived by careful logic from clearly stated assumptions to show us *why* the statement should be correct and how it identifies process or a *causal* relationship. For example, the statement "fat people eat too much" is usually an empirically correct statement of fact (a correlation), but it tells us little of interest about causality—why some people are fat, that is, why they eat too much. Often it is very difficult to uncover the process of causation that underlies a correlation we observe. In this case, what is the cause of overeating and therefore of fatness?

We also have to be very careful about the assumptions we make. It would not be very helpful to construct an elaborate logical theory about why people are overweight if one of our initial assumptions (e.g., "they start out with larger stomachs to fill") was empirically incorrect. Of course, we sometimes make simplifying assumptions that we know may not be correct or are not fully correct. For example, we can assume that people are rational, that competition in an industry is perfect, or that the speed of a falling body is not slowed by friction with the air. Sometimes these assumptions are close enough to reality that they do not affect our conclusions. Competition among thousands of grain farmers may be nearly perfect. The difference between the weights of iron and lead balls may not produce a significant difference in their speeds when they are dropped from the Leaning Tower of Pisa. It would take very careful observation to see any difference, and the differences would be so small that under most circumstances we would not care. But if the assumptions were wildly incorrect for a particular set of problems, the results could be disastrous. What if we assumed that competition in the international sale of petroleum was perfect? Or that air resistance would make no difference in the speeds between a feather and a lead ball dropped from the tower? A careful analyst, therefore, will always be alert to the nature of his or her assumptions, to how they may differ from reality, and to the conditions under which the difference may matter. A careful analyst will want to know what has been simplified and to have some sense of how that simplification may lead her predictions to depart from observable reality.

Much of scientific endeavor therefore requires systematic observation and precise measurement. A careful analyst will insist on a combination of logical deduction and accurate observation—empirical evidence—in evaluating the propositions put forth. Science thus is a systematic way of obtaining information and making generalizations.

> Scientific observation is deliberate search, carried out with care and forethought, as contrasted with the casual and largely passive perceptions of everyday life. It is this deliberateness and control of the process of observation that is distinctive of science, not merely the use of special instruments.[6]

---

6. Quotation from Abraham Kaplan, *The Language of Inquiry* (San Francisco: Chandler, 1964), p. 126. Quoted in, with further discussion by, Charles E. Lindblom and David K. Cohen, *Usable Knowledge: Social Science and Social Problem Solving* (New Haven, Conn.: Yale University Press, 1979), pp. 15–16.

In most social science, nevertheless, the statements we make rarely rest on a completely scientific basis. As some experienced social scientists point out, most of what we know about social phenomena is "ordinary knowledge" not derived from systematic scientific endeavors. Ordinary knowledge might include the fact that there are many countries in the world, that there is a war going on somewhere at virtually all times, and that very big states usually have larger armies than very small states. We must depend on many ways of knowing that are not scientific, since there are not enough resources to do all the desirable science. Yet we must also know when to doubt what passes as ordinary knowledge, when to question it, and how to supplant or supplement it by scientific knowledge when needed. Social science should be directed at key points of inquiry where ordinary knowledge is suspected to be wrong and where the consequences of being wrong would be serious.

Because so much of what we know is ordinary knowledge, we must be wary of accepting it too confidently. People long ago were sure that the world was flat. It is easy to become complacent about what we think we know. Dr. Benjamin Spock begins his world-renowned book, *Baby and Child Care,* with the words "You know more than you think you do." Maybe so, but in world politics the opposite is sometimes true: You know less than you think you do. Political decision makers take actions every day that determine the happiness and the lives of millions of people. They do not always know what the effects of their acts will be, nor do their advisors. While recognizing that action is necessary, we must retain a sense of humility about the knowledge base of our actions. In addition, we must be very self-conscious about the basis, in logic and evidence, of the propositions that guide our acts and our advice. In this book we shall try to identify the degree of confidence with which various assertions can be made, the reasons for that confidence or lack of it, and some criteria for you to use in evaluating logic and evidence.

FACTS AND VALUES

Similar humility (or at least self-consciousness) is needed for statements of *value*—what is beautiful and good. We make such statements all the time: One painting is more beautiful than another; one act is morally right and another wrong. We all make these judgments, though we make them with varying degrees of confidence, and we often disagree about them. The systems of thought by which we deduce statements about goodness and beauty may start from very different premises. A Buddhist, a Sunni Moslem, an evangelical Christian, and an atheist Marxist may well agree that certain elements of life, decent living conditions, and liberties constitute, in some sense, "basic human rights." But they will differ in how they arrive at those common conclusions, about the specific forms those rights should take, and about the relative importance of each. Some cultures value political liberty more highly than do others; poor people may rate decent living conditions as more important than political rights or more highly than would some affluent people who take comfort for granted. Thus, religion, ethical systems, other elements of culture, and living conditions influence people's values and ethical judgments. Whatever the basis of our ethical systems, we still must recognize their presence and the effect they have on our political beliefs and acts.

Moreover, they affect our positions as scholars or analysts of politics. Although we may try to keep our value judgments and our statements of empirical fact distinct, they are likely to interact in subtle ways. People living in a prosperous state threatened with war are likely to approve of a global system that promises to preserve their prosperity and peace. They may consider the most important problem of world politics to be one of balancing power among the big states so that war is avoided. They may in important ways look at the peoples of small states primarily as means of preserving the existing system. For those latter peoples, however, balance of power looks like a means of maintaining the great powers' dominance of the system. Superpower war may seem to be a rich person's problem; the problem of the people of small states is to achieve some level of independence and economic well-being in that system. People of small states will value détente (improving Soviet-American relations) differently, they will seek different goals, and they will develop different theories or explanations of world politics reflecting the search for different goals.

One illustration of ways in which values may subtly condition our ideas and especially our choice of phenomena to study is contained in Chapter 1, where we talked about how various aspects of the environment affect the system. In one example we contrasted a world system containing two great powers with a system containing four or five such powers. From the point of view of a person living in a war-prone world, especially a decision maker who must cope with such a world today and tomorrow (but not four years from now, when he or she will be out of office or retired), most attention may be directed at questions of how the system works and how to survive in it. For such people, their survival is highly valued.

But systems are not always stable; they change. Before World War II there clearly was a system with several major powers; after the war there were only two. Since the early Cold War years, the international system has again changed to some degree, lessening the influence of the two superpowers. We must be alert not only to the effects of aspects of a system at any one time, but to the dynamics of systems—how and why they change. Marxist dialectics—a perspective of systems changing as a result of internal "contradictions" of thesis, antithesis, and synthesis—is one such important perspective.[7] It stems from a desire to change the system to increase a value such as equality. Another perspective is that of the citizen who fears that the present world system is hopelessly war prone and riddled with injustice, who sees hope only in some quite different, alternative system. For such a perspective to be analytically sound and politically effective, that citizen must have a view not only of what the alternative system would be like but also of how to create it. Again, we would have an empirical focus on how systems change or might change stemming from a *value-based* focus on why systems ought to change.

THE USES OF A STUDY OF WORLD POLITICS

We can analyze a decision or event from the perspectives of different approaches to world politics and of several levels of analysis. In some of the next chapters we shall be focusing on characteristics of the global system (Chapters 4 and 5), of the relations between nation-states (Chapters 6 and 7), and of nation-states as actors (Chapters 8 through 10). This is an emphasis on large-scale, highly aggregated units of analysis, stemming from theorists' convictions that the most important, persistent influences on war and economic distribution are found at such levels. In this way it is part of the grand sociological tradition shared in different ways and with different theoretical details by such writers as Emile Durkheim and Karl Marx (and more recently espoused by Kenneth Waltz).[8] The case for this perspective is well argued by

---

7. See, for instance, Hayward R. Alker, "Dialectical Foundations of Global Disparities," *International Studies Quarterly* 25 (March 1981), 69–98.

8. See both Waltz's *Man, The State and War* (New York: Columbia University Press, 1959) and his *Theory of International Politics* (Boston: Addison-Wesley, 1979).

Nazli Choucri and Robert North in their analysis of the conditions that brought about World War I:

> The dynamics of national growth and expansion, the conflict of national interests, patterns of growth in military expenditures, alliance-formation, and violence-behavior . . . were not the immediate cause of WWI. The processes set the stage, armed the players, and deployed the forces, but they did not join the antagonists in combat. They created the conditions of an armed camp within which the assassination of the Austrian arch-duke was sufficient to trigger an international crisis and a major war.[9]

Even if the particular August 1914 crisis had been surmounted by wiser decision makers, from this perspective the underlying international dynamics of national expansion were certain to create further crises. With such repeated crises, one was sure to escalate out of control. Thus, it is important to understand the great forces that regularly produce situations fraught with the threat of war rather than to understand the behavior of decision makers alone. Although they may be able to extricate themselves from one crisis, they cannot be expected to do so repeatedly in an environment where basic systemic forces continually produce crises.

One influence determining the level of analysis someone considers important is whether he or she is a scholar pursuing scientific inquiry or a policymaker faced with immediate decisions. This difference can be illustrated by comparing the situation of a medical researcher with that of a practicing physician. Research scientists, for example, have established a variety of personal characteristics and environmental conditions that contribute to heart disease. They now know that an individual's probability of suffering a severe heart attack is greater if that person is male and middle-aged or older and if one or both of the person's parents suffered heart attacks. Personal characteristics that affect the likelihood of heart disease include being overweight, smoking, a diet high in cholesterol-rich fats, and too little exercise. High blood pressure also contributes to this likelihood, as does stress and anxiety in working or living environments. Finally, some people with aggressive, hard-driving, energetic personalities are especially prone to heart disease. To a scientist, all these influences may seem interesting, providing information that may at some point be important.

---

9. Nazli Choucri and Robert North, *Nations in Conflict: National Growth and International Violence* (San Francisco: W. H. Freeman and Company, 1975), p. 9. See also Richard K. Ashley, *The Political Economy of War and Peace* (London: Frances Pinter, 1980).

For the physician who must treat patients, however, different influences are not of equal interest. Some are beyond the control of the individual patient or doctor: The patient cannot stop growing older, is probably unwilling to change sex, and can't change biological parents. A patient may be able to change his or her life-style somewhat or even to quit a stressful job, but most people cannot do much about their basic personality types. A doctor may actually raise the danger of heart attack by frightening an already worried or anxious patient. Other influences, however, can be more readily controlled. High blood pressure, for instance, can be reduced by medication. You can tell the patient to lose weight, stop smoking, change diet, or get more exercise, as appropriate. It may be enough to control just one of these conditions, especially if two contributing influences interact (if, for example, smoking and obesity together posed a much greater danger than either one alone). Or your scientific information may be that in a particular case heart disease is "overdetermined"; that is, any of several contributing conditions is sufficient to produce a high risk of disease and therefore all must be eliminated. Here, very careful theory, as well as detailed understanding of a particular case, is essential for responsible treatment. If your patients refuse to take any steps to reduce their risks, you can at least advise them to keep their life insurance paid up—prediction is of some value even without control over the medical events! Finally, some normative considerations may also apply. Suppose a particular patient also suffers from a painful variety of terminal cancer. Would it be right to save him from a heart attack only to succumb to cancer shortly thereafter? Neither doctor nor patient can be indifferent to such a question, whatever their answer.

Returning to our concern with world politics, we have to take into account many considerations similar to those facing the physician. At some times the student of world politics proceeds chiefly with the kind of concern typical of scientists and at other times with that typical of policymakers, policy advisers, or citizen activists. A scientist wants to understand the causes of a particular phenomenon; he or she hopes to find those influences or variables that make the greatest difference in the outcome of some dependent variable (in statistical terms, to find the variable or variables that will account for a large proportion of the variation or variance). Practitioners of "pure science" are not so readily concerned with whether that difference (variance) can actually be controlled in practice, that is, whether the explanatory variables are themselves readily manipulable by policymakers. Although a good scientist will have theoretically based reasons for expecting a particular variable or level of analysis to be especially powerful, in principle there should be no reason for preferring an explanation in terms of a particular variable or level. The first step is understanding and perhaps prediction. Of course, since any scientific endeavor is driven by ethical or value preferences, the scientist will care about finding practical means of making a difference (say, in promoting peace). But he or she will neither necessarily expect the immediate application demanded by a policymaker nor need to serve the bureaucratic or political interests that constrain a policymaker's choice of goals and instruments.

The policymaker, by contrast, is concerned with predicting phenomena, especially with an eye toward changing outcomes from what they might otherwise be. Insofar as the concern is with *prediction*, the policymaker, like the scientist, should not in principle care what variable emerges as a good predictor, provided that it is one on which complete and reliable information can be gathered. But for *changing* outcomes, the policymaker must identify not just powerful variables but also manipulable ones. Explanations that identify something controllable are more interesting to policymakers than those that identify broad historical forces over which the policymaker has little control. Manipulability is of prime interest, prediction next, and simple understanding of little import. In this way, the policymaker is likely to be much more interested in explanations about how a crisis can be resolved short of war than in knowing about forces that brought about the crisis. The policymaker may have little control over the latter or at least not be willing to exercise much control. The role of pure scientist may not be a popular one, even if such a scientist's findings are accepted.

Suppose we proved that large, bureaucratically unwieldy states are more war prone, that great powers with systemwide interests are more likely to be involved in world-endangering crises, that the dynamics of capitalism or communism produce expansionist, aggressive, and warprone behavior. Would a policymaker for such a government want to take the steps that would reduce the power of the state or fundamentally change its socioeconomic system even if the steps could be identified? An explanation of how decision makers perceive and act under crisis conditions may seem more interesting. The decision maker may in fact have little control over the external environment but may believe that it is possible to exert substantial influence over the crisis decision-making system and improve it. Even if the perception variable was relatively weak in explanatory power, it would be attractive because of its potential manipulability.

Most people who deal in world politics share elements of the perspectives we have characterized (in extreme form) as those of scientists and policymakers. They want to understand and to change. In the long run, even the givens of politics are subject to change: Systems decay; powers rise and fall. Sometimes they may be given a nudge by citizens who care enough. Even policymakers may try to change basic conditions of the international system, as did those Americans and Europeans who, in the decades after World War II, promoted European political and economic integration.

In this book we are attempting to offer some understanding of world political phenomena without necessarily providing readily manipulable levers to solve problems. We shall address basic questions about war, peace, and justice—problems that will be around for many decades and that will require concerted, long-term effort. We shall look at explanations of why wars occur, how crises can be managed to peaceful conclusions, and why crises arise at all. We shall look at arms races and why they can escalate or be restrained and at problems of economic and political interdependence between the rich industrialized countries of the world and how inflation or depression can spread and constrain national governments. We shall look at relations between rich and poor countries; from one perspective they are seen as questions of access to resources and of promoting growth in national income, and from another as questions of dependence, national autonomy, and internal distribution of economic and political rewards. We shall also look at problems of global resource availability and distribution, population pressures, pollution, and alleged "limits to growth." Some of these problems would have been in a textbook written twenty years ago; others are quite new. Part of the change may be attributed to very important changes in empirical reality, in the world around us. Global pollution, for example, certainly is far more threatening now than it was a few decades ago. Yet pollution has been carried across international borders for centuries (e.g., industrial pollutants swept down the Rhine River in Europe) without being considered a major political issue. Small countries have always been dependent on big ones, but theories about the causes and consequences of that dependence have become widely adopted only with the great increase in the numbers of politically sovereign states during the recent decades.

Thus, facts change, values change, problems change, and theories change. At a very basic level, we shall try to teach you how to think about political phenomena without referring to particular contemporary problems. Given a set of analytical tools to apply to new problems many years from now, you will have to search for your own manipulable levers—levers appropriate to your circumstances, your political resources, your understanding, and your values.

3

INTERNATIONAL ACTORS: STATES AND OTHER PLAYERS ON THE WORLD STAGE

HUMANS IN GROUPS: NATIONALISM AND THE NATION

Now that we have provided some basic conceptions of world politics and how it is studied, one further preliminary issue must be discussed: Exactly what sorts of entities are we concerned with and whose behavior interests us? We must start our discussion of the actors on the world stage at the most basic level. World politics begins with the idea of *relations*, activities between entities. We must start with the notion of humans forming *groups*. Perhaps one of the things that make us human is our need to affiliate into groups. One major contribution to our knowledge of humans that comes from *ethology*, the study of animal behavior, is that humans are social animals. Although people's evolutionary heritage provides them with the genetic material most open to the forces and influences of the environment, they also appear to *require* a *social environment* for the brain and for potential skills like speech and written communication to be realized. Human beings as animals (physical and physiological creatures) appear to require some culture or group.[1]

Throughout history, humans have formed into groups. The comfort, security, and other advantages that a group provides for its members are central to the study of sociology and psychology. Along with the idea of the group goes the idea of *identification*. Individuals will identify with groups, give their loyalty to those groups, and act to maintain the character, security, and survival of those groups. We can say that a group of individuals has developed a group identification and a group loyalty when a certain amount of "we-feeling" exists—when members of a certain group of people feel more like "we" than some "they." As we shall see, this notion underlies group identification from the smallest organizations to that of nation-states. In fact, nationalism can be seen as a group consciousness that serves to hold together the *largest* groupings of people that have ever formed.[2] When people identify with groups, they are cut off from those people not in those groups. Much of what occurs in world politics boils down to this separation of "we" and "they"—they are different, therefore they are not normal, and therefore they are inferior in some way, and so on. They always want something we have. Can they be trusted? What do they really want?

Group Identification

In discussing the nation-state, we have started with the idea of a *nation*, a people who feel themselves part of some large identity group. Historically, the process of nationalism occurred in Europe over a period of several hundred years prior to 1648, when the Treaty of Westphalia

---

1. There is quite an extensive body of writing on this fascinating subject. On this specific topic, the following would be useful reading: Lionel Tiger and Robin Fox, *The Imperial Animal* (New York: Dell, 1971); Desmond Morris, *The Human Zoo* (New York: Dell, 1970). In addition to these popularizations, see Fred H. Wilhoite, "Primates and Political Authority," *American Political Science Review* 70 (1976), 1110–1126; Robin Fox, "The Cultural Animal," in J. F. Eisenberg and W. S. Dillon (Eds.), *Man and Beast, Comparative Social Behavior* (Washington, D.C.: Smithsonian Institution Press, 1971); Steven Nelson, "Nature/Nurture Revisited," *Journal of Conflict Resolution* 18 (1974), 285–335; 19 (1975), 734–761. Perhaps the most controversial work in this vein is Edward O. Wilson's *Sociobiology* (Cambridge, Mass.: Belknap, 1975).

2. These ideas were developed in Karl Deutsch's classic work, *Nationalism and Social Communication* (Cambridge, Mass.: MIT Press, 1953).

was signed, ending the Thirty Years War of religion. Kings and princes extended their central authority over territories that had previously been a disconnected hodgepodge of feudal fiefdoms. This process continued throughout Europe until World War I, with groups that had identified themselves as a people seeking to govern and represent themselves through the medium of the legal, sovereign entity known as the state. This was the dominant process until the end of World War II, so we shall discuss nationalism and the nation first and then the concept of the state and the meaning of the "Westphalian state system." But even here it should be pointed out that this process may be reversed. As in the post–World War II system, it is possible to have states (in the contemporary system, states created from the Western colonial empires) that exist without a nation. The process in this situation then becomes one of creating a nation—a we-feeling—to match the already existing state, rather than a nation seeking to obtain its own state.

So far nationalism has been discussed only in terms of "we-ness"—a psychological phenomenon, a state of mind, a feeling of identification or loyalty to some group of people. Still, this is probably the crucial factor, that people *feel* American or Italian or Canadian or Rumanian or Cuban. A nation is a group of people who feel this way—but *why* do they feel this way? A number of factors have been identified. One factor is a common territory or regionalism. People living and interacting in the same area, facing similar problems and challenges, have often developed a common feeling and identity. Closely related to regionalism is the factor of common economic activities: relying on the same resources, engaging in the same types of activities, and having common sets of economic interactions. These all provide people with a similar view of the world and common interests.

A second set of factors is related to cultural similarity. A common language is seen as an extremely important aspect of nationalism. Indeed, political leaders have even attempted to increase national cohesion by reinstituting languages that have been dead or only very sparingly used. The resurrection of Welsh by nationalists in Wales is a partially successful attempt to use a language to reinforce or create nationalistic feelings, while the use of Hebrew in Israel quite successfully drew a diverse people together. Similar factors include a common religion, a common culture, a common set of social rules, and a common ethnic background. Finally, and maybe most importantly, is the existence of a set of historical experiences and backgrounds that are perceived as a common history. Indeed John Stoessinger in *The Might of Nations* defines nationalism as "a people's sense of collective destiny through a common past and the vision of a common future."[3]

We have here the psychological element that leads a people to desire the territorial and legal aspects of the state. Without this psychological element, any government would have difficulty in ruling a group of people occupying its territory. This element is so important that many conflicts in contemporary international politics arise from threats (or perceived threats) to group identification and loyalty. Many would explain the Soviet reaction to American pressure for increased Jewish emigration from the USSR on these grounds. The critical reaction to Vietnam war resisters in the United States stemmed largely from the psychological threat of challenging the solidarity of the national group and appearing disloyal to the group. The swift and often vicious reaction of governments all around the world to regional, tribal, and other autonomy movements is based on the fear of such disloyalty spreading to other parts of their populations.

States have fought very intense civil wars to hold themselves together. The Ibo rebellion and attempt to establish Biafra was defeated by the Nigerian government in a war that lasted from May 1967 to January 1970. However, in Pakistan the secession was successful. East Pakistan rose in riots and a general strike in March 1971 after being denied victory at the polls. Though sharing a common religion, East and West Pakistan differed in ethnicity, language, and economic factors and were separated by approximately 1,000 miles worth of India. West Pakistani armed attacks on the East Pakistanis (Bengalis) led to the December 1971 war between India and Pakistan. The Indian victory permitted the Bengalis to declare their own independent state, Bangladesh.

Fears of a breakdown in nationalism are not confined to the less developed states or only to those states formed since World War II. While Pakistan still worries about other groups such as the Baluchis, and Iran and Iraq have continuing problems with the Kurds, France has its problems with the Bretons and Corsicans, Spain with the Basques, Britain with the Welsh and the Scots, and Belgium tries to remain one country despite being pulled between the Flemings and the Walloons. Canada's handling of the French-Canadian movement for a free Quebec is a good example of how an old and developed state could

---

3. John Stoessinger, *The Might of Nations*, 6th ed. (New York: Random House, 1979), p. 10.

be broken apart and the dilemmas that a democracy faces in such a situation.

One problem we have in discussing nationalism, however, is that none of the factors mentioned seems to be sufficient by itself to create and maintain the psychological element of we-ness and the individual's supreme loyalty to the national group. Although language is important, several viable nation-states exist with multiple languages, such as Switzerland with four languages (French, German, Italian, and Romansch) or India with many regional languages in addition to Hindi and English. India is the home of fourteen major language groups and over 1,600 languages. Other nations have several major religions, such as Germany, Nigeria, and the United States. Other nations have many regional differences, cultures, and ethnic backgrounds.

Perhaps the closest we came to a sufficient condition is the existence of a common history, though it is not always clear why some experiences are perceived as shared and others as limited to a subgroup. Sharing common historical experiences receives great emphasis in many of the new states that have gained independence since World War II, where we have states attempting to forge nations. This process of nation building is required to provide the loyalty and legitimacy needed by any government if it is to maintain internal control and rule in an efficient and acceptable manner. In the nineteenth and early twentieth centuries, Germany and Italy were states that had been created by pre-existing nations. Such nations also fought for independence from the Austro-Hungarian and Ottoman empires. But in the post–World War II system, states with no logic beyond the arbitrary lines drawn on maps by colonial powers are split by diverse tribal, religious, ethnic, and racial groups and are struggling to forge group loyalty from this diversity. In 1972 one scholar noted that only 12 out of 132 states could be described as being ethnically homogeneous. In 53 states (over 40 percent of the sample examined), the population had been divided into five or more significant groups. A study of states in 1975 found that well over 40 states had separatist movements that comprised over 10 percent of the population.[4]

---

4. The first study was reported by Walker Connor, "Nation-Building or Nation-Destroying?", *World Politics* 24 (1972), 320. The other findings can be derived from Charles L. Taylor and David A. Jodice, *World Handbook of Political and Social Indicators*, 3rd ed., vol. 1 (New Haven: Yale University Press, 1983), pp. 72–73.

THE STATE AS INTERNATIONAL ACTOR

Despite a number of trends to the contrary, the state (or the nation-state) has been and remains the primary actor in the global system. The number of states in the system has risen steadily since the end of World War II. One indicator is the growth in the membership of the United Nations: in 1945, there were 51 charter members of the international organization; in September 1983, St. Kitts-Nevis became the 158th member. The addition of 107 new members exemplifies the continuing desire of groups to achieve statehood status in the contemporary system.

Although there have been large-scale political organizations for 7,000 years, starting with the city-states and empires of the Tigris and Euphrates and the Nile, the state or nation-state in its present form is relatively new. Many scholars date the modern nation-state from 1648 and the Treaty of Westphalia. Some argue that until that time European history reflected the politics and interactions of cultures, religions, and princes rather than states. However, the end of the Thirty Years War brought with it the end of the medieval Holy Roman Empire. Authority for choosing the religion of the political unit was given to the prince of that unit and not to the Hapsburg emperor or the pope. No longer could one pretend there was religious or political unity in Europe. Authority was dispersed to the various kings and princes, and the basis for the sovereign state was established.

We can now begin to answer the question of why the state was and is the main international actor. The myth of separate secular and spiritual entities disappeared, and the authority that had been vested in both was assumed by the state. Consequently, the international norms and laws that developed then provided the state a status not enjoyed by any other actor. Perhaps the operative word here is *law.* The state is a legal entity; it has been invested with a legal status and a legal equality with all other states, which have been denied other actors on the international or global scene. Like a corporation, the state has no concrete existence; it is a legal abstraction. Through its government, and the representatives of that government, the state undertakes legal commitments such as signing treaties, joining organizations, and the like.

The state is also permitted by international law to do certain things denied other actors. In much the same way as the government of a state assumes a monopoly on legitimate violence within its society (through control of the police and the armed forces), the state has been given a *legal monopoly on the use of force* in the global arena by international law. Piracy was considered illegal because it entailed the use of force and violence by an actor other than a state. When implemented by a state, force can be pinpointed, responsibility can be assigned, and other rules of conduct can be invoked. For example, until the creation of the League of Nations, international law was concerned with how states behaved during a special legal condition called war. This condition only existed between two equal units—equal in the legal sense of being sovereign states. Once this condition existed, belligerents were designated by a declaration of war and neutrals by declarations to that effect. Each category had rights and responsibilities of behavior to other states, given the status they had declared. The various strictures of international law were rarely seen to apply to peoples who were outside the system of states, such as aboriginal populations and non-European areas that were to be conquered, colonized, and dominated by the European nation-states.

The state, in addition to its legal status, had two other important characteristics: people and territory. The government of the state represents a group of people who, in turn, inhabit a piece of territory. Commentators who argue that the state is no longer dominant in the world system ignore the fact that every person lives on territory that is controlled (at least nominally) by a state. No other form of international actor controls territory, and all the territory of the world (even Antarctica) has been divided among the existing states.

Let us summarize the core of the concept of the nation-state: The state is a legal abstraction with institutions (the government) to control a territorial area and the people who reside in that territory. This control is aided by and dependent on the cement that holds the people together and gives them a loyalty to that government and state—nationalism. The control over people and territory, without any external authority to which to answer, culminated in the development of the concept of sovereignty. Beginning with the Treaty of Westphalia, the concept of sovereignty has been crucial to the development of the state as the central actor. Ideally, it means that a state has complete control over the people and territory represented by its government. Ideally, it also means there is external autonomy: *No authority exists to order the state how to act.* All states are legally equal, and there is no actor with the legitimate authority to tell a state what to do. In principle, this means there is a monopoly over the control of the means of force within the state; no other authority has a right to exercise force or maintain order within the territory of the state. All of these features, but especially sovereignty and territoriality, provide the state with major advantages over nonstate actors in the global arena.

It is important to note, however, that this system of sovereign states has other consequences for state behavior that will become clear when we discuss such topics as the world system, power and influence, deterrence and arms control, and a number of global economic and environmental problems. Sovereignty means that states exist in a formally anarchic environment. That is, no legitimate or legal authority is empowered to control, direct, or watch over the behavior of the states (as, for example, the federal government of the United States does over the fifty states of the union). One consequence of such a system of sovereign states is that each state must in the end look out for its own protection and survival. Self-help in the international system means that each state must take measures to provide for its own defense.

One of the tragic flaws of the formally anarchic state system is that the secure environments of the various states are mutually exclusive: one state's security may be seen and defined as another state's insecurity. The means by which one state prepares to defend its territory and people may be perceived as threatening to others—as offensive and not defensive. (What does American defense preparation look like to the Soviet Union? What does Soviet defense activity look like to the United States?) This is the security dilemma—the phenomenon of insecurity that is built into the system by both the lack of authority above the state and the security that all states seek.[5] The security dilemma is central to many aspects of interstate relations and will reappear in several different forms later on. How states cope with this condition and create some degree of order out of anarchy will also be addressed throughout this book.

NONSTATE ACTORS IN THE CONTEMPORARY SYSTEM

We have already noted that states are the central actors on the world stage. However, there are a variety of other, nonstate actors that are increasingly involved in the crucial issues of world politics. These intergovernmental and nongovernmental (or transnational) actors form an important part of the global environment. We noted in the first chapter

---

5. Two excellent discussions of anarchy, order, and the security dilemma are Hedley Bull, *The Anarchical Society* (London: Macmillan, 1977); Robert Jervis, "Cooperation Under the Security Dilemma," *World Politics* 30 (1978), 167–214. See also Oran Young, "Anarchy and Social Choice: Reflections on the International Polity," *World Politics* 30 (1978), 241–263.

that the simplest division of levels of analysis is between the world system and the state: Influences on foreign policy that originate outside the state and influences that originate within the state. Nonstate or transnational actors are considered here to be at the world system level of analysis, because they influence the external environment of states and affect the possibilities and probabilities of state actions.

In viewing world politics, the global system can be seen as a chessboard and the pieces that move about on it. Or it can be analyzed using billiard ball models of entities caroming off each other in their pursuit of various objectives. Or, waxing Shakespearean, the world can be considered a stage, and those groups, organizations, and perhaps even individuals who interact on it as actors. We have used this term throughout, and it might be useful to explain some of our reasons. First, the word *actor* conveys a broad spectrum of interacting entities; it is large enough to encompass all the entities we wish to study. Second, our emphasis is on behavior, since we study international relations or world politics. The term *actor* helps convey the idea of an entity that is behaving or performing an action. More importantly, as we discuss nonstate actors, the term also helps to convey the idea that different actors have different roles, that some occupy center stage and are stars while others are bit players in the chorus. Yet they all interact in creating the finished production.

An obvious question concerns the criteria required to be considered an international actor. One formula contains the following three elements: (1) The entity must perform significant and continuing functions—significant in the sense that it has a continuing impact on interstate relations; (2) the entity is considered significant by the foreign policy makers of nation-states and is given significance in the formation of states' foreign policies; and (3) the entity has some degree of autonomy or freedom in its own decision making.[6] These and other criteria define other actors in terms of the dominant actor: the state. An entity may be seen as an international actor if it is taken into account in the calculations and strategies of the leaders of states.

It is important to remember that any organized unit that commands the identification, interests, and loyalty of individuals and that affects interstate relations becomes a major competitor of nation-states. As we survey the types of nonstate actors that exist, think of the various conflicts you have read about in the news between international organiza-

---

6. See Carol Ann Cosgrove and Kenneth J. Twitchett (eds.), *The New International Actors: The UN and the EEC* (London: Macmillan, 1970), pp. 12–13.

tions and states (e.g., between the United Nations and South Africa or the Soviet Union or between NATO and France) or between nonstate groups such as the Palestine Liberation Organization (PLO) and Israel or the IRA and the United Kingdom. In almost every case, the conflict arises from either the international organization challenging or trying to reduce the scope of the sovereignty of a nation-state or from the nonstate actor trying to wrest territory and/or population from a state. The dramatic rise in international terrorism by a wide variety of nonstate groups is another example of this competition—groups other than states employing force and violence in the global system in a direct challenge to the monopoly of force that international law has always granted to states.

Intergovernmental Organizations

Let us investigate the other international actors in the contemporary global system. The first are called *international organizations* or *intergovernmental organizations* (IGOs). The IGO label is often used because it stresses the fact that such organizations, like the United Nations, are composed of states—that the individuals who are sent as representatives to such organizations represent the interests and policies of their own states. Quite often these organizations have permanent staffs at a permanent home base, so there are also individuals whose primary loyalty is to the IGO and not to their state of origin. Thus, in the Secretariat of the United Nations exists an international civil service of individuals who put the organization ahead of their states. Again, this may cause an atmosphere of competition between the IGO and the state over the loyalty of individuals. The case of Arkady Shevchenko is illustrative. In April 1978, Shevchenko, the Under Secretary General for Political and Security Council Affairs (a post traditionally filled by a Soviet citizen), resigned from the United Nations and opted to stay in the United States because of "serious differences of political philosophy and conviction with the present Soviet system." At one point he refused instructions to return to Moscow on the grounds that the Soviet government had "no right to give such instructions to an official of the [UN] Secretariat."

IGOs may be usefully categorized according to the scope of memberships and the scope of their purposes. On the one hand, we have universal political organizations such as the old League of Nations and the United Nations, which aim to include as wide an international membership as possible. Such organizations are also general purpose in that they perform political, economic, developmental, military, sociocultural, and other functions for member states. Other general purpose organizations have more limited memberships. These include organizations such as the North Atlantic Treaty Organization, the Organization of American States, the Organization of African Unity, and several others. The British Commonwealth is not regional in the sense of its membership being grouped in any one geographical area but is limited to former colonial holdings of the British Empire. As with the League and the United Nations, these organizations perform a variety of functions.

There are a significantly greater number of organizations that perform more specific functions, which may be called *functional IGOs* or *limited-purpose IGOs*. The number of such IGOs doubled from 1945 to 1969, with more than 220 such organizations in 1969 and 360 by 1983. The steady growth of both IGOs and nongovernmental organizations (discussed below) is shown graphically in Figures 3.1 and 3.2. Many of these IGOs are affiliated with the United Nations or are related to the European Community. Those connected to the UN often have universal membership or aim for it. Many more have limited regional membership. Some stress military functions, such as the Arab League, NATO, and the Warsaw Pact in their early days. Others are related to primarily economic matters, such as the various organs of the European Common Market (now known as the European Community) or other organizations such as the Central American Common Market, the Association of Southeast Asian Nations (ASEAN), or the Soviet-established Council for Mutual Economic Assistance (COMECON) in Eastern Europe. Others provide various social services such as WHO (the World Health Organization) or the International Labor Organization (ILO). Others are involved with monetary matters and economic development such as the International Monetary Fund (IMF) or the World Bank. The list becomes almost endless if we think of IGOs with even more specific functional activities, such as the International Statistical Institute, the International Bureau of Weights and Measures, the International Wool Study Group, or the Desert Locust Control Organization for East Africa.

Without going into great detail on the workings of the various IGOs, let us review them as international actors. First, they do have a significant and continuing impact on interstate relations. The international role of many IGOs is clearly institutionalized in that states expect them to act in certain areas—for example, they expect the United Nations to

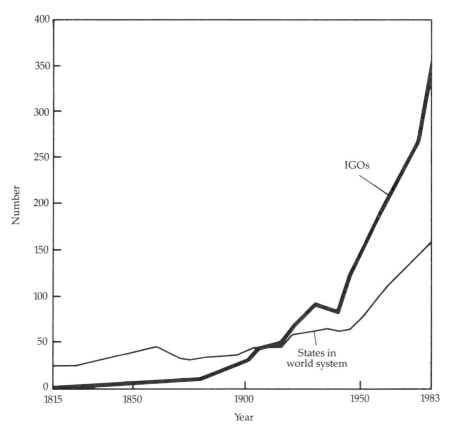

Figure 3.1
Growth in IGOs and states in the world system, 1815–1983. [Adapted from Michael Wallace and J. D. Singer, "Intergovernmental Organization in the Global System, 1816–1964: A Quantitative Description," *International Organization* 24 (Spring 1970), no. 2, p. 277.]

act in areas of perennial conflict, or they expected the Organization of African Unity (OAU) to act in Angola in 1976 or the Arab League to act in Lebanon in the late 1970s. When a state finds itself in serious economic trouble, it almost automatically looks to the World Bank or the International Monetary Fund for various kinds of aid. In addition, IGOs are actors in the sense that they continually affect the foreign policy behavior of their members, to the extent that member states join the organization and value the continuation of membership. Merely sending representatives to an organization, employing resources to maintain IGOs, or interacting with others through IGOs has an impact on the state. Perhaps most importantly, the IGOs may be considered ac-

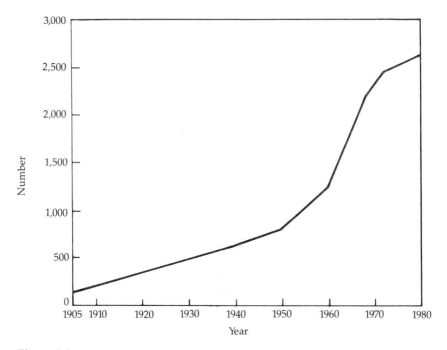

Figure 3.2
Number of international nongovernmental organizations (NGOs) in the world system, 1905–1980. [From Professor Robert C. Angell.]

tors because states and leaders believe that IGOs are behaving as international actors and must be taken into account in foreign policy deliberations. They are seen to affect where and how states interact.

IGOs have this effect in several ways. Most clearly seen in the United Nations, but common to many other IGOs, is the IGO function of acting as a forum for the member states to meet and communicate. The IGO may act passively as a line of communication or a meeting place or actively as a mediator. In a more active manner, IGOs perform a number of regulative functions across such areas as economics, health, communication, and transportation; examples range from the African Postal Union to the International Atomic Energy Agency. Here IGOs, with the consent of member states, regulate how members should interact to function smoothly, efficiently, and beneficially in the regulated area.

However, some IGOs also have distributive functions—distributing benefits and costs among states. Although organizations such as the World Bank spring most readily to mind, others such as the International Court of Justice, which dispenses legal decisions, are equally distributive. In these cases, states must take into consideration the pre-dispositions and power of the permanent staff of the pertinent IGO, which will decide how to distribute the costs and benefits that it has at its disposal.

Taking the distributive function a step further, a very small number of IGOs may be termed *supranational;* these have the power to make decisions that are binding on their members even if some members disagree. These IGOs can indeed take aspects of members' sovereignty away from them. Various organs of the European Community have such power and are the only true supranational IGOs in existence today.

Nongovernmental Organizations

IGOs, however, are not the only nonstate actors that have an impact on states, that states must take into account, and that constrain the range of state behavior. While IGOs are organizations composed of states, there are also a large number of organizations that are private interna-tional actors—nonstate, *nongovernmental organizations* (NGOs). The im-portant distinction regards membership: The members of NGOs are *not* representatives of the governments of states. They are organizations that cut across national boundaries and are made up of individuals or national groups, not official representatives of national governments. Many organizations come from below the level of state governments, either within a single country or from international nongovernmental organizations. International nongovernmental organizations are now very numerous, having increased from 134 in the year 1905 to 2,470 in 1972, and, according to one count, to over 4,700 by 1983. Like the IGOs, they deal with a great variety of matters. There are religious bodies, professional organizations, sports organizations, trade union groups, and political parties. Their membership may be composed either di-rectly of individuals (e.g., the International Political Science Associa-tion) or of various national societies, which themselves are composed of individuals.

Most often these organizations perform rather low-level tasks, pro-moting contact across state boundaries on matters of common interest and providing nongovernmental means of communication between individuals of many nations. NGOs help knit the global society to-gether in much the same way that private groups do within a state, although their total membership as a portion of the world's population is only a fraction of the comparable proportion of interest group members within an economically developed democracy. Sometimes they can function as pressure groups affecting national governments or international organizations. One example was the reaction of the International Civil Aviation Organization to the shooting down of a Korean Airlines plane by the Soviet Union in September, 1983. A great many NGOs are formally consulted by the international organizations concerned with their problems (such as health and medical organizations who are consulted by the World Health Organization). Some NGOs, such as the Catholic Church or, most strikingly, the Communist International, exert very important influences on the foreign policies of various states. Still, their political focus is usually on national governments, and they are effective through changing government policy rather than through direct action. Much of the same is true for purely *subnational* (as contrasted with international) organizations. The role of interest or pressure groups in foreign policy formation hardly needs emphasis, but only in rare instances (the Palestine Liberation Organization is one) do NGOs act directly, without the intermediary instrument of a national government. At the very lowest level, there are, of course, individuals. But individuals are virtually powerless in international politics except when they can, through an official or unofficial role, affect the policy of a government. For all their skills and charm, neither Lyndon Johnson nor Richard Nixon would have had much influence on global affairs as mere private citizens.

Multinational Corporations One important exception to this relative powerlessness of nonnational groups is the *multinational corporation* (MNC). There are at least 7,000 business corporations with subsidiaries in other countries; the number of subsidiaries runs to more than 26,000. The number and importance of MNCs has grown enormously in recent years. A selected group of 187 U.S. corporations owned a total of 107 foreign subsidiaries in 1901; by 1967, those same 187 firms owned nearly 8,000 subsidiaries. At least 42 of the corporations headquartered in the United States or Western Europe now have 30 or more foreign subsidiaries. Direct U.S. foreign investments were worth $65 billion in 1968 (or about twice the value of American earnings from imports), jumping to over $220 billion by 1982. The foreign sales of General Motors were roughly $4 billion in 1967, but over $16 billion by 1980. By 1980 the 350 largest MNCs had 25,000 foreign subsidiaries and a combined gross sales of $2.6 trillion, and they employed 25 million people. Clearly, giant corporations like these cannot help but affect the policies of many governments and the welfare of many people.[7] The oil companies, for instance, would still have tremendous impact with their pricing and marketing policies even if they did not try to change the policy or personnel of national governments. MNCs, in many ways, have emerged as one of the major competitors to the nation-state. While nonstate liberation groups, such as the IRA and the PLO, and the separatist groups, such as the Basques in Spain and the Quebecois in Canada, have challenged the military and political authority of specific nation-states, the MNC is a much more broad-based and subtle competitor.

Many multinationals predate the states that have been created since the end of World War II. MNCs also have their own spheres of influence through the division of world markets. They often engage in diplomacy and espionage, traditional tools of state interaction. Most importantly, MNCs have very large economic resources at their disposal, which give them an advantage over not only many of the newer and smaller states but also some of the older ones. For example, in 1980 Exxon Corporation had gross sales larger than the GNP of Switzerland and only slightly less than the GNP of Sweden. General Motors had gross sales exceeding the GNP of South Korea. Of course, GNP and gross sales are not directly comparable accounting terms; the most accurate comparison would be between GNP and "value added" by the corporation. Nevertheless, the comparison still suggests how very large some modern multinational corporations are compared with the often small, underdeveloped states with which they deal.

Nation-State Versus Nonstate Loyalty

Although there are competitors to the nation-state, some very formidable in special ways, the state continues on the whole to enjoy great advantages over the other international actors. In addition to the legal status of formal sovereignty, the state generally also possesses demographic, economic, military, and geographical capabilities unmatched

---

7. For further descriptive data, see George Modelski, "International Content and Performance among the World's Largest Corporations," in George Modelski (ed.), *Transnational Corporations and World Order* (San Francisco: W. H. Freeman and Company, 1979), pp. 45–65. Other sections of this book contain articles on effects of multinationals in the system, as well as on the regulation and future of multinationals. Similar, more recent material may be found in *Transnational Corporations in World Development, Third Survey* (New York: United Nations Centre on Transnational Corporations, 1983).

by other actors. Some IGOs or multinational corporations command the loyalty of some individuals, but the nation-state commands the loyalty of very large numbers of individuals through nationalism. One clear ramification of the combination of the nation with the state (which is what nonstate actors such as the PLO or the Basques attempt) is that the state comes to embody the nation and all it stands for through nationalism. That is, the government of the state is seen by the people as representing and protecting cultural values as well as history and tradition. Combined with the idea of sovereignty, this relationship is a powerful force indeed—a force that can rarely be matched by nonstate actors. Before the outbreak of World War I, the socialist parties of Europe, meeting together under the aegis of the Second International, called for loyalty to the proletariat and a refusal by workers anywhere in Europe to take up arms against other workers in the event of war. Here was a direct clash between an NGO and the states of Europe—a competition for the loyalty of the workers within the various European countries, especially Germany, France, and Britain. When the war came and choices had to be made, the workers rallied to the nationalist standards of their respective states and not to the Red Flag for a variety of reasons.

Nonstate actors also lack the territoriality of states, and this lack may be crucial. In his discussion of the territorial state, political scientist John Herz noted that, "Throughout history that unit which affords protection and security to human beings has tended to become the basic political unit."[8] The main factor in people's acceptance of authority and form of organization was the power of protection that states afforded. The basis of the state, argues Herz, was its ability to protect people through its size—its physical territory, which created a "hard shell" around the population in an era of gunpowder and the professional armies of centralized monarchs. Although nuclear weapons and modern delivery systems make the hard shell of the state obsolete, the territoriality of the state still protects the citizens of most states from most conflicts with other states.

Two concluding, if somewhat contradictory, comments are in order. The first is that states possess, in general, a far wider range of capabilities than do nonstate actors and thus have a much larger and more varied menu. Although there has been a tremendous growth in both

---

8. See "Rise and Demise of the Territorial State," *World Politics* 9 (1957), 473–493, as well as Herz's rethinking on the subject, "The Territorial State Revisited—Reflections on the Future of the Nation-State," *Polity* 1 (1968), 11–34.

IGOs and NGOs and the transnational interactions between them (and states), it is apparent that the nonstate interactions reflect the structure and distribution of power of the states in the global system and that the growth of nonstate activity both has mirrored and derived from the expansion of the state system itself in the postwar period.[9]

The second point, however, is simply that IGOs and NGOs exist: They are given attention by states, are components of the international or global environment that influence the state, and thus indeed affect the menu of constraints, possibilities, and probabilities of nation-states. Simply saying that the state remains the dominant actor does not mean it is the only international actor of interest or that it cannot be affected in crucial ways by other nonstate actors.

ALL STATES ARE LEGALLY EQUAL (BUT SOME ARE MORE EQUAL THAN OTHERS)

All states are juridically equal, but in practice some are more equal than others. One of the truisms in world politics is that nothing is distributed equally on the face of the globe—not people or their talents, not resources, not even climate, geographical features, technology, or air quality. In fact, many things are distributed in a most unequal manner. Nation-states are so different from each other in resources, capabilities, available menus, and their ability to exploit and choose from those menus that some observers find it difficult to call all of these units states. Thus, this section will outline some of the basic characteristics of states in order to indicate the extent of their differences.

All states are formally sovereign; they have achieved independent state status, and most have sought UN membership as an entrance ticket into world society. Even the smallest units have resisted pressures to continue as clients, colonies, or satellites to a larger state. We are faced, then, with the continued resurgence of nationalism and the nation-state in a world where the hard shell is eroding for many states

---

9. There is even some evidence that transnational actor activity has declined between 1948 and 1972. See the data presented in R. W. Mansbach, Y. H. Ferguson, and D. E. Lampert, *The Web of World Politics* (Englewood Cliffs, N.J.: Prentice-Hall, 1976), discussed by Michael Sullivan in "Competing Frameworks and the Study of Contemporary International Politics," *Millennium* 7 (1978), 93–110. The general arguments here are also expanded by R. Little and R. D. McKinley, "Linkage-Responsiveness and the Modern State: An Alternative View of Interdependence," *British Journal of International Studies* 4 (1978), 209–225.

and can hardly be seen to exist for the smaller members of the international community. One observer notes that

> sovereignty is the "Dracula" of international relations. It exists like a shapeless form with its origins in the medieval period. Just when rational men—scholars, idealists, even some politicians—declare its non-existence or its demise, a trickle of blood from the body politic will land on the Transylvanian sarcophagus and, lo and behold, sovereignty has risen from the dead and is alive and well in New York or London or Kampala. Those bitten by its fangs will join the select group of sovereign states and however weak their body, however lacking in the sinew needed for a modern industrial state, they still join the band of the living dead.[10]

The question of the relationship between small and large states has been a perennial one. Although there are any number of ways to divide states—to categorize and classify them—one division has always existed and been used in the interactions between states: a status hierarchy of size and power. We may always find large and small units, the strong and the weak, the influential and the ineffectual. Bruce Russett has studied the population of states through history to see if there were any trends toward states becoming larger or smaller. In fact, there has long been great disparity between the big and the small; the largest states of today are proportionately neither larger nor smaller than they were 2,000 years ago.[11] In Chapter 6 we shall discuss in detail the concepts of power and influence and the ways in which states attempt to exert their power and influence on others. The remainder of this chapter will deal with various measures of capabilities and characteristics of states.

As we noted, despite the fact of formal legal equality, states are unequal in all other respects. The British diplomat Paul Gore-Booth reminds us that, similar to the debates that occurred at the Constitutional Convention in Philadelphia over the representation of states in the American Congress, the major conflicts in setting up the United Nations were over size: "The basic argument in 1944–45 was not between the Russians and the Western Allies, although there were crises in that field too. It was between the big powers and the rest." The small

---

10. Dr. T. Clive Archer, University of Aberdeen, lecture, April 1979.

11. Bruce M. Russett, "Is There a Long-Run Trend toward Concentration in the International System?", in B. M. Russett, *Power and Community in World Politics* (San Francisco: W. H. Freeman and Company, 1974), pp. 122–138.

countries "contested very strongly any departure from the principle of one country one vote."[12]

Yet countries have been divided into many different categories. For years we simply had the first (the industrialized Western democracies), the second (the Communist bloc of Eastern Europe), and third worlds (everyone else). More recently, people have come to talk of the fourth and fifth worlds, labels based on levels of gross national product (GNP) per capita and the oil-producing capacities of states formerly classified as third world members. Additionally, observers now speak of "microstates," the very smallest of contemporary states (there is no agreement on how small a state must be to be called a microstate). In the mid-1970s the World Bank used five categories of states, based on various measures of economic size, development, and structure: low-income countries (income per capita less than $250), middle-income countries, industrialized countries, surplus-oil countries, and centrally planned countries. By the early 1980s the World Bank had revised its categorization as follows: low-income, middle-income oil importer, middle-income oil exporter, high-income oil exporter, and industrial. Some of the characteristics of these groups are presented in Table 3.1.

Table 3.1

World Bank's categories of states.

Countries	Population, 1980 (millions)	Average annual growth in GNP, 1973–1980 (%)	GNP per capita, 1980 (U.S.$)
Low income	2,174	5.1	250
Middle-income oil importer	640	5.2	1,562
Middle-income oil exporter	494	4.0	1,391
High-income oil exporter[a]	16	7.5	13,836
Industrial	715	2.5	10,340

Source: The World Bank Annual Report 1983 (Washington, D.C.: World Bank, 1983).
   [a]Includes Bahrain, Brunei, Kuwait, Libya, Oman, Qatar, Saudi Arabia, and the United Arab Emirates.

---

12. Paul Gore-Booth, *With Great Truth and Respect* (London: Constable, 1974), pp. 133–134.

Measures of Size

Notice from the above discussion that there seems to be no agreement on what makes a large or small nation-state. The United Nations Institute for Training and Research (UNITAR), in a study of microstates, used three variables to measure size—area, population, and GNP—which are quite basic concepts to most discussions of size, power, or status. Even those scholars who stress the perceptual aspects of smallness or largeness agree that the basic dimensions of power are territorial, demographic, economic, and military—and that a state's self-perception and the ways in which others view it are based to a large extent on its rankings along these dimensions.[13] Any map shows the disparity in geographical size among the world's states. The largest is the Soviet Union, with over 8.6 million square miles, or 17 percent of the world's total. Canada (3.8 million square miles) and the People's Republic of China (3.7 million square miles) comprise about 8 percent of the world's total each. The United States, the world's fourth largest state, covers 3.6 million square miles, 7 percent of the world's total. Britain and France, however, still thought of as major powers, cover only 94,000 and 213,000 square miles, respectively. Although a number of microstates, such as Barbados, Grenada, Malta, the Maldives, and the Seychelles, are in the 100-square-mile range, they are still giants compared to Liechtenstein's 62 square miles or Nauru's 8 square miles. Keep in mind also the existence of units such as Monaco (370 acres), San Marino (24 acres), or the Vatican (190 acres), which, though not nation-states in the sense of the others, are indeed international actors of a sort.

Just as we can map the geographical size of nation-states, we can also present graphically the relative size of states on other dimensions. Compare the physical size of nations to their size according to population, GNP, and energy consumption, as presented in the cartograms in Figure 3.3.

The disparity in population is as vast as that in land area. China, the Soviet Union, and the United States are again among the top four in population. China is the most populous nation on earth, with a 1980 population of over one billion people. India is ranked second with almost 700 million. The Soviet Union is a distant third with a popula-

---

13. An excellent review of small-state definitions and models may be found in Niels Amstrup, "The Perennial Problem of Small States: A Survey of Research Efforts," *Cooperation and Conflict* 11 (1976), 163–182.

Countries according to population

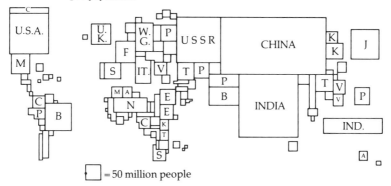

= 50 million people

Countries according to GNP

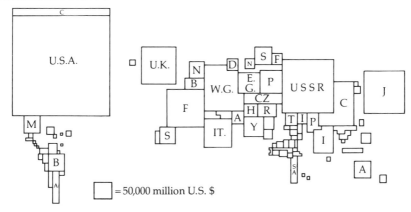

= 50,000 million U.S. $

Countries according to energy consumption

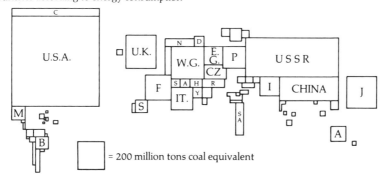

= 200 million tons coal equivalent

Figure 3.3
Cartograms of the world distribution of population, GNP, and energy consumption. [From *Oosthoek-Times Wereldatlas* (Times Newspapers Ltd./Kluwer, 1973, pp. 21, 24). Reprinted in Jan Tinbergen, *RIO: Reshaping the International Order* (London: Hutchinson, 1977), p. 20.]

tion of 265 million, and the United States is in fourth position with 228 million. Other states topping the 100-million mark are Brazil, Indonesia, and Japan. Britain had a population of 56 million in 1980, and France 54 million. At the other end of the scale, several dozen countries have less than one million people. Nauru has approximately 8,000 people—and had only around 6,000 when it became independent in 1968. Liechtenstein, which was admitted as the twenty-first member of the Council of Europe in September 1978, had a population of 24,000 at the time (and about 26,000 in 1982). A number of other states have less than 100,000 people, including the Seychelles with 67,000 people, the least populous member of the United Nations.

As Figure 3.3 indicates, similar disparities exist in GNP and energy consumption. Economic performance, economic size, and level of economic development are all concepts that people have tried to measure through GNP. Many observers, like the World Bank, have looked at the global system and categorized or ranked states on the basis of economic size. Economic performance is a good indicator of how well any state has mobilized and used its natural and human resources. Economic performance also provides a clue to the ability of a state to turn resources into military capabilities and the ability of that state to exploit its menu in general.

At one extreme of total national income we again find the United States, with a GNP of well over $2.5 trillion in 1980. By itself, the United States accounts for over one fifth of *all* the goods and services produced on the earth. A distant second is the Soviet Union, with a GNP of around $1.2 trillion, followed by Japan with a GNP of slightly over $1 trillion. West Germany leads Western Europe with $825 billion; France, $654 billion; and Britain, $516 billion. The top four nations— the United States, the USSR, Japan, and West Germany—represent almost half of the world's total GNP. The other 50 percent is distributed among all the other states of the world. Of those states, about two dozen still have an annual GNP of less than $1 billion, and some have yet to break the $200 million mark, such as Gambia or Equatorial Guinea (look ahead to Appendix B). The United States' GNP is almost 17,000 times as large as that of Equatorial Guinea!

Another way to compare GNP is to control for population and look at the GNP per capita (or income of the average person) for the various nation-states. When we do this, we find that the United States ranked only sixteenth in 1980, with a GNP per capita of $11,347. The leaders belong to that category called high-income oil exporters by the World Bank. With a small population and oil reserves generating great wealth, Qatar led the world in 1980 with a per capita GNP of over $28,000; in second was the United Arab Emirates with just under $28,000, and Kuwait was third ($24,400). Two small but industrialized and wealthy European nations were ranked fourth and fifth—Switzerland at $16,200 and Luxembourg at $14,300. At the same time, however, there are at least a dozen countries with a per capita GNP of $200 or less (with Laos under $100!). In some cases we have a tragic combination of a large population and a poor economic performance—for example, Bangladesh. Other countries with low GNPs per capita are Ethiopia, Mali, Chad, Burma, Nepal, and Vietnam.

Capabilities Cube Population, territory, and GNP are all basic indicators of the capabilities and potential of states. It is possible to create a capabilities cube to illustrate the relationship and distance between states high in these capabilities and those that are low. Figure 3.4 is such a cube. The upper left-hand corner contains the "superpowers"—states such as the United States and the USSR, which rank at the top in all

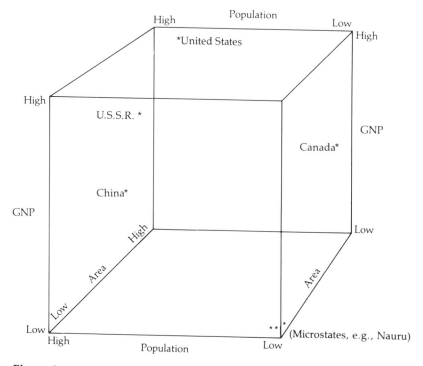

Figure 3.4
The "capabilities cube."

three categories. The lower right-hand corner contains microstates, such as Nauru, which rank at the bottom in these categories.

Another way in which to indicate the large differences that exist between the major powers and the rest of the nations is Table 3.2, which gives the "weight" of the great powers. Here, capabilities of the five great powers in the postwar period are summed and shown as a percentage of the total world capabilities for that year. As is the general practice, the list of great powers is comprised of the United States, the USSR, China, Britain, and France. Note also that these five are the only states with operational nuclear capabilities (India exploded a "nuclear device" in 1974). Table 3.2 also lists military expenditures. The military dimension is a most important aspect of the capabilities of states. Many indicators of this dimension can be investigated. In terms of people under arms, China, the Soviet Union, and the United States have millions—others, such as Iceland and some black African states, have no armies at all. One might also wish to count specific items in the arsenals of states, such as nuclear delivery systems, bombers, supersonic fighters, tanks, and so on. A useful summary measure that takes many of these things into account is defense expenditure. The Soviet Union and United States again far outdistance the rest of the world, spending over $130 billion annually on the military. China is a distant third at $28 billion, followed by West Germany, France, and Britain each spending about $26 billion.

Table 3.2
Major powers and the international system, 1950, 1965, 1980.

	1950		1965		1980	
	World	Major powers	World	Major powers	World	Major powers
Population (millions)	2,517	966 (39%)	3,276	1,229 (38%)	4,468	1,610 (36%)
GNP (billion U.S.$)	778	464 (60%)	2,135	1,278 (61%)	11,670	5,266 (45%)
Military spending (billion U.S.$)	47	38 (81%)	127	97 (76%)	543	355 (65%)

Sources: George Modelski and Robert Benedict, "Structural Trends in World Politics," *Comparative Politics* 6 (January 1974), 296; Charles L. Taylor and Michael C. Hudson, *World Handbook of Political and Social Indicators*, 2nd ed. (New Haven, Conn.: Yale University Press, 1972); Appendix B.
Notes: Major powers are the United States, the USSR, China, Britain, and France. Figures in parentheses represent the percentage of the major powers' share of the respective world figure.

The list of differences among nation-states could be expanded almost unendingly, particularly differences in living standards. We shall present that material in Appendix B, where data from several sources on national resources are reproduced. You should take some time looking over this comparative data. Simply looking at the United States, at the "best" and at the "worst," can indicate fairly well the range of differences in living standards and thus the potential and capabilities of the populations of the various states. For example, a number of developed Western countries have raised life expectancy into the mid-seventies: The United States in 1980 was ranked eighth, along with several other countries, with a life expectancy of 74; Iceland ranked first at 76. At the other end, Afghanistan, Cambodia, and Ethiopia had a life expectancy of forty years, only a little better than half that of the developed countries. Similarly, Denmark, Iceland, and Norway had the lowest death rate for infants (under a year old), with eight deaths for every 1,000 live births. However, in Cambodia, 212 infants die of every 1,000 born—twenty-six times the rate of infant deaths in the three Scandinavian countries. This discrepancy is related to factors such as the number of people per physician and the number of people per hospital bed. The United States ranks only twenty-sixth in the former measure, having 550 people per physician. Here, the USSR is first, with 270 people per physician, compared with Ethiopia, which ranks last with 69,600 people per doctor. The United States comes in only thirty-fourth in population per hospital bed, with 171; Iceland is first with 61, and Nepal ranks last with 5,865.

With well over half of the states in the world becoming independent since World War II, the United States (often thought of as a newcomer or young state), with its bicentennial in 1976, is rather ancient. The developed Western countries have more than two thirds of their populations living in urban areas; in the less-developed countries of black Africa, the comparable figure is around a quarter of the population or less. Yet another difference is racial composition. Only thirty-four countries, or less than a quarter of the international system, are composed predominantly of people of European origin. Roughly twenty countries are of mixed populations, largely Indian and Negro in Latin America. More than half are overwhelmingly of Asian or African peoples. Europeans' perspectives are therefore really very parochial. The majority of states in the world—and this means the majority of governments, prime ministers, and foreign offices—are very unlike those of Europe. They are recent ex-colonies, nonwhite, poor, and weak by most of the standard measures of national power. Also, parliamentary democracy on the Western model is a form of government found only in a small minority of cases. To comprehend international politics, we must have at least some awareness of these differences. We must also be aware of the differences among these ex-colonial, nonwhite, poor, and weak states. Their histories, perspectives, and goals vary enormously even among themselves and defy simple categorization. Different cultures, national experiences, governmental structures, or even different electoral systems may be highly relevant to particular circumstances or how governments behave on certain international issues.

MICROSTATES, SOVEREIGNTY, AND THE STATE OF STATES

Clearly the range of capabilities across state units is enormous. What states are capable of achieving—not only internally in regard to living standards but also externally in regard to foreign policy behavior—also varies greatly. Although all states are formally sovereign, it is also clear that many cannot exercise complete or even substantial control over their boundaries, territory, or population. No official authority controls states in the contemporary world system, but many are subject to powerful unofficial forces, pressures, and influences that penetrate the supposed hard shell of the state (as shall be discussed further in Chapter 6 and in detail in Chapters 16 and 17). This is especially true for the smallest of states, the microstates.

As stated earlier, there is no agreement about what makes up a microstate. Although it is easy to describe the vast differences in capabilities between the strongest and the weakest states in the world system, it is more difficult to draw a line between weak states, small or minor powers, and microstates. Most observers employ some measure of population as a cut-off point for microstates, such as one million or two million. International organizations have had to grapple with similar problems of categorization and status. Several years ago, with the membership applications of smaller and smaller units, the United Nations raised the possibility of a secondary status for certain small members. This issue raised such a cluster of problems, however, that it was soon dropped. The same issue arose in the Council of Europe, one of the first organizations formed in postwar Europe to deal with questions of common concern in political, social, legal, and economic matters. When Liechtenstein entered the council in 1978, a British representative warned, "If we let Liechtenstein join, we may face similar demands from other microstates like Monaco, the Faroe Islands, Guernsey, San Marino and all sorts of others."[14] More importantly, some members warned that if such microunits were to apply, the council might have to raise the whole question of what a state is!

As was noted at the time, Liechtenstein's application was mainly for prestige, but it is this same desire for the prestige and status of legal statehood that is fostering the declarations of independence of the smallest states and the breakup of many postcolonial federations, particularly island groups in the Caribbean and the islands of Oceania. Each new unit seeks UN membership to legitimize it among the community of nations. Though subject to a variety of pressures and hampered by a lack of resources in foreign policy, the microstate in the United Nations enjoys the same rights, privileges, and duties as the superpowers, particularly in terms of voting in the General Assembly and other UN bodies. The following quotation from former American diplomat George Kennan presents an extreme view of the negative impact of giving "state" status and UN membership to the microstates:

> Aside from bloating the various diplomatic corps across the world, this reckless squandering of the recognized status of unlimited sovereignty and independence has watered down the meaning of those very concepts. It has made a mockery of the fundamental principles of international organization, and has greatly reduced the usefulness of international entities—notably those of the UN and its associated agencies— which were set up to perform important and potentially constructive purposes. This prodigal scattering of the status of sovereign independence has led to the establishment, within a number of UN bodies (UNESCO, the ILO, and the World Health Organization are examples, but the outstanding one is of course the UN Assembly itself) of majorities, the irresponsibility and emotional instability of which is such that the potential value of the organizations in question has been seriously reduced.[15]

Nonetheless, the trend appears to be the creation of even more state units in the future. Along with a growing observance of international norms that outlaw war, especially by the strong against the weak, there is the phenomenon of "muscle-bound" nuclear superpowers. This is a world where there are two superpowers. Each attempts to deter the other from the capricious use of force outside of their own recognized

14. *International Herald-Tribune* (September 30, 1978).

15. George Kennan, *The Cloud of Danger* (London: Hutchinson, 1978), p. 30.

sphere of influence and to deter the other from nuclear blackmail of lesser military powers. Under these conditions, small states are generally free from such blatant actions as military takeovers by larger states or nuclear blackmail. In addition, the potential ruling elites seek the status and prestige of statehood, and, in so doing, the chance to have a country of their own to govern.

4

THE WORLD SYSTEM:
HOW IT CONSTRAINS BEHAVIOR

THE INTERNATIONAL ENVIRONMENT

Starting with the international system level of analysis, we have the most general picture of world politics, since the international environment surrounds nation-states and their foreign policy makers. It therefore provides a crucial component to the menu from which states and decision makers choose their behavior. How exactly does the international environment affect the menu? How does it affect what is possible and probable in state behavior?

The Location of States

Any nation-state exists within the context of many other states and other international actors. All of these actors are arranged in the international system in various ways. Some are large and some are small;

some possess great military and economic capabilities and others do not; some control important natural resources and others do not. The arrangement of states includes their political-geographical arrangement as well. First, this means that we care about the physical location of states; for example, China and the Soviet Union share thousands of miles of common land border, while the United States has a common land border with neither; Britain and Japan are islands off continents, while France and Germany touch many other states because they are continental states. In addition, some states are distant from the centers of international activity; Australia, for example, is at the periphery of international interaction. On the other hand, some states are located along historical trade routes or paths of invasion; such states include Egypt, Israel, and even Afghanistan.

The political-geographical arrangement includes not only geographical location (the sort of information provided by the maps at the front and rear of this book) but also topographical features. While states are concerned with and affected by their neighbors—how many there are, how close or how far (and how big or small)—they are also concerned with the features of land and sea. Being an island or a continental power; being at the end of a peninsula or at the center of a continental landmass; having long shorelines and good ports or being landlocked; having mountains, deserts, rivers, swamps, or other natural barriers as borders; or having open flat plains—all will affect the menu of a particular state. The arrangement of these physical features will limit the possibilities and probabilities of communication and transportation—the transportation of both economic goods and military capabilites.

The physical arrangement of the international environment also includes less obvious features. Useful natural resources are also unevenly distributed. These include potable water and arable land, as well as forests, animal life, and mineral resources. Usefulness is an important qualifying idea, since what is useful and what is irrelevant change over time: States that possessed uranium in the nineteenth century did not gain by it in either wealth or influence. Finally, climate varies across the globe. As parts of the physical arrangement and environment of all states, all of these factors affect opportunities for state interaction. Just as we can think of a chessboard (or any other gameboard) as influencing the possibilities and probabilities of movement by the pieces on the board, the international system also affects the behavior of states. The choices or options provided to states—what is possible or allowable to states and what is not—are all influenced by the international gameboard.

Location strongly affects interaction: States tend to get into wars more often with neighbors because they interact more with countries close by than with those far away.[1] One theory of the relationship between the closeness of states and their opportunities for interaction is that of Kenneth E. Boulding.[2] Boulding developed a "theory of viability" whereby any state's power is greatest at home but then declines along a "loss of strength gradient" as the distance from home is increased. This occurs because of the increases in the time and cost of transporting one's power. Because of this, Boulding asserts the axiom of "the further the weaker." We see then, that a state should be most concerned with its immediate neighbors and less concerned with those far away. Indeed, except for the interactions of and with some major powers, this is the case.

TECHNOLOGY AND THE INTERNATIONAL ENVIRONMENT

At any particular time, decision makers of a state are faced with a number of givens such as geography, the arrangement of neighbors, and distant states. Another one of these givens is the existing technology in the international system. As we noted when discussing opportunity in the last chapter, technology plays a major part in what is physically possible (Alexander could not communicate instantaneously with Darius, as could Nixon and Brezhnev during the 1973 Yom Kipper war crisis).

If we follow the definition provided by the Sprouts, technology is the application of human skills or techniques to accomplish human purposes.[3] Creative genius has continually led people to develop new technologies to overcome space and time, to generate power for economic and military purposes, to communicate and transport ideas and objects. Obstacles such as mountains, deserts, or distance are overcome by inventions such as the railroad, the automobile, or the airplane. Obstacles to the spread of ideas and ideologies have been overcome by the development of radio, television, and communications satellites,

---

1. For evidence of this effect, see Harvey Starr and Benjamin Most, "The Substance and Study of Borders in International Relations Research," *International Studies Quarterly* 20 (December 1976), 581–620; Starr and Most, "A Return Journey: Richardson, 'Frontiers and Wars in the 1946–65 Era,' *Journal of Conflict Resolution* 22 (September 1978), 441–467.

2. Kenneth E. Boulding, *Conflict and Defense* (New York: Harper & Row, 1962), chap. 4.

3. Harold and Margaret Sprout, *Towards a Politics of the Planet Earth* (New York: Van Nostrand Reinhold, 1971).

which bring events from all over the world into your home as they are happening (from events such as the first moon walk in 1969 to the Iranian seizure of hostages in the American embassy in 1979). Technology also permits us to overcome the obstacles of disease and age. Advances in medical knowledge and skills have played a large part in the explosive growth of population since World War II by lowering the rate of infant mortality and the death rate in general.

Technology can also overcome the obstacles and limitations imposed on states by the natural resources available to them. New technologies permit the extraction of resources such as oil, coal, and many other minerals previously out of reach. Synthetics, the products of technology, expand a menu limited by the earth's resources. One striking example is the German development of the Haber process to produce synthetic nitrates only one year before the outbreak of World War I. Germany had been dependent on Chile for the nitrates essential to any state's munitions industry. Without the breakthrough of technology, Germany could have been cut off from her source of nitrates by the British Navy—and thus cut off from her ability to fight a war. A less dramatic example was the development of synthetic rubber during World War II.

In sum, the technology that exists in the system at any time is an important constraint on what is possible. However, research and development by governments, industry, universities, and individuals—both through specific research projects and by accident—are continually changing the technological environment. Such change has been ever more rapid. It has been taking less and less time for new discoveries to become operational in our world. The gap between Marconi's first radio set and commercial broadcasting was thirty-five years, the atomic bomb went from discovery to use in six years, and the transistor in five years.

If, as we shall later argue, the menu of a state is intimately tied to its capabilities, influence, and power, then technology affects the bases of a state's power, the scope of that power, and the areas in which the state is interested in using that power. Remember one further point about technology as part of the international environment: The menu of any state is limited not only by the technology that exists at any point in time but also by the distribution of that technology in the system. Although the technology exists to create thermonuclear weapons that can be delivered by intercontinental ballistic missiles (ICBMs), only a few states in the system have the ability to take advantage of that technology. Often only the state that originates a new technological innovation possesses it for a period of time—for example, the U.S. monopoly on atomic weapons until the first Soviet atomic explosion in 1949.

CHARACTERISTICS OF SYSTEMS

We may speak of the structure of a system as the arrangement of various things in that system. In the first chapter we defined a system as a set of elements interacting with each other. A set of billiard balls being broken on a pool table constitutes such a system, for the balls interact with one another. An international system, infinitely more complex, is a set of states interacting with each other and with other behaving units or actors. Sometimes it is useful to treat the states as though they were billiard balls, considering the nation-state as the only type of actor or unit of analysis worth worrying about. Thus, we would concentrate on how the unit France interacts with other national units like Italy and China. But we said that the international system is infinitely more complex than a set of billiard balls. Why?

First, there are other actors, both within nation-states and among several states, that must be taken into account. Also, the kinds of interaction and the number of variables are much more numerous. The billiard balls act on one another only through the expenditure of energy, which can be measured on a single scale. If you know the initial location of the balls on the table, the energy-absorbing capacity of the balls and banks, the degree of level of the table surface, the friction created by the table covering, the amount of energy exerted through the cue, and the initial angles of interaction, it is possible to make a good prediction of where the balls will end up. That may sound like a tall order, but given the information, a competent engineer could perform the computations. It does require quite a lot of information, some of it very hard to obtain (such as the angles), but the number of different aspects or variables at issue is small (about six) and is theoretically manageable. Furthermore, these are the only variables that matter. If you had all the information for them, the effects both of chance and of ignored variables would be quite low. For instance, we can usually forget about the atmospheric pressure of the room (which influences friction). The typical billiard player is not an engineer and will not make the computations, but will recognize them as important variables and take them into account from experience and intuition. If the player "knows" the table, he or she will also have a good idea of how much force to use on the cue and the angle to try for to get the desired distribution of the balls. The player may not always be able to achieve it but knows what to try for.

The analysis of international systems requires, or at least seems to require, information about a great many more variables. We say "seems to require" because we are often not sure which variables exert a great deal of influence and which, like the atmospheric pressure, can be safely ignored without damage to most analyses. A system is defined by a combination of the attributes of its component units and their interactions. All of the following are important:

1. The *number* of state actors.
2. The relative *size* of the various state actors. The most relevant measure of size may be population, area, wealth, economic capacity (GNP), military capabilities, some other measure, or some combination of these.
3. *Nonstate actors*, in this instance principally international organizations. The United Nations would be one, especially when it is able to behave as an independent actor in international politics, mediating or resolving conflicts or intervening on the side of one party in a conflict. Other pertinent international organizations are military alliances among several states. Because of institutional bonds or other linkages, we also speak of a geographical or political *group of states* as an actor. This is the sense in which many observers commonly used the term *Soviet bloc*. They assumed that the linkages among these nations were so numerous and strong that the states would act as a unit, often delegating decision-making power to an intergovernmental organization or to one of their number. When such regional groupings, blocs, or alliances act together on a range of issues, they contribute to serious modifications in the structure of the international system from a set of states each acting entirely independently. The effect is in some ways analogous to that of a party organization that molds several fairly cohesive voting groups out of a body of individual legislators in a parliament. As with legislative bodies, there may be two or many such alliances, with great variation possible in their discipline and degree of cohesion. Bilateral (two-member) alliances typically do not set up formal organizations like NATO, but pairs of states with relatively long-term bonds can nevertheless be included under this heading.
4. Linkages or *interactions* among state actors, especially those that support alliances or otherwise help ensure that two or more nations act in concert. These may take the form of trade, foreign investments,

movements of citizens (tourism, migration, and student exchanges), communications between governments or private citizens (via mail or telegraph), or the mass media (radio and television). These links can be usefully classed together under the name of *transactions*, whether conducted by governments or by private citizens. From the viewpoint of the political analyst, any single event—a particular purchase, a single letter, one student fellowship—is rarely of any interest; rather it is the aggregate number of such acts that is of concern—the fact of whether the total volume of trade or communications is high or low. In addition, there is a class of events that may be of interest either in the aggregate or as a particular event. For this class we use the term *acts*, applying it primarily to government-to-government interactions. Acts include the signing or denunciation of treaties; visits by heads of state; messages of threat, concern, support, or approval transmitted between governments; and military actions (whether actually committing international acts of violence or merely moving and mobilizing troops) that convey a message to other governments. These are frequently measured and studied through the use of so-called events data; we shall deal with them in later sections of the book.

THE EMERGENCE OF A GLOBAL SYSTEM

It is the fact of interaction that makes a system out of otherwise separate units. As we have said, the kinds and amount of interaction among members can vary enormously. In addition, a great number of social, technological, economic, and political factors affect the rate and kind of interaction. Where interaction is much greater among a certain set of units than between those units and others outside the set, the interacting set is a subsystem. If the rate of interaction between members of the set and outsiders is extremely low, we may simply refer to the interacting set as a system rather than a subsystem. For example, there has not always been an international system of global scope. Before the sixteenth century, there was no global system but rather a number of regional systems. European states did not interact at all with the Western Hemisphere and in no significant way with Africa south of the Sahara or with East and Southeast Asia. Communication and transportation technologies were too primitive to permit interaction across long distances. This was largely true through much of the nineteenth century as well, for although there were some interactions between Europe and other parts of the globe, it was still possible for many non-European actors to ignore Europe for most purposes. This "splendid isolation" formed the basis for American foreign policy until the Spanish-American War.

Figure 4.1 shows what has happened in manned transportation since the early nineteenth century. Beginning with sailing vessels, and the earliest steamships which moved at about 5 miles per hour, the figure gives the maximum speed of human transportation over intercontinental distances achievable at various times. The graph rises to the speed attained by oceangoing passenger ships in the period between the world wars and then advances rapidly with the long-range jet bombers of the 1960s and the supersonic bombers and SST civil aircraft of the 1970s. Especially with the recent change, the whole world has become irrevocably bound into a closely knit system. America's isolation, which enabled America to avoid becoming enmeshed in Europe's wars for more than 100 years, is gone. What happens in Africa and Asia can

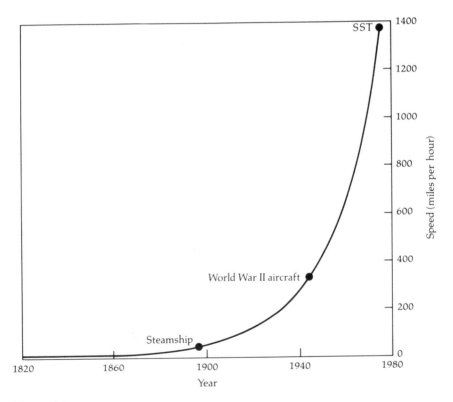

Figure 4.1
A shrinking world: maximum speed attainable for intercontinental travel, 1820–1980.

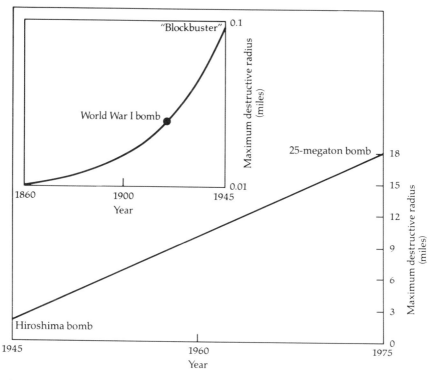

Figure 4.2
More bang for a bomb: maximum destructive radius of existing weapons, 1860–1975. [Calculated from U.S. Atomic Energy Commission, *The Effects of Nuclear Weapons* (Washingon, D.C.: U.S. Government Printing Office, 1962) and later data. Destructive radius is defined as sufficient blast overpressure (3 pounds per square inch) to collapse an ordinary frame house.]

affect anyone else in the world almost immediately. Indeed, all parts of the world are within 30 minutes' reach of intercontinental missiles from anywhere.

Much the same trend has taken place in the destructive capacity of explosive weapons. Figure 4.2 shows the increase in the radius of destruction of a single weapon, beginning with artillery shells during the American Civil War and continuing through the guns of the turn of the century, the largest conventional bombs dropped in World War II, and the thermonuclear weapons of the present. The measurements are approximate, but the general picture is clear. The best of the World War II "blockbusters" could seriously damage only those buildings within about 500 feet (one-tenth of a mile), but the Hiroshima atomic bomb destroyed most buildings within over a mile and a half. More recent scientific developments have raised this figure substantially, to about 18 miles for big 25-megaton Soviet hydrogen bombs.[4]

These technological developments have meant that, while wars are not more frequent in the international system now than they were 100 years ago, they certainly have become more destructive. Figure 4.3 shows the number of soldiers killed in all international wars since

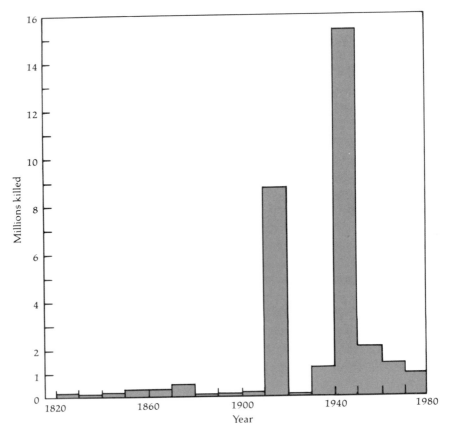

Figure 4.3
Deaths from international wars, 1815–1980. [Adapted from J. David Singer and Melvin Small, *The Wages of War, 1815–1965: A Statistical Handbook* (New York: Wiley, 1972); Small and Singer, *Resort to Arms* (Beverly Hills, Calif.: Sage, 1982).

4. The explosive power of weapons has increased at a much higher rate than indicated in Figure 4.2 for destructive radius, since increasing the destructive radius by 67 percent doubling the power of the bomb.

1815. The figures do not include civilian deaths; if they did, the number would be several times higher.

Coupled with the enormous growth in wealth of the industrial powers over the last century, the new technology provides the means for great powers to make their influence felt virtually everywhere and for the entire global system truly to operate as an interacting system. The major powers are particularly involved in interactions with one another. Each of the biggest powers has parts of the globe (or regional subsystems) that it dominates and within which it is able to limit sharply the influence of other major powers. The United States has

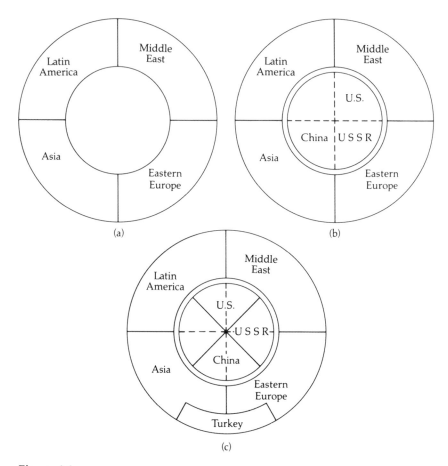

Figure 4.4
Several hypothetical international systems: (a) regional systems; (b) international system with major powers and regional subsystems (spheres of influence); (c) major power penetration across subsystems.

long been dominant in Latin America, and the Soviet Union in Eastern Europe. China is important in parts of East Asia but must compete with the USSR. Britain and France once had large spheres of influence in Africa and elsewhere, but no longer have as much power, relative either to their former colonies or to the United States and the USSR, to dominate these regions. Also, although certain major powers clearly predominate over others in particular spheres of influence (primarily in Latin America and Eastern Europe), most of the smaller powers within these areas maintain significant ties—economic, political, cultural, or military—with some other powers as well. Regional subsystems are thus penetrated by the big powers' global activities. Figure 4.4 illustrates several hypothetical international systems: a world with separated regional systems, a global system of major powers and spheres of influence, and major power penetration across subsystems.

Hierarchy in the International System

Another viewpoint stresses the degree of *hierarchy* in the international system: the extent to which all powers are linked together essentially as equals or only through the intermediary of one or more great powers. Several writers, notably Johan Galtung, have emphasized the allegedly *feudal* nature of much of contemporary and historical international politics. This means a world of several influence spheres, each dominated by a big power which interposes its own facilities between small powers within its sphere. For instance, telephone calls between Senegal and Gabon in West Africa once had to go through Paris. Each big power also limits as far as possible the penetration of other major powers into its own spheres.[5]

The spheres-of-influence perspective tends to emphasize interactions among great powers or limitations of each others' actions among superpowers in their spheres and looks at this in terms of *balance of power*. The perspective of hierarchy, on the other hand, looks at *structures of dominance* of the weak by the strong, and at the possibilities for limited autonomy or independence by those at the bottom, the "underdogs." This is what we meant earlier when we noted that the system

---

5. Many of the most important studies using this perspective have appeared in the *Journal of Peace Research*, published in Oslo, Norway. See especially Johan Galtung, "East-West Interaction Patterns," *Journal of Peace Research* 3 (1966), no. 2, pp. 146–176; Nils Petter Gleditsch, "Trends in World Airline Patterns," *Journal of Peace Research* 4 (1967), no. 4, pp. 366–407.

could produce constraints on behavior. Smaller states within a feudal system are highly constrained by larger powers, especially if they sit within the sphere of influence of a major power. If there are two super-powers, each superpower is limited by the other; each restrains its be-havior in anticipation (or fear) of the other's response. Having several major powers opens up the menu: The balance-of-power possibilities of coalitions or alliances increase as opportunities for interaction increase. These are just a few of the many possible constraints imposed by the system structure. Clearly, those states at the bottom of the international hierarchy have different menus from those at the top.

One way to picture a feudal pattern is illustrated in Figure 4.5, where the lines indicate substantial interactions that states have with one an-other. Thus, *A* and *B*, the "topdogs" or larger powers, interact most with each other and with small powers in their spheres of influence. Most importantly, *u, v, w, x, y,* and *z*—the small powers—interact least, even though they might be in the same geographical region and have many common interests. Robin Jenkins notes two basic ordering principles of the feudal system: (1) A state that ranks high on one dimension of power is likely to rank high on other dimensions; and (2) interaction tends to be dependent on average power. Thus, states that are powerful tend to interact more; powerful and weaker states interact less, and states that are weak interact still less.[6]

STATUS AND HIERARCHY IN THE INTERNATIONAL SYSTEM

Theories about spheres of influence or balance of power typically are "center-oriented" theories or "views from above," concerned chiefly with relations among the great powers. What goes on among the small powers at the periphery of the world system generally matters little except that the addition or loss of small states to a big power's alliance or sphere of influence affects the balance of power or the likelihood of war. In effect, the peripheries matter only as pawns in the arena of great power politics. Indeed, some theorists even praise the advantages of so-called "bipolar" systems, where two major powers or alliance sys-tems confront each other from positions of relative equality. Such theo-rists sometimes declare that a bipolar system will be stable in large part

---

6. Robin Jenkins, *Exploitation* (London: Paladin, 1971), pp. 82–83.

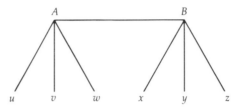

Figure 4.5
A feudal international system.

just because the great powers are able to dominate and control small states.[7] These perspectives are typical of most U.S. theorizing during the Cold War era and of Soviet theorizing as well. (We shall examine these and other theories about polarity and relative power among big states in Chapter 5.)

However, theorists in contemporary Europe and especially in the third world see the situation very differently. Their "view from below" is much more concerned with avoiding becoming arenas for superpower conflict and with obtaining some freedom of action for their countries. From below, balance of power looks like dominance within spheres of influence. Smaller powers looked upon Soviet-American détente with a mixture of hopes and fears for their own condition. A tacit Soviet-American understanding about spheres of influence might leave small powers even more under the control of the superpower in whose sphere they fall. Vigorous Soviet-American competition means competition for the allegiance of small powers—competition that may be manifested in offers of economic or military assistance to attract and hold small powers' allegiance. Under those conditions, and so long as the superpowers do not engage in proxy wars on their territories, big-power competition redounds to small powers' benefit. Soviet-American détente might reduce the likelihood of proxy wars in the third world, but at the same time it might reduce the flow of aid and other benefits to the third world. It is worth noting that from 1962 to 1983 the volume of American economic assistance to other countries declined from 0.8 percent of GNP to about 0.3 percent. During much of this period, Soviet-American relations improved significantly. In the earlier years, many third world countries were very good at playing one superpower against the other, extracting gains in aid from both. Now, as Soviet-

7. See Kenneth Waltz, "International Structure, National Force, and the Balance of World Power," in James N. Rosenau (Ed.), *International Politics and Foreign Policy*, 2nd ed. (New York: Free Press, 1969).

American relations have worsened, the aid from these superpowers has primarily taken the form of military equipment and sales programs.

Just as big-power theories look chiefly at horizontal relations among approximate equals, theories originating from small powers stress vertical relationships. As noted, some theories characterize international politics as essentially feudal; a related and especially popular kind of theory is concerned with *dependence*. Third world and European theorists examine the effects of big powers' economic, political, and cultural penetration on small powers. The effects at issue in such theories are also different—less concerned with war and international political alignments than are views by the superpowers and more concerned with patterns of economic and political development within third world countries. We shall examine such theories and the empirical evidence that can be brought to bear on them later in this book.

RELATIVE DEPRIVATION AND AGGRESSION

To gain a perspective on hierarchy in international systems, the distribution of goods and rewards among different states in the system must be examined, as must the linkages between the rich and the poor, the strong and the weak. "Topdogs" are likely to be feared, rich, and powerful. By looking at the distribution of various desired conditions (wealth, respect, and power) among nations in the system, we can find some clues as to which nations' leaders may feel deprived and hence prone to violent aggressive behavior.

Theories about status and feelings of deprivation are common in psychology, sociology, and political science. The most important versions assert that aggressive behavior stems from frustration arising out of a feeling of *relative deprivation*. That is, people may act violently or aggressively not because they are poor or deprived in some absolute sense but because they *feel* deprived relative to others or to their expectations of what they should have. Poverty alone is not sufficient to trigger feelings of anger and a desire to take strong action; poor people may fatalistically accept their lot as unchanging or as "God's will." For many of the world's poor, this has long been the case, but decreasingly remains so. Feelings of relative deprivation arise by comparing one's situation with that of others, or by comparing one's past, present, and expected future condition.

Most obviously, feelings of relative deprivation are likely to arise when a formerly prosperous individual experiences a severe economic setback. Such feelings are widespread during recessions and depressions and often result in severe political unrest. Karl Marx thought that revolutions would occur as the result of the increasing poverty of the working class. Prolonged, severe depression in Germany in the 1930s played a key part in preparing Hitler's rise to power. But in some cases, an improvement in people's material conditions can release unrest. Alexis de Tocqueville described the situation before the French revolution in these terms:

> "Thus it was precisely in those parts of Europe where there had been most improvement that popular discontent was highest. . . . Patiently endured so long as it seemed beyond redress, a grievance comes to appear intolerable once the possibility of removing it crosses men's minds."[8]

A more complicated hypothesis combines these two views and asserts that the most dangerous time for social unrest is when a sustained period of improving material conditions is followed by a sudden, sharp setback. The period of improvement may lead people to expect continuing improvement; thus, when the setback occurs, it causes more distress than if it had followed a period of unchanged conditions.[9]

The other perspective emphasizes the importance of people's comparisons with one another: "I may be satisfied, even with a bad lot, providing that you do no better. But to the degree I make comparisons with others and find my situation relatively poor, then I am likely to be dissatisfied." Here it is necessary to specify what group or individual is relevant for comparison. For the landless peasant in a traditional society, the condition of the rich landlord may be beyond the peasant's dreams, but the modest prosperity of the middle peasant (in Russia, for example, the *kulak*) may arouse acute feelings of relative deprivation. Generally, such feelings seem more severe for comparisons among people in close contact rather than for widely separated social groups or strata. Hence, poor whites may feel angrier and more threatened by the gains of blacks than angered about the privileges of rich whites, even though poor whites as well as blacks may be better off than their parents were.[10]

---

8. Alexis de Tocqueville, *The Old Regime and the French Revolution* (Garden City, N.Y.: Doubleday, 1955), pp. 176–177.

9. This hypothesis is most clearly stated by James Chowning Davies in his commentary and various contributions to his edited volume, *When Men Revolt and Why* (New York: Free Press, 1971).

10. Two important books utilizing relative deprivation theories are W. G. Runciman, *Relative Deprivation and Social Justice* (London: Routledge and Kegan Paul, 1966); Ted Robert Gurr, *Why Men Rebel* (Princeton, N.J.: Princeton University Press, 1970).

These two perspectives, emphasizing comparisons across time and across groups, can be usefully combined. The first suggests when serious discontent may arise, while the second suggests where in the social system it will be most manifested. Such a combination has been made by Johan Galtung, with his theory that discontent is likely to be most severe in periods of "status disequilibrium," across several different dimensions or measures of social status.[11] Galtung's theory is an intriguing amalgam of perspectives that stem both from the discipline of sociology and from a European and third world view very different from North American theories about international systems. Galtung's basic idea is that actors (individuals, groups, and nations) obtain status in different ways for different values. A person, for example, may compare himself or herself with another in terms of income or power or prestige. Galtung suggests that the greatest discontent is likely to arise when an actor's status on different values or dimensions is in disequilibrium, for example, an individual who is powerful or rich but held in low esteem, such as a newly rich person who is not fully accepted socially by those who have inherited wealth and status. Thus, one would look at any social system to find individuals whose status was in disequilibrium, especially those who might be strong on power but low on prestige, to find individuals who might act aggressively to improve their standing. A prime example of this sort of behavior is pre–World War I Germany. The newly formed German Empire (since 1870) under Kaiser Wilhelm was determined to gain the "place in the sun" it felt it deserved. A scramble for colonies, especially in Africa, and a naval arms race with Great Britain became preliminaries for the main event—World War I.

Social systems also vary in the degree of disequilibrium manifested. In long-established and stable systems, there is likely to be great congruence in individuals' status across dimensions: the rich will be powerful and respected. But in times when society is in flux, with individuals moving up and down the socioeconomic scale, individuals are more likely to be in disequilibrium across dimensions. Here is another way to identify periods of unrest as well as the actors most likely to manifest aggression.

Theories of relative deprivation, especially variants of Galtung's ideas, have received a good deal of attention in recent literature on

11. See his "A Structural Theory of Aggression," *Journal of Peace Research* 1 (1964), 95–119.

international relations. Part of the reason is doubtless that this seems to be a period of substantial change in international status and greater consciousness of differences in status. Many people in the slums and barrios of the Third World, for instance, are hardly better off economically than they had been—but thanks to transistor radios, television by satellite, and other wonders of modern communication, they are more aware of how well off people in other countries and elites in their own countries really are. This is what is meant by "rising expectations." Moreover, there seem to be some severe cases of status disequilibrium at the international level. The newly rich OPEC countries, for example, are by no means fully accepted or respected in world councils. In terms of size and to a lesser degree power, China is a major state, but at the same time it is still very poor and, at least until recently, not even recognized politically by the United States and many of America's allies. Israel, Taiwan, and South Africa are all relatively prosperous states, but for very different reasons each is denied full recognition or prestige in many parts of the world. By the general terms of the theory, this period, and perhaps especially these states, would seem likely candidates for aggression caused by feelings of relative deprivation.

WHO FEELS DEPRIVED?

The ideas at issue here are intriguing, but they must be further specified if they are to form the basis of a rigorous scientific theory. First, it is necessary to specify which dimensions are important and the effect of different kinds of disequilibrium. Are the relevant dimensions power, wealth, prestige, or other factors? Which of these are most important? Is the effect of ranking high on power and low on prestige the same as being high on prestige and low on power? One would assume not—the former case suggests the basis for a great amount of dissatisfaction and potential aggression, whereas the latter suggests a case where the actor should be very satisfied to be respected even if not necessarily powerful. This suggests an important distinction usually drawn by sociologists between achieved and ascribed status. The former includes such objective measures of possession as wealth and the material bases of power; the latter is a matter of prestige and social recognition, the subjective elements of status.

Second, it is necessary to move very carefully from identifying a case of apparent feelings of relative deprivation to a case where aggressive or revolutionary action is likely. For this second step to occur, we must know something about the actor's ability or inability to change a situation peacefully. So long as the potential for achieving greater status equilibrium by normal, peaceful channels is present (the leaders of the system, for example, may allow improvement through "reform" or rising members may be co-opted into a position of respect and authority), aggressive acts will be unnecessary and probably counterproductive. On the other hand, for aggression to be likely there should be some prospect that violent or aggressive action can succeed. If the secret police have thoroughly infiltrated the organization of the potential revolutionaries or the coercive state apparatus is extremely oppressive, revolt may seem utterly hopeless. Aggression, if it occurs at all under those circumstances, may more likely be turned against scapegoats, against fellow underdogs, or even against oneself in feelings of guilt and worthlessness. Thus the *political* context of deprivation is a central variable in any effort to move from sociological or psychological theories of aggression to political theories. In international relations, one would have to ask whether "deprived" states were so powerless as to make aggressive acts—at least those against great powers—hopeless. On the other hand, in a world where there was widespread feeling of deprivation and widespread access to nuclear weapons, we might very well see some dramatic acts of aggression rooted in that deprivation.

Another problem requiring much greater specification stems from the attempt to apply theories originally developed to explain the behavior of individuals to nations or other social aggregates. Here we have a level-of-analysis problem that illustrates the dangers in trying to jump from one kind of actor to another. For a theory of relative deprivation to be applicable, we must have a case where there are feelings of relative deprivation, not just a case where an outside observer can say that objectively there is deprivation or status disequilibrium. And if there must be feelings of deprivation—a subjective state—then who is to feel deprived? If we are talking about nonstate actors, then it may be enough for any small group of individuals—say, a few Palestinian refugees acting as terrorists—to feel deprived. But if this is to be a theory of state action, then we must focus not on isolated individuals or groups or even deprived masses, but on the elites who make state policy. Do they feel deprived? With which *other* individuals, groups, or nations do they compare themselves—industrialized European states who are very much better off, or their regional neighbors in Latin America, Africa, or Asia? What are the relevant dimensions to these decision makers, or do differences in cultural values matter so much that we cannot accurately speak about a single set of valued dimensions for the leaders of different nations? For leaders (elites), the assumption that they all share values of a single dominant world culture may be somewhat less problematic than for people at large. Then, too, should the relevant comparison be with other states at all or with their own people? The masses in most less developed countries live very poorly. But the elites typically live very well, with high incomes and access to foreign travel and to Western medical care and Western luxuries. (At a diplomatic reception they may "drink champagne on behalf of their people.") Such individuals, comparing themselves with their own populace, may feel very satisfied, with little disequilibrium and no serious desire (aside from some rhetoric designed chiefly for domestic consumption) to alter the existing international order.

These are serious theoretical problems that need to be resolved. Nevertheless, the theoretical perspective is intriguing and has generated some research indicating that we should take it seriously. One appropriate research design has been to look at all states in the world system (or at least the major powers) at various points in time (say, every five years over the past century and a half) and rank each nation by objective measures of the value dimensions that seem relevant (power, wealth, prestige, and so forth). We can then compute for each state a score for its status disequilibrium (the differences between its rankings on each of the dimensions) and, adding together the scores for each country, produce a summary score for the international system at each time period. (Thus, we use the distribution of nation attributes to characterize the system.) Then one can measure the amount of war occurring in the system at each time (using measures of frequency, severity, and duration of war, as appropriate) to see whether those periods with the greatest status disequilibrium had the most war or perhaps whether war tended to follow periods of great disequilibrium.

Analyses of this type have been performed. Although the results are not conclusive, they suggest what would be hypothesized from Galtung's theory: the greater the amount of status disequilibrium in a system, the more war, especially when one assumes a rather long time lag of ten or fifteen years between the period of disequilibrium and the outbreak of war. It would appear that time must elapse for the disequilibrium to seem urgent or perhaps for states to prepare themselves for battle.[12]

---

12. Michael Wallace, *War and Rank among Nations* (Lexington, Mass.: Heath, 1973); also, Manus Midlarsky, *On War: Political Violence in the International System* (New York: Free Press, 1975).

Again, there is much about this theory and research that leaves many questions unanswered. Although the results at the systemic level of analysis fit the theory, it is not at all clear whether nations most in disequilibrium are really the ones most likely to be involved in war or whether they or the existing powers initiate war. Nor have the necessary logical and empirical connections between the nation-state level of analysis and the actual perceptions and behavior of state decision makers been made. Still, in a period of rapid change in economic development and the availability of world resources, where rapid communication makes differences in value achievement obvious and the military is capable of vast destruction, this view from below about the causes of conflict deserves to be taken seriously.

We shall return to aspects of the international system's hierarchy and to some of the consequences of poor countries' dependence on rich, powerful countries for the economic and political systems of these poor countries. But for now, let us turn to aspects of relations among states near the top of the international hierarchy. How does the distribution of power among the leading states or alliances of the system affect the system's stability or the chances that major wars will arise?

5

THE WORLD SYSTEM: STRUCTURE, POLARITY, AND WAR

ALLIANCES AND NONALIGNMENT

"One is one and all alone." "Two's company, three's a crowd." In any social system, however small or simple, it makes a difference how many participants there are. Patterns of behavior differ greatly in different-sized groups. Thucydides of ancient Greece, many nineteenth-century European statesmen, and Henry Kissinger would all agree that the number of participants in the international system makes a great difference in the way the participants can and must behave, affecting the likelihood of war among them, and even their very survival as independent actors. Their concern with nation-states as actors in the pursuit of power is typical of realist analysis.

To characterize an international system, we need to know the structure of the system and how that structure affects the international relations within the system. To understand the structure of the system, we need to know the number of state actors, the relative size of those actors, and the existence of such nonstate actors as alliances built by various bonds or linkages between two or more states. Alliances tell us much about the political and military structure of the international system, about the distribution of friendship and enmity, and about the distribution of military capabilities. Alliances combine elements of cooperation and conflict. They involve interstate cooperation (between allied states), while addressing an existing or potential conflict with one or more other states.[1]

Cooperative behavior can be either formal or informal. Informally, two states are in alignment if they act in a similar way toward some third international actor. Again informally, states are said to be in coalitions if they act cooperatively, with common behavior and attitudes toward other actors and issues but without a formal agreement. Alliances are generally defined by at least two special characteristics: They are formalized in written treaties, and they are agreements to cooperate in security or military affairs. The agreements often specify the rights and obligations, the benefits and costs of the alliance members. The rights and obligations concern national security and military threats to that security. Alliances are distinguished from other forms of international cooperation because of the actual or potential existence of enemies, which promotes the risk of and planning for war. Indeed, over 2,000 years ago Thucydides observed that mutual fear of a third party is the only solid basis on which to organize an alliance. In sum, alliances involve the formal collaboration of states, generally for specified and limited periods of time in regard to some mutually perceived enemy or security problem.

Alliances and Power

The main reason throughout history why states enter into alliances is for the *aggregation of power*. Alliances permit states to augment their military capabilities by adding the military capabilities of others. When

---

1. Much of this section is drawn from Harvey Starr, "Alliances: Tradition and Change in American Views of Foreign Military Entanglements," in Ken Booth and Moorhead Wright (eds.), *American Thinking on Peace and War* (New York: Barnes and Noble, 1978), pp. 37–57. Two useful overviews of recent alliance studies are Michael D. Ward, *Research Gaps in Alliance Dynamics*, vol. 19, Monograph Series in World Affairs (Denver: University of Denver, 1982), and Brian L. Job, "Grins without Cats: In Pursuit of Knowledge of International Alliances," in P. T. Hopmann, D. A. Zinnes, and J. D. Singer (eds.), *Cumulation in International Relations Research*, vol. 18, Monograph Series in World Affairs (Denver: University of Denver, 1981), pp. 39–63.

states *A* and *C* are in conflict with each other, they may increase their own power, add the power of other states, or withhold from their competitor the power of other states. The aggregation of military power—or the addition of the military capabilities of two or more states—means that *A* allies with *B* so that *A* and *B* now have greater military capabilities relative to *C*. Alliance as a foreign policy strategy has been the vital component in the balance of power throughout history. The aim of the balance of power is first of all a deterrent one: to deter some opponent from engaging in some behavior—usually war—because the military capabilities of the alliance is equal to or outweighs those of the opponent (or will make war too costly to be of benefit). If deterrence fails, the aggregation of military capabilities permits the alliance to defeat the opponent. The formation of the two alliances before World War I—the Triple Entente of Britain, France, and Russia and the Triple Alliance of Germany, Austria-Hungary, and Italy—illustrates both these aspects of aggregation and balance of power. France and Germany each sought to offset the military capabilities of the other through diplomatic maneuvers that added new alliance partners to its side. In this situation deterrence failed (in part because it was not entirely clear that all the alliance agreements would be kept), and most of the alliances were then used to fight a war.

The addition of the power of others to one's own is not the only reason for alliance and may in some cases be quite secondary. Alliances may also be preemptive. States may accept others as alliance partners in order to deprive their opponents; *A* allies with *B* to prevent the addition of *B*'s power to *A*'s enemy, *C*. This maneuver ultimately affects military influence, not by making oneself stronger (although it might) but by making one's opponent weaker. A weaker opponent may be more vulnerable to the deterrent threat or more easily defeated in war. Adding the strength of others to one's own may develop new military and strategic capabilities. Preempting allies from opponents prevents opponents from similarly expanding their menu. For example, prior to World War I, France and Russia competed with Germany for Rumania as an ally. The competition was not so much to add Rumania's military might as to prevent its strategic location from falling into the hands of the opponent. The realist view of international relations argues that a state whose national security is threatened should ally with any state that will (a) help offset the power of others or (b) deny that state's power to the opponent. This choice of allies, realists argue, should not be affected by nonmilitary considerations, such as ideology, past relationships, or morality.

In fact, similarities between states, including bonds of cooperation, ideology, history, and outlook have had important influences on the alliance behavior of states. This is due to what Bruce Russett has called "responsiveness" between states: Similar states are often predisposed to respond to each other's needs and to comply with each other's wishes. Harvey Starr has found that similarity in ideology or "community" (shared values and interests) influences the size of war coalitions and the distribution of war spoils by the coalition.[2] When they want to form alliances, states try to aggregate enough military power to win. But in this search, states that are ideologically or culturally similar are usually chosen first. When distributing the payoffs of alliance, those with ideological or cultural similarity are usually treated best.

As noted in the case of Rumania, a state may be allied with because of its strategic location. The purpose is to increase one's security and military position, but not through the addition of the new ally's military forces. The new state, *B*, may provide an outlet to a body of water not bordered on by *A*, border on *A*'s opponent, or provide military bases such as the naval refueling stations so necessary in the past or air bases, which have been crucial to American strategic policy in the postwar era. In addition to denying the strategic location to *A*'s opponent *C*, *A* has improved its military position by the alliance. In doing so, it may have also achieved an important military advantage over *C*. This was possibly the major reason why Soviet leader Khrushchev placed missiles in Cuba in 1962. Although the Soviet Union had only a few long-range intercontinental missiles that could reach the United States, the Soviet Union could rapidly have increased its nuclear threat to the United States by placing medium-range missiles in Cuba—only 90 miles from the American mainland. Cuba is a good example of an ally, or coalition partner, taken on for strategic reasons.

Alliances are also used to strengthen deterrence by making international politics more predictable. Alliances have been created in the past through treaties in order to demonstrate clearly the political alignment of states in a formal manner. Some post–World War II American alliances, such as the Southeast Asia Treaty Organization (SEATO) and the Central Treaty Organization (CENTO) in the Middle East (both now defunct) were pursued by Secretary of State John Foster Dulles because he felt that the lack of such clear lines was one cause of the North

---

2. See first Bruce Russett, *Community and Contention: Britain and America in the Twentieth Century* (Cambridge, Mass.: MIT Press, 1963), p. 30; then see Harvey Starr, *War Coalitions* (Lexington, Mass.: Heath, 1972), pp. 22–26.

Korean invasion of South Korea in 1950. The logic was that the North Koreans were not deterred from such an attack because it had not been made clear that South Korea was an American ally and would be protected as such.

Credibility of Deterrence

Deterrence to protect third parties (and to expand one's sphere of influence) depends on the credibility of the threat. Alliances are thought to add to this credibility. Credibility depends both on capabilities and on the willingness to use them. This willingness is communicated in part through such activities as the signing of alliance treaties. The treaty tries to make clear to an opponent "this state is my ally; if you attack it you will have to deal with me also." Alliances, then, are intended to increase an opponent's belief that military aid will be rendered by state A to state B by making clear that state A identifies its security with that of state B.[3]

The strategic aspect of alliances also increases the credibility of deterrent threats. Alliances permit what is called the *projection of capability*. This happens when an ally A stations information-gathering facilities or elements of its military forces on the territory of others— perhaps even on the borders of its main opponent. The postwar American alliance network allowed the United States to have allies directly on the borders of both the Soviet Union and China; for example, NATO and CENTO ally Turkey, CENTO member Iran, and NATO ally Norway bordered the USSR, where Japan (bilateral treaty), Taiwan (bilateral treaty), and members of SEATO were very close to China. By projecting forces—by sending them to positions in allied states close to the opponent—these forces also become "trip wires." They not only

---

3. Studies of deterrence for the protection of third parties clearly show the enhanced credibility produced by various ties between the protector state and its protégé. These studies found that if the protector had close trade and political ties with the protégé, the odds of successful deterrence were twice as good as they were without such ties. A military alliance alone, however, added nothing to the chances of success. This is reported in Paul Huth and Bruce Russett, "What Makes Deterrence Work: Cases 1900 to 1980," *World Politics* 36 (July 1984), no. 3, 496–526. Simply declaring a formal alliance tie between states may not be enough if the opponent feels the tie is not strong enough—if the opponent feels there is a lack of community between the alliance partners. In fact, the existence of an alliance may even invite an attack on the would-be deterrer (A) if the attacker (C) wants very strongly to attack the protected state (B), believes the deterrer's threat, and therefore tries to get in the first blow (against A). See Bruce Russett, *Power and Community in World Politics* (San Francisco: W. H. Freeman and Company, 1972), chaps. 12–13.

demonstrate the ties between state *A* and its allies but also show state *A*'s resolve to protect its allies. U.S. forces in Europe, for example, have been called trip wire forces because a conventional Soviet attack on Europe would also have to attack American troops. This greatly increases the probability that the United States will carry out the threats that lie behind deterrence. In sum, the projection of troops to other areas says: "This is our ally. If you want to attack it, think twice, because if you attack this ally, you will also have to attack *my* troops that are stationed there. Do you really think I will allow you to attack my armed forces and do nothing?" The American system of alliances created in the late 1940s and 1950s was based on this sort of logic.

Alliances to Control Alliance Partners

Alliances have been used by large nations to control and dominate smaller alliance partners. They have also been used by smaller allies to manipulate larger alliance partners and to extract payoffs from them. An alliance leader may use alliances to create international order, an international environment where the alliance leader is safe, secure, and indeed a leader. Alliances permit this by adding to the leader's strength, denying this strength to the leader's major opponents, and increasing the credibility of the leader's deterrent threats. But order also requires organizing relations among the leader's allies—controlling or restraining the behavior of allies. Both the United States and the Soviet Union have used their alliances in this way, particularly in Europe. NATO was officially founded in 1949 as a means to protect Western Europe from Soviet invasion. The Warsaw Pact (or WTO, Warsaw Treaty Organization) was established in 1955 as a response to West Germany's entry into NATO. Both alliances have served the security interests of the United States and USSR, protecting the interests of each against the other in Europe. Both alliances have also been used to keep the lesser allies—especially the two German states—in line. This function of alliances may be more important than it seems. One researcher has found that wars between allies are common, three times greater than would be expected by chance. Another has found that more than 25 percent of one-time coalition partners go to war against each other some time in the future. Clearly, alliances are no guarantee of peaceful relations among states.[4]

---

4. See Bruce Bueno de Mesquita, *The War Trap* (New Haven, Conn.: Yale University Press, 1981); Harvey Starr, *Coalitions and Future War* (Beverly Hills, Calif.: Sage, 1975).

Alliance leaders can influence their partners by providing security. In the postwar world this has meant the extension of a "nuclear umbrella." Leaders may also provide economic and military aid or even use the alliance to justify supporting the domestic regimes of the allies. All of these positive rewards have been used to influence states to join alliances and to follow the alliance leader. The Soviet Union has used the coercive form of influence on its allies to a much greater extent than has the United States.

On the other hand, one danger for the leading member of an alliance is being dragged into conflicts by reckless smaller allies. It has been said that commitment is a seamless web—if a state does not honor its commitments to protect others or honor its deterrent threats, now, similar threats will become much less credible in the future. Small allies have often engaged their larger partners in war by trapping them in positions where the partners would either have to support their small allies or back down. Austria-Hungary's aggressive behavior toward Serbia and Russia before World War I illustrates this relationship. Germany felt forced into being a belligerent supporter of Austria-Hungary or losing its Austrian ally by backing down before Russia.

Large alliance partners have found it necessary to be particularly careful not to be trapped into this position. According to former President Nixon and former Secretary of State Kissinger, one of the most dangerous moments in U.S.-Soviet relations occurred in 1973, when the Soviets threatened to intervene in the October War to prevent their "ally" (informal coalition partner) Egypt from being defeated. This would have forced the United States to intervene on behalf of its client, Israel. During the Cold War, the United States had to restrain the Nationalist Chinese leader Chiang Kai-shek many times. Similarly, the Soviet Union found it had to be careful not to be dragged into the 1979 war between China and North Vietnam, a Soviet ally.

In sum, alliances permit the combining of capabilities, both adding elements of flexibility to state policy and making more complicated the calculation of relative power among states. Alliances affect the opportunities states have to add to their own capabilities by increasing their own resources or reducing those of an opponent. Alliances thus affect the menu of states by increasing opportunities as well as by altering their willingness to act. Decisions concerning the use of force or its threat are made much more complicated when one takes into account the capabilities of single opponents and the possible combinations of capabilities with other states. On the other hand, alliances may decrease uncertainty about others' intentions by indicating a readiness to use force if an ally is attacked.

Avoiding Alliances

States may also try to go it alone, avoiding alliances by some sort of neutral policy or by attempting to withdraw from the system of states as much as possible. Of course, a state's geopolitical position and the structure of the international system are important in selecting a strategy for security and survival. In the past a strategy of isolation was more useful for large countries that were self-sufficient and could draw inside themselves to develop. Japan was able to do this in the nineteenth century, and the Soviet Union to some degree during the 1920s. However, in the contemporary system, large countries with many economic and political ties and a network of economic, monetary, and resource interdependencies find it difficult to withdraw from the international system. China attempted to do so for a while, but it has chiefly been smaller countries on the geographical peripheries of international activity that attempt this strategy. The best example is Burma; possibly another is Cambodia, or Kampuchea, after the Communist victory in 1975.

Because of economic and political needs, many small states in the contemporary system have opted for a nonaligned foreign policy. The expression "third world" was originally coined to characterize all those less-developed countries that avoided alliance with the first world of the industrialized West or second world of the Communist East. Choices of alliance or nonalignment have been strongly affected by the post–World War II system structure. States had a choice of allying either with the Western bloc in some form or with the Soviet Union. As the two-bloc system loosened up, a few other possibilities arose, mostly in the form of small-state alliances. Of course, given the military superpower status of the United States and USSR, any other alliance would have to be considered a small-state alliance. The traditional reasons for allying with great powers have been security, stability, and status. In the postwar system, allying with one of the great powers has often brought just the opposite—fear of threat from the other superpower, internal instability through the clash of Western- and Eastern-oriented political factions (especially if the government opted for military links to one side), and a decline in status as a simple satellite or dependent of a superpower.

Then what about alliances with other small powers? Since two of the most important reasons for forming alliances have historically been to aggregate military power and to promote international order, this option has been unattractive. As noted, any military combination would be helpless to challenge either superpower or its military alliance. The

Arab League was formed to oppose a regional military antagonist and is the only example of a postwar small-power (non-European) military alliance. In the same way, an alliance of small, non-Western states could have little impact on the structure of international order—certainly less than could a group of nonaligned states that sought to pursue their interests through the United Nations and other international organizations. Through this channel, states can also escape the costs of alliances (possibly having to come to the aid of an ally) while appearing globally oriented rather than parochial.

So, although alliance has been a possibility, the international menu after World War II has made a nonaligned strategy attractive to small powers for several reasons. For states that recently achieved independence from a colonial status, it permits (at least the appearance of) an independent foreign policy stance. Nonalignment in the form developed by India and Yugoslavia, which is not simply fence sitting but an active and assertive policy directed toward independence, world peace, and justice, also gives smaller states a purposeful policy and a positive diplomatic identity. Nonalignment gives small, non-Western states a way to act as a third force in international organizations, not only as mediators between the blocs of the East and the West but also as a force to acquire aid and resources for their own development. Working through international organizations like the UN agencies in this way and employing the strength of the one-state/one-vote formula in these organizations, a nonaligned orientation can accomplish far more than any formal alliance structure outside the IGOs. Finally, as a nonaligned state keeping itself apart from the military webs of the superpowers, a neutralist state can also look to one of those powers if the other attempts coercion. Although not formally aligned with the protector, a nonaligned nation knows the protector superpower would be very reluctant to allow the other superpower to expand its sphere of influence.

MAJOR ACTORS AND THE POLARITY OF SYSTEMS

Perhaps the most important theoretical concept for classifying international systems concerns the *number of major actors* or *poles* in the system. A major actor or pole refers either to a single nation-state (major power) or to a tight and cohesive *alliance* of one or more major powers with other large or small allied powers. Thus, the number of poles in a system may or may not be the same as the number of major powers.[5] The pole or major actor is a center of military, political, and economic capabilities. The pole can act with significant independence from other major actors—it is its own master, with a wide selection of possible behaviors.

At one extreme is the system with only a single major actor that dominates all the small states. There never has been a *unipolar global system*, though a world empire would probably take such a form. Unipolar systems of less-than-global extent have been known in the past, with China and the Far East of several centuries ago being a good example.

A *bipolar system* has two major actors opposing each other—either two major powers or two stable opposing alliances. Bipolar systems are relatively common: Some famous ones include Athens and Sparta in ancient Greece; Rome and Carthage; and the United States and the Soviet Union during the first decades after World War II. The distinction between major powers as relatively independent actors and alliances as actors is often important. For example, in Europe of the late nineteenth century there were six major powers; there were some alliances among them but they were not very tight or permanent. It still made some sense to think of Europe as a multipolar system. But just before World War I in 1914, the alliances among most of those powers became so tight that it was accurate to speak of only two major poles in Europe: the Triple Alliance and the Triple Entente.

After World War I the basis for a *multipolar system* was greatly weakened. Austria-Hungary was fragmented into several small countries (Austria, Hungary, Czechoslovakia, and parts of Poland, Yugoslavia, and Rumania); Germany was defeated and disarmed; Russia was shattered by defeat and civil war. Nevertheless, the United States and Japan emerged as major powers in the world system, and by the 1930s both Germany and Russia had substantially recovered. This worldwide major power system was composed of states of similar power potential. But by the outbreak of World War II in 1939, its multipolar character had again shifted, as in 1914, toward a bipolar system, with Germany, Italy, and Japan allied against France and Britain. Both the United

---

5. Some writers, for example Kenneth Waltz, *Theory of International Politics* (Boston: Addison-Wesley, 1979) prefer to define polarity only in terms of the number of major states. Although a system polarized by two major powers is not the same in all respects as one polarized by two major alliances, we think that, at least for predicting wars, it is useful to treat both as bipolar.

States and Russia remained somewhat aloof from the others until they became drawn into the war.

When World War II was over, the basis for a multipolar system had been destroyed. Germany, Italy, and Japan were totally defeated. Though France was nominally a victor, it, too, was greatly weakened by its initial defeat and occupation in 1940. Britain was clearly a victor politically but drained economically and soon lost its major colonies. China was nominally a great power, but everyone recognized that in reality—being poor and in the midst of civil war between the Nationalists and the Communists—its "great power" status was a fiction. America and Russia both were clearly larger and more powerful than any other state in the world, a superiority strengthened and dramatized by the fact that even now they are the only two that possess large numbers of thermonuclear weapons (hydrogen bombs) and big, sophisticated missile systems necessary to deliver these weapons against a technologically advanced defender.

In addition to their own power, the two superpowers of the postwar system have been able to magnify the bipolarity of the global system by allying to themselves many small states, through NATO, the Rio Pact of Western Hemisphere states, the Warsaw Pact, and several other alliances. At the same time, quite a number of Asian and African nations, as well as a few European ones, have stayed nonaligned, apart from the rival alliance groupings. To the degree that (a) states stay apart from the two contending blocs, (b) states switch alignment from one bloc to the other, and (c) these states are fairly large with significant bases of power, the bipolar system can be considered loose rather than tight. In recent decades a combination of processes—the weakening of alliance ties; the recovery and growth of China, Germany, and Japan; the achievement of independence by many ex-colonies that choose nonalignment as their Cold War policy; the rise of OPEC; and the declining economic dominance of the United States—have somewhat loosened the initial U.S.-Soviet bipolar confrontation.

The U.S.-Soviet Bipolar System

Of course, real international systems never fit abstract models perfectly; for example, the U.S.-Soviet bipolar system was never one of two perfectly matched rivals, since the United States has always been richer and until recently possessed an overall military capability superior to Russia's. That superiority was never so great, however, that the American leadership saw fit to use it directly against the Russians. Though America between 1945 and late 1960s could almost surely have inflicted more damage than it received in a general war, the damage to the United States would still have been prohibitive except for the very highest stakes of national survival. And the Soviets at virtually all times have had the ability to destroy America's West European allies; knowledge of that fact doubtless helped restrain American leaders from casually utilizing their military superiority. Bipolarity was reaffirmed in 1968 when the United States did not resist the Soviet invasion of Czechoslovakia. That invasion spotlighted Soviet fear of potential shifts in the allegiance of East European states that would tip the balance of global bipolarity toward American dominance.

There is always a difficult analytical problem when trying to move from the idealized abstractions of deductive theory to an analysis of real-world conditions. How much of a departure from the theoretical norm of equal size can be tolerated without losing whatever the essential characteristics of a particular bipolar or multipolar system may be? And what are the relevant dimensions of equality? Population? Wealth? Military forces? Nuclear and thermonuclear weapons only? In weapons capable of mass destruction, only the United States and Russia can credibly threaten each other or threaten to obliterate any middle-range power. But if superpower nuclear weapons should be unusable in a quarrel between a superpower and a smaller state—either due to moral restraint or a fear that such use would only bring the other superpower in on the small state's side—the superpower might well find it hard to subdue a distant small state with conventional weapons only. Distances from the great power's bases, plus the logistical and morale advantages of fighting close to home, can nullify many of the superpower's advantages, contributing to a degree of multipolarity below the level of nuclear force. Similarly, under circumstances where military might is not easily used or threatened—and many such circumstances arise in negotiations, in UN discussions, and in disputes over raw material supplies and prices—the advantages of the big two can be diminished, and the political process often takes on many of the characteristics of multipolarity.

If one or more of the world's nonaligned states should develop great resources to the point where it could rival one of the superpowers of the bipolar system, then the system would be multipolar, analogous to the economic market system called *oligopoly*. The current international system, of course, is well below this point. Even though China has some nuclear weapons and a much larger population than any other nation (over one billion as compared with about 700 million in India), the country remains so poor in wealth and industry that it is unable to challenge even the Soviet Union militarily. It is probably capable of holding its own territory against virtually any assault and of defeating its potential regional antagonists, but China's army is ill equipped compared with America's or Russia's

The United States has tried to sustain Chinese independence from the Soviet Union (thus weakening the Soviet pole) without concluding a full alliance with China (which might provoke a very violent Soviet response). This leaves China in a rather unaligned position without the power base necessary to constitute a strong pole in the system. A European power composed of the present members of the European Community (Common Market) might be a more convincing rival, but a fully integrated political unit there neither exists nor is likely in the near future. Even if it were more unified, Europe could not qualify as a pole unless it achieved greater military independence from the United States. The same could be said for Japan, despite its powerful economy.

The military components for a fully multipolar system are not currently in prospect, but such systems have existed in the past. From the eighteenth to the early twentieth centuries, a precarious multipolar system existed in Europe. Occasionally it broke down through the dynamic and aggressive growth of one member (e.g., Napoleon's France) or rigidities introduced by very close alliances or longstanding and often ideologically based antagonisms. Around 1900, as we have said, there were several states of similar size and resources (Britain, France, Russia, Germany, Italy, and Austria-Hungary), but they became so commited to two rival groupings that the system was actually more nearly bipolar than multipolar. The prospect that two or more powers will gang up on another power or grouping stems from phenomena that are familiar in a variety of political situations and is an extremely serious source of instability in multipolar systems.

Finally, it is theoretically possible that there may someday be a large number of states in the world, none of which are especially more powerful than the others, and that no widespread or long-term alliances would form. Something like this exists within the United States, where neither New York nor California is in a position to lead a bloc of states. The economists describe such a market as one of perfect or near-perfect competition, where no single buyer or seller is big enough to affect the market conditions under which other buyers or sellers must operate.

But such conditions have not existed in any of the international political systems or subsystems in recent history, and the possibility remains one for speculation rather than empirical analysis.

CHARACTERISTICS OF SYSTEMS: WAR AND STABILITY

Since different systems provide different menus for states, both large and small, we may assume (although not much has been proven) that different systems are characterized by different patterns of state behavior. Are there any reasons to prefer one type of system to another, aside from the consideration that most people would probably prefer to live in a powerful and secure country than in a weak and vulnerable one? Is there anything about one type of system that makes it preferable to large states or to small states or the choice of most of the world's population, regardless of where they live? Some might prefer to inhabit a unipolar world; the world empire sounds like a stable and peaceful dwelling place. Probably it would be, almost by definition, for there would be no major sources of challenge to the imperial power; if such a system ever came about, it would surely last a long time. Such a domination, or *hegemony*, would allow the single power to establish a strong set of rules (often called a *regime*) for world trade and finance, thus permitting a degree of global prosperity and cooperation that could not otherwise occur. (We shall discuss regimes at length in Chapter 18). But it is hard to see how a unipolar system could evolve from our current world, except as the aftermath of a horribly destructive war, and it would almost surely be a highly unjust world, where it would be far better to be a citizen of the imperial state than of a subjugated nation. The bipolar and multipolar models are more applicable to the world in which we live and probably a little less uneven in the distribution of their benefits. For these models, we think especially of particular patterns of state behavior, or stability.

Stability

Stability in one sense is a matter of not being war prone. A stable system would be one with little war (and all things being equal, most people would prefer no war to war). Having little war, however, is a very ambiguous criterion: It might mean simply that wars are *infrequent*. But if the wars that did occur dragged on for many years into wars of attrition, the advantages of infrequency might pale. So *duration* is clearly another relevant aspect, as is magnitude or *severity*. One can easily imagine systems where wars are rare, but when they do occur they are savage, include most members of the system, and are fought to the point of unconditional surrender. If by frequency we mean simply the number of wars fought by a given number of nations in a particular period, and duration is the number of months or years each lasted, an acceptable index of severity would be the number of people (just combatants, or perhaps combatants and civilians together) who were killed.

These are not merely sterile academic distinctions among variables that are closely related in the real world. On the contrary, a survey of all interstate wars since 1815 has shown that the correlation between number of wars begun (frequency) within various three-year periods and the number of casualties is rather low. Furthermore, duration is also only moderately related to severity.[6] In fact, frequency and severity may largely be substitutes for one another, depending upon other characteristics of the international system. Bipolar systems, for instance, are characterized by the continuing confrontation of two major powers. Many bloody wars would quickly drain the two antagonists of their wealth and resources, either reducing them both to a level so near to the second-rank powers that the system became multipolar or destroying the weaker one and leaving the way open for a unipolar empire. If a system is to persist, its wars—at least among the major powers—must be either infrequent or not very severe.

In the post–World War II bipolar system, we have seen many crises and conflicts. But confrontations do not necessarily produce violent conflicts with military fatalities. On the contrary, there have been no acknowledged, direct, violent conflicts between the two superpowers, although it is likely that some American fliers and Russian antiaircraft crews killed each other during the Vietnam war without either party discussing the fact publicly. Clearly both sides fear that, should any such direct conflict begin, it would be very hard to contain it at a low level of intensity and would carry the risk of enormous damage to both sides if it could not be contained. Nor have there been violent conflicts between any of the major powers, save for a border skirmish between China and the Soviet Union in 1969.

---

6. Melvin Small and J. David Singer, *Resort to Arms: International and Civil Wars, 1816–1980* (Beverly Hills, Calif.: Sage, 1982), chap. 5.

Almost all the violent conflicts that have occurred since World War II have been in the third world. Many of these have been quarrels between a superpower and a small state. At least eleven of these conflicts have arisen since 1945, eight involving the United States (North Korea and China from 1950 to 1953, Lebanon in 1958 and 1983, Cuba in 1961, Indochina between 1961 and 1973, the Dominican Republic in 1965, and Grenada in 1983) and three involving the Soviet Union (Hungary in 1956, Czechoslovakia in 1968, and Afghanistan beginning in 1980). Most of these were quite limited and did not result in heavy casualties. (The Korean, Indochinese, and Afghanistan cases are exceptions. These were long and intense actions involving tens or hundreds of thousands of casualties.) The superpowers, however, have proved very successful in restraining conflicts among their own allies. With only a few exceptions—one or two in Central America, between Turkey and Greece over Cyprus, and one between Britain and Argentina over the Falklands Islands (Islas Malvinas)—wars between the allies of one superpower have been prevented.

Changing Fundamental Patterns of Interaction

Related to the concern with the amount and kind of violent conflict that may take place in a system is concern over the stability of the system. In one sense, of course, stability is the lack of violent conflict; other aspects include constancy in the number of major actors in the system, the patterns of linkage among members of the system, and even the identity of the major actors. Let us think of stability as the *lack of change in the fundamental pattern of interactions in the system*. Changes in the number of major actors affect stability only insofar as they affect that pattern.

For example, a unipolar system is marked by a pattern of dominance by and submission to the major actor. A bipolar system is characterized by competition and conflict between the two actors; hence, the pattern of interactions is very different from that of the unipolar system. A system with three major actors (where by definition each of the three actors retains its autonomy) is marked by shifting patterns of conflict and cooperation, both of which are manifested on all three sides of the triangle. If an alliance between two actors becomes tight and permanent, then it is no longer a three-actor system but a two-actor system, with substantial cooperation between the two formerly autonomous actors, both of which are in conflict with the third.

It may be that in politics as well as in love, three-actor systems are almost always unstable because they fall too easily into two-against-one alliances that end in the destruction of one of the original parties. Research by a number of scholars, especially sociologists, indicates that this is usually the case.[7] In the contemporary world, the Soviet Union and the United States continually fear that an alliance between the other and China will be cemented. For this reason, the addition of a fourth actor to any three-actor system eliminates the source of instability and perhaps makes a more reliable pattern of shifting conflict and cooperation. Nevertheless, there is always the possibility that the growth of many formal and informal linkages will create a bloc among two or more actors that formerly moved independently. What was once a multipolar system could become a bipolar one with several major powers, but those powers might now be combined into just two opposing alliances.

When there are more than four major actors, it is more difficult to know whether the addition of another would fundamentally change interactions. The difference in multipolar systems with four and with five actors might not be substantial. Beyond that point, however, as conditions approached those of perfect competition, the pattern of interactions might again be different.

By these criteria, a system might be stable if there were always four or more major powers within it, but the identity of these powers might change frequently as a result of wars, growth, or internal dissension in some states. When the number or identity of major actors (whether national actors or alliance blocs) changes, we say that the system has been transformed to a new system *only* if the changes seem to produce fundamentally different patterns of interaction.

CHARACTERISTICS OF SYSTEMS: POLARITY

There is a lively controversy over which type of system is likely to be less war prone and more stable. One fairly common viewpoint stresses the alleged success of bipolar systems in avoiding major war. This theory states that, despite the fears and hostilities likely to be built up between the two principal antagonists, a major war between them is improbable. One reason is that in a bipolar system, the two major pow-

---

7. See Theodore Caplow, *Two against One: Coalitions in Triads* (Englewood Cliffs, N. J.: Prentice-Hall, 1968) for theory and many examples.

ers are rather evenly matched, at least to the degree that neither has a good chance of easy victory. War would be long and costly, and the risks of losing, even for the side that may initially seem superior, would be substantial. After coexisting in the same system for a long time, the leaders of the two powers will have developed some skill in crisis management and learned what kinds of acts are likely to provoke dangerous reactions from the opponent. This is perhaps especially true in the contemporary nuclear bipolar system, but it may have also applied to others in the past.

Just as we found it essential to distinguish the amount of war by frequency, duration, and severity, to discuss the consequences of various systems we must make some careful analytical distinctions among various meanings of the concept of polarity.

First, from the previous discussion, we clearly must consider the *number* of poles or major actors. As we indicated, a pole may be composed either of a single nation or an alliance. Second is the *relative capabilities* of the various poles; hence, some observers distinguish between the bipolar system immediately following World War II and the bipolar system more characteristic of the 1970s. In the former, the United States was much stronger than the second-ranking power (the Soviet Union), and those two ranked far above any other powers. As alliances, moreover, the U.S.-led Western alliance was clearly stronger than the Soviet-led alliance. Despite the existence of two superpowers and two opposing alliance systems, one could speak of a system that tilted toward a unipolar dominance, or hegemony, by the United States. By the 1980s, the capabilities of America and the Soviet Union taken alone were much more nearly equal and still well above any other states. If, however, one includes in the American pole the substantial capabilities of its major allies—Western Germany, France, the United Kingdom, and Japan—and no longer considers China in alliance with the Soviet Union, the Western alliance remains stronger. Some data illustrating these points are shown in Table 5.1. Energy consumption is a generalized measure of the volume of economic production; military expenditures provide a very rough indicator of military capabilities.

Two other characteristics relevant to many theories are the "tightness" and "discreteness" of the poles. We may describe a system as tight if nearly all members of the pole are bound to one another by alliances or other linkages. It would be as though all members of the Rio Pact in the Western Hemisphere were allied not only with one another and with the United States, but also with the United States' allies in other

Table 5.1

Relative strength of major powers and alliances, 1955 and 1980–81.

1955

Energy consumption			Military expenditures		
Country or alliance	Million metric tons of coal or equivalent	Percentage of total	Country or alliance	Millions of current U.S. dollars	Percentage of total
United States	1,314	53.0	United States	35.8	48.7
Soviet Union	439	17.7	Soviet Union	26.4	36.0
United Kingdom	254	10.2	United Kingdom	4.4	5.9
W. Germany	175	7.1	France	3.3	4.5
France	114	4.6	China	3.1	4.2
China	97	3.9	Japan	0.4	0.6
Japan	88	3.5	W. Germany	0	0
U.S., U.K., W.G., France, Japan	1,945	78.4	U.S., U.K., W.G., France, Japan	43.9	59.8
S.U. and China	536	21.6	S.U. and China	29.5	40.2

1980–81

Energy consumption			Military expenditures		
Country or alliance	Million metric tons of coal or equivalent	Percentage of total	Country or alliance	Millions of current U.S. dollars	Percentage of total
United States	2,345	41.1	United States	144.0	36.7
Soviet Union	1,536	27.0	Soviet Union	130.0	33.2
China	572	10.0	China	28.0	7.1
Japan	421	7.4	United Kingdom	26.8	6.8
W. Germany	346	6.1	W. Germany	26.7	6.8
United Kingdom	259	4.5	France	26.5	6.8
France	220	3.9	Japan	10.0	2.6
U.S., U.K., W.G., France, Japan	3,591	63.0	U.S., U.K., W.G., France, Japan	234.0	59.7
Soviet Union	1,536	27.0	Soviet Union	130.0	33.2

Sources: 1955 data from Bruce M. Russett and Elizabeth C. Hanson, *Interest and Ideology: The Foreign Policy Beliefs of American Businessmen* (San Francisco: W. H. Freeman and Company 1975), p. 3. Energy data for 1981 from *U.N. Statistical Yearbook, 1981* (New York: United Nations, 1983), pp. 726–59. Military data for 1980 from Appendix B of this book. Military data for China and the Soviet Union are subject to error. Some other estimates of Soviet spending are higher.

parts of the world, such as NATO. A system is discrete to the degree there are no linkages across poles, with the two alliance systems completely separate. In terms of formal alliances there have been few changes in the international system since the mid-1950s, when the postwar alliance system was fully formed. A few states (Cuba, Iran, Pakistan) have dropped out of the Western alliance system, and Albania is no longer allied to the USSR, but neither the tightness nor the discreteness of the European alliance bonds, as we have defined those terms, have changed significantly. If we look beyond just the legal bonds of alliance to other kinds of linkages among nations, however, clearly there have been important changes. "Détente," even its limited version, meant the initiation of many linkages of trade, finance, travel, and cultural exchange between Eastern and Western Europe, between Eastern Europe and the Soviet Union on the one hand and between Africa and Asia on the other; and most dramatically, between China and the United States, reestablished while those between China and the Soviet Union have drastically diminished. An examination of these transaction linkages—measured by value of trade or numbers of travelers, for instance—would show very substantial reductions in both the tightness and the discreteness of the major power groupings.

Proneness to War

A look at a wide variety of international systems at different times in world history and at less-than-global systems in different parts of the world offers some empirical evidence of the degree of war proneness associated with different types of systems. Our concern with system structure stems from the question of how the opportunities of structure affect international behavior. For example, many researchers have asked whether the formation of alliances leads to war or peace. Although the results have been very mixed, there is little evidence that alliances are directly related to the occurrence of war.[8]

Similarly, we need to ask about the relationship between polarity and war, with alliances being one of the key factors in the determination of polarity. One study found that unipolar systems dominated by a

---

8. See, for example, Charles W. Ostrom and Francis W. Hoole, "Alliances and Wars Revisited," *International Studies Quarterly* 22 (1978), 215–236; Jack Levy, "Alliance Formation and War Behavior," *Journal of Conflict Resolution* 25 (1981), 581–613. Michael D. Ward, *Research Gaps in Alliance Dynamics*, vol. 19, Monograph Series in World Affairs (Denver: University of Denver, 1981), pp. 39–48, reviews this debate.

"peacekeeper," had very few wars; bipolar systems had few but prolonged wars; multipolar systems had both a larger number of wars and
a higher number of war casualties. Another study, examining systems
dating from 1824 to 1938, found a complex relationship. Instead of a
simple linear or straight-line relationship between the number of poles
and war, the authors identified what is termed a curvilinear relationship. Figure 5.1 illustrates these two kinds of relationships. In the
study described, they found that "the probability of war is moderately
large in the bipolar system" but much lower in a system with three
major poles. Then it is still higher "with the addition of more actors,
peaking at a system size five . . . and then declines again sharply" when
the system has six poles. Still another study, of the period between
1816 and 1965, found essentially no relationship between the number
of poles and the frequency or duration of war; however, the author of
that study looked only for a linear relationship, not a curvilinear one.
This same author, however, did look carefully for a relationship between differences in the tightness and discreteness of systems and
their war proneness, and found no linear relationship there either.[9]

These findings are neither entirely clear nor entirely consistent. Part
of the problem is simply that the set of cases, or sample, being examined is rather small for statistical analysis. (Though for human welfare
we can be glad there have not been more wars!) Also, each author has
used a somewhat different set of cases and somewhat different analytical or statistical tools. Thus, the evidence is inconclusive, and we cannot say with confidence whether systems with a certain number of
poles are more war prone than others. *No* simple hypothesis provides
an adequate explanation. Later in the chapter we shall turn to more
promising theories stating that *changes* in polarity are related to war
proneness. Nevertheless, there is some support here for the idea that

---

9. The relevant studies are, in order, Michael Haas, "International Subsystems: Stabil-
ity and Polarity," *American Political Science Review* 64 (March 1970), no. 1, pp. 98–124; C. W.
Ostrom and H. J. Aldrich, "The Relationship between Size and Stability in the Major
Power International System," *American Journal of Political Science* 22 (November 1978), no.
4, pp 743–771; Bruce Bueno de Mesquita, "Systemic Polarization and the Occurrence and
Duration of War," *Journal of Conflict Resolution* 22 (June 1978), no. 2, pp. 241–267. Manus
Midlarsky, "Power, Uncertainty, and the Onset of International Violence," *Journal of Conflict Resolution* 18 (September 1974), no. 3, pp. 395–431, also reports a curvilinear relationship, but the most marked difference in war frequencies is found for the difference
between unipolar and bipolar systems; above two poles the increase in war frequency is
small. Finally, Michael Wallace, "Alliance Polarization, Cross-Cutting, and International
War, 1815–1964," *Journal of Conflict Resolution* 17 (December 1973), no. 4, pp. 575–604,
found war more probable at very low and at very high levels of tightness of polarity and
less probable at middle levels.

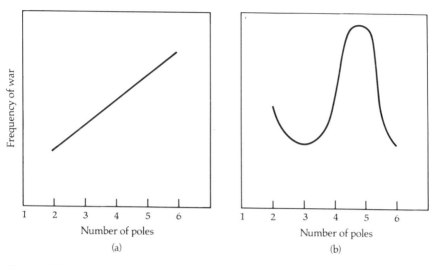

Figure 5.1
Number of poles and frequency of war. (a) Linear relationship between number of poles and frequency of war. (b) Curvilinear relationship between number of poles and frequency of war as reported by Ostrom and Aldrich.

systems with four or five poles may have more wars than bipolar ones and possibly more than systems with many poles. It may help to review some of the theories that have been put forth on the topic, again bearing in mind the different meanings of "amount of war."

In bipolar systems, wars may typically take the form of one pole nibbling at the periphery of the power sphere of the other. The Korean and Indochinese wars of recent decades fit this characterization. The system is likely to evoke intense competition, with pressure and counterpressure against each other's positions and strong feelings of threat and hostility that may get out of hand. Even wars that begin only as internal conflicts somewhere on the periphery of a power sphere may become transformed into struggles between blocs as one bloc leader fears it is about to lose an ally. Furthermore, there is always the risk in a bipolar system that if a war does break out between the two great antagonists, it will be terribly severe; even a rather low probability of conflict may, in the face of tremendous potential damage, seem frightfully high. Many deaths, even in only a few wars, would still mean enormous devastation. Accidents may occur from physical or human causes. Their consequences may seem very undesirable if the probability of an accident seems substantial. The result is a great emphasis on crisis management and efforts to avoid direct confrontation between the two major antagonists, although their proxies may fight. This last phenomenon, *proxy war,* has occurred frequently in recent decades, most prevalently in Africa (e.g., Angola and Ethiopia), where each of the superpowers has provided weapons and training to an ally but has avoided direct involvement of its own troops. Thus, there may even be many local, small wars that are not fought by the superpowers themselves. (Remember, however, that while such wars may seem small compared with one that pitted the two big powers against each other, they may not seem small to the states involved.)

At the other extreme from unipolar and bipolar systems is a system with *many* independent centers of power, none of which is strong enough to dominate the others. It is possible that such a system would both be quite stable—in the sense of maintaining the same pattern of interactions—and have little war. In a system with many states and no permanent polarities, the leaders of one nation must maintain proper relations with most of the others. Alignments are likely to shift frequently, so that an opponent on one issue today may be needed as an ally regarding some quite different issue tomorrow. In order to retain the possibility of future cooperation, it is important that a nation not let any temporary antagonisms get out of hand to embitter relations more generally. Multiple and cross-cutting ties of this sort are familiar to the student of stable democratic politics within nations and seem to be an important factor in promoting problem solving. The larger the system, the more numerous the possibilities are for coalition forming and the better the chances for this mechanism to work smoothly.

Two well-known analysts have suggested that cross-cutting ties might be a virtue of some international systems. In addition, they propose that for hostility to become severe and threaten to develop into war, a state or individual must devote a large proportion of attention to the disliked object; if attention must be scattered to keep watch on others, no single antagonism can become deep enough for violent conflict.[10] Hence, the more independent actors there are the less the chance of war. This latter point, however, depends on the assumption that with many states, attention will necessarily be diffused. In a real international system, this is hardly true. States will pay great attention to their immediate neighbors and perhaps to other states with whom they maintain especially important relations. Many other states will be

---

10. The argument is developed in Karl W. Deutsch and J. David Singer, "Multipolar Power Systems and International Stability," in James N. Rosenau (ed.), *International Politics and Foreign Policy,* 2nd ed. (New York: Free Press, 1969).

essentially ignored in order to permit that concentration of attention. The typical Central American state, for instance, may devote a great deal of attention to a neighbor with whom it has a border dispute but give little attention to Asian affairs. Thus, a big part of the hypothesized stability of a many-poled system rests on some rather shaky assumptions. If this hypothesis were true, however, it would have some interesting implications for one ideal-type international system. The small states of the world might like to see both the United States and the USSR each broken up into many smaller components to create an international system with many poles. If there were many wars in such a system, however, one would expect many defeated states to be eliminated and thus perhaps a gradual decrease in the number of actors over time.

BALANCE OF POWER IN A MULTIPOLAR SYSTEM

A many-poled system is hardly in prospect. A more relevant model shows a balance of power among several (but not many) states or groups of states. A balance-of-power system is characterized by a special pattern of state behavior. Basically, if several major powers are competing with one another, they will group together in ways that will prevent any one power or group from becoming dominant. Roughly equivalent capabilities among groups—and especially a willingness to shift alliances or even go to war to prevent any one actor from upsetting the balance of power—form the heart of this system. Efforts to maintain a balance of power have been common in various periods of history, but those efforts were by no means always successful and sometimes led to large as well as small wars. In an old but still important book, Morton Kaplan listed what he considered to be the essential rules that states *should* follow if a system is to be stable:[11]

1. Increase capabilities, but negotiate rather than fight.
2. Fight rather than fail to increase capabilities.
3. Stop fighting rather than eliminate a major power.
4. Oppose any coalition or single nation that tends to become predominant within the system.

---

11. Morton Kaplan, *System and Process in International Politics* (New York: Wiley, 1957), chap. 2.

5. Oppose any nation that "subscribes to supranational organizing principles," that is, one that promotes an ideology of subordinating nation-states to some higher authority.

6. Treat all major powers as acceptable partners. Permit a defeated power to reenter the system as an acceptable partner or replace it by strengthening some previously weak power.

If these rules are followed, states will compete with one another and there may even be fairly frequent wars (see the second rule). Yet the wars will not be terribly intense (rule 3), and the system itself will be stable in that the number and even the identity of the major powers is likely to remain quite constant.

Note that the war proneness of this multipolar balance-of-power system is not simply halfway between that of a unipolar or bipolar system and that of the many-poled system of Deutsch and Singer. With this kind of system, it is likely that rather frequent wars among the major powers could be tolerated without producing major changes in the system. Many such systems may have depended on frequent trials of strength, though perhaps limited in duration and intensity, to test the balance of power among their members and ensure that no nation grew disproportionately. This would account for the curvilinearity in war proneness mentioned above, where this type of system seems to have more wars than any other. The virtues of this system are supposedly in the relative restraint with which wars are fought and the stability of the system itself. The frequency of wars nevertheless makes it clear that a price is being exacted for the stability. The human and material cost of the total amount of warfare in the system is not necessarily less than in bipolar systems, which presumably have fewer but more intense conflicts. A preference for either system on this ground must await further theoretical refinement, more evidence, and a clarification of the values held by any particular observer.[12]

The hypothesized stability of multipolar systems has not been clearly demonstrated. True, there have been balance-of-power systems histori-

---

12. The theoretical case for preferring bipolar systems was made by Kenneth Waltz, "The Stability of a Bipolar World," *Daedalus* 93 (1964), no. 3, pp. 881–909. The distinction between frequency and severity of war in a bipolar system was well developed by Richard Rosecrance, "Bipolarity, Multipolarity, and the Future," in Rosenau (ed.), op. cit. Rosecrance suggests that something like a loose bipolar system (he terms it a case of "bimultipolarity") might achieve the best results, with fairly low frequency and severity of wars.

cally that were maintained for quite a long time. During most of the eighteenth and nineteenth centuries, Europe exhibited such a system, if we count the long and bloody Napoleonic Wars as an effort to dominate (or, from the viewpoint of Napoleon's opponents, prevent domination of) the system. This may be a relatively long duration. Nevertheless, it seems doubtful that the conditions for successfully maintaining a balance-of-power system could exist in the contemporary world. If some of Kaplan's rules for the balance-of-power system are ignored or broken, the system will break down. In that sense the rules prescribe how leaders ought to behave rather than describe how the leaders of nation-states do behave. If we examine these rules, we shall see how difficult it can be to follow them in reality and thus how fragile a balance-of-power system may be. Such examination will also lead us to note some more general considerations about system change.

Especially in an era of democratic politics and mass involvement in decision making, rule 6 (treat all major powers as acceptable partners) is especially hard to maintain. In the eighteenth century, with its aristocratic governments and close family and social ties between the elites of various nations, bitter warfare and harsh peace terms were rare. Since the French Revolution and the rise of nationalism, however, defeat in war can engender such hatred of the victor that the defeated nation is unwilling to ally with its conqueror in the future but instead presses for revenge. This is what happened in the French Third Republic after the war with Germany in 1870. Ideological fervor may inhibit certain alliances, as between Communist and non-Communist states. (For example, ideological differences delayed the rapprochement between the United States and China until a number of years after it first appeared to be in the two states' interest.) On the other hand, as we noted earlier in this chapter, states often prefer other states that are politically or ideologically similar as alliance partners. The passions resulting from mobilizing for total war in this century may lead to carrying out the first rule (fight rather than fail to increase capabilities) to extremes and to a demand for unconditional surrender that makes it difficult to observe rule 3 against eliminating a major power. Or the experience of fighting an unpopular and unsuccessful war (like the Vietnam war) may lead to the loss of the popular support necessary to increase capabilities, if necessary by fighting (rules 1 and 2). If public opinion swings sharply from interventionism to isolation and revulsion from foreign involvements, it may become difficult for decision makers to oppose effectively a dangerously growing opponent (rules 4 and 5).

Another source of instability arises from changes in states' capabilities that have little to do with the acquisition of new territories or allies (which may be opposed by other members of the system). A state's capabilities may increase with especially rapid economic growth, even without a conscious decision by its leaders to increase the state's power in the international system. Technological innovation may occur faster in one state than in another when a potent new weapon is developed and military capabilities consequently shift. (Such qualitative arms races have affected the relations between international actors throughout history, from the advent of the Macedonian phalanx to the contemporary development of ever more destructive, accurate, and protected nuclear weapons.) Changing economic needs may lead the commercial and industrial leaders of a nation-state to seek markets beyond their traditional alliance partners or sphere of influence, bringing new ties with the opposing alliance that diminish the tightness or discreteness of the system. Thus, a variety of economic, technological, or sociocultural changes may lead to the breakdown of one system and the emergence of another.

Yet another kind of risk stems directly from the frequent trials of strength that are such an integral part of the balance-of-power system. If wars do occur, sometimes a major power may be eliminated or fatally weakened because of a miscalculation, the state of domestic opinion in the victor, or the internal cohesiveness of the loser. For instance, at the beginning of World War I, none of the major enemies of Austria-Hungary envisaged the breakup of that empire and its disappearance from the ranks of major powers. But when a major power is eliminated, it may be very hard to find another state capable of filling the gap (rule 6). By mere chance—or at least by the influence of factors that can at best be considered nearly random—some big states will continue to grow bigger when others fail to restrain them. Thus, there are certain elements in any system that tend to eliminate some major powers and to strengthen others, making precarious the maintenance of the sensitive balance required in the long run.

In the contemporary world, the spread of nuclear weapons is likely to create a situation quite different from what would exist in the absence of nuclear power but with otherwise similar national power bases. Kaplan imagined a "unit veto" system, where each state in a multipolar system had the power to destroy others without being able to defend itself. It may well be that the possession of nuclear weapons instills a sense of caution and responsibility; the awfulness of nuclear war may restrain leaders from any major exercise of force out of fear that small wars will escalate into big ones. Nevertheless, the existence of nuclear weapons will probably make any war that does occur much more intense. Even if major wars would be somewhat less frequent in a nuclear multipolar system than in a conventional one, the high intensity of such wars would probably cancel out the gains from the diminution in frequency.

THE EFFECT OF SYSTEM CHANGE

We have begun to speculate about some of the reasons why international systems change. A further discussion of system dynamics— rather than of the characteristics of static systems—would address not only why and how systems change but also what the effects of system change are on the frequency and severity of war. Both some theoretical argumentation and the limited amount of careful empirical study suggest that periods of change may be especially dangerous. George Modelski has argued that there are 100-year-long "cycles of global politics." Modelski argues that global wars, fought by major powers, result in the establishment of a dominant world power and thus a high concentration of political, military, and economic capabilities. A number of factors lead to the neglect and overextension of the dominant power's concentration of capabilities; as its dominance wanes over the century-long period, the conditions for the next global war are created.[13]

A few studies that have found little systematic relationship between static characteristics of systems and war proneness have nevertheless found some relationship between *change* and war proneness. Most importantly, years when polarity tightened often were followed by war— according to one study, 84 percent of wars in the twentieth century were preceded by years of rising systemic tightness. By contrast, years of decreases in tightness, or of increases in the number of poles, were less likely to be followed by war.[14]

The reason for this may be rooted in the information-processing capacities of decision makers. Decision makers must estimate the relative

13. George Modelski, "The Long Cycle of Global Politics and the Nation-State," *Comparative Studies in Society and History* 20 (1978), 214–235. See also William R. Thompson, "Uneven Economic Growth, Systemic Challenges, and Global Wars," *International Studies Quarterly* 27 (1983), 341–355; Karen A. Rasler and W. R. Thompson, "Global Wars, Public Debts, and the Long Cycle," *World Politics* 35 (1983), 489–516.

14. Bueno de Mesquita, "Systemic Polarization," op. cit. and Frank Whelon Wayman, "Bipolarity and War: The Role of Capability Concentration and Alliance Patterns among Major Powers, 1816–1965," *Journal of Peace Research* 21, 1 (1984), 25–42.

gains or losses they can expect from various courses of action. A rational decision maker will choose the course of action promising the greatest gain or the least loss. That estimate of probable gain or loss is composed of two elements: the absolute gain or loss to be achieved if any act succeeds and the probability of success. Both of these elements—absolute value and probability—are included in the calculations political decision makers must make. The gain from a war fought in order to rule the world might be high if the war were successful, but most decision makers would consider the probability of success low and the losses in case of failure severe. Most decision makers, therefore, would not undertake such a war. Similarly, if you are offered a chance to win $1 million, the attractiveness of the bet depends on whether you think the odds of success are 100 to 1 or 10 million to 1.

In making such estimates, a political decision maker has to consider the relative power of his or her own state, enemies, and allies. The probability that allies will help and the probability that the enemy's allies will help the enemy must be considered. Tightening blocs imply greater clarity of alliance patterns, and hence increasingly predictable behavior. Increased tightness may come from upgrading already existing ties or from adding new, highly committed allies. The leader of one alliance may see his or her strength significantly increased and expectations of winning a war improved if his alliance is tightened but the opposing alliance is not. The leader thus becomes more willing to engage in war.[15] Notice that in this explanation we have interpreted a phenomenon—tightening or loosening of polarity—at the systemic level of analysis in terms of a characteristic of the states (power) and of a relation between states (alliance). We have then phrased the interpretation in terms of calculations by individual decision makers who are in charge of the states. In any theoretically satisfying explanation of international political phenomena, we have to specify the *process* by which various *levels are linked.*

The importance of changes in systems leading to war is supported by a careful look at pre–World War I Europe. Between 1900 and 1914 Europe was increasingly polarized, most notably by the addition of previously unallied England to the entente of France and Russia, by in-

---

15. Bueno de Mesquita, "Systemic Polarization," op. cit., p. 263. Bueno de Mesquita further develops these and related propositions in his book, *The War Trap* op. cit., and his article "Theories of International Conflict: An Analysis and Appraisal," in Ted Robert Gurr (ed.), *Handbook of Political Conflict: Theory and Research* (New York: Free Press, 1980).

creases in the tightness of the opposing alliance, and by a shift in relative capabilities in favor of the entente.[16]

States that are farthest apart on measures of power are least likely to become engaged in armed conflict. Both sides can easily calculate who would win in a military showdown, and the weaker is likely to give in to all but the most extreme demands. Of course, the weaker side does not always give in, as was apparent in confrontations between the United States and North Vietnam or the United States and Iran. Nor does the stronger state always win a war. As we shall see in Chapter 6, factors such as geographical distance, national morale, and a state's organizational ability make a difference and complicate simple calculations . International violence is more likely among states that are somewhat more equal on measures of power such as those reviewed in Chapter 3—area, GNP, military manpower, defense expenditure, and energy production.

Change during a Period of Near Equality

In a classic statement, A. F. K. Organski argued that "nations are reluctant to fight unless they believe they have a good chance of winning, but this is true for both sides only when the two are fairly evenly matched, or at least they believe they are."[17] Organski focuses on the period of "power transition," when a rising challenger approximates the power of the dominant state. "If great change occurs within a single

---

16. Alan Ned Sabrosky, "From Bosnia to Sarajevo: A Comparative Discussion of International Crises," *Journal of Conflict Resolution* 19 (March 1975), no. 1, pp. 3-24.

17. This and the following quotations are from A. F. K. Organski, *World Politics,* 2nd ed. (New York: Knopf, 1968), pp. 294, 480, 361. Evidence that wars are more common among states nearly equal in power is reviewed by Randolph Siverson and Michael P. Sullivan, "The Distribution of Power and the Onset of War," *Journal of Conflict Resolution* 27 (September 1983), no. 3, pp. 473-494. They find some reason to support this idea but term the evidence inconclusive. Thus here we do not attribute so much importance to the power balance as to changes in that balance. J. David Singer reports that while only 13 percent of all militarized disputes between major powers since 1816 escalated to war, the percentage rose to 75 where the parties were approximately equal in military power and there was a rapid military buildup in the three years preceding the dispute. See his "Accounting for International War: The State of the Discipline," *Journal of Peace Research* 17 (1980). Recent important work on the likelihood of changes in relative power leading to war includes A. F. K. Organski and Jacek Kugler, *The War Ledger* (Chicago: University of Chicago Press, 1981), chap. 2; Charles F. Doran and Wes Parsons, "War and the Cycle of Relative Power," *American Political Science Review* 74 (December 1980), no. 4, pp. 947-965. Robert Gilpin, *War and Change in World Politics* (Cambridge: Cambridge University Press, 1981) makes an important argument, with historical illustrations, supporting this view.

lifetime, both challenger and dominant nation may find it difficult to estimate their relative power correctly, and may stumble into a war that would never have been fought if both sides had foreseen where the victory would lie." It is the condition of change that affects calculations of relative power. The challenger may start a war because he thinks that now, for the first time, it has a good chance to win. Or the dominant power may foresee its own strength declining and thus calculate that it is better off fighting now while it still has some advantages, than to risk waiting until its position may be significantly worse. By this interpretation, it is the fact of change during a period of near equality that makes war likely, not just the fact of equality itself. Change makes calculations of power and war outcome difficult because the evidence is ambiguous (even though the decision makers may not see the ambiguity). Decision makers may miscalculate especially when the *rate of change is itself changing*, that is, when the rate at which an increase or decrease in relative power slows or speeds up. Miscalculation may then lead to the escalation of small wars, thus making this a time when major wars are especially likely.

Organski also suggests that "a rapid rise in power . . . produces dissatisfaction in itself." This means that the newly powerful state has not yet acquired respect or status as an equal power, so its leaders experience some status disequilibrium. Under these changing conditions it may be more willing to take the risk of going to war.

What do we make of this information in the current international system? As we noted, the post–World War II era has been a substantially bipolar system, but with some changes. The relative power of the two poles has changed from the U.S. pole being much stronger than the Soviet pole to the two poles being nearly equal. Recent changes in the relative strength of major poles come as much from differing internal rates of economic growth as from the addition or loss of allies. Nevertheless, there have also been decreases in tightness and the discreteness of the major poles. The former alliance between China and the Soviet Union has been broken. American allies in Europe and Japan have recovered both their economic strength and a degree of political independence from the United States. The shift in oil prices (more than a tenfold increase between 1972 and 1980) has given formerly dependent American allies, like Iran and Saudi Arabia, great economic power and the potential for substantial military independence.

If we look at static characteristics, there is some reason to fear that a multipolar configuration might be more war prone than present configuration. On the other hand, according to the findings of Bueno de Mesquita, recent changes toward a looser system of polarity are encouraging. Thus, so long as polarities continue to loosen, the chances of war do not increase and perhaps even diminish. But other elements—especially the rapid change in the relative power of the leading states— give grounds for concern. They suggest that rising Soviet strength and concerted efforts by the United States to curb increases in that strength could create a very dangerous period, demanding particularly careful and calm decision making.

SOME POSSIBLE CONSEQUENCES
OF POLITICAL CHOICES

At first glance, the structure of the international system might seem a "given" condition for policymakers, not something that is a "manipulable." It is not, however, entirely outside the long-term control of policymakers in the great powers. The superpowers strive mightily not only to match or surpass each other's military capabilities but to maintain bipolarity by insuring that their capabilities far exceed those of all smaller states. Their policies to prevent nuclear proliferation are also designed, in part, to maintain their own dominance.

Other kinds of decisions also illustrate how policymakers make choices that will ultimately make a huge difference in the kind of international system we inhabit. How to deal with China and whether to encourage or inhibit Sino-Soviet attempts to heal their rift had these implications. A similar choice was always at issue in American policy toward the European community and particularly in supporting the British application for membership in the 1960s. A world with a strongly united Western Europe, including Britain, has a far different structure than one where Europe remained politically fragmented. During most of the post–World War II years, most Americans have seemed to regard European unification as a good thing, but not necessarily on the basis of careful consideration of its consequences. Whether a united Europe would remain closely allied to the United States or how it would behave if it did not has rarely been asked in a rigorous and searching manner.

We see here how policy decisions have major implications for what might seem the most intractable and least manipulable of the major influences on international politics: the structure of the international system. The creative, daring, tenacious, and skilled statesman may be able to expand the menu.

In this chapter we have been concerned with characteristics of the international system, especially those that seem related to the frequency and severity of war between countries. As we looked at these characteristics, we found that the nature of the international system depended heavily on the alliances or other linkages between states. It is time, therefore, to shift our focus to a lower (that is, less comprehensive) level of analysis to consider the relations among states, and especially to questions of what *power* and *influence* really mean and how they are exercised in the contemporary world system.

6

RELATIONS BETWEEN STATES: BASES AND ANALYSIS OF POWER

FOREIGN POLICY AND POWER AS RELATIONSHIPS

Power as well as foreign policy can be thought of as a relationship. Each takes on meaning only as it affects a state's behavior toward another state or international actor. The menu of any state, then, is constrained or affected not only by its own capabilities, goals, policies, and actions but also by those of the state with which it interacts. Relationships between states can be seen in two ways, each of which will be described in our discussion of power. First, we can look at how two states compare on a set of national attributes or characteristics; the capabilities of a state become meaningful when they are compared with those of other international actors. Second, we can look at the actual set of interactions between pairs of states—how they behave toward each other. In discussing power we shall be concerned with both *attributes of power* and *power as a process* of interaction—how states influence others to behave.

International relations scholars have been concerned with studying the relationships between pairs of states, or *dyads*. They theorize that by looking at the "distances" or differences between two states in regard to certain attributes, they can predict how one state will behave toward the other.[1] These studies take into account both attribute space and behavior space. *Attribute space* means studying the different characteristics, or attributes, of states and trying to measure the differences or distances between them. *Behavior space* means studying the ways each of the states behaves toward the other.

Let us give just one example of using *dyadic interaction* to analyze foreign policy behavior. Using five nations—the United States, the USSR, Egypt, Syria, and Israel—over the period from 1950 to 1972, Edward Azar and colleagues found that simple "action producing reaction" models were able to explain much of the variation in the cooperative and conflictual behavior directed by one member of a dyad toward the other. That is, most of the hostile actions of, say, Israel toward Egypt could have been predicted by previous hostile actions of Egypt toward Israel, and vice versa. Even more notable, the researchers found that the interactions by a state with the others (e.g., Egypt with the United States, USSR, and Syria) were of little help in explaining interactions in the dyad (e.g., with Israel).[2]

So far, we have suggested that the two relational approaches to foreign policy and power can be useful in understanding the behavior of states. We need to review the specific processes, mechanisms, and tools that states use in their foreign policy interactions. Since it is basic to definitions of foreign policy, and since the concept is vital to understanding exactly what it is that states are tryng to do and why differences in certain capabilities should be significant, we begin our discussion by looking at power.

---

1. See, for example, Quincy Wright, *A Study of War*, 2nd ed. (Chicago: University of Chicago Press, 1965), chap. 35 or Appendix 40; Rudolph Rummel, *Field Theory Evolving* (Beverly Hills, Calif.: Sage, 1977); Michael P. Sullivan, *International Relations: Theories and Evidence* (Englewood Cliffs, N.J.: Prentice-Hall, 1976), chaps. 4–5; Jack Vincent et al., "Empirical Test of Attribute, Social Field and Status Field Theories on International Relations Data," *International Studies Quarterly* 17 (1973), 405–443.

2. Edward E. Azar, James P. Bennett, and Thomas J. Sloan, "Steps toward Forecasting International Interaction," *Peace Science Society, Papers* 23 (1974), 27–28. For a study that uses attribute distance to explain foreign policy behavior, see Rudolph Rummel, "U.S. Foreign Relations: Conflict, Cooperation and Attribute Distances," in Bruce M. Russett (ed.), *Peace, War and Numbers* (Beverly Hills, Calif.: Sage, 1972), pp. 71–113. Almost half of the variation in U.S. behavior to other states is explained by differences between the United States and the other state on a number of attributes.

POWER: ONE OR MANY?
WHICH METAPHOR TO USE?

Power plays a central role in the study of world politics. It means many different things to different people. "One or many" refers to the question of whether we should attempt to find a definition or meaning of power that is as general, unified, or multidimensional as possible or whether we should break the concept of power down into its many forms, deal with each of them, and then drop the word *power* from our analysis. Power has many broad meanings and is conceived of in different ways. To some it is best seen as a set of attributes; to others it is an influence process. It is seen by some as the ability to control—to control resources, other actors, events, and outcomes.[3] Some see power as the ability to control or reduce uncertainty in the environment. For some it is the means to an end, while for others power has come to mean causality, because explaining who has power explains why things happen. Others say power is like money in the sense that it can be saved and spent, while some see it as merely affecting the probability of outcomes. One view is that it is primarily a psychological phenomenon, that power exists if others think you possess it. The list could go on and on. But what do we mean by power? Let's break the concept down into more manageable sections.

As we noted in Chapter 2, realism is a view of international politics that sees people seeking power and desiring to dominate others. Hans Morgenthau, the most widely read exponent of this approach, stated the matter succinctly in his classic testbook, *Politics among Nations.* The section titled "International Politics as a Struggle for Power" opens with the following words: "International politics, like all politics, is a struggle for power. Whatever the ultimate aims of international politics, power is always the immediate aim." This view of power is centered on struggle and is characterized by the use and manipulation of military resources.

Other observers, however, came to object to the realists' stress on constant struggle and their highly conflictual, coercive, and military interpretation of the concept of power. They argued that although power is central to international politics, it takes many forms. To stress only the struggle aspects would distort how states actually behave and how they attempt to reach their objectives in international politics. As

---

3. See particularly Jeffrey Hart, "Three Approaches to the Measurement of Power in International Relations," *International Organization* 30 (1976), 289–305.

we stated earlier, there are a multitude of definitions of power. Let us use for now a simple, all-encompassing definition provided by Karl Deutsch: Power is *the ability to prevail in conflict and overcome obstacles.* This is useful because it indicates that power is the ability to get what you want—to achieve a desired outcome through *control* of one's environment (both human and nonhuman). The questions now are, first, how does one go about getting what one wants, and second, what do we mean by *conflict*? Conflict may not mean struggle or the threat of using or actual use of weapons. States, like people, come into conflict with others every day on a wide variety of issues. A decision to sell nuclear reactors to Brazil, the negotiations over the price of Mexican oil, and dealing with the effects of acid rain on Canada are all issues in which the United States comes into conflict with other states. The United States has its set of objectives, and the other states have theirs. As long as there are any incompatibilities between these sets of objectives, conflict will arise. But the manner in which these conflicts are resolved and the manner in which the United States attempts to prevail may have little resemblance to the concept of struggle and certainly will not involve the use of or the threat of the use of military force. It may not even involve coercion.[4]

Power conceived of as overcoming obstacles does not indicate how those obstacles are overcome. Power may mean achieving this state of affairs simply by the application of force to eliminate the opponent. There is still the relational element here: to get the Iranians to comply with American wishes during the hostage crisis, the United States could have simply removed Iran from the face of the earth with nuclear weapons (or it could do the same today with Cuba). The United States would then have acted toward another state and expected no behavior from the other—simply expecting it to be vaporized. The overwhelming majority of international interactions do not work this way. Most behavior requires other states or actors to respond, ideally in the manner desired. This form of power is called *influence.*

---

4. In fact, as Charles McClelland and Gary Hoggard show, in 1966 only one third of international behavior could be categorized as conflictual, one third cooperative, and one third neutral. Of the conflictual third, only a tiny percentage actually consisted of the use of force. See "Conflict Patterns in the Interactions Among Nations," in James N. Rosenau (ed.), *International Politics and Foreign Policy* (New York: Free Press, 1969), pp. 711–724.

INFLUENCE AND HOW TO GET IT

Power means getting one's way. *Influence* is one method by which people and states get their way. In its most general form, influence means *getting others to do the things you want them to do.* It is the ability to affect the behavior of others. This is the most relational aspect of power. Influence only makes sense when one is able to have some other actor behave in the desired manner in order to achieve some objective. In this formulation, *influence is a form of power.* If power is the general ability to prevail in conflict and overcome obstacles, influence is one way—in fact, the dominant way—states do this.

Influence itself takes many forms. To control others' behavior, a number of different objectives and procedures can be used. Sometimes we think of influence as actually changing the existing policy of another decision maker or country: leaving a rival's alliance and joining one's own, changing sides on a vote in the United Nations, or buying new tanks from one's own country rather than from a previous supplier. One form of this type of influence, especially in military situations, is called *compellence:* getting another country to stop an action it is already pursuing. For example, cases of attempted compellence include getting the North Vietnamese to withdraw from South Vietnam in the 1960s, getting the Cubans to leave Africa, or getting Iran to release American diplomatic hostages in 1979. As these examples suggest, compellence—because it seeks to reverse an established policy—can be very difficult to enact.

Other kinds of influence merely try to encourage another actor to continue doing things one likes, such as remaining in one's alliance and importing one's goods. If the emphasis is on persuading the other actor not to commit some act that would offend one's state, we speak of *deterrence.* Nuclear deterrence (which we shall discuss at length in another chapter) is the prime example of negative influence in the contemporary system. The United States influences the Soviet Union not to attack it with nuclear weapons (through fear of retaliation), and vice versa. Having the ability to stop others from doing what they want to do before they do it is a major element of any state's influence. There are many theories and speculations about deterrence but few satisfactory studies of deterrence in practice. It is easier (though still difficult) to look at the behavior one has influenced another state to perform than to observe the processes behind something that has *not* happened. For example, did NATO's strength deter a Soviet attack on Western Europe—or did the Russians never want to attack anyway? Somewhat related to negative influence is the idea of a *veto influence*, where one actor can simply prevent another from obtaining the desired goal. In the contemporary system, small states have the ability to prevent larger states from winning guerrilla wars. They can do this by not losing. North Vietnam, for example, could not win the Indochina conflict by forcing the United States to its knees, invading the United States, or the like. It could, however, simply not lose. It could keep the conflict going until the United States tired and withdrew from its involvement.

Another form of influence is *potential influence*. Some people think that influence exists only as a psychological phenomenon. What is important in international relations, they argue, are the *perceptions* of the capabilities and intentions of other states. Potential influence is based on the perceptions that the decision makers of a state have of a situation and of the influence of other states. If a state has potential influence, other states will not even attempt certain activities because they know that such activities will fail or be very costly. If one state recognizes that another has a stronger bargaining position or a better set of tools of influence, a hard bargaining situation may never arise. By avoiding the bargaining situation, where the state is likely to have to give in anyway, it avoids acrimony and the spending of resources (e.g., time and attention) that the bargaining process would require. Influence is likely to be greatest when its instruments do not have to be utilized openly or even in veiled threats. One may anticipate another's reactions, know what the other wants, and do it without any request being made.

This sort of influence, of course, is most difficult to measure. It means that state *A* has influence over state *B* if *B* does not even attempt to do something. *B* removes this option from its menu because it anticipates that it will lose in some way. This is the second "face" of influence that some students of power and influence have mentioned.[5] They argue that influence cannot be measured by the number of successes one achieves, because some actors have potential influence. Less powerful actors anticipate the reactions of more powerful actors and refrain from certain activities. How many times might Panama have wanted to demand that the United States leave the Canal Zone in the 1920s or 1930s? We have no idea because we cannot measure how many times the desire occurred and then was suppressed because of fear of American reaction.

---

5. Peter Bachrach and Morton Baratz, "The Two Faces of Power," *American Political Science Review* 56 (1962), 947–952.

One further problem in measuring any type of influence should be noted. An apparent success in influencing another state or international actor might have happened anyway. As we noted, this is especially important in cases of deterrence (deterring the Soviet Union from attacking Europe), but is true for compellence also. For example, did the United States get the Egyptians and Israelis to sign a peace treaty, or would they have done so without American mediation? The party one is trying to influence may have had its own reasons for its behavior, or some other international actor might have had the crucial role in the actual behavior taken. Simply because *A* wants *B* to do something and *B* does it, does not prove that *A* actually influenced *B*.

METHODS OF INFLUENCE

Influence means getting one's way by having others behave in the way that one wants them to behave. How can a state successfully achieve influence? Briefly, a state needs certain capabilities and the willingness to use those capabilities (to carry out threats or fulfill promises), and the opponent must be vulnerable in some way (have needs or weaknesses). A state's capabilities present that state's decision makers with a more or less restricted menu of what is possible; they also affect those behaviors that the decision makers feel will most probably be successful. The capabilities of a state affect not only its opportunities but also its willingness to exploit those opportunities.

How may those opportunities be used? K. J. Holsti lists six different tactics that might be seen as an influence ladder:[6]

- Use of force
- Infliction of nonviolent punishment
- Threat of punishment (the "stick")
- Granting of rewards (the "carrot")
- Offer of rewards
- Persuasion

Persuasion is based on having another actor behave as desired without the use of promises or threats. It is based on the ability to demonstrate to the opponent that a certain behavior is in its interest. Clearly there

---

6. See K. J. Holsti, *International Politics*, 4th ed. (Englewood Cliffs, N.J.: Prentice-Hall, 1983), chap. 6.

are many situations where it is in both parties' interests to behave in certain ways. International politics is not composed entirely of zero-sum games, where if one side wins, the other must lose. Many situations exist where both can benefit, and persuasion is based on being able to convince the opponent that this is the case.[7] For example, in getting the Soviet Union to agree to arms control measures, the United States did not threaten destruction or promise aid, but often demonstrated to the Soviets that they would benefit both economically and in security from such agreements. Persuasion, then, consists of trying to indicate where common interests exist and getting the other side to behave in line with those interests. An example would be having others join your alliance by getting them to see the security value in it or getting an opponent to place safety devices on its strategic weapons because it is in the opponent's own interest (as well as yours) that nuclear accidents do not occur. Especially during the 1960s, this was exactly the case with the United States and Soviet Union: influence through example and persuasion to make weapons—and thus the international system—safer.

Common interests may be more readily perceived if states share common values. Harold Lasswell and Abraham Kaplan wrote about "bases of influence"—things people value that can be used to get them to do other things. They list four "welfare" values—*well-being, wealth, skill,* and *enlightenment*—and four "deference" values—*power, respect, rectitude* (or rightness), and *affection.* Persuasion can occur when one appeals to the values that others hold dear. If one can demonstrate that one also holds these values or is trying to contribute to them, an appeal based on neither promise nor threat can still result in others doing what one wishes. For example, as the leader of an ideology like Communism or anti-Communism, you can establish the legitimacy of your request: "You are anti-Communist; my country, the United States, was the leader of anti-Communism here in 1954. The alliance I am trying to create is anti-Communist and is aimed at the security of all anti-Communist states in this region. Thus, would you want to join? Don't you think you should join?" All these values, of course, are open to manipulation through reward and punishment—all things that people need or value leave them vulnerable to such influence. The point here,

---

7. Anatol Rapoport, *Fights, Games and Debates* (Ann Arbor, Mich.: University of Michigan Press, 1960), in categorizing conflict into fights, games, and debates, would see persuasion as a form of debate.

however, is that values can be used in influence through persuasion without resorting to either the carrot or the stick.

Bargaining: Manipulating Rewards and Punishments

How else do we influence others? Many people, thinking as realists, stress the top of the influence ladder. In a violence-prone world, we may think of the *application of force*. As noted, this crude form of influence is relatively rare, and under most conditions it is the least important means by which states induce other states to obey their will. More important for achieving influence is *bargaining*. Bargaining is a process often used for persuading, and it is also the medium through which one can attempt to *manipulate rewards and punishments* to influence others. Following the conflict ladder, rewards may be promised or actually provided; punishment may be inflicted or merely threatened. Our discussion of rewards, however, is intimately tied in with the use of punishment in bargaining.

Punishment   Punishment, of course, includes the application of force. It may take many other forms, however, such as the withdrawal of some privilege, favor, or mutual contract that already exists. If punishment is actually meted out, it is intended to hurt the opponent in some way. This punishment can also be used to persuade the opponent that the punishment will occur whenever an act is performed that you dislike, or it may be applied as an example of further punishment that will be administered in greater degree if the opponent continues or expands on the disliked act. Thus, one may simply threaten punishment without applying it, apply punishment to harm the opponent, or apply some punishment as an implicit threat of further punishment. But the emphasis here is on punishment as a means of influence in bargaining, not as brute force to eliminate the opponent.

As one example, the American rationale behind bombing North Vietnam from 1965 to 1968 was less to destroy Hanoi's ability to carry on the war—it was generally recognized that strategic bombing of a poor, basically agricultural country could not have that effect—than to show the North Vietnamese government that the war was too expensive for attaining any goals it might desire and to call the conflict off even though Hanoi might still retain the physical capacity to fight. The Americans knew they could not prevent Ho Chi Minh's government from infiltrating men and supplies into the South but hoped to make the effort too costly. Also, at times the bombing was used to convey an implicit threat that, unless the North Vietnamese made peace, aerial bombardment might be extended to presently off-limits targets such as urban areas. Thus, force became an instrument of persuasion in attempted bargaining. Other more successful examples could be cited from earlier international history.

There are many possible ways to threaten or apply punishment in bargaining situations. Physical (military) force is obvious, but others are far more common. A developed state may withhold foreign aid from a poor one; an underdeveloped state may nationalize investment of the citizens of a rich country; either type of state may cut off trading relations with the other. Ambassadors may be withdrawn, diplomatic relations severed, or, much more mildly, one may withdraw support from another's position on a pet issue at the United Nations. A great many other forms of punishment can be imagined and are used at one time or another, but it is important to notice that in many cases the punishment (or threat of punishment) consists in withdrawing something that had been available; it cannot be withdrawn unless it was there in the first place. One cannot cut off trade or sever diplomatic relations unless they already exist. Thus, in refusing to carry on these normal channels of intercourse with another country over a long period of time, both sides in the pair deprive themselves of possible future instruments of influence over each other's policies. This is likely to be a special loss for the larger, more powerful state in the pair, since if the normal ties existed, the smaller and weaker state would be likely to be more dependent on them.

Rewards It may often be useful to establish a rewarding relationship with another party if only to provide a potential means of punishment later. A far more common use of *rewards* in bargaining situations is their immediate potential for influencing the other party. The would-be influencer must ask what it can do for the other side (other than simply stop punishing it). Consider a situation that quickly came to be considered appropriate for the predominant use of threat and punishment, but perhaps need not have been: American policy in Southeast Asia in the middle and late 1950s. As it turned out, almost all attempts to influence North Vietnam took the form of punishment; in the context of actual developments over the following years, it may be hard to imagine having used anything else. President Johnson's proposal in 1965 of massive economic aid to the whole Mekong Valley area—which was particularly meant to include North Vietnam—was quickly brushed aside by the Communists. The offer to bring the North Vietnamese into development programs and to provide substantial assistance for the development of all Southeast Asian countries was dismissed as just an imperialist bribe or an empty public relations gesture. But such an offer a decade earlier, before the war, might not have been perceived that way.

Of course, no one can say whether this policy would have worked or even whether it was better than some other approach, such as applying great force quickly or accepting Communist efforts to unify North and South Vietnam from the beginning. But certainly the step-by-step, punishment-oriented policy that was tried was no success, and it is intriguing to speculate about the possibilities of a reward-oriented effort. Within countries most people obey laws less out of fear of punishment than out of habit, convenience, and a conviction that the law is basically just. It is odd that so many conceptions of international politics concentrate on coercion, deterrence, and punishment.

Political Investments

Our discussion of a possible strategy for influencing North Vietnam leads us to another category of means of influence, one that is closely related to bargaining but deserves separate treatment. Influence may come as a result of *improving one's asset position,* of acquiring new resources and wider options in policy making. The would-be influencer obtains more—in quantity and variety—of the instruments of bargaining; in effect, it *invests* its power in order to increase its influence. The most obvious and perhaps the commonest strategy is a rather straightforward type of material investment, such as trying to foster economic growth, encouraging scientific research, or improving the level of education of the population.

A kind of political investment is to do favors, establishing political credits that can be cashed later. Or a state may try to see that its own citizens or those of its allies occupy key positions in an international organization like the World Bank. This kind of political activity is an important instance of using influence in order to increase one's influence base. But like most investments, there is always a chance of failure. Too obvious an effort to seize key political posts may lead to a counteraction that leaves the would-be influencer weaker than before. Despite the intention to invest influence, one may merely consume.

In international politics, the establishment of trade and aid relations with another country—so that one can withdraw something as punishment if necessary—is a subtler kind of investment. Much the same can be said for various kinds of military assistance or cultural and educational exchanges. A small country might quite deliberately allow a big one to establish a military base on its territory, so that the big power will become dependent on the base and later make concessions to the small one in order to retain the facilities. Turkey and the Philippines seem to have done this with the United States. Many years after their establishment, American retention of air, naval, and intelligence bases became a *quid pro quo* for hundreds of millions of dollars of military and economic assistance and for inhibiting any American efforts to make the domestic policies in these countries less repressive. In such situations as these, it may even be helpful for the small country to encourage a moderate amount of discontent toward the bases among its own populace. It can then point to popular pressure to close the bases as evidence that special concessions must be made by the stronger country to mollify the populace. Again, this example shades into the bargaining strategy; the emphasis, however, is not on overt bargaining but on creating a situation where, without overt threats, the other partner comes to realize that one has acquired a more favorable position.

Another means of influence arises in the *building of a community:* a sense of kinship, of common loyalties and values, and of belonging together. Individuals' perceptions of their self-interest can be greatly broadened; if individuals no longer think only in terms of their own self-image, they will be willing to make certain sacrifices regardless of whether those sacrifices are directly reciprocated. Family members will make sacrifices for the common welfare or the welfare of another member. The identification and affection may be so strong that on some matters a husband or wife comes to prefer to do what the spouse wants rather than what he or she had originally desired.

Community building in this sense involves a tacit agreement—tacit because if one has to state it openly it is a very fragile affair—not to coerce others and to limit the scope of bargaining. In effect, one gives up certain bargaining options without having to say so explicitly. One example is marriage between people who don't believe in divorce and remarriage. The partners in such a case are stuck with each other; they have little choice but to ride out the relationship, make it last, and make the best of it. They may occasionally threaten to break off the relationship, but not to marry someone else (which would be a more effective threat). They have given up this option, and the very fact that they have done so often predisposes them to try harder to build trust and to meet each other's requests without resorting to open bargaining and coercion. Naturally, everyone does bargain somewhat within marriage, but in a reasonably good relationship both partners recognize their common interest in keeping the bargaining limited and an altruistic desire not to coerce.

Again, this kind of influence within a community is much weaker in a tightly knit nation-state than in a small group, and it is usually even weaker between states. But it still happens. We speak of an Atlantic community or a European community; the relationship is stronger within some segments of the community at large, for instance, within Scandinavia or among the United States, Britain, and Canada. Certainly not all is love and affection between the United States and Canada, but there is something qualitatively different between that relationship and the U.S.-China relationship. These strong bonds of communication and attention are very important. We said above that a state might want to establish commercial relations or educational and cultural exchanges with another state to have a direct means of influence (such as rewards to offer or the threat to withdraw as punishment). Some of the most important functions of trade or other exchanges, however, may be their contribution to building and maintaining a sense of community between states and peoples.

Some means of influence are very subtle. A form of persuasion is changing the other person's (or country's) likes and dislikes so that the person will end up wanting the same things one wants oneself. If that happens, then directly persuading the other to do something one wants done will not even be necessary. For this reason, major powers engage in various kinds of cultural and information programs. The United States sponsors the Voice of America, Radio Free Europe, and many cultural activities through the U.S. Information Agency. Advertising by American corporations helps not only to expand the markets for their products but also to promote a pattern of consumption like that in the American free enterprise economy. The Soviet Union has Radio Moscow, national "friendship" societies, and cheap publications of Communist tracts, and it often sends Soviet artistic performers on tour. France spends large sums promoting the French language and French culture. All of these help to cultivate groups of people who think like Americans, Russians, or French people, wanting many of the same things as those people do and sympathizing with those major powers' political goals. Indeed, it is just this kind of influence that people in underdeveloped countries sometimes label "Coca-colonization" or, more generally, cultural imperialism.

POWER AND INFLUENCE AS ATTRIBUTES: CAPABILITIES AND THEIR MEASUREMENT

We opened this chapter with a few comments on how states compare on certain attributes and how these "distances" might influence their actions toward one another. We have also discussed activities specifically aimed at influencing other states. The examples provided give some idea of how military capabilities, economic resources, and wealth can be employed to influence the behavior of other states. We have said that national attributes or capabilities greatly influence the menu of activity available to states. Capabilities are directly related to the means at a country's disposal in implementing foreign policy. What is possible or probable relates to the means at one's disposal. This is especially important in gauging the activity of or reaction toward specific states. Here the relational aspect of power and influence is highlighted. Capabilities include any physical object, talent, or quality that can be used to affect the behavior of others. To affect behavior, remember, includes affecting how others perceive one's state, what one is able to do, and what one is willing to do.

Capabilities, then, are crucial to two different aspects of influence. First, for threats and promises to be useful as instruments of influence, they have to be *credible*. If someone is to believe a threat or promise, that person has to believe that the other is both able and willing to carry out the threat or promise. Capabilities are important in that one must indeed be *able* to carry out the threat or promise. The menu of the United States makes it possible to threaten or destroy another with nuclear weapons. This is a threat not available to Mexico or Sweden or Zambia. (Whether the United States is willing to carry out such a threat is another matter entirely.) Similarly, a promise of some sort must also be credible. In 1979, the U.S. promise to deliver economic aid to Egypt and oil to Israel if they would negotiate a peace treaty was credible because the United States had both the wealth and the oil to deliver on its promises. Again, most other countries could not make such a promise credible because they lacked the capabilities to carry it out.

We have also mentioned a second aspect of influence. If threats and promises do not work, often punishments must be inflicted—political, economic, or military. States require capabilities in order to coerce others, in order to impose the costs or the pain that they feel will force others to behave as they wish. Here capabilities are needed to influence others by actually imposing costs on them. But, by doing so—and by doing so effectively—a state also enhances its reputation as being willing to carry out threats in a way that gets results. If this occurs, then at some point in the future threats may not have to be carried out; the mere hint of punishment will bring about the desired action. It is useful here to point out that the actual use of military force in foreign affairs, while the hallmark of the realist view of power, may also be seen as a failure of influence. The use of the military instrument means that a state has failed to persuade another state to do something; it has failed in its promises and failed in its threats; it has had to resort to coercive force. The truly powerful state is like the officer in the military: When it expresses a wish to another state, it is taken as a command and obeyed.

The ability to get others to do one's bidding will differ with the object of one's influence. Remember that influence is relative—what the United States can do to the Dominican Republic, it cannot do to the Soviet Union; what the Soviet Union can get Bulgaria to do is much different from what it can get the United States to do; what China can get Vietnam or Thailand to do is different from what it can get Libya to do. Capabilities by themselves are of no use to our analysis of foreign policy and international politics. The capabilities of states take on meaning only when they are viewed *in relation to the objectives* of the state and *to the capabilities and objectives of others.* In studying a state's capabilties, the first question should concern the capability to do what. The second question should concern to whom. For example, if American nuclear capabilities are viewed in terms of the objective of obtaining mutual deterrence with the Soviet Union, they are quite adequate, and the United States may be said to have the capability to influence the Soviet Union through deterrence. If, however, the American objective is the ability to launch a "first strike" against the Soviet Union (attack first and disarm the Soviet Union with that strike, while having weapons left over to threaten the disarmed opponent), then American nuclear capability is woefully inadequate. The United States is unable to threaten or blackmail the Soviet Union as it would be able to do if it possessed a first-strike capability: This means of influence is not on the American menu. Similarly, Indian military capabilities are adequate for a war with Pakistan; if security in regard to Pakistan is the Indian objective, it is basically achieved. The same capabilities are inadequate, however, if India desires the same security from Chinese military power.

It is important to realize that the various elements of influence—

capabilities and instruments—can in some degree be substituted for one another and converted into other elements of influence. Some types of capabilities, like money, are especially capable of being exchanged for something else. Wealth, for example, can be used to obtain military capabilities, or knowledge (by putting resources into research and education), or a healthier population. Military capabilities can be used to influence others to give up territory or resources or simply to take these things. Either way, military instruments can be used to acquire wealth. Almost all bases of influence have some ability to obtain other influence capabilities, but the "exchange rates" can vary a great deal. It is hard, for instance (but maybe not impossible), to buy affection.

This problem of converting one base of influence into another base of influence creates many difficulties for realist analyses, where some measure of power is of the essence. When, under what conditions, and to what degree can such conversion effectively take place? Military strength, for instance, may have great value in deterrence but not in stabilizing a country's exchange rate or dissuading OPEC from raising oil prices.[8]

ELEMENTS OF A STATE'S CAPABILITIES INVENTORY

Earlier we attempted to indicate some of the differences between states by demonstrating the range of variation that existed on several attributes, especially size and economic development. The attributes we investigated, however, are also central to the power base of states. Almost all writers concerned with power and influence develop a set of attributes that form the base of a state's power—some sort of power inventory or power potential. It is not really important which specific term or scheme is used. What is important is that the analyst of interna-

8. See David A. Baldwin, "Power Analysis and World Politics: New Trends versus Old Tendencies," *World Politics* 31 (1979), 161–194, for a wide-ranging review of the concept of power, especially the ideas of convertibility and substitution. See Benjamin A. Most and Harvey Starr, "International Relations Theory, Foreign Policy Substitutability, and 'Nice' Laws," *World Politics* 36 (1984), 383–406, for the discussion of substituting foreign policy instruments, and Robert O. Keohane, "Theory of World Politics: Stuctural Realism and Beyond," in Ada W. Finifter (ed.), *Political Science: The State of the Discipline* (Washington D.C.: American Political Science Association, 1983), pp. 503–540.

tional politics has some such system for evaluating the universe of possible influence bases; without some systematic and explicit check-list, the analyst is likely to pay far too much attention to certain bases and to forget completely about others. For example, people pay a great deal of attention to the "deference" values of power and respect, but often neglect rectitude and affection. This is, in part, a legacy of the realist view of international politics. It ignores, however, the effects that bonds of friendship and affection between individual leaders may have (for example, between Sadat and Kissinger). Similarly, the moral stature of individuals like Pope John XXIII or Pope John Paul II has helped them have an impact on international politics.

Similarly, the "welfare" values of well-being, skill, and enlighten-ment are often slighted as people concentrate on wealth. International nongovernmental organizations like Amnesty International may, for instance, provide publicity (enlightenment) about alleged violations of human rights (rectitude). In doing so, they may affect the moral con-straints, domestically and globally, within which states must operate. We shall try, in this chapter, to touch on these neglected values.

The attributes of population, area, and GNP may be seen as major aspects of a state's base of power. The number of people within the state, the amount of territory it controls, and even the economic re-sources, goods, and services produced on that territory by those people are bases of power and influence. They constitute a small set of the tangible or measurable elements of power and influence capabilities that a state possesses. It might be useful to think of capabilities in terms of quantity and quality, tangible or intangible, or some similar catego-rization. The data in Appendix B are useful for gauging a number of these tangible measures of power and influence capabilities. A short list of such measures would include population and manpower, area, geography in the sense of defensible natural boundaries as well as the defensive depth that comes from a large territory, natural resources, industrial and agricultural production capacity, the size of the econ-omy, and various measures of military power. Of course, all capabilities involve a mixture of tangible and intangible qualities. For example, to understand the complexities of the Middle East and Israel's military success, we must note the advantages that a skilled, and healthy popu-lation gives to Israel over its neighbors. We shall first discuss those elements that are most tangible (noting their intangible aspects as we go along). Then we shall say a few words on those elements generally considered intangible.

Tangible Elements of Capabilities

Geography Geography includes not only the size of a state, but its topography (especially on its borders), its physical and political location, and its climate. Each of these factors may provide an advantage or a handicap or have no effect. Although sheer size by itself is not sufficient to make a state a great power (or today a superpower), it seems that it permits a fairly large population, a large industrial base, and large domestic sources of food and natural resources. Size also has the advantage of providing depth for military defense and isolation from neighbors; small countries are much more vulnerable to being overwhelmed by a sudden conventional military attack. Size, however, may also mean long borders. If these borders do not have natural defense features—rivers, swamps, and mountains—then size can also be a negative factor. The Soviet Union in World War II illustrates both these features. Its long and indefensible western border was an invitation to successful armored attack from Germany. However, the vast size of the Soviet Union provided it with the defensive depth required to absorb the Nazi invasion, to regroup, and to rearm for its ultimately victorious counteroffensive. It is also clear that area may have little correlation with the amount of regional military power a state possesses; for example, Israel or eighteenth-century Prussia as compared to Australia today or the Ottoman Empire of the past. A large area without resources, defensible boundaries, or arable land may be a great weakness.

Population Many of the same types of statements apply to population. Although a large population can be an asset or a liability, it seems difficult to become a great power or a superpower without a large population. A large population is required in order to have enough people with the range of talents required for the industrial, technological, and military capabilities required of a great power. Population must be looked at in a number of ways. We must be concerned with the age distribution of the population, the sex distribution, the spatial distribution (or density), whether the population is growing or declining, and the like. These measures of a population tell us about the size of the population that is productive, suitable for military service, and capable of reproduction. One illustrative comparison is that of France and Germany between 1870 and 1940. From approximately equal populations in 1870, the French gained only four million people, while the Germans gained twenty-seven million. Other aspects of population are qualitative, or intangible—the education, health, unity, and morale of a population.

Thus, we are also concerned with the quality of the human resources available to a state—not, of course, inherent human ability, but the degree to which a people's capabilities have been developed so that they can make a contribution to the state. Using Lasswell and Kaplan's terminology, one kind of capability may be called *enlightenment*—the extent of higher education and access to specialized knowledge in science, engineering, and the professions. Obviously, a state's military strength depends in large part on access to scientific knowledge; building modern weapons requires a body of scientific expertise that is unavailable to small, poor countries and is not uniformly available to big, rich ones. More broadly, a state needs physicians, architects, social scientists, lawyers, and administrators to run a bureaucracy, as well as many others with advanced training and ability. Many possible measures that tap aspects of this can be found, such as the number of students in higher education, the number of individuals in all age groups who have completed higher education, the number of scientists, or the number of scientific and technical journals published.

Many aspects of enlightenment are related to wealth and material development: Scientists are expensive to train and equip. The same is somewhat true for a more basic kind of knowledge we can call *skill*. Here we refer to the knowledge necessary to get along in modern life even at a rather low level of sophistication, such as literacy, familiarity with machinery, or a primary and secondary education. Literacy is especially important because it is required to learn so many other skills and other kinds of enlightenment; widespread literacy is both a resource base for a government and a means whereby the government can communicate information or propaganda quickly to its people. But universal education, even at the rather low levels required to produce literacy, is costly and difficult for a poor state to provide. One can also turn the argument around and say that only a literate and educated state can become rich. The relationships between GNP and GNP per capita on the one hand and these quality measures on the other can be seen in Table 6.1 and in Appendix B.

One more aspect of population quality is the health and well-being of the people. What access do they have to good medical care? How long do they typically live? How free is the country from various contagious diseases that are now in principle preventable? Does the state possess really first-class centers of medical treatment where the latest knowledge is available? How evenly distributed is good health

Table 6.1

Correlations among some indicators of a state's influence base, 1970.

	Size			Richness of life				Deference
	GNP	Area	Population	GNP per capita	Science journals	Literacy	Few infant deaths	Diplomats received
Size								
Military expenditures	.94	.38	.77	.57	.81	.60	.45	.86
GNP		.37	.81	.63	.87	.60	.42	.85
Area			.62	−.14	.23	−.26	−.25	.43
Population				.05	.61	.11	.05	.79
Development								
GNP per capita					.67	.84	.73	.36
Science journals						.73	.53	.72
Literacy							.78	.39
Infant death rate								.24

Source: Bruce M. Russett, *Power and Community in World Politics* (San Francisco: W. H. Freeman and Company, copyright © 1974).

throughout the population? Are there substantial minorities with markedly poorer-than-average facilities?

The health of a state's own population is an important base of influence. Military power depends in part on having a healthy population of young people. Here it is important that access to good medical facilities be available to the entire population, regardless of income. At the simplest level, poor distribution of health services results in physical and mental handicaps and consequently a significant number of people incapable of military service. One quite good measure that combines an average with equality of distribution within a population is the infant mortality rate. In almost all poor countries, many babies die in their first year of life simply because there is not enough good medical care and because public health standards (for water and food) are low. But in developed economies, the infant mortality rate is usually very low; these countries have the wealth and basic knowledge to bring the infant mortality rate near to the level of only 10 deaths per 1,000 births. Where this does not happen, it is virtually certain that some segments of the populace do not have adequate medical care and that their health conditions are markedly worse than average for the country.

Natural Resources Natural resources, especially since the 1973 oil embargo, are clearly an important dimension of wealth in the power and influence base of states. The concept of natural resources as capabilities is closely related to the idea that states with greater needs are most vulnerable to influence from other states that control or affect the resources that satisfy those needs. Natural resources, such as petroleum or other energy sources, such as coal and natural gas (even wood) are the most common examples. Many other resources are necessary to the industrial capacity of states—for example, uranium and other nuclear power materials and the metals related to ferrous metallurgy. Particularly in the area of resources, states have sought *autarky*, or self-sufficiency. Advances in technology (another hallmark of great power status) can be used to overcome resource deficiency to some extent through the development of synthetics and new industrial processes for refinement and extraction. If a state can be self-sufficient, it reduces its vulnerability to being influenced by others.

In recent years, the United States, the Soviet Union, and China have come closest to resource autarky. However, all countries are coming to depend more and more on resources found elsewhere. Of the United States, the USSR, and China, the United States is becoming the most vulnerable. For instance, the United States now has to import 40 percent or more of its petroleum, making it vulnerable to political pressures from Arab oil exporters. Japan and Western Europe are even more vulnerable; this shows up in their policies toward the Palestinian Liberation Organization (PLO) and Iran. Soon the Soviet Union may also become a net importer of energy for the first time.

Natural resources, along with human power and technology, all make up the industrial and agricultural productive capacity of states. This capacity is partially measured by GNP, but it goes beyond this. States often do not want to be in a position where they must purchase a great deal of their food, industrial equipment, technology, or energy from others (see Table 6.2). With all its influence and resources, the Soviet Union has had to make massive grain purchases from the United States and continues to try to purchase the most advanced computers and computer technology from the Americans (giving Americans the impression that a grain embargo in 1980 might be able to influence Soviet policy toward Afghanistan). A continuing debate that began in the United States in 1973 concerned whether the United States should manipulate its ability to grow and supply food to other states in the same way that the OPEC countries were using their control over petroleum as a basis of influence.

GNP or Wealth of a State We should also be concerned with the production of energy, electric power, and steel as indicators of industrial productivity in general. These indicators are also related to GNP—the wealth of a state. In regard to wealth, we should be interested in how much money and resources can be devoted to military capabilities. Fi-

Table 6.2
Energy production and consumption, 1981.

Country or region	Percentage of world production	Percentage of world consumption
United States	23	28
USSR	22	18
Arab OPEC countries	13	1
China	11	7
Western Europe	9	17
Latin America	7	4
Africa	6	4
Eastern Europe	5	9
Canada	3	3
Japan	0	5

Source: UN Statistical Yearbook, 1981 (New York: United Nations, 1983).

nally, we must also be concerned with the quality of the goods, services, and agricultural products produced. We must also be concerned with questions of how much is being produced in regard to what is needed: Are there surpluses or deficits in needed products, energy production, or food?

Military Capabilities The last area, and one most commonly thought of when investigating the capabilities of states for power and influence, concerns military capabilities. The most tangible and relational of such attributes are existing military capabilities (or military capability in being). Quantitative comparisons and descriptions can cover an endless array of things, from defense expenditure to the number of people in service to the number of aircraft, tanks, nuclear weapons, submarines, surface ships, and so forth. The point is that there are a variety of possible measures, each tapping different aspects and concerned with elements that are important in different circumstances.

Since 1945 we have primarily considered nuclear weapons: How many bombs does a state have and how many weapons are available and under what kinds of conditions? (Already we move beyond a simple count of bombs, and may wonder about whether they can be delivered only in a first-strike attack on another country or whether their delivery vehicles are relatively invulnerable to attack and so are useful as potential retaliation.) What other kinds and numbers of weapons does the state possess? How many people does it have under arms in the regular army and in reserves?

We might also compare the total military budgets of various states. There are great difficulties in comparing expenditures expressed in different national currencies, in obtaining reasonably full and accurate disclosures and in seeing that the same kinds of expenditures are counted in each case (for instance, border guards and internal security forces or expenditure for research and development on projects that may have both civilian and military uses). Still, the rough overall measure has great use if employed carefully. It is a better and more valid indicator than only the number of people under arms, for instance, because soldiers in an underdeveloped country may be poorly equipped and less effective in battle than the highly trained and splendidly armed soldiers of some industrial states. In Table 5.1, we noted the enormous differences between the two superpowers and all the rest of the world, even the other nuclear powers (China, Britain, and France). There we saw a basis for the military bipolarity prominent in the world today, even when we ignore the nuclear versus nonnuclear distinction among the smaller powers.

Various intangible factors, such as morale or even chance, come into play, however. One qualifying factor of special importance is distance. As noted in our discussion of Boulding's "loss-of-strength gradient" in Chapter 4, the effectiveness of military power declines with distance. The decline over distance, however, is not simple and certainly not linear. Cost and effectiveness vary greatly with topography. Because much of the cost of ocean transport is in the loading and unloading rather than the carrying, a great seapower like the United States can deliver conventional forces to the coastline of Asia at a cost that is actually not significantly greater than that of putting them onto an island in the Caribbean. And the United States is better able than the People's Republic of China to put forces on Taiwan, not because it is cheaper to ship from San Francisco to Taiwan than from the China coast to Taiwan, but because only the United States has the transportation capability to get large numbers of troops and supplies there. Thus, one has to severely discount the effectiveness of the millions of Chinese troops anywhere beyond the Chinese mainland.[9]

But even nuclear weapons lead to questions of quality as well as quantity. In nuclear matters, matters like accuracy, dependability, and the state of computer technology are important, as is quality in regard to all other weapons systems and the quality of both officers and enlisted personnel. The leadership and training of soldiers are more crucial than sheer numbers, as the quality of the technology of the weapons is more crucial than the sheer numbers of those weapons. Again, military capabilities can be seen as heavily dependent on the wealth and industrial base of a state, the level of education of its population, its level of scientific and technological advance, and the overall "quality" of its people (health, literacy, and morale).

COMBINING CAPABILITIES: INDEXES OF POWER

Although a number of qualitative or intangible factors have been mentioned, the above section has covered the most commonly discussed tangible elements of a state's capabilities for influence. Any pair of states may be compared on any single attribute, at a particular time or across time. For example, we could look across time to see how the

9. See Albert Wohlstetter, "Theory and Opposed-System Design," *Journal of Conflict Resolution* 12 (September 1968), no. 3, pp. 302–331.

United States compares with Britain on GNP per capita. In 1900 the United States ranked first and Britain second. This ranking was maintained through World War II. However, in 1950 Britain dropped to third behind the United States and Sweden. In 1960 the United States was still first, while Britain was fourth; in 1970, the United States was first and Britain tenth. By 1980, the United States had dropped to sixteenth while Britain had fallen to twenty-second. This comparison quickly indicates the consistency of American superiority up to 1970, and the steady decline of British economic performance after the onset of World War II. The rather abrupt decline in the American position by 1980 gave rise to fears that the American economy was suffering from the "English sickness."

Many people have recognized that power and influence are multifaceted and depend on a combination of capabilities. Several attempts have been made to devise indexes that are based on two or more indicators of national capabilities. We shall first investigate which attributes are employed in these indexes and why, that is, how the various capabilities are related to one another. Then we might see what the results of using different combinations of indicators are.

Table 6.1 is very useful in *illustrating* the relationships of capabilities to one another, since it shows the correlations between a number of indicators of national capabilities that have been mentioned above. The correlations indicate the relationship between pairs of indicators (from +1.00 to −1.00). The higher the positive correlation, the more likely it is that when a country's value on that indicator is high, its value on the other will be high. The highest correlation found is that between military expenditures and GNP. This indicates that economically big countries (measured by GNP) are likely to have large military expenditures. This reinforces the observation that a strong economic base is required for a strong military establishment—that wealth may be turned into military capabilities. (One reason why military aid and arms sales are so interesting is that military aid complicates the relationship between a state's wealth and the size of its military. Good examples are Israel, with its relatively small size, and Egypt, with its little wealth, and their very large military capabilities. Military aid has had a great impact on the military equation in the Middle East.) We see that population is also highly related to GNP, as well as territory and military expenditures. Such results reinforce our feeling that those types of indicators all measure approximately the same thing (but notice the much lower correlations between area and GNP per capita and military expenditures).

Other evidence indicates that these measures fit together in various ways. One study asked a number of people how powerful they perceived 122 states to be.[10] We noted that in regard to influence especially, it is the perception of other states' capabilities and will that is important (if threats and promises are to be believed). This study indicates that for many people, perceptions of power are highly related to the GNP or economic size of the state and to the military capabilities as measured by defense spending.

One of the most ambitious attempts at developing an index of world power was made by F. Clifford German in 1960.[11] He took four of the elements of power and influence that we have examined and refined them in various ways. German started with the area of a state, but modified this figure in terms of density (the "effectiveness of national occupancy") and by the quality of communications as measured by the relationship of railroad mileage to area. As an example of the effects of his modifications, before the modifications the area of the USSR in square kilometers was given as 22,403,000, and the United States as 7,828,000. After the modifications, the U.S value was 391.5 and the USSR value was 372—in other words, the United States was "larger," having a more useful land area.

German also corrected population for "working-age population" (15 through 60 years of age) and then for "technical efficiency" (energy consumption per capita), for a food supply factor, for the population engaged in manufacturing, and for a "morale factor." We begin here with a U.S. working-age population of 67.5 million (remember these data are for the late 1950s) and a Soviet working-age population of 75 million. After modifications, the U.S. population index is a 471.5-million equivalent, and the Soviet Union's is 322.5. Again, the qualitative corrections have reversed the original relationship.

The national economy is measured by industrial strength. German's index was based on the production of steel, coal, lignite, crude oil, and hydroelectricity. The last index was power based on straightforward measures of defense expenditure, people, and material. The grand totals, combining all four types of measures gave this result:

10. See Norman Z. Alcock and Alan Newcombe, "The Perception of National Power," *Journal of Conflict Resolution* 14 (1970), 335–343.

11. F. Clifford German, "A Tentative Evaluation of World Power," *Journal of Conflict Resolution* 4 (1960), 138–144.

United States	6459
USSR	6321
Britain	1257
China	999
West Germany	663.5

While practically equal, it should be noted that the United States and the Soviet Union were five times "stronger" than Britain, which was in third place.

For comparison, let us look at another index. Using a formula that is based only on energy production, steel production, and population, Karl Deutsch obtained the following ranks for 1963: The United States was equal to 100, with the USSR second at 68, then China at 26, West Germany at 14, Japan at 12, and Britain in sixth place at 11. In a later period, another index was created based on human resources, wealth, technology, trade, and military strength.

These different indexes show us at least two things: First, that they *are* different—they are tapping slightly different aspects of the capabilities or "power base" of states, which is part of the reason the rankings of the states are different. The second thing, however, is that they are measuring approximately similar aspects of this power base, in that the states that appear in the top group are the same for all these indexes (although it is most interesting to note the changes across time). We can support this last remark and gain an overview of the relationship between these various measures of power capabilities by looking at the states that rank at the top of these measures.

Look at Table 6.3. In this table, we want to do two main things. First, we want to show you the relationships between different bases of power, or state capabilities. Part A of Table 6.3 compares eight dimensions of power, as measured in 1965. Data for this year were selected because they are for approximately the same time period in which Deutsch measured states with his index (which is included in Part A). We can see, then, how the individual aspects compare to an index (Deutsch's) that combines these aspects.

Several other dimensions in Part A need comment. "Diplomats received" was included because some scholars have used it as a measure of the status, prestige, or respect of a state. States have only limited resources, and only a few have the need and ability to send diplomatic representatives to over 100 of the states in the contemporary system. Thus, the decision to send a representative to another state says something about which states any particular country feels are important to it, which states should be linked to it by a continuous diplomatic line of communication, and which states will give it a measure of prestige by having a representative in its capital.[12]

The second thing we can do with Table 6.3 is look at Part B and see the dynamics of changing power in the international system, to which we referred in Chapter 5. In Part B we have the top ten states in 1980 ranked on the first five dimensions of capabilities used in Part A. For this more recent set of data, we have also provided the actual figures for each state; as a basis for comparison, we have also included the figures for four small countries in South America, Asia, and Africa.

Note that despite its nuclear status and its continued high rankings in area and population, India is no longer ranked in terms of GNP or in military expenditures. Brazil, finally reflecting its own area and population, has taken India's spot in the GNP top ten. One can also see the continued rise of Japan's economic might, moving from sixth to third on the GNP list. This is also now matched by Japan's appearance as one of the top ten military spenders in the world. Change in the sources of the world's wealth—due mostly to oil—is reflected in the GNP per capita dimension (wealth per person in a society). Five of the 1965 top ten have dropped out, (all 5 are Western countries), including the 1965 leader, the United States. The top three are now oil-producing states. Similarly, West Germany has dropped off the population list. New entries are Nigeria and Bangladesh. The shifts in power distribution are also evident in military expenditure. Three of the bottom four states in 1965 are gone (India, Poland, and Canada), replaced by Saudi Arabia, Japan, and Israel. These are just some of the highlights. Study various specific relationships (such as those between the United States and the USSR) at your leisure.

A FURTHER WORD ON INTANGIBLES

Any state requires more than the mere existence of the resources that make up capabilities, as we noted in our discussion of population. The state must also maintain those political, social, and economic structures

---

12. Another new item on Table 6.3 indicates whether a state is a nuclear power and what that state's nuclear rank is. Despite the fact that India exploded a nuclear device in 1974, the five states listed remain the only powers known to have nuclear arms. The 1965 ratings are based on the size of nuclear arsenals. That order also happens to be the order in which each state first acquired nuclear weapons—the United States in 1945, the Soviet Union in 1949, Britain in 1952, France in 1960, and China in 1964.

Table 6.3

Ranking of top states by capabilities.

Part A 1965 data

Rank	Area	Population	GNP	Military expenditure	GNP per capita	Diplomats received	Literacy	Scientific journals	Deutsch index[a]	Nuclear rank
1	USSR	China	U.S.A.	U.S.A.	U.S.A.	U.S.A.	Denmark	U.S.A.	U.S.A.	U.S.A.
2	Canada	India	USSR	USSR	Kuwait	Britain	Finland	Japan	USSR	USSR
3	China	USSR	W. Germany	China	Sweden	W. Germany	Iceland	France	China	Britain
4	U.S.A.	U.S.A.	Britain	Britain	Canada	USSR	Norway	W. Germany	W. Germany	France
5	Brazil	Indonesia	France	France	Iceland	France	Sweden	USSR	Japan	China
6	Australia	Pakistan	Japan	W. Germany	Switzerland	Italy	Switzerland	Britain	Britain	
7	India	Japan	China	India	Denmark	Egypt	Belgium	Italy	India	
8	Argentina	Brazil	Italy	Italy	Australia	India	Canada	Poland	France	
9	Sudan	W. Germany	India	Poland	New Zealand	Japan	Czecho-slovakia	Sweden	Poland	
10	Algeria	Nigeria	Canada	Canada	Luxembourg	Brazil	E. Germany	India	Canada	

Part B 1980 data

Rank	Area (1,000 sq km)	Population (1,000s)	GNP (millions U.S.$)	Military expenditures (millions U.S.$)	GNP per capita (U.S.$)
1	USSR 22,402	China 1,006,712	U.S.A. 2,583,700	U.S.A 143,974	Qatar 28,034
2	Canada 9,976	India 693,578	USSR 1,212,030	USSR 130,000	U.A.E.[b] 27,975
3	China 9,597	USSR 265,542	Japan 1,048,168	China 28,000	Kuwait 24,434
4	U.S.A. 9,363	U.S.A. 227,704	W. Germany 824,886	Britain 26,776	Switzerland 16,188
5	Brazil 8,512	Indonesia 151,168	France 654,120	W. Germany 26,738	Luxembourg 14,297
6	Australia 7,687	Brazil 122,407	Britain 516,004	France 26,466	Brunei 14,162
7	India 3,288	Japan 116,782	Italy 393,925	Saudi Arabia 17,540	Sweden 13,962
8	Argentina 2,777	Bangladesh 88,052	China 300,000	Japan 9,990	W. Germany 13,399
9	Sudan 2,506	Pakistan 85,743	Brazil 245,110	Italy 9,598	Norway 13,357
10	Algeria 2,382	Nigeria 77,082	Canada 244,683	Israel 6,599	Denmark 12,504
Selected small states					
Barbados	0.4	249	822	9	3,301
Laos	237	3,458	300	n.a.	87
Gambia	11	591	227	0	384
Botswana	600	899	797	33	886

Sources: Part A, Charles Taylor and Michael Hudson, World Handbook of Political and Social Indicators, 2nd ed. (New Haven, Conn.: Yale University Press, 1972); part B, Appendix B.
[a] Based on energy production, steel output, and population, 1963.
[b] United Arab Emirates.

that will permit it to mobilize or to use the resources that exist within its borders. The question is one of mobilizing those resources to create the instruments of influence and then using the instruments to achieve the objectives of the state.

When looking at the political system of any state, we must ask whether that system efficiently administrates the nation-state's resources. That is, what is the quality of political leadership at all levels, especially the highest levels? Can the leaders move and motivate the people to support the government's politics, to sacrifice so that the state's resources can be devoted to military capabilities or heavy industry rather than consumer goods? Can the leadership achieve and maintain the support of the people and their continued loyalty to the nation and to the state? These issues involve how resources are molded into economic and political capabilities and then directing those capabilities toward obtaining the objectives of the government. Scholars have investigated the performance of a country's economic and political systems in mobilizing resources for war. Such cases as Israel and the Arabs, the Soviet Union during World War II, and Vietnam indicate the importance of the ability of governments to "extract" and use national resources.[13]

These intangibles can be crucial. As in sports, sometimes a weak team will beat one much higher up in the rankings. The weaker side does not always lose a war, and the stronger does not always win; examples of the latter case are the French in Indochina and later in Algeria and the United States in Vietnam. Neither do the more powerful states always win a diplomatic confrontation; for example, the diplomatic hostage incident between the United States and Iran. One scholar suggests that intangibles such as leadership, belief in a cause, and especially the cohesion caused by a threat to survival are important assets for smaller states in unequal, or "asymmetric," conflicts.[14] If one factor in "war power" is willingness to suffer and persevere, as suggested by another scholar,[15] then the weaker state, being willing to fight for survival against a larger adversary, increases its war power. The larger

---

13. See A. F. K. Organski and Jacek Kugler, *The War Ledger* (Chicago: University of Chicago Press, 1980), chap. 2.

14. Andrew Mack, "Why Big Nations Lose Small Wars: The Politics of Asymmetric Conflict," *World Politics* 27 (1975), 175–200.

15. Steven Rosen, "War Power and the Willingness to Suffer," in Bruce M. Russett (ed.), *Peace, War and Numbers* (Beverly Hills, Calif.: Sage, 1972), pp. 167–183.

state, although possessing greater capabilities, is often far away from the conflict and not threatened by the smaller opponent.[16] Since the larger state in colonial wars has often been a Western democracy, this lack of threat to its survival has been accompanied by a lack of will to mobilize its superior resources to pursue and win the war. The structure of the political system of a state is thus one aspect of the mobilization of resources. Another is leadership. In addition to domestic leadership, leadership also involves the skill with which a state's chief officials manipulate these capabilities in their ongoing attempts to influence other states. These are issues of the diplomatic and negotiating skills of leaders and will be discussed in the following chapter.

Other governmental intangibles involve the skill and efficiency of the state's bureaucratic organizations. The issues here include the size of the bureaucracy, how politicized it is or how protected it is from political influences, how it is organized and directed, the quality of the people who staff it in terms of education, training, and expertise, dedication to service (or to corruption), and how overloaded they are. Another question regarding mobilization and the use of resources goes back to the question of form of government: Are open or closed governments, democratic or authoritarian governments, better able to mobilize resources efficiently? Which form of government will elicit more sacrifice and higher-quality contributions from its citizenry? Which form of government will be better able to deal with other governments? To wield threats and promises with more effect? To be more flexible in its dealings? To be more ruthless? Although we do not have firm answers, it is important that such questions be kept in mind.

Finally, we come back to the notion of credibility mentioned earlier. The effect of influence attempts based particularly on promises or threats depends to a large extent not only on capabilities—the ability to carry out the action—but on the perception of a government's willingness to carry out the action. One major intangible, then, is the reputation that a government (or sometimes a people or state) acquires in its international dealings. If other states do not believe one's threats or promises, it is irrelevant how much capability one possesses. This issue will be raised in Chapter 7, when discussing diplomacy, negotiation,

---

16. One researcher notes that success in short-term outcomes is also subject to these asymmetries; will and recklessness on the part of the initiator were more important than capabilities. See Zeev Maoz, "Resolve, Capabilities, and Outcomes of Interstate Disputes," *Journal of Conflict Resolution* 27 (1983), 195–229.

and a state's bargaining reputation. Our general conclusion about political intangibles is a simple one. If a government—meaning its leadership, its bureaucracy, and the political system within which they both work—is so inadequate or inefficient that it cannot bring the state's capabilities to bear in a particular international situation, then those capabilities remain latent. Capabilities that are not mobilized cannot be used in exercising influence in the international arena.

Similar questions can be asked about the economic and social systems of a state. Does the economic system and structure reduce waste and loss? Is it efficient in the use of the state's resources? Does the social system, its values, and its structure promote a unified national effort, or are there major groups that feel alienated from the national society and are not willing to cooperate and coordinate their efforts? What are the values of the social system? Are they more oriented toward fairness and respect for human rights or toward some system of privilege? All these will affect how thoroughly, rapidly, and efficiently a society will be able to mobilize resources and present a unified front to the world in support of its government's foreign policies. Here some observers would speak of an even more ambiguous concept, that of "national morale." This is a very elusive notion, indicating something about the state of mind of a nation, about how committed the people of a state feel to the policy of the government.

Shifts in mood or morale do exist and can sometimes be traced through public opinion research. It is clear that shifts in national morale occurred in both France and the United States during their involvements in Indochina. In each country, as the war wore on, support for military involvement decreased and general governmental policy was increasingly challenged. Looking at the element of national morale, Vo Nguyen Giap, the North Vietnamese military strategist and minister of defense, stated bluntly that such Western powers would lose—that he could make the war go on long enough for the people of those states to tire of the war and its costs. Both the outcome and scholarly research have proved him to be correct.[17]

---

17. John Mueller has investigated the failure of American policy in driving the North Vietnamese to a breaking point. His findings indicate not so much an American failure, but an unprecedented willingness of the North Vietnamese to accept losses much higher than those of previous wars (e.g., battle deaths as a percentage of the prewar population were twice as high as those of the Japanese in World War II). See John Mueller, "The Search for the 'Breaking Point' in Vietnam: The Statistics of a Deadly Quarrel," *International Studies Quarterly* 24 (1980), 497–519.

THE INTANGIBLE OF INTELLIGENCE

A very different aspect of a state's intangible capabilities of power and influence are its capabilities for the collection and analysis of information: *intelligence*. In *The Nerves of Government*, Karl Deutsch observes that "it might be profitable to look upon government somewhat less as a problem of power and somewhat more as a problem of *steering*."[18] In the uncertainty of the anarchic international system, any government that knows how to get to where it wants to go has an advantage. Any government that can reduce the uncertainty of the international environment through knowledge of that environment has an advantage. Any government that can reduce the number of times it is surprised— that can provide itself with the time to plan for, prepare, and preempt the actions of other states—has an advantage.

Indeed, power may be steering. To know how to act, how to respond, and whether to continue one's policies or to correct them, a government needs information. To know how to influence other states or international actors, a government needs information on those actors and their vulnerabilities. We can break down the information that governments seek into three broad types. Earlier in this chapter we noted that in order to utilize their capabilities for influence, decision makers had to take into account their own goals and capabilities for influence *and* the goals and capabilities of others. The first type of information, then, deals with the goals, plans, and intentions of other international actors. We can steer more carefully through the international environment with foreknowledge or warning of the impending behavior of other states. The many books on World War II intelligence breakthroughs by the Allies indicate that advance warnings of German moves had great payoffs. It is the *failure* of intelligence-gathering organizations to provide warnings that shows how important such warnings are: Examples include American surprise at the Japanese attack on Pearl Harbor in 1941; Japanese surprise at the U.S. devaluation of the dollar by the Nixon Administration in 1971; American surprise at the North Korean attack on South Korea in June 1950; the unexpected building of the Berlin Wall by East Germany in 1961; the apparent failure of Israeli intelligence in the 1973 Yom Kippur war; the inability of U.S. intelligence to estimate accurately the conditions that brought

---

18. See Karl W. Deutsch, *The Nerves of Government* (New York: Free Press, 1963). p. xxvii (emphasis added).

down the Shah of Iran in early 1979. We cannot know how best to use our tools of influence—how best to use promises and threats—if we don't know the plans and intentions of others or if we are continuously surprised by the actions of others.

The same is true if we don't know the capabilities—and vulnerabilities—of others. This is the second kind of information: knowledge of others' military and economic strength, internal political situation, and domestic unrest. Knowing how strong an opponent is in these ways is helpful in knowing how to respond to the threats and promises of opponents and how to threaten, promise, and bluff ourselves. The largest portion of intelligence work is of this sort—the collection of a great deal of information about other states using readily available sources of information and using standard research techniques.

The last type of information, very important to the idea of steering, is feedback. This means that governments seek information on the effects of their own decisions and actions on others. Feedback permits a government either to continue its policies and behavior or to alter them. U.S. policy in Indochina during the 1960s can be seen as a classic case of the failure of information gathering and processing activities and the failure of U.S. leaders such as Lyndon Johnson to analyze feedback information correctly.

The intelligence process involves the collection, analysis, interpretation, and storage of information, as well as the transmission of information to top-level foreign policy decision makers. One reason we have placed intelligence capabilities under intangibles is the unreliability of this process. As we shall see in later discussions (e.g., the psychological aspects of decision makers), information may be "lost" or distorted within the government, it may be misperceived or disbelieved by policymakers, or important information may never be collected at all. All of these problems do not mean that governments are not trying. The United States and the USSR spend vast sums on intelligence activities, as do countries that have immediate and pressing security problems like Israel. (Israeli intelligence, despite the 1973 war, has often been touted as the best in the world.)

The United States, for example, spends well over $500 million annually on the Central Intelligence Agency (CIA). The CIA is clearly the most formidable intelligence organization in the United States in terms of secrecy, operations, manpower, and resources, despite efforts to rein in the agency during the 1970s. The head of the CIA is also the director of central intelligence and acts in a broad supervisory role over the entire American intelligence community. This includes the National

Security Agency, a code-breaking agency (with over 20,000 employees and a billion-dollar budget) that also monitors foreign communications. The State Department has the Bureau of Intelligence and Research, a very small agency. The Department of Defense has the Defense Intelligence Agency, a very large agency. In addition, the Army, Navy, and Air Force each have sizable intelligence organizations of their own, as do the FBI, the Treasury Department, and the Atomic Energy Commission. The Air Force also has the National Reconnaissance Office, which is responsible for both spy planes and the panoply of U.S. reconnaissance satellites that are now the single most important source of American intelligence data about the world, especially about the Soviet Union and China.

Before states can attempt to influence others, then, certain information about the world must be obtained. How well a state collects and handles information will affect the utility of all its other capabilities. How well a state collects and handles information will also affect the goals and objectives of the state and how it seeks to achieve them.

Once a set of objectives or goals exists, the foreign policy decision makers of nation-states must try to translate their capabilities into the influence required to achieve their objectives; they must implement their foreign policy decisions. As we have suggested, they have a wide range of tools, techniques, and methods with which to deal with other states. In the next chapter, we shall look at some of the methods through which states exercise influence.

7

RELATIONS BETWEEN STATES: INSTRUMENTS OF INFLUENCE

| WORLD SYSTEM |
| RELATIONS |
| SOCIETY |
| GOVERNMENT |
| ROLE |
| INDIVIDUAL |

DIPLOMACY AND BARGAINING

One British diplomat has observed that "Foreign policy is what you do; diplomacy is how you do it."[1] Although this is a good place to start, it is also incomplete. In one sense, *all* techniques for the implementation of foreign policy are, or should be, political. However, we can consider *diplomacy* as the central political technique because it involves direct, government-to-government interactions. The how of foreign policy regarding diplomacy is the direct communication between official representatives of two or more governments. It is direct in that it acts upon the people in other governments who would be able to do the things we want their states to do. In this sense, then, diplomacy is the central technique of foreign implementation—the only truly direct technique. That is, not only is it a technique in its own right, but it is an instru-

---

1. Paul Gore-Booth, *With Great Truth and Respect* (London: Constable, 1974), p. 15.

ment by which the other techniques used may ultimately influence target states. After a major military victory, it is usually through some diplomatic interaction that the defeated party indicates if it will surrender or modify previously held peace conditions. The military instrument in this case has had an effect on another state, but that effect can only be gauged and exploited through diplomacy. The same may be said for economic activities, such as embargoes and other sanctions that deprive a state of needed commodities.

The central feature of diplomacy is its communicative function. The basis for creating permanent diplomatic missions in the fifteenth century was the desire of kings and princes to have representatives in other courts to carry out continuous and systematic communication with other monarchs. Most of the legal trappings of diplomacy were established in order to maintain and facilitate communications and to reduce misunderstanding and distortion in interstate communication. Such rules as those of protocol, diplomatic immunity, and noninterference were established to reduce conflicts over rank and status among diplomats (and thus to permit them to get on with the business of diplomacy), to prevent host governments from interfering with the diplomatic representatives of other states, and to prevent diplomats from interfering in the domestic politics of their hosts. Such legal rules codified diplomatic interactions.

To what purpose have such interactions been directed? One observer has listed five "substantive" functions of diplomacy:[2] (1) *conflict management*; (2) *solving problems* facing two or more governments; (3) increasing and facilitating cross-cultural *communication* on a wide range of issues involving the countries; (4) *negotiation* and bargaining on specific issues, treaties, and agreements; and (5) general *program management* of the foreign policy decisions of one country toward another. Procedurally, these activities result foremost in communicating the views of one's government and in exchanging information. A diplomat must also try to ascertain the intentions and policies of the other government as well as bargain and negotiate with that government. This will be discussed in greater depth below. After such negotiation, diplomacy is often required to implement the agreements reached; lengthy and important talks may be held on exactly how agreements are to be executed. For example, after the Arab-Israeli ceasefire was achieved in

---

2. Leon P. Poullada, "Diplomacy: The Missing Link in the Study of International Politics," in D. S. McLellan, W. C. Olson, and F. A. Sondermann (eds.), *The Theory and Practice of International Relations*, 4th ed. (Englewood Cliffs, N.J.: Prentice-Hall, 1974), pp. 194–202.

1973, some very hard bargaining was required to separate Egyptian and Israeli forces on the Sinai Peninsula. The resulting Israeli-Egyptian talks on the Kilometer 101 disengagements of 1973 and the implementation of the less-than-precise peace treaty of 1979 are good examples of the importance of postagreement diplomacy.

So far we have been discussing diplomacy as a means by which one state directly influences another. But any discussion of the various functions of diplomacy cannot neglect another major function, which is aimed not at the other party but at third parties observing the diplomatic activities at hand. In this case diplomacy is used not to reach an agreement with the opposing party but to influence other parties through propaganda, undermining the position of the opponent, revealing the opponent's bargaining positions and other confidential information, or taking stances calculated to impress, frighten, or reassure third-party observers. Many of the U.S.-Soviet negotiations over the years have been aimed at their various allies, third world states, or China. Indeed, recent U.S. diplomacy with China seems geared to have as much impact on U.S.-Soviet relations as on China. The various talks between the Western democracies and Hitler, as well as those between the USSR and Germany before World War II, had third-party reactions as a major motivation.

Disagreement over how much diplomatic communication should be open or secret has been a major issue in the twentieth century. After World War I, there was a reaction to the old diplomacy of the great European powers. In addition to a general feeling that diplomacy was a devious and dishonest business, many people felt that the secret treaties that characterized the pre–World War I period and the formation of opposing alliances were responsible for the outbreak of the war. Idealists like President Woodrow Wilson attacked the immorality of secret treaties that offered territory if states would help others in their military offensives. Wilson called for "open treaties, openly arrived at." This "new" diplomacy was supposed to make communication public. The League of Nations helped with the idea of open treaties by publishing the text of treaties after they were negotiated. But the process of open negotiations almost ended the utility of diplomacy, because the propaganda function came more and more to the fore. One major example that continues today is the kind of speeches made in the UN General Assembly and Security Council. Here the propaganda function, as opposed to problem solving or conflict resolution, prevails.

After World War II, a hybrid form of diplomacy became most prevalent. It combined private negotiations between diplomats with public declarations of what had been achieved—through press conferences, joint statements, or the publication of agreements (usually by the United Nations). Former Secretary of State Henry Kissinger was a master of the private conversation and the public spectacle. He personified a return to the traditional diplomacy of the past, in the sense of hard bargaining in private and secret trips and agreements (which were revealed to the public after their completion) and a style that combined the use of force with the use of words to bring about an agreement with which every side could live but one that required every side to make concessions and compromises.

In the past the bulk of diplomatic communication, as well as most important talks, took place between the regular diplomatic representatives of the foreign services of states. Both day-to-day activity and major talks were handled by the diplomatic personnel of the embassies located in each state's capital. Today much of this activity, especially for smaller and less-developed countries, occurs in multilateral forums such as the United Nations. Called *parliamentary diplomacy,* this form of diplomacy includes both the regular meetings of the international body to which permanent representatives are assigned and the informal discussions that occur in a single location where a state's diplomats can meet representatives of many other states. At the other end of the scale, the larger powers have tended to skip over the embassy personnel and ambassadors and conduct more and more of their business through the use of special envoys and high-level officials such as foreign ministers or secretaries of state.[3] More frequent summit meetings between heads of government have also occurred. The development of instantaneous telecommunications has enabled governmental leaders and their foreign ministers to communicate directly and often, rendering many of the permanent diplomatic personnel irrelevant.

The American secretary of state regularly engages in "shuttle diplomacy" of some sort, flying between capitals of states in conflict, visiting allies, and engaging in discussions with major opponents. This became so routine that during the latter years of Henry Kissinger's tenure in office, leaders and officials in other countries often refused to deal with anyone else representing the United States, especially on crucial issues; ambassadors and assistant or undersecretaries of state would not do. To get anything accomplished, they felt only negotiations with the top decision maker was acceptable.

---

3. See Kissinger's memoirs, *White House Years* (Boston: Little, Brown, 1979) and *Years of Upheaval* (Boston: Little, Brown, 1982) for details of Kissinger's diplomatic travels and his employment as a high-level negotiator.

NEGOTIATION

Two Stages in Negotiations

The first stage of negotiation involves *negotiation "in good faith."* This means that both parties are negotiating in order to reach an agreement—that both sides want some sort of agreement. Often this stage requires one party convincing the other that an agreement of some sort would be in the interest of both sides.

Sometimes this is not such an easy task. As we have already noted, there are reasons for states to negotiate other than to reach a final agreement. States may negotiate in order to benefit from the side effects of the negotiation process. We have already mentioned one such negative or selfish side effect: negotiation to produce propaganda to support one's policies. As noted, a state can negotiate in order to influence a third party in some way.

Other reasons for negotiation include intelligence gathering and deception. In the former, a state will negotiate to gather information about the capabilities, aims, and problems of the other side. In the latter case, a state negotiates to give incorrect information about its own intentions and capabilities to the opponent. On the more positive side, states can also negotiate to maintain contact with the other side, even if chances of an agreement are slim. States may try to substitute diplomacy for the use of force, hoping that as long as the states are talking, neither will resort to armed conflict.

Once the first stage of negotiation is achieved, however, the parties must move on to the second stage: *bargaining over the actual terms of the agreement.* Before this happens some preliminary issues, often as important to both sides as the agreement itself, must be settled. These preliminaries involve issues of advantage or disadvantage to one side or the other. Quite often, procedural concessions actually involve substantive ones. Preliminaries include such issues as the location of the negotiations. States prefer a neutral site when bargaining with an adversary—such as Paris for the U.S.-North Vietnamese peace talks and Vienna and Helsinki for the U.S.-Soviet SALT negotiations. Similarly, the parties to be represented at negotiations can be a problem. Who participates involves fundamental questions regarding who has standing in the issue. In this era of nonstate actors trying to obtain territory or governmental status, simply recognizing their existence is a major *substantive* concession. Thus, by agreeing to their participation in negotiations, a state has made more than a procedural concession. This was a sticky point for the United States in Paris regarding the Viet Cong (even the shape of the bargaining table was an issue in these negotiations) and has been one of the major problems in the long history of the Arab-Israeli conflict. Until the dramatic breakthrough with Egypt in 1977, no Arab state even recognized Israel's existence. Israel, in turn, has refused to recognize the Palestine Liberation Organization.

The Business of Bargaining

Once these and other preliminary issues are settled, two or more states can get down to the business of bargaining. Because each side has different or conflicting objectives and interests, there is something to bargain over. The objective is to influence the opponent into agreeing with you as much as possible in achieving a solution to the problem. Each side wishes to minimize the costs to itself as well as the concessions it makes. In fact, to pass the first stage, each party must calculate that the benefits of negotiating some agreement outweigh the sacrifices that may be necessary in the negotiation. The authors of a study of bargaining, crisis, and conflict note that this often does not happen:

> There are many conflicts in international history that the parties have a common interest in resolving, but there is no attempt to resolve them by bargaining because both parties know that the sacrifice they would have to make to get a settlement is greater than the value to be gained in settling. A good example is the Alsace-Lorraine conflict between France and Germany after 1870. A settlement would have benefited both parties by improving their general relations and removing an obstacle to their alignment, which would have increased both states' bargaining power vis-a-vis third parties. But these prospective benefits were less than what each party would lose in accepting the other's minimum conceivable demand.[4]

Bargaining takes on features of both Rapoport's *debate* (where "opponents direct their arguments at each other" and "the objective is to convince your opponent, to make him see things as you see them"), and what Rapoport has labeled a *game* (where each party must take into account "the potentialities and evaluations of alternative outcomes; the object in a game is to outwit the opponent").[5] Thus, persuasion as well

---

4. Glenn H. Snyder and Paul Diesing, *Conflict among Nations* (Princeton, N.J.: Princeton University Press, 1977), p. 476.

5. See Anatol Rapoport, *Fights, Games, and Debates* (Ann Arbor: University of Michigan Press, 1960).

as threats and promises are employed in bargaining, as each side presents its conditions and demands and attempts to convince or coerce the other side to as many of these demands as possible. The threats and promises must be credible, and a vast literature exists on how this can be done. Each side must try to figure out how far to push demands and how far to push the opponent—when to make concessions and when to dig in and say, "I can't give in any further." In doing all of this, states employ specific threats and promises as well as deliberately vague threats and warnings ("We will not stand idly by . . ." and "You must bear the responsibility if . . ."). It is here that bargaining reputations become so important. A leader or a government's reputation for bluffing, standing fast, telling the truth, and honoring commitments all make up a state's bargaining reputation.

A feeling for the complexity of the bargaining process is given in this quotation from the work of Thomas Schelling, one of the pioneers in the study of international strategy and bargaining:

> Each party's strategy is guided mainly by what he expects the other party to accept or insist on; yet each knows that the other is guided by reciprocal thoughts. The final outcome must be a point from which neither expects the other to retreat; yet the main ingredient of this expectation is what one thinks the other expects the first to expect and so on. Somehow, out of this fluid and indeterminate situation that seemingly provides no logical reason for anyone except what he expects to be expected to expect, a decision is reached. These infinitely reflexive expectations must somehow converge on a single point, at which each expects the other not to expect to be expected to retreat.[6]

BARGAINING AND THE RESOLUTION OF CONFLICT

One of the substantive functions of bargaining and negotiation noted above was the resolution of conflict. A conflict can be resolved in many ways. A test of force is often the mechanism used to determine the outcome of a conflict—a situation where there are incompatible goals, values, or positions. Conflicts can then be resolved through conquest, forcible submission, or deterrence. However, conflicts can also be resolved through compromise, third-party arbitration, or adjudication of

---

6. Thomas Schelling, *The Strategy of Conflict* (New York: Oxford University Press, 1963), p. 70.

some sort (through international courts, third-party mediation, multi-lateral conferences, or international organizations).[7] In these processes, conflict situations are resolved through negotiations.

For successful conflict resolution, the first stage of the bargaining process is crucial. The parties involved must be willing to confront the issues in conflict in a rational atmosphere of some mutual respect and open communication. They must try to identify the issues involved in a realistic manner and not act merely to establish favorable conditions for the bargaining process. John Burton has even argued that a bargaining situation must be avoided. His view is that conflicts are based on misunderstandings and that the important thing is to get people sitting down face to face. In this situation, the largest issues may be set out in the presence of a mediator, who will help the parties see where their misunderstandings exist. Burton argues that once favorable conditions exist for analyzing the misunderstanding that underlies the conflict, the process of solving the conflict is well on its way.

Burton's view that most conflicts are based merely on misunderstandings is extreme, but his emphasis on the need to have the first stage of negotiations carefully approached and worked out is valuable. Our view, shared by others, is that many, if not most, conflicts are indeed concrete. *Objective incompatibilities* do exist in the global arena, such as the desire to occupy the same territory, to control the same governmental machinery, to fish the same waters, or to control the same sea lanes, or to disagree over the manner in which certain groups of people should be treated (coreligionists, or people of the same ethnic or linguistic background living within the borders of other states), and so on. Although most conflicts do have an objective basis, the process of conflict resolution is a highly subjective one, because of the complex nature of bargaining presented above. Even Roger Fisher, the best-known exponent of this view of conflict bargaining, advocates taking the game element out of conflict resolution bargaining and stressing the debate element.[8]

Fisher stresses trying to understand the opponent's view of the situa-

---

7. These are categories of resolution procedures developed by K. J. Holsti, "Resolving International Conflicts: A Taxonomy of Behavior and Some Figures on Procedures," *Journal of Conflict Resolution*, 10 (1966), 272–296.

8. See John W. Burton, "The Resolution of Conflict," *International Studies Quarterly* 16 (1972), 5–29. Roger Fisher has developed this point first in his handbook on international conflict situations, *International Conflict for Beginners* (New York: Harper & Row, 1969) and has presented it as a more general issue in bargaining in the more recent *Getting to Yes* (New York: Penguin, 1983), cowritten with William Ury.

tion and then attempting to figure out what can be done to make the opponent change that view. He specifically notes that "making threats is not enough"; how, then, does one try to influence the opponent? First, Fisher argues that one state must be very clear about exactly what behavior it wants the opponent to perform—what it wants the opponent to do. Then, always keeping in mind how the opponent sees the world, the choices offered the opponent should be made attractive and acceptable. Fisher's concern is that a bargainer's offers and positions appear sensible and legitimate in the eyes of the opponent. This is a hallmark of the debate. Fisher further argues that if making threats is the best you can do, and if punishment must be resorted to, your bargaining influence and your actions will appear to be failures. Coercion is seen to be a failure of influence.

Fractionation

An important aspect of Fisher's model of bargaining is the concept of *fractionation.* This simply means that problems should be broken down into smaller parts. Little issues should be kept little and not linked to larger issues. This, he argues, raises the probability that some issues will be settled, enabling the parties to see that they can resolve issues peaceably; that they can reduce hostility and conflict between them; and that they can get on to the other, usually tougher problems in an atmosphere of cooperation, success, and goodwill. Fisher, in effect, is concerned here with constantly renewing and reinforcing the positive elements needed to complete the first stage in the bargaining process. These recommendations are especially relevant to arms control negotiations.

Henry Kissinger's famed shuttle diplomacy in the Middle East after the 1973 Yom Kippur war provides an excellent example of many of Fisher's principles. Although criticized for failing to achieve an overall settlement, Kissinger aimed at fractionating the problem, getting the sides to withdraw from military confrontation (a useful conflict resolution procedure called *avoidance*), and working to settle issues that might then be settled. It is possible that those small settlements were necessary for the dramatic visit of Sadat to Israel in 1977 and the eventual Egyptian-Israeli peace treaty in 1979. Again, this treaty has been criticized as a failure to achieve a final settlement to the Middle East (read "Palestinian") problem. It has, however, calmed down one possible area of military confrontation. Even with the assassination of Anwar

Sadat and the cooling of Israeli-Egyptian relations over Lebanon and the West Bank, the continued observance of the treaty indicates to Israelis and Arabs alike that it is possible to work out problems through diplomatic means. The current political difficulties between Egypt and Israel, however, do point out that states must keep working at cooperative relationships.

The Use of International Organizations

Tentatively, we may conclude that in bargaining to resolve conflicts, the least coercive forms of influence appear initially most useful. Promises of rewards, persuasion, reliance on the legitimacy of claims, and opponents' awareness that you understand their position seem to be better methods of influence than are threats of force. Appealing to values held by the opponent through legitimacy is especially helpful. Fisher argues that you should be concerned with precedent and reciprocity to make your demands legitimate in the eyes of the opponents—to appear consistent with their principles. One way to do this is to use international law and international organizations. Of thirty-nine conflict situations that K. J. Holsti lists for the 1945-to-1965 period, twenty-three used international organizations to aid in conflict resolution. In an additional six cases, multilateral conferences, mediation, or judicial procedures were used. In the period as a whole compared with the 1919-to-1939 period (with thirty-eight conflicts), the use of conquest and forced submission declined as a method of conflict resolution. Compromise accounted for 13 percent of the settlements in the earlier period, but 26 percent in the later one.

Another study that surveys international organizations and the management of conflict in the postwar period supplements these findings. On the whole, no organization is very successful in managing conflicts between members of different Cold War blocs. However, the United Nations does better in managing conflicts between nonaligned countries and between a nonaligned state and one aligned with one of the major blocs. Regional organizations do well in managing conflicts that have no force involved, whereas the United Nations has done well with high-intensity conflicts.[9] Indeed, *referrals* of conflicts to the United Nations and regional organizations, which had dropped sub-

---

9. Ernst B. Haas, Robert L. Butterworth, and Joseph Nye, *Conflict Management by International Organizations* (Morristown, N.J.: General Learning Press, 1972).

stantially during the mid-1970s, had risen again to peak levels by 1980. But although states were bringing their disputes to IGOs, the rates of success for the United Nations (10 percent) and regional organizations (15 percent) in 1980 were the lowest for the whole 1945-to-1980 period.[10]

USE OF THE MILITARY FOR ACHIEVING INTERNATIONAL INFLUENCE

We have already noted that influence may be achieved through the application of force. Throughout history rulers have used war and violence to prevail in conflict and to overcome obstacles. Are military techniques for influence limited to war, especially in the contemporary era of nuclear weapons?

There is no doubt that the use of military capabilities is generally a coercive or punishment-oriented means of influence. It is, however, possible to use these capabilities for *rewarding* others. The most obvious rewarding activity is the use of military aid. States, particularly the larger states, may attempt to influence commitment to an alliance, UN voting, or general political orientation through the use of military aid. The supply of arms to the Arab states by the Soviet Union and to Israel and Egypt by the United States are two examples of military capabilities employed in this way. Powers such as the United States, the Soviet Union, Britain, and France have the technology, expertise, and capability to produce weapons that most of the world's countries are simply unable to produce. Through the arms-producing states, the other states may expand their menu rapidly through gifts or purchases; if they had to rely on their own resources, most states would be without tanks, aircraft, missiles, and most other modern weapons systems. Between 1978 and 1982, the Soviet Union supplied 37 percent of all major weapons supplied to third world countries, the United States supplied 32 percent, France 11 percent, and Britain and Italy 5 percent each. Non-European countries like Brazil, Israel, and South Africa are also beginning to be important suppliers of arms to the developing countries.

However, influence through providing weapons may be only temporary. Egypt illustrated how a recipient state can turn on its arms supplier when Sadat threw Soviet military advisers and other personnel

---

10. See Ernst Haas, "Regime Decay: Conflict Management and International Organizations, 1945–1981," *International Organization* 37 (1983), 189–256.

out of Egypt in 1971. A decision of this type is costly if one has to reequip one's armed forces or get technicians and spare parts elsewhere. Spare parts and maintenance linkages provide supplier states with their primary leverage over recipients. Still, the use of aid for influence is far from being an automatic process. Because there are usually at least two sources—the United States and USSR—and sometimes more, recipient states are less vulnerable to threats of cutting off such aid. Since military aid may be substituted generally without major difficulty, the ability of powerful states to influence third world governments is quite limited.[11]

Another way to reward states with military capabilities is to promise adding one's capabilities to theirs. This is a main feature of alliances. However, a formal treaty is not necessary for state *A* to aid state *B* by either threatening *B*'s enemy or actually using its military forces against *B*'s enemy. The American deterrent umbrella, whether for its allies or other states that know they will be protected even without a formal alliance (e.g., Austria and Sweden), exemplifies this form of influence through reward. Other examples are Taiwan and Israel, the former being the beneficiary of a formal treaty for most of the postwar period and the latter an informal coalition partner.

The Use of Force

Although this last form of influence (adding one's military capabilities to another's) involved the threat or use of force, it was not directed *against* the state being influenced. Most incidents employing the military tool of foreign policy, however, are based on the exploitation of the use or threat of using force. Force is coercive; it is the ability to destroy or kill or take away, to occupy and control through violence. As such, force directly affects the distribution of security, political control, territory, status, and wealth in the international system. Force is used because decision makers expect to benefit from the new distributions expected after it has been used. States are influenced by the threat of force because they fear what they will lose if others use force. The military technique of influence should be seen as another means to

11. See Bruno S. Frey, "Weapons Exports and Aid to Developing Countries," *Journal of Peace Science* 1 (1975), 117–126; David Sylvan, "Arms Transfers and the Logic of Political Efficacy," in James Kuhlman (ed.), *Military Policy Evaluation: Quantitative Applications* (Leiden, Netherlands: Sijthoff, 1979).

various political ends and not as an end in itself. The objective of using force is the same as that of the use of any other technique: influence to achieve objectives.

This view of force was most powerfully argued and popularized by the Prussian officer and military historian Karl von Clausewitz, who wrote the classic *On War* after his military service against Napoleon. Clausewitz clearly saw the military instrument as a means to an end, as a way to influence the opponent: "War is an act of violence intended to compel our opponent to fulfill our will." Clausewitz also argued that war could not be separated from the political ends of states and indeed must be subordinated to those ends. His famous dictum reads as follows: "War is therefore a continuation of policy by other means. It is not merely a political act but a real political instrument, a continuation, . . . a conduct of political intercourse by other means."

The political utility of force comes through two forms already identified: its actual use and its nonuse (including threats). The actual use of force involves *both power and influence.* We may speak of "brute force" where an obstacle is overcome simply by destroying it, as the Romans did Carthage in the Third Punic War. Rome employed force not to influence Carthage into desired behavior; there was nothing Rome wanted Carthage to do (there was no "yesable" proposition that Rome wanted Carthage to approve); Rome simply wanted to wipe Carthage from the face of the earth. The actual use of brute force, then, entails the destruction of an opponent. In these situations, influence is not the object. However, in most situations where force is used, influence is the aim. The use of force in these instances is meant to hurt the opponent; the aim is to break the opponent's will to resist any further.

We should now understand better why threatening to use force has been employed in the past and continues to have utility today. The threat of the use of force attempts to exploit the ability to hurt and inflict costs on the opponent. Military capabilities are exploited explicitly through diplomatic channels, especially when the aim is deterrence. The threat to the opponent is that one will use one's weapons if the opponent performs some specific behavior; one will refrain from using them as long as the opponent refrains from that behavior. The ability to influence an opponent away from taking some action requires diplomacy; the deterrer must make clear to the opponent just what actions are forbidden and what will happen to the opponent if those actions are taken. For the threat to be credible, the deterrer must also demonstrate to the opponent the military capabilities and willingness to carry out the threat. Although deterrence has been employed throughout history, it has taken on crucial new importance in the era of nuclear weapons. This topic will be further discussed in Chapter 14.

Beyond the threat of force, other techniques exist for the nonuse of military capabilities. These nonuse techniques are directed at influencing other states in the manner of potential influence discussed earlier. The aim is to convey to others the military capabilities that one possesses to influence their view of the world and their menu. Each state wants others to see it as a state that is militarily powerful, willing to use those capabilities, and thus as a state not to be challenged or thwarted. Just the possibility of such military resources being employed against them becomes enough to influence other states not to take certain actions, raise certain issues, or defect from alliances. This is what potential influence is all about. It may be implicit, or it may be explicitly achieved through the display of military capabilities—to impress others with one's military strength and to achieve status and prestige as a powerful state. In today's system, nuclear weapons are the most obvious element of military capabilities used for prestige or status. India's nuclear explosion in 1974 was motivated in substantial part by its search for a means to match the status and prestige of China, both in Asia and in third world countries around the globe.

Display of arms includes all those activities that demonstrate a state's military capabilities to outside observers: nuclear explosions, war games, military maneuvers (especially those near the borders of the states to be impressed), air shows, setting world records for speed or height of aircraft or for the size of any particular weapon, military parades such as those in Red Square on May Day, and sailing fleets around the world or into trouble spots. Navies have been used to indicate that a state's military power is mobile and can bring troops and firepower into every corner of the globe (one of the reasons the West has followed the Soviet naval buildup of the last fifteen years with such concern). Such activities as the mobilization of forces or putting forces on high-readiness alerts (as Nixon did with American forces during the 1973 Middle East war) can also be used to communicate to an opponent the seriousness of a situation. Here a state is not so much interested in demonstrating its capabilities as its *willingness* to use them in a critical situation; both are necessary to make threats credible.

One study has specifically investigated the use of American military force "short of war" as an instrument of influence (based on 215 cases that occurred between 1946 and 1975). The authors concluded that such limited use often had utility—to stabilize a worsening situation, to gain time, and even to defuse domestic American demands for more drastic action. On the other hand, the use of military force "short of war" did not produce long-term benefits. It was best used for deterrence, not compellence—to support existing friendly regimes rather than to change governments or their policies.[12]

The Nonuse of Nuclear Weapons and the Utility of Conventional Ones

It has been argued, nevertheless, that in the nuclear age military power has become obsolete—that nuclear weapons make Clausewitz's dictum meaningless. This argument is based on the view that the use of nuclear weapons has no political utility at all: Either the state that uses them is also destroyed by a retaliatory attack, or the devastation is so great that there is no territory, wealth, or population to be gained after their use. Nuclear weapons are of no actual use against guerrilla operations or terrorists, nor can they be used to seize territory. With victory indistinguishable from defeat in a war between two nuclear states, Kenneth Waltz's comment takes on added meaning in regard to a nuclear conflict: "Asking who won a given war . . . is like asking who won the San Francisco earthquake."[13]

Unless the aim of the war is to provide "the next Adam and Eve" when the dust clears (not one of the traditional foreign policy objectives of states), the large-scale use of nuclear weapons has no political utility. Some have even argued that any use of force is now debatable because of the risk of escalation. War has always been an unpredictable and risky business. In the nuclear age, one ever-present risk is that the war may spread to nuclear powers or to the use of nuclear weapons by a desperate loser. If used, nuclear weapons can cause such vast devastation in such a short time that the costs of war would far outweigh any possible benefits. Given the complex and vital interdependencies of modern society because of the importance of cities and their vulnerability to disruption, nuclear weapons would bring a society to a standstill—and within a few hours. Distance and time—elements that once protected states in war (for example, the Soviet Union and the United States in World War II)—are no longer operative. In a process

---

12. See Barry M. Blechman and Stephen S. Kaplan, *Force without War: U.S. Armed Forces as a Political Instrument* (Washington, D.C.: Brookings Institution, 1978).

13. Kenneth Waltz, *Man, the State and War* (New York: Columbia University Press, 1954), p. 1.

that began with the strategic bombing campaigns of World War II, nuclear weapons with their ballistic (and now cruise) missile delivery systems make it totally unnecessary to defeat an opponent's armed forces before being able to destroy its people and its wealth.

This argument is both right and wrong. Nuclear weapons have little utility if they must actually be used. Some strategists advocate the *limited* use of nuclear weapons—chiefly as a dramatic threat that the level of force can rise rapidly and dangerously. This is a very risky strategy, however, because it appears very difficult to maintain a controlled use of nuclear weapons. The main value of nuclear weapons still lies in nonuse—in deterring their use by other nuclear powers.

On the other hand, the actual use or threat of use of conventional military force against nonnuclear powers, particularly those not located in Europe, retains value. Force and the threat of force continue to be important characteristics of the present international system. War has been ubiquitous throughout history, and the use of war as a foreign policy tool continues to the present day. The legitimacy of force or the threat of force is maintained in a number of ways. The UN charter permits states, either individually or collectively in alliances, to use force for self-defense. The "collective security" function of the United Nations itself is based on the threat of the collective force of the UN membership against transgressors of international law (such as the North Koreans in 1950). Such staunch neutrals as Switzerland and Sweden base their neutrality on strong military establishments. Their military strength is a form of display to deter any would-be aggressor. The message is "it would be very costly and exceed any benefits to violate our neutrality." The Swiss would argue that this is exactly the effect their military capability had on Nazi Germany during World War II. Other states such as India, whose leaders had been the most outspoken in opposition to violence, have used force when it was convenient or necessary. In 1961 it was convenient for India to use force to take over the Portuguese enclave of Goa; in 1962 it was necessary to defend India from a Chinese attack (or vice versa).

There are still many instances, then, when the actual use of force or the threat of its use can be beneficial for obtaining political ends. Although the nuclear superpowers with their adversary relationship deter each other from using those nuclear weapons against one another or other states, and although they and their allies in Europe refrain from the use of force (conventional and nuclear) both within and without their blocs, these are not the only states in the system. A look at which states are engaging in conflict and in which parts of the world suggests that any argument about the obsolescence of the military tool applies mostly to U.S.-Soviet relations and East-West relations in Europe.

We must note at the outset that there is little agreement on what exactly constitutes a "war" in the post–World War II international system. With the disappearance of legal trappings such as declarations of war, different scholars have used different criteria to determine what events should be included on their lists of wars or violent conflicts.

One study of the period between 1945 and 1980 identifies 60 violent conflicts that qualify as major international and civil wars. As we would expect, most of these wars did not occur in Europe—only two, or 3.3 percent, took place in Europe. Another study identifies 106 cases of armed conflict between 1945 and 1983, including international war, civil war, and major civil strife. These wars are estimated to have caused 16,359,000 military and civilian deaths. Of these 106 conflicts, only three (or 2.8 percent) occurred in Europe, and they were estimated to have caused 175,000 military and civilian deaths.[14]

Since World War II, over 100 governments have been created. Because of the multiethnic or tribal populations of many of these states and the worldwide ideological clash between Western-oriented parties and Communist parties, governments have been under constant siege. Force has become a principal tool used by nonstate actors to challenge established governments for control of a state or a region that hopes to become a state of its own. The use of force by nonstate actors is one of the variety of challenges to the nation-state in the contemporary system. As noted, the concept of state sovereignty is the legal status that gives the state a monopoly on the internal and external use of force. This monopoly has been and continues to be severely challenged; for example, of those 106 wars mentioned above, 81 percent were civil wars, or violence within the territory of a state. A list of 2,700 incidents of international terrorism was compiled by the U.S. State Department for the period between 1968 and 1977.

The main forms of contemporary nonstate violence are guerrilla warfare and terrorism. Some observers have called these "new" forms of international violence, but each has a long history. What *is* new is the changing pattern of international conflict. According to some data, 80

---

14. The first data set was produced by the Correlates of War project and reported in Melvin Small and J. David Singer, *Resort to Arms: International and Civil Wars, 1816–1980* (Beverly Hills, Calif.: Sage, 1982). The second study is that of Ruth Leger Sivard, *World Military and Social Expenditures, 1983* (Washington, D.C.: World Priorities, 1983), p. 21.

percent of the wars between 1900 and 1941 were of the traditional sort, between the armed forces of two or more states. From 1945 to 1983, as noted, 81 percent were on the territory of only one state and were internally oriented.[15] Both guerrilla warfare and terrorism, then, are revolutionary activities, challenging the rule and authority of governments. The challenging forces are usually groups from within a state's population, though they often receive support of some kind from outside states.

If guerrilla warfare is the "weapon of the weak," then terrorism is the "weapon of the weaker." In both cases groups begin in a military position far inferior to that of the established government. Conventional military force is thus useful for both the government and the challenger. Outside parties often gain influence through military capabilities by providing aid either to the government or to the guerrilla or terrorist. Governments may provide support for other governments by supplying equipment, advisors, or expertise in handling the unconventional tactics of the challenger. Good examples of sharing expertise are found in the "antiterrorist" field. The Israelis, after the successful commando operation at Uganda's Entebbe airfield in July 1976, provided training to antiterrorist forces of other states. This included the West Germans, who later pulled off a similarly successful operation involving a Lufthansa airliner that had been hijacked to Mogadishu, Somalia, in October 1977.

This mutual support of governments has been called the "Holy Alliance" by Pierre Hassner. In contrast, he has called the support of each other's rebels by governments "International Civil War."[16] In either case, force is employed for political reasons and continues to be useful even in a nuclear age. Many of the conflicts in the Middle East, Asia, and Africa may be seen as proxy wars between the superpowers. Wary of confronting each other directly, the superpowers support clients that represent the East and the West in a local struggle—for example, the Arab-Israeli wars, stages of the Indochina conflict, and the conflict in Angola.

---

15. For the data on interstate wars, see Quincy Wright, *A Study of War*, 2nd ed. (Chicago: University of Chicago Press, 1965). For data on internal wars, see William Eckhardt and Edward Azar, "Major World Conflicts and Interventions, 1945 to 1975," *International Interactions* 5 (1978), 75–110.

16. Pierre Hassner, "Civil Violence and the Pattern of International Power," in *Adelphi Papers*, no. 83, "Civil Violence and the International System," Part II, "Violence and International Security" (London: International Institute for Strategic Studies, 1971), p. 19.

Having an international system filled with a large number of unstable, weak, or vulnerable governments is a more important factor in the exercise of force than the nuclear stalemate between the two superpowers. Indeed, a hallmark of both guerrilla warfare and terrorism is the primacy of the political element in the contest between challenger and government. Especially in guerrilla warfare, the military tool is to be constantly and consciously subservient to political ends. The guerrilla war theories of Mao Tse-tung particularly stress this point. The best example is his dictum that "Political power grows out of the barrel of a gun. Our principle is that the Party commands the gun and the gun must never be allowed to command the Party." Similarly, the political element is crucial in the use of economic techniques of influence.

INFLUENCE BASED ON ECONOMIC RESOURCES

States rely on each other for resources and commodities that enable them to develop and sustain their economies and the well-being of their peoples. One simple but striking example is the estimate that British farmers alone could support only 12 million people—not the 56 million that inhabit the British Isles. As K. J. Holsti says, "Needs that cannot be filled within national frontiers help to create dependencies on other states." Dependence conveys the idea of an imbalance, or asymmetry, in *costly effects.* Dependencies are thus vulnerabilities that leave states open to be influenced by others. Economic resources can be manipulated by those who possess them to influence those who do not. As was noted earlier, nothing in the international system is equally distributed. This, of course, applies to economic resources as well as the economic requirements of various states: Some states have far more of an economic resource or capability than is needed, and some have far less. In Chapter 3 we saw the range of the distribution of wealth in the international system. States that possess a surplus (or a monopoly) of resources may achieve greater economic influence. States that lack the resources and commodities they require are more vulnerable to economic influence.[17]

---

17. For a detailed discussion of dependence—what it means and how it can be measured and applied to interstate relations—see Bruce Russett, "Dimensions of Resource Dependence: Some Elements of Rigor in Concept and Policy Analysis," *International Organization* 37 (Summer 1984).

In comparison to diplomacy, economic means of influence may be considered indirect. In diplomacy, governmental representatives act directly on the representatives of another state's government; with economic means, the objective is to affect some aspect of the state's society—its wealth, production, or well-being. This is taken into account by the state's leaders and so influences their behavior (just as the defeat of an army on the battlefield is taken into account and then influences behavior). The blockade of food into a state during war influences decision makers not because they personally are in danger of starvation but because they must calculate the well-being of their people and the political reaction to a government that cannot (or can) protect the people from such hardship.

The manipulation of economic resources takes a number of forms. States can use trade, monetary policy, or international organizations to acquire more economic resources. As noted in Chapter 6, these resources can then be used to generate additional economic and military resources. The wealth from Iran's oilfields enabled the shah of Iran to purchase tens of billions of dollars worth of the most up-to-date and sophisticated weaponry from the United States during the 1970s. Indeed, from the 1973 Arab-Israeli war until the Shah's ouster in early 1979, Iran continuously pressed for higher oil prices in order to generate the wealth the shah desired for both his armed forces and his ambitious economic schemes for Iran. A state may also use economic techniques to acquire natural resources or goods that will then be denied to its adversaries.

Although the acquisition of economic capabilites can be viewed in much the same manner as the acquisition of military capabilities, the central use of economic techniques for international influence is the *exploitation of the vulnerability of other states.* As noted, all states have economic needs—and only a few can even attempt a policy of autarky, or self-sufficiency. States such as India, Pakistan, Bangladesh, even the Soviet Union often require more food, especially grain, than they can produce. Most states require petroleum, which is produced in only a handful of countries; Japan and the states of Western Europe are particularly vulnerable. But even the United States came under pressure from Nigeria in 1979, when Nigeria threatened to cut off its oil if the United States recognized what was then the white-dominated government of Zimbabwe-Rhodesia. (Shall we call this "petro-pressure"?) In the same way, certain metals and energy sources, such as uranium, are needed by most states; so are technology and the products of technology. Indeed, part of Kissinger's policy of enmeshing the Soviet Union within a web of world trade was a desire to make the USSR need more from other states and thereby become more vulnerable within the international system. It was hoped that the Soviets would be "more responsible" world citizens than they would be if they became totally self-sufficient. An autarkic state needs no one to help fill its needs and therefore has a much more open menu; consequently, it is less constrained by its own self-interests.

Rewards and Punishments

As with other types of influence, economic influence may be achieved through the use of rewards or punishment. That is, one state may take away, threaten to cut off, or fail to provide another with some economic resource, commodity, or service. The United States used such tactics against the Soviet Union in 1980 after the USSR invaded Afghanistan. The Carter administration renewed a grain embargo to attempt to influence the Soviets. Although the Reagan administration reversed this policy, it attempted to apply political and economic pressures on Western European nations to prevent them from cooperating with the Soviets on the Soviet gas pipeline. Trying to stop the pipeline was itself an attempt to punish the Soviets.

A state may also promise to provide, to continue to provide, or to increase its supply of some resource, good, or service to another state. In fact, however, it is rare for some economic good or service to be cut off completely. More often punishment and reward deal with the *level* of the good or service being provided or the *price* of that good or service. As we have seen in the industrialized West since 1973, the manipulation of the price of oil can bring clear-cut benefits or costs to the Western states. The Arab states have used this influence to good effect as judged by Western voting patterns in the United Nations, Western treatment of Israel, Western trade agreements, and other international areas.

No matter whether an economic good or service is being used to punish or reward another state, the success of the influence attempt and the amount of influence achieved depends on how vulnerable the target is to the manipulation of that economic good or service. The key issue here is *substitutability* and how dependent one state can make another state on the first state's economic goods and services. Writing on why economic sanctions failed in the 1960s and 1970s, Johan Galtung summarized a set of ideal conditions for economic punishment (or reward).[18] These conditions all relate to the issue of substitutability. The state being punished should already have important economic ties with the punishing state. One of the reasons that American economic sanctions against the USSR have been of limited use is exactly because these ties (in the form of limited trade) were so weak. If such ties do not exist, the threat of economic sanctions amounts to threatening to take away something one is not providing in the first place. Using the 1973 oil embargo and price rise by the Arab members of OPEC as an example, the countries of Western Europe had based their whole policy of energy resources and resource acquisition on the assumption of continued low-priced oil from the OPEC states that provided the overwhelming proportion of their oil.

Along with this, the state being punished must be unable to find a substitute for the sanctioned item—either in terms of goods or markets. When the United States under President Eisenhower attempted to punish Cuba by cutting the quota of Cuban sugar it would buy, Cuba was able to substitute markets by getting the Soviet Union to purchase the now-available sugar. Similarly, when the United States and the Western companies cut off Cuba's oil supplies, Castro again was able to substitute Soviet oil. On the other hand, when the Arab oil suppliers decided to embargo oil to the United States, Western Europe, and Japan in 1973, there was at least a visible short-run compliance by the European countries and Japan to Arab demands. The Arab states controlled such a large proportion of the oil supply that substitution was difficult; those oil-producing states that were not taking part did not have the capacity to provide the deficient supply. It is no accident that Galtung picked oil as the commodity closest to meeting his ideal conditions.

On the other hand, the punishing state must be able to substitute or be able to afford the cutbacks in supply or purchases. If the oil producers desperately needed every petrodollar garnered from oil sales, then the embargo would not have worked. But there were plenty of other states in the world willing to purchase their oil, and most oil-producing states could easily accept a reduction in oil revenues. In other words, the state doing the punishing must not be as vulnerable to the threatened disruption as the state being punished.

---

18. Johan Galtung, "On the Effects of Economic Sanctions, with Examples from the Case of Rhodesia," *World Politics* 19 (1967), 378–416; Richard C. Porter, "International Trade and Investment Sanctions: Potential Impact on the South African Economy," *Journal of Conflict Resolution* 23 (December 1979), no. 4, pp. 579–612. See also Albert O. Hirschman, *National Power and the Structure of Foreign Trade* (Berkeley: University of California Press, 1945), for one of the earlier discussions of these conditions.

While these conditions indicate how effective economic influence can be, they also indicate how difficult it is to achieve. The success of economic sanctions may be measured in terms of the objectives sought through sanctions: compliance, subversion, deterrence, international symbolism, and domestic symbolism. As noted, sanctions usually do not work in achieving compliance (what we earlier called "compellence") or in subverting the government of another state. Sanctions are also of limited use as a deterrent. However, they are very useful as international and domestic symbols of political support, opposition, or ideology. It is this success that explains why sanctions are still used by states.[19]

There are ways to fight back against economic sanctions. Galtung mentioned several defensive activities that states can take. It is interesting to note that in 1973 and 1974, seven years after Galtung's article was published, the Nixon Administration's energy policy for counteracting the Arab oil "weapon" matched Galtung's recommendations point for point. The major defensive strategy set out is one of self-sufficiency—just as Nixon announced that the American aim had to be self-sufficiency by 1980.[20] Until self-sufficiency is reached, it is suggested that a people learn to sacrifice, and even learn to like such sacrifice. One of the first suggestions by the Nixon administration was to turn down thermostats in homes; it added that cooler temperatures were healthier! The speed limit on American highways was cut to 55 miles per hour, and it was argued that in addition to saving fuel, this speed was also safer.

Galtung also suggested changes in trade with other parties and perhaps even some form of smuggling. At the time of the oil embargo, the United States organized the consumer states into the International Energy Agency as a means to coordinate energy policies, stockpiling, and aiding each other if another embargo occurred. The United States also intensified oil-oriented negotiations with non-Arab oil-producing states.

Finally, Galtung suggested that an economy restructure itself to absorb the loss of the embargoed material. The Nixon strategy contained

---

19. James M. Lindsay, "The Success of Economic Sanctions as a Policy Instrument: A Reassessment," Yale University manuscript, p. 2. A study of Peter Wallensteen, "Characteristics of Economic Sanctions," *Journal of Peace Research* 2 (1968), 248–267, supports this view. He reports that only two of eighteen attempts at total economic sanctions between 1918 and 1968 could be considered even partially successful.

20. Self-sufficiency may now be an outmoded strategy in a highly interdependent world, however. See Chapters 18 and 19.

not only energy-saving activities by individuals, industry, and government, but also plans for increased mining of coal and more emphasis on nuclear-generated electricity. In sum, just as one state aims for influence based on another's vulnerability, the vulnerable state attempts to cut down on the need for specific goods from specific sources (even if the policies do not work so well—as in the case of the Nixon administration's actions).

Controlling the Flow of Goods

There are a number of techniques that states use *to control the flow of goods, services, and resources between states.* These controls can be used either to punish or reward—either to cut down or expand the amount of the good being traded or to make that good more or less expensive. A state can impose *tariffs* on products entering its borders. Tariffs are taxes levied on imported goods to raise revenue or to control the flow of foreign goods into a country. This control is usually related to the protection of the country's domestic industries. If tariffs are raised, then a particular imported item becomes more expensive to purchase and fewer will be sold, particularly in relation to similar domestically produced goods. Low tariffs will encourage trade; high ones will discourage trade. Similarly, *quotas* control imports not through prices but through the amount of goods permitted to enter a country from a specific source for a specific time period. The United States, for example, used to impose strict quotas on sugar from Cuba, the Dominican Republic, and other sources. By shifting the quotas for different countries, some countries could be hurt and others helped. This is particularly effective in dealing with countries that depend heavily on one crop that cannot be stored and thus has to be sold relatively quickly.

States might also grant a special trade status, such as *most-favored-nation* (MFN) *status,* as a form of influence. MFN status is based on non-discriminaton in trade and means that any tariff reductions granted to any country will also be extended to the trading partner given MFN. The United States has attempted to encourage Polish economic independence from the USSR by giving Poland MFN. In 1975, U.S. Senator Henry Jackson and others attempted to influence Soviet policy on the emigration of its Jewish citizens through the manipulation of MFN. (The attempt failed; the Soviets, in fact, toughened their stance on emigration and refused an American treaty that granted MFN status to the USSR on the condition that the Soviets allow more Jews to leave.)

Other mechanisms exist for controlling trade. There are various sorts of *loans and credits* to stimulate buying by lowering prices, as well as monetary policy to make the goods of one state more or less expensive given the devaluation or revaluation of the state's currency. Additionally, there are devices that can be used strictly to punish other states. These include the *boycott,* by which states cease to buy the goods, resources, or services of another state. Boycotts cut the target state off from its markets. Similarly, an *embargo* entails stopping the sales of economic items to another state. An embargo cuts off the target state's supply of resources and products from the outside.

Foreign Aid

Finally, there is the whole question of economic aid to other states. Foreign aid is a major "carrot," or economic reward, technique. It involves the transfer of economic goods or services from the donor to the recipient. These might be any resource or commodity, money, service, or technical advice. In the newly independent and economically developing countries, the needs for development capital (money and goods) and for the technical and technological skills to build a modern economy are particularly high. The use of aid is therefore very useful in dealing with most of the states in the international system today. To give it or withhold it, to attempt to create dependencies through its use, and to attempt to substitute the aid from one state with that from another are all strategies for influence (or escape from that influence) employed today.

Aid may take any number of forms. It can be used for military assistance, economic development, or relief. *Bilateral aid,* which is provided by one state to another, is particularly liable to manipulation by the donor. The aid may come as outright grants, loans, sales, or technical assistance. In the 1950s and the 1960s, grants were the preferred form of aid. More recently, technical assistance and loans have assumed a greater role. With bilateral aid, dependence relationships can be created. One scholar has simply called much of foreign aid "bribery."[21] Bilateral aid has also been provided with "strings." *Tied aid* means that the recipient is forced to buy or trade for goods it does not want or need to receive the aid that it does desire.

---

21. See Hans Morgenthau, "A Political Theory of Foreign Aid," *American Political Science Review* 56 (1962), 301–309.

Donors may still find foreign aid a useful instrument. The greater proportion of *all* American economic assistance, for example, goes to two countries, Egypt and Israel. The assistance is provided for obvious political purposes. American aid to Egypt *did* displace Soviet influence. It was also useful for compensating the Egyptians for the loss of Arab economic aid as a result of the Israeli-Egyptian peace treaty. Recipients, on the other hand, typically prefer *multilateral aid*—assistance given through international organizations such as the World Bank, other UN agencies, or regional organizations such as the Inter-American Development Bank or the Asian Development Bank. This aid is less subject to donor manipulation, although the United States does have a great deal of influence over World Bank lending decisions (see Chapter 18). Third world recipients of aid have expressed their desire for much more aid but through multilateral agencies, because aid, like any other scarce resource that is valued, may be used to reward and punish in the pursuit of foreign influence.

This brief introduction to economic techniques for achieving influence will be expanded in sections of Chapters 16 and 17 on dependence and dominance relationships between the underdeveloped and developed states. The relevance of these brief and rather abstract concepts will be illustrated using contemporary economic and political relations between the poor and developing South and the rich and industrialized North.

CONCLUSION

In this chapter we have attempted to review some of the basic factors of how states interact. In studying foreign policy, we are concerned with how states deal with one another and exert influence over one another. Because of this concern, we looked at various techniques and instruments that states use to influence others. This, you must realize, was a very incomplete list. We have taken only a brief look at the major diplomatic, military, and economic methods for exercising influence; many related topics have only been lightly touched upon or even entirely skipped. Psychological techniques for exerting influence—propaganda through modern mass media—have become more widely used today than ever before. Since World War II, a good deal of money and resources have been devoted to this indirect technique, whereby states attempt to influence the values, attitudes, and behavior of the people (or specific groups of people) in other countries. The ideological overlay of the Cold War prompted a stepping up of this technique—for example, the use of radio and television (such as Voice of America and Radio Free Europe), films, and cultural materials aimed at the populations of opponents, allies, and neutrals alike. (Such propaganda was and is heavily directed at one's own population, also.) Propaganda is an important tool in raising other peoples' *respect* or increasing their images of your rectitude.

By now you should have a better idea about how states interact with one another and attempt to influence one another. A state's menu depends in large part on the array of techniques it possesses to influence other international actors. Its menu is also constrained by the attempts of others to influence that state. The tools for influence that a state possesses very much depend on its capabilities and how those capabilities stand in relation to the capabilities of others. In the next three chapters, we shall move within the domestic system of each state and look at the characteristics of the society and government. We have already provided a very general idea of how these domestic factors might influence the foreign policy menu of decision makers, but now we shall study these topics in depth.

8

DOMESTIC CONSTRAINTS: DO DIFFERENT KINDS OF COUNTRIES HAVE DIFFERENT FOREIGN POLICIES?

In the last four chapters, we discussed elements of constraint and opportunity that originate outside the nation-state—in the world system as a whole and in relationship with other states. In the next three chapters, we shall look at major aspects of the nation-state itself that constrain the possibilities and probabilities of behavior open to foreign policy decision makers. This is not a new idea; it has been discussed by many observers. As we noted earlier, Henry Kissinger said that statesmen are constrained by two sets of influences: the first consisted of the politics, power, and actions of other states; the second consisted of domestic constraints ranging from public opinion to the attitudes of the government and bureaucracy. The ideal statesman must be able to take both sets into account, deal with them, and master them. Commenting on all the statesmen whom observers claim (incorrectly) that he was trying to emulate, Kissinger said that those statesmen had in some way failed to take into account or deal with one of these sets of constraints. To be a great statesman, an individual must understand these constraints, master them, and transcend them—bending them to his own will.[1]

This chapter will consider the thoughts and research results of a number of scholars who have studied the domestic constraints and influences on making foreign policy. As such, it will be primarily addressed to some fairly general problems in the comparative analysis of foreign policy. We shall deal chiefly with *societal* influences, but we shall also refer at some point to influences operating from the *governmental* level of analysis. In Chapter 9 we shall consider a particularly important societal influence on foreign policy: the economic system of a society. In Chapter 10, we shall discuss aspects of governmental structure.

These domestic constraints—both societal and governmental—take several forms. They affect both opportunity and willingness, both what is possible and probable. In their analysis discussed earlier, the Sprouts related the idea of what is possible to "capability analysis." What is possible for a set of decision makers is constrained by their capabilities: the things that not only promote certain kinds of behavior but also ultimately allow certain kinds of behavior to occur. Decisions to mobilize or to turn potential capabilities into reality increase the range of possibilities and probabilities of certain kinds of behavior. One contemporary example of this is the rapid and striking growth of Soviet naval power during the 1960s and 1970s.

FOREIGN POLICY: WHAT IT IS AND HOW WE STUDY IT

First, however, we must briefly consider our dependent variable—foreign policy. What is it? How is it studied? How do people try to measure it? In the jargon of social scientists, a *dependent variable* is something we want to explain—something that varies and whose variation is of concern. We are interested in the differences among nation-states because we are concerned with the foreign policy of those states. We know that foreign policy activities are not the same—they vary from one state to another and from one *type* of state to another. Therefore, we are concerned with foreign policy as a dependent variable.

---

1. Kissinger expresses these sentiments in *A World Restored: Metternich, Castlereagh, and the Problems of Peace, 1812–1822* (Boston: Houghton Mifflin, 1957) and in the article "Domestic Structure and Foreign Policy," *Daedalus* 95 (1966), 503–529.

To be much less formal, foreign policy is the stuff of international relations. People do not agree on exactly what should be included here, but they are concerned with the policies that states declare, the decisions taken within governmental circles, the actions actually taken by governments, and the consequences of the behavior of governments and their official representatives. Foreign policy is the output of the state into the global system, the outcome of whatever foreign policy process exists within that state. As with the majority of important ideas in the study of world politics, there are almost as many definitions of foreign policy as there are political scientists writing on the subject.

One way to approach the concept of foreign policy is to break it down into its component parts—*foreign* and *policy*. We can think of policy as a decision or set of decisions or programs that act as a guide to behavior. Policy is a guide to an action or a set of actions intended to realize the goals an organization has set for itself. Policy itself, then, is rooted in the concept of *choice*—choosing actions to achieve one's goals. These choices should be reasoned in the minimal sense of comparing choices to see how well they achieve the desired goals.

The ideas of sovereignty and territoriality help us understand what *foreign* means. *Sovereignty* applies to the territory that exists inside the legal boundaries of the state. *Foreign* applies to anything beyond those legal boundaries, to areas where the state has no legal authority over people or territory. *Foreign policy* is thus a set of guides to choices being made about people, places, and things beyond the boundaries of the state. Although there are a wide variety of definitions of the term in the writing on world politics, it is possible to uncover several common features that are important in understanding what foreign policy is.

First, foreign policy—whether we are talking about the process of creating decisions, taking decisions, or implementing decisions—is *relational*. The intention of foreign policy is to affect the behavior of another actor from how it trades, to how it votes in the United Nations, to how it uses its weapons. The foreign policy goals of states have this relational intent, even if the intent involves a more general impact on how other actors relate to international organizations, how closely they obey international law, and similar behavior. Because nothing is distributed equally in the global system, every state requires resources, economic goods, military capabilities, political and strategic support, and cooperation of all sorts from other actors. Foreign policy thus concerns behavior toward some other actor for some reason. Whether the actual behavior taken by a state matches its intentions is another matter. Much of foreign policy analysis is directed toward this question of the links between the intentions of behavior and its consequences.

Many definitions of foreign policy are more specific about the *type* of relationship involved with other international actors. These definitions stress that foreign policy is based on the idea of continually trying to influence or control other actors—to get them to behave in ways beneficial to one's own state. Another point that should be stressed is that foreign policy is continuous—it does not end at a particular date or with the end of a specific government. The process of making and implementing decisions to get others outside one's boundaries to behave in a manner useful to oneself is never ending as long as there are states. Finally, keep in mind that foreign policy, as both process and output, is the link between what goes on inside a state and the world environment outside of that state. It puts any state into communication with the external world.

One final group of foreign policy definitions attempts to define foreign policy in a clear-cut and objective manner. For over a decade a group of scholars has been interested in "events-data" analysis. To this group, foreign policy is what states do; it is the actual foreign policy behavior directed across the borders of states, the activity actually performed by the official representatives of states. Lengthy and complex lists of types or categories of behavior have been developed to handle all the ways in which states actually behave toward each other either in the transmission of words (verbal and written communication in all their forms) or the transmission of objects (economic, military, and diplomatic) in all of their various cooperative or conflictual forms. For an example, see the categories used in the World Events Interaction Survey (WEIS) project, presented in Table 8.1. They represent the *acts* of states.[2] This view of foreign policy stresses what actually happens, rather than decisions not taken, decisions implemented differently from the original decision, or even how the foreign policy process

---

2. For a review of the WEIS project, see Philip M. Burgess and Raymond Lawton, *Indicators of International Behavior: An Assessment of Events Data Research* (Beverly Hills, Calif.: Sage, 1972). Another widely known and used events-data set is COPDAB, described by Edward Azar in "The Conflict and Peace Data Bank (COPDAB) Project," *Journal of Conflict Resolution* 24 (1980), 143–152. WEIS and COPDAB are systematically compared and evaluated by Llewellyn D. Howell, "A Comparative Study of the WEIS and COPDAB Data Sets," *International Studies Quarterly* 27 (1983), 149–159; Jack E. Vincent, "WEIS vs. COPDAB: Correspondence Problems," *International Studies Quarterly* 27 (1983), 160–168. Analyses of foreign policy based on the data from the Comparative Research on the Events of Nations (CREON) project are reported in Maurice A. East et al. (eds.), *Why Nations Act* (Beverly Hills, Calif.: Sage, 1978); Patrick Callahan et al. (eds.), *Describing Foreign Policy* (Beverly Hills, Calif.: Sage, 1982).

Table 8.1

Categories of foreign policy behavior (World Events Interaction Survey).

1. YIELD
011 Surrender, yield to order, submit to arrest, etc.
012 Yield position; retreat; evacuate
013 Admit wrongdoing; retract statement

2. COMMENT
021 Explicit decline to comment
022 Comment on situation-pessimistic
023 Comment on situation-neutral
024 Comment on situation-optimistic
025 Explain policy or future position

3. CONSULT
031 Meet with; at neutral site; or send note
032 Visit; go to
033 Receive visit; host

4. APPROVE
041 Praise, hail, applaud, condolences
042 Endorse others' policy or position; give verbal support

5. PROMISE
051 Promise own policy support
052 Promise material support
053 Promise other future support action
054 Assure; reassure

6. GRANT
061 Express regret; apologize
062 Give state invitation
063 Grant asylum
064 Grant privilege, diplomatic recognition; de facto relations; etc.
065 Suspend negative sanctions; truce
066 Release and/or return persons or property

7. REWARD
071 Extend economic aid (for gift and/or loan)
072 Extend military assistance
073 Give other assistance

8. AGREE
081 Make substantive agreement
082 Agree to future action or procedure; agree to meet, to negotiate

9. REQUEST
091 Ask for information
092 Ask for policy assistance
093 Ask for material assistance
094 Request action; call for
095 Entreat; plead; appeal to; help me

10. PROPOSE
101 Offer proposal
102 Urge or suggest action or policy

11. REJECT
111 Turn down proposal; reject protest demand, threat, etc.
112 Refuse; oppose; refuse to allow

12. ACCUSE
121 Charge; criticize; blame; disapprove
122 Denounce; denigrate; abuse

13. PROTEST
131 Make complaint (not formal)
132 Make formal complaint or protest

14. DENY
141 Deny an accusation
142 Deny an attributed policy, action, role, or position

15. DEMAND
150 Issue order or command, insist; demand compliance, etc.

(continued on page 194)

Table 8.1 *(continued)*

16. WARN 160 Give warning **17. THREATEN** 171 Threat without specific negative sanctions 172 Threat with specific nonmilitary negative sanctions 173 Threat with force specified 174 Ultimatum; threat with negative sanctions and time limit specified **18. DEMONSTRATE** 181 Nonmilitary demonstration; walk-out on 182 Armed force mobilization, exercise and/or display **19. REDUCE RELATIONSHIP** **(as Neg. Sanction)** 191 Cancel or postpone planned event	192 Reduce routine international activity; recall officials, etc. 193 Halt negotiations 194 Break diplomatic relations **20. EXPEL** 201 Order personnel out of country 202 Expel organization or group **21. SEIZE** 211 Seize position or possessions 212 Detain or arrest person(s) **22. FORCE** 221 Noninjury destructive act 222 Nonmilitary injury- destruction 223 Military engagement

works. For the purposes of the present chapter, an approach that looks at the actual behavior of states is useful if we are concerned with the differences in national characteristics and the way they affect state behavior.

Comparative Studies of Foreign Policy

This brings us to the idea of the comparative study of foreign policy, which compares the behavior of various state units to look for patterns associated with types of states in various types of situations. The question of what to compare may involve very basic decisions about the units involved in the comparisons. For example, does one compare the most different or the most similar units? Should one try to compare many states at one point in time? One state across many time periods? A large number of units across different time periods? The answers to these questions depend to a great extent on just what research problem one is confronting. Still, decisions of this type must be made.

The question of what to compare becomes most complex when selecting the independent variables. In trying to explain the variations in foreign policy behavior, what factors, influences, and characteristics—what variables—should we investigate? This may be approached in several ways. One ambitious attempt by the Dimensionality of Nations (DON) project attempted to list all the important independent variables thought to be involved in influencing foreign policy. This included the location and use of "marker" variables—variables that had been used in previous studies of the characteristics of states. Thus, faced with the question of what to compare, the project essentially said, "We don't know, but others have given us clues where to start." By assuming that there were patterns, the DON project and its director, Rudolph Rummel, applied a variety of statistical techniques to the data on states. Data from over eighty states for several years in the 1950s were collected for 230 independent variables. After statistical analysis, the mass of possible influences was found to cluster into a much smaller group of "dimensions": namely, economic development, political orientation, and size. In discussing the emergence of a small number of dimensions for a much larger group of independent variables, Rummel concluded that foreign policy is "highly patterned behavior. They [the small number of dimensions] mean that nations act similarly to each other and that these similarities can be resolved into a few basic dimensions. In other words international relations is structured behavior."[3]

Other *early* attempts at the comparative study of foreign policy that worked from more explicit theory came to much the same answer. The best-known theory, the "pretheory," of foreign policy was presented by James Rosenau in the mid-1960s.[4] Rosenau assumed that three aspects of the state took particular importance: size (he divided states into large and small), economic development (developed and underdeveloped), and the nature of the political system ("open" and "closed"). Rosenau then went on to make a crucial point: Until Rosenau's study, writers simply made lists of possible factors that influenced foreign policy; in

---

3. Rudolph J. Rummel, "Some Dimensions in the Foreign Policy Behavior of Nations," *Journal of Peace Research* 3 (1966), 201–223. See also his *The Dimensions of Nations* (Beverly Hills, Calif.: Sage, 1972).

4. James N. Rosenau, "Pre-Theories and Theories of Foreign Policy," in R. Barry Farrell (ed.), *Approaches to Comparative and International Politics* (Evanston, Ill.: Northwestern University Press, 1966), pp. 27–92. For other such attempts to study foreign policy, see Richard C. Snyder, H. W. Bruck, and Burton Sapin, *Foreign Policy Decision-Making* (New York: Free Press, 1962); David Wilkinson, *Comparative Foreign Relations: Framework and Methods* (Belmont, Calif.: Dickenson, 1969); Lloyd Jensen, *Explaining Foreign Policy* (Englewood Cliffs, N.J.: Prentice-Hall, 1982).

contrast, Rosenau noted that we must try to determine the "relative potencies" of these independent variables. That is, we must try to see which are most important and under what conditions. He claimed that all possible independent variables, or influences on foreign policy, could be classified into five categories: (1) idiosyncratic (having to do with the characteristics of individual decision makers), (2) role (of decision makers), (3) governmental, (4) societal, and (5) systemic influences (all the stimuli and influences impinging on the state from the outside). Except for our separation of relational from systemic influences, this is the level-of-analysis scheme we use in this book.

All of this may be translated into a question: Which part of the environment, or the menu, will be most closely studied by the decision makers of a particular state in formulating and implementing foreign policy goals? This analytical scheme is represented in Figure 8.1.

GOALS AND OBJECTIVES OF FOREIGN POLICY

We now require a brief introduction to the idea of foreign policy goals. It is difficult to identify specific goals of individual states at specific times in history, but we can broadly describe those things that leaders

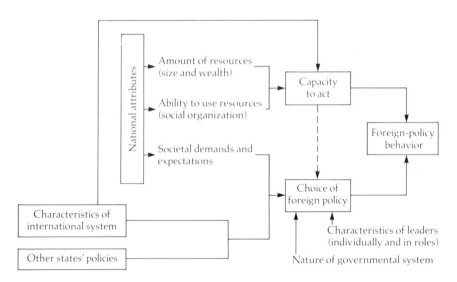

Figure 8.1
Relating global and national characteristics to foreign policy behavior.

of states pursue as foreign policy objectives. We must go beyond a vague notion of "national interest." The leaders of states have *different* and *changing* foreign policy orientations and role orientations. Along with these go evolving objectives and debate over how those objectives are best pursued. The phenomenon of foreign policy debate also points out the fact that there rarely is agreement or consensus within states over what the foreign policy interest should be.

Like K. J. Holsti and others, we prefer to discuss a set of foreign policy objectives, thinking of an objective as "an image of a future state of affairs and future conditions that governments through individual policy makers aspire to bring about by wielding influence abroad and by changing or sustaining the behavior of other states."[5] Objectives may be very concrete, such as Egypt's objective of recovering territory in the Sinai. Objectives may be much less concrete in terms of creating images or promoting a specific set of values—for example, raising one's prestige or popularity through certain behavior or "making the world safe for democracy" or working for the victory of the proletariat. Some objectives remain constant over long periods of time, such as geopolitical objectives like Russian possession of warm water ports or British command of the seas. Other objectives are quite transitory, perhaps changing from month to month—for example, monetary policy. Some objectives have consequences that affect the whole state—for example, the deterrence of nuclear attack as a security objective. Other objectives, especially in economic matters but also in political matters, that may keep a particular government in power involve the interests of only a small portion of society. Keep in mind that governments often pursue objectives that really are incompatible—private objectives that conflict, private and public objectives that conflict. For example, when the United States sold huge quantities of wheat to the Soviet Union in 1971 and 1972, the Nixon administration had to balance incompatible objectives. On the one hand, the deal would help improve relations with the Soviet Union and might ultimately help the administration disengage from the American involvement in Vietnam. On the other hand, the Administration also wanted to control inflation, keep food prices down, and increase the well-being of the American people. Also involved were less general objectives, such as being reelected in 1972

---

5. See K. J. Holsti, *International Politics: A Framework for Analysis,* 4th ed. (Englewood Cliffs, N.J.: Prentice-Hall, 1983), chaps. 4–5. The quote is from p. 124, citing the words of Snyder, Bruck, and Sapin.

and profit seeking by certain farm and food transportation groups. In sum, leaders of states seek a wide range of private and collective objectives, some concrete, some quite abstract and often in conflict with each other.

Holsti presents one scheme for classifying the objectives of states. Using three criteria—the value placed on the objective by the current decision makers, the time element placed on the achievement of the objective, and the types of demands that the objective makes upon other international actors—he comes up with three categories. The first is called *core objectives*, to which governments commit their very existence and which must be achieved at all times. These are usually related to survival of the state and are usually stated as basic principles to be accepted without question. In seeking survival, states are seeking to protect their sovereignty, autonomy, and territory and the lives and well-being of their people. How this is achieved obviously depends on the international environment and the capabilities of the state.

Core values are neither necessarily incompatible across states nor unchanging. From 1967 to 1979, most Israelis maintained that occupation of all the lands conquered in the Six-Day War was one of the core values involving security, protection, and territory. Nevertheless, the peace treaty between Israel and Egypt signed in 1979 provided for Israel returning the Sinai territory to Egypt. Clearly, even these core values are open to wide interpretation of means, achievement, assessment of danger, and so forth. The order that derives from states recognizing common interests, even within a condition of "anarchy," is illustrated by this peace treaty. Similarly, arms control agreements, such as the U.S.-Soviet SALT agreements, indicate that states need not constantly strive to be as militarily strong as possible in order to protect core objectives and values.

Compared with core objectives, the second type of objectives, *middle-range objectives*, are less important and less immediate to decision makers and require more cooperation from other states. There are many middle-range objectives, including such broad concerns as economic development and social welfare, which often require outside aid of some sort. *Long-range objectives*, the third type, are of least immediacy to decision makers and include "those plans, dreams and visions concerning the ultimate political or ideological organizations of the international system, rules governing relations in that system, and the role of specific nations within it." Though often having common core objectives, states can choose from various paths to fulfill those objectives.

DIFFERENCES IN THE FOREIGN POLICY BEHAVIOR OF STATES

Differences in the foreign policy behavior of states derive in part from different capacities to act. This refers both to the resources that any state has at its disposal and its ability to utilize those resources. Differences in states' capacities to act are affected, determined, and influenced by the characteristics of states, or *national attributes.* We are back to the question of what to compare. In both the traditional literature of international relations and in the more recent quantitative work, size, wealth, and political accountability emerge as the basic distinguishing characteristics of states. Which of these three attributes seems most important?

Of the three, Rosenau proposed that size would be "more potent" than either development or accountability. Although far from conclusive, a number of empirical studies have tended to support this view. Using the Comparative Research on the Events of Nations (CREON) data set for thirty-three states for the 1959-to-1968 period (and using almost 4,500 foreign policy events), researchers found that the physical size of a nation appeared to be most important in explaining the variations of foreign policy behavior of the states being investigated.[6] In another study Rummel concluded that dissimilarities in the size and the economic development of states are the most important determinants in explaining the variations in their behavior toward one another.[7] Size, as finally conceived by Rosenau and measured by others, included the physical area and population of a state. Size has an effect on capabilities and the capacity to act. Larger states have a greater range of options due to these greater resources.

In Rosenau's conception, small size in terms of people and area limits a state's resources and capacity to act. However, a lack of wealth or economic development limits a state's resources and capacity to act. The idea of a small state is often confused in this way, with some people meaning small in area and population and others meaning poor or less developed. Although both conditions limit a state's capacity to act, lack of development provides the more striking illustration. For

---

6. Maurice A. East and Charles Hermann, "Do Nation-Types Account for Foreign Policy Behavior?", in James N. Rosenau (ed.), *Comparing Foreign Policies* (New York: Halsted, 1974), p. 299.

7. Rudolph Rummel, "Some Empirical Findings on Nations and Their Behavior," *World Politics* 21 (1969), 226–241.

example, in one of the very rare empirical studies of the foreign policy administration in an underdeveloped country, Maurice East substantiated the importance of resources for the capacity to act. In studying the ministry of foreign affairs in pre-Amin Uganda, he found that the ministry had very little impact on or input into the foreign policy process. The lack of human resources seems to have been the main problem—for example, only two people were responsible for all of Africa and only one for the United Nations. In addition, most of the staff was inexperienced, young, and poorly trained.[8]

These findings fit with other findings that smaller states, especially less-developed non-Western ones, are more oriented toward employing joint action, particularly working through international organizations, as a way to conserve financial and human resources. Indicators such as the size of the delegation to the United Nations, sponsorship of UN resolutions, and having IGOs as targets of foreign policy behavior all support this view of small-state foreign policy.[9] Following East's arguments from several of his works, we get another aspect of the constraints on the menu. Not only are smaller states (in terms of land area, population, GNP, and military capabilities) restricted by a lack of resources and capabilities, but they are also restricted by a lack of information-processing capabilities. Although a lack of capabilities restricts what is possible or probable, a lack of information receivers and processors affects states in terms of what the Sprouts call *cognitive behaviorism*—the states do not know what is going on in the outside world well enough to respond properly or to shape policies to fit the environment. We have here the case of a potential diner sitting in a restaurant and not knowing how to order because he or she has forgotten to bring reading glasses and cannot see the menu (or, alternatively, the menu is written in a foreign language). Again, less-developed states seem to be more restricted in this regard than are developed ones that are simply small in population or area.

Larger states are not so restricted; they are able to monitor the world, react to it, and interact with it. Studies done by the Correlates of War

---

8. Maurice A. East, "Foreign Policy-Making in Small States: Some Theoretical Observations Based on a Study of the Uganda Ministry of Foreign Affairs," *Policy Sciences* 4 (1973), 491–508. Supporting evidence is also provided by Bruce Russett and J. Joseph Monsen, "Bureaucracy and Polyarchy as Predictors of Performance," *Comparative Political Studies* 8 (1975), 5–31.

9. See, for example, Robert Keohane, "Who Cares about the General Assembly?", *International Organization* 23 (1969), 141–149; Maurice East, "Size and Foreign Policy Behavior: A Test of Two Models," *World Politics* 25 (1973), 556–576.

project have demonstrated that the major powers receive the highest number of diplomatic representatives from other nations.[10] Diplomatic representation, in fact, has been used as a measure of "ascribed status," as discussed in Chapters 4 and 6. Table 8.2 gives some indication of how size relates to the *sending* of diplomatic representatives. Of the four most populous states, three have over 101 diplomatic missions and one lands in the 91–100 range. Of the microstates, only two have substantial diplomatic representation—one in the 71–80 range, the other in the 41–50 range. Nine maintain diplomatic relations only with the United States and/or Britain. Of the sixty-one states categorized as small, over half (thirty-four) have 20 or fewer diplomatic missions abroad. Remember, this table takes only population into account and not newness or state of economic development.

Researchers have confirmed that small states (small in terms of the four national attributes noted above) display low levels of overall participation in international politics and a rather narrow geographical and issue range of foreign policy concerns. It can also be demonstrated

Table 8.2

Number of diplomatic missions sent by states of different population size, 1975.

Number of missions sent	Population category			
	Micro	Small	Medium	Large
Over 101		2	8	6
91–100		1	5	3
81–90			3	
71–80	1		3	2
61–70		1	6	
51–60		3	8	
41–50	1	5	7	2
31–40		8	7	
21–30		7	8	
11–20		9	3	
1–10	9	25	1	
Total	11	61	59	13

Source: Elmer Plischke, *Microstates in World Affairs* (Washington, D.C.: American Enterprise Institute for Public Policy Research, 1977), p. 44.

---

10. See Melvin Small and J. David Singer, "The Diplomatic Importance of States, 1816–1970: An Extension and Refinement of the Indicator," *World Politics* 25 (1973), 577–599.

202 / Domestic Constraints

that large states act in just the opposite manner. One study using the World Event Interaction Survey (WEIS) data for 1966 (based on 5,550 event interactions) indicates that the twenty most active initiators of international activity accounted for 70 percent of all the world's activity for that year. The five great powers—the United States, the USSR, China, Britain, and France—accounted for over 40 percent of all the 1966 event interactions; the United States was the leader, responsible for 18 percent of all activities initiated in that year. The superpowers were also the leaders as *receivers* of international behavior—the United States received 16 percent of all interactional events and the Soviet Union 15 percent. The general relationship between size and level of international activity has been supported by other studies using other data sets.[11]

ECONOMIC AND POLITICAL DIFFERENCES

Decision makers act in the name of their states. As we have seen, countries differ in size, income level, and other characteristics that affect both their capabilities and their goals. They also differ in their histories as nations, in the ways their societies and economies are organized, and in the structure of their governments. Contrast, for a moment, the United States and the Soviet Union.

The United States is a country founded by immigrants who came to develop a vast and sparsely populated land and to construct a society in a wilderness. Most people came to the new land to realize hopes that were constrained in their home countries—hopes for political or religious expression or hopes for economic well-being away from overcrowded lands and famine. Their experience in America often rewarded individual initiative and offered a degree of equality of opportunity (for whites, at least) that exceeded what they had known in the Old World. Especially important for foreign policy, the new land

---

11. For example, Rudolph Rummel, "Some Empirical Findings on Nations and Their Behavior," *World Politics* 21 (1969), 226–241; Stephen Salmore and Charles Hermann, "The Effect of Size, Development and Accountability on Foreign Policy," *Peace Research Society Papers* 14 (1969), 15–30. We should take these figures only as suggestive ones, however. Because media attention is usually focused on the major powers, the data used tend to exaggerate major power activity. Also, one study indicates that size does not differentiate states in terms of their verbal/nonverbal behavior or conflictual/cooperative behavior; see Robert D. Duval and William R. Thompson, "Reconsidering the Aggregate Relationship between Size, Economic Development, and Some Types of Foreign Policy Behavior," *American Journal of Political Science* 24 (1980), 511–525.

was largely safe from external enemies. Once independence had been won from Britain, the limited transportation technology of the time insulated America from Europe's national wars and provided a security that prevailed for a century and a half.

The Soviet Union, by contrast, is a state inhabited by people who have traditionally lived in insecurity. The Russian state is epitomized by the wooden stockade fortresses that once dotted the harsh Eurasian plains. Russia was periodically conquered or invaded by Mongols, Poles, Swedes, Germans, and others. It was ruled by autocratic leaders whose chief virtue was their ability to provide a measure of national unity and strength to ward off attackers. In time the Russian state expanded to rule instead of being threatened by its neighbors. As a multinational empire, czarist Russia, and later the Soviet Union, governed or repressed many subordinate nations whose total population approached that of Russia alone. Economically czarist Russia was a relatively primitive society, following well behind Europe in the development of industry and the accumulation of capital. When the Communists took power in 1917, their revolutionary ideology seemed a threat to the entire capitalist world; indeed, they proclaimed the virtues of world revolution. European, American, and Japanese forces intervened indecisively on the side of the czarist counterrevolutionaries. The Communists ultimately consolidated their power, but only by confirming and deepening the Russian autocratic tradition. They built a modern, centralized, industrial state, one finally capable of providing security from invasion; at the same time, they became a constant threat to their neighbors.

Americans thus live with a tradition of security that allows them periodic forays into world politics but protects them from basic threats to national survival. Russians, by contrast, live with a tradition of insecurity and mutually threatening relations with others. Americans live with an economy developed by individual enterprise that provides an unusual measure of opportunity for many; economic development seems to proceed best when it is least fettered by state interference. Soviet citizens live in an economy where capitalist development began late and was cut short and where modern economic development is controlled and directed by the state bureaucracy. Americans live in a state where the government provided the religious and political liberty so many of its immigrants sought and the freedom for capitalist development. Russians live in a state where people welcomed state control; without control, there could be no unity, no security, and little prosperity.

The experiences of American and Russian citizens—and the selective memories they have of their parents' experiences—help provide the basic structure of belief and ideology through which these citizens view their place in the world and hence the appropriate roles and actions of their governments. These experiences also determine the structure of their economies and governments: capitalist and democratic in the first instance, socialist and authoritarian in the second. Furthermore, those individuals, groups, and classes dominant within both societies use their power to perpetuate belief systems that will reinforce their power. Americans are taught an ideology that praises freedom and extols capitalism as the engine of prosperity. Russians are taught an ideology that praises the state as provider of individual and collective security. If we exaggerate somewhat, we can say that in America the form of the economy shaped the kind of state that emerged—an economy of relatively decentralized, "plural" centers of power whose interest was best served by limiting state control. By contrast, in the Soviet Union the state—through state ownership of the means of industrial production, collectivization of agriculture, and centralized planning—determined the kind of economy that emerged.[12]

How much difference do these contrasting histories make for foreign policy? In the broadest terms, are states that are more democratic also more peaceful and less threatening to their neighbors? It would be reassuring for people who live in democratic countries to believe that their own freedoms made them readier to respect the freedoms of others and desirous only of enjoying their own freedom in peace. Many have thought this true. A famous American sociologist in 1960 dedicated a new book to his children, "that they may grow up in a more democratic and, therefore, more peaceful world."[13] Many have feared that autocratic states, because their rulers are less restrained by peace-loving citizens, may indulge their desires for foreign conquest or even try to unify their peoples behind them against a real or imagined foreign threat.

---

12. There is, in fact, an irony in that both nations were formed under conditions that no longer apply, and their structures therefore seem obsolete. America is no longer isolated in the world, the continent is no longer undeveloped, and threats to survival stem largely from the military, economic, and environmental interdependence between Americans and others. Russia has achieved an unprecedented degree of military security and economic strength; the state bureaucracy is now more clearly a burden on individual and national development.

13. Seymour Martin Lipset, *Political Man* (Garden City, N.Y.: Doubleday, 1960).

By contrast, others have feared a crusading spirit in many democracies; they have inverted Woodrow Wilson's wartime goal "to make the world safe for democracy," wondering instead how to make democracy safe for the world. Hypotheses about the effect of different systems of economic organization also abound. They range from propositions about the alleged need of capitalists for world peace and prosperity to statements about the alleged need of capitalists for forcible acquisition of foreign people, markets, and resources. Other theories—whose examination we shall postpone until Chapter 16—insist that the demands of foreign investors and domestic capitalists allied with foreign interests distort the economies, foreign policies, and domestic government of less-developed countries, gravely harming most of their citizens.

NATIONAL INTEREST, PARTICULAR INTERESTS, AND GOVERNMENT STRUCTURE

As noted, much theory stresses the role of "national interest" in determining states' behavior. Hans J. Morgenthau has long been the most prominent of such theorists; he has held that all states pursue certain interests, principally those of maximizing power.[14] Any government, whether democratically controlled or not, will pursue such interests in the anarchic world of each against all that power politics theorists see as being the true condition of international politics. One difficulty with such theories is that they can easily become mere tautologies, that is, statements that are merely definitions and hence impossible to refute. For example, one can construct arguments to prove that any action, whether initiating a war or keeping the peace, is intended to enhance or preserve the power of the nation-state.

Even when this kind of argument is avoided, however, we encounter the fact that within any given nation-state, different individuals, groups, and classes have different interests. Workers share some interests with factory owners (for instance, seeing that their products can be sold), but they differ sharply in others (such as who gains more from the production of those goods and whether it is better to manufacture goods with high-priced American labor or with cheap labor in a less-developed country). Some manufacturers are interested in selling food

---

14. Hans J. Morgenthau, *Politics among Nations: The Struggle for Power and Peace* (New York: Knopf, 1948).

or consumer goods in a world at peace; others want to sell armaments that have a market only in a world where states are at war or threatened by war. It then becomes essential to ask: *Whose particular interest is reflected in any particular governmental policy or act?* Which individuals, groups, or classes are most influential in determining government policy? Does this change from time to time or in different international or domestic circumstances? Are there some issues on which one group or class has a dominant influence and others on which some other group is dominant? These questions are absolutely central to political analysis and unavoidable in any political system where there are several individuals or groups and where each has different wishes or interests. Unless we know how these different interests are reconciled into a single decision, we can know nothing about what particular policy will result. Without more attention to this, our previous discussion of state goals and objectives is necessarily incomplete.

This problem has been well-known for a long time and has been elaborated in what is now known as *Arrow's paradox* of voting.[15] Some aspects of the problem can be seen if we imagine that Dick likes peanuts, Jane likes potato chips, and Spot likes dog biscuits. Dick finds a dollar, which with inflation will buy only one of the three desired foods. What do they buy? It depends on who is in charge and what his or her preferences are: If Dick is in charge because he found the dollar, and if he chooses to please himself, they will have peanuts. If he chooses to be generous and to please Jane, then they will have potato chips. If Jane is in charge (she is older and bigger and takes the dollar), then they will have potato chips. If either chooses to be generous, they may even have dog biscuits. (Spot, being a member of a weak and inarticulate class, cannot be in charge, so they are not going to have dog biscuits unless the person in charge chooses to be generous to Spot.) In any case, if we know who is in charge and whose taste that person wants to please, we know what that person will buy—but *only* if we know who is in charge (who is the dictator) or what decision rule is used.

If one can imagine Dick, Jane, and Spot in a perfect democracy (dogs and people have equal votes) and each holds out for his or her first choice, there is no way to identify a group interest that can be served. Only if we have additional information on preferences or decision making (e.g., they take turns, so Jane gets her way today and Dick

---

15. Kenneth Arrow, *Social Choice and Individual Values*, 2nd ed. (New York: Wiley, 1963).

tomorrow, or they both hate dog biscuits and Spot likes potato chips almost as much as dog biscuits, and they take second choices into account) can we begin to make a prediction or identify a way in which their different interests can be aggregated. The same is true with much larger social systems like countries: We must know how individual preferences become collective choices—who is in charge, how compromises are reached, how these decision-making procedures differ in different times and circumstances—if we want to talk about what a government may do. That is why we consider it vital to know what the structure of the government of a state is. Whose particular interests will it serve at any particular time? Does the structure of the economy give particular groups or classes (such as finance capitalists or the managers of state-owned enterprises) particular clout on a particular issue? The concept of a national interest may indicate certain core values or goals that most citizens share to some degree (such as peace, prosperity, and security), but until we know how different actors' interests are combined, we know very little about the *priorities* of the various values or goals or about how they will be pursued in international politics.

There is little evidence to support claims for the superior peacefulness of any particular form of societal, economic, or governmental organization. Various studies of large numbers of states, either in the contemporary international system or over the past two centuries, have found no consistent relationship between frequency of engaging in international war and having a democratic or an authoritarian political system or a capitalist (largely private enterprise) or socialist (state-owned factories and farms) economy.

One conclusion of the pioneering peace scientist Lewis Richardson was that individual states vary greatly in frequency of war involvement over their individual histories. States cannot be characterized as inherently warlike or peaceful. Richardson's analyses were based on all the "deadly quarrels" he could identify from 1820 to 1949. The Correlates of War project, studying the period between 1816 and 1980, identified 118 large-scale international wars. The top three states in war involvement were the same ones that Richardson found—France, Britain, and Russia. France was involved in 19 percent of the Correlates of War conflicts, and Britain and Russia in 16 percent.[16] Clearly, simply being a democracy does not keep a state out of war.

---

16. See Lewis F. Richardson, *Statistics of Deadly Quarrels* (Chicago: Quadrangle, 1960); Melvin Small and J. David Singer, *Resort to Arms: International and Civil Wars, 1816–1980* (Beverly Hills, Calif.: Sage, 1982).

Are democracies more peaceful? As the above data indicate, if we simply look at the frequency of participation in war, democracies (or "bourgeois democracies" as termed in the Correlates of War studies) were *not* more peaceful over the period studied, especially when "extrasystemic" colonial or imperialist wars and interventions in the internal conflicts of other countries in the post–World War II period are considered. However, if these extrasystemic wars are excluded, and if the focus is on the pair of countries—do democracies fight against democracies?—then we can conclude that democracies are more peaceful.[17] In sum, the results are mixed, as indicated by Quincy Wright's summary of his findings on this subject:

> Statistics can hardly be invoked to show that democracies have been less often involved in war than autocracies. France was almost as belligerent while it was a republic as while it was a monarchy or empire. Great Britain is high in the list of belligerent countries, though it has for the longest time approximated democracy in its form of government.... More convincing statistical correlations can be found by comparing the trend toward democracy in periods of general peace and away from democracy in periods of general war. This correlation, however, may prove that peace produces democracy rather than that democracy produces peace.[18]

The ability of a government to control society and the ability of specific interests in society to communicate their needs and demands to government are both related to the openness of government. *Openness* means the extent to which a government is subject to influences from society. This means that a government is accountable: It must satisfy the people of a society, or it can be removed from office by regular, agreed-on procedures that are by some criteria fair. Being open means that *opposition groups in society can contest groups in government* for the right to control the government through some type of electoral procedures. Being open means that such opposition groups can present their positions and ideologies to the people through a free press and other

---

17. See Steven Chan, "Mirror, Mirror on the Wall . . . : Are the Free Countries More Pacific?", *Journal of Conflict Resolution* 28 (1984); Melvin Small and J. David Singer, "The War-Proneness of Democratic Regimes, 1816–1965," *Jerusalem Journal of International Relations* 1 (1976), 50–69. Similarly complex findings are reported by Jonathan Wilkenfeld, "Domestic and Foreign Conflict Behavior of Nations," *Journal of Peace Research* 5 (1968), 56–69.

18. Quincy Wright, *A Study of War,* 2nd ed. (Chicago: University of Chicago Press, 1965), p. 841.

media. Being open means that no group in society is systematically prevented from acting as an opposition. (Remember that in open societies, the opposition also has responsibilities. Just as the government allows fair procedures that decide who is to run the government, the opposition must also agree to contest for office in a fair manner. That is, if the opposition loses a fair election, it doesn't run off to start a guerrilla war!)

Earlier we introduced three dimensions of a state that were thought to be important to foreign policy: size (large or small), economic development (developed or developing), and accountability (open or closed governments). A number of studies have provided evidence that size, development, and accountability are related to foreign policy behavior. Characteristics of a society (societal variables) will be more influential in affecting foreign policy in truly open or democratic societies than in closed societies. Governmental factors should be more "potent" in explaining foreign policy in closed states.[19]

For states where the political process is more authoritarian or closed, it will be more useful to look at characteristics of the government and its structure rather than at attributes of its society to explain foreign policy. Being closed, public opinion and political interests will be less likely to have an impact. These sorts of relationships between government and society are supported in studies of whether conflict within states results in external or international conflict behavior by states (or perhaps whether international conflict results in internal strife and conflict).

The first major empirical research studies concluded that, in general, there is no systematic relationship between the domestic and foreign conflict behavior of states. However, when states were studied in terms of type of government, it was found that information on particular types of internal conflict helped to predict two different forms of external conflict for different types of government. Three categories were used: (1) *polyarchic*, or democratic governments, (2) *personalist*, or military-type authoritarian regimes, and (3) *centralist*, or Communist-type governments, the latter two being closed systems.[20] The differences

19. For example, see David W. Moore, "Governmental and Societal Influences on Foreign Policy in Open and Closed Nations," in James N. Rosenau, *Comparing Foreign Policies* (New York: Halstead, 1974), pp. 171–199.

20. The basic studies may be found in Rudolph Rummel, "Dimensions of Conflict Behavior within and between Nations," *Yearbook of the Society for General Systems* 8 (1963), 1–50; Raymond Tanter, "Dimensions of Conflict Behavior within and between Nations, 1958–60," *Journal of Conflict Resolution* 10 (1966), 41–64; and Jonathan Wilkenfeld, "Domes-

that showed up in the analyses were explainable partly in terms of how open the domestic system was.

Briefly, domestic conflict was distinguished according to three basic kinds: (1) *turmoil* (nonorganized, spontaneous conflict such as riots or demonstrations), (2) *revolutionary conflict* (overt and organized), and (3) *subversive conflict* (secretly organized, such as guerrilla war or assassinations). Foreign conflict was also reduced to three dimensions: (1) *war*, (2) *"diplomatic conflict"* (measured by such activities as nonviolent troop movements or the expulsion of ambassadors), and (3) *"belligerent activity"* short of military action (such as breaking diplomatic relations or antiforeign demonstrations). Different types of government showed different relationships between domestic and foreign conflict. For instance, with polyarchic states, domestic turmoil is related to all three types of foreign conflict. For personalist states, all three types of internal conflict lead to diplomatic foreign conflict. For states with centralist governments, revolutionary internal conflict is related to foreign war.

More important to our discussion of governmental and societal influences on foreign policy is a major difference between centralist governments and the other two types. For personalist and polyarchic states, there are mutual relationships in that some forms of internal conflict appear to lead to external conflict and some forms of external conflict appear to lead to internal conflict. Sometimes governments may use foreign conflict as an excuse to rally their own people behind the government. In times of domestic turmoil or conflict, they may pick a quarrel with a foreign enemy in an effort to unify their people and divert them from their domestic conflict. Alternatively, sometimes involvement in foreign wars may create domestic protest and dissension. In the United States, the Vietnam war led to domestic turmoil, not vice versa. Democracies, where governments may be unwilling or unable to repress dissent effectively, are especially prone to foreign conflict lead-

---

tic and Foreign Conflict Behavior of Nations," *Journal of Peace Research* 5 (1968), 56–69. In Appendix B, along with data on population, area, and other societal characteristics, we present a code for political system type, or degree of political freedom as those freedoms are known in democracies. The code, from the annual survey of Freedom House, *Freedom in the World: Political Rights and Civil Liberties 1981* (Westport, Conn.: Greenwood Press, 1981), characterizes states as "free," "partly free," or "not free" on the basis of whether free, honest, and competitive elections are held, whether civil liberties such as free speech, free assembly, and assurance of a fair trial are present, and whether political terrorism is largely absent. The characterizations are of course comparative—no society is entirely free. By these characterizations, only about 36 percent of the world's population lives in the 31 percent of the world's countries that were "free" in 1981.

ing to domestic conflict, rather than vice versa. For centralist states, however, external conflict rarely leads to overt domestic conflict—dissent can more easily be controlled.

> On the one hand, we have highly centralized nations, in which decisions concerning foreign conflict behavior are in some cases generated by the types of internal conflict behavior it is experiencing, but in which external conflict decisions are made in *relative isolation from internal reactions.* On the other hand, in the polyarchic nations, and to a lesser extent in the personalist nations, neither internal nor external are taken in isolation from each other.[21]

Yet these large-scale statistical studies, however useful as preliminary explorations, do not substitute for more carefully stated hypotheses linked to particular historical contexts and kinds of systems. In the next chapter, we shall pay particular attention to certain widely quoted theories attributing particular international policies to certain alleged economic causes. In Chapter 10, we shall consider the role of public opinion—what the content of that opinion is on some key foreign policy issues, how that opinion may be formed, and what effect it is likely to have on foreign policy choice in a democracy. This focus on public opinion in democracies comprises part of the larger question of the effect of different modes of government organization on foreign policy.

---

21. Wilkenfeld, op. cit., p. 67 (emphasis added). For a general review of the relationship between internal and external conflict, see Michael Stohl, "The Nexus of Civil and International Conflict," in Ted Robert Gurr (ed.), *Handbook of Political Conflict* (New York: Free Press, 1980).

9

DOMESTIC CONSTRAINTS: ECONOMICS AND SOCIETY

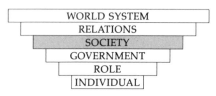

We have reviewed the effects of differences in size and wealth on states' foreign policy. These are both societal-level variables in our scheme. It is now time to focus on some more specific propositions about societal constraints or influences, specifically some major economic influences. We shall look in detail at various ideas that are central to political science. How does the organization of a state's economic system affect the foreign policy "outputs" of that state? More precisely, do particular modes of economic organization—for example, capitalism in advanced industrial societies like the United States—produce foreign policies that are more aggressive or war prone than those of states with other modes of organization, such as socialism? We shall review several major bodies of theory on the topic and test their hypotheses with empirical evidence where possible.

IMPERIALISM AND CAPITALISM

Both conventional and Marxist traditions assert that there is something very special about the advanced capitalist economies dating from the industrial revolution. Some elements of conventional theory emphasize features in capitalism that are alleged to promote world peace, but other elements of liberal theory and certainly most of Marxist thought claim that capitalist countries are likely to have particularly aggressive foreign policies. This concern is not limited to acts of war. Capitalism is sometimes blamed for a variety of *imperialist* acts, loosely defined as efforts to exert political or economic control over smaller or weaker states. Political and military interventions in less-developed countries are of special interest. Other foci of attention include military spending, "militarism," and arms races.

The theories differ substantially on the particular aspects of capitalism that are considered to cause imperialism or war. Some describe the alleged needs of the entire capitalist economy—that the capitalist system *as a whole* (or at least the capitalist economy of any major nation-state) is dependent on military spending or on continued access to foreign markets for goods or investment opportunities. Other theories cite the interests and power of *particular groups or classes.* Foreign investors, the military-industrial complex, or other economically defined groups may have an interest in an aggressive or expansionist foreign policy that can potentially yield great gains for them, even though many other members of the system—capitalists as well as workers—suffer net losses from such a policy. A minority of economic interests, therefore, may successfully maintain a policy that benefits them but is not required by and may even be detrimental to the capitalist economy as a whole. Finally, some theories are addressed less to readily definable material interest than to *value structure,* that is, the ideology of capitalist systems. According to these theories, this value structure, concerned as much with the desire to preserve the capitalist system as to extend it, produces behavior that is excessively responsive to economic growth and the incentive of material rewards. The resultant foreign policy is thus both expansionist and hostile to socialist states with different value structures, whose adoption by major segments within the capitalist system would undermine the system's viability and the privileged place of the capitalist classes within it.

Contradicting these theories are others that stress the relative unimportance of economic motivations in influencing foreign policy; as an explicit refutation, they emphasize political and cultural ends and other kinds of ideological motivations. The whole question of economic causes of foreign policy is extraordinarily broad, and we could not possibly provide a comprehensive overview here. We shall, however, consider a number of variants within each of the three categories just identified, including some counterarguments as well as economically oriented theories. Our attention will be devoted mainly to the economic theories, and we shall at least mention most of the major ones.

Most of the classical economic interpretations attribute imperialism to demands arising from the organization of production in capitalist economies. Many eighteenth- and nineteenth-century economists believed that the profit rates in industrialized countries tended to fall over long periods. They had differing explanations for this phenomenon, but J. A. Hobson, the liberal English economist writing at the end of the nineteenth century, developed the argument and linked the phenomenon to imperialism. He saw the very unequal distribution of income and wealth in capitalist countries—especially England—as leaving the poor unable to consume much. This, in turn, forced capitalists to invest their capital abroad and to compete with others to control foreign markets. The capitalist system of the time was to blame, but according to his theory imperialism was not inherent in capitalism.[1] If there were a more equal distribution of income, insufficient domestic consumption—and thus the export of capital—could be avoided.

Karl Marx himself had comparatively little to say about the international consequences of capitalism, but many writers of the early twentieth century developed extremely influential theories of imperialism that were in the Marxist tradition. Most famous is the work of Lenin. According to him, *surplus capital* inevitably arises from the processes of monopolistic capitalist production; no feasible redistribution of income could avoid it. Industrial and banking capital (*finance capital* in the phrase of Rudolf Hilferding) merges to gain effective control of the state. Thus, the drive to export surplus capital becomes a competition among nations rather than simply a competition among corporations. The capitalist nations, in turn, divide the world among themselves, and their competition for territory ultimately leads to war among the capitalist powers.[2]

Like Lenin, Nikolai Bukharin and Rosa Luxemburg believed militarism and colonial expansion to be inherent in capitalism. "Imperialism is the political expression of the accumulation of capital in its competitive struggle for what remains still open of the non-capitalist environment." Manifested in political expansion, violence, and war, "imperialism grows in lawlessness and violence, both in aggression against the non-capitalist world and in ever more serious conflicts among the com-

1. J. A. Hobson, *Imperialism: A Study* (London: Allen and Unwin, 1902).
2. V. I. Lenin, *Imperialism* (New York: Vanguard, 1929).

peting capitalist countries."[3] Both Luxemburg and Bukharin also gave attention to capitalist countries' need for market outlets for their products as well as their capital and to their continual need for new sources of raw materials.

All these theories were designed essentially to explain the phenomenon of European colonialism, which was at its height in the decades preceding World War I. The theories have been the subject of intensive criticism; on a variety of grounds they are said to explain the phenomenon poorly. A number of studies have pointed out empirical evidence that contradicts the theories. For example, Hobson's underconsumption theory suffers from the fact that during the nineteenth century, most British exports were in industries established especially for the export market, not by firms with full warehouses of goods that they had been unable to sell within England. Although economic interests may have provided a powerful incentive to overseas expansion, the mechanism was not quite as Hobson imagined. Another difficulty with classical theorists stems from the fact that income from overseas investment *exceeded* capital outflow for Great Britain (the chief capitalist and imperialist power) during most of the nineteenth century and up to 1914—hardly consistent with the idea of ever-expanding surplus capital at home. Moreover, most of British foreign investment did not go to the African and Asian colonies or other less-developed countries; instead, more than three fourths went to the United States, predominantly white-settled countries of the British Commonwealth, and other advanced capitalist countries, which should have been plagued by surplus capital conditions similar to those that were supposed to have been occurring in Great Britain. Then, too, the formation of monopolies in Great Britain took place mainly toward the end of this period, not during the time of greatest colonial expansion.[4]

Some prominent writers incorporated economic motivations into their analyses of the period, but not in the way of Hobson or the Marxists. For William L. Langer, British imperialism of the late nineteenth century was basically reactive and protective, as witnessed by the fact

---

3. Quotations from Rosa Luxemburg, *The Accumulation of Capital* (New Haven, Conn.: Yale University Press, 1951). Also see Nikolai Bukharin, *Imperialism and World Economy* (London: Merlin Press, 1972).

4. For examples of this counterevidence, see A. K. Cairncross, *Home and Foreign Investment, 1870–1912* (Cambridge: Cambridge University Press, 1953); Herbert Feis, *Europe: The World's Banker, 1870–1914* (New Haven, Conn.: Yale University Press, 1930); D. K. Fieldhouse, *The Theory of Capitalist Imperialism* (London: Longmans, 1967); for an acknowledgment of the force of this argument by one now writing in the Marxist tradition, see Michael Barratt Brown, *After Imperialism* (London: Heinemann, 1963).

that other countries imitated earlier British imperial expansion and erected trade barriers in their new colonies to keep British goods out:

> At bottom the movement was probably as much economic as anything else. It resulted from the tremendously enhanced productive powers of European industry and the breakdown of the monopolistic position of England through the appearance of competitors. The feeling that new markets must be secured was very widespread and the need for new fields of investment, though not much discussed at the time, was probably even more important. These needs, however, had been met in the past without any corresponding expansion of territory. It was the embarkation of France, Germany, and other countries on the course of political control that brought the British to the conviction that only political control could adequately safeguard markets.[5]

Other theorists have offered primarily political or strategic explanations for imperialism, taking account of economic factors but putting them in a relatively subordinate place. Diplomatic and strategic rivalries among European powers assume prominence. Eugene Staley, for instance, believed the typical situation was one of investments in the service of diplomacy, not vice versa:

> Private investments have usually, in actual practice, been subordinated by governments to factors of general political or military strategy which have a more direct bearing on power. Thus it is that private investors have received strong, even outrageously exaggerated governmental backing where they have been tools and agents of power and prestige politics, while other investors whose projects seemed to run counter to the government's line of political endeavor have experienced official indifference or even active opposition.[6]

Other writers, carefully examining British actions in Africa, declare that their object was political and strategic, not economic.[7] Karl Polanyi, acknowledging the responsibility of commercial interests for

---

5. William L. Langer, *The Diplomacy of Imperialism, 1870–1914* (New York: Knopf, 1935), p. 95.

6. Eugene Staley, *War and the Private Investor* (Garden City, N.Y.: Doubleday, 1935), pp. 361–362.

7. R. E. Robinson and John Gallagher, *Africa and the Victorians* (New York: St. Martin's, 1961). But the strategic interests arose for Britain because of its *existing* imperial holdings in India, which leaves open the possibility that the basic motivation was to protect the economic interests there.

many fairly small wars, noted their concern for avoiding large-scale violence among the colonial powers:

> Actually, business and finance were responsible for many colonial wars, but also for the fact that a general conflagration was avoided. Their affiliations with heavy industry, though really close only in Germany, accounted for both. For every one interest that was furthered by war, there were a dozen that could be adversely affected. International capital, of course, was bound to be the loser in case of war; but even national finance could gain only exceptionally, though frequently enough to account for dozens of colonial wars, as long as they remained isolated. Every war almost, was organized by the financiers; but peace also was organized by them.[8]

The Marxist Karl Kautsky (explicitly attacked later by Lenin) also hoped that the international cartels might become a force for peace, a "superimperialism" that would dominate the world and impose peace and order. Liberal, nineteenth-century English advocates of free trade, such as Richard Cobden and John Stuart Mill, also developed this view, as did Saint-Simon and many other French liberals and socialists. A prominent modern writer, though frequently critical of multinational corporations, held out a similar hope:

> The growing number and internationalist ideology of the corporations means that the number one nation no longer has the discretion traditionally associated with national sovereignty. Schumpeter's analysis of the modern capitalist is vindicated. The interest of the leading corporations is indeed in peace, and, increasingly, the corporate managers are coming to see it. That being so, the power of the corporations will serve as a restraining influence on military adventurism.[9]

Best-known of the noneconomic theories is surely that of Joseph Schumpeter. Although he acknowledged that some monopolists have an interest in the conquest of lands producing raw materials and foodstuffs, he regarded it as "a basic fallacy to describe imperialism as a necessary phase of capitalism, or even to speak of the development of capitalism into imperialism."[10] Some capitalists may gain, but only a small minority. The gains from war for capitalists as a class are more

---

8. Karl Polanyi, *The Great Transformation* (Boston: Beacon Press, 1957), p. 16.

9. Richard Barnet, *Roots of War* (New York: Atheneum, 1972), p. 235.

10. Joseph Schumpeter, *Imperialism and Social Classes* (New York: Meridian Books, 1955), p. 84.

than offset by their losses and burdens. Though economic interests play a part, imperialism is primarily an affair of politicians and military personnel, not capitalists. Basically, imperialism is the result of attitudes and behavior patterns among the militarists, a group that evolved historically, in the precapitalist era, to defend the state and establish its security. Leftover psychological dispositions and social structures, having outlived what Schumpeter called their "meaning and their life-preserving function," retain an interest in war itself rather than in the material advantages to be gained by conquest.

Despite the relative age of these theories, the fact that they were developed mainly to explain the acquisition of overt political control of colonies, and the empirical difficulties posed by many of them, they most certainly are not dead.

In their careful study of World War I, Nazli Choucri and Robert North used the term "lateral pressure" to characterize the Great Powers' colonial expansionism. Colonial expansion—especially once the Southern Hemisphere was just about fully carved up among the imperialist states—led to increasing clashes over colonial borders and spheres of influence. The colonial conflicts increased the incentives of the Great Powers to maintain large armies and navies so that they could hold and defend their colonies. Moreover, the colonial conflicts, coupled with the arms races they stimulated, led to increasingly violent relations among the Great Powers, creating repeated crises of which the last, in August 1914, resulted in World War I. Choucri and North, in examining changes in each country's colonial holdings, military expenditures, and so forth, find substantial evidence for each of the chains in this link. Furthermore, they find that economic pressures, stemming from rising income, population, and trade, produced pressures to obtain foreign markets and raw materials that led to the acquisition of colonies.[11]

Although not fully a Marxist interpretation, this evidence is compatible with those theories which assert that imperialism, and ultimately war among imperial powers, had important economic roots. In addition, this evidence is still fully compatible with evidence that individual capitalists did not want large-scale war. A quite different study, for example, has shown a very high correlation between leaders' percep-

---

11. Nazli Choucri and Robert C. North, *Nations in Conflict: National Growth and International Violence* (San Francisco: W. H. Freeman and Company, 1975). This perspective has been applied to contemporary U.S.-Soviet-Chinese relations by Richard K. Ashley, *The Political Economy of War and Peace* (London: Frances Pinter, 1980).

tions of hostility and the outflow of gold from London in the 1914 crisis. Prices on the security markets of all the major powers collapsed at the same time, because financiers were horrified by the impending war.[12] Thus, although *individual capitalists* may have genuinely desired peace at a particular time and place, economic expansion (under a capitalist economic and social *system*) may have produced political pressures that led to war-inducing crises. It is essential in this kind of thinking to distinguish a capitalist's desire for peace from the perception that the national economy must expand with access to markets and resources. That expansion may generate conflict with other nations' interests. If war then looms, no one may want it—but in the crisis, decision makers may find their menu so constrained that they must take actions they would prefer to avoid.

MODERN THEORIES ABOUT THE IMPERATIVES OF CAPITALISM

Few modern theories accept the full surplus capital version of the classical Marxist tradition, though several employ major aspects of it. Baran and Sweezy express the neo-Marxist position well. Their basic argument is that heavy military expenditures serve the capitalist purpose of maintaining prosperity at home while fighting socialism abroad. According to them, monopolistic capitalism does generate a surplus, which must be absorbed. This can only be done by government spending and taxing. "It is to the interest of all classes—though not of all elements within them—that government should steadily increase its spending and taxing." Some "welfare state" spending is broadly acceptable, but not to the point of damaging work incentives in the labor market or providing major competition to private enterprise. The scope of government activity is limited by capitalist desires not to lose potential areas of productivity to public enterprise and by the need to maintain capitalist ideological premises that social welfare is best provided by the private production of goods and services. Thus, neither private demand nor public spending for civil purposes can sustain the economy. Under these circumstances, military spending is entirely acceptable because it does not compete with any vested private interests, and

---

12. Ole R. Holsti, *Crisis Escalation War* (Montreal: McGill-Queen's University Press, 1972), chap. 3.

it has the extra advantages of quick obsolescence and effective central control over levels and locations of economic activity.[13]

It is difficult to test these ideas satisfactorily. Nearly everyone agrees that rearmament for World War II provided a stimulus to the American economy that brought it out of the Depression. Since World War II, military spending as a proportion of GNP has been at a level unprecedented during peacetime—coinciding with a long period of prosperity. But other kinds of government spending, taxation, and monetary policy, as influenced by modern economics, probably deserve more credit as causes of that prosperity. Some other countries—notably Japan and West Germany—have had even more expansive economies with much less military spending. Nevertheless, it is now well-known that political leaders like to increase government spending just before elections to create at least short bursts of prosperity that will impress voters favorably. Military spending is relatively easy to increase and at most times is considered a proper function of government. Arthur Burns, chairman of the Council of Economic Advisors under President Eisenhower, was described as advising the following in March 1960:

> Burns' conclusion was that unless some decisive governmental action were taken, and taken soon, we were heading for another dip [in the economy], which would hit its low point just before the elections.... He urgently recommended that two steps be taken immediately: by loosening up credit and, where justifiable, increasing spending for national security.[14]

In an analysis of year-to-year changes in military spending in the postwar United States, Miroslav Nincic and Thomas Cusack found that "military spending cut back at an expected rate of $2 billion per annum after on-year [presidential] elections and expanded at a similar rate in the two years prior to those elections."[15]

A different explanation, but also with roots in Marxist-Leninist theory, states that foreign trade and investments are essential to contem-

---

13. Paul A. Baran and Paul M. Sweezy, *Monopoly Capital: An Essay on the American Economy and Social Order* (Harmondsworth, England: Pelican, 1968); see especially chaps. 6–7.

14. Richard M. Nixon, *Six Crises* (New York: Doubleday, 1962).

15. Miroslav Nincic and Thomas Cusack, "The Political Economy of U.S. Military Spending," *Journal of Peace Research* 16 (1979), no. 2, pp. 101–115. The more general hypothesis about spending increases before elections is made by Edward Tufte, *The Political Control of the Economy* (Princeton, N.J.: Princeton University Press, 1978).

porary industrial capitalism and that the attempt to secure foreign markets or commodities leads to "neocolonialism" and clashes over spheres of influence with other great powers. However, in terms simply of their proportion of the economy, foreign trade and investment have not been all that important to the United States in recent decades. Only recently has either come to exceed 10 percent of GNP; more than two thirds of this is with other industrial countries, not the less-developed countries that were the focus of classical imperialism. The rise of the United States to superpower status, in fact, coincided with a period when trade and investment were a smaller proportion of GNP than earlier in the century.[16] The old arguments about an advanced capitalist economy's dependence on foreign investment or trade to absorb surplus capital thus encounter some difficulty, although it is still possible to argue that this foreign-oriented activity is critical to the economy's health.

Another line of attack thus is to emphasize the crucial nature of foreign economic activities. For example, Staley noted that the British purchase of control over the Anglo-Persian Oil Company was impelled by the Royal Navy's need for oil; he quoted Churchill: "The supreme ships of the navy on which our life depended, were fed by oil and could only be fed by oil. . . . A decision like this involved our national safety as much as a battle at sea." This is consistent with Staley's general view that the government intervened more often to promote investment or exploration for political or strategic purposes than to act as the subordinate agent of private enterprise. Something like this might surely be going on now, given the substantial and very rapidly growing dependence of the industrialized countries on foreign sources of raw materials, including chromium, nickel, cobalt, bauxite, and tin, as well as oil. Figure 9.1 shows the situation for many of these materials in 1980; American overseas dependence has been increasing and is expected to continue to increase for each of these materials. Any industrial economy, whether capitalist or socialist, would be dependent on these sources, but it is alleged that the existing capitalist economy is particularly vulnerable for two reasons: the especially high valuation that is placed on growth (and hence requiring ever-greater resource needs) and the global rivalry with the socialist states. Any danger that developing countries will adopt socialist governments and then either

---

16. Data supporting these statements can be found in Figures 15.2 and 15.3 of Chapter 15. Also see Benjamin J. Cohen, *The Question of Imperialism* (New York: Basic Books, 1973), chap. 4.

UNITED STATES

	Percentage	Major Foreign Sources
	0% 25% 50% 75% 100%	
Columbium	100	Brazil, Canada, Thailand
Diamond (industrial stones)	100	Ireland, South Africa, Belgium, Luxembourg, U.K.
Graphite (natural)	100	Mexico, South Korea, Madagascar, USSR
Mica (sheet)	100	India, Brazil, Madagascar
Strontium	100	Mexico
Manganese	98	South Africa, Gabon, France, Brazil
Bauxite and alumina	94	Jamaica, Australia, Guinea, Suriname
Cobalt	91	Zaire, Belgium, Luxembourg, Zambia, Finland
Tantalum	91	Thailand, Canada, Malaysia, Brazil
Chromium	90	South Africa, Philippines, USSR, Finland
Fluorspar	85	Mexico, South Africa, Spain, Italy
Platinum-group metals	85	South Africa, USSR, U.K.
Asbestos	80	Canada, South Africa
Tin	80	Malaysia, Thailand, Bolivia, Indonesia
Nickel	72	Canada, Norway, Botswana, Australia
Potash	68	Canada, Israel
Zinc	67	Canada, Mexico, Spain, Australia
Cadmium	63	Canada, Australia, Mexico, Belgium, Luxembourg
Tungsten	52	Canada, Bolivia, China, Thailand
Antimony	51	South Africa, Bolivia, China, Mexico
Silver	50	Canada, Mexico, Peru, U.K.
Selenium	49	Canada, Japan, Yugoslavia
Barium	43	Peru, China, Ireland, Morocco, Chile
Titanium	43	Australia, Canada, South Africa
Vanadium	42	South Africa, Chile, Canada
Mercury	39	Spain, Algeria, Japan, Italy
Iron ore	28	Canada, Venezuela, Brazil, Liberia
Iron and steel	19	Japan, Europe, Canada
Lead	10	Canada, Mexico, Peru
Gold	7	Canada, USSR, Switzerland
Copper	5	Chile, Canada, Peru, Zambia

Figure 9.1
Percentage of the raw materials consumed that are imported by the United States, European Community, Japan, and major exporting countries, 1980.

cut off the resource flow for Cold War reasons or divert the resources to their own development could be particularly threatening. Low prices, as well as adequate supplies, are at issue.[17]

Surely the idea of intervening to assure access to strategic raw materials is not dead, though whether capitalist systems are especially prone to such acts is not clear. That view will not explain every case of intervention in a less-developed country, but realistically, no single theory should be expected to explain every case. Sensitivity to particular needs, rather than mechanically looking at percentages of GNP,

17. Eugene Staley, *War and the Private Investor* (Garden City, N.Y.: Doubleday, 1935), p. 76. For more modern interpretations along these lines, see Harry Magdoff, *The Age of Imperialism* (New York: Monthly Review Press, 1969); Gabriel Kolko, *The Roots of American Foreign Policy: An Analysis of Power and Purpose* (Boston: Beacon Press, 1969).

EUROPEAN COMMUNITY

JAPAN

Percentage

Percentage

Columbium	100
Cobalt	100
Chromium	100
Tantalum	100
Platinum-group metals	100
Nickel	100
Selenium	100
Titanium	100
Vanadium	100
Molybdenum	100
Manganese	99
Gold	99
Copper	99
Phosphate rock	99
Silver	98
Tin	95
Antimony	91
Mercury	86
Bauxite and alumina	84
Graphite	84
Mica (all types)	83
Asbestos	82
Iron ore	79
Tungsten	77
Zinc	71
Lead	70
Cadmium	53
Strontium	30
Aluminum (smelter)	28
Fluorspar	18
Potassium (potash)	1

Columbium	100
Mica (all forms)	100
Bauxite	100
Cobalt	100
Tantalum	100
Fluorspar	100
Nickel	100
Antimony	100
Titanium	100
Vanadium	100
Phosphate rock	100
Chromium	99
Asbestos	99
Iron ore	99
Molybdenum	99
Platinum-group metals	98
Manganese	97
Tin	96
Gold	94
Copper	87
Lead	75
Tungsten	75
Silver	73
Zinc	59
Barium (barite)	43
Aluminum	31
Alumina	13
Cadmium	
Selenium	
Mercury	
Iron and steel products	

Figure 9.1 *(continued)*

ought to be a major element in any theory. The monetary value of some products may be relatively slight, but the products may be very hard to do without. To capitalists, governments aiming to abolish private ownership and private enterprise may be

> objectionable not only because their actions adversely affect foreign-owned interests and enterprises or because they render future capitalist implantation impossible; in some cases this may be of no great economic consequence. But the objection still remains because the withdrawal of any country from the world system of capitalist enterprise is seen as constituting a weakening of that system and as providing encouragement to further dissidence and withdrawal.[18]

18. Ralph Miliband, *The State in Capitalist Society* (New York: Basic Books, 1969), p. 86. A variety of studies have looked at many instances of intervention to try to discern a pattern of apparent motivation. Although the difficulties in inferring a causal role (or

THE MILITARY-INDUSTRIAL COMPLEX

In his last public address as president, Dwight Eisenhower, once a general, warned about the political influence of a newly powerful "military-industrial complex":

> We have been compelled to create a permanent armaments industry of vast proportions. Added to this, three-and-a-half million men and women are directly engaged in the defense establishment. We annually spend on military security alone more than the net income of all United States corporations.
>
> Now this conjunction of an immense military establishment and a large arms industry is new in the American experience. The total influence—economic, political, even spiritual—is felt in every city, every state house, every office of the federal government. . . . In the councils of government, we must guard against the acquisition of unwarranted influence, whether sought or unsought, by the military/industrial complex. The potential for the disastrous rise of misplaced power exists and will persist.

The phrase *military-industrial complex*, especially if interpreted broadly to include labor unions and political leaders, such as U.S. representatives from districts with defense industries or military bases who would benefit directly from military spending, is now a common expression. It represents the understanding that whether the entire capitalist system benefits from aggressive foreign or military policies, certainly particular interest groups do benefit. Even if the American economy as a whole could prosper without military spending, some industries and some geographical areas would suffer severe short- or medium-term damage from any reduction in military expenditures. A cutback in military purchases, disrupting production and marketing in these industries and forcing them to make alternative products and find buyers for them, would cause sharp, temporary losses. Defense industry corporations, aided by the technical and political knowledge

---

absence thereof) by such methods are formidable, there nevertheless appears to be a small, but only small, importance for economic interest. See John Odell, "Correlates of U.S. Military Assistance and Military Intervention," in Steven J. Rosen and James R. Kurth (eds.), *Testing Theories of Economic Imperialism* (Lexington, Mass.: Heath, 1974); Frederic S. Pearson, "Geographic Proximity and Foreign Military Intervention," *Journal of Conflict Resolution* 18 (1974), no. 3, pp. 432–459; Frederic S. Pearson, "American Military Intervention Abroad. A Test of Economic and Non-Economic Explanations," in Craig Liske (ed.), *The Politics of Trade and Aid* (Beverly Hills, Calif.: Sage, 1975); John Eley and John Petersen, "Economic Interests and American Foreign Policy Allocations, 1960–69," in Patrick J. McGowan (ed.), *Sage International Yearbook of Foreign Policy Studies* I (Beverly Hills, Calif.: Sage, 1973).

of former military officers who become defense industry employees (see Table 9.1), try hard to maintain their business and to add new contracts. They are helped by government policies that seek to maintain a "mobilization base" in defense industries, especially the aerospace industry. It is important, for instance, to have several firms capable of manufacturing modern military aircraft. When one of Lockheed's aviation contracts is finished, a new contract will be needed if the company's experience, skilled labor, and capital equipment is not to be scattered and lost.[19] Increasingly, sales of arms abroad, especially to allies and the third world, rival in economic importance the sales of many countries' arms manufacturers to their domestic governments. Britain, France, and the Soviet Union are all heavily dependent on foreign arms sales.

Certainly someone stands to gain from every dollar spent on arms; some industries do benefit from military spending and would suffer from its reduction. The important question for military-industrial complex theories is how broad and how deep that suffering would be compared with the benefits to other industries if resources were taken away from military ends. The damage to military industries (and prob-

Table 9.1

Personnel Transfers between the Department of Defense and Major Military Contractors, 1970–1979.

Company	Total flow	Flow to company		Flow to Department of Defense
		Military	Civilian	
Boeing	388	316	35	37
General Dynamics	238	189	17	32
Grumman	88	67	5	16
Lockheed	304	240	30	34
McDonnell-Douglas	200	159	12	29
Northrop	360	284	50	16
Rockwell	223	150	26	47
United Technologies	73	50	11	12
Total	1874	1455	186	233

Source: Adapted from Gordon Adams, *The Iron Triangle: The Politics of Defense Contracting* (New York: Council on Economic Priorities, 1981), p. 84.

19. See James R. Kurth, "Aerospace Production Lines and American Defense Spending," in Steven J. Rosen (ed.), *Testing the Theory of the Military-Industrial Complex* (Lexington, Mass.: Heath, 1973). A good review of arms industry competition worldwide is Anthony Sampson, *The Arms Bazaar* (New York: Viking, 1977).

ably to certain regional labor markets as well) caused by disarmament would exceed the gains made by any other single sector of industry; that is, although military spending does not necessarily benefit the economy as a whole, the gains from defense spending are greater for a few industries than are the costs to any one sector when spread among all the sectors of the civilian economy. Toy makers, citrus growers, and home builders all lose a little business when more money is spent for fighter planes. But if less money was spent for fighters, McDonnell-Douglas Corporation would lose heavily—and resist mightily. In democracies, pressure groups concentrate their activities on those issues that promise them the greatest gains and will not deeply resist efforts of other groups pursuing their most important special interests when those efforts involve modest costs (as long as the prospective costs remain modest). Each group seeks to gain something for itself and tolerates similar activities by others.[20]

This essentially political explanation would account for continuing excessive levels of military spending (and perhaps even maintaining an ideological climate of fear and hostility to support such a defense posture), despite the fact that economic gains were limited to a small segment of the economy. This view is entirely consistent with the findings of a major study of American businessmen's attitudes toward tariff issues. According to the study, "The men who feared loss from a tariff cut were more in favor of raising tariffs than were those who explicitly asserted that they would gain by the increase. We see that fear of loss is a more powerful stimulus than prospect of gain."[21]

ELITE ATTITUDES AND BEHAVIOR

In all these different perspectives on economic causes of politics, it is assumed that the beliefs, attitudes, and policy preferences of individuals, groups, and classes on matters of foreign and military policy will differ sharply. They will differ according to their "objective" interests and according to their views of those interests. These various actors may also have different views on what is in the "national interest,"

---

20. See Stanley Lieberson, "An Empirical Study of Military-Industrial Linkages," in Steven J. Rosen (ed.), *Testing the Theory of the Military-Industrial Complex* (Lexington, Mass.: Heath, 1973).

21. Raymond A. Bauer, Ithiel de Sola Pool, and Anthony Dexter, *American Business and Public Policy: The Politics of Foreign Trade* (New York: Atherton, 1963), p. 142.

since there are no clear ways of understanding how various individual interests will be reconciled.

The perspectives, however, lead to quite different predictions and hypotheses. Some suggest that capitalists as a class will have different beliefs and attitudes than will members of other classes (according to some theories, the capitalists would be more favorable to military spending or to expansionist or imperialist foreign policies; according to others, overseas interests would lead capitalists to strenuously avoid at least those kinds of foreign activities that might lead to war). Other perspectives implicitly or explicitly emphasize differences among different types of capitalists, for example, those whose businesses are entirely domestic versus the leaders of multinational corporations or defense industry executives versus the rest. On these matters, there is some reasonably hard evidence about the beliefs of different kinds of leaders, or prominent individuals. Two major studies of leading individuals were conducted in the 1970s, one by a group at Columbia University and another by researchers at Yale University. Table 9.2 shows the answers of different kinds of leaders to questions about foreign policy.

Clearly, business leaders were among the more hawkish of all the groups. (The labels *dove* and *hawk* have value-laden meanings that we do not intend to convey here. We nevertheless use the terms as a generally understood shorthand for different sets of beliefs. The first favors and the second opposes détente with the Soviet Union and accommodation to socialist governments. The terms also refer to attitudes against and for special reliance on military instruments of national power, respectively.) The businessmen in the Yale sample were significantly more dovish than senior military officers on defense expenditures and alliances, but markedly less so about the balance of nuclear weapons and the third world issue. The Columbia sample of businessmen was a bit more dovish overall and significantly more so than the Yale military sample on all items except third world nationalism. Comparing the views of the business executives with those of other important civilian elite groups within the Columbia sample shows that businessmen were always more hawkish than the average leading Democratic politician, civil servant, voluntary organization leader, and major figure in the mass media. Businessmen in both the Yale and Columbia samples, however, were more dovish, or liberal, on third world nationalism than were the labor leaders; both business samples were often more dovish than were Republican politicians (party officials, officials of the Nixon administration, and legislators),

Table 9.2
Percentage of various leaders holding "dovish" positions on foreign policy.

| Questionnaire item | Yale sample | | Columbia sample | | | | | | |
	Military	Business	Business	Republican party	Democratic party	Labor	Civil service	Voluntary organizations	Media
1. Reduce defense spending	12	51	63	43	71	76	74	78	79
2. Dismantle alliances	22	34	47	32	52	55	53	51	62
3. Keep U.S. ahead in nuclear— disagree	26	22	30	28	38	31	40	57	63
4. U.S. contributed to Cold War	58	52	65	37	77	81	70	74	82
5. Third world revolutions nationalistic	84	74	70	77	72	60	84	83	91
6. Accept socialist governments	78	78	81	78	83	83	88	87	93

Sources: Yale sample: Bruce M. Russett and Elizabeth C. Hanson, *Interest and Ideology: The Foreign Policy Beliefs of American Businessmen* (San Francisco: W. H. Freeman and Company, 1975), p. 71. Columbia sample: Allen H. Barton, "Conflict and Consensus among American Leaders," *Public Opinion Quarterly* 38, no. 4, pp. 507–530 and further provision to Russett. Similar conclusions from a more recent survey are reported by Ole R. Holsti and James N. Rosenau, "Cold War Axioms in the Post-Vietnam Era," in Ole R. Holsti, Randolph Siverson, and Alexander George (eds.), *Change in the International System* (Boulder, Colo.: Westview, 1980).

Note: The percentages show which portion of each group held the dovish position strongly or with qualifications. The questionnaire items were:
1. In the next 5 years should the level of U.S. defense spending be (raised, reduced, kept about the same, etc.)?
2. The United States should seek agreement to mutually dismantle alliances such as NATO and the Warsaw Pact.
3. The United States must always keep ahead of the Russians in strategic nuclear weapons.
4. The United States has sometimes contributed to the escalation of the cold war by overreacting to Soviet moves or military developments.
5. The revolutionary forces in the "third world" are now basically nationalistic rather than controlled by the USSR or China.
6. The United States should be prepared to accept Socialist governments in Latin America even if the Communists play an important role in them.

especially on defense spending and the alleged U.S. contribution to the Cold War.

Businessmen as a class are clearly on the hawkish end of the foreign policy spectrum, but not more so than senior military officers and leaders of the Republican party. To some degree, these results support the arguments of Marxist theories, but the support is hardly overwhelming. They are more consistent with broader military-industrial complex theories that stress alliances of businessmen with other bureaucratic and political leaders who share a preference for hawkish policies. They certainly do not support the idea that businessmen as a class are more supportive of détente or accommodation.

An analysis found that by 1967, prices of shares on the New York Stock Exchange rose in response to events that gave promise of peace in Vietnam and fell when the war was escalated. Evidence like that was found about the London gold market in 1914, indicating that business and finance generally did not see these major wars as furthering their economic interests. In the years before 1967, however, when the Vietnam war was less severe and less burdensome to the American society and economy, there was no clear association between war events and stock prices. This suggests that although business interests may abhor large wars, they do not so overwhelmingly object to smaller wars for limited goals.[22]

The differences among capitalists, depending on the nature of businessmen's interests, are more ambiguous. The Yale survey provided some information on the executives' firms: those selling a large proportion of their product to the Defense Department, those selling or investing substantially abroad, and those with expectations of large markets in the Soviet Union and China. Not surprisingly, executives from firms that sold to the Defense Department were more likely to believe that the level of U.S. defense spending should be raised, but they were not more likely to approve of the Vietnam war or to be more hawkish than other businessmen on other foreign policy issues. Nor did other indications of foreign interest on the part of their firms make any systematic difference in the businessmen's attitudes being either hawkish or dovish. Thus, hypotheses viewing capitalism as promoting an aggressive foreign policy and those viewing capitalism as generally a force for peace were both unsupported.[23]

These empirical studies neither definitively refute nor strongly support economic interest theories. However, they do suggest that the

---

22. Bruce M. Russett and Elizabeth C. Hanson, *Interest and Ideology: The Foreign Policy Beliefs of American Businessmen* (San Francisco: W. H. Freeman and Company, 1975), chap. 5.

23. Bruce M. Russett and Elizabeth C. Hanson, *Interest and Ideology: The Foreign Policy Beliefs of American Businessmen* (San Francisco: W. H. Freeman and Company, 1975), chap. 4. Furthermore, in the stock market analysis, stocks of firms oriented toward sales to the Defense Department or to less-developed countries on the whole behaved no differently in response to ups and downs in the Vietnam war than did the general stock index.

interests of particular groups and classes are complex and not perceived by individuals in any easily predictable manner. The most ca-
sual perceptions make it obvious that many people who advocate anti-
Communism, interventionism, or national preparedness stand to gain
little from their views materially. More important, individuals' perceptions of their self-interest vary even within groups in which each individual has the same material stake in an outcome. The definition of
one's self-interest is a very complex matter, subject to a variety of influences from colleagues, friends, the media, pressure groups, and, of
course, one's experiences and political socialization. Bauer, Pool, and
Dexter are very explicit about this at repeated points in their book:

> A pressure group's function is, in large part, to define the interests of its
> partisans. Interests may not be self-evident, and a pressure group may
> define interests in such a way as to gain supporters it would not other-
> wise have; a firm or businessman may go to either side depending on
> how the definition is set up for him. . . .
>   Unlike our friends who told us, "Tell me a man's interest and I will tell
> you his stand," we would say, "Tell us where a man stands and we will
> tell you what perceptions of his interests will serve to make that stand a
> self-consistent and stable one." There are perceptions of self-interest
> available to bolster any stand by any individual.[24]

IDEOLOGIES AND COHERENT BELIEF SYSTEMS

In the study we mentioned of American business executives and other
leaders, the contribution of identifiable economic interests to predicting foreign policy attitudes proved rather small. A much better predictor was the set of attitudes on domestic policy: attitudes on civil rights
for blacks, civil liberties (legalizing marijuana or the role of the police
and FBI), and income inequality. People's views on domestic issues
tended to be quite uniform across the entire set; that is, to be liberal or
conservative on almost all of the issues. More important for our discussion here, if we knew whether a person was a liberal or conservative
on domestic issues, we had a very good idea about whether he would
be a dove or hawk on foreign policy issues. We could predict his domestic policy preferences much better than we could have by simply

---

24. Raymond A. Bauer, Ithiel de Sola Pool, and Anthony Dexter, *American Business and
Public Policy: The Politics of Foreign Trade* (New York: Atherton, 1963), quotations from pp.
398, 142–143.

knowing he was a businessman or the kind of firm he represented. Conservatives tended to be hawks, and liberals doves. Thus, we have a picture of a general ideological view of public policy in the sense of closely related beliefs.

Such a coherent and organized set of beliefs helps a person to make sense of new pieces of information or to adopt an opinion on a new problem. In this sense, all of us have ideologies of some sort so that we do not have to deal with each issue on a purely ad hoc, isolated basis. In politics we understand this when we use such broad-brush terms as *liberal, radical, reactionary, hawk, pacifist,* and others. Of course, some people's ideologies are much more tightly organized and coherent—not to say rigid—than others. Here we use the term *ideology* in much the same way as Ole Holsti uses *belief system:*

> A set of lenses through which information concerning the physical and social environment is received. It orients the individual to his environment, defining it for him and identifying for him its salient characteristics. . . . In addition to organizing perceptions into a meaningful guide for behavior, the belief system has the function of the establishment of goals and the ordering of preferences.[25]

We shall discuss belief systems in greater detail in a later chapter. But here the significant point is the joining of liberal-dove views and conservative-hawk views across a broad range of domestic and foreign policy issues. Such a joining has been found repeatedly in recent research on opinions in the United States—for example, in surveys of the general public and in several studies of voting in the U.S. Senate and House of Representatives in the 1960s and 1970s.[26] This close association of domestic and foreign policy views is strengthened by the belief that money for new armaments comes at the expense of domestic programs that would benefit minorities and urban areas.

---

25. Ole R. Holsti, "The Belief System and National Images: A Case Study," *Journal of Conflict Resolution* 6 (September 1962), no. 3, p. 245. Some people tend to use the word *ideology* in a pejorative sense; "I have a carefully considered and flexible set of beliefs, you have a [rigid and emotional] ideology."

26. On the general public, see Norman Nie, Sidney Verba, and J. R. Petrocik, *The Changing American Voter* (Cambridge, Mass.: Harvard University Press, 1979); for data on Congress, see Bruce Russett, *What Price Vigilance? The Burdens of National Defense* (New Haven, Conn.: Yale University Press, 1970), chap. 3; Wayne Moyer, "House Voting on Defense: An Ideological Explanation," in Bruce Russett and Alfred Stepan (eds.), *Military Force and American Society* (New York: Harper & Row, 1972); Robert A. Bernstein and William W. Anthony, "The ABM Issue in the Senate, 1967-71. The Importance of Ideology," *American Political Science Review* 68 (September 1974), no. 3, pp. 198–220.

The Congressional voting studies cited in footnote 26 also show some association of economic interests with foreign policy attitudes. Representatives with military bases or defense industries in their districts will, of course, vote in favor of appropriations that will benefit their constituents. But beyond those very narrow issues, defense-related interests do not affect a representative's voting record very much. Again, views on civil rights and civil liberties are much more closely associated with foreign policy beliefs. We cannot confidently say that one causes the other, but whatever it is—personality, life experience, position in society, or information and acquaintance network—that creates a generally coherent ideological position is a stronger influence than direct economic interest.[27]

Particular policy preferences have various motives; although direct economic interests doubtless play a significant role in many instances, there is surely more involved. Often, as in the case of the conservative ex-military officer now working for an aerospace corporation, several influences converge and his foreign policy beliefs are "overdetermined." Of course, this happens with liberals as well as with conservatives, and it happens in very different political systems.

Similar interests are powerful in the Soviet Union. Although there are no capitalists in that economy, certainly state industrial managers have interests in promoting the growth, power, prosperity, and technological preeminence of the arms manufacturing plants that they control. They, too, share interests with their clients in the Red Army and Strategic Rocket Forces and with hawkish ideologues in the Communist party. A Cold War—though not necessarily a hot one—helps to maintain their privileges and central roles in Soviet society.[28] In both countries, therefore, entrenched economic and political interests maintain the momentum of established hard-line policies and resist change. In a perverse way, the military-industrial complex of each country helps the other. Each embodies the foreign threat that its counterpart in the other country needs to justify its own activities.

---

27. For evidence that defense industry workers who have served in the military tend to have more hawkish attitudes than those who have not, see Nancy Adelman Phillips, "Militarism and Grass-Roots Involvement in the Military-Industrial Complex," *Journal of Conflict Resolution* 17 (December 1973), no. 4, pp. 625–655.

28. For instance, see Vernon V. Aspaturian, "The Soviet-Military-Industrial Complex: Does It Exist?" in Steven J. Rosen (ed.), *Testing the Theory of the Military-Industrial Complex* (Lexington, Mass.: Heath, 1973).

STATE INTERESTS

People frequently pursue economic interests, and governments pursue the economic interests of some of their citizens. Sometimes, however, government officials act for their own reasons—personal interests or perhaps ideological or strategic considerations—while clothing their actions in the language of economic interests to broaden their support. They may attempt to enlist the support of appropriate economic interests for policies on which they have already decided for quite other reasons. If we see only the policy output, it may be virtually impossible to decide what is the driving motivation, who is initiating a policy, and who is being used to lend support and legitimacy.

We noted one aspect of this in Staley's discussion (quoted earlier) of the role of private investors in overseas diplomatic intervention. Another manifestation appears in a discussion of a famous statement by Assistant Secretary of State Dean Acheson to a congressional committee in 1944. Acheson declared that America must for economic reasons follow a much more internationalist political policy, because the economy required expanding markets abroad to absorb its "unlimited creative energy" and to avoid stagnation of the domestic economy. This statement and others like it are frequently referred to by radical and neo-Marxist opponents of American foreign policy. But to quote Robert W. Tucker:

> Why may we not argue that such statements as the one above [i.e., Acheson's] obscure far more than they reveal the true sources of policy, that their purpose is largely to elicit support for a policy that is pursued primarily for quite different reasons?[29]

The assertion that all states pursue similar basic strategic interests is common in the literature on national interest and in several recent works on foreign policy.[30] Theories of national or strategic interest thus attribute the actions of American policymakers to their perceptions of security requirements and *realpolitik*. By this explanation, American policymakers think in terms of military security, balance of power, containing Soviet expansionism, containing power centers in general,

---

29. Robert W. Tucker, *The Radical Left and American Foreign Policy* (Baltimore: Johns Hopkins University Press, 1971), p. 61.

30. One of the best is Stephen Krasner, *In Defense of the National Interest: Raw Materials, Investments, and U.S. Foreign Policy* (Princeton, N.J.: Princeton University Press, 1978).

and the importance of honoring commitments to defend one's allies. This perceived need to match, contain, or repress rival world powers stemmed in part from, or at least was reinforced by, the experience of World War II—most especially the failure of British Prime Minister Chamberlain's effort to appease Hitler at Munich in 1938. By this line of thought, the fact that Russia is Communist is only incidental; that powerful country would be a formidable opponent and threat under any government. Policymakers holding strategically oriented views are basically concerned with containing any rival power center regardless of its ideology or form of domestic organization. An almost perfect example of this line of reasoning is this comment in the *Washington Post* by columnist Joseph Alsop in 1974:

> The choice the British and French made in 1939 was to fight like cornered rats rather than to submit to Adolf Hitler. But with the vast tilt in the power balance that had then occurred, the same choice would have had to be made even if Adolf Hitler had been miraculously replaced by another German leader of undoubted rectitude. The mere presence of overweening power almost always begets this choice.

Certainly such views are common among American leaders, and the survey of leaders discussed above found such views especially common among hawks. The belief in national power and national interests as inevitable causes of conflict was closely associated with hawkish beliefs.

Eventually one encounters the argument that ideology is a "false consciousness," a superstructure manufactured, deliberately or otherwise, to justify international conflict in the interest of particular groups. According to this view, the capitalist economic system in Western industrial countries generates an ideological superstructure of anti-Communism "that lends political legitimacy and moral energy to the system's foreign policies." According to a nineteenth-century historian:

> Everywhere the first impulse to social action is given as a rule by real interest, i.e., by political and economic interests. But ideal interests lend wings to these real interests, give them a spiritual meaning, and serve to justify them. . . . Interests without such "spiritual wings" are lame; but on the other hand, ideas can win out in history only if and inasfar as they are associated with real interests. . . . Wherever interests are vigorously pursued, an ideology tends to be developed also to give meaning, reenforcement, and justification to these interests.[31]

---

31. Otto Hintze, quoted by James Kurth, "Testing Theories of Economic Imperialism," in Steven J. Rosen and James R. Kurth (eds.), *Testing Theories of Economic Imperialism*

At one level there can be no solution to the problem as posed this way. How can we possibly sort out the real motivations from the manufactured ones when both are expressed? If we cannot get inside a person's head, we cannot know why that person does what he or she does; even the individual may not know, and even psychoanalysts disagree about unconscious motivations. Nor would it help much to look at temporal priority, for leaders and attentive segments of the public are likely to express beliefs and policy preferences before the public at large does so; but that is no proof that such beliefs and preferences are imposed, or whether they are imposed to serve narrow material interests.

At another level, however, we can suggest some relevant evidence. If an economic interpretation is to have validity, we should expect that those whose interests are allegedly served by such beliefs will express themselves most frequently or most strongly. That is, if an assertive, aggressive, or vigorously anti-Communist foreign policy does indeed serve the interests of the capitalist class, then we should expect capitalists to support that policy even more than do other groups or classes. Doubtless writers, politicians, administrative officials, labor union leaders, and others will also, with substantial strength or frequency, support the policy. But generally speaking, there ought to be some diminution in that support as we move further away from the interests of capitalist entrepreneurs. We are thus driven back to our earlier evidence that corporate executives as a group (with substantial variation within the group) fall on the hawkish end of the foreign policy spectrum, but not at the extreme.

Many business people see their economic interests as being served by hawkish policies; many political leaders and military officers must see their bureaucratic and career interests as being served by them, too. This view does not imply that they deliberately subordinate the welfare of their own society or of the world at large to those interests. They may hold a set of beliefs for reasons quite independent of those

---

(Lexington, Mass.: Heath, 1974), p. 12. One of the best-known arguments is that by Marc Pilisuk and Thomas Hayden—that the Cold War anti-Communist consensus was hardly spontaneous but imposed and manipulated by the elites through their control over education and the mass media; it was a "false consciousness" made to serve parochial interests. See their "Is There a Military-Industrial Complex Which Prevents Peace?", *Journal of Social Issues* 21 (July 1965), no. 3, pp. 67–117. A more recent liberal discussion of the power of economic elites to shape society's discussion of policy issues and fundamental economic structures is Charles F. Lindblom, *Politics and Markets* (New York: Basic Books, 1977), chap. 15. The power of elites over opinion is of course even greater in authoritarian states, where the government or ruling party directly owns or controls the media of mass communication.

interests, and we cannot lightly dismiss the possibility that their beliefs about the general welfare may be correct. Some beliefs are, to an important degree, independent of immediate material interests. Yet interests do help to support a broader ideology. At the least, interests provide a reason for failing to challenge ideological beliefs under circumstances when some of the basic intellectual underpinnings might seem questionable to an objective, outside observer. Interests may not, therefore, be the cause of an ideology, but they may, in ways not necessarily traceable to conscious reasoning processes, prevent, delay, or diminish the abandonment of that ideology.

Finally, there is a version of economic determinist theories to which our discussion of businessmen's attitudes is basically irrelevant. It asserts that their attitudes are not the cause of governmental behavior; rather, government officials are sensitive to the needs of the capitalist system they serve and frequently anticipate any particular demands from the business and financial community. Such officials would recognize the symptoms of capitalism in crisis and, on their own initiative and out of responsibility to the system, would take up and pursue the aggressive, expansionist policy needed to sustain that system. According to this explanation, government officials or political leaders might well be more hawkish than businessmen; certainly they might express a set of hawkish perspectives not in fact held or yet fully crystallized by the business community.

10

DOMESTIC CONTRAINTS: GOVERNMENTAL STRUCTURE AND THE ROLE OF PUBLIC OPINION

CONSTRAINTS AND SUPPORT

The primary concern of the previous chapters was to describe societal constraints on foreign policy. We might say that we have simply been looking at how various aspects of the domestic or societal setting influence foreign policy, but it is more than that. In Chapter 3 we looked at the basic capabilities that a state can possess—area, population, economic size, military strength, and the like. We noted that these impose constraints on foreign policy decision makers as they increase or reduce the alternatives open to decision makers. The main effect of such capabilities is to limit or expand the ability to act—the opportunity to act, or what is possible in terms of physical resources.

Similarly, by looking at how societies differ, we considered how societies differed in past experience, values, beliefs, and, as stressed in the preceding chapter, ideologies. We also discussed differences in economic systems and economic structures. This led us to see that economic interests differ within societies as well as between societies. Thinking about different economic systems and interests led us to thinking about what sorts of groups exist within and compete for control of states, for example, the military-industrial complex. In the course of discussing theories about the effect of certain forms of economic organization (chiefly industrial capitalism) on foreign policy, we asked whether people with different economic interests tend to have different foreign policy preferences. In discussing military-industrial complex theories, we also began to ask a second question: Does public opinion, outside of the opinion of a small set of interest group leaders, really have much influence over policymaking?

What influence does the public have? Here we come back to the idea of constraints. The way these ideologies, interest groups, or public opinions affect foreign policy is through their impact on governmental decision makers. As we noted when talking about state interests (see also Chapter 11), people in government have their own interests: to keep or increase their political positions and political power, to keep or increase their wealth and economic position, to keep or increase their position or status within society, and to promote their ideological values, beliefs, and ideals. These and other interests lead governmental leaders to seek societal support in order to remain in office, gain control of government, and then implement their policies. In order to do this, governments must hear and respond to the demands and needs of society. By meeting societal demands and needs (e.g., high tariffs for protection of certain industries, marines to protect foreign investments, and hard-line policies toward the Soviet Union to protect freedom and defeat Communism), governmental leaders are constrained just as they are by the state's capabilities.

Such demands, as we have seen, limit a leader's menu. Some things are just not acceptable to the populace as a whole or to the elites that control society and government. For example, in the early 1960s, President Kennedy expressed the desire to begin friendly relations with Communist China but did not do so, supposedly because it was "just not acceptable" to the American people. One major societal-governmental relationship that constrains governmental leaders, then, is the desire not to lose office—not to lose an election or a power struggle or to be overthrown by a revolution. Interests must be attended to. To gain the support of those interests, some policies will not be feasible, and others will be.

Closely related to this last point is another major theme addressed in this chapter, Robert Dahl's famous question "Who governs?"[1] One way to see which interests governmental leaders will listen to and which interests they will support is to see who the governmental leaders are. In today's world this question translates into some of the following questions: What tribe are they from? What language do they speak? What religion are they? What is the color of their skin? What region of the country are they from? How much money do they have? What family do they belong to? What class or social group do they spring from? What political party are they affiliated with? What ideology do they believe in? By knowing the answers to these sorts of questions, we gain some idea about what section of societal interests will be taken into account in the formulation and implementation of foreign policy.

Willingness and Capabilities

There is another relationship between societal support and government that we should note. So far we have discussed support in terms of the tenure of the governing officials—how they will have to gain support to remain in office. But we can also look at society in terms of how societal interests support specific foreign policy positions of the government. Just as society's resources give decision makers the opportunity to act, societal support helps provide the "willingness." As noted earlier, human power and resources and economic and military capabilities do not count for much if a government cannot mobilize them. Governments do not just passively respond to societal needs and demands; they also try to shape and control them. If a government cannot persuade a people to get behind its policies and use those capabilities to support its policies, the capabilities are useless. If a people are not willing to act (for example, to send military aid to countries such as Vietnam in 1975 or to El Salvador in 1984 for fear that the aid would lead to another Indochina-type involvement for the United States), this is transmitted to the government. In the case of Vietnam, Congress reflected the general public feeling and refused to authorize the money that President Ford wanted for military aid.

An unwilling public affects a country's foreign policy in many ways. When discussing power and deterrence, we noted that to be effective, a state had to be able to make credible threats and promises. Credibility

---

1. Robert A. Dahl, *Who Governs? Democracy and Power in an American City* (New Haven, Conn.: Yale University Press, 1961).

was described as the actual willingness to use the capabilities at one's disposal in the ways threatened or promised. If societal support is lacking and prevents a government from pursuing certain policies or using certain capabilities, the credibility of that government declines in the eyes of other states. Its ability to influence them shrinks as its reputation as a bluffer grows. In all probability, its foreign policy menu will also shrink.

In sum, societies affect foreign policy in several ways through their effects on government. First, society affects the amount of resources available to a government. Clearly, the greater the resources available, the longer the menu. Second, government officials decide how they want to use those resources based on their own background (which societal group or elite they most represent), as well as their own view of what society wants or should want. Lastly, society places political limits on how such resources can be used through interest group pressures and public opinion. How important these may be is related to how accountable a government is—how open or closed it is to societal influences.

POWER ELITES VERSUS PLURALISM

We must now investigate the degree of public influence over policy-making. Although we still will not be able to give any hard and fast answers, we can provide a little more guidance by further considering the content of public opinion and by asking how public opinion is expressed or shaped within different governmental forms. In this consideration we shall move from the societal level to the governmental level of analysis. For example, in what way does it make sense to say that the foreign-policy decisions of a democracy result from public opinion? What opportunities to shape public opinion, as well as needs to be constrained by public opinion, are presented to the leadership of a democracy? We shall look mostly at ideas and information about the United States. That choice is both the result of the wealth of information available and the fact that the United States, as a major democracy, is the kind of country where we would expect public opinion to have a relatively significant effect. We shall also look at some data on the West European democracies.

One major perspective on American public affairs starts with the proposition that interests among the leadership groups in American society converge. By this "power elite" view, political and major societal leaders fundamentally agree on what the national goals should be. Attitudes among most of the public are thus not even relevant. In the words of the most famous proponent of this view,

> The conception of the power elite and of its unity rests upon the corresponding development and the coincidence of interests among economic, political, and military organizations. It also rests upon the similarity of origins and outlook and the social and personal intermingling of top circles from each of these dominant hierarchies.[2]

By this view, those who occupy the leading positions of power in American society (that is, those who occupy positions of authority in key economic and political institutions) basically agree on the fundamental principles by which American society is organized. Although they may disagree about details or the implementation of particular policies, their commitment to the principles of a market economy, regulated yet also protected by the ruling political structures, provides a basic common denominator. These like-minded individuals are held together by common upper-class origins, educational experience in "elite" schools and colleges, and social and professional mingling.

The contrasting "pluralist" view is typified in this comment:

> A substantial part of the government in the United States has come under the influence and control of narrowly based and largely autonomous elites. But these elites do not act cohesively with each other on many issues. They do not "rule" in the sense of commanding the entire nation. Quite the contrary, they tend to pursue a policy of non-involvement in the large issues, save where such issues touch their own particular concerns.[3]

The proponents of the pluralist view argue that for every major issue (defense, education, environment, and others) there are specialists and that different groups fight and win different political battles. Their argument emphasizes the diversity of opinion and the unpredictability of particular political outcomes rather than any fundamental consensus on the form of political and economic order.

In a real sense, the conflict between these two perspectives is irreconcilable. One emphasizes a diversity, unpredictability, and clash of

2. C. Wright Mills, *The Power Elite* (New York: Oxford University Press, 1956), p. 292.
3. Grant McConnell, *Private Power and American Democracy* (New York: Knopf, 1966), p. 339. The best-known proponent of the pluralist view is undoubtedly Robert A. Dahl. See especially his previously cited *Who Governs?*

opinion that surely is real. (Will the defense budget be increased? Will the MX ever be built?) The other dismisses this diversity as trivial and stresses the fact that certain values—liberal democracy, free enterprise, and the support of free enterprise by the government—are common denominators for most people in elite positions in America (or, for that matter, in Japan or Western Europe). Advocacy of alternative forms of economic or political order (extensive socialism and fascism) is clearly outside the mainstream, done only by a small minority and without the sound perspectives essential for one who would be thought responsible in a high position of public trust.

In fact, both views are correct. There are important differences within and between elite groups. At the same time, by long-term historic or global standards the spectrum of "respectable" opinion on major public policy issues in America is not especially wide. There has, however, been some periodic widening of that spectrum. Before World War II, isolationism—the idea that America could and should isolate itself from European quarrels—was widespread; until the Japanese attack on Pearl Harbor, it retained many adherents from both conservative and leftist (socialist and progressive) circles. By the 1950s the number of proponents of this view had shrunk to a small minority, which was held in ill repute by the elite. There was instead a substantial consensus on an internationalist policy of military alliances, a strong defense, some foreign aid (at least to pro-American and pro-capitalist states), and a general active involvement of the United States in world affairs. This policy consensus began to break down during the Vietnam war years, as opposition to American military involvement in foreign countries came into question. After the Vietnam war was over and the United States seemed to suffer a series of policy reversals with respect to the Soviet Union and its allies in the third world, opposition to an active American foreign policy again became less common and less respectable. The fluctuations in this kind of opinion are illustrated by a public opinion survey question that has been asked repeatedly for more than forty years. Although the wording of the question has varied slightly, its basic form has been quite stable: "Do you think we are spending too much, too little, or about the right amount for national defense and military purposes?"[4] Figure 10.1 shows the results.

You can see here substantial fluctuation in the early years of the Cold

---

4. For a discussion of the rise in particular elements of conservative ideology, including an increase in anti-Soviet and anti-Communist sentiment and a rise in support for a stronger military establishment, see Louis Kriesberg and Ross Klein, "Changes in Public Support for U.S. Military Spending," *Journal of Conflict Resolution* 24 (March 1980), 79–111.

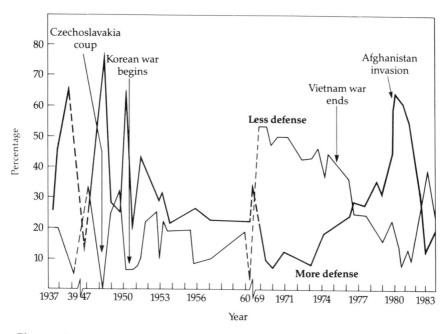

Figure 10.1

Percentage of Americans favoring more or less defense spending, 1937–1984.
[Data from Bruce M. Russett, "The Revolt of the Masses: Public Opinion on
Military Expenditures," in Bruce M. Russett (ed.), *Peace, War, and Numbers*
(Beverly Hills, Calif.: Sage, 1972), pp. 302–306; Bruce Russett and Donald
DeLuca, " 'Don't Tread on Me': Public Opinion and Foreign Policy in the
Eighties," *Political Science Quarterly* 96 (Fall 1981), no. 3, p. 383. Data since Janu-
ary 1981 from surveys for NBC, CBS/*New York Times*, and the American Insti-
tute of Public Opinion.]

War, before a popular and elite consensus was established. Then a long
period of stability ensued, when more people preferred increasing
rather than reducing defense spending, but where the majority of the
population was content with the existing level (not indicated in the
figure). This consensus was shattered by the antipathy toward the military generated by the Vietnam war, and since then opinions on this
matter have proved very changeable. The antimilitary mood of the
early 1970s faded and was then abruptly reversed by worsening relations with the Russians, the Iranian seizure of American diplomats as
hostages in 1979, and finally the Soviet invasion of Afghanistan. But by
1982 that mood, too, had passed, leaving about half the population satisfied with the existing levels of military spending (which were mark-

edly higher than in the 1970s); the other half was more or less evenly split between wanting more and wanting less. The volatility of American opinion toward the military contrasts sharply with opinion in other democratic countries. In Britain, for example, the percentage favoring increased military spending between 1968 and 1983 varied only between a low of 12 percent and a high of 40 percent (see Figure 10.2).

Segments of the American Public

In considering public opinion in general and the opinions of leaders in particular, it is useful to distinguish carefully among various segments of the population. About 30 percent of the American public, for instance, has little or no interest in or information about foreign affairs. They typically are unaware of most international events, although they know matters of major importance to the nation as a whole. For example, in June 1979, 82 percent of all Americans professed to have heard of the SALT II treaty then being considered by the Senate.

Perhaps another 40 to 50 percent of the population can be described as at least being aware of many major events. This group is often labeled the *attentive public*, though their attentiveness and knowledge is not deep. (For example, in June 1983, only one quarter of all Americans

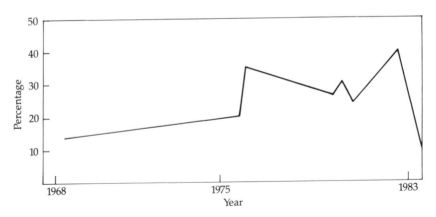

Figure 10.2
Percentage of Britishers favoring more defense spending, 1968–1983. [*Source:* Bruce Russett and Donald DeLuca, " 'Don't Tread on Me': Public Opinion and Foreign Policy in the Eighties," *Political Science Quarterly* 96 (Fall 1981), no. 3, p. 383; *Gallup Political Index* (Britain) 276 (August 1983), p. 20.]

knew that their government sided with the government of El Salvador in the civil war in that country.)

The remaining 25 percent or so of American adults are generally knowledgeable about foreign affairs, say they follow news about other countries, and have attitudes that are fairly stable over time. Many of these people discuss foreign affairs with others and communicate their own positions. Because of their interest and, to a lesser degree, their social roles (such as teachers, clergy, and those active in civic affairs), these people can be characterized as *opinion leaders*. Within this last group is a small segment of the population, people who give money or time to political activities and communicate their opinions beyond their personal acquaintances. Often these people, sometimes called *mobilizables*—or, used in a weaker sense than in power elite theory, *elites*—write, speak in public, or otherwise reach an extended audience.[5] Constituting no more than 1 or 2 percent of the populace, this group primarily includes party politicians, business and labor union executives, senior civil servants, leaders in the mass media, and leaders of economic, ethnic, religious, professional, or other interest groups involved in political activities.

The Content of Elite Opinion

Not surprisingly, membership in the opinion leaders or mobilizables is closely correlated with education, income, and professional status. People who have a lot of information and who are politically active tend to have reasonably consistent attitudes that form a relatively cohesive ideology; those who have a sizable amount of accurate political information and a high degree of interest will relate various facts and principles to produce a coherent set of beliefs. A recent study reported only a moderate relationship between education and coherence of political attitudes, but a much stronger one between political interest and coherence.[6]

Americans of higher social and economic status have tended to support official policy even more strongly than the average Amer-

---

5. These categorizations are taken from Barry Hughes, *The Domestic Context of American Foreign Policy* (San Francisco: W. H. Freeman and Company, 1978), pp. 23–24.

6. Norman Nie, Sidney Verba, and J. R. Petrocik, *The Changing American Voter* (Cambridge, Mass.: Harvard University Press, 1979).

ican, whatever that policy has happened to be. In the 1950s and early 1960s, when an active foreign policy and a strong defense were popular, highly educated, professional, upper-income Americans were more pro-defense than were people of lower status and more supportive of foreign aid and the Vietnam war. When a withdrawal from some overseas commitments and a smaller defense establishment became popular later in the Vietnam period, high-status Americans held those views disproportionately to the total population. When SALT II was still fairly popular nationwide and looked as though it would be ratified by the Senate (June 1979), higher-status people especially favored it. In the 1980s, upper-income and educated people tend to favor foreign aid programs (economic and military) and are generally more inclined than the average American to send troops or military assistance to American allies if they should be attacked. In Western Europe, college-educated people—and also older people—are much more likely to favor their countries' continued membership in NATO than are their less-educated or younger fellow citizens, who often endorse a policy of neutrality toward the two superpowers.

Furthermore, higher-status people are more discriminating in their judgments, as should be expected of individuals with more information at their disposal. For example, when Americans were offered a list of countries that might be attacked and asked which ones they would be willing to assist with troops, many people in the general populace gave the same answer for every country; on the other hand, American leaders were much more likely to pick and choose which countries to help—principally those to which the United States was bound by a formal alliance commitment. Table 10.1 shows these results.

Upper-status Americans did diverge from official policy in several important areas. They overwhelmingly opposed restricting trade between the United States and the Soviet Union and were more likely

Table 10.1

Support by U.S. elites and the general public for sending U.S. troops to help areas if invaded by Soviets, 1982.

Area invaded	Leaders	General public
Western Europe	92%	65%
Japan	78	51
Poland	6	31
China	6	21

Source: John E. Reilly (ed.), *American Public Opinion and U.S. Foreign Policy 1983* (Chicago: Chicago Council on Foreign Relations, 1983), p. 31.

Table 10.2

Positions on military issues of the U.S. public according to income and education group.

Issue	Annual income		Education	
	High	Low	High	Low
Ratification of SALT II (June 1979)				
For	48%	34%	56%	22%
Against	23	16	25	15
No opinion	29	50	19	63
Defense spending (November 1982)				
Too little	17	14	15	16
Too much	44	35	50	30
About right or no opinion	39	51	35	54
Verifiable freeze (March 1983)				
For	76	63	75	56
Against	21	20	22	18
No opinion	3	17	3	26

Sources: Gallup Report 167 (June 1979), 11; *Gallup Report* 208 (January 1983), 12; *Gallup Report* 212 (May 1983), 25.

Note: High income is $25,000 and above in 1983 and $20,000 and above in 1979; low income is $5,000 to $9,999 in 1983 and $3,000 to $6,999 in 1979. High education is having completed college; low education is not having gone beyond grade school.

than lower-status people to favor arms control agreements, to favor "an immediate, verifiable freeze on the testing, production, and deployment of nuclear weapons," and to prefer lower levels of defense spending. Table 10.2 shows some of these results.

Women at all levels of the population were especially critical of the Reagan administration's foreign policy, even more than of most of its domestic programs. For example, a national survey done for the *Los Angeles Times* in September 1983 found that only 40 percent of women (as compared with 54 percent of men) approved President Reagan's handling of foreign affairs, 30 percent of women (22 percent of men) believed his policies increased the risk of nuclear war, and 55 percent (40 percent of men) favored the withdrawal of American marines from Lebanon.

Faced with this and similar evidence, a number of scholars believe that the general support for official American foreign policy among American leaders has been shattered. Some point to a fourfold division of opinion among Americans in general, categorizing people very broadly as "isolationists" versus "internationalists" on one dimension and as "hard-liners" versus "accommodationists" on Soviet-American relations on a second dimension. Although these scholars find internationalists and accommodationists somewhat more common among the elites than among the general public, all variants are to be found at all levels. Two other authors also find a fragmentation of opinion among American leaders, which they attribute to the impact of the Vietnam war. In their survey of American leaders, they found that 16 percent wanted to seek a complete military victory both at the beginning and at the end of U.S. involvement. Another 17 percent tended to favor a complete withdrawal from Vietnam not only at the end but also when the war first became a political issue. These two groups, the extreme hawks and doves, remain large and opposing on a wide range of foreign policy beliefs and attitudes. Even within the two thirds of the leaders who tended to feel in between the two extremes of military victory and withdrawal or who changed their positions in the course of the war, very different conclusions have been drawn about the war, and very different preferences for future policy are held. Although these nonextremists in some sense make up the center of opinion, they show no unity of opinion. By these data, there is no longer (if there ever really was) an elite consensus on some basic issues of the *means* by which foreign policy should be pursued.[7] Whether that lack of consensus extends also to what *goals* should be pursued or whether a consensus will reemerge under the threatening conditions of the 1980s, remains to be seen.

Interactions among the Elite

The power elite perspective also stresses a system of interpersonal relations, past and present, that serves to maintain the unity of opinion among the powerful. Several writers have noted the common social origins (raised in the East and upper-class) of many—but not all—holders of positions of power in America.[8] Common origins, however,

7. Eugene Wittkopf and Michael Maggiotto, "Elites and Masses: A Comparative Analysis of Attitudes toward America's World Role," *Journal of Politics* 45 (May 1983), no. 2, pp. 307–333; Ole R. Holsti and James N. Rosenau, "Vietnam, Consensus, and the Belief Systems of American Leaders," *World Politics* 32 (October 1979), no. 1, pp. 1–56.

8. William Domhoff, *The Higher Circles: The Governing Class in America* (New York: Random House, 1970); William Domhoff, *The Powers That Be: Processes of Ruling-Class Domination in America* (New York: Random House, 1978). On Britain, see Anthony Sampson, *The New Anatomy of Britain* (New York: Stein and Day, 1972).

are not enough to maintain a consensus on values. For that to happen, elite members would have to interact frequently on a wide scale. They would need a dense network of current communication from knowing and seeing one another professionally and socially (on boards of directors, in social clubs, and through civic, private, or professional organizations).

To examine this, one scholar looked at the network of direct personal contacts among people identified in the Columbia survey of American leaders discussed earlier. She found that for two thirds of the leaders, the network of contacts was fragmented into small, relatively isolated groups in which members tended to share interests with one another only on specific issues. The remaining third, however, all were found to be part of a single large cluster of frequently interacting people. In this "central circle," the contacts were broad—not limited to specific issues—and dense, with members having an average of 8.7 different kinds of contacts with one another. In addition, this central circle was connected with many of the small, issue-based circles. Even more than that, members of the central circle were especially visible and potentially influential. They wrote more, spoke in public more, and were more likely to belong to federal advisory committees or such policy-planning organizations as the Council on Foreign Relations or the Committee for Economic Development.

> Circle members are more active than their noncircle colleagues in serving on federal advisory committees, testifying before congressional committees, and serving as members of important policy planning organizations. Wide visibility, as measured by level of communications output, is far higher for members than nonmembers of the central circle in nearly all sectors. This potential influence over public opinion strongly distinguished circle members from nonmembers. Reputation for influence is much greater among persons who are members of the central circle than among their noncircle colleagues.

These findings suggest that although the allegations that America is ruled by a power elite may well be exaggerated, there does exist a social basis whereby "the central circle directly and indirectly integrates leaders of a wide variety of institutions into a network capable of discussing and resolving issues of national concern."[9] Whether this potential is in fact achieved, especially in foreign policy, we cannot yet say. We do not at present have information relating social contacts to

---

9. Gwen Moore, "The Structure of a National Elite Network," *American Sociological Review* 44 (October 1979), 673–692.

specific views among members of the central circle; more important, we do not have information on whether their access to one another and their potential for influence is really converted into influence and power. At this point, we hit the old political science problem of trying to infer effective influence from mere attempts to influence, a problem we discussed in Chapter 6.

THE EFFECT OF PUBLIC OPINION IN AMERICAN GOVERNMENT

We certainly cannot exhaust the topic or provide final answers, but some further observations are worth making, especially concerning American governmental institutions. First, we can ask *how* public opinion, or at least attentive public opinion, affects policy; second, we can ask *when* that effect may be greatest.

How Public Opinion Affects Policy

1. *By setting broad limits* of constraint and identifying a range of policies within which decision makers must choose if they are not to face retaliation in competitive elections. These constraints are clearly quite broad, though they are likely to be felt more intensely the closer a particular decision time is to a national election. Of course, this still begs the question about how strongly mass opinion is itself merely shaped or controlled by elites who command public attention and the mass media.

2. *By constraining policy execution.* Top decision makers must depend on subordinates, from military officers and high-level civil servants down to foot soldiers and clerks, to carry out their policies. Subordinates have many ways to "drag their feet" or sabotage policies that they do not like.

3. *By distorting or selectively screening information* given to top decision makers. Top leaders must depend on their subordinates not only to execute policy but also to provide the information on which decisions are made. The specific interests or general ideological views of subordinates—perhaps extending quite far down in the information-handling chain—will affect the completeness, kind, and interpretation of information that these people pass upward. An information "screen" lets some information through and holds other information back; think, for

example, of a secretary who lets only some phone calls into the boss's office and tells other callers that "the boss isn't in." Screens may be found in organizations within the government, and within individuals' own minds as they consider what information to pay attention to and what to ignore. These concerns will be touched on below when we consider the effects of governmental structure. In the following chapter also, in the section on individuals and their roles in government, screens and other information-processing concepts will be discussed in greater detail.

4. *As part of the climate of opinion* eventually shaping the top decision makers themselves. The *recruitment base* from which future leaders will be drawn is the broad set of today's middle-echelon figures.

When Public Opinion Affects Policy

1. It matters greatly whether the policy is *important to a specific minority* of citizens or leaders, especially a high-status and thus potentially influential minority. Some issues directly affect important ethnic or religious groups. (Polish-Americans were very concerned about the situation in Poland after the communist government's crackdown on the Solidarity worker's movement in 1981; Mexican-Americans worry about the status of new immigrants; many Jews, as well as other Americans, are strongly committed to Israel's security.) Other issues affect farmers (grain sales to Russia), auto workers (imports from Japan), arms manufacturers (policy on arms sales abroad), and other economic interest groups. Others are the focus of groups concerned with protecting the environment ("Save the Whales").

2. Not only the specific issue, but *broad classes of issue* probably make a difference. Most matters of foreign economic policy (trade, for example) are of primary interest only to the kinds of interest groups just noted. These issues are not usually matters of concern to the mass public or the attentive public in general. In contrast, issues of military or political security (SALT, sending the Marines into Lebanon, the fate of the hostages in Iran) are much more likely to capture the attention and concern of broad segments of the public. Table 10.3 presents one categorization of various kinds of issues.

3. *The time frame* matters. Issues that can or must be resolved quickly, before opinion can be changed or rallied, are not likely to be very constrained by mass public opinion. The longer an issue stays alive, the more public attitudes are likely to matter. This must first be qualified,

Table 10.3

A typology of foreign policy decisions with examples.

Economic Considerations Important				Economic Considerations Relatively Unimportant			
Security issue		Nonsecurity issue		Security issue		Nonsecurity issue	
Decision time long	Decision time short	Decision time long	Decision time short	Decision time long	Decision time short	Decision time long	Decision time short
Size of defense budget	Marshall Plan	Tariff structure	Chile's copper nationalization	Support El Salvador government	Korean invasion	Policy on West Bank	UN vote to oust South Africa
Vietnam war deescalation	Foreign oil embargo	International whaling restrictions	Peru's fishing extension	Arms limitation treaty	Cuban missile crisis	Admission of China to United Nations	Arrest of prominent American citizen
Extent of trade with Communists		Restricting Japanese auto imports		Iranian hostage affair	Send Marines to Lebanon	Japanese peace settlement	
MX missile deployment		Immigration from Mexico			Berlin airlift	Adherence to World Court decisions	

Source: Adapted from Barry B. Hughes, *The Domestic Context of American Foreign Policy* (San Francisco: W. H. Freeman and Company, copyright © 1978). p. 201.

however, by our earlier point about proximity to elections. Fear of retaliation by voters after opposition political leaders have had a chance to make a long and detailed public case may constrain leaders from doing something even though they may fear no immediate reaction.

Congress is said to be especially sensitive to the needs and demands of particular, narrow interests. More precisely, particular members of Congress are likely to be especially sensitive to the needs of major interests in their constituencies or other interests that provide them with support at election time. Defense industry representatives can expect a favorable hearing from the U.S. representative in whose district they employ many workers. Representatives from Iowa will care about grain sales to the Soviet Union. Moreover, the chair of the House Merchant Marine Committee is likely to be solicitous of shipowners, shipbuilders, and merchant seamen. Whether or not those interests are located in the representative's district, they can provide (or withhold) financial and other support at election time.

In matters of more general policy, it is difficult to be sure how much the opinion in a representative's or senator's district constrains his or her actions as a legislator. One major study was done by Warren Miller and Donald Stokes. They compared the policy positions of 116 representatives—as determined through interviews and a study of their voting records—with the opinion of the constituents in their districts, as measured by public opinion surveys. They discovered that the relationship between constituency opinion and the foreign policy votes of representatives was very low. (They observed a correlation of only .32, indicating that only about 10 percent of a representative's voting record could be predicted by knowing what his or her constituents said on the opinion survey.) The authors concluded that representatives vote their own preferences, or perhaps the preferences of the president or congressional leaders or various interest groups. In any case, they did not seem to have or to seek much knowledge about their constituents' foreign policy views. (The correlation between representatives' votes and their *perception* of opinion in their districts was even lower, .25, than the correlation between their votes and the survey of attitudes.)

However, Miller suggested in another study an important qualification to the first study. He compared the results for representatives from safe districts (where they are reasonably sure of being reelected) with those for representatives from marginal or closely contested districts. He found that Republican and Democratic representatives from safe northern districts vote very differently from each other, but in marginal districts they vote very much alike. This fact suggests that representatives are more sensitive to constituency opinion when they have to be, though it is not clear whether the difference between Republican and Democratic representatives from safe districts reflects the freedom of such representatives or merely the differences in their districts. (Northern Democrats' safe districts are usually in cities; Republicans' districts are usually rural or suburban.)[10]

Sometimes a president can persuade Congress to adopt an important defense or foreign policy measure even if public opinion opposes it. For instance, President Carter in 1978 urged senators to do the "statesmanlike" thing and support the Panama Canal treaties, despite sentiment against the treaties as measured by most polls. Two thirds of the Senate did support the treaties, and they were ratified. The next year, however, Carter met with failure. The second Strategic Arms Limitation Treaty (SALT II) was favored by more people than opposed it (in a July 1979 survey, 39 percent favored it and 22 percent opposed it), but many people either had no opinion or had never heard of SALT II. With such lukewarm approval in the mass public and a worsening international atmosphere, a majority of the Senate remained unconvinced. After Carter's electoral defeat, President Reagan withdrew the treaty from consideration.

Some kinds of public preferences cannot be reflected by appropriate congressional action because policy is already in accord with those preferences. For instance, if public opinion shifts toward stronger opposition to a draft for the armed forces, Congress cannot adopt a policy *more* in conformity with that opposition because there is no draft anyway! But a review of public opinion and government policy changes between 1935 and 1979 found that in two thirds of all cases (including foreign policy issues) where there was a shift in public opinion and a subsequent change in public policy, the policy change was in the same direction as the public opinion change. Moreover, the government was more likely to shift in the direction of public preferences than vice versa. This seems to indicate that the American democratic form of

---

10. Warren E. Miller and Donald E. Stokes, "Constituency Influence in Congress," in Angus Campbell, Philip E. Converse, Warren E. Miller, and Donald E. Stokes (eds.), *Elections and the Political Order* (New York: Wiley, 1966), p. 363; Warren E. Miller, "Majority Rule and the Representative System of Government," in E. Allardt and Y. Littunen (eds.), *Cleavages, Ideologies, and Party Systems* (Helsinki: Transactions of the Westermarck Society, 1964).

government is fairly responsive to the will of the general public.[11] We must nonetheless be cautious with this interpretation, because we do not know why public opinion changes. It may well be that public opinion changes because opinion leaders and elites—including government officials—first express a preference and then persuade the attentive public and the mass public to voice that preference. Then Congress, including some of the very people who helped change public opinion, can "respond" to that public change. Certainly this possibility often seems more plausible than the simple notion of Congress merely being obedient to the "voice of the people." The interaction between opinion change and policy change is complex.

THE CHIEF OF STATE

The chief of state—the president, prime minister, monarch, or general secretary, as the case may be—embodies the national interest more than anyone else. He or she is at the top of the political pyramid, responsible for somehow bringing together all the separate individual and group interests. Personal characteristics—personality, experience, leadership style—surely matter in determining what choices a leader makes. So, too, does the relationship he or she has with advisers and subordinates—people who provide information, help make decisions, and are responsible for carrying out decisions. We shall look intensively at these considerations of individual characteristics and role relationships in the next chapter; here we want to ask another kind of question: How constrained is the top leader by the general structure of mass and elite opinion in the society? Does public opinion matter to the chief? If so, when and how? We shall concentrate on the attention that scholars and other citizens have paid to public constraints on foreign policy making during the Vietnam war.

Mass Opinions

According to one view, mass opinions set limits on the range of actions that a political leader may safely take. One version of this view stresses the importance of ideological anti-Communism among the masses on

---

11. Benjamin Page and Robert Shapiro, "Effects of Public Opinion on Policy," *American Political Science Review* 77 (March 1983), no. 1, pp. 175–190.

the freedom of action of leaders in the United States. American policy-makers feared a backlash of militant anti-Communism by the general populace in reaction to major foreign policy reverses. They remembered, for example, the domestic political costs resulting from the trauma of losing China incurred by the administration in the late 1940s and the witch-hunting of the Joseph McCarthy era, which was so hard on both liberals and radicals in the United States. In the words of former Senator Sam Ervin, "You can't believe the terror that man [McCarthy] spread among politicians."

Thus, politicians feared to loose a popular anti-Communism that would punish them for foreign policy defeats and were therefore constrained by popular anti-Communism even though they themselves were too sophisticated to believe all its premises. Believing that the people would not tolerate the "loss" of Vietnam, senior officials in Washington resolved that Vietnam would not be lost—at least not during their terms in office. They would hang on and escalate where necessary to avoid defeat, even though they knew the long-term prospects for holding the country were poor. They could hope to postpone the day of reckoning until a time when they themselves would not be held responsible, perhaps hoping against all available evidence that events would break favorably so that the ultimate outcome would not be disastrous. According to some analysts, this kind of thinking can be found in every administration from Truman to Nixon.[12] The remains of it could perhaps be seen in the fears of Democratic representatives that if they did not support President Reagan's policy in Central America, they would ultimately be blamed for "losing Central America."

Support from the Populace

A very different point of view, however, maintains that the leader has great potential support among the populace for virtually any kind of foreign policy initiative. A leader can take either hawkish or dovish initiatives and, with the authority and respect he or she commands,

---

12. This is basically the interpretation of Daniel Ellsberg, "The Quagmire Myth and the Stalemate Machine," *Public Policy* 19 (Spring 1971), no. 2, pp. 217–274. See also Leslie Gelb and Richard Betts, *Vietnam: The System Worked* (Washington, D.C.: Brookings, 1979). To an important degree, popular anti-Communism was built up by policymakers themselves, as in Senator Vandenberg's advice to Truman that he must "go and scare hell out of the country." Once this force was unleashed, policymakers felt more constrained by it than they wished to be.

still be backed by a substantial portion of the population. Some analysts, for example, maintain that for most of the Vietnam war (at least until opposition to the war because overwhelming after 1970), the president of the United States could have obtained considerable support for deescalation of the war as well as for escalation. In a national survey conducted in March 1966, shown in Table 10.4, people were asked whether they approved of various possible initiatives. The results are shown in Table 10.4. (The various options were mixed together and not labeled "hawk" and "dove," as we have done in the table.)

Table 10.4
Public approval of various policy options in Vietnam, March 1966.

Hawk options	Percent approval	Dove options	Percent approval
Bomb military targets in North Vietnam	77	Negotiate with Viet Cong	88
Send 200,000 U.S. troops to Vietnam	61		
Fight the Chinese in Vietnam if necessary	56	Permit free elections, even if Viet Cong might win	54
Send 500,000 U.S. troops to Vietnam	45	Allow a coalition government including Viet Cong	52
All-out mobilization	40	Gradual withdrawal and let Vietnam work out own problems	39
Fight the Chinese in China if necessary	32		
Fight an atomic war with China	29	Let Viet Cong eventually gain control	28
Fight an atomic war with Russia	22		
		Immediate withdrawal	15
		Withdraw even if it means Communist takeover in Thailand and Laos	13

Source: Sidney Verba et al., "Public Opinion and the War in Vietnam," *American Political Science Review* 61 (1967), no. 2, pp. 313–333.

At first glance the answers in this table may seem foolishly incompatible: If 77 percent of the population wanted to bomb North Vietnam, and 88 percent also were willing to negotiate with the Communist Viet Cong (neither initiative was policy at the time), simple arithmetic shows that nearly two thirds of the population answered yes to *both* of these questions. Yet the two policies seem *contradictory*. Simple arithmetic further shows that some people (at least 10 percent of the populace) were willing to fight the Chinese in Vietnam and/or to permit truly free elections so the Viet Cong might win! The point, however, is not that people were muddled; rather, they were ready to pursue *either* hawkish or dovish policies. Thus, there really was a great deal of flexibility available to the president, who could have built a majority coalition behind him regardless of the course of action he followed, provided he was pursuing a relatively moderate course of action. Only the extremes (fighting the Chinese in China or atomic war on one hand, or withdrawal and permitting the Viet Cong to control South Vietnam on the other) were rejected by large majorities. Nor did many people take *consistently* hawkish or dovish positions even on questions falling near the middle. Only 6 percent gave hawkish answers to all four of the middle questions: (bombing North Vietnam, sending 500,000 troops, and opposing free elections or coalition government), and only 12 percent gave dovish answers to all four. President Johnson may not have perceived this degree of freedom—and he still might have had to cope with a backlash from a disappointed minority of the populace holding strong opinions—but it probably was there.

The ability of a president to gather support for a variety of foreign policy initiatives, so long as he is perceived as doing something, has been termed the "rally-round-the-flag" phenomenon and can be seen in the experience of almost all recent American presidents.[13] Figure 10.3 illustrates trends and fluctuations in a standard American Institute of Public Opinion survey question asked about twice every month: "Do you approve or disapprove of the way [Carter] is handling his job as President."

Both the trend and fluctuations are the result of many influences, including domestic events and the state of the economy as well as

13. The term comes from John E. Mueller, *War, Presidents, and Public Opinion* (New York: Wiley, 1973). A later analysis of data on presidential popularity, refuting some of Mueller's conclusions but confirming most, with a systematic sampling of foreign policy events, is Samuel Kernell, "Explaining Presidential Popularity," *American Political Science Review* 72 (1978), no. 2, pp. 506–522.

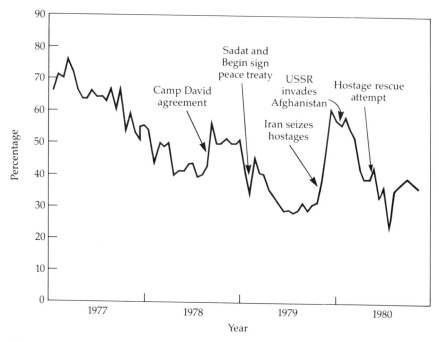

Figure 10.3

President Carter's popularity. [*Source:* Adapted from *Gallup Opinion Index* 183 (December 1980), 6–7.]

foreign policy and international events. Nevertheless, the rise in Carter's popularity coinciding with major international events is striking. Certainly Carter's image in the minds of the American people was enhanced by his role in concluding the Camp David agreement between Egypt's President Sadat and Israel's Prime Minister Begin and their later signing of the peace treaty. But he also was helped, very temporarily, by the unsuccessful American attempt to rescue the hostages held captive in Iran in 1979. Almost any action increased public approval, even if, like the hostage rescue, it was a failure. Seeing a similar increase in his public standing after the Bay of Pigs fiasco in 1961, President Kennedy remarked, "The worse I do, the more popular I get." For him, both Cuban crises (the Bay of Pigs and the missile crisis in late 1962) were followed by an immediate jump of ten points or more in his popularity. The biggest reversal in the downward slide in public approval of President Carter, moreover, came from the two major international events of his administration: Iran's seizure of the American embassy and the Soviet invasion of Afghanistan in December 1979. Carter shrewdly converted these events into a general challenge to America's willingness to resist aggression, a challenge that he felt Americans should meet.

The rally-round-the-flag phenomenon had become so well-known to scholars and journalists by 1980 that many of those people expected President Carter to make another dramatic diplomatic or military move to free the hostages in the autumn of that year, right before the election. If he had made such a move, many of them were ready to interpret it as a cynical political act. In the end—and possibly to avoid losing votes by too transparently seeking them—Carter made no such move, and there was no rally to him. On the contrary, a year of national frustration and humiliation, brought home almost every evening on millions of television screens, hurt his reelection campaign badly. The ultimate effect of the Iranian hostage affair was to feed many Americans' sense of frustration about their country's apparent weakness in international affairs. That sense contributed mightily to Jimmy Carter's defeat.

We now have some evidence that presidents are more likely to use military force if they are seeking reelection at a time when there is a developing or ongoing war. When this is the case (as during the Korean and Vietnam wars), a president knows that voters will be more concerned than usual about foreign affairs and will therefore be especially likely to hold the war against him if things go badly. Thus, the temptation to use more force to resolve the conflict may be strong. If the year has been a relatively peaceful one, the risks that a use of military force may backfire often seem great enough to discourage such acts.[14]

As you can see in Figure 10.4, President Reagan's popularity rating during his first three years in office was much steadier than Jimmy Carter's or that of most preceding presidents. The most dramatic shift came in March and April of 1981, almost certainly reflecting widespread sympathy for him when he was shot and nearly assassinated. After that, it showed the fairly smooth decline typical of most presidents, although it leveled off and even showed an upswing in 1983 and 1984 as the economy improved. Most of the fluctuations were small and may have been nothing more than chance variations. (The polls, of course, just take opinions from a random sample of Americans, and there is a chance that the percentage expressing an opinion in any

---

14. Richard J. Stoll, "The Guns of November: Presidential Re-Elections and the Use of Force," *Journal of Conflict Resolution* 28 (June 1984), no. 2, pp. 231–246.

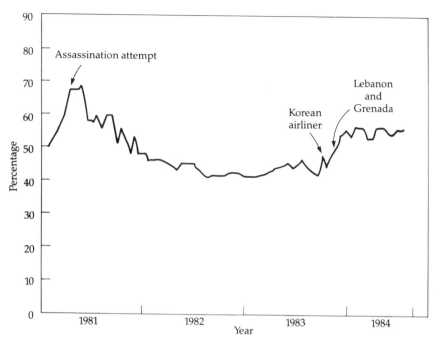

Figure 10.4

President Reagan's popularity. [*Source: Gallup Report* 207 (December 1982), 29; subsequent Gallup press releases.]

survey will differ from that of the preceding survey merely because of chance differences in the sample. Analysts usually do not treat differences of 3 percent or less between two surveys as statistically significant.) There were, however, two clear rally-round-the-flag effects in 1983. The first was in September, when the Soviet Union shot down a Korean airliner with many American passengers aboard, and President Reagan directed some very strong words toward the Soviets. The second stemmed from two events that occurred in close sequence in late October: a terrorist attack on the U.S. peacekeeping force in Lebanon, which killed 241 American Marines, and the American invasion of the island of Grenada only three days later to overthrow a Marxist government aligned with Cuba and Russia.

Limits of Presidential Support

The ability of the president to shape public opinion and thus to generate support in a crisis is usually short-term. It did not prevent the long-term erosion of Johnson's political position, caused by an unpopular war. Carter's popularity declined sharply early in 1980. The life of bursts of popular support is four or five months at the most, and more often only two or three. By the end of that time, support usually returns to its previous, lower level. The reason for this may be related to the reason for the rally in the first place. In the first week or two after a sudden military action or major diplomatic event, criticism of the president, even by opposition political leaders, is usually muted. The president has the most information about foreign policy and security affairs, especially in fast-breaking crises. Opposition leaders who criticize him risk being shown up as being poorly informed. Since "responsible" political leaders do not immediately criticize the president's actions, the mass media (newspaper columnists and television commentators) have few critical comments to report. The absence of criticism looks like bipartisan support to much of the public, and so ordinary people are also reluctant to criticize. But in time, as the president's policy begins to falter or less favorable information about the circumstances becomes available, opposition political leaders become bolder, and their renewed criticism is picked up by the media and then by the general public. The rally effect then decays.[15]

The shorter the decision time available to a leader—and short decision time is one element in the definition of a crisis—the less constrained by public opinion he or she is likely to be. The short-term rally effect helps powerfully. This is especially strong in national security affairs, because people tend to feel that the commander-in-chief has secret information and special competence. We saw this effect after the invasion of Grenada. But as the challenge or crisis drags on, as in Lebanon, dissenting voices become more widely heard, and constraints built into the political structure become more effective.

If the president wishes to respond militarily to a foreign challenge, the president can try to mount an action with existing military forces and without prior approval from Congress. A majority of the public will probably support him and if the action is successful it may be widely applauded. The year-in–year-out maintenance of military action abroad, however, requires congressional approval and the appropriation of funds under circumstances where the trade-offs with domestic welfare become much more apparent and politically salient. The War Powers Act of 1973, passed by Congress in reaction to Vietnam, allows the president to use American military forces in a national emergency,

---

15. Richard A. Brody, "International Crises: A Rallying Point for the President?" *Public Opinion*, 6, 6 (December/January 1984), pp. 41–43, 60.

but he must immediately report such use to Congress. At the end of sixty days (extendable to a total of ninety in some circumstances), however, he must withdraw the forces unless Congress specifically authorizes their involvement.

A survey of over 2,000 American leaders in 1976 produced overwhelming support among almost all groups for the statement "If foreign interventions are undertaken, the necessary force should be applied in a short period of time rather than through a policy of graduated escalation." Domestic constraints appear, therefore, to limit the president's menu of choice in a crisis—not necessarily encouraging or discouraging the use of military force in general, but, if the decision is to use force at all, favoring those forms of military action (possibly even nuclear weapons?) that might bring quick results rather than protracted warfare.[16]

International and security issues are remote for most Americans, even those of the upper socioeconomic classes. Only a small proportion of the population directly benefits from the military-industrial complex; in any given year, relatively few Americans travel abroad and even fewer obtain much information relevant for evaluating complex foreign policy issues. People know they can be incinerated instantly in a nuclear war, but few of them can apply immediate experience in formulating a policy for dealing with that threat. The kinds of issues that the general public is likely to have had some experience with are economic (unemployment or inflation) or even social (race or abortion). Foreign policy is thus a prime candidate for what Donald Kinder and his colleagues have termed "symbolic" politics.[17] In an earlier era, Americans depended heavily on personal contact with "opinion leaders," who relayed information and interpreted events.[18] In the electronic era, Tom Brokaw, Dan Rather, and Peter Jennings bring informa-

16. Ole R. Holsti and James N. Rosenau, "Vietnam, Consensus, and the Belief Systems of American Leaders," *World Politics* 32 (October 1979), no. 1, pp. 1–56. If asked directly whether they would approve the use of nuclear weapons in the event of attack on an American ally, however, the proportion of the populace saying yes is very small. See also Bruce M. Russett and Miroslav Nincic, "American Opinion on the Use of Military Force Abroad," *Political Science Quarterly* 91 (Fall 1976), no. 3, p. 425.

17. Donald R. Kinder and R. D. Kiewiet, "Economic Discontent and Political Behavior: The Role of Personal Grievances and Collective Economic Judgements in Congressional Voting," *American Journal of Political Science* 23 (1979), no. 3, pp. 495–527; D. O. Sears et al., "Self-Interest vs. Symbolic Politics in Policy Attitudes and Presidential Voting," *American Political Science Review* 74 (September 1980), pp. 670–685.

18. Elihu Katz and Paul Lazarsfeld, *Personal Influence* (New York: Free Press, 1955).

tion and interpretation directly into people's living rooms without going through any intermediary.

Rallying round the flag is most common among people with high income, social status, and educational attainment. However, high-status people are quicker to change their minds when official policy seems to be working badly. For example, in the early stages of the Vietnam war, high-status Americans were more likely to favor American participation. But as the war dragged on into the 1970s, these same individuals were more likely to change, especially if they were greatly exposed to the mass media.[19]

People may support a policy for any of three reasons: (1) because doing so satisfies basic personality needs, (2) because on the basis of available information they perceive the policy as consistent with certain interests and beliefs, and (3) because the segment of their social environment most meaningful to them reaffirms support. Although high-status people are no more or less likely than others to have certain basic personality needs, they are more likely to be linked with a broad social environment where international affairs are considered important. Thus, when cues in their environment change, high-status people are more likely to change their opinions for two interacting reasons. First, new information that a given foreign policy is inconsistent with personal beliefs and interests is especially likely to reach them, thus prompting them to reassess their beliefs. Second, because this likelihood applies to all members of the high-status group, the general support from the social environment for the old beliefs will decrease.

A different kind of perspective emerges from looking at attitudes toward security policy in Western Europe. As we noted, support for official NATO defense policy is strongest among the elites there. Lower-status people are less committed to NATO and to specific poli-

---

19. Richard F. Hamilton, "A Research Note on the Mass Support for 'Tough' Military Initiatives," *American Sociological Review* 33 (June 1968), no. 3, pp. 439–445; Andre Modigliani, "Hawks and Doves, Isolationism and Political Distrust: An Analysis of Public Opinion on Military Policy," *American Political Science Review* 66 (September 1972), no. 3, pp. 960–978; John E. Mueller, *War, Presidents, and Public Opinion* (New York: Wiley, 1973), chap. 5; James D. Wright, "Life, Time, and the Fortunes of War," *Transaction* (January 1972), no. 3, pp. 47–52. Controlling for socioeconomic status, the higher the exposure to the mass media, the more likely a person was to turn against the war. See Richard Brody and Benjamin Page, "The Impact of Events on Presidential Popularity: The Johnson and Nixon Administrations," in Aaron Wildavsky (ed.), *Perspectives on the Presidency* (Boston: Little, Brown, 1975); Peter Braestrup, *Big Story: How the American Press and Television Reported and Interpreted the Crisis of Tet 1968 in Vietnam and Washington* (Boulder, Colo.: Westview, 1977).

cies concerning the use of nuclear weapons. For instance, despite near-solid government support for deployment of new intermediate-range missiles during 1983, the general public was very skeptical. Also, official NATO policy has always been that although NATO will never start a war, it will follow a policy of "flexible response" if the Russians invade Western Europe. That is, if the Russians seemed to be winning, even with a purely conventional (nonnuclear) attack, NATO forces would retain the option of escalating the conflict by a first use of nuclear weapons. But most ordinary Europeans are extremely worried about the consequences of using nuclear weapons in that densely populated region of the world. Fewer than 20 percent of them in the big countries (Britain, France, Italy, and West Germany) say they approve of a first-use policy.[20] What their verbal disapproval really means in political terms is unclear; they are not necessarily willing, for example, to spend the money necessary to establish credible nonnuclear defense forces. Nevertheless, this long-standing tension between elite and mass attitudes in Europe may ultimately pose problems for Western security policy and the unity of NATO. Similar problems may arise in the United States out of fear of nuclear war.

Overall, our view of the importance of public opinion is complex, depending very much on the kind of *issue*, the *circumstances*, the *level of government* at which the decision is made, and other specific features of the political context. Certainly there is no close, immediate connection, even in a democracy, between public opinion and foreign policy. Political decision makers are skilled leaders of opinion, with ready access to television, newspapers, and other media. They shape opinion as well as respond to it. Always we are bedeviled by the problem of making inferences about power and of differentiating between the *activity* of people or pressure groups and their *influence*. If any summary statement is in order, perhaps we cannot do better than to quote the conclusion of a major review of evidence on the question, which notes "the paradox that a policy making system which seems to have mastered all the modes of resistance to outside opinion nevertheless seems, from a long run perspective, to accommodate to it."[21]

20. Bruce Russett and Donald R. DeLuca, "Theatre Nuclear Forces: Public Opinion in Western Europe," *Political Science Quarterly* 98 (Summer 1983), no. 2, pp. 193–195.

21. Bernard Cohen, *The Public's Impact on Foreign Policy* (Boston: Little, Brown, 1973), p. 205.

GOVERNMENTS AS INFORMATION PROCESSORS

In addition to being open and closed, governments differ in many other ways. Most of these differences involve the acquisition, processing, and movement of information. Governments differ in the types and number of organizations and institutions within them, the distribution of influence among these organizations and institutions, the numbers and types of personnel in those institutions, and the societal interests they represent. Some governments are large, made up of many organizations and staffed by hundreds of thousands of people; some are small with few people to staff the few organizations involved. Some governments centralize powers in one institution or group; others distribute governmental power among a number of institutions. Some have strong executives, who make most foreign policy; some have weak executives or executives restricted by other groups. Governments also have different forms of executives. In the United States there is a president, who shares foreign policy powers with Congress. In France there is also a president, but with much more centralized control over the French parliamentary body and the foreign policy process. There are parliamentary systems run by a cabinet and a prime minister, as in Britain. There are systems ruled by single parties or single individuals, as in Communist governments or military dictatorships.

Although scholars have discussed how governments differ and have described those differences, we still have little systematic evidence about how the governmental structure actually affects foreign policy. Some observers have proposed that closed centralized governments can act more quickly and efficiently. Others have argued that democracies can get the most out of their societies. Some argue that although democratic governments work more slowly, they produce better foreign policy because they get more diverse and accurate information from society about society's capabilities and about the constraints in both the domestic and foreign environments. We have mentioned "information processing" because how well information is collected and used may be the most useful way we have for comparing governmental structures and how good their foreign policy is. We can begin to compare how fast, how accurately, and how efficiently governments process information—how well they "learn" and adapt to the world.

However, we still do not have the evidence needed to support or refute any of these propositions. We still can only agree with Harold and Margaret Sprout when they some time ago observed: "There remains a hard core of disagreement as to what forms of government are best, or least, adapted to cope with the ever more complicated problems which confront governments everywhere these days."[22]

We can, as have many scholars, look at information from other perspectives. One of the most thoroughly studied has been how information is handled by individuals in making decisions. Individuals, especially those occupying foreign policy roles in government, have their own impact on foreign policy and produce their own sets of constraints. Decision making within governments is discussed in Chapter 11, and individual perception and decision making in Chapter 12.

---

22. Harold and Margaret Sprout, *Foundations of International Politics* (New York: Van Nostrand Reinhold, 1962), p. 212.

11

ROLE: COMMUNICATION AND DECISION MAKING

INTRODUCTION: ON SEEING THE MENU AND MAKING CHOICES

As we noted earlier, foreign policy decisions are made by people acting either as individuals or as part of a group. The individual foreign policy decision maker is surrounded by several "layers" of environment, or context, and each environment affects the choices, possibilities, and probabilities open to the decision maker. Both the external environment and the domestic environment constrain and limit what the decision maker is able to do or is likely to do in a number of ways. The resources and capabilities of the decision maker's country—its people and territory—are vital to a state's foreign policy orientation, objectives, and choice of tools by which to influence others. Capabilities and characteristics of a state are intimately involved in the power and influence that a state possesses, and through those processes, in what a state is able and is likely to do. In preceding chapters we discussed states in terms of other aspects of the domestic menu, such as the societal elements of public opinion, interest groups, ideology, and form of government—as factors affecting the mobilization and use of the state's capabilities.

Each of the various factors blends into others that sandwich it. There are a number of connections between the systemic and societal factors, between societal and governmental factors, and between governmental and role factors. In this chapter and the next, we shall investigate the final two factors: role and individual (or idiosyncratic) influences. These impinge directly on the individual who plays a part in the development and execution of foreign policy.

By looking at individuals we have moved from the broadest context—the systemic or the global system—to the narrowest, the individual involved in the foreign policy process. Earlier we mentioned several types of relationships between an entity and its environment. One of these was called cognitive behaviorism, referring to "the simple and familiar principle that a person reacts to his milieu as . . . he perceives and interprets it in the light of past experience." Individuals, then, have perceptions or *images* of the world. What is actually "out there" is of less importance than what the decision maker *thinks* is out there. The possibilities and probabilities provided by the domestic and global environments will only affect plans and decisions as they are perceived and understood by decision makers.

A number of constraints on the foreign policy menu of any state thus derive from the perceptions and images of individuals in the government of that state. If the menu cannot be read; if the individual reading the menu sees only what he or she wants to see or argues with the "waiter" later on because he or she was sure the menu said that wine was served free of charge (when clearly it wasn't); if the decisions on what to order are made by a group so that no one really gets their preference; or if the individual feels pressured to order something because of the preferences of everyone else—then the range of possibilities and probabilities will be affected. This influence and constraint on behavior comes from within the individual as a pressure to see the world in certain ways. Our concern here is with those things that affect how the individual perceives the world and how the individual makes foreign policy decisions. We are concerned with willingness rather than opportunity. What makes an individual or a small group of individuals who make foreign policy willing to decide on a course of action? What influences their perception of an opponent, a situation, or themselves?

These influences can be divided into several basic groups. Moving down our series of levels of analysis, we shall discuss the role factor. One of the important characteristics of individuals who help make foreign policy is their position within the government. Where a person fits in the government and what duties, responsibilities, and loyalties are connected with that position will affect the individual's images of the world and his or her foreign policy decisions. We must continue our discussion of governments and information by bringing in small groups and individuals and how they handle information.

Just as governments do, individuals must process information—a vast, ongoing wave of incoming signals, facts, and noise. Just like governments, an individual cannot process, handle, and understand all available information—especially an individual in a high-level governmental position. As do all organizations, individuals must *screen* out some of the information directed at them from the environment. Some information is simply ignored; some is altered to not upset existing views or beliefs; some is looked at quickly and then either thrown out or buried. Many of the psychological processes that we all use are designed specifically for this screening process. Governmental organizations do the same thing. Bureaucracies may similarly be used to screen information. One's role may be used as a way to be involved in some things and not others, to ignore or bias the flow of information. The line between organizational and psychological screening may sometimes be very fine.

Both role-organizational factors and individual-psychological factors affect how people make decisions. These are then implemented in some form or another as foreign policy events, which have consequences for the global system. The real world becomes important at this point, because when an action is taken it will then become (sometimes painfully) clear how different the real world is from the decision maker's image that produced the decision. The world then provides *feedback*—information on the consequences of one's actions—giving the decision makers a chance to reevaluate their policies, decisions, and images and to change them if necessary.

Before we discuss role factors, it is important to have an overview of what we mean by decision making—what it is and how it has been studied. The impact of specific role factors and that of *small-group decision making* will be discussed after decision making.

DECISION MAKING: AN OVERVIEW

Some Definitions and the Ideal

In trying to define *foreign policy,* we noted that the *policy* indicated something about choice and choosing from various courses of action. We also noted that the foreign policy process is constantly in motion. Furthermore, all parts of that process involve the decisions and actions of people. Decision making focuses on the people involved in the foreign policy process and on the part of the process that deals with choosing among alternative courses of action. (Remember, *not choosing* to make a decision is also part of the decision-making process.) *Decision making* itself should be thought of as a process, the result of which is the choice of some course of action directed at achieving the objectives of the decision makers. The main questions, of course, include what *kind* of process decision making is, what factors influence how decisions are made, and what decisions are actually taken. The study of decision making involves descriptions of how people behave as well as how people should behave to get the "best" decisions.

Many ideal decision-making processes stress the idea that the best decision is the most rational decision. There are many ongoing debates about exactly what *rationality* means. The simplest way is to think of rationality as a relationship between means and ends—that actions are taken to achieve some goals. Exactly how closely means and ends are related, with what certainty they are related, and how closely the actual consequences of behavior match the consequences desired are all questions that go back to our original question of what kind of process decision making is. We shall outline the *ideal rational* model of decision making that a number of people have developed. This model is rational decision making as people would like it to be. It is a decision-making process that actual decision makers try to achieve. Unfortunately, though people attempt to meet this ideal, they never really succeed; many times they do not even come close. Maybe even more unfortunate, some people who spend their time analyzing foreign policy still think that foreign policy decisions are really made in this ideal way.[1]

One scholar of decision making, Charles Lindblom, has given us the following version of the ideal model. Faced with a *given problem,* the

---

1. This point is central to an excellent review of alternative perspectives on decision making by Donald R. Kinder and Janet A. Weiss, "In Lieu of Rationality," *Journal of Conflict Resolution* 22 (December 1978), 707–735.

rational decision maker first *clarifies* his or her *values, goals, and objectives* and then *orders* them in some way (usually in a transitive, most-to-least desired ranking). Then the decision maker *lists* all the important possible ways to achieve those goals. Then the decision maker *investigates* all the important consequences of each alternative identified in the previous step. Now the decision maker *compares the consequences* of the various alternatives. Finally, the decision maker *chooses* the decision or policy alternative with the consequences that most closely match the goals.

Before we go look at the reasons why this is an ideal process and the problems in achieving it in the real world, let us look at one other version of this ideal. Irving Janis and Ralph Mann list seven criteria for achieving what they call "vigilant information processing." These steps, though a bit more detailed than the steps outlined above, also loosen the ideal requirements somewhat. The decision maker, to the best of his or her ability:

1. Thoroughly canvasses a wide range of alternative courses of action.

2. Surveys the full range of objectives to be fulfilled and the values implicated by the choice.

3. Carefully weighs whatever he or she knows about the costs and risks of negative consequences, as well as the positive consequences that each alternative could produce.

4. Intensively searches for new information relevant to further evaluation of the alternatives.

5. Correctly assimilates and takes into account any new information or expert judgment to which he is exposed, even when the information or judgment does not support the course of action he initially prefers.

6. Reexamines the positive and negative consequences of all known alternatives, including those originally regarded as unacceptable, before making a final choice.

7. Makes detailed provisions for implementing or executing the chosen course of action, with special attention to contingency plans that might be required if any of various risks materializes.

These are the steps in the ideal decision-making process, along with some less stringent information-processing requirements.[2] But whether

---

2. For a full discussion of these processes, see Charles E. Lindblom, *The Policy Making Process* (Englewood Cliffs, N.J.: Prentice-Hall, 1968); Irving Janis and Ralph Mann, *Decision Making* (New York: Free Press, 1977).

one is talking about a single individual or about groups, it should be clear that there are many problems in achieving these ideals. For example, let's look back at our initial summary of the ideal, where we spoke about a given problem. Decision makers are not faced with problems; they must look out into the world and identify and formulate problems. For instance, even at the time of the Cuban missile crisis in 1962, when the Kennedy administration discovered that the USSR had secretly placed medium-range missiles in Cuba despite assurances that they would not do so, there were some members of Kennedy's ExComm (Executive Committee) who did not think this was so important. For example, Secretary of Defense Robert McNamara is reported to have said at the first meeting of the ExComm, "A missile is a missile. It makes no difference if you are killed by a missile fired from the Soviet Union or from Cuba." The point is that different people in different parts of government, or different people occupying the same position (role) in government at different times, may not see the same situation as a problem. Individual, role, ideological, and political factors will all combine to make a person see a problem. Since these factors vary across individuals, not all people, and especially not the relevant foreign policy people, will see the same problem at the same time.

The Ideal and the Rational Decision Maker

After identifying a problem, the "rational decision maker" clarifies and orders his or her values and goals. This task is very difficult; think of all the competing values and goals in the relatively simple task of purchasing a new automobile—cost, size, comfort, safety, durability, passenger and luggage capacity, gas mileage, as well as the more intangible things such as appearance, status, and so on. The rational decision maker must order these values: which is most important, next important, least important. These values must also be transitive. This means that if *A* is preferred to *B*, and *B* to *C*, then *A* should be preferred to *C*. (This would not be the case, however, if you would prefer a blue car over a yellow one and a yellow car over a white one, but if you had to choose between blue and white, you'd choose white!)

If these ordering tasks are difficult for individuals, then they are almost impossible for governments. Graham T. Allison, in a very important work on different models of decision making, set out three "conceptual models" for understanding foreign policy activities and decisions.[3] His first model, Model I or the "Rational Actor" model, is

---

3. See Graham T. Allison, *The Essence of Decision* (Boston: Little, Brown, 1971).

the one that he says analysts use most of the time. It is a model that makes a number of these ideal assumptions. Because these assumptions are not satisfied, Allison argues that the Rational Actor model must be supplemented by others. One who uses the Rational Actor model has to assume that governments are *monoliths*—that is, they speak with one voice, hold one view, have one set of agreed-on values, and one set of agreed-on goals. From our very brief discussion of foreign policy goals and governmental influences on foreign policy, we know that this is not the case. Allison develops the fact that governments are made up of different organizations and individuals with different views, values, and goals in his alternative two models. Recall that in discussing domestic constraints, we used Dick, Jane, and Spot to illustrate the difficulties of finding group interests and acting to achieve them. A *non-monolithic* government composed of different organizations and individuals presents us with similar problems but on a more massive scale.

Before making a choice, the ideal rational decision maker must first identify alternatives, list the consequences of those alternatives, and then compare the alternatives with goals to be achieved. The ideal decision maker must look at all the important alternatives and their consequences. This requires the individual or group making the decision to have perfect information. However, there are time limits for making decisions, and there are limits on the human resources and money that can be spent on acquiring the information needed. Unlike academic observers, decision makers must act at some point. There will always be a trade-off between the time and resources devoted to gathering more information and the need to take action in the global arena. In the end, one can never be sure that one has all the relevant information. In international politics especially, there is a great deal of secrecy about a state's capabilities and intentions, as well as uncertainty over and just plain ignorance of events, capabilities, and intentions.

As we have noted, both individuals and organizations set up screens to filter information. This is one of the important effects of having a government broken up into various organizations—these organizations will often pass along only information that is beneficial to them and not all the information that might be relevant; an example was the actions by the CIA during the Bay of Pigs fiasco in 1961. Because of individual psychological screens and organizational screens, decision makers do not have perfect information but only a collection of selected data. The psychological screens are interesting because, along with problems in processing information, they may lead decision makers to ignore or fail to grasp the significance of important information they do have. A study of why the American forces at Pearl Harbor were surprised by the Japanese attack in 1941 shows that all the important information needed to indicate that an attack was coming was in the hands of American decision makers. However, because there was so much noise (unimportant, irrelevant pieces of data), the true signals were missed. Those signals that did get through to decision makers, especially those stationed at Pearl Harbor, were dismissed through the working of psychological screens.[4]

Shortcomings of the "Ideal"

In sum, then, the ideal model falls short of its aims for many reasons, especially because of constraints on achieving perfect or even near-perfect information. The requirements of an ideal rational decision also lead to a paradox. One requirement is for perfect information (at least very large quantities of information even for minimally complex decisions), but we also know that as a decision maker is bombarded by more and more information, more and more screens, both bureaucratic and psychological, are used to eliminate information "overload." Few individuals or organizations have the capacity to be rational in the ideal sense, because they lack the ability to adequately process all the information required by the ideal rational model. The paradox occurs because all screens distort the world in some way. Thus, in order to function, decision makers must distort their perceptions of the real world. The issue then becomes what degree of distortion is acceptable and how we can recognize and deal with it.

Perhaps even more important is the assumption that decision makers actually want to make ideal decisions—decisions where they find the optimal choice or try maximizing all their goals and values through the best possible decision. The Nobel Prize–winning economist Herbert Simon, in a famous formulation, pointed out years ago that the decision maker does not maximize but *satisfices*. This means that the decision maker searches for an acceptable choice, one that is good enough to meet a minimal set of requirements. Instead of reviewing all alternatives and then choosing, the satisficer will usually pick the first alternative that meets the minimal set of requirements. Simon argued that this approach derives from the limited information-processing capacity

---

4. See Roberta Wohlstetter, "Cuba and Pearl Harbor: Hindsight and Foresight," *Foreign Affairs* 43 (1964–1965), 691–707.

of people, and as such, people were creatures of "bounded" or "limited" rationality who used a simplified conception of the world.[5] Again, we shall find that there are different methods, mechanisms, or models for simplifying the world (or explaining how people simplify the world). We shall also see that other approaches to decision making may be viewed as responses to the ideal model. A summary comparison of the ideal and real processes of decision making is presented in Table 11.1.

Decision Making: Some Alternatives to the "Ideal"

Simon told us that people try to simplify the world through the bounded rationality of satisficing. Charles Lindblom studied how people make decisions and said that people simplify the world not by looking for grand solutions but by "muddling through." Lindblom observes that decision makers often work in an incremental manner as one way to cut down on uncertainty and risk, to rely on the familiar, to

Table 11.1
Decision making: the "ideal" and the "real."

Task	Ideal performance	Actual performance
Scanning for information	Comprehensive, perfect in detection	Imperfect in detection, covers only some things
Transmitting information	Instantaneous, undistorted	Delayed, distorted, loses information
Storing and recalling information	Infinite storage, instant recall	Memory lapses, distortion in recall
Identifying alternatives	Exhaustive	Limited
Implementing decisions	Instantaneous, coordinated, efficient	Subject to lag, lacking coordination, wasteful of resources
Feedback	Instantaneously self-corrective	Imperfect in detecting feedback, imperfect correction of error

Source: Modified from Patrick Morgan, *Theories and Approaches to International Politics*, 2nd ed. (Palo Alto, Calif.: Page-Ficklin, 1975), p. 148.

---

5. See Herbert Simon, *Models of Man* (New York: Wiley, 1957).

reduce the number of alternatives to be examined, and to reduce the complexity of an analysis. That is, instead of grand decisions that review the total situation as it existed, a decision maker makes small changes that are only slightly different from decisions and actions already taken. This incremental approach is based on taking routine, small steps in order to cut down on the costs of decision making and the cost of making mistakes. Incremental decisions are thus described as remedial—they can be easily reversed or changed if they prove wrong. Similarly, they are serial in that they build on what has gone before and what is presumably acceptable. They are also exploratory in that one can move into new policy areas to explore new avenues and still pull back if they look to be costly or ineffective. An observer of American foreign policy, who himself was a decision maker in the Kennedy administration, says this about the way foreign policy is made:

> Rather than through grand decisions or grand alternatives, policy changes seem to come through a series of slight modifications of existing policy, with new policy emerging slowly and haltingly by small and usually tentative steps, a process of trial and error in which policy zigs and zags, reverses itself and then moves forward.[6]

The incremental view of decision making can nevertheless have some clearly negative effects. Just because the steps are small and easy to reverse if necessary, it is possible after a time to find oneself deep in a policy that was never intended. Some have asserted that this was the case with the American involvement in Vietnam—small foreign policy activities that led to a massive involvement that was not supposed to have happened. Incremental decision processes can actually be a way of "deciding without really deciding" because policy is not reviewed on a large scale.

Thus, we have one model of people making decisions based on the large view of the situation, attempting to find the optimal or most rational choice and trying to control the situation as much as possible. The other model describes people who make small, marginal choices primarily based on what had previously taken place—a process of "muddling through." How can scholars observing decision making come up with two such divergent explanations for the behavior of

---

6. This is Roger Hilsman's observation in *To Move a Nation* (New York: Dell, 1964), p. 5. It is similar to the process described by Lindblom in "The Science of 'Muddling Through,' " *Public Administration Review* 19 (1959), 79–88.

decision makers—as well as several other intermediate positions?[7] One answer is that there are different forms of the decision-making process. Because of the inability to meet the ideal rational decision making process outlined above, and because of the need to simplify the world, people have come to make decisions in other ways than the intellectual process of sitting down, gathering information in the ways just discussed, making calculations, and then choosing one of the alternatives. Because there are different processes and different types of decisions to be made and because each decision is actually a series of decisions, different observers have seen different aspects of foreign policy decision making and have thus come to describe what appear to be very different things.

THREE DECISION-MAKING PROCESSES

Three different types of decision-making processes can be identified. The rational model, where individuals sit down and work their way through a series of intellectual steps to choose among alternatives, may be called the *intellectual process* of making decisions. We have already seen lists of the sorts of steps the intellectual decision maker goes through to come to a decision. Because the decision maker is assumed to be rational, and because we like to think that decisions (especially in foreign policy) are made rationally, Allison argues that the Rational Actor model is the most frequently used model for explaining foreign policy. Again, if one is trying to explain why a set of foreign policy decision makers did something, the easiest thing to do is to assume that

---

7. We have already touched on some of these intermediate views. The steps listed by Janis and Mann require less information and searching than the ideal "synoptic" process described by Lindblom. The notion of satisficing, as a form of bounded rationality, is an intermediate view that sees a decision maker as purposive and trying to find a useful alternative, but not the best one—a satisfactory one will certainly do. Another intermediate approach is one developed by Amatai Etzioni called "mixed scanning," which is related to satisficing in many ways. He is concerned with agreement or consensus within a decision-making group or bureaucracy. For periods of noncrisis, he suggests the incremental approach. For periods of crisis, a wider and more intensive search for alternatives should be used. The alternative search and evaluation process we have already discussed is summed up by the word *scanning*. By "mixed scanning," Etzioni means that the scope of the scanning should change, depending on whether one is engaged in a fundamental policy decision or in the clusters of minor decisions that must be made after the fundamental issues have been decided. For the former, a more synoptic or rational approach should be used; for the latter, a far more incremental approach should be used. See Amatai Etzioni, "Mixed-Scanning: A 'Third' Approach to Decision-Making," *Public Administration Review* 27 (December 1967), 385–392.

they are rational; then you can try to put yourself in their shoes and see what possible goals they could have had to select the actions they did. Assuming others go through this intellectual process implies that they are purposeful and rational and have thus made their choice because it will further some foreign policy goal. It also implies that the government of the other actor is a monolith and that—most important for the analysis of foreign policy—important events have important causes. (The assumptions of both monolithic behavior and chosen, purposive, rational behavior are challenged by Allison's other two models, set out below). The Rational Actor analysis can be done with little information. Because you assume the actor being analyzed is rational, you can attempt to follow the same intellectual steps that have been taken to understand how a decision was reached.

We have seen, however, that the ideal rational process takes place only with great difficulty. Because of this difficulty, people satisfice, practice mixed scanning, and decide incrementally. Also, a foreign policy decision taken may not be accurately reflected in foreign policy implementation—the actual event that occurs may not be the one that was decided on.

Mechanical and Social Processes

In addition to an intellectual process there are also *mechanical* (or quasi-mechanical) and *social processes* of decision making. In a social process, there is an active social interaction among several decision makers that results in the decision produced. In Allison's second and third models, "Organizational Process" and "Governmental Bargaining," we see that governments, including those portions involved in the foreign policy process, are made up of many parts—both individuals and organizations. Because of this, decisions are not the products of a rational intellectual process but of the interaction, adjustment, and politics of people and organizations—social and quasi-mechanical processes. Roger Hilsman, in his book on the foreign policy of the Kennedy years, notes very simply that "policy making is politics." Foreign policy emerges from the normal political process of bargaining, compromise, adjustment, arm twisting, favor trading, and so on. This is the heart of the social process of decision making. Allison's Model III, Governmental Bargaining, presents a very different picture of decision making from that of the Rational Actor. Events are not the result of rational choices but the "resultants" of various "bargaining games" among the "players" in the government. Model I may be seen as rational economic man at work; Model III involves a social process where some market mechanism is at work.

What we have, then, is a process where each individual player is trying to act in a rational way. Each player—the president, prime minister, first secretary, advisers, senators, foreign ministers, generals, and cabinet members—tries to set goals, assess alternatives, and make choices through an intellectual process. And each individual player fails.[8] But this failure is not crucial, because there are other people involved in the process. Each brings some information into the process, along with individual goals, alternatives, and calculations of the consequences. With all these people participating, most of what should be considered is put into the process. Each participant or player sees a "different face" to the issue under consideration, each has different stakes in the game, and each takes a different stand. This includes the chief decision maker, such as the president or the prime minister. For example, part of John Kennedy's perspective on the Cuban missile crisis was his desire not to endanger his political position in the upcoming off-year elections by appearing to be weak in handling the Russians.

The foreign policy behavior of a state is not that of a monolithic actor, which has an important goal in mind and then acts to achieve it. It is the result of a set of "decision games" and then "action games." Participants first play bargaining and political games and come out with some resultant, which is government policy. Then there is another set of games by which the decision is implemented—action games. The result of the action games, as noted, may or may not reflect the decision finally made. Whatever the case, the important event that occurs, such as the construction of a new weapons system (e.g., the Polaris submarine, the cruise missile, or the B-36 bomber in the late 1940s), may be far removed from a single, monolithic governmental goal. Some advocates of the "bureaucratic politics" school even argue that most if not all foreign policy is developed with an eye to domestic political problems—keeping special interests happy, balancing off organizations and institutions within the government, keeping a particular administration in power. Hilsman pictures the American foreign policy process as a series of concentric circles, with the president (as much a bureaucratic actor as the others) at the center. He is surrounded

---

8. This is what Hilsman calls "politics," and what Allison calls "governmental bargaining." Charles Lindblom has labeled this process "partisan mutual adjustment." See Lindblom, *The Intelligence of Democracy* (New York: Free Press, 1965).

by rings of players—the inner rings having the most important play-ers, the further ones having players less likely to have the ear of the president or to be consulted by him. Foreign policy decisions, it is argued, emerge from the structured bargaining and bureaucratic games played by these participants (see Figure 11.1).

Decisions may also be made through a quasi-mechanical reference to past decisions, precedence, routines, or governmental role—the "stan-dard operating procedures" of organizations. Organizations within governments all have a catalog of past behavior to draw on. Organiza-tions are also basically conservative and rarely try anything new; they are happy with incremental changes based on past decisions and be-havior. One way to cut down on the complexity of the world and to cut down uncertainty is to act as one has acted before. Organizations tend to have rule books, guides, and so on that indicate how things should be done by that organization. As Allison notes in his discussion of Model II, Organizational Process, what will happen at time $t + 1$ is

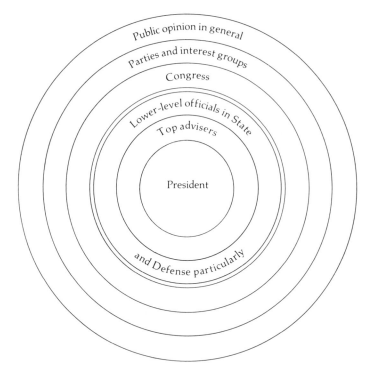

Figure 11.1
The concentric circles in American foreign policy.

best explained by looking at what happened at time *t*. This is a neat summary of the cautious and remedial incremental model. Model II may be summarized by three main points: (1) A government is made up of a "conglomerate of semi-feudal loosely allied organizations"; (2) governmental decisions and behavior should be understood not as rational choice, but as the "outputs of large organizations functioning according to standard patterns of behavior"; and (3) each organization, with its SOPs (standard operating procedures), routines, or programs, will behave today substantially as it behaved yesterday—and will behave tomorrow much as it behaved today. Again, a quasi-mechanical process affects both the decision that is made and the implementation of that decision.[9]

DECISION UNIT, TYPE OF DECISION, AND DECISION STAGES

Regarding the three different processes or models that focus on different units of analysis—governments personified (Model I), bureaucracies (Model II), and individuals in group interaction (Model III)—it is apparent that how any individual affects a foreign policy decision and its implementation depends on governmental role factors as well as individual factors. Where each person stands in the government, within which organization, how close to the central decision maker (such as the president or the prime minister), and what the decision unit is are all factors that must be taken into account. The decision unit is particularly important. This refers to the specific group of individuals involved in making a foreign policy decision. This may range from the president alone (or prime minister or first secretary) to the president and one or two advisors (such as Nixon and Kissinger) to large sections of the foreign policy bureaucracy. How many and what sorts of people are involved will influence the effect of the individual, given that individual's role in the government and personality. The size and composition of the decision unit will affect the social and quasi-mechanical processes at work. We do not expect the entire State

---

9. For a general overview of how organizational process might affect national security policy, see Harvey Starr, " 'Organizational Process' as an Influence on National Security Policy," *International Relations* 4 (1972), 176–186. For a useful application of organizational process to the outbreak of war, see Jack Levy, "Non-Rational Factors in Decisions for War: Organizational Routines and the Causes of War," paper delivered at the annual meeting of the American Political Science Association, Chicago, 1983.

Department to be involved in a crisis decision such as the Cuban missile crisis, nor do we expect the president and his top advisors to be concerned with many of the day-to-day decisions regarding the running of embassies, the technical details of weapons systems in the SALT negotiations, and so on.

This alerts us to several other aspects of a decision that we must consider to understand how decisions are made and implemented: The decision unit will change depending on the decision being made. Although there are many ways in which we could categorize decisions, a rather standard typology sets out crisis decisions, general foreign policy decisions, and administrative decisions. The *crisis decision* generally involves a few very high level decision makers. It is a special situation with certain qualities, such as a finite or specified decision time. Usually this time is very short. The situation also involves a major threat to the decision makers and their state, and there is little warning—they are surprised by the event (see Figure 11.2).[10]

General foreign policy decisions set out future foreign policy, looking at the present and into the near future (and often beyond). Deciding on a U.S. policy toward petroleum producers and other third world providers of natural resources, reevaluating U.S. policy toward the Soviet Union and China in the early years of the Nixon administration, or the Carter administration's decision to make a commitment to human rights as part of American policy toward other countries are all examples of general foreign policy decisions. *Administrative decisions* are concerned with very specific situations, usually handled within a specific part of the foreign policy bureaucracy. They are routine situations, calling for the application of the expertise and standard operating procedures of foreign policy organizations. Whereas the participants in a crisis are of the highest level and are relatively few in number, general foreign policy decisions usually involve a large number of medium-level officials interacting with one or two of the high-level foreign policy players. Administrative decisions usually involve low-level officials.

Because of the number of people, the seriousness, and the short time involved, some scholars have observed that crisis decisions look more like the intellectual decision-making process than do other types of

---

10. The three-dimensional definition of crisis—short time, high threat, and surprise—is most closely identified with Charles Hermann; see, for example, *International Crises* (New York: Free Press, 1972). Our modification of the time element derives from Michael Brecher, "State Behavior in International Crisis," *Journal of Conflict Resolution* 23 (1979), 446–480; and from Irving Janis and Ralph Mann, *Decision Making* (New York: Free Press, 1977).

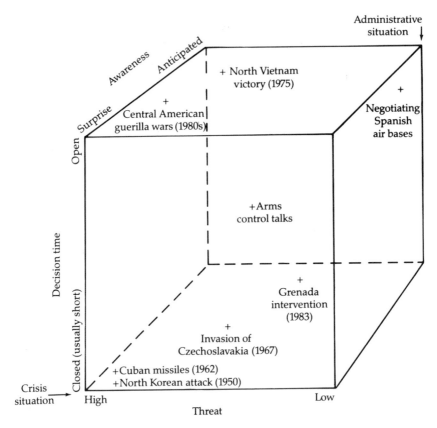

Figure 11.2
A modified "crisis cube." [See also Charles F. Hermann, "International Crisis as a Situational Variable," in James N. Rosenau (ed.), *International Politics and Foreign Policy* (New York: Free Press, 1969)].

decisions, and recent research has supported this view: In crisis situations, policymakers use an analytic, intellectual, rational model of decision making.[11] We must keep in mind, however, that some of the small-group interactions involve interesting social processes and that quasi-mechanical processes can also be crucial in determining what information reaches top-level decision makers. General foreign policy decisions, however, are characterized mostly by social processes. Because there is much less time constraint and because the general direc-

---

11. See Zeev Maoz, "The Decision to Raid Entebbe: Decision Analysis Applied to Crisis Behavior," *Journal of Conflict Resolution* 25 (1981), 677–707.

tion of foreign policy is of concern to so many sections of the government, these types of decisions generate a high degree of governmental conflict—and thus bargaining and compromise, as competitors try to make policy reflect their personal views or those of the organization they represent. Although the other two processes are also involved, the social processes tend to dominate these general foreign policy decision situations. Finally, administrative decisions are characterized primarily by quasi-mechanical processes.

It should be clear now how various observers come up with different descriptions of how people make decisions. Several different decision processes exist. They generally involve different groups of decision makers (or different decision units) as well as different types of foreign policy decisions. In fact, we can make this even more complicated if we look at different *stages* of any particular decision. James Rosenau has suggested that any decision might be broken down into a predecisional stage, a formulation stage, and an implementation stage. The *predecisional stage* involves the collection of information and views and the scanning of the foreign policy horizon for possible problems and issues. The *formulation stage* involves the actual selection of an alternative after evaluating the possibilities. In the *implementation stage*, the decision has been translated into some form of action or foreign policy behavior.

Because high-level decisions are usually put into effect by officials at much lower levels in various governmental organizations, the implementation stage is often affected by bureaucratic screening and the selective action of bureaucrats. The predecisional stage seems to be most important for general foreign policy decisions and administrative decisions; the formulation stage for general foreign policy decisions and crisis decisions; and the implementation stage for crisis and administrative decisions. Again, which decision units one studies may shift even within the process of a single decision. The study of decision makers may reveal several kinds of decision-making processes going on simultaneously within a foreign policy establishment, even for the same decision.

Although this analysis may seem very complicated, it is necessary if we are to investigate the place of the individual in making foreign policy. We must remember that the individual will be involved in some decision unit, surrounded by very few, several, or many other participants. We must also remember that the individual and these others may be predominantly involved in intellectual processes, or they may be most strongly influenced by their organizations (role and Model II, Organizational Process), or they may be involved in highly political games within the government. All these factors affect the impact an individual has on the foreign policy process, and they also affect the individual's perceptions, image of the situation, values, and beliefs.

INDIVIDUALS IN GOVERNMENT: ROLE, DECISION MAKING, AND SCREENS

The foreign policy decision maker is embedded within the government and, even more immediately, within the governmental organization or bureaucracy for which he or she works. The individual decision maker is an information-processing system. So is the government as a whole, however. The information received and passed on will thus be affected by organizational and role influences, as well as the decision maker's own psychological characteristics. Information that any individual receives (or does not receive) will also affect the individual's image of the world. Too much information, as well as too little, will be an important factor in forming this image. Where this information is coming from, as well as where it is going, will also be important to the individual's view of the world. Before we talk about an individual's role or how that role places him or her in a decision-making position, in affecting what information comes to him or her, and in affecting his or her image of the world by acting as a screen, we should briefly touch on the area of *cybernetics*—the study of communication and control.

Information and Screens

As Karl Deutsch has pointed out, communication is the cement of all social organization; all groups or collectivities are held together by communication.[12] Communications transmit pieces of information and are involved in the control of the flow of information. Social systems, such as societies, governments, and bureaucracies, may be called "self-controlling" systems in that they have goals and are able to respond to stimuli from their environments. For such systems, and particularly for governments, the main question is one of *steering*. Steering refers to such questions as where are we going, through which choices, why,

---

12. Karl Deutsch's classic, *The Nerves of Government*, 2nd ed. (New York: Free Press, 1966), provides the basis for much of the material presented in this section.

and how. Control of steering, says Deutsch, is the real problem of government. We have seen a similar view in the idea of incremental decision making.

We are now approaching topics that we have already discussed from a slightly different perspective. We can think of organizations, individuals, or any self-controlling system as having to react to the environment—to steer through it by learning. Learning involves the receipt of information and the use of the information to help us steer. This is the concept of feedback. Positive feedback amplifies or reinforces your behavior, encouraging you to respond or act in the same direction—basically, to continue your behavior. If feedback indicates that you are moving away from your goal or missing it by ever greater distances, then your behavior must change to bring it back toward the target. This is negative feedback. How much of this information gets back to us, how it is screened on the way (by governmental organizations or by individuals) will affect our image of the world and how to behave in it. This is precisely why we are interested in role influence and the effects of the interests of organizations. In the early 1960s, when the United States was becoming involved in Vietnam, in what direction should the United States have steered? Should it have *continued* involvement (positive feedback)? Or should it have *changed* course and disengaged (negative feedback)? (Similar questions concerning steering—of taking small steps that ultimately lead away from one's goals—were raised about American policy towards Central America in the 1980s.)

One important influence on the decision makers in Washington was the information they received about the effectiveness of the American involvement in Vietnam. As David Halberstam points out in his account of the Vietnam war and the Kennedy administration, *The Best and the Brightest*, military and intelligence organizations with an interest in continuing and expanding the involvement sent back information supporting a continued increase in military involvement. Individuals with a strong anti-communist ideology and other beliefs that made such involvement seem beneficial also sent back positive feedback. More importantly, Halberstam shows how information that opposed increasing involvement—negative feedback—was suppressed or eliminated. Such information was screened out at various bureaucratic and individual points. Even when it managed to get through, the information was ignored if individuals did not want to believe it.

Information and images are so important because it is only through feedback that decision makers are able to steer their states through the troubled waters of the international system. As noted, not only are we concerned with too little information, but also with too much. Because of information overload, decision makers must cut down on the amount of information received so that they can function. Remembering that there are over 160 states in the global system, hundreds of IGOs, and thousands of NGOs—each sending out information through words and deeds, with hundreds of diplomats reporting back on this activity, as well as intelligence-gathering agencies—one can see how decision makers in the contemporary system can be overwhelmed with information. Overload forces decision makers to decide what to decide. By paying attention to one issue, situation, or crisis, others have to be ignored.

Some critics charged that by paying so much attention to the Middle East and the U.S.-Soviet-Chinese triangle, Kissinger ignored what was happening in Africa and even with America's European allies until problems arose. This was probably the case. Overload forces us to choose what to consider—a major form of screening. Overload may obscure true signals by hiding them in noise. This was the case in the surprise attack on Pearl Harbor, where the Americans were able to read all of the Japanese messages because they had broken their code. Instead of being a help, the information-processing system of the American intelligence bureaucracy was swamped. The Allies' strategy for locating the World War II D-Day landings in Europe was a consciously similar one—to overload the Germans with a great deal of information, much of it false. In this way, they hoped that the Germans would miscalculate the invasion site, which was exactly what happened.

In a rather roundabout way, we come back to how individuals see the world: the need for information to make decisions and the fact that there exist screens to channel or distort the information received by decision makers. Although there are many aspects of an individual's governmental role that we could investigate, let us evaluate *role* as one factor that acts on the systematic omission of information.

Role and Screens: Organizational Process and Decisions

The word *role* has been used in several ways in this book, but the meaning has always involved an image of how a state, a government, or an individual thinks it should be acting. *Role* has been defined by Rosenau as "any aspect of the actor derived from his policy-making responsibilities and which is *expected* to characterize *any* person who fills the same position," (emphasis added). We can think of a role as the interaction between the individual and the political system. They come together in a role—the expectations of that system working on the individual. The individual, however, also must perceive and interpret these expectations. So although the role may constrain what an individual might do, it also has to be interpreted by the individual in light of that individual's personality and idiosyncracies.

For any position within a government, an individual comes into a situation where there already exists precedent, or the behavior of previous individuals who held that office. Role and individual elements are mixed in a complex fashion. A strong personality may overcome the constraints of precedent—someone unafraid to innovate or shock or to take political risks. Others may find it comfortable to tread a well-worn path. In Chapter 1 we noted that during his first six months as president, Harry Truman appeared inexperienced, unsure of himself, and strongly bound by the precedents set by Franklin Roosevelt (who had been president from 1933 until his death in April 1945).

An even trickier question is when does an idiosyncratic element become a role element? Nehru, for example, was responsible for Indian foreign policy for many years. Indeed, he was the foreign policy minister for the Indian Congress Party for over twenty years before India achieved independence in 1947. Because there had been no one before him, Nehru had great leeway in stamping his own personality and interpretation on Indian foreign policy. But as the years wore on and he behaved in accordance with his own previous actions, was he acting according to role or to his own idiosyncratic characteristics? Questions such as this apply to any individual who was the first to hold a certain position and did so for a long time; another example is Mao Tse-tung in China. One example of awareness of the power of precedent can be found in the behavior of George Washington. He was constantly aware that, as the first president, his actions would set precedents for those who followed. To show how this can be taken to extremes, Charles Frankel, writing of his experiences in the State Department, noted that "once things have happened, no matter how accidentally, they will be regarded as manifestations of an unchangeable Higher Reason."[13]

One's role is also defined by very specific statements of what an individual should be doing, such as legal statutes, constitutions, job descriptions, and one's position within an organization. These clearly set out an individual's duties and responsibilities. These are not as

---

13. See Charles Frankel's fascinating account of his experiences, *High on Foggy Bottom* (New York: Harper & Row, 1968).

important, however, as the expectations of an individual's fellow workers, both superiors and subordinates. Clearly, one is most concerned with the expectations of those people who are responsible for one's promotion within an organization or whose support is required to maintain one's position. We are now getting into the matter of the organizational setting and Allison's Organizational Process model. Individuals who want to retain their positions or to advance their careers are likely to behave as they think others expect them to behave.

The individual who performs a specific role is often expected to follow the needs and requirements of his or her organizational setting rather than his or her personal convictions. Before World War I, Winston Churchill deplored the naval arms race between Germany and Britain—recognizing that both states were spending large sums of money and raising international tensions in a competition to build more and better battleships. He also recognized that when the process was over, both sides would be in approximately the same relationship as before and thus it would all be futile. However, as first lord of the Admiralty, he went before Parliament and requested more funds for naval construction. Other examples of subordinating personal convictions to those of the organization include George Marshall, who as chief of staff of the U.S. Army opposed the State Department proposal to use aid to influence the Chinese government to institute reforms; however, in the late 1940s, as secretary of state under Harry Truman Marshall defended such a use of aid in China against challenges by the new chiefs of staff. When Samuel Hoare was the British secretary of state for air in the 1920s, he fought against naval control of the air forces within the Fleet Air Arm; ten years later, when he became first lord of the Admiralty, he argued exactly the opposite.

Clearly, the behavior expected by those in control of an organization limits the range of behavior of individuals within that organization. In addition, members of different organizations see different sides of a situation, depending on how that situation affects (and perhaps threatens) their organization. As Allison says, "Where you stand depends on where you sit." An individual's priorities and self-interests are seen to derive in large measure from his or her organization's self-interests. The "parochial" nature of organizations is one of the core concepts of the Organizational Process model. This means that each organization within a government has a narrow range of interests and priorities. The mission of that organization requires capabilities—the organization needs money and people. To get these, the organization needs influence within the government, especially on budget decisions and decisions that distribute new programs and responsibilities to government organizations. Each organization—and subgroup within that organization—sees its interests as being similar to and necessary ingredients of some national interest. They define the reason for their organization's existence in terms of "essence"—what missions an organization *should have*. For example, the essence of the U.S. Army is a ground combat capability. Various subgroups of the Air Force must struggle over the definition of the organization's essence—those involved in missiles see missiles as the main way to deliver nuclear weapons against the USSR, while another group sees combat airplanes as the main delivery system. The Navy sees its essence as maintaining combat ships to control the seas. The only problem is that people in submarines think this should be achieved by subs, air power proponents support the use of aircraft carriers, and sea power advocates stress surface combat ships.

Organizations are deeply concerned with "organizational health"—the protection (and often an expansion of the scope) of essence, defined in terms of budget allocations and human resource allocations. Because of this, members of the organization are expected to enhance the organization's health. For instance, an Army officer who opposes increases in the Army budget would find it more difficult to be promoted than one who followed role expectations. Organizational health can also be protected by demonstrating how successful the organization is (or, more commonly, its lack of mistakes). One reason why organizations follow standard operating procedures is to cut down on uncertainty and risk. Organizations behave incrementally for the same reason. But—and this is crucial for us at this point—the protection of the organization also entails providing information to decision makers that shows the organization in the best light. This involves withholding information that would embarrass the organization and implementing top-level decisions in a way that meets the best interests of the organization, not necessarily in the spirit of the decision handed down to the organization for implementation.[14]

---

14. In order to see that this is not simply an American phenomenon, read the famous diaries of the British Labor cabinet minister Richard Crossman, who describes how ministers are trapped, manipulated, ignored, and infuriated by bureaucrats who presume to know what is best for the ministry and hence the government and the country. See Anthony Howard (ed.), *The Crossman Diaries, 1964–1970* (London: Methuen, 1979). For example, see pp. 7–10 and pp. 92–98, where Crossman sums up his first six months as minister.

Morton Halperin, another advocate of the bureaucratic politics approach, summarizes our discussion with a list of things "every President should know":

> Organizations have interests. Career officials in these organizations believe that protecting these interests is vital to the security of the United States. They therefore take stands on issues which advocate these interests and maneuver to protect these interests against other organizations and senior officials, including the President.[15]

Halperin also summarizes four areas in which organizational parochialism affects policy. All of these call for role occupants to behave in the interest of the organization rather than in the interest of the state as a whole or out of individual conviction:

1. Organizations acquire information to protect their interests, supply others with information that will protect the organization, and get decision makers to see the situation in the way the organization desires.

2. Similarly, when the organization presents options, it attempts to give decision makers a "menu" of options, each of which will support and further the organization's essence.

3. The organization will also attempt to prevent top decision makers from selecting options from other organizations that will threaten the organization's interests.

4. The organization will implement decisions on the basis of organizational interests—it will delay, alter, and often disobey top-level directives.

In addition to the examples given us by students of bureaucratic politics (e.g., the way the Air Force reported bombing results in Vietnam, often using highly unreliable pilots' reports, which exaggerated bomb damage, rather than satellite or reconnaissance photographs or the withholding of crucial information by the CIA in the Bay of Pigs operation), there are numerous anecdotes of presidents giving up in despair at trying to get various sections of the bureaucracy to do what was wanted. Franklin Roosevelt was particularly vexed by the Treasury and the Navy; John Kennedy called the State Department a bowl of

---

15. See, for example, Morton H. Halperin, *Bureaucratic Politics and Foreign Policy* (Washington, D.C.: Brookings Institution, 1974), especially chaps. 2–4, 11, and 15.

jelly; FDR likened the Navy to a feather pillow (which, no matter how hard or long one punched it, always came out the same).

We have gone into Allison's models in such detail because the core of the Organizational Process model is the self-interested parochialism of organizations (of course, this is not limited to foreign policy or governmental organizations, but a well-known finding applicable to organizations in general). This parochialism is a major determinant of the expectations for a particular role. If individuals are indeed interested in getting ahead in their roles, then they will tend to meet those expectations—to support the parochial interests of the organization and to see the world as the organization sees it.

Although we will view the question of role-individual relationships from the other side in the next chapter, we should also briefly look at the conditions under which individuals break out of or reshape their role constraints. The longer a specific role exists, the more precedents are set, and the expectations for people holding the role become more widely held by other members of the government. Thus, as an institution becomes older and more complex, it is more difficult for an individual to shape a role in that institution. When Rosenau introduced the idea of role as a pretheoretical factor, he thought that role would be more important in developed countries. By this he meant the older, industrialized Western states, those with greater political (as well as economic) development. We noted above that new positions in government provide much more leeway for an individual to shape a role rather than be constrained by it. But also, the higher the role position in the government hierarchy, the less the role influence on the individual. The higher one goes, the fewer superiors one has and the more likely one is to be confronted with new or unexpected situations. Such situations are also more open to individual influences than those of a role.

Whether an individual can modify or shape a role, then, depends on factors such as the degree of precedent, the organizational context, and how old the role is. However, the impact of a role also depends on the individual's personality and especially his or her political skills. The Governmental Politics model (Model III) goes beyond the organizational background of the players to the personality and ability of the individual players to get their way in the various decision and action games played. Model III concerns the "power and the skill" of the individual players. Much of the power derives from an individual's position in government, or role, but this power can be expanded or reduced on the basis of the personality and skill of the players involved. Although William Rogers was secretary of state for most of the Nixon years, Henry Kissinger was the unquestioned primary adviser to the president on foreign policy and national security matters. Similarly, for John Kennedy it was the Secretary of Defense Robert McNamara who was dominant in foreign affairs, not Secretary of State Dean Rusk. Although the office of the secretary of state did not undergo any real role alteration, the strength and skill of its officeholders varied, as did their individual relations with their respective presidents.

Role and Small-Group Interaction

How an individual behaves within the constraints of his or her role is also affected by the immediate environment of the decision unit. As noted earlier, finding the decision unit may tell us a great deal about the decision being made. People studying organizations and social psychologists studying small-group behavior have found that being a member of a small group can affect both the perceptions and behavior of the individual very strongly. More specifically, there are pressures on the individual to conform to the view of the group and not to challenge it. In this process, the perceptions of the individual—in terms of both situation and role—may be altered to fit the collective views within the group. Here is an example not only of social decision processes (mostly through pressure on members to come to a consensus of some kind), but of a failure of those processes. One idea behind "partisan mutual adjustment" was that although each individual had limited information, perceived alternatives, and so on, when that individual interacted with others, a wide range of information and alternatives was considered. We shall see that this need not be the case.

A number of laboratory experiments run by psychologists demonstrate the pressures to conform that a small group can have on its members. One experiment had a group of six to eight people comparing visual stimuli—the length of two lines, for example. However, only one member of the group was actually being observed; the others (unknown to the single subject) had been instructed to give false answers. The subject, then, heard the others in this small group saying that the shorter line was longer, the smaller cube was larger, and so forth. At first, subjects acted puzzled and upset. But the experiments indicated that they then began to conform and to describe the stimuli as the others did![16]

---

16. See, for example, S. E. Asch, "Effects of Group Pressure upon Modification and Distortion of Judgment," in D. Cartwright and A. Zander (eds.), *Group Dynamics, Research and Theory* (Evanston, Ill.: Row, Peterson, 1953), pp. 189–200.

On version of the individual's conformity to small-group views has been studied by Irving Janis—a phenomenon he calls *groupthink*.[17] In his study, Janis looked at a number of American foreign policy decisions, such as the Bay of Pigs invasion in 1961, the response to the North Korean invasion of South Korea in 1950, the decision to set up the Marshall Plan, the decisions to escalate the war in Vietnam, the decision making about Pearl Harbor prior to the attack, and the Cuban missile crisis of 1962. Janis sums up his central theme as follows: "The more amiability and esprit de corps among the members of a policy-making in-group, the greater is the danger that independent critical thinking will be replaced with groupthink, which is likely to result in irrational and dehumanizing actions directed against outgroups."

Janis comes up with a number of major symptoms of groupthink. In terms of self-image, a close and amiable group will produce an *illusion of invulnerability*. This feeling and view of one's group is overly optimistic and encourages risks. Other research has identified the phenomenon of the "risky shift." Studies have shown that by themselves, individuals respond to real and hypothetical situations in a more conservative way than when they are in a group. For a variety of reasons, the same individuals are willing to take much riskier behavior when asked about the same situations in a group setting, despite individual or role factors.

A second symptom also involves self-images. This is the group's unquestioned belief in its own morality. The group setting leads the individual members to feel that this group of decent fellows could not be anything but good. This symptom will foster group screening by leading the group members to ignore the ethical or moral consequences of their decisions; the assumption is that the group is moral, and therefore the decisions of the group will be also. At the same time, the third symptom is a stereotyped view of the opponent's leadership as being too evil or stupid to negotiate with on a good-faith basis.

The groupthink process, then, leads to a shared illusion of unanimity (often overcoming role influences). This symptom derives from several other symptoms. Groupthink leads to efforts to rationalize the group's decisions—to justify them no matter what they might be. This helps to screen out any warnings or counterinformation that might lead the group to reconsider its decisions. Groupthink also leads to direct pressure on any individual who argues against the stereotypes that the

---

17. Irving Janis, *Groupthink*, 2nd ed. (Boston: Houghton Mifflin, 1982).

group produces; it leads to *self-censorship* of doubts and counterarguments (much as the perception experiment described above).

The conditions that promote groupthink derive from group cohesiveness—how well knit the group is, how well it sticks together. This also includes isolating the group from outsiders and outside views, as well as information that might challenge the images of the group. Finally, the appearance of a group leader who promotes a preferred solution is another major influence on the creation of groupthink. It is not necessary for the others in the group to be mere toadies or "yes men" for this effect to take place. A person becomes a leader because of a number of personal and role characteristics; others in the group will go along with him or her because of shared values or because of the leader's control of promotion decisions.

A good example of this is the American decision to send military aid immediately to South Korea after the administration was informed of the North Korean attack. President Truman walked into the meeting of his advisers and approved the plan presented by Secretary of State Acheson. The rest of the discussion was based on that view rather than any other. Indeed, one of the reasons so little groupthink occurred during the Cuban crisis was because John Kennedy consciously removed himself from a number of the sessions of the ExComm so that his presence would not inhibit the broadest possible review of options and views (an interesting mixture of the intellectual and social processes at work). Other aspects of the Cuban decision are also interesting. Groupthink was avoided because each participant acted as a generalist—*not* as a representative of a particular role. He was also supposed to be as skeptical and challenging as possible in a very informal atmosphere without a formal agenda or rules of protocol.

A variety of possible remedies for groupthink have been suggested by scholars, from "devil's advocacy" (having an individual whose job is to challenge all assumptions and decisions) to multiple advocacy. In the latter, chief executives are advised to ensure that individuals with a range of views are encouraged to advocate those views and to make sure that they all can be heard.[18] Such phenomena as groupthink probably cannot be eliminated, but they can be reduced, and decision makers can be alerted to their existence and the effects such phenomena can have on decisions and actions.

---

18. See, for example, Alexander L. George, "The Case for Multiple Advocacy in Making Foreign Policy," *American Political Science Review* 66 (1972), 751–785.

CONCLUSION

A number of scholars have combined the Organizational Process model with the Governmental Politics model to get a bureaucratic politics model that takes on the organizational and political components of each. The bureaucratic politics model can be summarized in three questions about the foreign policy process: Who plays? What determines each player's stand? How do these different positions merge to yield governmental decisions and actions? Role is very important in answering the first question. Both role and idiosyncratic factors are important in answering the second. Both of these plus governmental factors (communications channels and structures, the institutional hierarchy, and so on) are important for answering the third.

In the bureaucratic politics model, what a government does in any particular situation should be seen largely as the result of bargaining among the players. These players should be seen as being positioned hierarchically within the government (role factors). The bargaining follows regularized "circuits" (role and governmental factors). Finally, the bargaining and the results, the decision games and the action games, are affected by a number of constraints, especially the organizational processes (roles) and the individual political skill of the players (idiosyncracies). This is yet another indication of the complex and close interaction between an individual's role position and personal idiosyncracies. Another indication is the picture presented by the results of two studies using the same data. James Rosenau looked at American senators and their behavior toward Secretaries of State Acheson and Dulles. Rosenau concluded that party and committee roles were the primary influences at work. Subsequently, Glenn Stassen reanalyzed the data and concluded that the belief systems of the senators (based on attitudes of isolationism and Cold War images) were the primary explanatory factors, accounting for behavior that could not be explained by the role variables used by Rosenau.[19] This close connection between role and individual factors will be further examined in Chapter 12, where we shall look at general statements concerning how individuals perceive the world about them and how idiosyncratic differences affect the foreign policy process.

---

19. James N. Rosenau, "Private Preferences and Political Responsibilities: The Relative Potency of Individual and Role Variables in the Behavior of U.S. Senators," in J. David Singer (ed.), *Quantitative International Politics* (New York: Free Press, 1968), pp. 17–50; Glenn H. Stassen, "Individual Preferences Versus Role-Constraint in Policy-Making: Senatorial Response to Secretaries Acheson and Dulles," *World Politics* 25 (1972), 96–119.

12

INDIVIDUALS AND WORLD POLITICS: PERCEIVING THE WORLD

LOOKING AT THE INDIVIDUAL

We are now concerned with the impact of individuals—their needs, desires, and images—on government and on foreign policy decisions. This entails the differences between the images of the world that decision makers hold and the real world. To quote the observations of scholars who have studied how people perceive enemies in politics:

> In a striking section of *The Hero in History,* Sidney Hook tries to imagine "A World without Lenin" in order to demonstrate the historical importance of what he calls the "event-making man." In political science, no less than history, we must also confront the problem with which Hook wrestles. Stated more formally, we are concerned with the impact of personal as well as institutional, cultural, social, and economic factors on the conduct of politics.[1]

---

1. David J. Finlay, Ole R. Holsti, and Richard R. Fagen, *Enemies in Politics* (Chicago: Rand McNally, 1967), p. 233.

In Chapter 11 we tried to highlight factors that influence a person involved in decision making; several more factors will be reviewed in the sections below. We shall look at the personal characteristics of individuals that are relevant to diplomacy and intragovernmental bargaining. This relates to the study of the leader and leadership itself. The study of the images held by foreign policy decision makers—the *psychological environment* of foreign policy leaders—involves the study of their belief systems and how their images of other peoples, states, leaders, and situations affect their decisions and behavior. Here we recognize that the psychological environment limits the menu just as the other environments do. We recognize the need to look at the cognitive constraints on rationality.

Before studying these things, several assumptions must be made. The first is that foreign policy is made and implemented by people. In other words, we are taking a kind of decision-making approach; we do not see states as monolithic, impersonal creatures that somehow behave on their own. The second assumption is that individuals can make a difference in the foreign policy process of a given state. This means that the governmental structure, as well as the basic processes of policymaking, permit individuals to have an impact on foreign policy. This is the point that Hook was making in the quotation above. Presidents, secretaries of state, prime ministers, foreign ministers, revolutionary leaders, and dictators can strongly influence the foreign policy process of their own states and of others'. Although he never admitted that he could be analyzed either psychologically or psychoanalytically, Henry Kissinger was a firm believer in the importance of the individual statesman in history; as a practicing diplomat, he felt he had to know and understand the psychological makeup of foreign diplomats and decision makers. In addition to this view (which prompted him to have American intelligence services draw up psychological profiles of the foreign leaders with whom he negotiated), he saw individuals as important to the outcomes of diplomacy and history: "But when you see [history] in practice, you see the differences that the personalities make. The overtures to China would not have worked without Chou En-lai. There would have been no settlement in the Middle East without Sadat and Golda Meir or Dayan."[2] Special Counsel Theodore Sorensen noted that on Sunday, October 28, 1962, after hearing that Khrushchev agreed to all of Kennedy's terms about Cuba, there had

---

2. Quoted in Hugh Sidey, "An International Natural Resource," *Time* (February 4, 1974), 24.

been speculation over "what would have happened . . . if John F. Kennedy had not been President of the United States."

The third assumption derives from the first two: given that foreign policy is made by people and that individuals can have an impact, how these people see the world should be important. What affects how they see the world? Is it something called "human nature"? The constitution of UNESCO contains the famous phrase "Since wars begin in the minds of men, it is in the minds of men that the defenses of peace must be constructed." All of this goes into the study of what we called the *individual factor*. The unique characteristics that affect an individual's decision making and behavior include a number of things that are relatively easy to study and some that are quite difficult. An individual's idiosyncrasies are made up of values, personality, political style, intellect, and past experience. They work together, creating the individual's set of images about the world or the belief system.

Some of the data on individual idiosyncrasies may be difficult to obtain, however, and once they are obtained, they may be difficult to interpret. We require biographical information on decision makers, but we also want information on their world views, their values and opinions, their personalities, and their styles of behavior. In particular, we need to know how these factors are used to form images and how the images work. For foreign policy decision makers, we have a very difficult problem of "access"—how do we get to them while they are embedded within the vast and overlapping governmental structure of the modern state? In a well-known observation, political scientist Richard Brody inquired, "How can we give a Taylor Manifest Anxiety Scale to Khrushchev during the Hungarian Revolt, a Semantic-Differential to Chiang Kai-shek while Quemoy is being shelled, or simply interview Kennedy during the Cuban missile crisis?"[3] The answer, of course, is that we cannot.

The psychological or *psychohistorical* study of individuals requires imagination and creative research programs. Interviews with the subjects themselves are most useful, but sometimes the best available method is interviewing people close to the subject.[4] There have been psychoanalytic studies of written and spoken materials and the psychoanalysis of biographical and historical details of an individual's life.

---

3. Richard Brody, "The Study of International Politics Qua Science," in Klaus Knorr and James N. Rosenau (eds.), *Contending Approaches to International Politics* (Princeton, N.J.: Princeton University Press, 1969), p. 116.

4. For example, Bruce Mazlish has done this in his psychobiographical study of Henry Kissinger, *Kissinger: The European Mind in American Policy* (New York: Basic Books, 1976).

Access may also be achieved by *content analysis*—a systematic study of the communications produced by an individual that makes inferences from the subject's words. This may be done in a highly formal, quantitative fashion or in a less formal fashion, such as operational-code analyses (described below). Other analyses use content analysis or similar techniques (such as questionnaires) to determine psychological characteristics of an individual and then correlate those characteristics with behavior. Finally, there are a number of *artificial* techniques by which one tries to study the behavior of people in general under certain conditions. This can be done in the psychologist's laboratory or in simulations and gaming activities run by governments, political scientists, or others. These include all-human role-playing games, simulations that combine people with complex computer-generated information, and all-computer simulations. The results of these experiments are then used to form hypotheses about how decision makers might behave under similar conditions and to help guide research on decision makers—what we should look at, what we should look for, and how we might explain what we find.[5]

The Operational-Code Approach

As one example of these approaches, let us review the operational-code approach. In the early 1950s, Nathan Leites reviewed Russian literature and the writings of the Bolsheviks in order to reconstruct the belief system of the Russian Communist leaders—to discover their images of the outside world. His aim was to determine the Bolshevik image of reality, and from this to try to understand the behavior of the leaders. This approach has since been modified into a set of ten questions asked about a subject as a way to get at the subject's view of the world. There are philosophical questions, such as "Is the political universe essentially one of harmony or conflict?", "Is the political future predictable?", and "How much control or mastery can one have over historical development?" There are also instrumental questions concerning one's style of behavior in the political world, such as "What is the best ap-

---

5. For a review of the applicability of various content analytic approaches to the study of foreign policy decision makers, see Harvey Starr, "The Kissinger Years: Studying Individuals and Foreign Policy," *International Studies Quarterly* 24 (1980), 465–496; for a full study that actually employs a variety of these techniques, see Harvey Starr, *Henry Kissinger: Perceptions of International Politics* (Lexington: University Press of Kentucky, 1984).

proach for selecting goals or objectives for political action?" and "What is the best timing of action to advance one's interests?"

The operational code has been applied to a number of foreign policy decision makers. It is especially useful in studying individuals who wrote a large number of books and other works before reaching high office. These writings should reveal a broad set of beliefs about the political world in general. By looking at views set out before taking office, it is possible to match those views with the individual's behavior after taking office. Studies of a number of American secretaries of state, such as Dean Acheson, John Foster Dulles, and Henry Kissinger, have followed this procedure.[6]

In addition to access, different interpretations of the same data pose another problem. This latter problem affects the analysis of operational-code studies and is particularly vexing in psychoanalytic studies, where different observers may interpret events in an individual's life in a number of ways. But the question of interpretation returns us to the question of whether individual factors are really important or whether role influences are the ones that matter. Here we take up the question of role and individual factors addressed earlier from a different angle, by looking at the circumstances or conditions under which individual traits are likely to affect decisions. For example, just as Rosenau proposed that the role would be more important in economically developed states, he proposed that idiosyncratic factors would be more important in underdeveloped states—societies that are generally new and small and lack established roles or highly structured bureaucracies. He also proposed that idiosyncratic factors would be at work more in closed societies than open ones—where the leader is less constrained by the influence of public opinion and interest groups. Idi Amin's rule in Uganda was a good example of a new state, small in many ways and underdeveloped both economically and politically, where one man and his idiosyncrasies dominated a system.

---

6. See Nathan Leites, *The Operational Code of the Politburo* (New York: McGraw-Hill, 1951); Alexander George, "The Operational Code: A Neglected Approach to the Study of Political Decision-Making," *International Studies Quarterly* 13 (1969), 190–222. See also David McLellan, "The 'Operational Code' Approach to the Study of Political Leaders: Dean Acheson's Philosophical and Instrumental Beliefs," *Canadian Journal of Political Science* 4 (1971), 52–75; Ole R. Holsti, "The 'Operational Code' Approach to the Study of Political Leaders: John Foster Dulles' Philosophical and Instrumental Beliefs," *Canadian Journal of Political Science* 3 (1970), 123–157; Stephen G. Walker, "The Interface between Beliefs and Behavior: Henry Kissinger's Operational Code and the Vietnam War," *Journal of Conflict Resolution* 21 (1977), 129–168.

Research also indicates a number of other circumstances where idiosyncratic variables have a greater effect on decisions and behavior and where knowledge of these factors are useful. As we noted before, in nonroutine situations such as crises, which require more than the quasi-mechanical application of standard operating procedures, the idiosyncracies of decision makers are more in evidence. Again, decisions made at the top of a governmental hierarchy, where the individuals are less constrained by pressures for promotion or by superiors, will have more idiosyncratic influences on them. Other situations containing uncertainty or ambiguity are also open to individual influences—the subjective guesses of what should be done and a greater reliance on the values of the decision makers (what *should* be done?). Long-range planning, for example, involves a good deal of uncertainty and involves questions such as "What is important?" and "What is likely?" These decisions look like the general foreign policy decisions discussed in Chapter 11. As primarily social decisions, they also call on the individual skill of decision makers—including their political style and their ways in dealing with interpersonal relations. Those situations involving very poor or very scarce information will also depend a great deal on an individual's existing images and beliefs. At the other extreme, in situations of information overload, images come to the fore as screening mechanisms; again the values, beliefs, and images of the individual will highly color the decisions and actions taken. Very complex situations can cause this form of overload; such situations are then handled by the use of simplified images and beliefs.

Many of these points are summarized in Figure 12.1, which indicates how the nature of a situation relates to the decision maker, his or her idiosyncracies, and his or her place in the government's foreign policy apparatus.

BELIEF SYSTEMS: IMAGES AND PERCEPTIONS

Three things have to occur before a situation exists for the foreign policy decision maker—that is, before there is a problem, which is the first step in the ideal decision-making process. First, there has to be some sort of *stimulus* from the environment—a "trigger event." That stimulus then has to be perceived in some way. *Perception* is the second thing that must occur. It is a process by which an individual selects, organizes, and evaluates incoming information about the surrounding world. *Interpretation* of the perceived stimulus is the third thing. Both

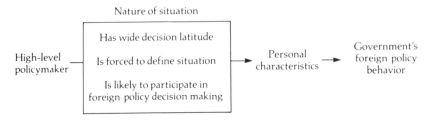

Figure 12.1
The conditions under which individual factors are expected to affect foreign policy behavior. [*Source:* Margaret G. Hermann, "Effects of Personal Characteristics of Political Leaders on Foreign Policy," in Maurice East et al. (eds.), *Why Nations Act: Theoretical Perspectives for Comparative Foreign Policy Studies* (Sage Focus Editions, vol. 2) copyright © 1978, p. 54, by permission of the publisher, Sage Publications, Inc. (Beverly Hills/London).]

perception and interpretation depend heavily on the images that already exist in the mind of the individual decision maker.

Ole Holsti has provided us with a diagrammatic representation of perceptions and their relationship to images and the belief system (Figure 12.2). Many scholars have noted that an individual's response to some situation—some *stimulus*—will be based on his or her *perception* of that situation or stimulus and not necessarily on the objective nature of the stimulus itself. Decision makers, like all other human beings, are subject to the many psychological processes that affect perception—

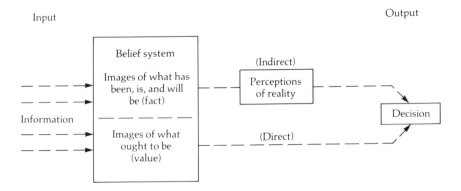

Figure 12.2
The relationship between the belief system and foreign policy decision making. [*Source:* Ole R. Holsti, "The Belief System and National Images: A Case Study," *Journal of Conflict Resolution* 6 (1962), 245. By permission of the publisher, Sage Publications, Inc.]

defense mechanisms, reduction of anxiety, rationalization, displacement, and repression—and many other psychological processes and characteristics that make up our individual personalities.

Our images affect our perceptions in a number of ways. Initially, a person's values and beliefs help determine his or her attention—what is selected as a stimulus and what is actually looked at and attended to. Then, on the basis of previous attitudes and images, the stimulus is interpreted. An *open image* means that new information, contradictory information, or modifying information is incorporated into existing images, changing them to fit reality. A *closed image* is one that, for a number of psychological reasons, resists change and thus ignores or reshapes contradictory information or selects only the little bits and pieces that might be used to support the image already held. But whether open or closed, *images are screens*. Each of us is attentive only to part of the world around us, and each of us has a different set of images for interpreting incoming information. Perception, based on images already held, is a selective process. As Anatol Rapoport notes, "Since we must select, we must be blind to what we have left out."[7] A *belief system* is the collection of beliefs, images, or "models" of the world that any individual holds: "The belief system is composed of a more or less integrated set of images which make up the entire relevant universe for the individual. They encompass past, present, and expectations of future reality, and value preferences of 'what ought to be.'" Thus, the belief system performs some very important functions for the individual; it helps orient the individual to the environment, organizes perceptions as a guide to behavior, helps establish goals, and acts as a filter to select relevant information in any given situation.[8]

Returning to our ideal rational model developed in Chapter 11, we see that even if we could obtain perfect information about alternatives and consequences, problems of perception make meaningless the notion of an ideally rational choice of alternatives. From all that information, only some of it will be perceived or selected. The *interpretation* of the information will depend on the individual decision maker's belief system and images. It is not clear what *rational* means, if two or more individuals in the same situation, receiving the same information,

---

7. Anatol Rapoport, *Fights, Games and Debates* (Ann Arbor: University of Michigan Press, 1960), chap. 16. Note that Rapoport sees the object of debate as modifying the image the opponent has of the situation and oneself.

8. Ole R. Holsti, "The Belief System and National Images: John Foster Dulles and the Soviet Union," Ph.D. diss., Stanford University, 1962, pp. 5–6.

make different choices because they see and interpret the information differently on the basis of different images. *Misperception* means that, for any number of reasons, the behavior of one state or its decision makers is seen to diverge from what has actually taken place or diverges from the meaning of the act intended by the state or decision makers taking that action. Studies of the European leaders in the weeks immediately preceding the outbreak of World War I strongly support this observation.[9] Another scholar, John Stoessinger, wrote a book based on thirteen case studies of situations between the United States and the USSR and China where misperception had important effects on foreign policy. Stoessinger was interested in four types of perceptions (and the images that guided those perceptions): each state's self-image and each state's perception of the adversary's character, power and capabilities, and intentions.[10]

Mechanisms of Selective Perception

Misperception really means that images are screening out important signals in some way—either ignoring them completely, interpreting them incorrectly, or changing the information to fit existing images. Images act as *intervening variables,* mediating between the incoming information and the behavior based on that information. Let us point out several psychological processes and mechanisms by which decision makers process information and select it on the basis of held images.[11]

One important consideration has been highlighted by Robert Jervis (and also by Ole Holsti in his study of John Foster Dulles). The various information-screening processes that occur in the course of perceiving the world are *normal processes.* We mean *normal* in both senses—that they are found widely among people and, in particular, among decision makers and found not only among "madmen" who distort their images of the world. In order for decision makers to act at all in a

---

9. See, for example, Ole Holsti, *Crisis, Escalation, War* (Montreal: McGill-Queen's University Press, 1972).

10. John G. Stoessinger, *Nations in Darkness: China, Russia and America* (New York: Random House, 1971). Jack Levy has also looked at misperceptions of capabilities and intentions in theorizing about the causes of war in "Misperception and the Causes of War: Theoretical Linkages and Analytical Problems," *World Politics* 36 (1983), 76–99.

11. Perhaps the most inclusive work in this area is Robert Jervis' excellent book, *Perception and Misperception In International Politics* (Princeton, N.J.: Princeton University Press, 1976); much of this section is based on Jervis' study.

complex world of information overload (or at least one filled with tremendous amounts of noise), they must use screens, including the perceptual ones. Keeping this in mind, what are some of the major reasons and ways in which decision makers perceive the world selectively? People try to achieve *cognitive consistency*. This means that the images they hold do not clash with or contradict each other. Sometimes new information forces an image to change so that it contradicts other images; this often happens when information contradicts a negative stereotype of a group of people or of an enemy. Rather than change one image and cause a reappraisal of others, a person may simply ignore or reshape the new information. John Foster Dulles, according to research by Holsti, did this to maintain his image of the Soviet Union as being aggressive, imperialistic, and cooperative only when weak or frightened.

Another mechanism that influences selective perception is the *evoked set*. People perceive and evaluate the world according to what they are concerned with at the moment. Rapoport has called this the "blindness of involvement." The use of historical analogies, though often imperfect, also leads to selective perception—looking for those details of a present episode that look like a past one, while ignoring the important differences.[12] One of the most famous examples of this mechanism is the "Munich syndrome." Decision makers in the United States and Britain who had been active during the 1930s, when the Western democracies attempted to appease Hitler (of which the Munich agreement was the main symbol), tended to use this traumatic event as an analogue for many postwar events that only partially resembled it. The Suez crisis of 1956 was generated in part by the selective perceptions of British Prime Minister Anthony Eden, who saw Nasser of Egypt as another Hitler and thus one who could not be appeased. The historical analogy necessitated selecting certain aspects of the situation and ignoring others. A study of the effect of Reagan's belief system on his dealings with the Soviet Union suggests that he has been similarly affected by the Cuban missile crisis, which has served as his main historical analogy.[13]

Another related process that affects perception is the process of *wishful thinking*, the influence of fears and desires on perception. We often see either what we fear or what we wish to be the case. In a content

---

12. See, for example, Ernest R. May, *"Lessons" of the Past* (New York: Oxford University Press, 1973).

13. See Russell Leng, "Reagan and the Russians: Crisis Bargaining Beliefs and the Historical Record," *American Political Science Review* 78 (1984), 338–355.

analytic study of the chief European decision makers in the period immediately before World War I, it was seen that the Kaiser feared England, which had been ruled until recently by an uncle whom he had also feared. Apparently the Kaiser also perceived the events that he was afraid would come true. Simply hearing that the British felt they still had freedom of action caused the Kaiser to write: "The net has been suddenly thrown over our heads and England sneeringly reaps the most brilliant success of her persistently prosecuted anti-German world policy." Similarly, leaders who wished to see peace thought they saw it when Chamberlain returned to Britain from Munich exulting that there was "peace in our time." The strong desire for peace led many of the conservative followers of Chamberlain to see the carving up of Czechoslovakia as the act that would indeed placate Hitler and preserve the peace—although there was really no evidence at all that this was the case.

Returning to the work of Robert Jervis, we may also briefly set out some of the common misperceptions that have been found to recur in foreign policy. First, foreign policy decision makers often underestimate how *unclear* a message, speech, or other communication may be to someone else (in spite of the sender's efforts). Second, decision makers often do not realize that their behavior may not convey what they *intend* to communicate. They assume that others will understand their actions and behavior much more easily than is the case.

These two observations are directly related to the more substantive misperceptions common in foreign policy. An important one is the tendency for decision makers to see other states, particularly adversaries or competitors, as more hostile than they are. Again, perception leads one to select the information that supports hostility or to interpret behavior as being hostile. Because others are seen as more hostile, some of the phenomena related to the image of an enemy take place (to be discussed below). One sees the behavior of other states as more centralized and coordinated than it really is. One ignores or underestimates the role of chance, mistakes, and particularly the influence of bureaucratic politics when looking at the behavior of other states. This result derives from the use of the Rational Actor model—which sees the other state as monolithic, acting in a rational, single-minded way, and every event having a good reason for occurring. When others act in the way you want, the tendency is to overestimate the influence you had on the opponent's behavior (such as "cold warriors" in the United States taking credit for the lack of a Soviet-initiated war in the past thirty-five years: "We deterred them from doing what they wanted").

On the other hand, when the adversary does something undesired, the tendency is not to say, "It seems I have no influence with him," but to find other, usually internal forces to explain the behavior. When the United States was unable to achieve a strong and stable state in South Vietnam, it was considered not due to U.S. failure or to the lack of will and capability in the South, but to external intervention from the North.

Psychological Processes Affecting Perception

We have already touched on another psychological process, that of seeing others as opponents or enemies. Once this happens, the opponent labeled "enemy" takes on certain characteristics—and we then behave toward that state in certain ways. As several observers have shown, this view is a powerful influence on the perceptions and behavior of the leaders of states.[14] Some of the psychological processes that distort reality are *defense mechanisms.* These act to protect the individual from things that would otherwise make him or her uncomfortable and anxious. One defense process is called *projection*—where we project onto others feelings, characteristics, and desires that we cannot admit exist in ourselves.

A major factor in projection is the existence of a *scapegoat*—an excuse for failings we cannot admit. An enemy acts as a scapegoat in that it is accused of the things that one dislikes in oneself. The accusation is used to justify one's own behavior, which is similar to that of the opponent. In foreign relations an enemy is usually seen as being aggressive and seeking dominance and conquest—a state capable of evil and brutality (Dulles saw the Soviet Union as atheistic and evil). Being able to crusade against such an enemy brings great psychological satisfaction. One can ignore one's own behavior and preserve one's self-image because no matter how badly one is behaving, the object of that behavior is an even more evil enemy. Much of this sort of behavior was observed in the United States during the Vietnam war, when some Americans refused to question various U.S. tactics such as napalm bombing, the torture of prisoners, or the My Lai massacre.

---

14. See David J. Finlay, Ole R. Holsti, and Richard R. Fagen, *Enemies in Politics* (Chicago: Rand McNally, 1967); Arthur L. Gladstone, "The Concept of the Enemy," *Journal of Conflict Resolution* 3 (1959), 132–137; Ralph K. White, *Nobody Wanted War: Misperception in Vietnam and Other Wars* (New York: Doubleday, 1970). Much of the following discussion is based on the work of Gladstone.

Having an enemy allows one the satisfaction of recognizing one's own moral superiority—of having a cause and being needed by that cause to oppose and defeat the enemy as well as having the satisfaction of being able to hate and kill without being bothered by one's conscience. Having an enemy permits one to see the world in easy (non-anxiety-producing) black-and-white images—clear-cut distinctions of good and evil. It helps to define the "we" by having a nasty "they."

Ralph White, in a study of the two world wars and the Vietnam war, has spoken of a "Black-White Diabolical Enemy Image." Included in this is a "virile self-image"—the positive self-image already noted. But the image of the enemy also distorts the view of the opponent. By seeing the opponent as something evil, there is a lack of empathy, the inability to see the world as the opponent might see it. This gives only a very incomplete view of a situation—and a dangerous one at that—by not seeing how virtuous behavior may appear to the other party and how it may worsen a situation. In addition, seeing one as an enemy often screens out any conciliatory, cooperative, or tension-reducing behavior of the opponent. Ignoring this may result in ignoring chances to stop a war before it starts or to end a war already begun.

This has indeed been the result discovered in several studies. A major content analysis study of the European decision makers in the period prior to the outbreak of World War I indicated that the decision makers of each state perceived threats of hostile behavior (whether correctly or not) from the states in the other alliance; these perceptions led to hostile behavior toward the opposing states. Stated differently, other states were seen as enemies—they were in opposing military alliances and had engaged in arms races and in competition for colonies. Those who were enemies were then seen as behaving in a hostile manner (whether they were doing so or not). This hostility was then matched by the perceiver's hostility. This type of process is known as a *conflict spiral* and can escalate a minor incident (or, indeed, one that might not have even happened) into a war. Ralph White's study of the Vietnam war similarly found that misperception of the adversary led to the escalation of hostile activity.

When such images are held by each side in a conflict, then there is a *mirror image situation*. Each side sees the other as an enemy or a devil, and each sees itself as moral, virile, and so on. The term "mirror image" was popularized in a study that looked not at decision makers, but at the images that ordinary people of the Soviet Union and the United States held of each other. Each side saw the other as aggressors, as having a government that exploits and deludes its people, as being a

country where the mass of the people do not support their government, as being a country that cannot be trusted, and as having a policy
that bordered on madness. A study of the protracted Arab-Israeli conflict also indicates that a major factor in the continuation of the hostility is the set of perceptions held by the people in the region. One side's
perception of the other is a classic image of the enemy, and each side
returns these feelings in a classic mirror image situation.[15]

The mirror image nature of the Soviet-American relationship has
been supported by a study of foreign policy events. A number of models of the Cold War were studied using chronologies of U.S.-Soviet
foreign policy events. The results indicated an exact mirror image
model. Both the United States and the Soviet Union exhibited the same
pattern, interpreted as follows: "I am a 'consolidationist' [a state that
seeks only to preserve what it has and not to expand]; he knows that I
am consolidationist; but he is an expansionist."[16] As with the conflict
spiral, a mirror image such as this may keep a conflict going for a long
time and make it that much more difficult to end.

A number of writers hope that the analysis of such selective perception or misperception may sensitize decision makers to the dangers
that exist. Robert Jervis has said that he would like to make decision
makers "more thoughtful" about how they communicate to others, interpret others' behavior, and feel their own behavior appears to an
opponent. Decision makers should be made aware that they do not
make unbiased analyses but are influenced by the images they hold.
Because such images are held, the theories they generate should be
made as explicit as possible, so that decision makers and others understand the basis for decisions and actions. Being explicit will also help
decision makers see if they and other governmental groups have tied
their decisions to a specific set of images. It will also help them look at
the situation and the decision differently.

Other advice to decision makers has included such things as trying
to put oneself in the place of the opponent and seeing what the sit-

---

15. See Uri Bronfenbrenner, "The Mirror Image in Soviet-American Relations," *Journal
of Social Issues* 17 (1961), 45–56. A partial report of the Middle East study is Edward E.
Azar and Chung-In Moon, "Protracted Social Conflict in the Third World," paper presented at the annual meeting of the American Political Science Association, Washington,
D.C., 1984.

16. William Gamson and Andre Modigliani, *Untangling the Cold War* (Boston: Little,
Brown, 1971). Possible support for this analysis may be that even at the height of Cold
War tension, war did not break out. Such a nonevent may be the result of successful
deterrence. It might also, however, be the result of two states that were not expansionist
but simply trying to protect existing spheres of influence.

uation looks like from the other side—"seeing with the eyes of the other."[17] Related to this is the attempt to understand how things work on the other side—to go beyond the Rational Actor model. A critical evaluation of policies should be built into the system. This would help evaluate decisions from a framework outside the images and beliefs of one person or a small group of people. Following these sorts of suggestions (including the devil's advocate or multiple-advocacy procedures noted in Chapter 11), may begin to correct the selective self-images and images of others that pervade foreign policy analysis.

The following excerpt describing how American decision makers view the United States and the Soviet Union is a good example of all the pitfalls described. It also fits into Stoessinger's study of self-image and the image of the opponent's intentions and capabilities.

> I have heard it argued: "Oh, well, they [the Soviets] know we [the U.S.] have no aggressive intentions. They know we have no idea of using these arms for an attack on them." To this there are two things to be said. When one attempts to explain to people in the Pentagon and to like-minded civilians that perhaps the Russians are not really eager to attack the West—that they have very good reasons for not planning or wishing to do anything of that sort, one is met with the reply: "Ah, yes, but look at the size of their armaments, and concede that in matters of this sort we cannot be bothered to take into account their intentions—intentions are too uncertain and too hard to determine; we can take into account only capabilities; we must assume the Russians to be desirous, that is, of doing anything bad to us that their capabilities would permit them to do." Now it is our view that *we* should take account only of *their capabilities*, disregarding *their intentions*, but we should expect them to take account only of *our* supposed *intentions*, disregarding *our capabilities?* . . . If we are going to disregard everything but their capabilities, we cannot simultaneously expect them to disregard everything but our intentions."[18]

AFFECTING THE IMAGE: PERSONALITY AND PERSONAL IDIOSYNCRACIES

Recently there has been a marked growth in various psychological, psychoanalytical, and personality studies of individual foreign policy decision makers, as well as "comparative foreign policy" studies of

---

17. See, for example, Joseph DeRivera, *The Psychological Dimension of Foreign Policy* (Columbus, Ohio: Merrill, 1968); Alexander George et al., *The Limits of Coercive Diplomacy* (Boston: Little, Brown, 1971); Irving L. Janis, *Groupthink*, 2nd ed. (Boston: Houghton Mifflin, 1982).

18. George Kennan, *The Cloud of Danger* (Boston: Little, Brown, 1978), pp. 87–88, (emphasis added).

leaders compared on the basis of personality characteristics. In the study of political leaders and personality, many people find most interesting (or most fascinating) examples of aberrant personalities—the psychotic leader and his or her impact on policy. One of the classic studies of this type was done by Alexander and Juliet George on Woodrow Wilson. The Georges suggest that Wilson's approach to a number of issues related to power and control over others, such as his unwillingness to compromise with political opponents in crucial situations (such as the ratification of the Treaty of Versailles, where the Senate's failure to ratify killed Wilson's dream of American participation), were consequences of his childhood relationship with his father. Wilson's need to dominate others stemmed from his competition with and aggression toward his father. They say that "political power was for him [Wilson] a compensatory value, a means of restoring the self-esteem damaged in childhood."[19]

Studies of Hitler and Stalin also reveal basic personality disturbances. Stalin's paranoia was matched in the early Cold War period in the United States by that of James Forrestal, the first secretary of defense, who tragically committed suicide. Extreme personality disturbances are relatively rare among leaders of large bureaucratized organizations like nation-states, especially under normal conditions where a potential leader has to work his or her way up through the organization over a long time. People who think or act very peculiarly will be weeded out of positions of leadership or will fail to be promoted.

A person with a severe personality disturbance is likely to spend so much energy coping with psychological problems that he or she will be unable to perform at the level required for high achievement in a large organization. During times of great social and political upheaval, however, a person with very unusual personality characteristics may achieve power when normal people are unable to cope with social problems. Hitler, for instance, came to power after terrible inflation and unemployment in Germany; Stalin during the upheaval following a revolution and civil war. Moreover, a leader—especially one entrenched for many years in an authoritarian system—may become much more abnormal in behavior over time. Both Hitler and Stalin seemed to become even more aberrant after ten years or so in power.

In countries and times where the accession to power is more routine, the range of personality types found in office is substantially narrower.

---

19. Alexander and Juliet George, *Woodrow Wilson and Colonel House: A Personality Study* (New York: Dover, 1964), p. 320.

Even so, there is enough variation to warrant the use of psychoanalytic techniques to study foreign policy decision makers, sometimes through the use of a categorization system. The most famous of these is James David Barber's categories created for the study of *The Presidential Character: Predicting Performance in the White House*.[20] Barber asserted that the character and style of any president are rooted firmly in his political experiences very early in his career. The experience and style of the individual are molded in the "first independent political success" and go far in determining whether the individual is "active" or "passive" (how much energy is given to the job) and whether the individual is "positive" or "negative" (whether the individual actually enjoys his or her job). An active and confident president who enjoys his job—an active-positive—would be one like Franklin Roosevelt or John Kennedy. The opposite, a president with little liking of the office and low activity and self-confidence, is a "passive-negative," such as Calvin Coolidge or Dwight Eisenhower. Some of our recent presidents have been active-negatives—almost compulsively active in office but not deriving much pleasure from the job because of low self-esteem and confidence; examples are Lyndon Johnson and Richard Nixon.

Recently several psychobiographical studies of Henry Kissinger have been written that attempt to link his past experience to his personality and style, which affect his behavior in the foreign policy arena. One observer sees the trauma of Kissinger's boyhood world crumbling about him in Nazi Germany as the main influence on his personality and style. The "inner chaos" that resulted motivated his search for external order, his search for the "strong individual"—even if it is an opponent. This also explains, it is argued, his ambivalent attitude toward taking risks. Another psychohistorian goes back to Kissinger's quest for order as the basis for his quest for power. This quest shaped his style of interacting with others, such as identifying with an opponent (getting on better with America's enemies than with its allies was a charge frequently leveled at Kissinger during his White House days). Thus, he cultivated powerful patrons to help him and yet acted alone as the solitary hero. This, it is argued, is the basis for Kissinger's effective negotiating technique.[21] The picture that emerges is of an "active-

---

20. James D. Barber, *The Presidential Character* (Englewood Cliffs, N.J.: Prentice-Hall, 1972).

21. See, respectively, Dana Ward, "Kissinger: A Psychohistory," *History of Childhood Quarterly* 2 (1974–1975), 287–348; Bruce Mazlish, *Kissinger: The European Mind in American Policy* (New York: Basic Books, 1976). See also Dan Caldwell, ed., *Henry Kissinger: His*

negative"—a man of incredible energy and drive who never succeeds in dispelling unease over the chaos that might reoccur at any time. Perhaps it is not unusual that two active-negatives such as Nixon and Kissinger were able to work well as a foreign policy team.

These are just a few examples of in-depth psychological and personality-oriented research applied to the analysis of foreign policy making. All hark back to the classic formulation of Harold Lasswell—that there is a displacement of *private* motives onto *public* objects. Just as all people take out their emotions, frustrations, and personality quirks on the world around them (e.g., kicking the dog when you're angry with your spouse), decision makers will also displace the private (idiosyncratic) personality drives they have onto the world around them. In their case, this world is also the world of diplomacy and foreign policy decision making.

Private Motives and Public Objects

Another way to study private motives and public objects is to match indicators of various types of personalities to the behavior most likely to be associated with that personality. For example, scholars have been concerned with the personality attributes associated with the willingness to take risks, to cooperate, or to go to war. Some of these studies have used content analysis of decision makers to isolate such personality characteristics. Margaret Hermann, for example, looked at the following personality characteristics: the need for power, conceptual complexity, trust and distrust of others, need for affiliation, belief of control over events, and nationalism.[22] Her studies provide results such as the following: The greater the need for power exhibited by the decision maker, the more aggressive his or her government will tend to be; the more cognitively complex (the ability to see various sides to issues and not see things in simple black and white terms) the decision maker is, the more cooperative his or her government will tend to be. In updating her research to include Ronald Reagan, she has reinforced

_____

Personality and Policies (Durham, N.C.: Duke University Press, 1983); Harvey Starr, *Henry Kissinger: Perceptions of International Politics* (Lexington: University Press of Kentucky, 1984).

22. See, for example, Margaret G. Hermann, "Leader Personality and Foreign Policy Behavior," in James N. Rosenau (ed.), *Comparing Foreign Policies* (New York: Halsted, 1974), pp. 201–233; Margaret G. Hermann, *A Psychological Examination of Political Leaders* (New York: Free Press, 1976).

these findings. Compared with previously studied heads of government, Reagan was highly nationalistic, among the highest in the need for power, and low in cognitive complexity.[23]

Such studies have also been done on people at lower levels, such as the foreign policy bureaucracy. Lloyd Etheredge studied over one hundred foreign policy specialists in the U.S. State Department. Although it is often more fascinating to study people who are close to madness, the processes of selective perception and misperception are normal occurrences in normal persons. Etheredge has studied the relationship between personality factors and the willingness to use force. He notes that the "men I studied bore little resemblance to the sort of primitive, aggressive, authoritarian personalities that are often portrayed by social psychologists as the instigators of international violence."[24] He found that those who were mistrustful, who had low self-esteem, who liked to compete with others, and who were active and ambitious were more likely to advocate the United States using force in specified situations. Interestingly, if people combined ambition with high esteem, they were also more likely to advocate the use of force.

Finally, we note an example of a study that used both content analysis and simulation to study the impact of personality on foreign policy. Charles and Margaret Hermann ran two simulations with students playing the roles of decision makers. Each student was set up to match the role of a European leader before the outbreak of World War I, but the situation was "masked" so that the students did not know they were participating in a World War I simulation. On the basis of the content analysis studies done by Robert North and the group at Stanford who researched the European decision makers in the pre–World War I crisis, the Hermanns outlined the personality characteristics of the actual European decision makers. After tests were made on the students, they, too, were classified on characteristics such as dominance and self-control. In one simulation, students were matched to the roles of decision makers on the basis of similar personality characteristics. In the second simulation, personalities were not matched. Where personalities were matched, the students' perceptions of the events that occurred correlated quite highly with those of the actual decision makers in 1914. In addition, the events that occurred were quite similar to those of 1914,

---

23. Margaret G. Hermann, "Assessing Personality at a Distance: A Profile of Ronald Reagan," *Mershon Center Quarterly Report* 7 (1983), 1–8.

24. Lloyd Etheredge, "Personality and Foreign Policy: Bullies in the State Department," *Psychology Today* (March 1975), 38.

and the simulation led to the brink of war with alliance configurations similar to those of 1914. The close fit between events and perceptions did not occur in the simulation where personalities were not matched.

Belief System, Personality, and Perception: The Case of John Foster Dulles

One of the most famous studies done in this field is that of Ole Holsti on John Foster Dulles, Eisenhower's secretary of state from 1953 through 1959. Holsti's study addresses many of the issues and factors noted in this chapter. Holsti studied Dulles's "image of the enemy"— how Dulles perceived the Soviet Union across time and along several dimensions. This study dealt with some of the basic psychological processes involved with the closed image and the screening of information. One part of the study, for example, clearly demonstrates projection as discussed earlier. Holsti used an operational-code approach to analyze Dulles's writings before he became secretary of state. Two of Dulles's instrumental beliefs about how one should act in foreign policy were that when one's opponent is strong, avoid conflict; when one's opponent is weak, be willing to run risks. These beliefs were culled from a number of books written on foreign policy. Yet when Dulles later became secretary of state, he asserted that the Soviet Union was only cooperative or friendly when it was weak or afraid. Here is a good example of an individual projecting his beliefs onto the actions of another.

Holsti's research included a full study of Dulles's belief system and personality and how those factors were related to his perceptions of the Soviet Union. This study is a good example of the effect that psychological variables can have on an individual who is not aberrant but with a normal (if strong) personality.

Decision makers, as we have discussed above, behave according to their images of a situation and the other parties involved. If the image or the theory is too tightly held, however, the images become stereotyped and unchanging. Holsti was interested in how this process might be related to the image of the enemy: "Enemies are those who are defined as such, and if one acts upon that interpretation, it is more than likely that the original definition will be confirmed."[25] The thrust of

---

25. Ole R. Holsti, "Cognitive Dynamics and Images of the Enemy," *Journal of International Affairs* 21 (1967), 16; see also Holsti's "The Belief System and National Images: A Case Study," *Journal of Conflict Resolution* 6 (1962), 244–252.

Holsti's presentation is that cognitive processes exist that maintain images of an enemy. He then goes on to describe Dulles's images of the Soviet Union and demonstrates that not only was the picture a very negative one but one that resisted change.

Part of Holsti's study involved a content analysis of all of Dulles's public statements while he was secretary of state. The various speeches, press conferences, statements, and congressional hearings produced 434 documents for study. In these documents Holsti searched for Dulles's evaluations of the Soviet Union. He divided these evaluative statements into four groups: evaluations of Soviet capabilities, Soviet success, Soviet hostility, and a general evaluation. Each of the over 3,500 evaluations was placed into one of these four categories and rated (determined by a set of rules) on scales between $+3.00$ and -3.00 from strength to weakness, success to failure, friendship to hostility, or good to bad.

Dulles's general view was that the Soviet Union was atheistic, totalitarian, and Communist. He held an "inherent bad faith" image of the Soviet Union—that it could not be trusted and would only act in a friendly way when weak or afraid. His images included the view that the Russian people were "good," but that the Communist leaders were "bad." The Russian national interest was evaluated as a much better thing than the interests of international Communism. The Russian state was also evaluated in a much more favorable manner than the Communist party.

Although over the years Dulles's view of Soviet capabilities, success, and hostility did change, nothing seemed to change his general evaluation of the Soviet Union. As we can see from Figure 12.3, the other three categories rise and fall, but general evaluation is almost a straight line at the bottom of the graph. The other three categories correlate with each other (e.g., when Dulles saw the Soviet Union being less successful or decreasing in capabilities, he saw it as less hostile, and conversely). Dulles's general evaluation, however, did not correlate with any of the others. Holsti uses this as evidence to support the conclusion that Dulles had a closed image of the Soviet Union: "Dulles interpreted the very data that would lead one to change one's model in such a way to preserve that model." Information contrary to Dulles's image, especially of the kind that led to a decrease in hostile acts and the perception of this decrease, was reinterpreted to leave the original image intact. For example, cuts in the size of the Soviet armed forces were attributed to Soviet economic weakness and to bad faith (he felt that the men released from service would be put to work building

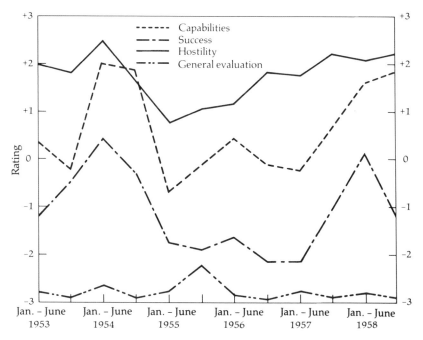

Figure 12.3
John Foster Dulles's perceptions of the Soviet Union, 1953–1958. [*Source:* Ole R. Holsti, "The Belief System and National Images: A Case Study," *Journal of Conflict Resolution* 6 (1962), 249. By permission of the publisher, Sage Publications, Inc.]

more lethal weapons!). The study revealed a textbook case of images leading to a selective perception of information—an image of the enemy acting as a screen that ignored some information and reinterpreted other information. This process is similar to stereotyping and other processes that permit an individual to maintain a consistent belief system. The psychological consequences of admitting that the Soviets could be good or act cooperatively out of any motive other than fear or weakness would have opened up to question other parts of Dulles's belief system.

A useful comparison may also be made here with Harvey Starr's study of Henry Kissinger. The Kissinger study was explicitly modeled on that of Dulles so that the effect of idiosyncratic variables could be systematically compared. If we look at the images that Kissinger held of the Soviet Union, the differences from Dulles's view are striking (see Figure 12.4). In addition to his evaluations being far more positive, Kissinger had an open and flexible image of the Soviet Union. How

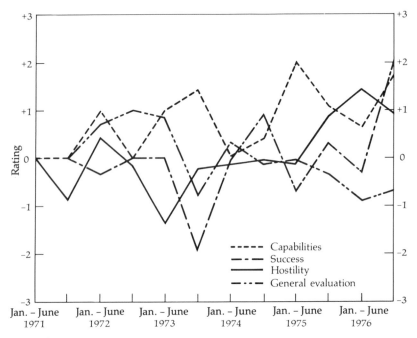

Figure 12.4
Kissinger's perceptions of the Soviet Union, 1971–1976.

good or bad the Soviets were seen to be was related to their behavior—
the friendlier Soviet behavior appeared to be to Kissinger, the better
his general evaluation of the Soviet Union. Kissinger, who was able
not only to negotiate the SALT arms control agreements with the Soviet Union but also to begin a period of détente, had a more positive
and more flexible view of the "enemy." He was able to modify that
view according to the behavior that the opponent exhibited. Although
we have to take into account the fact that Dulles was operating in a
period of Cold War and Kissinger dealt with the USSR during a period
of détente, we also know that individuals may have some impact on
foreign policy and that they can, if they desire, slow down or accelerate
changes in the direction of foreign policy when they take office. Dulles
may have had to deal with the Soviets during the Cold War, but he was
also responsible for helping to continue that state of affairs; Kissinger
not only worked within a period of détente, but was largely responsible for continuing and accelerating a trend that existed when he took
office.

AFFECTING THE IMAGE:
THE DECISION MAKER AS
A PHYSIOLOGICAL ANIMAL

If we look at foreign policy and foreign policy decision as the product of human behavior, then it would be foolish to overlook the fact that decision makers are physical beings, influenced by their physiology and possibly, as some assert, their genetic heritage. On a very simple level, whether information is received and the degree to which it is understood and interpreted depend on the physical ability of the individual. Thus, the physical as well as the mental health of decision makers can affect foreign policy and the decision-making process. The strain of high public office is great. You can see this for yourself by looking at photographs of almost any U.S. President since World War II, comparing his appearance before taking office and a few years after. The effect of this strain often breaks down the health of the leader. This is even more important when we remember that many political leaders, particularly the heads of governments and senior ministers, are older individuals and thus even more susceptible to the strains of office. Men such as Mao Tse-tung (who died at age 84), Charles De Gaulle (age 79), Jomo Kenyatta (age 85), Tito (age 88), and Leonid Brezhnev (75) remained in office to a very advanced age. The average age of the Soviet Politburo (often called a geriocracy) for example, is over 70; the Chinese leadership is similarly well advanced in age.

Humans today are basically the same physical creatures that evolved as plains hunters tens of thousands of years ago. Human physiology is built so that in a stressful situation (one provoking fear, anger, or anxiety) the body is geared for "fight or flight." All the physical reactions that accompany a situation of high stress—increased heartbeat, pumping adrenalin, movement of blood to the muscles—are directed to getting the body ready for combat or for running away as fast as possible. The stress that builds up in the body is released by this physical action. The foreign policy decision maker of today reacts to stress in exactly the same way physiologically but not behaviorally. He doesn't go running in circles around the White House lawn but sits in conference or talks on the telephone or broods alone in his study. Physical stress is not released as it was supposed to be and impairs the health of the decision maker. In addition, stress such as that during a crisis broadly affects the performance of people—how they see the situation to be decided, how they narrow the number of alternatives they see available, how they may decline in their level-headed thinking, and so on.[26]

A study by Hugh L'Etang of the medical histories of twentieth-century political and military leaders indicates the extremely high rate of medical disabilities that occur among this group.[27] These ailments and the drugs and other treatments taken for them have a number of purely physiological effects on the individual that could affect his or her perception of the world and decision-making procedures. Even common psychoactive drugs such as alcohol, caffeine, tranquilizers, and sedatives can affect perceptions and mood without individuals knowing it; for example, alcohol can increase risk taking and recklessness, tranquilizers can increase hostility, and cocaine can induce feelings of euphoria and increased strength.[28] Perhaps the best example of this is the behavior of British Prime Minister Anthony Eden during the Suez crisis of 1956. From a variety of sources, it was clear that Eden was ill at the time, suffering from hypertension and other nervous disorders. Other reports claim that he was also taking pills, such as benzedrine, that give the feeling of control and confidence. We do know that Eden's decision-making activities at that time differed markedly from those he used in other cases. He was much more secretive and consulted only a very small group of colleagues. He suffered a physical breakdown right after the crisis.

Critics of Franklin Roosevelt claim he was too ill during the 1945 Yalta Conference to negotiate effectively with Stalin. Some claim Roosevelt gave in on points so that he could rest from the grueling bargaining sessions. We also know that Woodrow Wilson's stroke, which occurred after the stress of campaigning unsuccessfully for approval of the Treaty of Versailles, weakened his control over the decisions of government. No one really knows how decisions were made at that time, but the consensus is that his wife was the actual president during that time.

---

26. Thomas Wiegele, "Decision-Making in an International Crisis: Some Biological Factors," *International Studies Quarterly* 17 (September 1973), 295–355; see also Ole Holsti and Alexander George, "The Effects of Stress on the Performance of Foreign Policy Makers," in C. P. Cotter (ed.), *Political Science Annual*, vol. 6 (Indianapolis: Bobbs-Merrill, 1975), pp. 255–319.

27. Hugh L'Etang, *The Pathology of Leadership* (New York: Hawthorn, 1970). Studies have also been done on the effects of drugs in decision making. See, for example, Allen H. Stix, "Chlordiazepoxide (Librium): The Effects of a Minor Tranquilizer on Strategic Choice in the Prisoners' Dilemma," *Journal of Conflict Resolution* 18 (September 1974), 373–394.

28. See Roy Lubit and Bruce Russett, "The Effects of Drugs on Decision-Making," *Journal of Conflict Resolution* 28 (1984), 85–102.

Eisenhower's heart attacks also weakened his control over policy, and he turned the government over to Vice-President Nixon, which partly prompted the adoption of the constitutional amendment on presidential disability and succession in 1967. Just about every president and high-level decision maker has had major physical problems. Thus, health is important, since the death or inability of top decision makers to function can bring the decision-making processes of government to a halt or cause great disruption. Leonid Brezhnev's continual health problems in the late 1970s added another source of uncertainty to the analysis (and running) of Soviet foreign policy.

Looking at humans as physical creatures has taken other forms. People have always been concerned about human nature—whether humans have built-in instincts for violence or aggression or domination. The debate over "nature and nurture" is an old one: What accounts for human actions—innate genetic characteristics or the cultural environment? The debate also continues between ethologists and anthropologists. *Ethology* is the study of animal behavior (or "comparative psychology," as it is sometimes called). It has been popularized by Konrad Lorenz (*On Aggression*) and Desmond Morris (*The Naked Ape* and *The Human Zoo*).[29] The most extreme ethologists say that there is a strong biological basis for human behavior and that we can find the causes for that behavior in studying the evolutionary ancestors of *Homo sapiens*. They claim that biological influences on behavior are very powerful. More moderate exponents claim that ethology provides us with a few interesting insights and analogies between mechanisms found in animals and similar mechanisms found in human societies and cultures. Opponents of this view claim that the genetic or biological impact is either extremely small or nonexistent.

For animals higher on the evolutionary ladder, the influence of the environment is greater. Each animal has a "program," "template," or "biogram" built into its genes. For the oldest and least complicated forms of life, much if not all behavior is guided by such a program. However, more of the behavior of higher animals depends on stimuli from the environment—whether hearing its parents sing the proper bird song or watching a lioness mother hunt. Humans have by far the most open and flexible program of all. It seems that group life itself may be a biological necessity, built into human genes, along with things such as language.

---

29. See also the works cited at the beginning of Chapter 3.

But what group one lives with, what culture one is surrounded by, what language one speaks are all completely undetermined. Anthropologists have demonstrated that just about any conceivable type of behavior, in almost every conceivable combination, can be found in the groups of humans that live and have lived on earth. This debate was given new life by a book published in 1975 by Edward Wilson called *Sociobiology*, which systematically discusses the biological basis of sociality. Critics of Wilson and this approach claim it is *biological determinism*—that human behavior derives primarily from genetic sources. However, a careful reading of the book indicates that Wilson feels that at most 10 percent of social behavior has some genetic basis.

For our purposes, we should not despair that war, violence, and aggression are somehow built into humanity and thus can never be prevented. Although ethology does provide us with some interesting analogies and explanations for human behavior, it cannot explain decisions to go to war or to act cooperatively in international relations. We cannot fall back on human nature to explain foreign policy behavior; we are all humans, and thus we all share the same human nature. Yet behavior varies greatly among people, situations, and time. Some societies are much more peaceful than others. A few, like the !Kung (a tribe in Africa), have no war. Human nature or our biological heritage cannot explain this variation. We shall do much better to look at how certain types of situations affect individual perception and individual and group decision making.[30]

AFFECTING THE IMAGE: CRISIS SITUATIONS

One type of situation studied extensively by students of international relations is the *crisis*. We noted that a crisis is characterized as a *high-threat situation* that was not anticipated and that requires action in a short time. This is exactly the type of situation that places a decision maker under the most stress. Studies have shown that stress is indeed greatest in crisis situations; thus, what we said about stress in the preceding section also applies to crisis. The important point is that the

---

30. In his 1973 article, Wiegele suggests that we investigate a variety of factors related to the physiological response of decision makers, such as weather conditions. One of the authors investigated the effect of weather on pre–World War I decision makers and concluded it was indeed the crisis situation that had the major effect on behavior. See Harvey Starr, "Physical Variables and Foreign Policy Decision Making: Daily Temperature and the Pre–World War I Crisis," *International Interactions* 3 (1977), 97–108.

crisis situation in which decisions have to be made will affect the perceptions of decision makers differently from noncrisis situations such as general foreign policy decisions or administrative decisions. The decision processes will also tend to be different, and the constraints (mainly psychological) will also be different. A crisis situation presents a decision maker with a different menu and makes the decision maker see that menu in a special way.

Quite often, because of the time pressure, a crisis is a period of information overload on the decision maker—messages come in from observers on the spot, from aides that have been asked to find out what is happening, from ambassadors, and from others. The combination of stress and information overload (although sometimes the situation is exactly the opposite: there is no information about what has happened) will usually lead decision makers to overreact or underreact. Again, this comes down to screens and the psychological processes that set up those screens. The distorted view of the world will reduce the decision maker'ʳ ability to interpret and the quality of the interpretation. For example, we have already discussed the "blindness of involvement."

A crisis caused by high threat is also a situation of high involvement. One study of the pre–World War I period, the Cuban missile crisis, and the Vietnam war looked at the intensity of involvement. As this intensity grew, there was the tendency in World War I and the Vietnam war for decision makers to take tangible and specific issues and to make them more symbolic.[31] Thinking back to the bargaining analyses of Roger Fisher, we can see that as issues became more intangible and symbolic, they become more difficult to bargain over and resolve. Indeed, in both World War I and Vietnam, war either broke out or escalated. Neither of these things happened in Cuba. Another study that compared the pre–World War I crisis and the 1962 Cuban crisis demonstrated other differences. The United States and the Soviet Union perceived each other's behavior far more accurately than was the case in prewar Europe. Somehow the problematic effects of perception in crisis (to be noted below) did not happen in Cuba. Why not?

Several possible explanations may be offered. One version of the "advice to decision makers" we discussed in a previous section did occur. John Kennedy had read Barbara Tuchman's history of the period preceding the outbreak of World War I, *The Guns of August*. Although

---

31. Michael P. Sullivan, "Commitment and Escalation of Conflict," *Western Political Quarterly* 25 (1972), 28–38.

Kennedy did not explicitly state his argument in terms of misperception and conflict spirals, he did recognize that these processes were
largely responsible for the onset of war. Memoirs of the missile crisis
point out that he wanted to be careful to avoid such mistakes—he did
not want a book entitled *The Missiles of October* to be written. A second
possible factor was the clear knowledge of the disastrous consequences
of failing to control the crisis. In 1914 many decision makers saw the
possible war as a replay of the Franco-Prussian War of 1870—a brief
war of several sharp encounters. This possibility did not frighten them
as would a picture of trench warfare lasting four years, causing almost
ten million battle deaths and the destruction of the German, Russian,
Austrian, and Turkish monarchies. Kennedy and Khrushchev had no
illusions about the consequences of losing control of the crisis and engaging in nuclear war. The stakes were so high that extra caution was
employed as an antidote to the usual misperception induced by crisis.

Very briefly, studies of World War I, the Korean war, and the Cuban
crisis have indicated the following sorts of effects on perception: During a crisis, *communications tend to become shorter and more stereotyped* as
stress increases. Stereotypes not only distort but also tend to cast things
in black-and-white images and to foster the creation and maintenance
of the image of an enemy. Not surprisingly, then, crisis also can lead to
an *overperception of the level of hostility* and violence of one's opponents;
in other words, one sees hostility where it might not exist (wishful
thinking or the self-fulfilling prophecy). On the other hand, one *under-
perceives the hostility and violence in one's own actions.*

In addition, if a state sees itself as the object of hostility, it will express hostility to that state. With this process we are back in a *conflict
spiral*—a mirror image situation between two states that perceive each
other as enemies. Perceptions of anxiety or fear are likely to increase in
these conditions; as they do, they might also lead decision makers
to ignore perceptions of capabilities. The desire to break the tension
through any end to the crisis—even war—could lead to ignoring the
strength or weakness of oneself, one's allies, and one's opponents.
Luckily, this did not happen in the Cuban crisis. Neither Kennedy nor
Khrushchev called nuclear weapons "paper tigers" (as the Chinese did
before they acquired them), nor did they underplay the destructiveness
of such weapons. Each went out of his way to stress the consequences
of their use. The last general point (and this point is related to other
general perceptions of the opponent as a rational monolith) is that as
the crisis grows, decision makers increasingly feel that their *own range
of alternatives becomes more restricted.* The crisis, therefore, cuts down

their perceptions of available alternatives. At the same time, decision makers see the *alternatives of their opponents as expanding:* "Although we have no choice but to go to war, they could avoid war by doing any of a number of things."

Since crisis situations can have these sorts of effects on decision making, it is important that the advice on perception given above be taken into account in crisis situations. Especially since crises are most likely to call forth intellectual processes rather than social ones—because only one or two persons or a small group try to work out a solution to the problem—the decision will be based on images of the world distorted by the pressures of the crisis situation itself. The study of crisis management thus becomes very important.

Table 12.1
The sources of foreign policy.

Systemic aggregation continuum	Time continuum		
	Sources that tend to change slowly		Sources that tend to undergo rapid change
Systemic sources		Great power structure Alliances	Situational factors: external Issue areas Crises
	Size Geography	Technology	
Societal sources	Culture and history	Economic development Social structure Moods of opinion	Situational factors: internal
Governmental sources		Political accountability Governmental structure	
Idiosyncratic sources			Values, talents, experiences, and personalities of leaders

Source: James N. Rosenau, "The Study of Foreign Policy," in James N. Rosenau, Kenneth Thompson, and Gavin Boyd (eds.), *World Politics* (New York: Free Press, 1976), p. 18. Copyright © 1976 by The Free Press, a division of Macmillan Publishing Co., Inc.

CONCLUSION

A few concluding comments are in order here, as we finish the material in Part I. We have spent our time looking at a series of environments, contexts, or sources of influence and constraint on the foreign-policy-making process. We began with the global system and concluded with a look at the individual and his or her psychological environment. These sources are presented in Table 12.1, which also provides some idea of the degree to which these sources can change in time.

The place of the individual and the idiosyncratic factors affecting perception may be highlighted by looking closely at Table 12.1. Although the other factors exist in the real world and change slowly, the perceptions of these other factors by a changing set of decision-making individuals can shift very rapidly. The present chapter stresses the existence and significance of the psychological environment. By looking at the psychological environment, we can then compare that environment with the reality of the other environments and investigate the crucial disparities between the real and the perceived. As we have seen, even in the most normal of decision makers, selective perception is an important influence on policy making.

PART II

CONTEMPORARY AND FUTURE PROBLEMS OF WORLD POLITICS

Our emphasis so far has been on general tools of analysis, with relatively wide-ranging theories and abstract statements. Often we have illustrated propositions by referring to particular phenomena of contemporary or recent world politics. Nevertheless, the discussion has been very different from what you might encounter in an issue-oriented study of current events. This has been deliberate—partly because what seemed current when we wrote the textbook probably would be dated by the time the book was published and found its way to your classroom. However, the more important reason for a relatively abstract and theoretical presentation has been to help you establish a set of principles for thinking about the world politics. To do that, you need a discussion of theory rooted in real political problems and political structures. You need historical information and concrete illustrations. Yet you also need to see the utility and the beauty of more general and abstract theoretical inquiry.

We cannot envision in any detail the kinds of problems that you, as a citizen of your country and of the world, will see in your lifetime. Our crystal ball is almost as clouded about the nature of future problems as it is about solutions. Nevertheless, we do have some idea about what kinds of problems will endure, so you need a more concrete examination of problems. In Part II, therefore, we shall examine four kinds of problems, combining a discussion of historical detail with an exposition and evaluation of contemporary theory and research relevant to those problems. In doing so, we shall look at various conflicts in the international system and examine different theories about the causes of war and peace. The four problems are as follows:

1. *Arms races, deterrence, and arms control* (aspects of the eternal quest for security and the role of force in enhancing or diminishing that security, with special attention to the threat of mass destruction in a nuclear war).
2. *Peaceful relations among the industrialized countries* (how the interdependence of industrialized nations has shaped the ability to achieve security without war but has also helped make common problems out of previously individual ones).
3. *Dependence of less-developed countries on the industrialized world* (especially as that view is seen by the developed countries and how it can shape the quest of citizens of less-developed nations for decent living conditions and political liberties).
4. *The ecology of the world system* (incorporating the pressures and needs for growth with the constraints of resource limits, the pollution-absorbing capacity of the environment, and the political dilemmas of achieving some order in an often anarchic world).

As we examine these problems, we shall frequently move from one level of analysis to another, illustrating how understanding these problems requires taking analytical perspectives from virtually all levels. We shall also note the differences in power of various levels of analysis when dealing with different problems. Questions, values, explanations, and proposed solutions are also very different for rich or powerful countries and weak countries—and also for rich and powerful people contrasted with poor and weak people within countries. As a result, we have chosen a set of broad problems that (though hardly including all that you will see in the world politics of your lifetime) are both important and varied.

13

CONFLICT AND COOPERATION
IN ARMS RACES

A BRIEF HISTORY OF THE
SOVIET-AMERICAN ARMS RACE

International politics, like all social life, involves a mixture of conflict and cooperation. In all our relations, even with friends and family, we both compete and cooperate. Usually in personal affairs the competitive elements are kept under control because it is so important to maintain the cooperative relationship. As a result, we occasionally give in to a friend's or relative's interest when it conflicts with ours. With someone we love and with whom we share a sense of identity (a spouse, a parent, a child, or a close friend), it is sometimes a pleasure rather than a sacrifice to give up something for that person. In international politics, however, there is little affection or sense of shared identity. Common interests and the need to maintain a cooperative relationship may seem less immediate; thus we tend to emphasize the elements of competition much more. But we should remember that both conflict and cooperation are there and that any effort to achieve our own goals must include both. This applies even to war or to threatened war, as in arms races.

We shall examine some of the interactions of conflict and cooperation in the arms race between the United States and the Soviet Union. First, we shall outline a brief history of the strategic arms race and then analyze the interactions.[1]

1945-1950: The Period of U.S. Nuclear Monopoly

After World War II, both the United States and the Soviet Union had substantially disarmed from the high levels of World War II, though the Soviet Union did so to a lesser degree. During this time, the atomic bomb was the central element in America's policy of deterrence. Although the Soviet Union retained large land forces—forces that might have threatened Western Europe—the Russians had for practical purposes no atomic weapons. They exploded their first bomb in 1949, but it took several years for them to build up a stockpile adequate for fighting a war; in any case, they lacked intercontinental bombers capable of reaching the United States. The Americans did have the ability to bomb the Soviet Union and inflict substantial damage, though the number of American bombs was not large (probably only about 300, even at the end of this period), and they were *fission* (atomic) weapons rather than the much more devastating *fusion* (thermonuclear or hydrogen) weapons that followed. Still, with the disease, famine, and economic dislocation to be expected after any attack, the prospective damage was enough to deter the Soviet Union from any great adventures—especially given that country's great and vividly remembered suffering from World War II and its twenty million casualties.

1951-1957: The Period of American Nuclear Dominance

June 1950 marked the beginning of the Korean war, with the attack of Communist North Korea on U.S.-supported South Korea. The Soviet leaders apparently did not expect any substantial American response to this invasion, but in fact the United States did intervene militarily in a

---

1. For a general history of this period emphasizing weapons developments, see George Quester, *Offense and Defense in the International System* (New York: Wiley, 1977).

massive way. Furthermore, as the Americans turned the tide of battle in their favor and later in the year penetrated deep into North Korean territory, the Chinese Communists intervened to protect their North Korean allies. This result was a very large land war on the Korean peninsula. Coupled with previous serious incidents in the emerging Cold War (the Communist takeover of Czechoslovakia and the Berlin blockade in 1948, a Communist victory in China, and the Russian atomic bomb explosion in 1949), the Korean war initiated a great American program of rearmament, during which annual U.S. defense expenditures nearly tripled.

The Korean war was a painful experience for the United States in domestic as well as international politics, and American leaders vowed not to fight another such major land war against a Soviet ally. Therefore, the American secretary of state, John Foster Dulles, declared that the United States would respond to any further Communist attack on "free world" nations "in a manner and at a place of our own choosing." He simply meant that the United States would feel free, in the face of any such "proxy war," to strike not at the small Communist ally but directly at the Soviet Union, a "massive retaliation" with nuclear weapons. Such a threat was credible because the United States had by then built up a very large stockpile of nuclear weapons and an intercontinental bombing force to deliver them. With the development of the hydrogen bomb (first tested by the United States in 1952), the amount of damage that could have been inflicted on the Soviet Union was very great indeed, including tens of millions of potential deaths. Although the Russians exploded a multimegaton thermonuclear device in 1953, they lacked either very great numbers of the weapons or adequate means of delivering them to the North American continent. (The Americans had the advantage of bases in Europe and Asia that are quite near their opponent, an advantage always denied to the Russians.) The ability to inflict damage was so greatly imbalanced in favor of the United States that we can speak of this as the period of American strategic dominance. In the face of this capacity, the Soviet leaders pursued a very cautious and generally unprovocative foreign policy.

Nevertheless, they, too, embarked on a major rearmament effort in response to that of the United States. Figure 13.1 illustrates American and Soviet defense expenditures throughout the post-World War II period in constant (inflation-adjusted) 1979 dollars. The estimates of Soviet military spending are very rough and quite controversial, since the USSR does not publish accurate military budget data. Consequently, various problems arise in estimating total Soviet expenditures

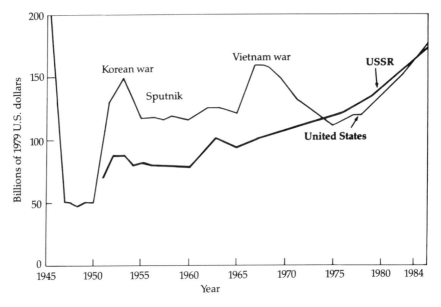

Figure 13.1
Military expenditures of the USSR and the United States, 1945–1984 (billions of 1979 U.S. dollars). Our estimates of Soviet spending are derived from several sources and are subject to large error. See footnote 2 in this chapter.

expressed in dollars. The figures here reasonably indicate upward and downward trends, but the actual level in recent years could differ by 20 percent or more from the figures given.[2]

1958–1966: The Period of American Preponderance

The degree of American dominance over the Soviet Union decreased from 1958 to 1966, as reflected in the new term describing American superiority. Still, it was a period when the United States could consider

---

2. CIA estimates are higher than those given in Figure 13.1, and SIPRI estimates are lower. See U.S. Congress, Joint Economic Committee, *Allocation of Resources in the Soviet Union and China* (Washington, D.C.: U.S. Government Printing Office, annual) and *World Armaments and Disarmament: SIPRI (Stockholm International Peace Research Institute) Yearbook* (New York: Taylor and Francis, annual). A respected independent assessment is Franklyn D. Holzman, "Soviet Military Spending: Assessing the Numbers Game," *International Security* 6 (Spring 1982), no. 4, pp. 78–101; Holzman suggested that the Soviet Union underspent the United States until 1977 but passed it, at least temporarily, in 1980.

the option of a first strike (that is, the initial use of nuclear weapons) on the Soviet Union in response to a proxy war started by a Soviet ally. Despite Soviet rearmament, the Americans retained a substantial edge in the strategic weapon competition. Any temptation to relax this competition was eliminated by the shock that Americans received in 1957 when the USSR became the first country to put a satellite (Sputnik) into orbit around the earth. The Russians could do that only because they had perfected very large rockets—rockets that could be used equally well as intercontinental missiles, the delivery vehicles for nuclear and thermonuclear bombs. The United States was slightly behind in this technology, and there were widespread fears that the Soviet Union would build so many missiles (ICBMs) that they could rapidly destroy American bombers, on which the United States still relied for its deterrent. Although this "missile gap" never in fact materialized, the fear of it led to a new crash program of development and deployment of American land- and sea-based intercontinental missiles.

American preponderance was thus maintained, although the Soviet Union was increasingly developing a capability of doing much war time damage to the United States—at least in retaliation if not in a first strike because of an anticipated overwhelming American retaliation. The casualty levels in a war might have been on the order of five to ten million American deaths compared with perhaps fifty million Soviet deaths. To remedy this imbalance cheaply, the Soviets in 1962 put a variety of nuclear-armed missiles and bombers into Cuba, less than 100 miles from Florida. Even though the United States still had a very substantial nuclear edge over the Russians, the American leadership thought this act sufficiently serious to consider it a crisis. In that ten-day crisis, President John Kennedy instituted an air and naval "quarantine" of Cuba and demanded that the Soviet Union remove all its nuclear-weapons-carrying forces. He made it clear that the United States was prepared to launch a nuclear first strike against the forces in Cuba and perhaps against the USSR if these forces were not removed. Because the United States had such overall nuclear predominance—as well as local nonnuclear superiority in an area of vital importance to it, the Caribbean—the Russian leaders believed the American threat and withdrew their missiles and aircraft.

In reaction to this very public demonstration of their weakness, however, the Soviet leaders began a new program of strategic armament, developing and ultimately deploying a whole new range of missiles and aircraft. This effort showed up in a steadily rising level of Soviet military expenditure after 1965.

The Period of Essential Equivalence

From 1966 until 1975, the United States was deeply involved in another long, painful, and costly land war in Asia, this time in Vietnam. The effort, which was finally lost, was to prevent a takeover of the government of South Vietnam by North Vietnam–supported Communist guerrillas. During the war American military expenditures climbed to new heights. But by the time of gradual American withdrawal, public revulsion with the war and with some of the excesses of the Cold War produced a broadly based desire to cut the military budget. As a result, by 1973 American military expenditures had dropped below the pre-Vietnam level and remained there until 1977, then resuming a slow climb once more. Meanwhile, the Soviet Union maintained its military buildup in conventional as well as nuclear arms. By the 1970s, it was spending about as much as the United States, and since then it has substantially been on par with the United States in strategic nuclear forces. Although there remains substantial controversy over the precise nature of the Soviet-American strategic balance during most of this period, most observers characterize it as one of "essential equivalence" when all elements of strategic weapons are taken into account.

Table 13.1 illustrates the essential facts about the changing strategic balance during this period. You can see that at the beginning of 1963 the United States maintained a clear quantitative superiority in all classes of strategic delivery vehicles: ICBMs (land-based missiles like Minuteman), SLBMs (submarine-launched missiles from vessels like the Polaris, Poseidon, and in the 1980s Trident submarines), and long-range bombers such as the B-52. Furthermore, in most dimensions of quality (for instance, relatively undetectable submarines and high-accuracy missiles) the United States also was superior. By the 1970s, however, the Soviet effort had borne fruit, and the USSR had surpassed the United States in numbers of ICBMs. The Russians also developed very large rockets and warheads.

The apparent Soviet advantage in large warheads was not as important as it seemed, however, because a single large warhead is relatively inefficient compared with several smaller ones. As we noted in Chapter 4, doubling a bomb's power does not double its destructive capability. Instead of producing big missiles with single warheads, the United States concentrated on building missiles having *multiple* (3 to 10) *independently targeted warheads* or *reentry vehicles* (MIRVs) of high accuracy. These advantages in the number of reentry vehicles and accuracy,

Table 13.1

Soviet and American strategic nuclear forces, 1963–1986.

	1963	1972	1981	1986 with SALT II	1986 without SALT II
ICBMs					
United States	424	1,054	1,052	1,052	1,052
Soviet Union	90	1,533	1,398	1,200	1,604
MIRVed ICBMs					
United States	0	139	550	550	550
Soviet Union	0	0	652	820	1,190
ICBM warheads					
United States	424	1,332	2,152	2,152	2,152
Soviet Union	90	1,533	5,354	6,080	9,110
SLBMs					
United States	224	656	576	640	712
Soviet Union	107	437	950	950	1,016
MIRVed SLBMs					
United States	0	160	496	640	664
Soviet Union	0	0	192	380	444
SLBM warheads					
United States	224	2,096	4,656	6,344	6,584
Soviet Union	107	437	1,334	2,470	3,740
Intercontinental bombers					
United States	630	457	348	348	348
Soviet Union	190	156	156	100	150
Strategic cruise missiles					
United States	0	0	0	2,600	3,400
Soviet Union	0	0	0	0	100
Total delivery vehicles					
United States	1,278	2,167	1,975	4,688	5,512
Soviet Union	387	2,110	2,504	2,250	2,870
Total force loadings (warheads and bombs)					
United States	?	5,598	9,000	13,100	13,260
Soviet Union	?	2,282	7,000	8,750	13,150

Source: 1963 data from Bruce Russett and Bruce Blair, eds., *Progress in Arms Control? Readings from Scientific American* (San Francisco: W. H. Freeman and Company, 1979), pp. 6, 7; 1972–1986 data adapted from Herbert Scoville, Jr., *MX: Prescription for Disaster* (Cambridge, Mass.: MIT Press, 1981), p. 67. All are originally derived from U.S. Department of Defense reports.

coupled with the remaining American advantage in long-range bombers, basically compensated for Soviet advantages in size and number of missiles.

The result was a situation in which neither side could attack the other without suffering enormous damage from the opponent's retaliation. According to Department of Defense estimates, each side had the ability to destroy at least one third of the other's population and 60 percent of its industrial capacity in a strike. This gave both sides a "mutual assured destruction" (sometimes abbreviated as MAD) capability. It ensured that, for all intents and purposes, neither side could win a nuclear war.

Different aspects of this essential equivalence can be seen in Figure 13.2, which shows the strategic balance in terms of numbers of warheads, equivalent megatons (EMT), and hard-target kill (HTK) capability. Equivalent megatons is a widely used measure that takes into account the number of warheads and their explosive yield. Just as the United States is credited with an advantage in the number of warheads (mostly because so many of its missiles are MIRVed), the USSR has an advantage in equivalent megatonnage because of its preference for

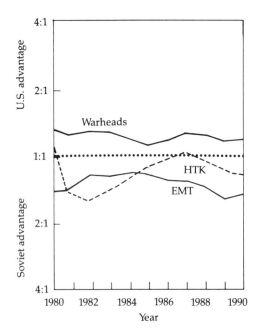

Figure 13.2
The Soviet-American strategic balance in the 1980s. EMT = equivalent megatons; HTK = hard-target kill. [*Source:* U.S. Department of Defense, *Authorization for Appropriations for Fiscal Year 1982, Hearings before the Committee on Armed Services of the United States Senate*, 97th Cong., 1st sess. (Washington, D.C.: U.S. Government Printing Office, 1981), p. 144.] "Warheads" include bombs.

very large warheads. Hard-target kill capability weights the equivalent megatonnage of each warhead by its accuracy. It shows an increasing Soviet advantage in the early 1980s as their new MIRVs came on-line, followed by a substantial diminution of that advantage with the deployment of new American systems. Important to the American position are the large-scale deployment of new cruise missiles, a new force of Trident submarines and missiles, and the retro-fitting of some older Poseidon subs with longer-range Trident missiles carrying eight large MIRVs each. The improvements to the SLBM force much more than make up for the retirement of a few old Polaris submarines with un-MIRVed missiles, which began in 1981.

Each of the different measures (warheads, EMT, and HTK) addresses different aspects of the strategic balance and the relative advantage either side might have in a war or crisis. But by none of these measures can either side now, nor can it in the future, command a substantial lead (all the ratios of advantage are well under two to one), and none would be likely to matter very much in the course of a nuclear war. Also, though the graph assumes deployment of the MX missile, the improving American military position in the mid-1980s is not affected, since even the first MX missiles would not become operational until late 1986.

Look again at the picture of overall military spending of the two superpowers presented in Figure 13.1. Expenditure levels, even allowing for the difficulties in determining Soviet expenditures, are a very imperfect way to measure military effort or capability. For one thing, they include all sorts of expenditures—for conventional (nonnuclear) forces, such as surface ships and armored vehicles, as well as for strategic nuclear arms, and for troops' payrolls as well as for weapons. The totals are compiled once a year (with the annual budgetary cycle), although a more frequent evaluation might better reflect a response to immediate international tensions.

Expenditure totals lag greatly behind civilian and military decisions to acquire weapons. For instance, in the U.S. political system, the process begins when the military services *request* a certain level of expenditure. Their request is then *approved* or modified by the Joint Chiefs of Staff and the Secretary of Defense and then is approved or modified again by the White House and the Office of Management and Budget. The expenditure must then be *authorized* by Congress. After that still another procedure, managed by a different set of congressional committees, is necessary to *appropriate* the funds. Only then can the funds be spent. Of course, with buying something as complex and expensive as a modern strategic weapons system, it is usually several years before all the funds are spent to produce a finished weapon. Thus a long time goes by between an international event that prompts an upsurge in military spending and the actual expenditure of large sums. Furthermore, strategic arms represent only a small fraction (about 15 percent) of the typical military budget. These factors make it difficult, but not necessarily impossible, to see any connection between what two countries do.

Also, in the real world, even superpowers react not just to each others' moves but to the acts of other states as well. For instance, the Soviet Union is clearly worried about China as well as about the United States. For the past twenty years it has maintained about fifty modern divisions on its frontier with China, and about 20 percent of all Soviet military spending is directed toward the Chinese threat. As for the United States, the big burst of spending during the late 1960s was due to its involvement in Vietnam, not to any sense of direct menace from the USSR.

Despite all this, some patterns do emerge from looking at Figure 13.1 in light of other knowledge about the international situation. First, you can clearly see the upsurge in American military spending with the onset of the Korean war. At the beginning, those expenditures were mainly just to fight the war itself, but they very soon turned into a much broader rearmament. Second, there is a much smaller but still discernible upsurge in American spending shortly after 1960—a response to *Sputnik* and the alleged missile gap. At about the same time as both of these American upsurges, the Soviet Union also raised its spending, though by lesser amounts. Later, you can see a steady rise in Soviet spending beginning after 1965 and reflecting decisions taken after the Cuban missile crisis. This increase has been maintained ever since, despite the American restraint demonstrated after the end of the Vietnam war. Finally, you can see a renewed American effort beginning in 1976 and continuing to the present. This continuing, parallel increase in military spending by both powers since the mid-1970s is what some people mean by the term "arms race"—an image of the two superpowers racing against each other and reacting to each other's exertions in an upward spiral. The term is not always apt in describing the long history of Soviet-American superpower relations, however, because the United States has occasionally decreased its spending.

CONFLICT AND COOPERATION
IN THE ARMS RACE

We now look at the competition in a way that derives from the theory of games and is especially popular in the form called the *prisoners' dilemma*. It shows how people (including the leaders of states) can become trapped in self-defeating acts. It stresses interdependence of each side's choices in the combination of conflict and cooperation found in many social situations. Game theory, if used carefully, can allow us to think in terms of the equivalence of roles: "How would my behavior look if I were in the other person's shoes?" It may at least avoid the perspective that simply says, "We can only be provoked; he must be deterred."

We begin by thinking about conflict and cooperation situations as mixed-motive or non-zero-sum games. This means situations where the combined value of the outcomes to each of two players totals something other than zero. These are situations in which it is possible to have many outcomes where both players lose or gain. By contrast, in zero-sum games one person's gain equals the other's loss; added together, the net change is always zero. (We are assuming that gains and losses can be measured in some common unit. In many situations, that is a serious simplification; in others, where one may speak of gains and losses in money or, as below, as years in prison, the simplification is less distorting.)

In most of the games we play for sport, such as chess or tennis, winning or losing is not everything. Even when we lose the match, we presumably gain from the exercise and the pleasure of the competition. In international relations, too, it is a *fundamental mistake to think of most conflicts as zero-sum situations.* On the contrary, two countries often gain something by staying at peace, and both usually incur serious losses by going to war. Peaceful coexistence is precisely such a situation. Both big powers continue to compete and to gain or lose power at the expense of the other, but they also have an interest in keeping the competition from becoming militarily or economically destructive to both of them. We shall explore some conditions that may encourage or hinder cooperative behavior, starting with an imaginary example of criminal behavior and then applying it to situations of international politics.

In the basic story of the prisoners' dilemma, two people are arrested. Each is held incommunicado in a police station after an armed robbery and murder have been committed. Each person is presented with a pair of unattractive options, and each is questioned separately and given a choice by the police official: "I'm pretty sure that you two were responsible for the killing, but I don't have quite enough evidence to prove it. If you will confess first and testify against the other prisoner, I will see that you are set free without any penalty, and he will be sentenced to life imprisonment. On the other hand, I am making the same proposal to him, so if he confesses first, you will be the one to spend life in prison and he will go free. If you both confess on the same day, we will have a little mercy. But you still will be badly off, because you will both be sentenced to twenty years in prison for armed robbery. If you both want to be stubborn, we cannot convict you for a major crime, but we can punish you for a small crime you committed in the past—one that carries a one-year prison term. If you want to take a chance that your fellow prisoner will keep quiet, go ahead. But if he doesn't—and you know what sort of criminal he is—you will do very badly. Think it over."

In order to analyze these problems, we shall illustrate the dilemma with a simple table (Table 13.2). Each box represents all the possible outcomes for the two players, Ron and Kon. The first number represents the outcome for Ron; the second, for Kon. A 4 is the best possible outcome; a 1, the worst. The letters represent the payoffs (again, the first for Ron and the second for Kon). *R* is reward received; *P* is joint punishment received; *T* is the temptation to defect when the opponent cooperates; and *S* labels the opponent as a sucker (or a saint, if you prefer).

What will the prisoners do in the situation described? Since they cannot communicate with each other, each must make the best possible choice regardless of what the other does. In terms of rational self-interest according to the theory of games, each should act so that he will get the better of the two possible outcomes for each of his opponent's choices. Consider Ron's options, for example: If Kon should confess (that is, defect from his partnership with Ron), Ron will get a twenty-year term (a 2) if he, too, defects but life imprisonment (a 1) if he keeps quiet (that is, tries to cooperate with Kon). Hence Ron is better off if he defects. If, on the contrary, Kon should cooperate, Ron receives a one-year sentence (a 3) if he, too, cooperates but gets off free (a 4) if he defects. Again, Ron is better off defecting. In fact, *whatever* Kon does, Ron does better by defecting; so, by this logic, he will confess. Kon—in the same situation—will also confess. As a consequence of their cold-blooded rationality, both will receive twenty-year sen-

Table 13.2
Prisoner's dilemma.

		Kon	
		Cooperate	Defect
Ron	Cooperate	3, 3 (R, R)	1, 4 (S, T)
	Defect	4, 1 (T, S)	2, 2 (P, P)

tences! Jointly, they will end up much worse off than they might have had they been able to coordinate their strategies and depend on the other to cooperate. This is the prisoners' dilemma.

This basic style of analysis can be applied to many kinds of international politics problems, especially arms races and crisis behavior.[3] To do so, however, we must move from a situation with easily measured outcomes (years of prison sentence) to one with outcomes that are much harder to measure. In war we may speak about billions of dollars of damage done or thousands of people killed, but it is hard to combine dollars and people into a single sum. And, of course, there are other values (such as justice, freedom, and maintaining a culture or civilization) that dollars and casualties measure very imperfectly. But despite these difficulties, we generally prefer certain outcomes to others and to varying degrees. For our purposes here, we need only assume that we can say which outcomes are better; we do not have to assume that we can say how much better one is than another.

In applying this analysis to an arms race, for example, the worst outcome is usually when the other side has a much more effective capability than one's own. This is especially true when it has a credible first-strike capability. To be at the mercy of such a force is the sucker (S) outcome; to have such an advantage is the temptation (T) outcome. To reduce an arms race and so to be able to devote more resources to domestic needs is quite a good outcome—one of reward (R). In a highly competitive and ideologically charged situation, perhaps it is less desirable than being able to wipe out your opponent, but it is clearly better than the joint punishment (P) of a mutual arms race carried on at substantial expense.

---

3. For the basic ideas, see especially Anatol Rapoport and Albert Chammah, *Prisoners' Dilemma* (Ann Arbor: University of Michigan Press, 1965); Anatol Rapoport, *Two-Person Game Theory: The Essential Ideas* (Ann Arbor: University of Michigan Press, 1966); Steven J. Brams, *Game Theory and Politics* (New York: Free Press, 1975).

Thus the payoff situation is just the same as for the hapless prisoners who are asked to confess. Given the conditions laid down for the prisoners' dilemma—that the relative payoffs are as described, that there is no communication, and that this is a one-time, single-play situation—the rational choice for each player acting alone is to take the temptation to defect. That assures him or her of the better outcome, no matter what action the other takes. If the second player also defects, the first gets P, which is bad but still better than S; if the second does not defect, then our first gets T, which is even better than R. There is no effective incentive to cooperate; hence, both prisoners will defect and both will end up with quite a bad outcome (P), though not the very worst that might have happened to either if one cooperated while the other defected (S). Thus, in the prisoners' dilemma, the players defect whether their motives are aggressive or defensive: The results are the same.

THE SECURITY DILEMMA

Given the relative payoffs in a prisoners' dilemma, are two nations in an arms race condemned to the risk and waste of a never-ending, costly arms competition? In 1950 that seemed to be the case. President Truman's scientific advisers told him that they could build a powerful new weapon, hundreds of times more powerful than the atomic bomb: This was to be the hydrogen bomb. It would be an awesome weapon, and any war in which it was used would surely leave millions dead. Some Americans would have liked best to be sole owner of the new bomb (T) but would have settled for a situation where no country had it (R). But the Russians had all the same basic scientific knowledge that the Americans had, and neither power would consider allowing the other to have such a fearsome weapon unless it also had one. It seemed better to go ahead and build the hydrogen bomb if the Russians were going to build it also (P). Even though building a hydrogen bomb would leave both countries exposed to its dangers, it seemed better than being at the mercy of the Russians without a counterweapon (S). Lacking any prospect of an enforceable agreement that neither would build hydrogen bombs, both sides felt forced to build a weapon that they wished didn't exist.[4] This is the essence of the security dilemma: One may lose

---

4. See Herbert York, *The Advisors: Oppenheimer, Teller, and the Superbomb* (San Francisco: W. H. Freeman and Company, 1976).

greatly by failing to trust the other, but one risks losing even more if the trust proves misplaced.

Yet this is not always the outcome, because unlike the prisoners, national governments sometimes find it possible to communicate and to commit themselves to cooperate. A formal agreement, perhaps a treaty, that includes a provision to verify whether the agreement is being kept, provides the instrument for commitment. It takes a long time to build and deploy enough modern weapons to be militarily decisive—unlike the act of defection in prison, which requires only a moment. With good inspection techniques, one nation can detect betrayal before it becomes effective; thus, at worst, it would end up with a P payoff rather than with an S. That inspection may be agreed on and jointly executed (with inspectors permitted to roam about each others' countries) or unilaterally executed by mutually tolerated means (observation satellites and perhaps spies). But only if each has reliable information about the other's activities—and knows that the other has information—can two nations make and keep a commitment.

Not all arms race situations fit the prisoners' dilemma model, though communication is still critical to any effort to cooperate. The previous example assumed that strategic parity was a reasonably good solution for both countries—the second best of four solutions. Probably a different situation applied to the American-Soviet rivalry during the 1950s and early 1960s. The Russians were in a position of strategic inferiority; they could not credibly threaten war against the United States except in response to the most dire threat to their interests in Eastern Europe. Although they had the military means to deter any unprovoked American attack, they dared not do anything that might endanger the American global position and thus tempt the U.S. government to use nuclear weapons.

For the Russians, the payoffs may well have stayed like those of the prisoners' dilemma. But this was not the way the Americans saw things. The temptation (T) of spending heavily to widen American superiority was not very attractive because it promised to be expensive and offer few real gains. Thus, Americans were satisfied with the existing state of armament (R). A reversal of American superiority (S) was, of course, least preferred but highly unlikely given the American ability to keep track of Russian armaments by means of space satellite photograpy and overflights by U-2 planes. (Officials in the American executive branch with access to secret information from these sources did not share the worries of others about the so-called missile gap.) With this information and the wealth and scientific resources of the

Table 13.3

The arms race in the 1950s.

		Soviet Union	
		Limit arms	Race harder
United States	Limit arms	4, 3 (R, R)	1, 4 (S, T)
	Race harder	3, 1 (T, S)	2, 2 (P, P)

American economy, the United States did not see Soviet dominance as a real threat (see Table 13.3).

Because the Americans preferred the rewards of cooperation to the costs of trying to widen or even fully maintain their own superiority, the situation differed from the prisoners' dilemma. Nevertheless, the Americans were quite prepared, as the second best approach, to punish the Russians (and of course themselves) if Moscow refused to cooperate. The two countries could reach a cooperative solution if the Americans could show that (1) they were fully aware of Russian missile-building efforts, so the Russians could not push the S outcome on the Americans without the Americans' knowledge, and (2) the American payoffs were indeed as described—that is, America was prepared to go to great lengths to match new Russian missile building with enough of its own so as not to fall behind. The Americans also had to be able to show that (3) their political system was strong enough to undertake such a project (that is, that American taxpayers would support it with very high expenditures) and that (4) their economy was strong enough to carry the burden.

Ultimately, of course, the Russians did catch up, in effect because the Americans permitted them to do so. Why? By the mid-1960s, the relative number of weapons on both sides meant far less than it had; even with numerical inferiority, the Russians were strong enough to retaliate with sufficient force to discourage any American attack. Under those circumstances, it made little difference whether the Russians had only a third of the American number of missiles or as many—it was no longer worthwhile for the Americans to increase expenditures to the point required to restore the old ratio. The situation changed and a new set of outcomes was accepted because American perception of the payoffs changed even further from that of a prisoners' dilemma. For the United States, S became a much more acceptable result, which was really no worse than P (provided that the outcome of S was parity and not a reversal of superiority, which many people began to fear by the 1980s).

A very important way in which both players can avoid undesirable outcomes, therefore, is through changes in the payoff table. This often occurs because of technological or economic developments that make formerly preferred outcomes costlier or more difficult to achieve. In this case, it became almost impossible to achieve an advantage in strategic weapons that would lead to any real military or political advantage. There was also some shift in values, and many people in America—fatigued by the Vietnam war—decided that a military advantage was not more desirable than parity. Also, note the importance of technological change in facilitating communication: Observation satellites and aircraft made it possible for each side to check immediately on whether the other was building its capabilities too fast.

PROMOTING COOPERATION

Confrontations between the same parties occur repeatedly in international politics. When that happens, each country's actions in any single round of the game have consequences not only for the payoffs in that round but in later rounds as well. It is a logical next step, then, to consider what happens when a prisoners' dilemma situation occurs within what the participants think will be a string of relationships. Many experimental psychologists and other experts, including Anatol Rapoport and his colleagues, have examined situations like this under laboratory conditions. Their studies now include thousands of players with from fifty to several hundred plays by the same individuals. There is a typical sequence that many players adopt, which we shall now describe.

At the beginning participants often play cooperatively, with each partner being rewarded. After a short while, however, one partner becomes tempted to defect. His partner will usually retaliate after being betrayed once or twice, so both take the punishment outcome. At this point each may try to reestablish cooperation, but, without means for overt communication, it is a difficult business. A would-be cooperator may well continue to suffer the sucker's penalty. He may interpret this as betrayal and so return to defection.

In international politics, too, it may be very hard to change to cooperative behavior. The first initiatives may not be seen as cooperation at all, or, if perceived as such, they may be interpreted as weakness and thus be exploited. After a good deal of trial and error, however, many players do in fact succeed in cooperating consistently again, but it may be a long, painful time before this favorable pattern is established.

Under these conditions, each play is eventually seen not as an end in itself but as a means of communicating one's hope of promoting joint cooperation on later plays. In this way the game resembles the on-going politics among nations, where cooperation breeds expectations of cooperation and defection breeds expectations of defection. Ultimately, over many plays, it becomes possible to develop trust as the players become increasingly confident that they know how each other will behave.

Similarly, a nation-state may observe an agreement (such as an arms control treaty), even when in the short run it might seem in its interest to violate the agreement—and the nation-state may observe it out of self-interest rather than out of ethics or morality. International law is, of course, violated frequently, but in normal day-to-day procedures (such as those concerning transportation, communication, respect for the persons of ambassadors, and travel between nations), governments far more often observe the accepted conventions. Especially if their acts can be easily observed by others (again, communications between nations are crucial), nation-states pass up the immediate benefits of seizing a valuable cargo or person because they cannot afford the reprisals and disruption of future traffic that would surely follow. Thus, it becomes in the Russians' interest to observe an agreement; we trust them only to serve that interest, not be be honest or moral.

Let us note a few of the other circumstances that affect the frequency with which players, under experimental conditions, choose cooperative rather than competitive strategies. We can then apply these observations to international politics. Of course, it is a long jump from the laboratory to the world of national leaders, but the findings about variations in experimental procedures are nonetheless stimulating. They are important, too, because of an inherent difficulty in any analysis of the real world of international politics. We can only examine what has been done; if we want to speculate on the future we shall have to look at behavior under other conditions and try to make analogies where appropriate.[5]

1. Experimental evidence clearly shows that competitive strategies are more common where there are no means of communication

---

5. These and other relevant findings are regularly reported in several journals: *Behavioral Science, Journal of Conflict Resolution, Simulation and Games,* and *International Journal of Game Theory.*

between the players. Many kinds of information need to be communicated: Activities, reasons for those activities, intentions, and preferences (i.e., payoff structures) matter in varying degrees. Formal government-to-government communication facilities are a key part of this, but so are trade and various person-to-person contacts, such as tourism and cultural exchange.

2. When players do communicate, it seems essential that the communication be honest. If one player uses the opportunity to deceive the other, the result is often a longer run of mutual defection and double-crossing than happens when no communication is permitted. President Carter's decision to impose economic sanctions on the Soviet Union because of its invasion of Afghanistan stemmed partly from anger that Brezhnev had lied to him. Apparently, Brezhnev had told Carter that Afghanistan leader Hafizullah Amin had "requested the assistance" of Soviet troops—troops who then supervised Amin's deposition and assassination.

3. Competitive strategies are more common when the first player can reverse a decision about a particular play even after the decision has been made and communicated to the second player. When it is possible to change one's mind after seeing the other person's choice, it is much more common for players to change a previously announced noncooperative act to a cooperative one in response to the other's cooperation than for players to switch a cooperative choice to betrayal so as to exploit an opportunity.

4. Competitive strategies seem more common when players' decisions are made consecutively (without a chance to reverse them) than when both players communicate their decisions at the same time. This is probably because the player who has to move first often hesitates to expose himself to the sucker's penalty by leading with a cooperative play.

5. Some of these principles have been employed in a strategy developed by social psychologist Charles Osgood, who calls his strategy "Gradual and Reciprocated Initiatives in Tension-reduction," or GRIT. He says one side should make some limited conciliatory gestures unilaterally (such as not building or even abandoning some weapon), communicate the fact to the other side, and then look for some similar move by the other in return. If the other side seems to be taking advantage of your apparent weakness by escalating, then you retaliate with a step carefully matched to the other side's escalation. You may later try other conciliatory gestures. With this strategy, actions may start off as

unilateral, but they are limited and continue only if the other side responds favorably.[6]

6. It helps to have some experience in doing things together to gain some common reward. A famous "robbers' cave" experiment, performed by several psychologists in a boys' camp, supports this point. The leaders divided the boys into two rival groups and deliberately encouraged rivalry between them. After the two groups had become quite hostile, the leaders tried to see how the tension might be reduced. They tried bringing the groups together for enjoyable events, but that did little good. Then they created situations where the two groups had to cooperate in order to obtain something they both wanted. After reluctantly taking part in the latter activities, the boys eventually developed a new spirit and antagonisms eased. This experiment suggests that a major cooperative action by hostile governments has an importance that goes far beyond the immediate goal that the government may be trying to reach. Joint activities in space might have long-term effects that promote broader cooperation; so might joint activities to control global population. Long-term efforts to develop trust and avoid the prisoners' dilemma might lead to some sense of shared interest as well as to the specific benefits of whatever concrete steps were undertaken.[7]

7. It makes a difference how the experimenter describes the purpose of the game to the players before they begin. He can present it as (1) each player doing the best he can do regardless of what happens to the other player, (2) each player doing better than the other, or (3) both players doing well. Not surprisingly, people cooperate least often when the experimenter emphasizes doing better than the other. The game description becomes a self-fulfilling prophecy. Similarly, it may matter very much what preconceptions people bring to the analysis of international politics. People can be taught to think about joint rewards and to care about others. Those who have been taught—informally or in school—to think of the world in stark realist terms as "red in tooth and claw," where the overriding goal is to maximize the national interest of one's own state over all others, will be less ready to cooperate when they choose policies. What should be non-zero-sum situations

---

6. Charles Osgood, *An Alternative to War or Surrender* (Urbana: University of Illinois Press, 1962). See also Amitai Etzioni, "The Kennedy Experiment," *Western Political Quarterly* 20 (1967), 361–380, for an example of a GRIT process that actually took place.

7. Muzafer Sherif et al., *Intergroup Conflict and Cooperation: The Robbers' Cave Experiment* (Norman: University of Oklahoma Press, 1961).

may be interpreted so that the player's only concern is to maximize his or her own well-being (and result in producing mutual misery).

Professor Robert Axelrod conducted a tournament among thirteen social scientists to see whose computerized strategy for playing repeated prisoners' dilemma games would be most successful. Of all the strategies played, he found that *tit for tat* (cooperating after the opponent cooperated, defecting after a defection) was most successful, especially when coupled with *optimism* (opening with a cooperative move) and being somewhat *forgiving* (punishing once, then trying again to cooperate). But in analyzing the results carefully, he found that being somewhat more forgiving would have been even more successful; that is, all the social scientists played more competitively than would have been best.[8]

Thinking back on our prisoners in the police station, imagine how different their situation would have been if one or both of them had held some principle of "honor among thieves," possessing a prickly conscience that made it painful to betray the other. Suppose that both were in fact innocent—and moral, at that. Each might well prefer to accept a long prison term rather than to condemn the other unjustly to an even longer term. The payoffs thus would not coincide merely with jail terms. Under these circumstances (where the pangs of conscience associated with the temptation of defecting make T a very undesired outcome), the prisoners would actually get what would for them be the highest possible payoff when both refused to defect and thus received the very short jail sentence (R). In international politics, it is often easy to dismiss the effect of morality, since not too many people are prepared to say "Better me dead than both of us" when considering deterrence of a country perceived as an enemy. But such considerations should not be ignored. Many Americans and Russians might hesitate to annihilate each other's civilian population centers with nuclear weapons.

We must recognize from the beginning that international politics requires both conflict and cooperation. This is a fundamental argument that has been made against excessively realist strategic thinking about Cold War problems. One side alone cannot make all conflicts go away; yet if we insist on seeing the world as a constant struggle, we shall indeed make it more so.

---

8. Robert Axelrod, *The Evolution of Cooperation* (New York: Basic Books, 1984).

THE CAUSES OF ARMS ACQUISITION

Why do countries arm themselves, and how can an arms race be controlled? We have already discussed the prisoners' dilemma and an action-reaction arms race. Those ideas represent an advance over the ideas prevalent in the early Cold War years, when it seemed to many Americans that the action-reaction phenomenon was all one way—that is, America was reacting to Soviet militarism and aggressive behavior. But when the period of isolation under Stalin drew to a close and Soviet and American scientists began to make contact with each other, it became apparent that Soviet citizens typically held the mirror image of that perspective; that is, they saw the Soviet Union as simply reacting to American threats. From this exchange, people developed a more general understanding that in some real sense each side was reacting to the other and that it was extraordinarily difficult to sort out particular causes, especially once the action-reaction process was well under way. Several scholars then took up this understanding and saw that it fit some mathematical models of arms race behavior set out by Lewis F. Richardson years before and published in book form after his death.[9]

After the onset of the Cold War just after World War II, the Soviet and American arms levels were more or less constant for a long time, not showing a clear move upward until the 1960s. An arms race, of course, need not imply an upward spiral. It does imply competition; but if two long-distance runners maintain a steady pace, we nevertheless consider them in a race just as much as if their speeds were continually increasing. It is the element of *competition*, or *interaction*, that *characterizes a race*. To some degree, that interaction seems to be present in Soviet and American behavior—not a steady activity, but one that moves in fits and starts in response to particular acts that seem especially provocative. The notion of a race surely does not explain every element of this behavior. It may tell us about the fact of interaction in arms spending but not the level at which that interaction takes place. Thus, the Soviet-American arms race might occur at spending levels of less than $50 billion a year instead of more than $100 billion. Something other than mere interaction must be affecting that level. Moreover, the idea of interaction does not explain what happened in the 1970s. Interaction suggests that the Soviet Union would have moderated its military spending once the Americans slowed down their

---

9. Lewis F. Richardson, *Arms and Insecurity* (Chicago: Quadrangle, 1960).

after Vietnam. No such moderation took place; rather, quite the contrary. Again, something else was going on.

International hostility may help start and maintain an arms race, but various kinds of domestic influences also help maintain high levels of military spending. To understand further what drives this infernal machine, we must move down to some lower levels of analysis. It will be helpful to look at a diagram (Figure 13.3) prepared by Nazli Choucri and Robert North that identifies the causes of war; it provides an especially comprehensive framework for the causes of World War I.[10] The authors were not very concerned with explanations at the individual level of analysis, that is, how particular decision makers chose and behaved as they did during the August 1914 crisis. Rather, they were trying to identify the conditions at the governmental, societal, relational, and international system levels that brought about the crisis. In our terms, they were looking at the constraints that were imposed on decision makers and trying to understand the causes of those constraints.

This is a very complex diagram. But as you have discovered by now, international politics is very complex; there are few shortcuts to understanding. If you look at the diagram carefully, however, you will see that we have at one point or another in this book discussed most of the influences identified there. Each of the arrows with a plus sign indicates a causal relationship, where an increase in one factor or variable helps produce an increase in the variable to which the arrow points. Changes in some variables, of course, are caused by two or more other variables. Although this diagram includes more variables than we want to look at here—it pertains to causes of war (or "violence behavior" in the diagram), not just military expenditures—it provides us with many useful points of discussion. It also reminds us of another question to which we must eventually return: Do arms races lead to war?

The box labeled "military expenditures" has six arrows pointing to it. One on the right is from "military expenditures of nonallies." Considering that the Soviet Union and the United States are certainy nonallies, we have a reference to the type of arms race that we have been discussing. Obviously the largest, most important, and potentially threatening nonallies are most relevant to military-spending decisions. The broad term *nonallies* reminds us, however, that we should not see all arms races as purely bilateral phenomena. As we noted, in the contemporary world the Soviet Union also has to be concerned with the power and

10. Nazli Choucri and Robert C. North, *Nations in Conflict: National Growth and International Violence* (San Francisco: W. H. Freeman and Company, 1975).

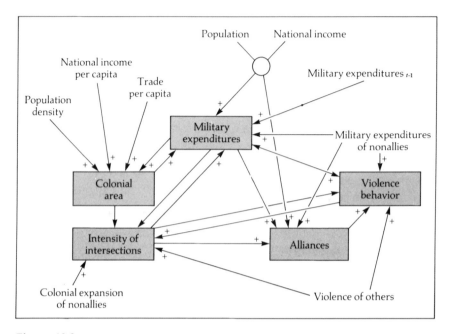

Figure 13.3
A model of the dynamics of international violence. [*Source:* Nazli Choucri and Robert C. North, *Nations in Conflict: National Growth and International Violence* (San Francisco: W. H. Freeman and Company, copyright © 1975), p. 168.]

behavior of its close neighbor, China, and devotes a significant part of its military effort to coping with that problem. And it was not many years ago that U.S. strategic delivery vehicles were pointed at China so that the United States could strike at China as well as at Russia in case of a Soviet attack on America.

Conflicts over Spheres of Influence

Two other arrows to the military expenditures box come from the left-hand boxes labeled "colonial area" and "intensity of intersections." For Choucri and North, the latter term refers to "the intensity of violence in specifically colonial conflicts between the actor state and other major powers." In the late twentieth century, there are few colonial territories as such; most areas of the world are composed of formally sovereign states. Yet most major powers clearly do have spheres of influence that include states over which they exert substantial control. The Western

Hemisphere (excluding Cuba and Nicaragua) is such a sphere for the United States. Most of Eastern Europe, with Communist states that are often referred to as *satellites* of the Soviet Union, is the major USSR sphere of influence. But the two powers compete sharply with each other in these and especially other areas of the world. They are deeply involved in this competition, using economic, political, and military means in Africa, the Middle East, and Asia. States often move from one power's sphere of influence to the other's, often in a process that includes a great deal of military violence. Or one power may repulse an effort to shift a state out of its sphere of influence, often using substantial military force.

The Vietnam war is the most vivid example of such a use of force, but there are many others. Within the past few years, Ethiopia has shifted from being an American to a Soviet client, and its enemy and neighbor, Somalia, made the opposite shift in the course of a long and devastating war between them. After a long national liberation struggle, Angola ceased to be a colony of America's NATO ally Portugal. Its struggle was heavily assisted by the Russians and the Chinese, each of which supported different and bitterly opposed local leaders. The United States and France later intervened to preserve their influence on Angola's African neighbor, Zaire, when there seemed to be some threat to it from Angola. Zimbabwe (Rhodesia) was long wracked by civil war. The government was dominated by the white minority, which looked to the West for help (not always successfully), and the black guerrillas, who were helped but not dominated by the USSR. Western-backed Yemen fought Soviet-supported South Yemen on the Arabian peninsula. Of course, the United States and the Soviet Union have been deeply enmeshed in the Arab-Israeli conflict, sending arms to various and changing allies. The Soviet Union helped engineer a coup in its favor against a fairly neutralist regime in Afghanistan to bring that country securely into its sphere of influence. The new regime proved highly unpopular, and the Russians found themselves increasingly drawn into a civil war there. In Indochina, the Soviet Union helped the Vietnamese overthrow a government in Cambodia that had been allied with China. Dominant powers—or would-be dominant powers—in the international system require large armed forces.[11]

---

11. Erich Weede, "National Position in World Politics and Military Allocation Ratios in the 1950s and 1960s," *Jerusalem Journal of International Relations* 2 (Spring 1977), no. 3, found that being a major power, having a land border with a state not a member of its own bloc, and having a territorial dispute with such a state all contribute to relatively

In thinking about conflicts of interest or intensity of intersections, recall the discussion in Chapter 5 about how various configurations of polarity in the global system can influence the frequency and severity of war. Multipolar balance-of-power systems, we noted, are likely to have a substantial amount of war. In fact, war is one of the most important means whereby some major powers try to prevent other big states from expanding their power. War, especially in peripheral or colonial areas, is supposed to be a key instrument in maintaining an acceptable balance. In a bipolar system, the two major powers are likely to be in constant competition and conflict of some sort out of fear that one will attain a decisive advantage. Although under most conditions the major powers may be deterred from fighting each other directly, they may feel obliged to carry on proxy wars in various parts of the world. Experiments by social psychologists with people playing non-zero-sum games have found that two-person games are more likely to be played competitively than games with three or more players. This suggests that cooperation may be harder to achieve in a bipolar world than in a multipolar system, perhaps because it is easier to compare one's own achievements with those of a single other player and thus to perceive him or her as an opponent.

These influences help to produce colonial or sphere-of-influence expansion and intense intersections and feed demands for more military expenditures. If a big power has colonies or spheres of influence, it will need troops to police them. They may be troops of the big power itself or local client forces armed and supplied by the big power. If wars are going on or are threatened in various parts of the globe, the big states need arms and troops. If they don't fight directly, they still need arms to supply their small-power clients and money to support their clients' armed forces in war.

Moreover, notice that in each of these two relationships (military expenditures and colonial area, and military expenditures and intersections) there are two arrows running between the paired boxes in Figure 13.3, one arrow in either direction. This indicates that two variables interact with each other in a positive way, creating feedback whereby high intensity of intersection creates a need or demand for more arms and military expenditures create the possibility of further intense in-

---

high military expenditures. Other research indicates that *colonial* borders are strongly related to the occurrence of war; see Harvey Starr and Benjamin A. Most, "A Return Journey: Richardson, 'Frontiers' and War in the 1946–65 Era," *Journal of Conflict Resolution* 22 (1978), 323–356.

tersections. With a large, well-trained, well-equipped, and mobile military establishment, there comes a potential and perhaps a temptation to use it. Here, capabilities create an opportunity as well as increase the willingness to take advantage of the opportunity. Such capabilities expand a state's menu; for example, it can conquer new colonies or spheres of influence, if necessary, against other expansionist powers. Many critics of American foreign and security policy maintained that the Vietnam war was made possible and in some sense perhaps caused by the fact that the United States had developed a great capacity for fighting counterinsurgent, or antiguerrilla, wars in faraway places. These critics therefore tried to reduce the size of the American military establishment, especially its capacity for fighting conventional wars, as a means of making it less likely that the United States would get involved in such wars. Whatever the merits of their evaluation of the Vietnam situation, it does seem reasonable that local conflicts are made possible by, as well as stimulate, military expenditures.

Domestic Influences

Shift now to the variable at the upper right corner of Figure 13.3 labeled "military expenditures$_{t-1}$." The subscript is simply a way of referring to a previous time period $(t - 1)$. Here the figure indicates that the level of military expenditures at any time depends in part on previous levels of military spending. Pressures to maintain and to increase military expenditures arise within a country in at least three different ways. The first reflects *bureaucratic pressures* and inertia within the government. As we have seen in earlier chapters, the leader of any large organization must be deeply concerned with the interests of his or her organization. A leader is most reluctant to see the size of the organization shrink or its budget cut. Furthermore, the leader is likely to feel that the organization is doing important jobs for society—if he didn't think so, he probably would do something else for a living. If the organization is doing an important job and fulfilling an important function, then it would do even better with more people and resources at its disposal. Moreover, the leader's own power in the government and in society at large depends heavily on the size of the organization. Leaders of big and growing organizations receive more respect than do leaders of small or shrinking ones. A leader will therefore vigorously resist any effort to cut the budget or staffing level of the organization and do his best to expand them. Research on budget making has long established that just about the best predictor to the size of any organization's current budget is the size of its last budget—and, especially in an expanding economy, adding an incremental increase.[12]

Military organizations are by no means exceptions to this observation. Personal self-interest, interest in the organization one leads, and images of societal self-interest all come together. After all, if the Air Force chief of staff doesn't speak up to be sure that the Air Force gets a fair share of society's resources, who will? This also means that when one major weapons system becomes outmoded or obsolete, there will be a built-in interest group pressing either to modernize it or to replace it with something else that will do a similar job and keep the same people and resources employed.

When the B-52 bomber becomes obsolete, Air Force generals will look around for a new bomber, such as the B-1, to replace it. They think the bombing mission is important and vital to American security. How can there be a good Air Force if there are no big, glamorous planes to fly? Who would enlist in the Air Force only to be a missile command officer in a silo hundreds of feet underground? Air Force evaluations of the merits of a proposed new strategic bomber are unlikely, therefore, to be entirely objective and disinterested. To the degree that a major Air Force mission is to provide strategic nuclear deterrence through its land-based missiles, Air Force generals will be loath to see land-based missiles abandoned as being obsolete. They will look hard for something like the MX and a means to deploy it. Once a weapon has gone far through the process of research and development, it becomes politically and bureaucratically very difficult not to produce and deploy it in large numbers. For example, the MIRV was developed largely to ensure that some American retaliatory vehicles would be able to penetrate Soviet defenses even if the USSR should deploy an effective ABM system. The 1972 ABM Treaty between the United States and the USSR, however, very sharply limited ABM construction and made MIRVs unnecessary for the main purpose for which they were designed. Nevertheless, production and deployment of MIRVs went ahead.

---

12. The most important early work on this topic was Otto Davis, M. A. H. Dempster, and Aaron Wildavsky, "A Theory of the Budgetary Process," *American Political Science Review* 60 (September 1966), no. 3, pp. 529–547. This was applied to the Department of Defense by John Patrick Crecine and George Fischer, "On Resource Allocation Processes in the U.S. Department of Defense," in C. Cotter (ed.), *Political Science Annual, 1973* (Indianapolis: Bobbs-Merrill, 1973). Also see Morton Halperin and Arnold Kanter (eds.), *Readings in American Foreign Policy: A Bureaucratic Perspective* (Boston: Little, Brown, 1973); Arnold Kanter, *Defense Politics: A Budgetary Perspective* (Chicago: University of Chicago Press, 1979).

The Navy, too, has its own interests. Admirals like to maintain big surface ships like aircraft carriers, as well as the limited-mission and not-so-glamorous nuclear submarines. It's hard to "join the Navy and see the world" from under the sea.

This argument does not imply that military leaders are corrupt or that their advice to maintain or acquire a weapons system is necessarily mistaken. Their evaluation of the national interest and that of most objective observers might well coincide. But it does imply that the allocation of resources within a government is strongly resistant to reduction or elimination. This year's military budget is a good predictor (along with such external factors as intersections and opponents' spending) of next year's military budget.

The second kind of pressure, one that arises from the society and economy at large, is what we discussed in Chapter 9 as the *military-industrial complex*. In broad terms, many elements of society have a stake in maintaining and expanding a high level of military spending. Labor unions, defense contractors, politicians, and government bureaucrats all stand to benefit. Boeing Aerospace Corporation—and its subcontractors and their employees—make missiles. If the Minuteman is phased out, they need contracts for an MX or something like it to stay prosperous. Although the structure of its economy is somewhat different, similar pressures and interests exist in the Soviet Union.

The third kind of pressure is *technological momentum*. Military research and development employs a half million of the best-qualified scientists and engineers worldwide and absorbs one third to one half of the world's human and material resources devoted to research and development. The research is intellectually challenging—and highly competitive. Individuals compete with one another, corporations and military services compete with their counterparts, and, of course, their countries compete. The incentives, privileges, and rewards are high. The work, however, takes a long time. Lead times of ten years or more are typical from conceptualization through design, model production, improvement, repeated testing, evaluation, prototype production, training, and final deployment. This scientific inertia intertwines with bureaucratic inertia to make it very difficult to halt a promising project once it gets under way, even if its initial purpose (as with MIRV) has been lost.

The MIRV system had its origins in satellite-launching systems of the early 1960s. It began principally in government organizations: the Advanced Research Projects Agency of the Department of Defense, the Space Technology Laboratory, and the Air Force Space and Missile System Office. Once many of the pieces were available, it then became almost inevitable that they would be put together as a multiple-warhead delivery system, and private aerospace companies combined with the government laboratories and military chiefs to promote the project. As Herbert York, who observed the process from inside, remarked, "Once the technology was developed MIRV assumed a momentum of its own; the chances of halting it were by then slim."[13]

These three influences help explain why the lines for military spending shown in Figure 13.1 generally maintained their previous level or rose. Periods of significant reduction, while not totally absent, were rare. Usually a "ratchet effect" occurs from a war; after the level of military effort has been geared up to a high wartime level, a ratchet of bureaucratic and political-economic pressure keeps it from dropping to its prewar level. The new expenditure floor is usually well above the previous level. This phenomenon can be observed in the United States after all its major wars in the last ninety years (Spanish-American, World Wars I and II, and the Korean war) except the Vietnam war.

Finally, note the other arrow leading into the military expenditures box in Figure 13.3, from the interaction between "population" and "national income." We have not talked much about this particular influence, though it suggests various domestic societal-level influences. Here it chiefly implies that economic and population growth provide the means for an expanding military establishment. A big country can support a big army. In a growing economy, more resources can be devoted to military purposes without reducing anyone's share of the expanding pie. Maintaining large armed forces becomes relatively painless.[14] These factors of population and income growth also remind us of other explanations of imperialism—more completely captured by Choucri and North in the influences leading to the growth of colonial area shown in Figure 13.3. Growth provides not only the possibility of military expansion, but also the need for it: a need for the control of resources, a need for assured food supplies to feed a growing population, and a need for assured raw materials to feed a growing economy. Colonial expansion in turn feeds into military spending.

---

13. Herbert York, "Multiple Warhead Missiles," *Scientific American* 28 (1973), no. 2, pp. 14–25. See also Ted Greenwood, *Making the MIRV* (Cambridge, Mass.: Ballantine, 1975).

14. Gernot Köhler, "Toward a General Theory of Armaments," *Journal of Peace Research* 16 (1979), no. 2, pp. 117–135. By the same token, economic *stagnation* exerts a *negative* effect on arms growth, especially at high levels of military spending where the trade-offs become painful.

Together, domestic influences seem so strong that some analysts have maintained that military establishments are essentially "autistic" actors. They take this image from the psychology of autistic children, who shut themselves off almost completely from outside social stimuli and respond overwhelmingly just to their own internal psyches. By this characterization, the arms race is not really a race at all if by *race* we mean that the runners really care about each other's positions. The governmental and societal leaders in an autistic system maintain a level of military capability almost solely as a result of demands and pressures from within their own countries, not as a result of international incidents or military gains by the other racer. By this explanation, we are racing against ourselves; international events are irrelevant except as they provide an excuse for societal elites to demand sacrifices for military purposes. What the enemy is doing thus becomes useful domestic propaganda to support policies that leaders desire on other grounds. Such an explanation certainly does not rule out some collusion between the elites of two ostensibly competing countries. About the time when budgetary appropriations or authorizations are drawn up, the so-called enemy might act aggressively or show off a new weapon to assist the elites of their "enemy" to extract more military funds—and then expect the same favor in return.

A preoccupation with Soviet and American military spending may obscure another fact: Many countries have military establishments that are ostensibly directed toward external enemies but in reality are chiefly directed toward internal enemies. They are not instruments of foreign war but instruments of internal repression. This is most obviously the case in many third world countries, but even for the Soviet Union this view should not be ignored. Political dissidence still calls forth repression. Half of Soviet citizens are not Russians, but members of other European and Asian ethnic groups with a potential for nationalist separatism. The Soviet government needs a substantial army just for internal security.

Which Influences Are Most Important?

It is one thing to list the various influences that may promote military spending or militarism, and quite another to assess the truth of the assertions or their relative importance. Most of the explanations seem plausible, and there is some evidence for each. Choucri and North report that for most of the major powers in the years before World War I, most of the contributing factors to military expenditures shown in Figure 13.3 are significant. But they see domestic factors as more powerful than international ones:

> The primary importance of domestic factors ... does not preclude the reality of arms competition. Two countries whose military establishments are expanding largely for domestic reasons can, and indeed almost certainly will, become acutely aware of each other's spending. Thereafter, although spending may continue to be powerfully influenced by domestic factors, deliberate military competition may increase and even take the form of an arms race (although the race may be over specific military features and may be a very small portion of total military spending).[15]

Other research efforts have concentrated on the post–World War II Soviet-American and NATO-Warsaw Pact arms increases. These results do not point clearly to the dominance of either domestic or international influences. Rather, it is clear that both matter under conditions that vary at different times and for different participants. Action-reaction conditions may occur only in episodes, not in response to normal increases in the opponent's military spending but to major changes.

The United States did react with increased military expenditures to international political reversals on certain occasions: It rearmed after the North Korean attack on South Korea in 1950; it started a crash program in the late 1950s when Soviet space achievements suggested—erroneously—that Russia was about to get an ICBM first-strike capability; and American foreign policy reversals in the late 1970s, especially in the Middle East, helped stimulate the most recent American arms buildup. The Soviets may have boosted their military spending in the 1970s in response to the visible and rather humiliating defeat they suffered in the Cuban missile crisis. Yet even in all these cases, many domestic interests had already demanded the increases in arms spending. The external political reversals provided a rallying cry, an excuse, as much as a true impetus.

Many problems arise in trying to do a good arms race analysis. The results are rarely conclusive, and the time for analysis is relatively short. The data available are highly aggregated; usually one must deal with total military spending rather than, say, spending for strategic arms, which might be the most relevant figure to an arms race hypothesis. The quality of the data on Soviet military spending is very poor,

---

15. Nazli Choucri and Robert C. North, *Nations in Conflict: National Growth and International Violence* (W. H. Freeman and Company, 1975).

subject to rather wide differences in interpretation. The lags between request and authorization and appropriation add further difficulties, as we noted. As a result, any analysis is bound to contain substantial error. Moreover, both the bureaucratic politics and arms race explanations lead us to expect very similar behavior—namely, steady or gradually increasing expenditures by both sides. Given these problems, it is very hard to separate different causes and to document those differences in a convincing way.[16]

Given the present state of our art and science, we can only say that both domestic and action-reaction influences operate, and they often *reinforce* each other. It also matters who the decision-makers are. Some leaders or administrators may be more tolerant of military spending by the other side or less willing to divert funds from domestic civilian needs than are others. The Reagan administration has shifted spending from civilian to military purposes to a degree that is unprecedented for the United States. This was a deliberate political choice, though observers disagree about the degree to which it reflects the change in the administration per se and the degree to which it reflects a broader shift in domestic political preferences—of which the administration would be only the agent—that in turn may result from the higher level of international political tensions. Some might argue, furthermore, that high international tensions themselves have resulted from the change in the administration. Cause and effect are not readily distinguishable.

Since the empirical results are not conclusive, and since each of the independent or causal influences is itself caused by other factors in the chain, it becomes very hard to suggest effective ways to reduce arms expenditures and slow what we call the arms race. Some people, accepting one version of the autism argument, insist that only a drastic change in domestic economic, social, and political institutions can make a difference. But since both the United States and the Soviet Union behave similarly despite their very different domestic systems, that viewpoint is questionable. Obviously, some shift in popular and elite preferences and in the sense of threat could help slow the arms race. But how much? We saw in Chapter 10 that the Vietnam-period shift toward preferences for lower military spending proved transitory. Further attention to governmental and bureaucratic factors in the mo-

---

16. The arms race literature is reviewed in Bruce Russett, "International Interactions and Processes: The Internal vs. External Debate Revisited," in Ada Finifter (ed.), *Political Science: The State of the Discipline* (Washington, D.C.: American Political Science Association, 1983). See also Dina A. Zinnes, "Three Puzzles in Search of a Researcher," *International Studies Quarterly* 24 (1980), 315–342, on the general puzzle of interstate interaction.

mentum behind arms spending is in order. For instance, it might be easier to restrain scientific research and development than to head off bureaucratic pressures to deploy newly developed systems.

A future leader hoping to conclude an international arms control or disarmament agreement might draw the following conclusions about the importance of domestic influences:

1. Any agreement has to be sensible politically as well as just strategically. Bureaucratic and domestic interests will have to be satisfied, and the agreement may not be worth the price. (President Carter, for instance, approved development of the MX in a largely vain effort to satisfy domestic critics of the SALT II agreement.) It may therefore be easier to reach tit-for-tat informal agreements with the Soviet Union than to negotiate a formal treaty that must get a two-thirds majority in the Senate.

2. It is probably impossible to achieve any long-term improvement in the nuclear arms competition without some East-West understanding about what kinds of acts in the other's sphere of influence are permissible and what kinds are not. Otherwise the fears stimulated by sphere-of-influence military clashes may lead to the rejection of arms control efforts.

3. Beware of agreements that cannot be adequately verified. Even if a violation does no real harm to the military balance, it is likely to alarm domestic critics and make it harder to keep the country united in support of other arms control agreements.

WHAT'S WRONG WITH ARMS RACES, ANYWAY?

At this point you may feel we have skipped past a deceptively simple question: Why should we care about arms races at all? Are they really so bad? After all, states are faced with a security dilemma in this anarchic world of each state against all. Perhaps the continuing, competitive acquisition of weapons may be the only way to find a measure of security; arms purchases might provide a necessary and otherwise unobtainable deterrent: "If you would have peace, prepare for war."

The case against large-scale arms acquisitions rests on three assertions:

1. It is wasteful, imposing an enormous financial burden and squandering resources.

2. It ensures that if war ever does occur, it will be much more destructive than if such great accumulations of killing power had not taken place. Conceivably such a war could mean the end of humanity.

3. The continued accumulation of weapons increases international tension and therefore increases the likelihood of a major war. Arms races are a cause of war.

We shall examine each of these assertions in turn.

Waste

The amount of money the world spends on military purposes in one year alone now exceeds the value of the entire output of the world in 1900 (measured in constant dollars—that is, not counting the effects of inflation). In 1913, immediately before World War I, roughly 3 to 3½ percent of total world output was devoted to the military; now the proportion is about 5 percent of the world output (gross national product of all countries). Current world military expenditures equal the value of the gross national product of all South Asian and African countries combined, or total worldwide government expenditures on education or health. What this means in terms of world opportunities foregone—in terms of misery, ignorance, starvation, and disease—cannot be measured precisely, but it can be imagined. As a general and Republican president, Dwight Eisenhower once said, "Every gun that is made, every warship launched, every rocket fired signifies, in the final sense, a theft from those who hunger and are not fed, those who are cold and are not clothed. This world in arms is not spending money alone. It is spending the sweat of its laborers, the genius of its scientists, the hopes of its children."

Many people have argued that military spending drains the economy of productive potential, that by diverting funds and skilled manpower to the dead end of the military establishment, investment and technological innovation in civilian sectors are lost. Defense industries, working under contracts with the Pentagon that provide for a profit margin above whatever the producer's costs may be, can afford to pay whatever salaries are needed to attract skilled workers. Civilian industries' products must compete in the market with other domestic and foreign goods; therefore, those industries have to worry about their costs and the prices they can get for their products. As a result, they often cannot pay the high salaries offered by the defense sector. They either risk pricing themselves out of the market or simply fail to hire enough high-quality labor. High-technology enterprises and top-flight scientists who might otherwise produce goods and services that could be sold abroad to compete with Japanese and German industry never get to produce those goods.

In the long run, the problems of universities are as serious. Currently, for instance, there is an extreme shortage of Ph.D.'s in computer science, and universities cannot remotely match the salaries offered in the defense industry. Without computer science Ph.D.'s to train new computer scientists, the supply of skilled personnel may never catch up to the need. In effect, the defense industry risks eating the "seed corn" (the productivity of future generations) necessary for both its own long-term survival and the competitiveness of high-technology American industry.

It is easy to point to the much lower military expenditures of Germany and Japan (3.2 and 0.9 percent of GNP, respectively, in 1980) than the United States (5.3 percent) and their substantially higher growth rates over a long time period. Since World War II, the United States has carried a substantially higher military burden (military spending as a percentage of GNP) than any other industrialized capitalist country. Such a long-term absorption of high-technology resources for what are economically unproductive uses must have bad effects. Arthur Burns, chairman of the Council of Economic Advisers under President Eisenhower, put it this way: "The real cost of the defense sector consists, therefore, not only of the civilian goods and services that are currently foregone on its account; it includes also an element of growth that could have been achieved through larger investment in human or business capital." Systematic evidence tends to support this argument. Short-run effects on the economic growth rate are hard to find, but it does seem clear that military expenditures reduce investment and capital formation (and hence future growth and future military power) in virtually all kinds of economies: developed capitalist countries, less-developed countries, and the Soviet Union.[17]

Of course, there is no guarantee that a cut in military spending would result in much more investment, much more money spent on health and education, or satisfying human needs. The allocation would

---

17. The quotation is from Arthur F. Burns, "The Defense Sector and the American Economy," in Seymour Melman (ed.), *The War Economy of The United States* (New York: St. Martin's, 1971), p. 115; a report on the relation between military spending and growth is Ron Smith and George Georgiu, "Assessing the Effect of Military Expenditure on OECD Economies: A Survey," *Arms Control* 4 (May 1983), no. 1, pp. 3–15.

depend on economic conditions and especially on conscious political choice.[18] But we do know that the savings from lower military spending would not all be consumed as beer and swimming pools.

Sometimes, military spending is justified as a means to create employment—people can be put to work building weapons or serving in the armed forces. This happened in 1940 and 1941, when the United States began to arm for World War II and, in the process, completed its recovery from the Great Depression. People and factories that would otherwise have been idle were put to work. But that was an exceptional time: The government was willing to engage in deficit spending in order to rearm; it was much less willing to do so for obvious civilian make-work projects or even for large-scale expenditures on behalf of civilian well-being.

Since that time, however, the situation has rarely been so simple. In recent years many people have been out of work, but the country has also been plagued by inflation. Deficit spending may help create employment opportunities, but it also fuels inflation. The government has tried to hold down nondefense spending and avoid increasing taxes. Under these circumstances, the military increase comes at the expense of government spending for civilian purposes, and military spending reshuffles jobs rather than creates them. Some workers (such as engineers and draftsmen), industries (such as aerospace, munitions, and shipbuilding), and parts of the country (especially the Sun Belt) gain jobs; others (unskilled workers, home construction, and the Midwest) lose jobs.

Because of the types of jobs gained and lost, military spending actually produces a net *loss* of jobs when it substitutes for civilian expenditures. Military purchases go mostly for high-technology goods made by highly skilled and highly paid workers. The salaries are higher, but the number of jobs is smaller. Careful studies have demonstrated that almost any other kind of spending, either private or public, would create more jobs. The assumptions and methods of these various studies differ, so the details of their results differ, too (see Table 13.4). But they all come to the same basic conclusion: Military spending produces fewer jobs than does virtually any other kind of spending, private or public (except for the space program).

---

18. See Bruce Russett, "Defense Expenditures and National Well-Being," *American Political Science Review* 76 (December 1982), no. 4, pp. 767–777; William Domke et al., "The Illusion of Choice: Defense and Welfare in Advanced Industrial Democracies, 1948–1978," *American Political Science Review* 77 (March 1983), no. 1, pp. 19–35.

Table 13.4
Four estimates of employment-creating effects of defense and other expenditures.

---

1. Number of jobs created by alternative expenditures as compared with spending on the B-1 bomber, 1977:

Tax cut	+10,000
Housing	+30,000
Welfare and Public works	+20,000

2. Number of jobs created or lost by changes in defense budget of 30 percent, compensated by opposite equal change in education, health, public assistance, and environmental programs, 1980:

Defense increase	−1,300,000
Defense decrease	+2,000,000

3. Number of jobs created by $1 billion spent for various purposes, 1977:

Defense	45,800
Civilian production	53,000
Antirecession aid to state and local governments	71,000
Public service employment	98,000

4. Number of jobs created by $1 billion spent for various purposes, 1974:

Defense (military personnel)	58,000
Firemen	70,000
Policemen	73,000
Nurses	85,000
Teachers	76,000
Job Corps	145,000

Sources: 1. Chase Econometric Associates, *Economic Impact of the B-1 Program on the U.S. Economy and Comparative Case Studies* (Cynwyd, Pa.: Chase Econometric Associates, 1975), table 14, T2.

2. Roger Bezdek, "The 1980 Economic Impact—Regional and Occupational—of Compensated Shifts in Defense Spending," *Journal of Regional Science* 15 (1975), no. 2, pp. 183–197.

3. "The Pentagon as Job Creator," *The Defense Monitor* 6 (September–October 1977), no. 7, p. 3.

4. Marion Anderson, *The Empty Pork Barrel* (Lansing: Public Interest Research Group in Michigan, 1978), p. 1.

Destructive Potential

Waste is not the worst of sins: We might tolerate it if the arms race did not threaten our very existence. The destructive potential of modern weapons needs little emphasis. Before World War II, military aircraft had a combat radius of but a few hundred miles and could carry only a ton or so of high-explosive bombs. But now bombers and missiles reach halfway around the globe, carrying payloads whose explosive power can be nearly 100 million times that of a pre–World War II bomber.

A large-scale Soviet attack on the United States, using thousands of warheads to attack urban and industrial targets, would be devastating. Various studies by U.S. government agencies produce various estimates of "prompt casualties" (those occurring within the first thirty days of the attack), depending on assumptions about shelters, wind and weather conditions, and the nature of the blasts (air burst or surface burst). But all the estimates are high, ranging from a top of from 155 million to 165 million (75 percent of the American population) to a low of from 76 million to 85 million. If the urban population could be evacuated before the attack, the prompt *fatalities* might still be 20 million to 55 million. Although these estimates were made for a Soviet first strike, the USSR could produce very nearly the same number of deaths in a retaliatory strike.

Even restricted counterforce attacks would still produce very heavy casualties because of the large number of targets that would have to be hit. An attack on only the existing 1,052 ICBM silos, 46 Strategic Air Command bases, and 2 bases for missile-launching submarines would result in seven million to 15 million prompt deaths and as many wounded.

The loss of essential medical facilities probably would make things even worse. If only one city were hit, patients could be shipped to nearby areas, and doctors could come in from nearby. If all major cities were hit, there would not be much outside from which help could come. Take, for instance, the effect of an attack on the seventy-one largest urban areas in the United States. About 55 percent of the American people live there, but those same areas contain 70 percent of all American physicians. The ratio of still-living casualties to surviving physicians would at first be around 1000 to 1, but then drop as more people died. This compares with an average daily patient load for each doctor of, at most, 25 to 1. Casualties could exceed available hospital beds by 30 or 40 to 1. These fatality estimates are just for the short term, preceding "the worst epidemic that could ever be." Critical damage to the economy and society would soon appear.

If, in addition to hitting the seventy-one urban areas, a "mere" 200 hundred-kiloton warheads were used against the centers of three remaining industries—iron and steel, other metals, and petroleum refining—only 2 percent of the entire national capacity in those industries would survive. Gas pipelines, oil pipelines, and electricity grids would be fragmented. Without fuel, the entire American transportation system would be crippled. Railroad lines would be chopped up. Water supply and sewage facilities would break down all over, creating epidemics and further straining the already impossibly overburdened doctors and hospitals. Antibiotics and other medical supplies would be quickly exhausted. Radiation damage would lower people's resistance to disease. If food were still available in agricultural areas, it could not be processed and shipped, since those facilities are generally in metropolitan areas. Food would rot on the farm while remaining supermarket shelves, which normally contain only a week of stock, would be immediately emptied. Starvation would be widespread. No possible level of preparation or civil defense could significantly ease this disaster.

We have not even mentioned long-term ecological results, such as depletion of the ozone, selective destruction of some plants and animals and the survival of the hardier forms, cancer from radioactive fallout, etc., etc., etc. Worse yet, a major scientific report in 1983 raised the likelihood of "nuclear winter" and global climatic catastrophe. Dust and especially soot from fires following nuclear explosions might bring on a period of darkness (much too dark to see, even at midday, for a week) and a temperature drop of 20 degrees Celsius in the Northern Hemisphere; the temperature, even in summer, would remain below freezing for three months. An entire growing season for crops might be lost. The precise effects from this climatic shock would vary depending on the size and targeting of the nuclear strike. These estimates are for 5,000 megatons of explosive in strikes against cities and missile bases that, while great, is well below the maximum possible. (Total Soviet and American nuclear megatonnage is around 15,000.) The specter raised is that of the end of civilization, and perhaps of all human life.[19]

If the arms buildup had been halted two or three decades ago, civilization-threatening levels of nuclear destruction would not exist. But it wasn't, and they do. The threat will remain with us until the arms race is dramatically reversed.

Likelihood of War

If we could be sure that these destructive capabilities would never be used—that the "balance of terror" would be reliably stable—they might be tolerable. But there can be no such assurance. Technological change

---

19. See U.S. Congress, Office of Technology Assessment, *The Effects of Nuclear War* (Washington, D.C.: U.S. Government Printing Office, 1979); Arthur M. Katz, *Life after Nuclear War* (Cambridge, Mass.: Ballinger, 1982); Carl Sagan, "Nuclear War and Climatic Catastrophe: Some Policy Implications," *Foreign Affairs* 62 (Winter 1983/84), no. 2, pp. 256–292.

and the spread of nuclear weapons to other countries could easily make war more likely. Despite all precautions, accidental or unauthorized firings of nuclear weapons by an insubordinate military commander or a terrorist group could trigger destruction. Increasing the number of weapons also immensely complicates the problems of command and control involved in any effort to limit nuclear war once it has begun. These problems will be more severe as poor countries, unable to spend billions of dollars on good command and control systems (like those of American and the USSR), acquire such weapons. Nuclear war *can* happen.

Research on the question of whether arms races lead to war has, until recently, been inconclusive. People have taken sides on the issue with evidence that was no better than the maxims of conventional wisdom (such as "If you would have peace, prepare for war") and selectively referring to contradictory examples. Some people have argued that there is no evidence that arms races typically result in war. On the other hand, Choucri and North concluded that military expenditures played a significant role in promoting international violence in the period before 1914.

More generally, a study of great powers since 1815 found that the great majority of disputes arising during accelerating arms races did, in fact, end in war, whereas only a small number of serious diplomatic disputes not combined with arms races ended in war. This evidence is basically correlational—that is, it shows that arms races tend to be followed by war—and not persuasively causal. Therefore, it is possible to argue that states engaged in arms races were experiencing such conflict and tension that they would have gone to war anyway, whether or not they were engaged in an arms race. By this argument, the arms race was a symptom, not a cause, of the conflict that ended in war. Also, the results depend somewhat on how an arms race is defined: how much interaction and whether one party is far ahead of the other and whether the gap is closing.[20]

We do know enough to say that engaging in an arms race is certainly not a very reliable way of preventing a war. Knowing the fears that must inevitably arise during an arms race—fears that the other side

---

20. The general study is Michael Wallace, "Arms Races and Escalation: Some New Evidence," *Journal of Conflict Resolution* 23 (March 1979), no. 1, pp. 3–16. It has been subjected to several critiques that qualify without fully refuting its conclusions. See Paul Diehl, "Arms Races and Escalation: A Closer Look," *Journal of Peace Research* 30 (1983), no. 3, pp. 205–212.

will obtain some decisive advantage—it is hard not to believe that an arms race increases tensions that may, especially in periods of crisis, result in the outbreak of violent conflict. Indeed, the problem of instability in crisis, when tensions may cause fear, threats, and violence to spiral rapidly, lies at the heart of many analysts' concern about contemporary deterrence. In their view, the assumptions on which deterrence theory rests apply best to periods of relative calm between nations. By their understanding, deterrence works best when it is least needed! To comprehend and evaluate this argument, we must now turn to an extended discussion of deterrence theory.

14

DETERRENCE
AND ARMS CONTROL

CONTEMPORARY ARMS
AND STABLE DETERRENCE

In Soviet-American experiences of the past decades, the stability of
deterrence in crisis (no sudden escalation to nuclear war) and the relative stability of the arms race (few very sharp increases in spending)
both depended on the fact that neither side had a first-strike capability.
Because of existing technology, neither side's nuclear retaliatory forces
were highly vulnerable. If either side had been highly vulnerable, the
situation would have been quite different. It also would have been
different if both sides' forces had been vulnerable; that is, if who struck
first would have made a significant difference in the outcome of a war.
Knowledge of that fact could have been highly dangerous in a crisis
and fueled the arms race.

Understanding the difference between first- and second-strike capability is crucial to understanding the arms race and also to deterrence
theory. A first-strike capability means that one can attack and destroy

the other's retaliatory (second-strike) capability and suffer only minimal damage. It can thus become very tempting to make the attack. Under conditions of stable deterrence, each side has only a second-strike (retaliatory) capability, not a first-strike force. Each has an assured capability to inflict enormous destruction on an attacker; thus, neither is tempted to attack the other. It is this situation with which most American and perhaps most Russian decision makers have become content. In order to protect their second-strike capabilities, both sides have spent many billions of dollars on the research, development, and procurement of advanced weapons. The steps they have taken include:

1. Producing large *numbers* of delivery vehicles so that an attacker will not be able to destroy all of them. Both the United States and the Soviet Union have built 2,000 or more ICBMs, SLBMs, and bombers.

2. *Dispersing* delivery vehicles widely, again to multiply the number of targets an attacker would have to hit, making it impossible for one attacking warhead to wipe out more than one delivery vehicle. Thus, bombers are widely dispersed among many airfields, and ICBM silos are separated. If there is warning of a possible attack, bombers can be further dispersed by having them take off, since planes are much harder to destroy in the air than on the ground.

3. *Hardening* the launching sites of delivery vehicles. For example, American missile silos are enclosed in enough steel and concrete to withstand the blast of a near miss.

4. Making the delivery vehicles *mobile,* since a moving target is hard to track and hit. Submarines for launching missiles take advantage of this feature, as would a proposed American land-based missile (Midgetman) that is small and mobile.

5. *Concealment* of missile launching sites. Until the era of satellite photography, the United States did not know where most Soviet land-based ICBMs were located. Now concealment has to take other forms. Submarines, operating hundreds of feet below the surface of the ocean, are well concealed. Antisubmarine warfare is not sufficiently advanced to detect submarines with any reliability. In fact, the submarines for launching American SLBMs (now the Poseidon and the new Trident series of subs) form the most dependable and secure American second-strike force.

Another possible way to protect second-strike capabilities is the active defense of retaliatory forces. Interceptor aircraft may attack intruding bombers, and a system of antiballistic missiles (ABMs) could, in theory at least, knock down incoming ICBMs. The ABM Treaty of 1972 between the United States and the Soviet Union essentially eliminated this option, which was not very technically feasible anyway. Recently, new kinds of ABM systems, including space-based lasers and particle beam weapons, have received attention, but they would be enormously expensive and may not even work effectively.[1]

Another possibility is to adopt a "launch on warning" policy or (a more reassuring label) a "launch under attack" policy. By this means, land-based ICBMs that were vulnerable to a first strike would be launched before they could be struck by incoming missiles. This would be desirable only if we could be confident of avoiding false alarms (although it might not be desirable even then).[2]

All these ways to protect nuclear retaliatory forces require intensive and costly efforts to provide secure means of command and control from headquarters to the numerous, dispersed, movable, and well-concealed launching sites. The military chiefs must be able to ensure that retaliatory forces would be launched when they were so ordered, that they would be directed to the proper targets, and that they would not be launched unless the order was given. And the civilian leaders— in the United States, the president—must be confident that they have secure command and control facilities from which to deal with the military chiefs and that the military people operate only on orders from the civilian commander-in-chief.

By the end of the 1970s, a combination of technological change and a shift in values made it questionable whether the apparent stability of the arms race achieved in the earlier period would be maintained. The Soviet Union had continued to build large numbers of land- and sea-based missiles, surpassing the U.S. figure. More seriously, the Soviet Union began to deploy a new generation of high-accuracy missiles that were equipped with MIRVs. Since the Soviet rockets had always been substantially larger than their American counterparts, the combination of big missiles able to carry many MIRVs with multimegaton warheads with great accuracy looked very threatening to the United States. Specifically, it endangered the ability of even very hardened American land-based missiles to survive a Soviet attack.

---

1. See Hans Bethe, Richard Garwin, Kurt Gottfried, and Henry Kendall, "Space-based Ballistic-Missile Defense," in Bruce Russett and Fred Chernoff (eds.), *Arms Control and the Arms Race Readings from Scientific American* (New York: W. H. Freeman and Company, 1985).

2. See John Steinbruner, "Launch under Attack," in Russett and Chernoff, eds, op. cit.

A part of the American answer to this danger is to produce MXs, each of which will be bigger than the Minuteman and have ten MIRVs instead of the three on the Minuteman rockets. But no one has been able to devise an invulnerable way to base the MX, so its usefulness as a second-strike weapon is in doubt.

Also, the MX presents problems because of its vulnerability combined with its first-strike potential. It will have a larger warhead than the Minuteman (335 kilotons versus 170 on each Minuteman MIRV, compared with less than 20 kilotons in the Hiroshima bomb). The MX also has great accuracy; each warhead will be able to hit, within a few hundred feet of its target, even when launched from another continent. The MX therefore will be an effective first-strike weapon, able to destroy most or all of the Soviet land-based missiles. Thus, for land-based missiles at least, both sides might have effective first-strike forces (and by definition neither would then have a secure second-strike force). This could be a very dangerous and unstable situation, especially in a crisis. Many Americans are very worried about this situation.

In evaluating such a danger, you must bear several facts in mind. First, most of the calculations about relative "survivability" of strategic weapons assume a perfectly coordinated attack (bombers, ICBMs, and SLBMs all arriving on target at just the right time, though they must be launched from many different places at different times). Also, all warheads and delivery vehicles are assumed to be highly reliable—they will do everything they are technically capable of doing. Both of these assumptions are in fact highly unrealistic and exaggerate the worst case that a defender might face.[3]

Second, remember that land-based missiles are not the only element in American or Soviet strategic forces. Each side also has a large number of bombers capable of attacking the other's home territory (intercontinental bombers and, in the case of the United States, American bombers stationed in Europe or on aircraft carriers). Most important, each side has many SLBMs on submarines. Together, aircraft, land-based missiles, and submarine-based missiles form a *triad* of weapons. This notion of a triad of different kinds of weapons, each having different capabilities and each protected in different ways, has formed a central part of American (and Russian) strategic planning. Even though

---

3. See Matthew Bunn and Kosta Tsipis, "The Uncertainties of a Preemptive Attack," and Bernard Feld and Kosta Tsipis, "Land-Based Intercontinental Ballistic Missiles," in Bruce Russett and Fred Chernoff (eds.), op. cit.

one or even two parts of the triad might become vulnerable through technological change, the other elements will still be secure. So long as there are no major breakthroughs in antisubmarine warfare, those SLBMs can be depended on to devastate the other side. So long as the SLBMs are secure, neither side can really have a complete first-strike capability, and deterrence will remain reasonably stable.[4]

To counter any emerging Soviet threat to strategic forces, several kinds of actions have been taken. One was an American program to build cruise missiles—essentially unmanned, rocket-powered aircraft. These are much cheaper than ballistic missiles and, like airplanes, travel over land at low altitudes. Equipped with a new kind of guidance system that can "read" the terrain below and compare it with electronic maps, cruise missiles are highly accurate, perhaps coming within 50 feet of a target. Large numbers of these, launched from aircraft or ships, would be able to overwhelm Soviet air defenses and so provide a new kind of strategic weapon. The Americans seem to be well ahead of the Russians in developing this technology, yet it promises to be something of a mixed blessing. Might it not simply fuel a new round of acquisition and counteracquisition in the arms race? It also imposes new problems in information-gathering abilities for both sides. Can each side reliably count the number of cruise missiles of its opponent? Will this new weapon be so accurate and dependable as to become a new kind of first-strike weapon?

Other actions to counter the Soviet threat included a series of Soviet-American negotiations. The Strategic Arms Limitation Talks (SALT) were begun in 1969 and led to several important agreements, some of which we shall discuss below. In 1979 they led to a treaty (SALT II) that was never ratified, but both sides have said they will observe its terms. It sets limits on the number and kinds of strategic weapons each side can deploy. For example, the treaty calls for each side to have a total of no more than 2,250 launchers of all types (missiles and bombers) and a ceiling of 1,200 on MIRVed missiles. Except for the 2,250 limit on all Soviet launchers (they had about 50 launchers above that limit at the time the treaty was signed), these limits are all higher than the number of launchers then deployed. Nevertheless, they have placed a ceiling on the quantities, if not the quality, of weapons.

---

4. This is the conclusion of the commission appointed by President Reagan and chaired by General Scowcroft; see *Report of the President's Commission on Strategic Forces* (Washington, D.C.: U.S. Government Printing Office, 1983).

DETERRENCE AND CRISIS INSTABILITY

We must now step back from the details of Soviet and American military hardware to consider the theory of deterrence and how it may
work in a crisis. We shall begin by discussing the "normal" situation of
deterrence, the "balance of terror," using the prisoners' dilemma described in Chapter 13. The true prisoners' dilemma is probably not a
common situation in international politics. However, under some circumstances there are grave risks that a previously safe non-zero-sum
situation may turn into a dangerous form of the prisoners' dilemma.
Nuclear deterrence always carries this risk to some degree.

Table 14.1 represents the relative values that the U.S. and Soviet
governments might attach to the use of nuclear weapons in a typical
noncrisis situation. For both participants, the best outcome is where
both wait—that is, where peace is preserved. Even under the best of
conditions, war would leave both parties much worse off than at present. Given the capabilities of each side to retaliate, the first strike is a
very unattractive course of action.

Remember that in the prisoners' dilemma, one is better off defecting
(in this case, attacking) whether the other side defects or cooperates.
In this example, however, although each side is better off attacking if
the other intends to attack, each is also clearly better off waiting if the
other also waits. Since the payoff for peace (*R*) greatly exceeds the
temptation to hit first (*T*), this is no prisoners' dilemma. Neither side
will attack, and peace will be preserved. This is essentially what a situation of stable deterrence looks like. It was also the condition of the
world for most of the last three decades.

Yet a policy of restraint is acceptable only as long as neither side has
a first-strike capability and as long as each side is confident that the
other also sees a first strike as poor policy. Stability can be shaken by a
number of possible developments. A great technological breakthrough
for one side, such as an extremely effective ABM and air defense sys-

Table 14.1

Noncrisis decisions by the United States and the Soviet Union about using
nuclear weapons.

		Soviet Union	
		Wait	Attack
United States	Wait	4, 4 (*R, R*)	1, 3 (*S, T*)
	Attack	3, 1 (*T, S*)	2, 2 (*P, P*)

tem and very accurate MIRVs, might raise the gains from a first strike (T); that is, it might reduce the damage expected from the opponent's retaliation. Even the information—correct or mistaken—that the enemy was about to achieve such a breakthrough might suddenly change the estimates of the country receiving the information. If the enemy seems about to gain the ability to attack you, a preemptive attack might seem the rational thing to do.

However, technological change alone is unlikely to make much difference in deterrence stability as long as both superpowers maintain heavy research and development programs and keep a varied set of strategic weapons (SLBMs, manned bombers, and perhaps land-based ICBMs); under these circumstances, a single technical breakthrough by one side cannot be decisive. But a much more plausible set of events that would upset the deterrent balance can be imagined in a crisis— perhaps one like the Cuban missile crisis of 1962, but with some variations. This would happen if one power violated a principle laid down by Henry Kissinger:

> If crisis management requires cold and even brutal measures to show determination, it also imposes the need to show opponents a way out. Grandstanding is good for the ego but bad for foreign policy. Many wars have started because no line of retreat was left open. Superpowers have a special obligation not to humiliate each other.[5]

As it happened, in 1962 President Kennedy was careful to give Khrushchev an opportunity to withdraw the Russian missiles with some dignity. Kennedy termed the outcome a victory for peace, not a victory for the United States. But suppose he had dramatized the situation as an American victory and a great loss of prestige for the Russians, claiming that it proved the Russians were unable to deter any serious American pressure against the Communist world. Then suppose Kennedy had followed up with efforts to overthrow the Castro government. Under these circumstances, the value of peace (R) to the Russians—and especially to the humiliated Khrushchev, who would have faced immediate ouster as leader of the USSR—would have dropped sharply; the stability of the whole Communist system would have been at risk. At the same time, Khrushchev might have interpreted Kennedy's actions as indicating that the Americans had much

---

5. Henry Kissinger, *Years of Upheaval* (Boston: Little, Brown, 1982).

Table 14.2
Possible crisis options for the Soviet Union.

		Soviet Union	
		Wait	Attack
United States	Wait	2(R)	1(T)
	Attack	4(S)	3(P)

greater confidence in their first-strike capability than he had previously thought. That might have led the Russians to raise substantially their estimates of the damage that the Americans could inflict (S) and of the likelihood of an American attack. Thus, even though a Russian first strike would still have resulted in a bad outcome for the Russians (T unchanged), using even a moderate first-strike capability might have looked better to the Soviet Union than continuing to live in humiliation with the Americans. Whether the Americans would have attacked or waited, the situation for the Russians would have become a prisoner's dilemma, and attacking the United States would have been the better of each pair of generally bad outcomes for the Soviet Union (see Table 14.2).

Alternatively, we could suppose that President Kennedy, who in our scenario acted rashly and claimed a victory over the Russians, then thought the matter over more calmly and realized the risks he was running. He then might have decided that he had prompted the Russians to make a preemptive attack and felt required to preempt the preemption! The point is that, in the course of a crisis, previously stable conditions can be suddenly upset.[6]

The scenarios just sketched may seem improbable, but they are not. President Kennedy is reported to have said at the time of the Cuban missile crisis that he thought the chances of nuclear war were about one in three. Perhaps he was mistaken, though in a very real sense such a belief can become a self-fulfilling prophecy. Thinking war is near can bring it near through pressures for preemption, just as thinking war is near can also bring greater efforts to avoid disaster. The problem of crisis stability is especially serious because of how fallible

---

6. The point about anticipation ("He will do this because of what he thinks I will do because of what I think he will do), as well as many related points about strategic decision making, is developed by Thomas C. Schelling, *The Strategy of Conflict* (Cambridge, Mass.: Harvard University Press, 1960). A valuable discussion of strategy, with historical examples, is Robert Jervis, "Cooperation under the Security Dilemma," *World Politics* 30 (January 1978), no. 2, pp. 167–214.

human leaders are and how easily they can misperceive each other's intentions—especially under the enormous pressures of a nuclear crisis (as noted in Chapter 12). The problem will become clear by looking at some assumptions about decision making that were implicit in the previous discussion of deterrence in crisis but that are not necessarily correct.

1. *The assumption of a single event.* In a real crisis, of course, decision makers must consider not just what is happening now but what has happened in the past and especially what may happen in the future. If I behave reasonably now, will my opponent take that as a sign to moderate his or her demands in the future? Or on the contrary, will my opponent see my reasonableness as a sign of weakness to be exploited by still greater demands in the future? Will my allies, as well as my enemies, interpret my reasonableness as an unwillingness to take risks to defend them? The specter of Prime Minister Chamberlain's effort to appease Hitler at Munich in 1938 still haunts contemporary leaders. We noted this kind of consideration in our discussion about repeated plays of the prisoners' dilemma and in Chapter 7, where we discussed a state's bargaining reputation.

2. *The assumption of symmetry in values.* To simplify matters, we usually assumed that both parties had the same valuation of the various outcomes. This is, of course, not necessarily true. A power favoring the status quo will value peace more than will leaders who feel their country has been deprived of status. (Remember our Chapter 4 discussion of status and relative-deprivation theories.)

3. *The assumption of unitary actors.* We must now shift levels of analysis. In a real crisis, several decision makers will be involved on each side, giving advice and, in the case of military chiefs, having some direct control over the outcome. Each actor will be concerned with his or her own personal and organizational interests, as well as his or her perception of the national interest. Problems in group decision making and groupthink determine how those various interests will be used to form one final decision. Even the president is not immune from such considerations. A political leader must worry about being returned to office in the next election. The temptation to take short-term gains or to avoid short-term losses, even at the risk of greater long-term costs to the country at large, may be very strong, especially if the public does not understand the probability of long-term losses. The political leader cares about preserving his or her own power now, and he or she may rationalize this with the view that his own continuation in office is

really in the country's best interest. In the Cuban missile crisis, President Kennedy felt that any display of weakness was likely to damage his party badly in the Congressional elections only a month away.[7] If, on the other hand, he had sensed a great popular fear of war, Kennedy might have grasped at "peace in our time" even at the risk of later war. As the great economist John Maynard Keynes said, "In the long run we are all dead." In any case, different decision makers will have different values for the various outcomes and different attitudes toward risk taking. It matters who is making the decisions (Chamberlain or Thatcher, Hitler or Kohl). A sophisticated understanding of organizational politics, domestic politics, and psychology all are helpful here.

4. *The assumption of only two choices.* In a real crisis, a decision maker has to choose not simply between two options—attack and no attack— but from several options, if he or she looks carefully. Those options will range from cooperation to competition. No leader or group of leaders can hope to consider all possible alternatives, for under the best of circumstances he or she must choose within a limited time span and within the limits of human frailty. The quality and scope of a search for different options and the definition of the problem differ for different decision makers and for different organizational constraints. We discussed some of the determinants of search and problem definition in Chapter 11. Still, a good political decision maker can both consider a wide range of possible options and make a good initial selection of options to look at more carefully. The options he or she calls to mind are unlikely to be picked out of the air at random but rather are likely to reflect his or her search procedures. A good chess player is not someone who just chooses well from a given set of options but someone who knows how to pick out the most promising strategies for more careful consideration in the first place. For instance, in the early stages of the Cuban missile crisis, President Kennedy's advisers quickly converged on a choice of two options: a "surgical" air strike against the Soviet missile emplacements or a landing in Cuba by American troops. Kennedy disliked the implications of both choices and insisted that his advisers come up with something else—which eventually became the blockade.

5. *The focus on threats, especially military threats.* Naturally, military leaders will be involved in military decisions. Both they and political decision makers may overemphasize the role of military instruments in

---

7. Graham Allison, *Essence of Decision: Explaining the Cuban Missile Crisis* (Boston: Little, Brown, 1971), p. 194.

solving the problem. A common criticism of traditional international politics is that it concentrates too heavily on military means, on conflicting rather than cooperative acts, and on threats or punishments rather than on inducements or rewards.[8] Very high threatened punishments, or punishments, may arouse great fear and stress in decision makers, interfering with their ability to assess probabilities and their own and others' values. By arousing irrational behavior, threats may be counterproductive.

6. *The assumption of nonstressful perception and behavior.* The preceding points remind us of the difficulty in understanding and assessing other people's motives and behavior. This is especially difficult in cross-cultural assessments, as when capitalist Americans have to think like Communist Russians or Chinese. It becomes even more difficult in times of crisis. In Chapter 12 we showed that behavior under stress is typically different from behavior under normal conditions. The rational person in the prisoners' dilemma has a difficult time at best. We nevertheless assume that he is able to perceive his options clearly, calmly consider the probable actions of his opponent, and carefully weigh the values he attaches to possible outcomes. Small or moderate amounts of stress may make him work harder and more effectively if he believes in the possibility of finding a satisfactory policy, if he has sufficient time to consider options, and if he has the resources to devise and implement such a policy. But great stress is likely to bring procrastination, shifting of responsibility to others, and "bolstering"—that is, an exaggeration of favorable consequences and minimization of unfavorable ones. Highly stressed decision makers may react fatalistically and become more prone to anger and despair. In the World War I crisis of 1914, for instance, some tired, tense, overworked leaders simply stopped searching for further ways to escape war, even though they certainly did not want it.

AVOIDING THE ESCALATION OF CRISES

There are a number of ways in which nuclear war between the superpowers could erupt. Table 14.3 lists the most important possibilities. The last two possibilities are the least likely: Terrorist or third-party

---

8. On some of the difficulties with deterrence theory, see especially Alexander George and Richard Smoke, *Deterrence in American Foreign Policy* (New York: Columbia University Press, 1974); Patrick M. Morgan, *Deterrence: A Conceptual Analysis*, 2nd ed. (Beverly Hills, Calif.: Sage, 1983).

Table 14.3
How a nuclear war might erupt.

Deliberate escalation by top leaders in the face of military or political losses.

Preemption by top leaders in anticipation of an enemy's deliberate escalation.

False warning from misinterpreting enemy alert procedures.

Computer or human error in information systems.

Unauthorized firing by lower-level military officers, such as submarine commanders or field commanders in Europe.

"Catalytic" war begun by smaller nuclear power or terrorists.

Physical accident involving warhead or delivery vehicle.

---

use of nuclear weapons is certainly plausible, but it could probably be identified accurately and not be blamed on a superpower; technical improvements make the explosion of a nuclear weapon by physical accident quite improbable. The other possibilities, however, are very real.

To avoid nuclear war over decades of confrontation will require policymakers to take a number of steps with the support of their citizens. Among these steps are the following:

1. Very careful, calm statesmanship, with attention to developing standard operating procedures that minimize stress, maximize the search for alternatives, and control the distortions of judgment that can arise from group decision making and organizational politics.

2. The building of a sense of predictability, identity, and mutual interest among top decision makers and, perhaps even more importantly, among those members of the elite and the attentive public below the top decision makers whose support is needed for policies of restraint. Predictability of each other's behavior is essential, because uncertainty may lead to actions aimed just at avoiding worst-case outcomes, even though such outcomes may be very unlikely. A sense of identity and mutual interest help in developing conscience, which produces a beneficial shift in values and hence in the payoff structure. Here it is a matter of realizing that the other person's welfare is also important. Narrowing the "human distance" is an effective way to discourage violence. When victims have no discernible characteristics or identity or when people and suffering cannot be seen (as when a missile is sent across the globe), it is easier to give or obey orders to inflict pain. The ease with which very ordinary and normally moral people

will inflict pain on a faceless victim has been demonstrated in laboratory experiments.[9]

3. Deliberate efforts to build weapons systems that do not make a first strike inordinately advantageous—perhaps even self-denial in not building weapons that might give a good first-strike capability.

4. Technological improvements to strengthen information processing and control over weapons to avoid human and mechanical error.

5. Arms control and disarmament steps, including efforts to share information that could assure the other side that no first strike is contemplated.

6. A good deal of luck.

ARMS CONTROL EFFORTS SINCE WORLD WAR II

Table 14.4 lists the major arms control agreements since 1959. The final column indicates whether they were bilateral U.S.-USSR agreements or multilateral agreements. A quick review of them will indicate their principal goals and methods.

Most of the U.S.-USSR bilateral agreements have been directed toward the avoidance of nuclear war between the superpowers. The hot line agreements of 1963 and 1971, the nuclear accidents agreement of 1971, the high seas agreement of 1972, and the nuclear war prevention agreement of 1973 are all devoted principally to providing both sides with information—particularly on intentions in time of accident or crisis, when such information is most crucial. The SALT II agreement of 1979 also provides for some means of verification to assure each side that the agreements on limitations of types and numbers of weapons are being kept.

The 1972 ABM agreement (modified in 1974) sharply limited and ultimately reduced each side's acquisition of antiballistic missile systems. If effective, an ABM system might have provided substantial protection for population centers. Although that may sound benign, it contradicts the principle of "mutual assured destruction," whereby each side's own population becomes hostage to that side's responsible

---

9. For descriptions of some very interesting laboratory experiments that illustrate the ease with which very ordinary and normally moral people will inflict pain on a faceless victim, see Luc Reyschler, "The Effectiveness of a Pacifist Strategy in Conflict Resolution: An Experimental Study," *Journal of Conflict Resolution* 23 (June 1979), no. 2, pp. 228–260; see especially Stanley Milgram, *Obedience to Authority* (New York: Harper & Row, 1974).

Table 14.4
Major arms control agreements since 1959.

Signed	Agreement	Provisions	Multilateral (M) or bilateral U.S.-USSR (B)
1959	Antarctic treaty	Prohibits all military activity in Antarctic area.	M
1963	Partial nuclear test ban treaty	Prohibits nuclear explosions in the atmosphere, in outer space, and under water.	M
1963	"Hot line" agreement	Establishes direct radio and telegraph communications between the United States and the USSR for use in emergency.	B
1967	Outer space treaty	Prohibits all military activity in outer space, including the moon and other celestial bodies.	M
1967	Treaty of Tlatelolco	Prohibits nuclear weapons in Latin America.	M
1968	Nonproliferation treaty	Prohibits acquisition of nuclear weapons by nonnuclear nations.	M
1971	Seabed treaty	Prohibits emplacement of nuclear weapons and other weapons of mass destruction on ocean floor or subsoil thereof.	M
1971	"Hot line" modernization agreement	Increases reliability of original hot line system by adding two satellite communications circuits.	B
1971	Nuclear accidents agreement	Institutes various measures to reduce risk of accidental nuclear war between the United States and the USSR.	B
1972	High seas agreement	Provides for measures to help prevent dangerous incidents on or over the high seas involving ships and aircraft of both parties.	B

Year	Agreement	Description	
1972	SALT I ABM treaty	Limits deployment of antiballistic missile systems to two sites in each country. Reduced to one site by 1974 agreement.	B
1972	SALT I interim offensive arms agreement	Provides for five-year freeze on aggregate number of fixed land-based intercontinental ballistic missiles (ICBMs) and submarine-launched ballistic missiles (SLBMs) on each side. Later extended to 1980.	B
1972	Biological weapons convention	Prohibits development, production, and stockpiling of bacteriological and toxic weapons and requires destruction of existing biological weapons.	M
1973	Nuclear war prevention agreement	Institutes various measures to help avert outbreak of nuclear war in crisis situations.	B
1974	Threshold nuclear test ban treaty	Prohibits underground tests of nuclear weapons with explosive yields greater than 150 kilotons. *Not ratified.*	B
1976	Peaceful nuclear explosions treaty	Bars explosions greater than 150 kilotons for "peaceful purposes," such as excavation or mining. *Not ratified.*	B
1977	Environmental modification convention	Prohibits military or other hostile use of environmental modification techniques.	M
1979	SALT II offensive arms agreement	Limits numbers and types of strategic nuclear delivery vehicles. *Not ratified.*	B

behavior. A successful ABM system could have destabilized the balance of terror by reducing one side's confidence in its ability to retaliate. The SALT I and II offensive arms agreements were also intended to contribute to strategic stability by limiting the types and numbers of weapons that could be deployed. This would slow the possible destabilizing effects of technological change and also limit the wasteful effects of arms race spending.

Neither SALT I nor SALT II, however, called for any significant degree of *disarmament*. They limited and controlled arms but required almost no destruction or dismantling of existing arms. (The 1974 agreement called for dismantling one ABM site—but that was a system both parties had already decided would not be effective anyway.) *Arms control is not necessarily disarmament*. Arms control is a process that produces agreements on weapons and the use of weapons—types, deployment, characteristics, safety conditions to prevent accidents, and so forth. Many arms control agreements are concerned with the creation of stability in the sense that neither side is tempted (as in the *T* of the prisoners' dilemma) to use weapons first. The aim of disarmament is to reduce the numbers of weapons. Thus, arms control may be seen as a distraction from the quest for disarmament. Alternatively, some kinds of disarmament could work against stability (as by reducing second-strike capabilities). These possible contradictions produce serious conflicts within the ranks of those who wish to reduce the threat of war.

Generally, multilateral treaties have different aims from those of bilateral agreements. Their goals—still largely regarding arms control— are to prevent the spread of weapons of mass destruction to places and countries where they have not already been deployed. Thus, the Antarctic, outer space, seabed, and environmental modification treaties all provide that signatories will continue not to do something they have not yet done. The biological weapons convention called for destroying some stocks of weapons, but most analysts of modern warfare techniques agree that both biological and chemical weapons are generally inferior to nuclear weapons as a means of killing large numbers of people; that is, if a state already has large stocks of nuclear weapons, then chemical and especially biological weapons are largely superfluous except for small encounters. Thus, the most important targets of the biological weapons convention are the nonnuclear states.

The focus of multilateral arms control agreements on nonnuclear states is clearest in the Treaty of Tlatelolco (for a Latin American nuclear-free zone) and particularly in the nonproliferation treaty (NPT). Most countries have signed and ratified the NPT, but thirty-two have not. Many of the nonsignatories are important: France and Spain; China, Vietnam, and North Korea; Algeria; Israel and Saudi Arabia; India and Pakistan; South Africa; and Cuba, Argentina, Brazil, and Chile. States that do not already have nuclear weapons but are parties to the treaty promise not to acquire them, and states that do have nuclear weapons agree not to transfer them to nonnuclear states. Surely this is directed toward reducing the risk of nuclear war, both war between nonnuclear states and catalytic war (a war initially involving third parties that draws in a superpower). The acquisition of nuclear weapons by Middle Eastern states is especially feared because of the likelihood that any nuclear war between Arabs and Israelis would lead to a Soviet-American confrontation. But nonproliferation agreements also help to maintain the overwhelming superiority of the two superpowers over everyone else. Even among the superpowers, this superiority is evident. In 1983, the United States had over 9,000 deliverable strategic warheads; the Soviet Union, about 8,000. The equivalent number for the next tier of nuclear powers (Britain, France, and China) was less than 300 apiece. Nonproliferation agreements, if effective, ensure that there will be no challengers to the nuclear might of the two superpowers.

Leaders of nonnuclear countries, even when they see the dangers of nuclear proliferation and support limitations, often resent the superpowers' nuclear dominance. Many have demanded that continued enforcement of nonproliferation agreements depend on the superpowers' willingness not just to pursue arms control but also to accept some measure of nuclear disarmament. They refer to the superpower arms race as "vertical proliferation." The message of Alva Myrdal's book, *The Game of Disarmament: How the United States and Russia Run the Arms Race,* is contained in its title.[10] Myrdal charges: "Behind their outwardly often fierce disagreements . . . there has always been a secret and undeclared collusion between the superpowers. Neither of them has wanted to be restrained by effective disarmament measures." For her, the reason is rooted in international politics: "Military competition results in an ever-increasing superiority—militarily and technologically—of the already overstrong superpowers, thus sharpening the discrimination against all lesser powers." To her, the game is *duopoly* with the superpowers: They do not merely stimulate each other to acquire ever more

---

10. Alva Myrdal, *The Game of Disarmament: How the United States and Russia Run the Arms Race* (New York: Pantheon, 1976).

expensive and sophisticated weapons but continually outpace any military force available to any other state or combination of states by an enormous margin.

To support her argument, Myrdal notes the failure of the SALT agreements to produce any disarmament by the superpowers or even to limit effectively the acquisition of more horrendous weapons systems. According to her, "Only when the arms race has reached a point where some type of bomb or delivery vehicle is obsolete or further weapons development has lost any military usefulness to the superpowers will a gesture of 'disarmament' be made." Myrdal also notes that the United States retains, as key elements of both doctrine and preparation, the option of first use of nuclear weapons in response to conventional (nonnuclear) attacks by the Soviet Union or its allies anywhere in the world (for example, Europe, the Middle East, or Korea). Whether this argument is basically correct, much of the world agrees with it. K. Subrahmanyam, former director of the Institute for Defense Studies and Analyses in New Delhi, India, wrote that the price of the superpowers' strategy "is to convert the nuclear issue into a confrontation between North and South, and make the development of nuclear technology a symbol of declaration of autonomy from neocolonialist dependence."[11]

Aspects of the Proliferation Problem

The proliferation problem has two distinct aspects. One is the acquisition of material and know-how by governments to make bombs. New nuclear powers will lack the experience of existing nuclear powers in controlling the use of such weapons and will lack the resources to manage the elaborate command and control capabilities required (this is especially true of the less-developed countries). Also, many of these governments will be involved in serious local conflicts, which increases pressures to use such weapons in warfare.

The second aspect is the opportunity for terrorists to gain control of nuclear material (which may have been acquired by governments for "peaceful" purposes) or finished weapons. Such terrorists may be based

---

11. "The Nuclear Issue and International Security," *Bulletin of the Atomic Scientists* 33 (February 2, 1977), 20.

within the countries in question or may be based far away, simply taking advantage of opportunities to acquire nuclear materials from governments who are unable to take sufficient security precautions.

To meet the threat of proliferation, several different kinds of incentives for proliferation must be recognized. For some countries, the problem of security against present nuclear powers may be paramount (for example, the case of Taiwan and China or Pakistan and India). More often, however, security is sought against local powers that are not yet nuclear (for example, by Israel and South Korea). For still other states, military security is not a primary concern; rather, they may wish to obtain the prestige of a big power or the technological information that can be obtained from the development of peaceful and military nuclear capabilities (as in the case of Argentina). For still others, perhaps all three kinds of incentives are involved (for example, Iran under the shah).

Although some further proliferation is inevitable, there is nothing inevitable—in speed, extent, or form—about its extent. Because there are so many facets to the problem, control must proceed along several fronts.[12] It also is worth remembering that a war among small nuclear powers, however horrendous, would not approach the catastrophe of nuclear war among the superpowers. Only the superpowers can destroy civilization in the Northern Hemisphere. Their first responsibility is to reduce that possibility.

Many people—scholars, citizens, and governmental leaders—have devoted their energies to reducing the prospects of war and reducing the levels of arms with which war might be fought. Nevertheless, our review of arms control and disarmament efforts since World War II leaves us with a mixed and not very reassuring picture. By some standards there has been progress. At least the world has not blown up; no nuclear weapon has been exploded in anger since 1945. By historical standards, that's a long time without a major war. Despite common fears, in 1984 the number of states with nuclear weapons may have been only seven. (Acknowledged nuclear states were the United States, the USSR, Britain, France, and China. India has exploded a "peaceful

---

12. On nuclear proliferation, see Lewis Dunn, *Controlling the Bomb: Nuclear Proliferation in the 1980s* (New Haven, Conn.: Yale University Press, 1982); Stephen Meyer, *Nuclear Proliferation: Models of Behavior, Choice, and Decision* (Chicago: University of Chicago Press, 1984).

nuclear device," and Israel is generally believed to have had untested nuclear weapons for years.) There have been international agreements to bar nuclear weapons from many environments (Antarctica, outer space, and the seabed), as well as to prohibit atmospheric testing and proliferation (these agreements have not been accepted by all relevant states, however). Various U.S.-USSR agreements have established procedures for consultation and some quite high limits on weapons deployment.

Yet this progress is extremely limited when compared with the dangers that nuclear weapons pose to humanity. Proliferation of nuclear weapons now appears much more likely during the next few years. Several treaties drawn up in the 1970s were not ratified, others (like the ABM treaty) may be abandoned, and negotiations on several arms control measures have been suspended. U.S. military spending is increasing again, and Soviet military spending increased throughout the period when American spending declined. If anything, the dangers of an upward spiral in the arms race seem greater now than at any time since détente began after the Cuban missile crisis. Superpower crises no doubt will occur again, perhaps over control of parts of the Middle East. In any major crisis, there remains the real possibility of a wide-scale nuclear war.

ETHICS AND WAR

In our discussion of arms races and deterrence, we have concentrated on such factors as the historical record, analytical perspectives that illuminate our understanding, and empirical evidence supporting propositions set forth about the causes and consequences of arms races. Occasionally we have alluded to moral and ethical considerations as possible restraints on behavior, but that has been the extent of our discussion of ethics and morality. We have not considered such issues as what actions are moral or ethical or what moral and ethical principles should guide our behavior and the behavior of our leaders both in peacetime and in war.

Moral or ethical propositions concern how people *ought* to behave rather than how people *do* behave. Ethical reasoning is basically deductive reasoning. One starts with a very few given principles and deduces from them a set of propositions. Although people often make ethical statements without proceeding carefully and logically, the same is also true about many empirical statements. Ethical deductive reasoning can be as rigorous as mathematical or other formal reasoning. Yet it is typically avoided in most social science textbooks, and we have avoided it up to here. Why?

Most social scientists are principally concerned with asking how people behave and why they behave that way. In earlier periods of social science, questions of "is" and "ought" were less differentiated than they are now. An older book on world politics might be composed of a mixture of empirical statements and moral exhortations to prevent war or to seek justice. Many modern social scientists rightly take pride in their ability to separate those two types of questions. This does not mean that social scientists are amoral or that they are insensitive to moral questions. They do act from moral bases; their choices of research topics (avoiding war, reducing world poverty, or preserving freedom) clearly reflect moral judgments; their choice of remedies for such problems reflects some mixture of what they see as feasible and what they see as right. Value-free social science is simply not possible. Nevertheless, it is useful and very important to distinguish ethical statements from empirical statements or other kinds of analytical proposition.

Another reason why social scientists are so reluctant to engage in ethical discussions is the great difficulty we have, in modern industrial societies, in establishing a common frame of reference. We do not live in a culture where a single value system is dominant. Although most of our values are heavily influenced by Greek and Christian-Judaic traditions, there is no commonly accepted authority and only a few propositions shared across most contemporary religions and other ethical systems. Humanists, Marxists, agnostics, and atheists share some common ground with religious believers, but that ground is not very extensive. Even within many of the major traditions, authority is repudiated and a wide variety of opinions is tolerated. Under these conditions, it is either a brave or a foolhardy person who ventures very far into ethical discussion in a book intended for a wide readership.

However, we cannot completely ignore such issues in a chapter on deterrence and war. Instead, we shall discuss the historical tradition and the background of discourse on the limits to be observed in warfare and consider how these might apply to modern nuclear war. Are there circumstances under which nuclear weapons should not be used? Are there targets that should not be attacked according to widely accepted ethical precepts? Our purpose here is not to insist on answers— we're not at all sure we have the right ones. But we do offer this discussion to open up these issues to discussion.

The Realist Position

At one end of the spectrum of ethical thought about warfare are the views that any act in war is justifiable if it seems to serve the "national interest" and that rightness depends solely on the ends sought rather than on the methods used to obtain those ends. The first view implies that if in some sense the populace as a whole desires something (we should nevertheless be wary of attributing preferences to a whole group or class), leaders should seek to obtain it with whatever means are available. This version of realism holds that, regardless of the moral restraints that bind our interpersonal behavior, international politics is so anarchic—a war of each against all—that mere self-preservation requires the abandonment of moral inhibitions. For those who hold to the second view, there are legitimate and illegitimate goals in world politics; however, if your goals or ends are just, any means may be employed to reach them.

Although many people may express such viewpoints, it is not clear how many people *really* believe they are guides to action. Most adults come to believe that the law is important; it should be obeyed most of the time, and if it is disobeyed, it should not be disobeyed lightly. Civil disobedience is permissible, but only for some higher moral purpose.[13] International law is generally regarded as one of the least authoritative and least effective forms of law, but even it is given some respect and observance, and not solely out of self-interest. When occupying the Vietnam village of My Lai, Lieutenant William Calley deliberately ordered and supervised the killing of hundreds of innocent, noncombatant civilians. This action might have safeguarded a few American troops from Communist Vietcong guerrillas disguised as civilians (though this was a rather far-fetched possibility). Nevertheless, his act violated U.S. Army regulations, international law, and most people's moral sense of what was right and wrong. Calley was tried and convicted by an Army court.

Similarly, after World War II many German and Japanese wartime leaders were tried by Allied military tribunals at Nuremberg and Tokyo. They were charged with the deliberate killing of civilians and prisoners of war and with "waging aggressive war." Some of these acts, such as killing prisoners of war, were clearly forbidden by international law, such as the Geneva Convention. Others, like "waging ag-

---

13. See Richard H. Hersh, Diana Pritchard Paolitto, and Joseph Reimer, *Promoting Moral Growth: From Piaget to Kohlberg* (New York: Longman, 1979).

gressive war," were less clearly outlawed; yet it was widely agreed that the enemy leaders had committed acts that were morally if not legally outrageous. Many of the leaders were convicted and executed. Most people act as though they believe legal, moral, or ethical restraints are relevant to international behavior.

The Pacifist Position

A very different position from the realist's "anything goes" is that of the pacifist. A completely pacifist position may result from a philosophical and moral predilection for nonviolence, a rejection in principle to the use of force as an instrument of national policy, a belief in the spiritually regenerative effect of a nonviolent response to violence, or an overriding concern for the preservation of human life.

Pacifism has deep roots in a number of secular and religious traditions. It seems to have been the dominant view in the early Christian church before the Roman emperor Constantine converted to Christianity. The Roman Empire was pagan and often persecuted Christians; no Christian could in good conscience serve in the army of such a power. Pacifism is not the dominant tradition in contemporary Christianity, but it is still a common and respected view in many Christian churches. It is a basic principle of the Society of Friends (Quakers) and was practiced by Martin Luther King, Jr., in his program of civil disobedience against racial segregation. Mohandas Gandhi blended part of this Christian pacifist tradition with Hinduism in his resistance to British colonialism, and his example has had great influence worldwide. A position that is pacifist for all practical purposes may emerge from the conclusion that, in any modern thermonuclear war, the costs necessarily outweigh the gains. Plans for nonviolent resistance—a war without weapons against a would-be conqueror—are commonly discussed and sometimes practiced.[14]

Intermediate Positions

Between these two extreme views are a variety of positions. For those who accept the use of force as a legitimate instrument of state policy in many but not all circumstances, there are two principal moral consider-

---

14. Gene Sharp, *The Politics of Nonviolent Action* (Boston: Porter Sargent, 1973); Anders Boserup and Andrew Mack, *War without Weapons* (New York: Schocken Books, 1975).

ations in determining limitations. One is concerned with the norms that govern the *resort* to war, and the second with the norms that govern the *conduct* of war.

The first limitation, which concentrates on what conditions justify an initial resort to physical violence, is typically less concerned with how the conflict is conducted once it is begun. In the American philosophical tradition, the only just war is one undertaken in self-defense. Self-defense by this definition includes (1) defense of one's allies in keeping with a formal commitment; (2) assistance to a small power under the principle of collective security when authorized by an international organization, such as the United Nations, even if there is no treaty commitment; or (3) assistance to another government in response to its request for aid. Furthermore, the "self" to be defended is generally defined broadly to include not only the physical territory but also the values and way of life believed to characterize the nation. No other grievances, however severe, would justify the initiation of war; grievances should always be addressed only through negotiation or arbitration, or they should be endured in the hope they will become more tolerable as circumstances evolve. This position can become a very conservative one politically and is rejected by people who declare that oppression and exploitation must be resisted by force if necessary. Furthermore, once a war in self-defense is undertaken, limits on both the political objectives to be achieved and the means used to pursue them become very hard to establish.

The most common Marxist view holds that a war need not be undertaken in self-defense to be justifiable; it can be perfectly right if its purpose is to redress class oppression or national subjugation. In this respect, it differs widely from the classical American doctrine. Even for the Marxist, however, a just war must not have a reactionary effect. Thus, a nuclear war that would annihilate capitalist and socialist civilizations would not be initiated. Not just any hypothetical war undertaken by a Communist or third world country would be permissible. Differing interpretations of the likely result of nuclear war were partly responsible for the public differences between Russian and Chinese leaders during the past few decades.

Analysis of a Just War

A quite different position stems from Christian moralists, which is embodied in the "just war" tradition. This tradition has origins in ancient Greek and Roman thought, was developed in the Middle Ages and later refined, and now is the predominant Christian view. It also provides a foundation for very similar positions taken by some non-Christian thinkers today. The just war tradition begins with strong doubts about the legitimacy of violence and establishes very strict constraints both on the circumstances under which a resort to violence can be considered just and on the actions that can be taken in fighting a just war. We shall illustrate just war thinking here by a pastoral letter from the U.S. Catholic bishops that attracted much attention in 1983.[15]

Three elements of the just war tradition are especially important to questions about nuclear war. The first is the requirement of *discrimination*, or observing the principle of noncombatant immunity. Especially in modern warfare, it is often hard to distinguish civilians from combatants. Workers in weapons factories, for instance, are hard to classify. But many kinds of people are clearly civilian noncombatants, such as children, old people, people in hospitals, women at home, farmers, and so forth. The requirement of discrimination forbids direct, deliberate attacks on civilians. Quoting the bishops, "Under no circumstances may nuclear weapons or other instruments of mass slaughter be used for the purpose of destroying population centers or other predominantly civilian targets. . . . No Christian can rightfully carry out orders or policies deliberately aimed at killing noncombatants." This is a strong statement. It implicitly condemns the bombing of Dresden (a city with no military significance), the firebombing of hundreds of thousands of Japanese civilians in World War II, and the atomic bombing of Hiroshima and Nagasaki (cities that were chosen as civilian, not military, targets). According to this principle, the fact that these bombings may have hastened the end of the war and possibly even have reduced the total number of civilian casualties from what they might otherwise have been is not sufficient justification. Using this principle, the direct killing of civilians as a means to achieving some good end or avoiding some evil is never morally permissible.

This position directly opposes policies adopted by all the nuclear powers. Until 1973 American *declaratory* policy always emphasized

---

15. U.S. Catholic Conference, *The Challenge of Peace: God's Promise and Our Response* (Washington, D.C.: U.S. Catholic Conference, 1983). For a more extended commentary on the letter, see Bruce Russett, "Ethical Dilemmas of Nuclear Deterrence," *International Security* 8 (Spring 1984), no. 4, pp. 36–54. Similar though less prominent and comprehensive statements have been made by other religious groups. For an earlier Protestant statement, see Paul Ramsey, *The Just War* (New York: Scribner's, 1968); for a secular but closely related view, see Michael Walzer, *Just and Unjust Wars* (New York: Basic Books, 1977).

countercity deterrence, that is, the ability to destroy a large fraction of any enemy's industry and to kill a large fraction of the enemy's population in retaliation for any attack on the United States or its allies. After 1973 there was a gradual shift in public statements; in recent years, American officials often say things like, "We do not in our strategic planning target population centers as such." American *operational* policy (what in fact is in the war plans) never concentrated on civilian targets, despite the declaratory policy. One war plan from 1948 (charmingly known as "Broiler"), for example, called for the use of thirty-four bombs against targets in twenty-six cities. The targets of these plans included military sites, "military-related industry," transportation centers, and electricity-producing facilities. But most targets were in major population centers, and bombing them would have resulted in a large number of civilian deaths. Some decision makers saw these deaths as unintended but unavoidable; to others they were "bonus effects" that strengthened deterrence.[16]

A second aspect of the just war analysis is called the principle of *proportionality*. By some (inevitably subjective and uncertain) calculation, the harm done by an act, even unintentionally, may not be disproportionate to the good intended to be gained or to the evil to be avoided. The principle of discrimination forbids counterpopulation warfare; the principle of proportionality sharply limits counterforce warfare. The latter principle recognizes that in almost any war, some civilians will unavoidably be killed if military targets are hit. Thus, some civilian deaths can be accepted as a by-product of striking a military target. But just because civilians are not killed intentionally does not mean they can be killed without limit. Specifically, the bishops' letter expresses very grave reservations about the massive civilian casualties that would surely occur in any nuclear exchange, even one directed only to military targets. The section of the letter on deterrence is filled with references to how military facilities and civilian living and working areas are interspersed and to the fact that the number of civilians who would necessarily be killed in hitting the military targets is "horrendous." The section also cites admissions by the Reagan administration that "once any substantial numbers of weapons are used, the civilian casualty levels would quickly become truly catastrophic." The principle of proportionality thus says that discrimination alone—

---

16. David Alan Rosenberg, "The Origins of Overkill: Nuclear Weapons and American Strategy," *International Security* 7 (Spring 1983), no. 4, pp. 3–71.

merely limiting a nuclear strike to counterforce targets—is not enough to make that policy morally acceptable.

Many strategists and government officials have maintained that improvements in strategic weaponry are movements in the direction of greater moral acceptability. Specifically, improvements in accuracy, coupled with the elimination of the very large warheads placed on older missiles, have the effect of limiting damage. The number of (supposedly greatly reduced) civilian casualties sustained when military targets are hit could therefore be judged appropriate for some aims of war or deterrence. Nuclear deterrence could then be said to be both discriminating and proportionate. Modernization of the strategic arsenal, with more accurate weapons like the MX, is therefore morally permissible and even required! Similar claims are made for "small," tactical nuclear weapons used on the battlefield.

On first encounter, it is hard to disagree with this assessment. A reduction in unintended civilian deaths would be consistent with traditional moral principles. But on examination the problems are immense. As mentioned in Chapter 13, any large-scale nuclear exchange, even of discriminating weapons, would inevitably result in millions or tens of millions of civilian casualties. The combination of immediate casualties from blast and radiation, with longer-term casualties from fallout, disruption of the medical, sanitation, transportation, and communication systems, ecological devastation, climatic effects, and so forth, would be very great—even if attacks were limited to strictly military targets. Furthermore, the Defense Department's current list of military and militarily related industrial targets (40,000 of them, including 60 in Moscow alone) includes industries and utilities essential to the economic recuperation of the Soviet Union.[17] If the Soviet economy is destroyed, tens of millions of Soviet citizens will die of hunger and disease (of course, the same applies if the American economy is destroyed). The effect would hardly be different than if population centers had been specifically targeted. There are not many causes to which such deaths would be proportionate.

One problem is therefore the illusion that any large-scale nuclear exchange could in any real sense be limited in its consequences. The other problem is the expectation that nuclear war could be fought in some precise fashion of strike and counterstrike—that in any major

---

17. Desmond Ball, *Targeting for Strategic Deterrence,* Adelphi Paper no. 185 (London: International Institute for Strategic Studies, 1983).

nuclear exchange the war could be restricted to a limited number of strictly military targets. There are people who imagine that such a war could be waged with acceptable consequences. The majority of analysts, however, consider the likelihood of such limitation, under wartime conditions of anger, confusion, ignorance, and loss of control, to be extremely small. One cannot definitively rule out the possibility, but neither should one bet the future of civilization on it. One of the most knowledgeable experts on this matter is John Steinbruner. In his words:

> Once the use of as many as 10 or more nuclear weapons directly against the USSR is seriously contemplated, U.S. strategic commanders will likely insist on attacking the full array of Soviet military targets. . . . If national commanders seriously attempted to implement this strategy (controlled response) in a war with existing and currently projected U.S. forces, the result would not be a finely controlled strategic campaign. The more likely result would be the collapse of U.S. forces into isolated units undertaking retaliation on their own initiative against a wide variety of targets at unpredictable moments.[18]

In a nutshell, limitation of nuclear war fails a third principle of the just war: *reasonable chance of success.* Thus to many people the idea of "winning" or "prevailing" in a nuclear war seems only a dangerous fantasy, as would any notion of "sovereignty and continued viability of the United States and of the Western democracies as free societies" after such a war.[19]

So much for what could—or could not—be done in war. Is deterrence—as contrasted with what one actually does in war—different? After all, the purpose of deterrence is to prevent war. The trouble is that, whatever our good intentions, deterrence may fail. If we make plans—build weapons, set up strategic programs, proclaim doctrines, instruct commanders—on the basis of principles that we are not willing to act upon, we may be called to act upon them anyway. Many things happen almost automatically in any war or defense establishment. In the 1914 crisis the powers had competitive mobilization plans that worked automatically, making World War I almost unavoidable.

---

18. John Steinbruner, "Nuclear Decapitation," *Foreign Policy* 45 (Winter 1981–82), 22–23.

19. See the exchange between Theodore Draper and Defense Secretary Caspar Weinberger in *The New York Review of Books* 29 (November 4, 1982), no. 17, pp. 26–31, and 30 (August 18, 1983), no. 13, pp. 27–33. The quotation is by Secretary Weinberger.

Or, we may contemplate recent talk about launching nuclear weapons on warning. Plans adopted in the name of deterrence may be activated, whatever our desires at the time. If war should come as the result of some uncontrollable crisis or a physical or human accident, plans calling for morally unacceptable acts in the name of deterrence would very likely be realized as morally unacceptable acts.

Another aspect of strategy is brinkmanship, or what Thomas C. Schelling called "manipulating the shared risk of war."[20] Schelling recognized that a would-be deterrer might well threaten to do something that he would not want to carry out in the event deterrence failed. The United States might *threaten* all-out nuclear war if the Soviet Union should occupy West Germany. If the Soviet Union did occupy West Germany, the United States government might not want to carry out its threat. In fact, a government fully in control of its military forces probably would not want to initiate all-out nuclear war. One way to deal with this situation would be to build some variant of a "doomsday machine": commit oneself to an act of mutual destruction that one would not want to carry out if one has a choice at the time. Almost everyone rejects the doomsday machine solution as grossly imprudent and disproportionate.

A less drastic solution is to build into a situation an element of unpredictability and uncontrollability. In practice, a Soviet invasion of West Germany might very well trigger all-out nuclear war whether or not the American government wished it to do so. The United States has nearly 5,000 nuclear weapons based in Europe, the Soviet Union an equivalent number, and the French hundreds more. In a condition of high alert, those nuclear weapons would probably be dispersed from their storage "igloos" even before war began. To keep them at their storage centers would leave them too vulnerable to a first strike. Yet their dispersal would likely be accompanied by release of the permissive action link (PAL) codes, which permit the use of those weapons. At the point of dispersal and decentralization, control over nuclear weapons would pass to low-level army officers—including those of allied countries, not just America. With such authority delegated, controlled escalation and bargaining would become impossible. Neither the President nor the NATO commander (always an American) could prevent the use of the weapons. A batallion commander, surrounded

20. Thomas C. Schelling, *Arms and Influence* (New Haven, Conn.: Yale University Press, 1966), p. 99.

and endangered, could use them. The prospect of these events could trigger a Soviet preemptive strike.[21]

The problem here represents a fundamental dilemma of nuclear command and control. Control should be tight and centralized in the hands of the very top civilian and military leaders. But centralization runs the risk that, if the top leadership is incapacitated, there will be no nuclear response at all; hence the certainty of response, essential to successful deterrence, is degraded. The weapons and PAL codes could be released to avoid this horn of the dilemma. Some balance must always be struck, but it is never likely to be very satisfactory.

The uncontrollability of nuclear weapons in Europe perhaps makes a terrific deterrent strategy—it deters any rational Soviet leader from making any military move against Western Europe. It implies that, in the event of war, even if we wished to avoid the use of nuclear weapons to save our own skins, we could not. As long as all Soviet leaders are fully rational—and always fully in control of their own military forces and political events—that may be a good strategy. But if political crises are not always controllable or avoidable, (such as the situation in 1914, or a revolt in Eastern Europe that somehow attracts support from the West, or a political breakdown in Yugoslavia that draws in regular or volunteer fighters from East and West), the uncontrollability of weapons does *not* seem prudent. In the apt words of a distinguished historian, military forces must serve two purposes: They must deter enemies, and they must reassure friends.[22] Nuclear deterrent systems that depend on their uncontrollability are not reassuring to one's friends.

Yet another question is whether one can threaten to perform acts that one cannot morally do or intend. On practical grounds, deterrent threats of the indiscriminate or disproportionate use of nuclear weapons do not seem to be prudent. For one thing, if the threatener was known to adhere to other aspects of the just war tradition, it would be an obvious bluff—the threatener simply would not be believed. If the threatener was not known to adhere to the just war tradition, the threat would gain greater credibility. But to be credible, the threat would have to be supplemented by public orders and plans for the use of nuclear weapons *if* deterrence failed. Declaratory policy would have to be contrary to operational policy, with only a very small circle of

---

21. Paul Bracken, *The Command and Control of Nuclear Forces* (New Haven, Conn.: Yale University Press, 1983).

22. Michael Howard, "Reassurance and Deterrence," *Foreign Affairs* 61 (Winter 1982/ 83), no. 2, pp. 309–324.

policymakers aware of the difference. It is very unlikely that such a policy would succeed. On the one hand, the fact that the threat was only a bluff would probably become known through leaks or espionage. Even if the secret was kept, the automaticity inherent in strategic nuclear planning might take over in the event of war, especially if war included (as it very likely would) a "decapitating" attack that removed the commander-in-chief. The use of nuclear weapons would then probably follow the lines of the declaratory policy rather than the secret operational policy—and nuclear weapons would be used in a "morally unacceptable" manner. Those dovish critics of U.S. limited-war policies who rely on extreme versions of MAD (mutually assured destruction) counterpopulation strategies thus have no good solution to the moral and practical dilemmas either. They lack an acceptable answer to the question of what to do *if* deterrence fails.[23]

No First Use

The central problem for deterrence is not deterrence of an attack on the United States. The United States adopted nuclear deterrence years before the Soviet Union had any serious nuclear capability at all. (The Soviet military only acquired operational weapons in 1952.) The real problem, then and now, is "extended deterrence": deterrence of attack on allies or neutrals under American protection. Furthermore, nuclear deterrence has broadened to include deterrence of *conventional* attacks on American allies, a policy promoted by the relatively low cost of nuclear weapons (more "bang for the buck," in the phrase of Charles Wilson, President Eisenhower's Secretary of Defense) and the difficulties for NATO in raising adequate conventional defense forces against what are often seen as the "Eastern hordes." We do live in a world where the use of military force is contemplated, where values of freedom, justice, and a democratic way of life need to be defended, and where vital national interests may sometimes be at stake.

Many analysts have come to advocate a policy of "no first use" of nuclear weapons as a way of easing the dilemmas posed by deterrence. By this policy, the defense of allies and vital interests against nonnuclear threats would be undertaken predominantly by conventional military forces. Nuclear weapons would be used only in reply to nu-

---

23. This is apparent in Draper's reply to Weinberger (see footnote 19).

clear attack. Readiness to use conventional forces would be coupled with a doctrine of preparation, of physical capability, and of public declaration that the United States would not be the first to use nuclear weapons. In June 1982, Secretary Brezhnev of the Soviet Union made precisely this pledge. It could be in the interest of the United States to do so even if the Soviet Union had not. But so far the United States has refused.

No-first-use is not a prescription guaranteed to be popular. It could be expensive. Although it would require the elimination or much more secure storage of some nuclear weapons, it would require new expenditures for conventional forces. Nevertheless, these costs should not be exaggerated. Part of the solution lies in changing force structures, tactics, and types of weapons (for example, more antitank missiles than tanks) rather than just buying more weapons. Nor is NATO inferiority in Europe severe even now. Warsaw Pact divisions are more numerous than are NATO's, but they are smaller. In actual ground manpower on the central front, the pact has an advantage of only 110,000 troops. Of the fifty-eight Warsaw Pact divisions, fifteen are Polish and ten are Czechoslovakian—and of doubtful sympathy to the Soviet cause. (Perhaps they should be subtracted from the Soviet total rather than added to it.) In time, Soviet forces from Russia could reinforce troops on the central front, but there are limits to this ability both in readiness and in the need to keep large forces on the Chinese border. NATO forces would also bring in reserves, and troops from America would be met with preplaced supplies and equipment in Europe.

The conventional defense of Europe is very far from hopeless. Although not advocating no-first-use, the Supreme Allied Commander in Europe does support stronger conventional forces so as to raise the threshold of conflict before nuclear weapons had to be used. He reports a NATO study that adequate conventional defense could be achieved by a 4 percent real increase in NATO military spending over six years. In the words of four former national security advisers, "Even if careful analysis did show that the necessary conventional posture would require greater funding, it would be the best bargain ever offered."[24]

---

24. See General Bernard Rogers, "The Atlantic Alliance: Prescriptions for a Difficult Decade," *Foreign Affairs* 60 (Summer 1982), no. 5, pp. 1145–1156; McGeorge Bundy, George F. Kennan, Robert McNamara, and Gerard Smith, "Nuclear Weapons and the Alliance," *Foreign Affairs* 60 (Spring 1982), no. 4, pp. 753–768; see also the rejoinder in the next issue by four German analysts. Finally, see John Steinbruner and Leon Sigal, eds., *Alliance Security* (Washington, D.C.: Brookings Institution, 1983).

Other objections to a no-first-use policy require attention. The United States might again need a draft to provide enough manpower. The governments of some allies would have to make substantial expenditures and sacrifices that they had been able to avoid while sheltered under the American nuclear umbrella. Europeans do not want to fight a conventional war in Europe either, for good reason. It would tempt nonnuclear nations to create their own nuclear forces and thus lead to nuclear proliferation. It is not a policy to be embraced lightly or with enthusiasm. But neither is the continued acceptance of policies that seriously contemplate limiting the unlimitable—nuclear war.

WHAT KIND OF FUTURE?

Primary reliance on conventional weapons, rather than nuclear ones, for extended deterrence fits in well with the kind of analysis we outlined above. It avoids the need for quick-reacting, highly accurate silo-busting first-strike forces that could endanger stability in a crisis. The risks of escalation would be serious in any superpower confrontation. If the other side should begin nuclear war, some of those risks would already have been taken. To deter a nuclear attack and to bring a war to a negotiated halt just as soon as possible, we would plan certain very restricted forms of nuclear retaliation. But the risks of first use of nuclear weapons are too great to justify ever beginning it ourselves. At the same time, our analysis implies that less dire threats are terrible enough. Relatively milder threats would avoid the horrors of bombing population centers and *somewhat* reduce the dangers of escalation. A shift to less severe threats is required because of the ever-present and not fully controllable chance that deterrence may fail, forcing us to make good our threats.

The continued buildup of nuclear weaponry (for example, the projected increase in the stockpile of American nuclear warheads to 29,000 by 1990) is a step in the wrong direction. Mutual reductions— not just a freeze, though that could be helpful if adequate means of verifying compliance could be found—are important. The Reagan administration has in principle endorsed "deep cuts" in nuclear weaponry, perhaps by a process of "builddown" (removing two older weapons from the arsenal for every new one deployed). New weapons that are primarily suitable for a first strike endanger stability in a crisis, but they are being deployed by the Americans (Pershing II in Europe and the MX) and the Russians (SS-20 missiles and Soviet submarines close to the American coast, which can hit American targets in five to ten minutes). There is a role for both negotiations and self-restraint. Brinkmanship and risk taking in a crisis rather than building up nonnuclear means of defense are folly. Proposals to establish a joint U.S.-USSR military communications center and to upgrade the hot line from a teletype to direct voice communication make good sense for crisis control.

Most of the measures that we have discussed come under the heading of arms control, with some elements of disarmament. They call for reducing and controlling the risks associated with nuclear deterrence but not for abolishing it. They imply resigning ourselves to generations or centuries of continued reliance on nuclear deterrence in some form. It is a harsh prospect. People are prone to error, and machinery to accidents. The usual belief is that the risks simply have to be accepted: Nuclear weapons have been invented, and hundreds of thousands of people know how to build them. That knowledge cannot be unlearned, and the problems of verifying any really substantial cuts in weapons are staggering. (With, say, 10,000 weapons on each side, cheating on an arms control agreement by 500 weapons would not give either side a decisive advantage. Cheating at that level, though not desirable, might be tolerable to achieve other goals. But if each side agrees to reduce its inventory to 500 weapons and then one side cheats by 500, the balance would be upset.) We may have no choice but to live forever in a nuclear world.

Yet the prospect is repellant, a terrible legacy to leave our descendants. Many people will not resign themselves to it. Some declare themselves pacifists, or at least nuclear pacifists, and say that nothing can justify the use or even continued possession of nuclear weapons. Others search for acceptable paths to disarmament. (One proposal suggests that although the knowledge of nuclear weapons cannot be unlearned, maybe that very knowledge and the threat to act on it will serve as the necessary deterrent to violation of a comprehensive disarmament program.)[25] Ultimately, we see no perfect or even good solution overall. Every possibility contains moral and practical dangers.

---

25. A representative statement of resignation to arms control and a nuclear future is Albert Carnesale et al., *Living with Nuclear Weapons* (Cambridge, Mass.: Harvard University Press, 1983), and the proposal for total nuclear disarmament, with rearmament deterred by the threat of counterrearmament, is Jonathan Schell, "The Abolition," *New Yorker*, January 2, 1984, pp. 36–75, and January 9, 1984, pp. 43–94.

But neither is the situation hopeless. We have, after all, come this far without nuclear war. Many people in 1945 did not expect that much success. The success—such as it is—has not come by accident. It has come because people have puzzled and struggled. Some of those people are scientists, government officials, and military officers. Others are ordinary citizens who, by their votes and their protests, have forced leaders to take their fears seriously. There is no choice but to continue wrestling with the dangers and contradictions of our nuclear dilemmas.

15

CAUSES OF PEACE AMONG INDUSTRIALIZED COUNTRIES

THE ACHIEVEMENT OF PEACE AND PROSPERITY

Many of the achievements of the past three or four decades in the rich industrialized countries of the world are very impressive indeed. Despite periods of recession and the more recent combination of reduced economic growth and inflation, these countries have experienced a period of economic well-being unrivaled in history. Despite serious inequalities and remaining pockets of real poverty within many industrialized countries, prosperity has been widespread—truly a mass phenomenon not true in most of the great empires of the world which benefited only the elite.

All this has happened in spite of the enormous loss of life and physical destruction caused by World War II, at the end of which the economies of Japan, Germany, and many other states were in ruin. Moreover, the whole world—but especially the industrialized countries—is now tightly linked by a network of trade, investment, communications, and travel to a degree also unprecedented. If they wanted to do it, most citizens of Europe and North America could readily afford an intercontinental trip and arrive at their destinations within less than half a day. The prospering economies of these countries are tightly interdependent: growth, inflation, and recession are readily transmitted from one country to another with little control.

Equally important but not noticed as often as the achievement of prosperity is the achievement of *peace*. Among the developed market economies—the industrialized countries of the OECD (the Organization for Economic Cooperation and Development, composed of all the capitalist countries of Europe, the United States, Canada, Japan, Australia, New Zealand, and Yugoslavia as an associate member—there has been no war or other violent conflict since 1945. Not only has there been no war among OECD countries in nearly forty years, but there has been little expectation of or preparation for war among them either.[1] The seemingly most permanent hostility—between France and Germany—appears well buried since the 1960s. Individual German and French citizens may not love one another, but neither do they expect the other's state to attack or wish to mount an attack. Europeans, Americans, and Japanese may still fear an attack from outside the OECD (as from the Soviet Union); they may continue to use or threaten to use military force against small, Communist, or poor states to retain their spheres of influence. But among countries within the OECD area, peace and the confident expectation of peace are the norms.

This is an extraordinary achievement by the standards of recent history. Until 1945, war or the expectation of war among these countries was the norm. These were the instigators and major combatants of both world wars, which resulted in the deaths of tens of millions of people. The preceding century saw many major wars among these same countries, beginning with the extended Napoleonic Wars among all the major states of Europe (and provoking the War of 1812 between Britain and America) and including several wars involved in Germany's unification in 1870. Even in periods of peace, everyone recognized that peace was precarious, depending on constant watchfulness, readiness and ability to fight, and maintenance of a balance of power. Crises and

---

1. A marginal exception to these statements is the brief, limited conflict between Greece and Turkey over the control of Cyprus in 1974. Greece and Turkey, however, are virtually the least wealthy and least industrialized countries of the OECD, an important fact in light of the explanations of the phenomenon of peace that we shall offer below.

war scares were common; several conflicts threatened to provoke a general European war before one finally did occur in August 1914.

Peace among the OECD countries is also an extraordinary achievement by the standards of world history. The countries involved contain a total population of over 800 million, spread over a geographic area equal to nearly half the land of the Northern Hemisphere. By both measures it is a larger "zone of peace" than has ever existed before. These are simple facts—but facts that cry out for explanation. If we could understand why such a large set of peoples, who only recently fought bitterly and bloodily, now live at peace with one another, we would know something very important. Looking for the causes of peace is merely the opposite side of the common question "What are the causes of war?" If we could answer it for the OECD countries, we might have a key to promoting peace over a wider area, even the entire globe.

Peace: *Salaam* or *Sulah?*

We must begin with a clear meaning of a common but often misused term: *peace.* To some, *peace* is simply the absence of war, the absence of organized violent conflict. For most of us, however, that is not enough. One cannot, for example, "make a desert and call it peace." The kind of peace we want is not a world where every individual or group who could conceivably resort to violent conflict is simply destroyed: that would include everyone who is not a pacifist. Ideally, we wish to achieve a "stable peace" like that among the OECD countries: the *absence of preparation for war or the serious expectation of war.* If we prepare for or expect violent conflict—or if we repress violent conflict by force—we have what Kenneth Boulding calls "unstable peace."[2] An unstable peace can be enforced by deterrence, the fear of violent retribution, where we continually fear for the continuation of peace under a "mutual balance of terror."

If there is no balance—if deterrence is merely one-way rather than a mutual relationship between two hostile parties—then we talk of *repression.* By some values and for some people (especially the most privileged), the absence of violent conflict achieved by repression and coercion may be better than the outbreak of violent conflict, but it is hardly

---

2. Kenneth Boulding, *Stable Peace* (Austin: University of Texas Press, 1979).

anyone's ideal. Repressive and coercive relationships can be found between powerful and weak states as well as between powerful and weak groups within states. People may be deprived of political liberties, made materially poor, or allowed to die from sickness or starvation without direct physical violence. Some analysts thus refer to "structural violence"—deprivations enforced by coercive social and political systems or structures—in contrast to direct or physical violence, such as in war or even imprisonment.[3] Structural violence is in fact a very slippery and emotion-laden term, and much of the time it is hard to devise a definition with which all observers would agree. Nevertheless, the central distinction between stable peace under conditions that are basically acceptable to both sides and a situation of nonwar maintained only by threats (whether unilateral or reciprocated) is clear enough. It corresponds roughly to the Arabic terms *salaam,* which means an enduring peaceful relationship based on mutual respect, and *sulah,* which means only the end of hostilities or a truce.

One of the most prominent theorists about the conditions of peace is Karl W. Deutsch. He characterizes an area where peace is expected as a security community:

> A *security community* is a group of people which has become "integrated." By *integration* we mean the attainment, within a territory, of a *"sense of community"* and of institutions and practices strong enough and widespread enough to assure . . . dependable expectations of "peaceful change" among its population. By sense of community we mean a belief . . . that common social problems must and can be resolved by processes of "peaceful change."[4]

Note the emphasis on peaceful change—an ability and willingness to accommodate new demands and needs, not merely to maintain a status quo that may be unjust. It is a situation where participants have a relationship that is reasonably equal and symmetrical, frequently harmonize their interests, compromise their differences, and reap mutual rewards. There still may be conflict, but the use or threat of force to resolve conflict is absent.

---

3. This perspective is common, especially among contributors to the *Journal of Peace Research* and the *Bulletin of Peace Proposals,* both published by the Peace Research Institute of Oslo, Norway.

4. Karl W. Deutsch et al., *Political Community and the North Atlantic Area* (Princeton, N.J.: Princeton University Press, 1957), p. 5.

These conditions have essentially been met within the OECD area. We may speak of injustice and of governmental coercion and repression within many industrialized and democratic countries—and conditions of injustice, coercion, and repression do indeed exist there. But compared with many other parts of the world, it is fair to say that a security community largely exists both among and within the OECD countries. The greatest exceptions are within rather than between countries. The most significant cases of violent political deaths within the last decade or so have been within the United Kingdom (the continuing conflict in Northern Ireland) and Spain (violence by Basque separatists). In both of these cases, the violent acts involve people who do not wish to be subjected to a common government and seek either independence (the Basques) or inclusion in another country (Ireland). There are also a few other separatist movements where the possibility of violence is not high but nevertheless cannot be completely ignored—for instance, in Canada (Quebec separatists) and Belgium (between the Dutch-speaking Flemish and the French-speaking Walloons). Violence directed at existing governmental institutions by separatists thus seems to be more of a threat than does violence among OECD governments—a point to which we shall return.

THE MOVEMENT FOR EUROPEAN UNITY

The achievement of peace by integrating smaller political units into larger ones has long been a goal of political theorists and policymakers. The Roman Empire brought peace, the *Pax Romana*, to much of the world for several centuries. Although there were some revolts within the empire and continuing battles with the "barbarians" on its borders, the Roman Empire did give its subjects a remarkable era of peace as well as of prosperity. Of course, it was largely a peace of domination—not the kind of stable peace or security community capable of peaceful change to which we aspire. Dante, writing in the fourteenth century, nevertheless looked back on the Roman Empire as being far better than the situation of almost constant warfare among the Italian city-states of the Renaissance. He argued that "in a multitude of rulers there is evil" and hoped for the emergence of a unified Italy under a single crown.

Following the devastation of World War II—the second enormously destructive war in only thirty years—some people adopted the principles of "world federalism," with the idea that permanent peace could be achieved only by establishing a world government. In Europe, many statesmen vowed that wars among Europeans had to cease and saw some form of European unification as the means to secure that goal. In May 1950 Robert Schuman, the foreign minister of France, announced:

> The French Government proposes to put the whole of the Franco-German coal and steel production under a joint High Authority, in an organization which is open for the other European countries to enter. . . . It will change the destiny of these regions which for so long have been used for making weapons of war of which they have been most frequently the victims. The solidarity between the two countries established by joint production will show that a war between France and Germany becomes not only unthinkable but materially impossible.

He further declared that his plan would "establish the basis for a European Federation . . . indispensable for the safeguarding of peace." From this initiative the European Coal and Steel Community was born a year later, including not only France and Germany but also Belgium, Luxembourg, the Netherlands, and Italy. This was the first major European supranational institution, that is, an institution with powers to overrule the member national governments on some issues.

Promoting interdependence among the heavy industry parts of the European economies seemed a good way to limit the independent war-making ability of individual states. Wider economic union could do so even more effectively. Another French leader, Jean Monnet, wrote:

> There will be no peace in Europe if countries build up their strength on a basis of national sovereignty. . . . The countries of Europe are too limited to assure their people the prosperity that modern times afford. . . . Larger markets are needed. Prosperity and vital social development are inconceivable unless the countries of Europe form a federation or a European entity which in turn creates a common economic union.

This kind of thinking led to another major Western European institution, EURATOM, to undertake collectively the enormously expensive but promising development of nuclear power. It ultimately led to the signing of the 1957 Treaty of Rome, which established the European Economic Community, or Common Market, among the same six countries that had formed the Coal and Steel Community and EURATOM. These separate institutions were then merged into the European Community (EC) with broad powers to abolish tariffs and other restrictions on trade within the community; to regulate working conditions, environmental controls, and marketing practices within the community; to establish a common set of trade restrictions on outside countries; and to provide free movement of persons (particularly workers) and financial capital within the community. Now the community institutions include an executive commission, a court of justice, and a parliament directly elected by the people (but so far with little power).

In Monnet's vision, the economies and ultimately the people would be bound inextricably by economic union, making war "unthinkable." Notice, however, that in Monnet's statement another motive appears. In addition to providing peace, European unity would bring prosperity. Europeans had experienced not only war but terrible economic destruction and deprivation afterward. Even before World War II, the economies of the separate states suffered from various trade restrictions that severely limited commerce among them and, by dividing the continent into many small markets, made impossible economies of scale of the kind that helped make American enterprise so efficient in the enormous U.S. market. For example, economic disunity contributed to competitive trade restrictions and currency devaluations that worsened the Great Depression of the 1930s. True prosperity seemed to require creating a large European market without internal barriers; for such a market to work effectively, a wide range of controls on goods, capital, and labor had to be coordinated.

Finally, many Europeans had another motive in addition to internal peace and prosperity: external security. Big countries have great power, and only big countries are great powers. In a world dominated by the Soviet and American giants, each with several times the population and wealth of any single European state, Europeans could have the benefits of great-power status *collectively* if not individually as France, West Germany, or England. Thus, Europeans, who retained great concern for their military security because of Russia and who did not trust the United States to observe its NATO commitments indefinitely, wanted to see Europe as a united political and military unit.

This aim largely motivated the attempt to create a European Defense Community (EDC) in 1950. With the continued deterioration in relations with the Soviet Union, made still more threatening by the outbreak of the Korean War earlier in 1950, many Europeans and Americans came to the conclusion that the military security of Western Europe could not be guaranteed unless West Germany could be rearmed. Germany at this time was still occupied (by America, Britain, France in the west and the USSR in the east); it had no army and no control over its foreign policy. Because of their recent Nazi experience, the Germans were still intensely distrusted. The EDC, therefore, was conceived as a way to harness German personnel and industrial strength to the common defense. It would have also controlled German militarism by uniting all the member states' armies under a single commander. The EDC would have also had a directly elected European parliament and an executive that could be dismissed by the parliament—virtually a "United States of Europe." The Germans need not be feared if they had no independent military might; at the same time, a powerful common European unit, able to pursue a united foreign policy and to cooperate militarily with America as a near equal, would be formed.

In the end the European Defense Community idea was rejected. Not enough Europeans (especially the French) were ready to give up such sweeping powers to a supranational institution. To this day, the major missing elements in European unification concern military security and international politics. Europeans make various efforts to coordinate foreign and military policy and to pursue some common military activities, along with other powers, within NATO (however, the French limit their participation). Of the three goals behind European unification—goals that different Europeans rank differently in importance—great-power status remains the most elusive.[5]

TRYING TO EXPLAIN PEACE

World politics scholars cannot answer confidently or definitively why there is peace within the OECD area. We lack a solid body of tested theory. We can, however, make some suggestions. We shall proceed in the following manner, which is perhaps the most productive way a social scientist can work:

1. We start with some observations or some facts that need explaining. In this case, we begin with the fact of OECD peace.
2. We offer some tentative hypotheses.
3. We see whether available facts support our hypotheses.

---

5. For instance, the European states have not evolved a common strategic nuclear deterrent force or even been able to pursue a unified policy toward OPEC. For a study finding that regional integration in Europe had no significant consequences for the international system, see James A. Caporaso, "The External Consequences of Regional Integration for Pan-European Relations: Inequality, Dependence, Polarization, and Symmetry," *International Studies Quarterly* 20 (1976), no. 3, pp. 341–392.

4. If these facts do support the hypotheses, we look for some implications—general propositions that we can deduce from the first hypotheses and facts.

5. We test such propositions on the first case or on new cases.[6]

Analysis along these lines is sometimes referred to by the German term *gedankenexperiment,* or "thinking experiment." It is a purely analytical exercise, unlike the clinical or laboratory experiments where one may vary conditions to see what effect the changes have. With citizens and nations—real people—we simply cannot conduct an empirical experiment. In our analysis here, we shall necessarily proceed very tentatively, developing hypotheses that will require much more theory and research; we shall not proceed through all the above steps with creation of rigorous data or documentation. The exercise can, however, produce some intriguing suggestions.

Cohesion in the Face of Outside Threats

Hypothesis 1: Peace in the OECD area is a consequence of nations coming together in response to a *common threat* by an external enemy—in this case, the Soviet Union.

Some Further Facts and Their Implications Most, though not all, citizens of the OECD countries have indeed felt a security threat from the Soviet Union since World War II. A desire for common defense, the strength that derives from a joint effort, was one of the motivations behind the European unity movement and, of course, behind NATO. The perceived need to act together helped produce a determination to overcome differences within the OECD community and was important in the beginning. Yet the sense of threat was greatest in the early years of NATO, the 1940s and the 1950s. This threat may have helped bring peace within Europe initially and spawned NATO. But the threat has not been necessary to sustain peace among these countries nor was the threat urgent enough to establish the EDC. During Soviet-American détente in the 1960s and early 1970s, people in the West no longer thought a Soviet invasion of Western Europe or a Soviet attack on the

---

6. Charles Lave and James March, An Introduction to Models in the Social Sciences (New York: Harper & Row, 1975), Ch. 1.

United States was very likely. It was still seen as possible, but not as the real and immediate threat that it had seemed earlier. If the sense of external threat was the principal cement holding the OECD countries together in peaceful relations, we should have seen a decline in stable peace during the 1960s. Actually, quite the opposite occurred: People also became more confident in the maintenance of peace between the traditional enemies among the industrialized countries. Possibly one might claim that "peace" among America's allies was enforced by the United States itself, so as not to weaken the common defense. But except for the conflicts between Greece and Turkey, enforcement simply has not been needed in Western Europe. By contrast, the Soviet Union has repeatedly intervened militarily, as well as threatened to do so, in the affairs of its East European allies.

Also, we find that the OECD case does not very well meet the set of conditions under which social psychologists have found that an external threat promotes internal cohesion. These conditions include a sense that there is an ability to counter the threat, some prior experience in acting as a group, and the view by all parties that the threat is common, affecting all members of the group equally.[7]

The first of these conditions was present in this case. The members knew that if they could act together they certainly had the resources—population, wealth, and technological sophistication—to counter any Soviet threat. The second condition, however—prior experience as a group—was not present. There was little experience of close cooperation among OECD countries before World War II; during World War II the group was clearly divided. Nor could it be said that the threat affected all members equally. Some, like Japan and West Germany, were very close to Soviet military power and the threat of invasion; others, like the United States and Britain, were protected by distance and natural barriers. Peace among these countries, therefore, does not seem the result of any uniform experience of a common external threat. Indeed, we know that in some cases an external threat can fracture cohesion. The possibility that the Austro-Hungarian empire would be invaded in World War I was seen not always as a danger but rather as an opportunity for some of the subjugated Slavic peoples (Czechs, Slovaks, Poles, Croatians, and Slovenes) to free themselves from Austrian and Hungarian domination. The external threat thus became an external ally for the prosecution of revolt. Similarly, a perceived common

---

7. See Arthur Stein, "Conflict and Cohesion: A Review of the Literature," *Journal of Conflict Resolution* 20 (1976), no. 1, pp. 143–165.

threat from Israel has not brought peace among all the Arab countries. Clearly, other factors are at work.

Institution Building

Hypothesis 2: Peace in the OECD area is a consequence of the construction of governmental *institutions,* especially the supranational institutions binding together several countries. The best examples are the political and economic institutions of the European Community (EC).

For some theorists, the important aspect of institutions is that they can forcibly keep the "peace." They are the wielders of the only legitimate instruments of violence—the army and police—and as a result they can impose order and compel obedience for the common good. For other theorists, who have been more influential in recent decades, specific institutions attending to particular needs or *functions* of society can create habits of obedience and cooperation. This group of theorists owes much to the functionalist ideas of David Mitrany, and their ideas are also well expressed in the early work of Ernst Haas.

Perhaps Haas's greatest contribution was to focus attention on the political process of transferring *loyalties to new institutions* rather than simply on institution building alone. Two quotations from his classic study, *The Uniting of Europe,* make this clear: "Political community, therefore, is a condition in which specific groups and individuals show more loyalty to their central political institutions than to any other political authority." Defining political integration as the process leading to the transfer of loyalties, "the existence of political institutions capable of translating ideologies into law [is] the cornerstone of the definition."[8] For Haas it is particularly the loyalties of elites—those involved in or with the government—that matters, not so much the loyalties of the mass public.

In his study of the operation of the Common Market bureaucracy, Peter Busch found that whereas individuals in the different EC countries still look to their national economic interest groups for political

---

8. Ernst Haas, *The Uniting of Europe* (Stanford, Calif.: Stanford University Press, 1957), pp. 4, 7. More recently Haas moved away from his earlier concerns with institutions to look at multidimensional patterns of interdependence both within and outside regional groups. See his "Turbulent Fields and the Theory of Regional Integration," *International Organization* 30 (1976), no. 2, pp. 173–212.

activity, the interest groups themselves operate not so much with the national bureaucracies as with officials of the EC. Regardless of the focus of mass loyalties or attention, major political actors know that the action is to be found at EC commission headquarters in Brussels.[9] There they can obtain the rewards to satisfy their followers. Other authors have also focused on institutions. For example, Leon Lindberg said, "The essence of political integration is the emergence or creation over time of collective decision-making processes; i.e., political institutions to which governments delegate decision-making authority and/or through which they decide jointly via more familiar intergovernmental negotiation."[10]

For functionalists, the important aspect of what happens is the "spillover" of activities from some functions (e.g., the coal and steel industry), creating the impetus toward more integration. One analyst defines *spillover* as

> the process whereby members of an integration scheme—agreed on some collective goals for a variety of motives but unequally satisfied with the attainment of these goals—attempt to resolve their dissatisfaction either by resorting to collaboration in another, related sector (expanding the *scope* of mutual commitment) or by intensifying their commitment to the original sector (increasing the level of mutual commitment) or both.[11]

Thus, Robert Schuman could say, "Europe will not be built in a day nor as part of some over-all design. It will be built through practical achievements that first create a sense of common purpose." Many theorists thought that spillover might be automatically progressive as well as irreversible, leading inexorably to full European integration. We now can see, however, that it need not be so. The current level of European unification seems secure, but further steps will probably be slow and difficult at best.

Some Further Facts and Their Implications It certainly is true that stable peace has been achieved among members of the EC (the original six, plus Britain, Ireland, Denmark, and Greece). For countries now so

---

9. Peter Busch, "Germany in the European Community: Theory and Case Study," *Canadian Journal of Political Science* 11 (1978), no. 3, pp. 545–573.

10. Leon Lindberg, "Political Integration as a Multidimensional Phenomenon Requiring Multivariate Measurement," *International Organization* 24 (1970), no. 4, pp. 649–731.

11. Philippe Schmitter, "Three Neo-Functional Hypotheses About International Integration," *International Organization* 24 (1969), no. 1, p. 162.

highly interdependent, the EC institutions are probably essential in solving members' common problems and perhaps in preventing tensions that could endanger the peace. Yet the area of peace includes all of the OECD countries. Although there are a variety of important institutions like the Council of Europe, NATO, and the OECD itself, these are not in any significant way coercive organizations. Save for the powers of the EC to set common standards, make regulations, and assess contributions from its members, these institutions have few coercive powers. Principally, they must work by negotiation and consensus among members, not by enforcement.

For instance, in peacetime the NATO Supreme Headquarters does not command the troops of the constituent countries. The military and civilian leaders of the NATO countries meet annually to set military capability and spending targets, but NATO cannot tax its members or demand a specific military contribution from each. These therefore are not coercive institutions to enforce peace or even to enforce common sacrifices as normal national governments do.

A national government, for example, coerces all of us by requiring us to pay our taxes. We may grumble, but on the whole we accept this coercion so long as it is applied reasonably equally among people. Because we want most of the benefits—health, education, defense, and so forth—that a modern government provides, we are more or less willing to be coerced to pay our share so long as others are equally required to pay. Most OECD institutions lack this kind of power. Rather, they largely facilitate mutual attention and problem solving among its members. This is very important and probably essential for interdependent countries. But it is a far cry from a common government.

In addition, the only serious expectation or actuality of violent conflict within the OECD area is within countries, that is, among people already bound by a common government—chiefly in Northern Ireland and in Spain (the Basques). It is not simply a matter of an institution—the common government—being unable to prevent violence; rather, the fact of common government is a *cause* of the violence. The separatists want to be free of the common government. There have been many cases of civil war or secessionist revolution in history. The revolt of the thirteen American colonies and the later unsuccessful secession attempt by the Confederate states well illustrate the fact. One of the most significant contributions of Karl Deutsch's 1957 book on international integration was to point out what should have been obvious: People may fight against a common government but then subsequently live in peace as separate states. Common institutions are no panacea for peace; thus, neither is any simple prescription of world government. For

Deutsch the integration goal is peace; institution building at best contributes to that kind of integration but is often irrelevant or even destructive to it.

Deutsch's book went on to examine seventeen cases of attempted security community formation in order to see whether certain conditions were more often associated with success than with failure. We cannot look at all those conditions here, but some of them provide the bases for useful hypotheses.

Economic Ties and Social Communication

Hypothesis 3: Peace in the OECD area is a consequence of strong economic ties and *links of social communication.*

The importance of economic and communications links is strongly emphasized by Deutsch and others with his perspective. These links become facilities for attention to each other and for identifying their interests with others'. One cannot help meet the needs of another without knowing what those needs are—without a large continuous flow of information. There is a social fabric between as well as within nations that is built from such bonds as trade, travel (migration and tourism), cultural and educational exchange, and the use of communications facilities such as the telephone and television. These ties communicate the needs and perspectives of one group of people to others; they strengthen the sense of a collective identity within the collectivity. In the tradition of sociological theory, these community bonds are part of the *gemeinschaft* (common loyalties and values, a feeling of belonging together) as contrasted with the *gesellschaft* emphasis on competitiveness, contractual arrangements, and institutions. It is a focus not just on the elites but on the attitudes and beliefs at all "politically relevant strata" of the population, which include the mass public in democracies. Deutsch terms the relevant sense of community

> a matter of mutual sympathy and loyalties; of "we-feeling," trust, and mutual consideration; of partial identification in terms of self-images and interests; of mutually successful predictions of behavior . . . in short, a matter of a perpetual dynamic process of mutual attention, communication, perception of needs, and responsiveness in the process of decision making.[12]

---

12. Karl W. Deutsch et al., *Political Community and the North Atlantic Area* (Princeton, N.J.: Princeton University Press, 1957), p. 36.

Two pieces of evidence illustrate the contribution of such ties to predicting each other's behavior and accurately communicating desires. In a study of French businessmen's attitudes toward the European Defense Community (EDC), Daniel Lerner found that businessmen who engaged in no foreign trade whatever tended to favor the establishment of the EDC by a margin of 2 to 1, but individuals whose firms did at least half their business in foreign trade favored EDC 6 to 1. Similarly, American senators with personal ties or constituent economic ties to Britain were twice as likely to take a pro-British position on political issues than were senators with no known ties. Correspondingly, British members of Parliament with ties to the United States were twice as likely to be pro-American than were those who lacked such ties; those with two or more ties were three times as likely to be pro-American as were those with none.[13]

In both these studies, the issues at stake were broad and diverse, going well beyond the direct economic interests of the individuals involved. All these contacts become general channels of communication, opening individuals up to information and viewpoints they would not otherwise receive. In reviewing the literature on international exchange and attitude change, Herbert Kelman concluded:

> These are not necessarily changes in general favorableness toward the host country, but rather changes in the cognitive structure—for example in the complexity and differentiation of images of the host country. Such changes are probably more meaningful in the long run than total approval of the country would be; they indicate a greater richness and refinement of images and a greater understanding of the other society in its own terms.[14]

Donald Puchala ties the argument to learning theory: "Learning during regional integration is a direct result of mutually rewarding actions among regional partners."[15]

Of course, trade, tourism, and migration can also serve as irritants, though they usually seem to bind nations or social groups together.

---

13. Daniel Lerner, "French Business Leaders Look at EDC," *Public Opinion Quarterly* 20 (1956), no. 1, p. 220; Bruce Russett, *Community and Contention: Britain and America in the Twentieth Century* (Cambridge, Mass.: MIT Press, 1963), chap. 9.

14. Herbert Kelman (ed.), *International Behavior* (New York: Holt, Rinehart and Winston, 1965), p. 573.

15. Donald Puchala, "The Pattern of Contemporary Regional Integration," *International Studies Quarterly* 22 (1968), no. 1, p. 51.

The most important qualification—and it is a serious one—is that the exchanges must be mutual and on a basis of relative equality. Ties perceived as exploitative or colonial, however strong, do not seem to bring groups together. Contacts that are involuntary for one party (an extreme case being the payment of reparations) are not facilitative; nor would be highly status conscious relations, such as those between employer and employee.

Contacts between highly disparate cultures are also as likely to arouse conflict as to bring the cultures together. Tourists from rich countries to poor countries, for instance, may create animosities among their hosts and distress in their own minds. Thus, the nature of the contacts in each particular case must be examined before any firm conclusions about their effects are made. A theory that ignored this fact might be simpler but would surely be misleading. Fortunately, some very general observations can be made: Ties between nations that are culturally similar and perhaps geographically close are more likely to be favorable. Again, the presence of ties itself does not prove anything, but as Arend Lijphart notes about relationships within a common government, a high level of political contacts requires a high level of social contacts for the relationship to be mutually rewarding.[16]

Economic interdependence also provides the simple result of giving one party a material stake in the prosperity and stability of the other's economic system. One cannot sell goods or services to others unless the others can afford to buy them. When strong economic links work both ways, each party has an important stake in the other. The oil trade between Arab producers and industrial-country consumers illustrates this point nicely. American-based multinational corporations like Exxon reap substantial profits from the high price of oil—it is not only the Arab governments who gain. All American and European consumers have a stake in the economic and especially the political stability of the Arab oil-producing states. If they slide into chaos, as did Iran in 1979, they will not produce; hence, they will not be able to export oil and prices for the remaining supplies will shoot up. On the other side, the Arab producers have a stake in high prices, of course, but not so high as to produce economic instability in the consuming countries. A serious recession or depression would reduce their markets.

Moreover, many OPEC states have been unable to use their oil-derived revenues fast enough and have invested them in banks, securi-

---

16. Arend Lijphart, "Consociational Democracy," *World Politics* 21 (1969), no. 2, pp. 207–225.

ties, and land in the industrialized countries. An economic crash in the consuming states would mean a crash in the value of their investments.

Some Further Facts and Their Implications On the whole, economic and other types of international ties, especially among the OECD countries, have been increasing. The increase has been especially strong since World War II. Table 15.1 gives information on imports and exports for all the economies of the developed countries for more than twenty years. You can see that trade among these countries usually totaled about 70 percent of their total international trade and sometimes more. The growth suggested by the dollar figures is deceptive because of inflation and because of the need to control for growth also in the domestic economies. The ratio of foreign trade to GNP is a useful indicator of the degree of interdependence—how important foreign exchange is to the overall level of economic activity. During the 1960s

Table 15.1
Developed market economies' trade: Destination of exports and origin of imports, 1960–1982.

	Exports to		Imports from	
	($ bil.)	(%)	($ bil.)	(%)
Developed market economies				
1960	58.8	69.2	58.8	72.2
1970	172.5	77.0	172.5	78.0
1977	517.8	70.9	517.8	68.4
1982	861.0	70.2	861.0	69.3
Developing market economies (incl. OPEC)				
1960	21.2	24.9	19.8	24.3
1970	41.9	18.7	40.7	18.4
1977	172.7	23.7	208.9	27.6
1982	308.2	25.1	332.8	26.0
Centrally planned economies				
1960	3.0	3.5	2.8	3.4
1970	8.4	3.8	7.8	3.5
1977	34.4	4.7	29.9	4.0
1982	55.6	4.5	58.4	4.7
World				
1960	85.0	100.0	81.4	100.0
1970	224.1	100.0	221.0	100.0
1977	729.9	100.0	756.6	100.0
1982	1227.0	100.0	1242.4	100.0

Source: UN. Monthly Bulletin of Statistics, December 1982, and earlier issues. 1982 figures are year-long estimates based on the first six months.

and 1970s, the total GNP for these countries more than doubled, and trade among them nearly quadrupled.

Figure 15.1 shows the value of U.S. exports from 1964 to 1982 to various groups of countries. Figure 15.2 illustrates U.S. foreign trade as a percentage of the U.S. GNP since 1860. This figure shows that, historically, the U.S. foreign trade levels of the 1980s are extraordinarily high—above even the levels reached around World War I.

Another indicator of economic interdependence among the industrialized countries is foreign investment. In the nineteenth century, the United States was heavily dependent on capital investment from Europe to finance its development, and American investors sent little money abroad—much like the situation of some underdeveloped countries today. This changed dramatically after World War I, when American capital was invested abroad. Several countries, especially Britain, financed much of their effort in World War I by selling their investments in the United States. As shown in Figure 15.3, after World War I, American investments abroad rose very sharply, as did foreign investments in the United States after some lag. World War II saw a sharp gain in both figures. Since World War II, investment here and abroad

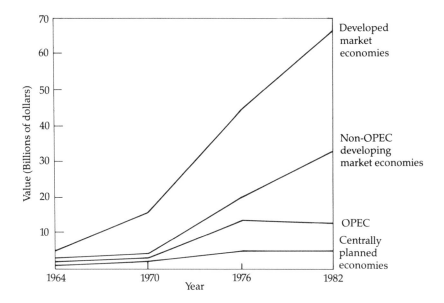

Figure 15.1
U.S. exports to groups of countries. [*Source: UN Monthly Bulletin of Statistics,* December 1982, and earlier issues.]

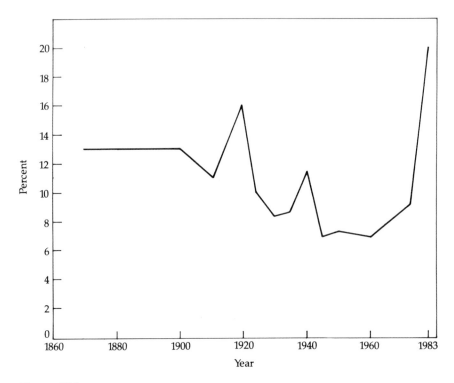

Figure 15.2
U.S. foreign trade as a percentage of GNP. [*Sources:* U.S. Bureau of the Census, *Historical Statistics of the United States, Colonial Times to 1970* (Washington, D.C.: U.S. Government Printing Office, 1975); *Survey of Current Business*, October 1983.

has continued to rise and is now at roughly the same level, relative to the American GNP, as the peaks earlier in the twentieth century.

Like foreign trade, around two thirds of this investment goes into or comes from other industrialized countries. Receipts from the profits of foreign investments now equal about one sixth of the total value of U.S. exports. Many American, European, and Japanese manufacturing firms prefer to establish foreign subsidiaries to produce goods abroad rather than to export finished products. The sales of such American-owned subsidiaries now amount to almost three times the value of U.S. exports of manufactured goods. Figure 15.4 shows the percentage increase in the number of foreign branches of major U.S. banks and of manufacturing subsidiaries abroad of the 187 largest U.S. manufacturing corporations. These companies and similar European and Japanese enterprises constitute the world's multinational corporations, which have operations in dozens of different countries.

Overall, international trade and investment seem high by the stan-

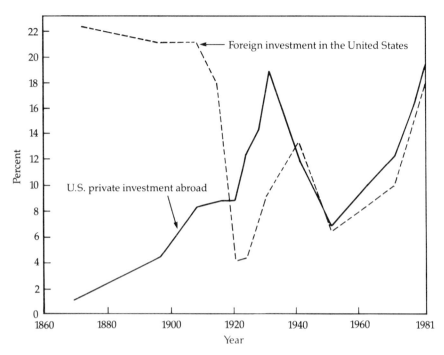

Figure 15.3
U.S. investment abroad and foreign investment in the United States as a percentage of U.S. GNP. [*Sources:* U.S. Bureau of Census, *Historical Statistics of the United States, Colonial Times to 1970* (Washington, D.C.: U.S. Government Printing Office, 1975); U.S. Bureau of Census, *Statistical Abstract of the United States, 1982–83* (Washington, D.C.: U.S. Government Printing Office, 1983).]

dards of recent decades but not especially high by historical standards. Economic ties among the developed-market (or industrialized) countries seem strong, but we should not forget that the industrialized countries make up the largest share of the world economy. They account for about 65 percent of gross world product, so trade among industrialized countries, at 46 percent of all world trade ($1,894 billion), is not especially high. The economic ties represent vast wealth and link great numbers of people, but they are not as strong as the ties between many developed countries and less-developed countries.

The relatively weak economic ties within the industrialized world in the 1930s may help explain the political tensions that culminated in World War II. But the current level of such ties is not so high, according to the standards of other times or with other countries, that we can cite it as a major cause of peace in recent decades. Peace among the

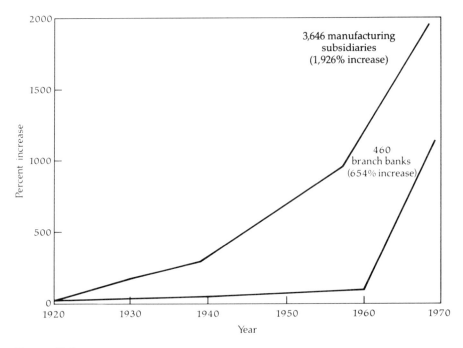

Figure 15.4
The number of U.S. branch banks and manufacturing subsidiaries in foreign countries from 1920 to 1970. [*Sources:* Raymond Vernon, *Sovereignty at Bay* (London: Longmans, 1971), p. 62; Uolevi Arosalo and Raimo Varynen, "Industrial and Financial Oligarchy," *Journal of Peace Research* 10 (1973), no. 1–2, p. 17.]

industrialized countries was well established before the high levels of economic interdependence were achieved in the 1970s.

Economic Benefits

Hypothesis 4: Peace in the OECD area is the result of the achievement and continued expectation of substantial *economic benefits* to all the members.

This hypothesis reflects Deutsch's findings that conditions that promote a security community include superior economic growth, the expectation of joint economic rewards, and a wide range of mutual transactions. Although Deutsch found these conditions merely "helpful" to what he called "pluralistic security communities" (including several independent countries without a common supranational government), he suggested that they might be essential conditions for a security community where various peoples were united under a common government. Economic growth provides the resources to compensate people who lose some of their traditional markets or benefits. If the total pie is growing, they may be able to find new ones.

Some Further Facts and Their Implications   Certainly a high level of economic activity and a high rate of economic growth are prominent features of the OECD. Virtually all the OECD countries experienced rapid economic growth after World War II. This was especially true for the defeated states, Germany and Japan, who benefited from various forms of American assistance and, by 1960, had totally recovered from their devastation. From 1960 to 1981, the average rate of growth in GNP per capita for the developed-market economies was 3.4 percent a year, compared with 2.9 percent for low-income economies.

By contrast, the negative economic growth during much of the 1920s and 1930s for most OECD countries—the Great Depression—was probably a major cause of World War II. Germany's economic difficulties, including rampant inflation followed by mass unemployment, led directly to Hitler's accession to power in 1933. Many of the industrialized countries, in an effort to maintain their own balance of payments, adopted various protectionist measures to restrict imports from other industrial countries. The result was a set of "beggar thy neighbor" policies, which reduced international trade and led to a further decline in everyone's income. Conflicts over economic policies were a major cause of international tension and contributed to Japanese expansionist political and military actions. So we have had a good example of low or negative growth severely damaging the prospects for peace.

We must also be aware, however, that in several important theories about the causes of international violence, economic growth plays the villain's role. According to some theories of imperialism, the constant search by growing economies for new markets for goods or investment capital and for new sources of raw materials leads to war. Choucri and North, in their explanation of the causes of World War I, point to "lateral pressures" created by the growth of income and population and resulting in clashes over colonial acquisitions. Within less-developed countries, some of the theories that we shall examine in the next chapter specify that rapid economic growth, especially if its benefits are distributed very unequally, leads to serious domestic conflict. If some people are gaining little or actually losing while others are visibly enriching themselves, economic growth may well produce feelings of relative deprivation and make revolutionary movements popular. Thus, the distribution of economic rewards is an important element in determining whether growth contributes to peace.

Here we see another of Deutsch's conditions, that of a need for joint economic reward. On this ground, the OECD countries of the past thirty or forty years fare very well. Except for a few oil-rich OPEC countries, the OECD countries are by far the world's richest, with an average GNP per capita of about $9,000 in 1980, when the average for the world was about $2,600. Moreover, these high living standards apply quite equally among the various developed industrialized countries. Whereas GNP per capita ranged in the world from $87 in Laos to $28,034 in Qatar, the range within the OECD was much narrower: from $1,327 in Turkey to $16,188 in Switzerland.

Income is also distributed relatively equally within these countries. Figure 15.5 shows the distribution of income in the United States, which is fairly typical of developed-market economies, and of Brazil, a less-developed country. In the developed countries, the poorest 20 percent of households typically receive 5 percent or more of the income of all households in the country; the richest 10 percent of households do not receive more than about 30 percent of all household income. In less-developed countries, the poorest of the poor, the lowest 20 percent, may get less than 3 percent of all the income of the country, whereas the richest 10 percent may take in as much as half. Certainly there are serious inequalities even within the industrialized countries, particularly among ethnic or racial minorities or in particular geographical regions. But compared with most less-developed countries, OECD countries distribute their income quite equitably.

Within the OECD, however, equality is not a sufficient condition for peace. Economic inequalities, while significant, do not constitute the main grievance in Northern Ireland, where conflict is based on religious and cultural differences. The Basque district is in fact one of the most prosperous parts of Spain; again, the conflicts are over cultural and linguistic autonomy rather than over economics. These few exceptions are not enough to indicate that economic inequality is irrelevant to peace, but they do suggest that it is not a sufficient condition. Without equality, a state of nonwar is likely to be imposed by the dominance of the rich over the poor. Thus, the trade relations between rich and poor countries may be significant, but if they are not seen as producing equivalent rewards on both sides, they will not promote peaceful relations. It is tempting to extend the requirement of equality to

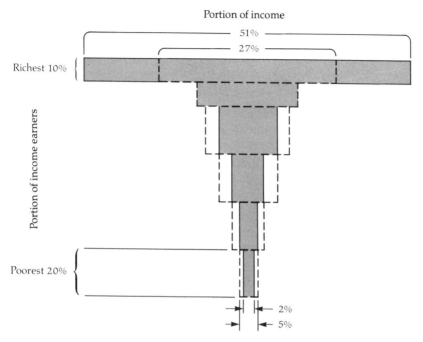

Portion of income

Figure 15.5
Household income distribution for Brazil (shaded outline) and the United States (dashed outline) in 1972. [*Source:* Data from World Bank, *World Development Report, 1979* (Washington, D.C.: World Bank, 1979), p. 173.]

additional, noneconomic values—for example, to status and respect for cultures—to account for the Basque and Northern Ireland cases.

High levels of wealth and equality mean that all citizens would have a great deal to lose in a war. The level of destruction from a big war among industrialized countries would be far greater than the gain realized from any victory.

This suggests that perhaps a combination of moderate growth (not so great as to produce rapid social change and dislocation or to stimulate imperialism greatly), plus equality, plus a high level of economic activity together constitute a set of conditions for peace. This makes sense if most decisions to go to war are rational acts, that is, if war is initiated by decision makers who calculate, to the best of their ability, the probable costs and benefits of their acts. Of course, decision makers value many things (honor, prestige, cultural autonomy, their own political positions, and so forth) as well as material things. Moreover, they often calculate poorly, on the basis of incomplete or erroneous information.

What may look like an act that will produce more benefits than costs may turn out to do quite the opposite. Nevertheless, decision makers attempt to make such calculations. For a war among OECD countries, the prospective gains would not be high (existing equalities mean that a conquered "rich" country would not be so much richer than its "poor" conqueror). The costs of such a war, however, would likely be very high—economic growth would be interrupted, many buildings and capital equipment would be destroyed, and existing wealth would be severely eroded. With such great prospective costs, war with another developed-market economy just does not look cost-effective at all. Any rational wars, with other kinds of countries, will be limited and distant, where the expected losses would be low.

Thus, we have one plausible hypothesis—stable peace can be maintained under conditions of *moderate growth, equity,* and a *high level of economic activity.* Where such conditions do not exist, peace is more likely to be maintained, if at all, only through deterrence (mutual or one-sided). This leaves us with an unanswered question: Why do we not have stable peace (rather than a peace maintained only by deterrence) between the OECD countries and the Soviet Union and Eastern Europe? Perhaps there still is not quite enough equity between the two sides. For instance, in 1980 the average GNP per capita in centrally planned economies was well under $5,000, compared with $9,000 in the OECD countries. Or perhaps we have reached the limits of arguments about economic conditions as causes of peace or war and must now look for additional explanations.

DEMOCRATIC PRACTICE AND BELIEF

Deutsch suggests two additional conditions that are essential for achieving a security community: that the major *values* held by the populations in question are compatible and that a situation of *mutual responsiveness* exists among these populations. However, neither of these conditions sounds like an independent cause. We suggested earlier that mutual responsiveness was likely to arise when there was a high level of communications and transactions between countries; without such links creating a community, there is insufficient knowledge about one another to make responsiveness possible. Compatibility of major values sounds like a condition that would contribute to responsiveness and not merely be incidental. Actually, both responsiveness and compatibility appear to arise in large part because of the ties of community. They can then contribute to peace and be firmly established by the condition of peace. But neither seems like an independent factor contributing to peace.

Furthermore, compatibility of major values sounds like a circular argument: If there is no peace, major value differences seem to explain its absence. Without very carefully specifying what constitutes a major value (whether religion, political system, culture, or kind of economic structure), it is too easy to twist facts to make them fit. Thus, the OECD countries are very similar on some kinds of values (every OECD country except Yugoslavia is now a constitutional democracy and a market economy rather than a socialist one), but very different on other kinds that in the not-too-distant past were the cause of major wars. In the sixteenth-century religious wars in Europe, Catholics and Protestants slaughtered each other by the millions. Consequently, it is not convincing to say that Christianity constitutes a compatible major value. Even more damaging to the significance of a compatible major value are the very great cultural differences that still exist between Japan and the rest of the OECD countries, whose cultures are of European origin. This difference is very substantial, yet it does not prevent Japan and the others from living in a condition of stable peace. This may, nonetheless, suggest a value that, if widely held, would contribute to peace:

Hypothesis 5: Peace in the OECD area is a consequence of the widespread acceptance in all countries of the value and institutions of *constitutional democracy.*

Some Further Facts and Their Implications Since the restoration of democracy in Greece, Portugal, and Spain in the early 1970s, all OECD countries but Yugoslavia have democratic forms of government. Their governments are, by worldwide standards, relatively nonrepressive—certainly less repressive than is typical of the less-developed world or of Eastern Europe. In this respect the present OECD governments differ markedly from many of their governments in the late 1930s. At that time Germany, Italy, Japan, Spain, and Portugal were all ruled by fascist dictatorships. Also, a study of the frequency of war over the past two centuries showed that, although democracies were as likely to be involved in war as countries with other kinds of government, the experience of democracies did stand out in one respect: Democratic countries were *very unlikely to fight each other.*[17]

---

17. This is the clear consensus of the articles (by Small and Singer, by Rummel in 1983, and by Chan) cited in footnote 17 of Chapter 8.

It is this particular form of government that seems to matter. If similarity of form of government were enough, then we would expect to see peace between the Soviet Union and China, between the Soviet Union and its Eastern European neighbors, or between China and Vietnam. Despite important differences in political values and organization among the Communist countries, they are much more like one another (especially in values or ideology) than like the democracies or even like right-wing dictatorships. Yet war or the threat of war between these countries is commonplace.

As we noted, democracies may often fight wars, but they almost never fight each other. Perhaps our elites cannot persuade us to fight other peoples who we imagine, like us, are self-determining, autonomous people—people who largely control their own political fate. People will fight to obtain a form of government that provides this autonomy—hence all the "national liberation" movements in the former colonies of the third world and revolts by some ethnic groups like the Basques and Northern Ireland Catholics within OECD countries. People have been willing to die for democracy or even to die for the king but rarely to die for the institution of monarchy. And if people already have an image of autonomy or self-determination for themselves, they may be unwilling to fight others who also have that self-image and are seen to have it.

CONDITIONS FOR GLOBAL PEACE

We surely cannot say that we have confirmed any of our hypotheses, since we have not made a thorough, systematic test of any of them. Even if we had, further tests or additional cases might still lead us to question our conclusions. We did largely reject Hypothesis 1, attributing OECD peace to the existence of an external threat. Hypotheses 2 and 3 were not so clearly rejected. Institutions and community ties surely make important contributions to achieving and maintaining OECD peace, but there is peace among OECD countries with low as well as high institutional bonds, and there was peace in the OECD area before the 1970s, when interactions reached a high level.

The two remaining hypotheses still seem promising and worth further investigation. These are Hypothesis 4, which we restated as a requirement for moderate growth, equality, and a high level of economic activity (that is, the achievement and continued expectation of mutual economic rewards), and Hypothesis 5, the acceptance of the values and institutions of constitutional democracy. The concepts of constitutional democracy might be broadened slightly to include institutions for self-determination and autonomy that do not completely match the patterns of Western parliamentary democracy. Although it is difficult to give convincing examples from current world experience, it is possible that institutions and practices of self-reliance in the third world, on local and national levels, might also promote peace.

Notice that we looked at influences operating at all levels of analysis. At the individual level, we noted the important role that people of vision, like Jean Monnet and Robert Schuman, played at key moments. Although their vision would not have been sufficient if underlying conditions had not been right, nothing would have happened if there had not been people able to conceive and carry out the plans. Conversely, we might have talked about the power of particular individuals to delay or divert integration schemes—for example, French President Charles De Gaulle's veto of British entry into the EC, delaying British participation for nearly a decade. Governmental structures or institutions constitute important sites of communication and negotiation, whether or not supranational institutions also exist. We suggested that economies had to be capable of growth and exhibit reasonably equitable distributions of income and wealth. Institutions for popular participation in government and self-determination are important and are not found in all states. At the levels of relations between states and the international system, we have all the questions about supranational institutions and transnational linkages of trade and social communications.

The vulnerabilities created by interdependence can very easily create conflict among states. But in stable peace, the states and peoples involved gain mutual benefits from their interconnectedness. These positive aspects outweigh the costs of vulnerability. Many international interactions—if not international relations as a whole—are ventures where collaborative or cooperative interests outweigh competitive ones. Cooperation is the only way to manage interdependence among states without domination or constant warfare. As the magazine *The Economist* said, "The EEC comes up with its most promising internal compromises when two or more of its members spot the makings of a deal which gives something to each of them."[18]

---

18. Quoted in Robert O. Keohane and Joseph Nye, "International Interdependence and Integration," in Fred Greenstein and Nelson Polsy (eds.), *Handbook of Political Science*, vol. 8, *International Relations* (Reading, Mass.: Addison-Wesley, 1975), p. 386.

We now can speculate on whether the experience of the OECD countries gives us any basis to hope that a stable peace based on something more than just dominance or mutual deterrence can be achieved in other parts of the world or by the OECD countries with other states. For example, can relations with the Soviet Union ever be like those within a security community? The socialist countries' partial separation from the global economy and the web of interdependence weakens one of the favorable if not essential conditions for peace. More serious doubt stems from the apparent importance of political liberty. If political liberty is important to a security community, stable peace is possible only if the government of the Soviet Union becomes more democratic than it is under the current "state socialism." Liberalization will not be easy to achieve, as various Soviet dissidents and exiles will testify. Liberalization in Czechoslovakia in 1968 was seen as a major threat to the Soviet leaders' control in Eastern Europe and within the USSR itself. At the beginning of the book we suggested that fear was one of the major motivations behind the Soviet military intervention in Czechoslovakia.

The prospects for major liberalization in the Soviet Union are dim, because it is not just the political control of the current leaders that is at issue—or even the maintenance of socialism versus some restoration of capitalist institutions. The very unity of the USSR itself is at stake. A major barrier to liberalization by the Soviet government is the suppressed desire of ethnic groups or nationalities for self-determination. Liberalization could revive these separatist movements, leading to the breakup of the world's last great colonial empire.[19] If to have stable peace we must have liberalization and self-determination in the Soviet Union, then that is a tall order.

Similarly, the requirements for economic growth and the equality of economic distribution worldwide are very demanding, given the experience of the third world over the past few decades. We shall look at this problem in much greater depth in the next chapter. For now we can note that economic stagnation has been the lot of some less-developed countries; although others have strong records of growth by conventional measures, like GNP per capita, the record of equitable distribution within those countries is very mixed. Often economic in-

---

19. In the scenario sketched by the best-seller *The Third World War,* the war ends with a proclamation of independence by the Ukrainian Republic and the dissolution of the Soviet Union. Although this seems a bit farfetched, the underlying problems for the Soviet regime are certainly real. See John Hackett et al., *The Third World War* (New York: Berkley, 1980).

equality is maintained by authoritarian and coercive political institutions—a further departure from the conditions observed in the industrialized countries. On this basis, although it is possible to imagine stable peace arising in a few areas of the third world where conditions are favorable, it is much harder to imagine its achievement worldwide. It poses the intriguing but daunting possibility that stable peace, economic equality, decent living conditions, and political liberties may be bound together in an inseparable package; thus, to strive for one requires us to strive for them all. We shall return to these considerations at the end of the book.

Some theories about the causes of underdevelopment and authoritarianism in the third world actually lay much of the blame on poor countries' dependence on and penetration by the rich, industrialized countries. Such theories allege that growth, relative equality, and political peace within rich countries are obtained only by exploiting the working classes of the poor countries through multinational corporations and other means. The governments of some countries have therefore explored the possibility of withdrawing from the world economy. If these theories should be correct, stable peace within the industrialized countries is impossible without such exploitation. Moreover, stable peace in one part of the world would prevent the establishment of stable peace worldwide. For most of us living well in rich countries, this would be a very painful conclusion. We shall discuss this kind of issue in the next chapter, but we shall not be able to provide firm answers. For the moment, this consideration serves to illustrate how interconnected many seemingly separate questions of world politics really are, and how uncertain predictions of the future or major policy recommendations are.

16

DEPENDENCE IN THE LESS-DEVELOPED COUNTRIES

DEVELOPMENT AND DEMOCRACY: COMPLEMENTARY, CONTRADICTORY, OR IRRELEVANT?

For large portions of the world's poor, development and democracy are ever-retreating mirages. Reality is a parched existence in the midst of physical misery and political oppression. Two thirds of the people of the earth live in low-income countries. Although the privileged elite in those countries live very well indeed, the average person must survive on a per capita GNP of under $400 (in 1980 dollars) compared with more than $9,000 for the average citizen in a developed industrial country. Moreover, a person in a poor country does not live as long either; in such countries, the average life expectancy for a newborn child is 57 years compared with 75 in the developed countries.

Just as the lack of economic rights is the normal state of affairs in poor countries, so, too, is the lack of political rights. Liberal democratic governments are the exception; authoritarian regimes are the rule. Co-ercion and repression are part of daily life, especially for anyone who dares to challenge the existing distribution of power and wealth.

Most Western social scientists, particularly North Americans, did not expect the persistence of poverty and repression in less-developed countries. Everyone, of course, knew that economic development in poor countries would be slow and difficult, the result of a long process of accumulating capital investments and human skills. But most of these analysts did not expect the gap between the rich and the poor in these countries to widen so rapidly; the upper classes have made very sharp gains while the condition of the poor majority has remained virtually unchanged. Everyone, of course, knew that the acquisition of political power by the world's poor would be difficult. According to the accepted wisdom of political science, political development is the establishment of stable democratic regimes, which is possible only if certain prerequisites of democracy are met. These prerequisites are enough income and wealth to create a literate population, informed by newspapers, radio and television, and other mass media. They also in-clude a sufficiently healthy economy to provide reasonable stations in life that can be attained through industry, commerce, agriculture, or intellectual activity—that is, there are sources of wealth and power other than simply controlling the government and looting the public treasury. Such private sources of power provide checks on authoritar-ian government and provide respectable sources of employment and status for defeated politicians, therefore making it possible for them to accept electoral defeat with reasonably good grace. Economic develop-ment is thus not only a way to escape the misery of poverty; it is also seen as good for promoting, or at least solidifying, political liberties.[1]

In comparing countries in the world, the strength of the theory of the economic prerequisites of democracy lies in the fact that high-income industrial countries are, without exception, all political democ-racies. Among them, those with the most recent history of nondem-ocratic rule (Greece, Portugal, Spain, and Turkey) have the lowest incomes within the OECD. No advanced industrial economy outside of Eastern Europe and the Soviet Union (and for these countries, the accu-racy of the label "advanced industrial" is questionable) is governed

---

1. For critical reviews and a citation of North American development theories, see J. Samuel Valenzuela and Arturo Valenzuela, "Modernization and Dependency: Alterna-tive Perspectives in the Study of Latin American Underdevelopment," *Comparative Politics* 10 (1978), no. 4, pp. 7–8.

otherwise. A few of the oil-rich Arab OPEC states have higher per capita incomes (and certainly are not democracies), but typically this new wealth has not been reflected in high rates of literacy or improved living conditions for the whole populace. Among the nearly 40 very poor states (under $500 per capita), only a very few—India, Sri Lanka, and Gambia—have operated as reasonably stable democracies.

Some analysts have taken the argument a step further, contending that short-term political repression may have to be tolerated for the sake of immediate economic development and therefore the chance to establish the prerequisites for democracy. Weak government, it is claimed, cannot satisfy the needs of a population that makes major demands on it. Trouble arises from rapid social change and the participation of new groups and classes in politics, coupled with the slower development of political institutions. Many less-developed countries typically have large urban populations, especially in the capital city. It is not unusual for a quarter of the population of a small- or medium-sized less-developed country (LDC) to live in the capital. Many of these people come in from the countryside looking for work, only to be unemployed or to work sporadically at part-time jobs, living a marginal existence. Nevertheless, in the city they are exposed to the mass media and see people in the rich sectors of the city living very well. Their expectations rise without being fulfilled. Because they are in the capital, they can participate in political activity: riots, general strikes, and street demonstrations. The demands of these people, who can be mobilized by activists for political participation, may be nearly impossible for a weak government to meet or repress.

A stable government, it is contended, requires a strong administrative capacity and political institutions capable of channeling or, if necessary, repressing these popular demands. The institutions of authority might take the form of a mass political party like the Congress Party of India, founded in 1885, and the highly capable and well-organized Indian Civil Service. More commonly, they would not be institutions so clearly associated with democratic rule, instead more nearly resembling the authoritarian structure of Ayatollah Khomeini's religious organization in Iran or the Communist party. Also associated are organizations capable of enforcing authoritarian rule and coercing malcontents whom the government cannot or will not satisfy—that is, an efficient police force and army. One scholar puts the argument in these terms:

The primary problem [in many modernizing countries] is not liberty but the creation of a legitimate public order. Men may, of course, have order without liberty, but they cannot have liberty without order. Authority has to exist before it can be limited, and it is authority that is in scarce supply in those modernizing countries where government is at the mercy of alienated intellectuals, rambunctious colonels, and rioting students.[2]

This may sound very much like an endorsement of authoritarian rule. It is not a long step from such an analysis to the argument that traditional Western ideas of political rights and liberties must be put aside in the interest of economic development. Development cannot occur without order. Furthermore, development requires large-scale sacrifice on the part of the masses. If there is to be investment in modern industry and agriculture, somehow that investment must be paid for. Without massive foreign assistance, the resources for that investment can only be obtained by reducing consumption. People must be forced to reduce their consumption or at least not to increase it for the sake of future generations. In a very poor country with widespread misery, such "forced draft" modernization can occur only by repressing discontent. Agricultural prices (and thus farmers' incomes) have to be kept low, and urban people, where they cannot be satisfied, must feel the arm of the state in discouraging protest. By these arguments people in poor countries must choose essentially between political liberty and decent material conditions; they cannot have both, and it is a parochial Western prejudice to insist on traditional Western concepts of political rights.

THE RECORD

The trouble with the economic prerequisites argument is simple: It does not fit the facts of recent experience in the third world. Certainly development has not brought democracy. There has been no trend toward an increase in political liberties in the third world as a whole. The average income level has risen about as fast as in the developed countries, but there are many exceptions—both stagnant economies and very dynamic, fast-growing economies. In many of these countries, however, that income has typically been skewed sharply in favor of the rich and has had no discernible effect in promoting political liberty.

---

2. Samuel P. Huntington, *Political Order in Changing Societies* (New Haven, Conn.: Yale University Press, 1968), pp. 7–8.

Almost all the former British and French colonies entered their era of independence with governments that were chosen by reasonably free elections and had the forms of parliamentary democracy. Very few have free competitive elections or the institutions of free speech and free assembly today. Perhaps five or six countries in Africa and another four or five in Asia can be termed democracies in the Western sense. In some countries the suppression of political liberty has brought economic growth, but in many others it has not.

Even more devastating for theories of political development is that in some of the most prosperous less-developed countries, the turn away from democratic government to coercion has been most vicious. Uruguay and Chile in the 1960s were relatively rich and had long histories of a stable democracy. (Chile had had uninterrupted democratic government since 1927, and Uruguay since the 1930s. Along with Argentina and Venezuela, these countries were the most prosperous of the twenty Latin American countries.) The Philippines were fairly prosperous for a South or Southeast Asian country and had a high literacy rate. For several decades the Philippines had developed the institutions and practices of political democracy with free elections, first under American colonial rule and then as an independent state after 1946. By the theory, these countries all should have been able to maintain and deepen their democratic patterns. But they were not. Their democratic governments were overthrown (in 1973 in Chile and Uruguay and in 1972 in the Philippines) and replaced by some of the most repressive, coercive regimes in the entire third world. Argentina, with a highly sophisticated, literate population and sporadic periods of democratic government, similarly slipped back into authoritarian military rule for almost a decade.

Of course, theories of economic and political development are not nearly as simple as the preceding presentation implies. Some emphasize the strains put on a political system in multiethnic societies, where people from different tribes, with different languages, or belonging to different religions are all concerned with maximizing gains for themselves and seeing to it that their tribe, language, or religion is dominant, favored, or at least secure. Much of the political instability in Nigeria, Iran, and many other third world countries has its roots in such conflicts; India is unstable with its 14 major language groups and Hindu-Muslim divisions. Other theories of political modernization concentrate on the citizens' attitudes; these theories describe a participant civic culture, where people see themselves as taking part in a governmental process responsive to their needs, or they describe a set of modern attitudes toward society, politics, and economic activity. But these variants are not much more helpful than the simpler economic prerequisites arguments for explaining cases such as Chile and Uruguay, which are remarkably homogenous ethnically and had substantial experience as stable democracies.

Other theories take note of the fact that Argentina, Chile, and Uruguay, though prosperous by third world standards, nevertheless were economically stagnant by their own historical experience. They had passed through more than a decade of little or even negative growth in GNP per capita and were wracked by inflation rates sometimes exceeding 100 percent in a year. This economic "stagflation" put enormous strains on social and political systems, bringing economic gains to a few and widespread deprivation and poverty to many who had once been prosperous. Under strains like these, it is not surprising that democracy failed.

Although a useful concept to add to theories about economic prerequisites, stagflation shares a weakness with the other perspectives we have discussed; it focuses too much on domestic causes of development (or non-development) and excludes international forces. Without careful attention to the fact that virtually all third world states are now deeply affected by external influences, one cannot really understand economic or political development in those states. Some more recent theories have paid attention to the role of these external forces in affecting internal development with some success—as we shall see later in the chapter. For now, it may be enough to emphasize the great diversity of experience in the third world. Some countries have experienced rapid economic growth, some little or none. Some have had democratic governments, others (the majority) various kinds of rightist or leftist authoritarian regimes.

Within the third world (that is, excluding the rich industrial democracies and the Soviet-bloc countries), there is only a very limited relation between the type of political system and the level of economic activity. Only a very few really poor states are democracies, but among the middle-income third world countries, there is really no relationship between income and type of political system. Nor is there much systematic relationship between political system and the rate of growth in economic activity.

Table 16.1 shows several economic and political characteristics for selected LDCs in the 1970s. It roughly classifies countries according to democratic or authoritarian political systems and specifies economic growth records and the distribution of income. For each country, the first number given is its rate of growth in GNP per capita during the decade of the 1970s; the second number (in parentheses) shows the percentage of total household income received by the richest 10 percent of households. Because the data for this second number were not always available, we made informed estimates on the basis of various studies.

As we emphasized above, the experience of different countries varies enough to make it clear that simple explanations will not do. Most of the countries with very rapid growth rates during the period had basically authoritarian regimes, but the overall economic performance of relatively democratic Malaysia and Turkey during the period was also very creditable. Certainly, having an authoritarian system is no guarantee of rapid economic growth, as you can see from the table entries for Cuba (Communist), Peru (populist military dictatorship), Chile (right-

Table 16.1
Economic and political characteristics of some less-developed countries.

GNP per capita growth, 1970–1979	Income distribution		
	Egalitarian		Inegalitarian
	Democratic political systems		
High ↑		6.4 Malaysia (40)	
		4.3 Turkey (41)	
	4.0 Sri Lanka (28)	3.4 Costa Rica (40)	
		2.3 Venezuela (36)	
		1.6 Mexico (41)	
Low ↓		1.5 India (34)	
	Authoritarian political systems		
High ↑	8.4 South Korea (28)		7.8 Saudi Arabia
			5.9 Iran[a]
	5.7 Taiwan (25)		5.7 Brazil (51)
	5.0 China		
			2.8 Uruguay
	1.0? Cuba		1.1 Kenya (46)
		0.3 Peru (43)	−1.0 Chile
Low ↓			−3.4 Uganda

Sources: GNP per capita growth rates from *UN Yearbook of National Accounts Statistics, 1980* (New York: United Nations, 1983) and *UN Statistical Yearbook, 1983* (New York: United Nations, 1983). Income distribution data from World Bank, *World Development Report, 1983* (New York: Oxford University Press, 1983).

Notes: First number is the GNP per capita growth rate; second number in parentheses (where present) is the percentage of total household income held by the richest 10 percent of households. Some growth rates are estimated or for shorter periods.

Democratic rule is often limited: India, Malaysia, and Turkey all suspended parliamentary government for "national emergencies" during part or all of the decade; although Mexico is formally democratic, the same party wins all the major elections.

[a]Prerevolutionary.

wing military dictatorship), and Uganda (corrupt personal dictatorship of Idi Amin). Iran and Saudi Arabia owed their economic success less to wise policy than to their good luck in living over large pools of oil.

This table also shows that the internal distribution of economic rewards varies markedly from country to country, again showing only a moderate relationship with political systems or economic growth rates. Many authoritarian regimes have pursued economic growth through policies that have forced the lower classes to carry most of the burden. Brazil is an excellent example, where the distribution of income was shifted markedly in favor of the upper classes. Saudi Arabia and the shah's Iran did not have to squeeze the lower classes as the Brazilian regime did, but certainly the gains from the rise in oil prices (accounting for Saudi Arabia's and Iran's rapid growth during the period) went mostly to the elites and upper middle class. On the other hand, many authoritarian regimes, dominated by a small oligarchy, have preserved a very inegalitarian distribution of wealth and income without achieving rapid growth. In fact, many such governments have not even sought rapid growth, knowing that the rapid social change that might result could create new expectations and new demands and thus destabilize their rule.

Although inegalitarian income policies have been followed by a variety of third world governments, some states have succeeded in achieving growth while maintaining relative equality. The governments have not necessarily been democratic but have nevertheless allowed, and to some degree even encouraged, a pattern of rewards that has benefited many sectors of the populace. Both South Korea and Taiwan vigorously pursued rural development following earlier land reform programs, thus permitting the rise of a substantial landowning, prosperous rural peasantry. We shall continue to look at the relationships among economic development, equality, and democracy throughout much of this chapter, but for the moment we can offer tentative answers to two of the questions we have been posing:

1. *Are equality and rapid development incompatible?* Not necessarily. It is possible to pursue development at the expense of equality. But there are real possibilities for achieving growth while preserving relative equality if the government chooses to pursue such a policy and can retain the support of key social and political groups.

2. *Are democracy and rapid development incompatible?* Certainly a high level of development helps to make democracy possible. In that sense they are eminently compatible. Also, democracy is rare—but not un-

known—in very poor countries. Even within the many countries that are not democracies in the Western sense, there are different means and different degrees of enabling the majority of the populace to have some control over their government, at least at the local level. The rare cases of democracy within very poor countries suggest that in the right social, economic, and cultural circumstances, mass poverty need not prevent the establishment of democracy—though it may not be possible to have rapid economic growth in a context of both poverty and democracy. On the other hand, a relatively high income level or the past achievement of rapid economic growth does not necessarily bring democracy. As of 1984, economic growth in Brazil and Taiwan had brought some moderate relaxation of governmental repression, but hardly full liberalization.

HISTORICAL VIEW OF DEPENDENCE

To some observers, the failure of Western theories of economic and political development to anticipate economic stagnation and political repression in much of the third world was not surprising. Theorists from Latin America, Africa, and other parts of the world took a view of development that was much more attentive to international influences on development than most Western theory. For these people, a crucial flaw in Western theory was its treatment of political and economic development as being determined essentially by domestic forces. They thought that political and economic structures within LDCs were primarily determined by the role LDCs played in the world market. Without understanding the effect of foreign penetration of third world economies and polities and how that penetration helped shape relations between social classes in those countries, one could understand little.

Some of these theories take a historical perspective that extends back to the creation of a world system in the sixteenth century. The colonial "center" powers (Spain, Portugal, and later Britain, Holland, and France) had created a world division of labor between themselves and the territories of the "periphery." Commerce and manufacturing were established largely in the center, and the colonies of the periphery provided food and minerals for the world market. The native populations of the periphery were often subjugated and made into landless peasants working on big farms or as slavelike labor in the mines. In some areas, especially in the Caribbean, the native populations were largely exterminated and replaced by slave labor imported from Africa. Governmental control was exercised from the center or, more commonly in those days of slow communication, by the big landowners and urban merchants who sold their products to the world market. Most of the colonial world was thus established as a producer of raw materials for the European center, ruled by an upper class who imported their manufactured goods from Europe. The ruling elites had neither the power nor the interest to resist European penetration and this global division of labor.[3]

When these peripheral countries became politically sovereign in the nineteenth and twentieth centuries, the ruling elites maintained close economic links with the world market. In some instances their interests coincided closely with those of European capitalists who came to invest in the periphery, and they prospered by providing services and local expertise to the Europeans. In other instances their interests diverged, but still the peripheral states lacked strong central governments that could effectively resist or control European penetration. There were sometimes deep and violent conflicts between landowners and urban entrepreneurs, between domestic and foreign capitalists. Nevertheless, the masses of people in the countryside usually remained poor and powerless. Some urban workers in favored industries did reasonably well, but most remained poor, unemployed or underemployed, and politically weak. Sharp inequalities in income distribution meant that, except in a few big countries (such as Argentina, Mexico, Brazil, and much later India), there could be no large mass market for domestically manufactured goods. The result was economic stagnation and relegation to the role of primary producer for the world economy.

In some areas where significant local industry had existed before the colonial era, that industry was stifled. The most famous instance is nineteenth-century India. The British colonial government deliberately destroyed the Indian textile industry; it built a railway system through India with the express purpose of opening up the country so that the textile manufactures of Lancashire in England could be sold to the Indian population. Another famous example is that of the Belgian Congo in the late nineteenth century, where the colonial rulers wanted to use the local population as a labor force in the mines. Streams were poisoned so that the Africans could not live from fishing. Then the

---

3. See Immanuel Wallerstein, *The Modern World System* (New York: Academic Press, 1974).

natives were required to pay taxes in money, and they could earn money to pay taxes only by working for very low wages.

This much is historical background for the twentieth century. There are important differences of interpretation about the colonial era. In Chapter 9 we discussed theories of imperialism. We established that, although there are conflicting theories about how important economic motives were in promoting imperialism and precisely what economic mechanisms were involved (a search for markets, for raw materials, or for outlets for surplus capital), economic motives in general were a major influence. A world division of labor between an industrial center and a periphery producing primary goods (with some states in a "semiperipheral" status) did arise. Associated with this division of labor were powerful groups and classes in all parts of the world with a great stake in maintaining the basic structure. But what these historical facts mean for patterns of development in the twentieth century, what the significance is of some of the exceptions to the general picture that did exist, and what the prospects are for third world development in the late twentieth century are issues involving much more controversy.

VIEWS OF DEPENDENCE THEORISTS

In the view of some theorists, the world division of labor could not be changed and stagnation was inevitable so long as the peripheral economies remained bound to the world market. One perspective, important twenty or thirty years ago, originated with economists working with the UN Economic Commission for Latin America (ECLA). They accepted most of the description of the past that we have just laid out and saw these peripheral economies as consequently being plagued by vulnerabilities imposed by the world market—low wage rates, persistent inflation, low but variable prices for raw materials, and political institutions too weak to deal with these conditions.

Figure 16.1 shows the deterioration in the terms of trade for some principal commodity exports of LDCs. By "terms of trade" we mean essentially what can be obtained for one's exports. If the relative terms of trade improve for an LDC, it can obtain a greater volume or value of manufactured imports in exchange for a given amount of the primary commodity it exports. The graph in Figure 16.1 shows the relative value of all nonoil primary commodities (that is, minerals and agricultural products) as compared with the UN index for the value of manufactures exported by developed countries. Of course, the value of spe-

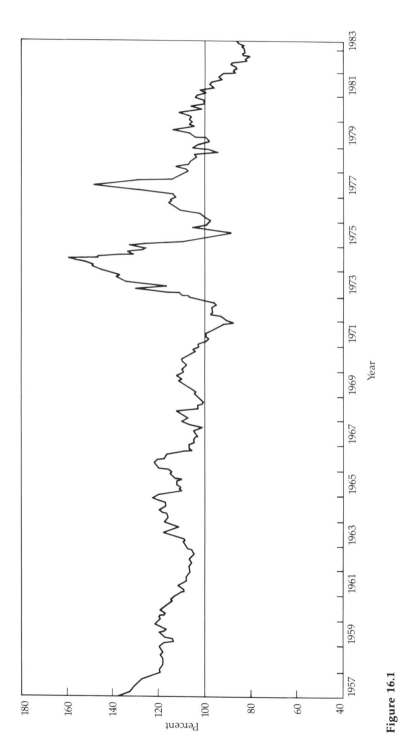

Figure 16.1
Value of nonoil primary commodities imported as a percentage of the value of manufactured goods exported by developed countries. [*Source: World Economic Outlook, 1983* (Washington, D.C.: International Monetary Fund, 1983), p. 155.]

cific products can change by more or less than the value of the index. For example, in 1955 it took 6.3 bags of coffee or 7.9 tons of tea to buy 100 tons of steel products from the United States or Britain; by 1972 it took 12.1 bags of coffee or 14.1 tons of tea.

It is important to be aware that there is a good deal of controversy about calculations like these. It makes quite a difference which commodity we are speaking about (the relative value of oil has changed very differently from that of coffee!), what base year we use for our calculations (the decline in the terms of trade for primary commodity exports from 1973 to the present looks much worse than from 1971), and what kind of grouping of industrialized countries' exports we use for comparison. Nevertheless, it is widely believed that there has been a long-term decline in the terms of trade for many, though not all, agricultural and mineral exports common to LDCs.

The aggregate value of commodity exports has also fluctuated. Sudden price declines for some commodities have been especially severe. Drops of 25 percent or more from one year to the next for cocoa, rubber, sugar, copper, lead, and zinc have been common. With prices fluctuating like that, producers have a very hard time planning future production and sales. Bad weather may reduce the volume of exports but drive up the price of what is left. Producers who increase their acreage or mining capacity to take advantage of higher prices in future years may overdo it, creating an excess supply that lowers prices and earnings instead of raising them.

Countries that are heavily dependent on earnings from commodity exports to provide foreign exchange for development can also be hit hard. If export earnings fall, key development plans may have to be eliminated or postponed or loans may have to be obtained. The International Monetary Fund described how commodity-exporting economies were hit even harder by the decline in prices for their products than by the shrinkage of their export volume because of the recession in 1981–1982:

> Exports of primary commodities of the non-oil developing countries averaged about $120 billion a year in 1979–80. The impact of the price decline that occurred is therefore responsible for a reduction of about $20 billion in export earnings in 1981 and for a further $15 billion decline in 1982. In other words, at 1980 commodity prices, and with import values and export volumes unchanged, the current account deficit of the non-oil developing countries as a group might well have been well under $60 billion, instead of the $87 billion actually recorded.[4]

---

4. *World Economic Outlook, 1983* (Washington, D.C.: International Monetary Fund, 1983), p. 155.

Most big, populous countries can have reasonably diversified economies and are therefore not too vulnerable to fluctuations in commodity prices. Also, a number of big and middle-sized LDCs have become partly industrialized (sometimes called the *newly industrialized countries,* or NICs); South Korea, Taiwan, Mexico, and Brazil are examples of industrializing states that are no longer very dependent on commodity exports. But some middle-sized countries and many small ones are still very dependent on commodity prices, and often on a single commodity. In the early 1970s, for example, Zaire derived 68 percent of all its export earnings from copper, and 47 percent of Egypt's earnings came from cotton. Other countries with similar problems were Cuba (84 percent from sugar), Ghana (62 percent from cocoa), Sri Lanka (60 percent from tea), Panama (56 percent from bananas), and Bolivia (52 percent from tin). Figure 16.2 shows how much more dependent on primary commodity exports developing market economies LDCs are than are developed market economies.

To eliminate excessive reliance on commodity exports, the ECLA theorists advocated a strategy of development by promoting industrialization that would substitute domestic manufactures for imported ones. For the larger countries with a reasonably big domestic market, this worked for a while. But the limits to this effort soon became apparent—these still were relatively poor countries, with an income distribution heavily favoring the rich and therefore without a really big mass market for consumer goods. Even the reasonably big domestic markets were, because of their poverty and inequality, much smaller than in European countries of comparable populations (see Figure 16.3 on the distribution of wealth in Latin America). Also, further industrialization required foreign loans and direct investment by multinational corporations. Although the kind of goods produced did change, the countries were still heavily penetrated by foreign interests, with ruling groups still consisting of externally oriented interests and domestic interests allied with foreign capitalists. Severe social and political tensions resulted from these alignments.

Another important theoretical perspective, related to the above but especially sensitive to differences among LDCs—differences in their resource endowments, the nature of colonial penetration, and their subsequent social and economic development—is represented in an influential book by Fernando Henrique Cardoso and Enzo Faletto.[5]

---

5. Fernando Henrique Cardoso and Enzo Faletto, *Dependency and Development in Latin America,* trans. by Marjory Mattingly Urquidi (Berkeley and Los Angeles: University of California Press, 1979).

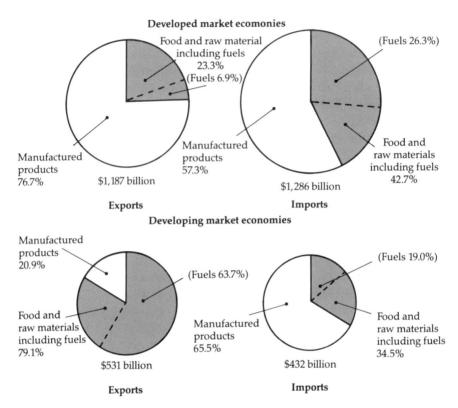

Figure 16.2
Imports and exports for developed- and developing-market economies, 1980. Excludes trade with centrally planned economies (less than 5 percent of the total). [*Source: UN Statistical Yearbook, 1981* (New York: United Nations, 1983).]

Cardoso is a Brazilian scholar who went into exile after the military coup in Brazil in 1964 and then returned to run for the senate when the regime became more liberal in the late 1970s. In this and in some of his earlier work, Cardoso notes that, especially in the larger peripheral countries, economic stagnation is by no means as certain as some earlier theorists imagined. He is well aware that manufacturing may become the basis for new export growth, as in Brazil or Korea, especially as some manufacturing activity becomes transferred from the industrialized center to some of the peripheral countries. As this occurs, the governments in the LDCs usually have to become much bigger and play a more active role in the economy.

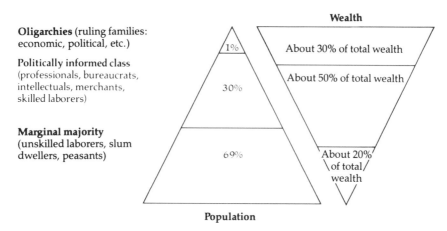

Oligarchies (ruling families: economic, political, etc.)

Politically informed class (professionals, bureaucrats, intellectuals, merchants, skilled laborers)

Marginal majority (unskilled laborers, slum dwellers, peasants)

Figure 16.3
Distribution of wealth in Latin America. [*Source:* Ervin Laszlo et al., *Goals for Mankind* (London: Hutchinson, 1977), p. 37. Copyright © by The Research Foundation of The State University of New York. Reprinted by permission of the publisher, E. P. Dutton.]

Nevertheless, policymaking about the usefulness of exports or local production often remains heavily influenced by multinational corporations. The government is not identified with a national interest but rather with a particular class of government bureaucrats (sometimes called a *state bourgeoisie*) as well as with domestic and foreign capitalists. The technology of new heavy industry is typically capital intensive, of the sort developed in rich industrialized countries, that is, where high wage rates force manufacturers to use more complex machinery (capital equipment) and fewer workers. Government intervention is essential to stabilize markets and ensure that these heavy investments will be profitable. In markets that are not large, the government restricts competition by limiting the number of firms operating in the industry. Even where the public sector becomes large, "those who control the state sector come to act more as public entrepreneurs than as implementers of a populist policy to promote income redistribution. . . . The state ceases to be a populist state and is transformed into an entrepreneurial state."[6] Income inequality thus means that broad segments of the working class and the middle class are not rewarded, not "coopted" into the system as were the working and middle classes in the ad-

---

6. Ibid, p. 165.

vanced industrial market economies. If the loyalty of these classes cannot be assured by a wide distribution of economic and political benefits, then the state is condemned to securing grudging acquiescence through political coercion. Ultimately the state becomes both economically active and politically repressive.

Important differences exist among dependence theorists. Some see LDCs as doomed to stagnation; others see possibilities of "dependent development" that can make possible rapid growth in GNP per capita but in economies that are fundamentally distorted and highly inegalitarian. Writers differ on the relative importance of domestic class relations as contrasted with external forces; their theories often derive from varying mixtures of "liberal" Keynesian economics and Marxist analysis.[7] Yet, despite their differences, all dependence theorists agree that economic, social, and political conditions in peripheral societies are inextricably linked and that the appropriate levels of analysis are not only the nation-state but also transnational and international actors in the global system. Poor countries are dependent on rich countries when the two-way aspects of interdependence are minimal. Especially in terms of vulnerability, the situation is unbalanced. Acts by the governments of developed center countries or by multinational corporations based in those countries affect what happens in peripheral countries much more than almost any action in a peripheral country (especially a small, poor one) can affect what happens in a rich industrialized country. Poor countries are dependent, penetrated, and vulnerable.

AN OUTLINE OF DEPENDENCE THEORY

The core of dependence theory can be summarized as follows: Foreign penetration and external dependence lead to large-scale distortions in the structure of peripheral economies, which in turn result in intense social conflict and ultimately in harsh state repression in dependent societies. A more elaborate statement, drawing on some of the previous discussion but expressing it more systematically, is presented in outline in Figure 16.4. Nearly all third world countries are now deeply penetrated by, and in important ways dependent on, the industrial

---

7. A good recent collection of dependence theory and related perspectives is Samir Amin, Giovanni Arrighi, et al., eds., *Dynamics of Global Crisis* (New York: Monthly Review Press, 1982).

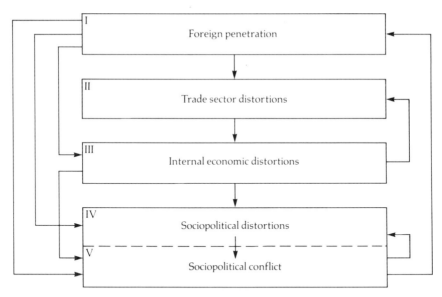

Figure 16.4
A simple flow model of dependence theory.

world and especially the world economy.[8] Penetration can occur in a variety of economic, political, and cultural modes and at different periods in a country's development.

Economic penetration can be by financial or technological means. In relatively early stages of development, the most common way is by direct foreign investment, where multinational corporations establish subsidiaries involved in mining (Kennecott Copper in Chile, British Petroleum in Iran), agriculture (United Fruit in Guatemala, Firestone Rubber in Liberia), manufacturing (Volkswagen in Brazil), and commerce (Sears, Roebuck and Coca-Cola in Korea—and almost everywhere else).

Individual foreigners may also invest some of their capital in local enterprises, often using that beginning to raise much more finance capital from local investors. Subsidiaries of multinational corporations (MNCs) typically use technology developed in the industrial economies. If this technology is not used immediately, then it comes after

---

8. This exposition of dependence theory is presented in greater detail in R. Duvall, S. Jackson, B. Russett, D. Snidal, and D. Sylvan, "A Formal Model of 'Depencencia' Theory: Structure and Measurement," in R. Merritt and B. Russett (eds.), *From National Development to Global Community* (London: Allen & Unwin, 1981).

some delay as part of a "product cycle." In this cycle, previous production processes are transferred to the periphery, where labor is cheaper, after a new process is introduced in the world center. MNC subsidiaries, therefore, are likely to import capital equipment (computers, transportation equipment, and other machinery) from the advanced countries. Local manufacturing facilities that MNCs set up are likely to use the processes developed in the center and thus carry foreign patents, licenses, copyrights, and trademarks. Even if the industries become predominantly locally owned and operated, their need to compete with MNCs may still lead them to adopt foreign technology. Economic assistance (foreign aid) from industrial countries often requires the purchase of goods or services from those same countries.

Political and cultural penetration may also come in material or symbolic "packages"—books, television programs (reruns or ABC news by satellite), newspapers and magazines, and motion pictures. Or it may come more abstractly through people who become "carriers" of foreign cultures. Young people are sent from the periphery to the educational institutions of the center; they return having adopted important elements of Western industrial culture—ways of thinking and behaving, ideologies, values, and appreciation of Western consumer goods. Tourists coming into the peripheral countries also bring their cultural values and expect their wishes to be satisfied (for instance, concerning cleanliness, quick and efficient service, and various consumer goods). Students may dislike many aspects of the countries in which they study. Tourists may inspire hatred as well as envy or emulation. Either way, the exposure to advanced countries' culture deeply shapes and often overwhelms local cultural values. People may come to want consumer goods readily available in advanced industrial economies but which only a small minority in poor countries can afford—private automobiles, refrigerators and air conditioners, and color television sets. Manufacturing enterprises in less-developed countries may thus turn toward this small market of upper-middle class Westernized consumers, producing familiar products with well-established technologies, rather than aiming toward a working-class market with many people but little purchasing power. To the degree that they establish a capacity to serve the upper-middle-class market, LDC manufacturers have an interest in preserving and expanding that market rather than the mass market. This means, in effect, that industrial and commercial interests support a distribution of income that favors the well-to-do classes rather than an egalitarian distribution of income that would produce a mass market for basic consumer goods (bread rather than beef, mass transit rather than private cars, and village doctors rather than urban medical specialists).

Governments as well as private organizations and individuals import political and cultural products that shape the way they perform their tasks and how they define their tasks—importing, for example, advanced military armaments, police training programs, and computers. By all these means, peripheral countries' values regarding consumption and production become deeply conditioned by penetration from the center. These aspects of long-term continuing penetration are grouped together in the first box of Figure 16.4.

The historical and continuing fact of penetration, it is alleged, led to a pattern of economic activity characterized by large-scale foreign trade and the development of economic enclaves within LDCs devoted primarily to production for export (box II in Figure 16.4). Foreign trade became increasingly important to LDC economies, and that trade often became highly dependent on one or a few industrial countries. LDC exports consisted of only a few products—generally, but not exclusively, products from the mineral extractive and agricultural sectors. Over time, the enclaves typically become less reliant on exports of particular commodities and on industrial countries, but LDCs tend to diversify trading partners very slowly. Even long after achieving formal independence, most ex-colonies still trade predominantly with their former colonial powers (most Latin American states trade predominantly with the United States). Although in some respects there is certainly a world market, there are also various divisions of that market where, by experience, custom, special needs, or formal tariff or other trade agreements, not all trading partners are equally favored.

Distorted Development

Patterns of penetration, dependence, and trade are perhaps most important in their interaction with various conditions *within* the economies of LDCs; they promote, and in turn are promoted by, a kind of economic growth marked by severe internal structural "distortions" (box III in Figure 16.4). First, development is uneven, being much greater in the export enclaves than in other sectors. Second, the economy is poorly integrated, meaning that the various sectors tend to be poorly connected. For example, even though a substantial manufacturing sector may develop, it will be little oriented to producing capital goods such as tractors for the agricultural sector. Rather, the industry may use some raw materials from the countryside but produce primarily for urban customers. Third, the economy is marked by severe differences of reward from one sector to another. Wages for labor in particular will be much higher in some sectors, such as manufacturing or possibly mining, than in others like agriculture.

Dependence theory asserts that foreign capital is attracted primarily to the dynamic sectors of a peripheral country's economy, thus spurring uneven development by reinforcing those sectors while ignoring backward sectors and increasing wages only of a small but skilled "labor aristocracy." Capitalist penetration is also usually seen as increasing economic growth. However, growth will be reduced if the export enclave is large and ultimately diverts capital out of the economy through profits sent back to the countries where MNCs have their headquarters. Growth is also reduced through repayment of debts to foreign governments and banks.

Examination of the experience of LDCs tends to support most of these propositions, though not all of them convincingly or completely. The effects of penetration or uneven development, disintegration of the economy, and differences in wage rates are complex, often indirect, and vary greatly in different kinds of countries. A country's previous colonial history, its size, relative level of wealth, and natural resources all influence what effects penetration will have. The effects of penetration on overall economic growth rates are somewhat clearer. In the short run, foreign investment and foreign aid usually stimulate growth. But in the long run, repatriation of profits by MNCs and the effects of large-scale public debts can sharply reduce growth.[9] Some LDC governments get themselves deeply into debt and run up huge bills just to pay the interest on their debts.

---

9. For evidence on penetration and structural distortions, see David Sylvan, Duncan Snidal, Bruce Russett, Steven Jackson, and Raymond Duvall, "The Peripheral Economies: Penetration and Economic Distortion, 1970–1975," in William R. Thompson (ed.), *Multiple Perspectives on the World System* (Beverly Hills, Calif.: Sage, 1983); for evidence on growth rates, see Bruce Russett, "International Interactions and Processes: The Internal vs. External Debate Revisited," in Ada Finifter (ed.), *Political Science: The State of the Discipline* (Washington, D.C.: American Political Science Association, 1983). The evidence is discussed more extensively in Bruce Russett, Raymond Duvall, Steven Jackson, Duncan Snidal, and David Sylvan, *Penetration and Repression in the Global System* (forthcoming). Three diverse but useful case studies are Thomas Biersteker, *Distortion or Development? Contending Perspectives on the Multinational Corporation* (Cambridge, Mass.: MIT Press, 1979); Colin Leys, *Underdevelopment in Kenya: The Political Economy of Nationalism, 1964–1971* (Berkeley and Los Angeles: University of California Press, 1975); A. Quijano, *Nationalism and Capitalism in Peru: A Study in Neo-Imperialism* (New York: Monthly Review Press, 1971).

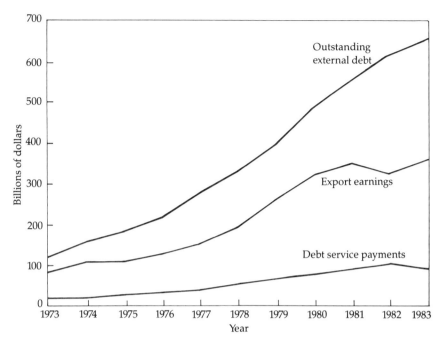

Figure 16.5

Outstanding debt, export earnings, and debt service of nonoil-exporting developing countries, 1973–1983. [*Source: World Economic Outlook, 1983* (Washington, D.C.: International Monetary Fund, 1983).]

Figure 16.5 shows how LDC debt has risen; for some countries, it is enormous. At the end of 1982, the foreign debt of Argentina, Brazil, Chile, Mexico, and the Philippines alone totaled $318 billion, with interest payments taking virtually half of their exports. Most of these countries, in fact, simply could not meet their interest payments; to avoid default, they had to negotiate a "rescheduling" (postponement) of their payments with the international agencies and especially the commercial banks that had lent them the money. These rescheduling agreements are the only reason for the slight downturn in debt service payments in 1983. As a result of the rescheduling, the indebted govern-. ments had to institute deflationary austerity policies and accept declining incomes. (Real income per capita in Latin America declined for the third successive year in 1983, with about a 10 percent decline over the three-year period.) As even more-advanced LDCs become heavily dependent on exports and foreign loans, the option of pursuing a strategy of national self-reliance or diminished linkage with the world economy becomes unavailable.

Looking back at Figure 16.4, notice the arrow pointing up from "Internal economic distortions" to "Trade sector distortions." This reflects the view of recent dependence theorists that reduction of the export enclave is a difficult matter and not just a short-term phenomenon. The export enclave may change its emphasis from raw materials to manufacturing, taking advantage of cheap labor. Thus, in Korea and some other Asian countries, industrial exports have become very important. Still, their markets are abroad, not necessarily in a growing domestic market—unless the country is either rather large or has a sufficiently egalitarian distribution of income to create a mass market for consumer goods.

This pattern of distorted development has been recognized by a wide variety of theorists—not only dependence theorists but also many quite conventional economists. Dependence writers nevertheless interpret the phenomena in distinctive ways. First, they compare this pattern of development with a somewhat idealized image of an economy that is growing quite slowly but in a balanced, integrated, homogeneous manner. (In fact, many of the economic distortions of current LDCs also occurred in nineteenth-century Europe.) Second, they attribute distortions of development to a pattern of dependence and penetration, and, as we noted, there is some evidence that penetration and distortion are positively related. Third, and most important for students of international politics, they link penetration and economic distortion with additional distortions in the social and political systems. As a consequence, the economic growth of the typical peripheral state often does not lead to the development of liberal democracies but rather to the establishment of dictatorships. These theorists see a state bureaucracy that controls the government and perhaps substantial state economic enterprises (in transportation, public utilities, banking, and possibly manufacturing) eager to consolidate power. According to this view, the state bureaucracy forges an alliance with foreign interests and some domestic capitalists and makes ample use of political repression. Also, violence—both direct and "structural," as defined in the preceding chapter—is an *inherent consequence of economics and politics in the periphery and the periphery's linkages with the world economy and political system.* We now can consider how these forces are alleged to operate, referring back to the final box in Figure 16.4.

POLITICAL CONFLICT AND REPRESSION

External penetration in the form of capital-intensive investment reduces the need for large numbers of workers. Because of the use of a relatively small number of skilled workers, even an expanded industrial sector may employ no more industrial laborers than before expansion. Other workers are left unemployed, only partially employed, or working full-time on unskilled jobs for wages that give them a marginal existence. The larger the "reserve army of the unemployed," the greater the downward pressure on wage rates for workers in general (workers who demand too much can readily be replaced). In many instances, MNCs will pay relatively high wages, but the potential supply of workers is likely to be so large—in part due to mass migration from the countryside into the cities in search of work—that wage rates in other sectors are not likely to be affected. Rather, these high wages in MNC subsidiaries contribute to increasing income inequalities within the working class.

These inequalities within the working class, as well as enormous inequalities elsewhere in the economy—between the cities and the countryside, between businessmen or professionals and the unemployed, between large landowners and peasants—lead to increasing government intervention in the economy. Insofar as the government is directly dominated by either foreign or domestic investors, it will reflect their interests in stabilizing costs by keeping wages down and thereby maximizing profits.[10] To the degree that the government bureaucracy reflects state interests and attempts to expand the sphere of publicly owned enterprises, it similarly acquires an interest in holding wages down to stabilize or minimize costs for the government enterprises. Thus, whether the state is dominated by capitalists or begins to take on its own major economic role in the public sector, its actions are likely to intensify economic inequalities in the society.

As we noted in Chapter 4, theories that relative deprivation fosters conflict are common. Unequal distributions of the national pie tend to induce conflict, as some groups or classes see others moving ahead

---

10. For evidence of the relation between foreign penetration and income inequality see Bruce Russett, "International Interactions and Processes: The Internal vs. External Debate Revisited," in Ada Finifter (ed.), *Political Science: The State of the Discipline* (Washington, D.C.: American Political Science Association, 1983); Bruce Russett, Raymond Duvall, Steven Jackson, Duncan Snidal, and David Sylvan, *Penetration and Repression in the Global System* (forthcoming).

rapidly while they themselves gain little or in some instances even slip backward. In highly inegalitarian societies, any appreciable change (either positive or negative) in overall national income will stimulate greater conflict over how the expanded or contracted pie should be divided, but there will be most conflict during periods of economic decline.

Chile in the early 1970s, under Marxist President Salvadore Allende, experienced economic stagnation and even some declines in real income due to mismanagement by Allende's government and economic sabotage by Allende's domestic and foreign (especially U.S.) enemies, who wanted to see him fail. When Allende tried to pursue policies of redistributing income at a time of overall growth failures, the result was work stoppages by key groups, riots, demonstrations, and eventually a right-wing military coup against him. Iran in 1978, by contrast, had experienced a decade of unprecedented growth in its national income. But these economic rewards were distributed very unequally and left a variety of groups—peasants, urban workers and urban unemployed, followers of traditional religion, and some intellectuals—very dissatisfied. Social conflict erupted, culminating in the shah's overthrow.

Societies marked by relative equality respond somewhat differently to changes in the level of economic activity. In such societies, economic growth is less likely to foster conflict (for example, the seemingly low but perhaps deceptive levels of violent social conflict in Taiwan and, during the 1970s, South Korea). Reductions in overall income, however, clearly promote conflict. One of the most vivid examples here is Uruguay, which until 1973 was a quite egalitarian welfare state. Once it had also been one of the highest-income countries in the Western Hemisphere, on a par with a number of Western European countries. But decades of stagnation and economic decline brought severe social tensions, the rise of radical urban guerrilla groups, and ultimately a right-wing military coup to "impose order."

The Spiral of Conflict and Coercion

In a democratic political system, social unrest may suddenly erupt in the form of strikes, demonstrations, and even riots. Democratic governments typically are anxious to maintain the reality (or at least the appearance) of civil liberties and do not immediately respond with repression. Rather, they respond with attempts to defuse the opposition, to meet reasonable demands or those put forward insistently by power-ful groups, and to try to satisfy the most important opposition leaders. If the underlying causes of social unrest are severe, however, this policy may not suffice; it may, in fact, embolden critics of the govern-ment, to make even stronger demands. If criticism of the government mounts with increasing violence (in the worst case, urban guerrilla warfare), economic as well as political instability is likely to follow—massive strikes may disrupt production. The democratic government under these circumstances may well alternate between a policy of try-ing to appease critics and mild efforts at repression and coercion (per-haps outlawing strikes, censoring newspapers, and arresting or even assassinating opposition leaders). But these policies are not likely to be sufficient against widespread, deeply felt grievances. Half-hearted po-litical repression may introduce a new set of grievances, feeding a spi-ral of protest.

After extended periods of unrest, economic and political disruption, and perhaps terrorism, the more conservative elements of society (with potentially the most to lose) are likely to lose patience. Landowners, business people, the army, and perhaps the middle class in general may demand strong action. These are the circumstances when a mili-tary takeover of the government becomes acceptable or even attractive to people who previously had supported democratic institutions.

Conflict and coercion thus feed on each other until the existing gov-ernment either cracks down or is replaced by a regime that will do so. Widespread arrests, outlawing of normal political activity, the suspen-sion of parliament, and bans on free speech and assembly may occur. It may take a while for these repressive efforts to be fully implemented. It takes time, after all, to build a strong apparatus for state coercion—police and soldiers have to be trained, and military and surveillance equipment has to be manufactured or imported. For a while, therefore, government repression may increase to the point where the state can instill fear, silence opposition, and track down and arrest (or torture or execute) dissidents.

Once this coercive political apparatus is in place, it may take a very long time—long after the emergency is past and long after much overt opposition remains—before repression is relaxed. New political struc-tures may be created to channel and control dissent. For instance, inde-pendent labor unions may be replaced by state-sponsored labor organi-zations, and collective bargaining rights may be severely restricted. A strong police and military bureaucracy will have been created, staffed by people who think their work is important and enjoy it. Political authorities may lose control of the secret police and fear that the police would turn on them if they tried to limit police activities. The police and government may become widely hated, yet deeply feared. As a result, a plateau of strong coercion and suppressed protest may be reached, with a government unwilling to relax repression for fear that protest or revolution will burst out again. Coercive government becomes habit forming. A government's success in repressing dissent will depend substantially on the coercive resources it can employ. A regime that is already authoritarian—perhaps in the traditional style of a "banana republic" dictator like Somoza of Nicaragua was—will crack down on dissent sooner and more sharply than will a fairly democratic regime. But both types of government must ultimately have the necessary force to make coercion stick. A relatively advanced economy (like Argentina's) or one with a lot of surplus readily available to the government (like oil-rich Iran) may be able to develop its own coercive apparatus without too much external help. The government of a less-developed state may have to depend more on purchases or gifts from abroad.

This reference to foreign assistance reminds us that we are primarily speaking usually about relatively poor, small, and penetrated societies. Foreign investors (MNCs), banks, and other financial lending institutions like the International Monetary Fund may insist on "responsible" economic and political policies as a condition for making or renewing investments. They may insist, for example, that prices (and of course wages) be brought down and that wildly fluctuating inflation rates be stabilized. High but stable inflation rates may be much more tolerable to investors, who understandably dislike uncertainty, than would sharp annual changes in the inflation rate. To do this, discipline must be enforced, and sacrifices must be made. Well-organized but poor urban workers who are asked to give up subsidized food or public transportation, for instance, will not accept sacrifices lightly. As a result, whether or not it is their intention, the demand of foreign interests for economic discipline really becomes a requirement of political "discipline"—that is, repression. This is one of the mechanisms by which some theorists link economic and political conditions in the third world back to theories of economic imperialism like those discussed in Chapter 9.

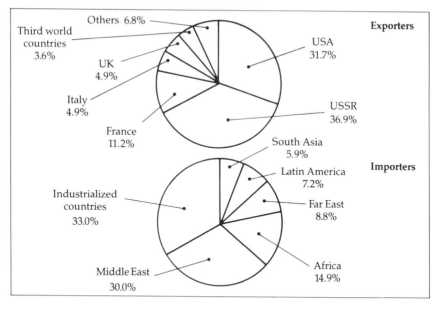

Figure 16.6

Shares of world exports (by country) and world imports (by region) of major weapons, 1978–1982. [*Source: World Armaments and Disarmament: SIPRI Yearbook 1983* (New York: Taylor and Francis, 1983).]

THE INTERNATIONAL ARMS TRADE

LDCs can obtain military and police assistance from Western Europe, the United States, the Communist countries, or even other third world states, depending on government policies and opportunities. Figure 16.6 shows the relative shares of the international arms trade by exporting countries and importing regions. Figure 16.7 shows the sharp increase in arms imports by LDCs during the 1970s as well as the recent slight decline in such imports forced by the fall in many states' oil earnings. Almost two thirds of these arms imports are by military governments.

Arms exports are often promoted by industries in the developed countries. Foreign sales can make the difference between short production lines—building perhaps a few hundred tanks per year at high cost—or longer production lines—turning out a thousand or more tanks with the lower unit costs of mass production. These efficiencies of scale are especially important to smaller countries like France, who could not buy enough for their own armed forces to keep costs at a

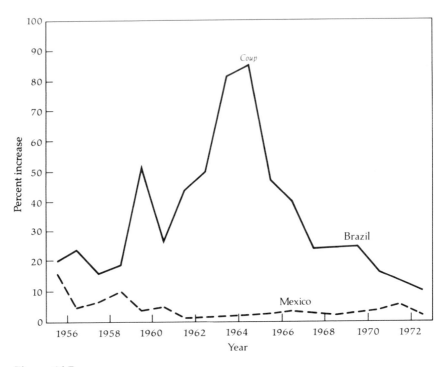

Figure 16.7
Third world imports of major weapons, 1963–1982. [*Source: World Armaments and Disarmament: SIPRI Yearbook 1983* (New York: Taylor and Francis, 1983).]

competitive level. Arms sales are also useful to help the balance of payments. American and European arms sales to Iran before 1979 and to the Arab states helped to pay the increased cost of oil imports from those same countries. Both to sustain a healthy domestic arms industry and to help the balance of payments, governments of exporting countries often encourage arms exports at the same time that for other reasons, such as the recipients' authoritarian regimes, they want to discourage them.

The demand for arms is stimulated by the many, sometimes overlapping arms races (between Israel and Arab countries, between different Arab countries with long-standing hostilities, between Iran and its Arab neighbors). The governments of exporting countries usually want to use arms sales or military assistance programs to build up their foreign allies: South Korea and Saudi Arabia are very important allies of the United States, and the demands of American national security seem to override misgivings about arming governments that will use those arms at least partially to suppress their own populations. Any government policy that tries to limit the scope of international arms sales always bumps up against these political and economic realities. In addition, if one country (the United States, for instance) refuses to sell arms to a third world state, some other country (like France or the Soviet Union) will gladly oblige the would-be importer.

Thus, a variety of pressures help maintain a heavy flow of military sales and assistance to third world countries, even without the incentives provided by links of dependence and penetration. In addition, the many third world governments desire modern arms and police primarily as instruments to control their own populations (rather than to deter their neighbors), and industrialized countries want to help prop up the governments of their "friends" (such as the USSR in Afghanistan, Angola, and Ethiopia and the United States in Morocco, the Philippines, and Zaire). Thus there is a powerful convergence of interests that maintains one of the world's biggest industries.

Moreover, there are innumerable military assistance programs for training foreign soldiers and technicians. Sometimes American, European, Russian, and Cuban military personnel go to third world countries to train local personnel or even to operate complex weapons systems for which local personnel cannot be trained fast enough. Alternatively, third world military officers go to the industrialized countries for intensive training programs, sometimes in the use of weapons, sometimes in the military and political philosophies of the industrialized countries.

The Problems of Dependence

We must now return to the problems of dependence. Because of such factors as the demands of lending institutions and the world commerce in arms and military training, dependence theorists say that penetration by foreign interests ultimately results in a long chain of economic and ultimately sociopolitical distortions, culminating in authoritarian government. "Growth in GNP, diminished inflation, and fewer strikes may be achieved but at a huge cost in terms of repression, income redistribution, elimination of national entrepreneurship, increased poverty of the urban and rural popular sectors, and alienation of intellectuals and students."[11] Although dependence theory may not be entirely

---

11. Guillermo A. O'Donnell, *Modernization and Bureaucratic Authoritarianism: Studies in South American Politics* (Berkeley, Calif.: Institute of International Studies, 1973), p. 103.

correct for all countries, it makes clear to us the fact that the achievement of equitable economic and political development is far more complicated than merely a matter of promoting foreign investment in LDCs.

In addition, foreign penetration (through military aid and investors' requirements for responsible economic policy) and coercive government may feed on each other, as local governments become ever more dependent on foreign support to maintain control over the social unrest that economic developments have created. The condition of peripheral countries in the world economy thus is quite different from that experienced a century or so ago by Europe and North America or even by Japan. Today's LDCs cannot simply copy the development patterns of the OECD world. Most European countries already had a stronger tradition of representative government than exists in most LDCs, though there are exceptions. (Uruguay probably had a stronger democratic tradition than did imperial Germany.) More important is that political authorities lacked the instruments of effective repression that are now common—sophisticated surveillance technology for the police, powerful modern armed forces—and foreign sources from whom these instruments of repression can be obtained.

Thus, even though most European countries experienced periods in their industrialization when income and wealth were very unequally distributed, most of them ultimately were obliged to make concessions and come to some peaceful terms with their peasants and working classes. (Those who waited too long, like the czars of Russia, simply lost everything.)

Now, however, many repressive governments may not have to make concessions. Their linkages to the world economy and political system may enable them to institutionalize an unequal distribution of income and power in a way that their earlier European counterparts could not. This accounts for the arrow leading from the lower box of Figure 16.4 back to a reinforcement of foreign penetration. It represents the nightmare of many who live in or observe the third world—a choice between the misery of economic stagnation and economic growth at the price of extreme inequalities and political repression. In some countries economic development may never lead to democracy.[12] Thus, the fail-

---

Two good discussions of O'Donnell's arguments, emphasizing how complex these phenomena are, can be found in David Collier (ed.), *The New Authoritarianism in Latin America* (Princeton, N.J.: Princeton University Press, 1979); Richard R. Fagen (ed.), *Capitalism and the State in U.S.–Latin American Relations* (Stanford, Calif.: Stanford University Press, 1979).

12. Much of the current mainstream theory of economic development recognizes most of the same phenomena and processes that we have labeled "economic distortions" (boxes I, II, and III in Figure 16.4) and can be accommodated within our discussion.

ure to find a way to combine moderate growth with relative equality requires the continued imposition of domestic order through coercion—not the stable peace of constitutional government.

ONE EXAMPLE: BRAZIL, 1950–1984

We introduced some of Brazil's political and economic problems in Chapter 1. We return to Brazil's experience because it provides an example of a development policy in a highly penetrated peripheral state in the world economy that was remarkably successful in increasing GNP per capita and laying the foundations of a large, modern industrial sector. It also offers an illustration of the price that was paid to achieve the "Brazilian economic miracle"—a highly unequal distribution of income and the suppression of political liberties.

At the beginning of the 1960s, Brazil had acquired the reputation of a country "with a great future behind it." It seemed a potentially rich country: it is the fifth biggest country in the world in area, with a large population, a variety of valuable natural resources, and, at least in cities like Rio de Janiero and São Paolo, a sophisticated and cosmopolitan population. It had emerged from World War II with a developing industrial base to go with its agricultural exports and followed that with new earnings from the boom in demand for primary commodities during the Korean war. It appeared to be at the point of takeoff to sustained economic growth.

But the takeoff did not occur. In the decade after the end of the Korean war (1953), economic growth was first erratic and then just plain slow, not very much above the rate of increase in population. Foreign investors became disillusioned with Brazil's economic prospects, and new external capital investment began to fall off. By 1963 annual payments on Brazil's foreign debt exceeded 40 percent of the country's export sales, frightening foreign bankers about prospects for the country's financial solvency. Inflation became a very severe problem—rarely less than 20 percent a year and sometimes 50 percent or

---

Dependence theorists, however, go a step further to link economic and social phenomena (boxes IV and V). Dependence theorists voice concern that an institutionalization of power will make permanent most of these economic distortions. For a good review of the economics, see the main text of the World Bank, *World Development Report 1979* (Washington, D.C.: The World Bank, 1979). The most common versions of dependence theory do not discuss the economic and political distortions that may arise from penetration by Communist states like the Soviet Union, even though those distortions may be as harmful or more so. Dependence theory is concerned with development under capitalism; attention to the distortions of Communist rule requires another set of concepts.

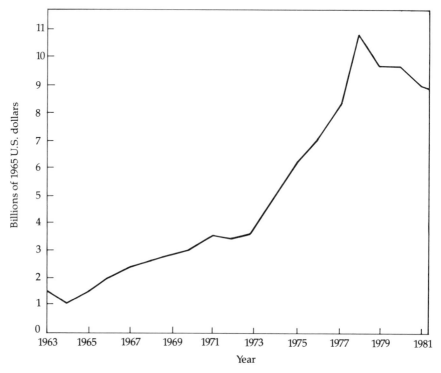

Figure 16.8
Annual increase in consumer prices in Brazil and Mexico, 1955–1972. [*Source:* Adapted from Guillermo O'Donnell, "Change in the Bureaucratic Authoritarian State," *Latin American Research Review* 13 (1978), no. 1, p. 14.]

more. The combination of high, erratic inflation with slow growth led to severe unrest among both workers and employers. New foreign investment dried up. (See Figures 16.8 and 16.9, comparing Mexico's experience with that of Brazil before and after the military takeover in 1964, which we shall discuss below.)

Brazil also had a history of alternating between democratic government and dictatorial rule. Nevertheless, Brazil had a sustained if shaky period of democratic rule from 1945 until March 1964. In 1961, however, President Janio Quadros resigned after failing to deal with the country's economic and political problems. Despite substantial apprehension in military and other conservative quarters, Vice-President João Goulart—a man with a leftist and populist following—was allowed to succeed to the presidency in a more or less constitutional fashion. Goulart at this point had three main problems. First, Brazilian political figures were split along left-right lines about how much to

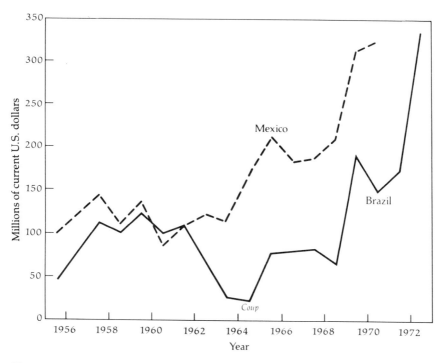

Figure 16.9
Direct foreign investment in Brazil and Mexico, 1955–1972. [*Source:* Adapted from Guillermo O'Donnell, "Change in the Bureaucratic-Authoritarian State," *Latin American Research Review* 13 (1978), no. 1, p. 21.]

encourage or discourage foreign investment. Goulart chose to accept an investment law in 1963, that was opposed by the American ambassador to Brazil, Lincoln Gordon, requiring reinvestment of profits (rather than their return to the center countries). Second, violence in the countryside became common, chiefly between landless squatters, who tried to occupy unused land for agriculture, and real estate speculators. Goulart ineffectively tried to introduce a land reform measure. Third, inflation and the balance of payments deficit became worse than ever. Both the International Monetary Fund and the U.S. Agency for International Development effectively withheld further economic assistance until "financial discipline" was imposed.

Faced with these problems, Goulart moved further left in his rhetoric, and in March 1964 he promised to expropriate and redistribute large agricultural land holdings and to take over the Brazilian (not foreign owned) oil refining industry. When he sided with the enlisted men in a brief insurrection against navy commanders, the majority of the Brazilian military command had had enough. They seized power in a coup, suspended the constitution, and tightened control. The U.S. embassy in Brasilia clearly was well informed about the impending coup. Although the United States may not have actively supported the coup, it certainly did nothing to discourage it and immediately recognized the new government. A renewal of U.S. economic and financial assistance shortly followed. Many middle-level and senior Brazilian officers had been trained in the United States, and they had developed an anti-Communist ideology of "national security."

The military government dissolved all political parties in 1965. Strikes were outlawed, and the labor unions were tightly controlled. A world-renowned economist, Professor Roberto Oliveiro Campos, became finance minister and adopted orthodox economic policies to stabilize prices and especially wages and to encourage foreign investment. Later, the government moved to establish and expand various publicly owned enterprises, developing substantial public enterprise sectors in heavy industry, including transportation vehicles and ultimately armaments. In this later period, foreign investors, while still encouraged, faced somewhat stricter controls and greater Brazilian competition. Economic growth was rapid until the first rise in oil prices in 1973.

The benefits of this economic boom, however, were distributed very unevenly. Industrial workers' wages were unchanged. Income inequalities sharply increased; the poorest 60 percent of the population gained little or nothing during this burst of economic growth, and many of the poorest citizens actually endured worsening living conditions. The infant mortality rate in the poorest regions was 250 per 1,000 births—a level typical of the poorest states in Africa.

The Brazilian government discouraged programs to curb the rate of population growth. Part of its motivation included its ideological commitment to becoming a great power (which would require not only industrialization but also a large population). But it also is worth noting that a rapid rate of population growth, especially in the countryside, means before long a rapidly growing supply of labor—and a large labor force helps keep wages low.

In December 1968 the president assumed virtually unlimited powers. Repression was not too severe at first but gradually intensified. At one point hundreds of people in the public eye who were not political leaders—people such as entertainers and sports and media figures—simply disappeared for several weeks; when they returned, they would not discuss their absence. This was intended as a powerful deterrent, a demonstration of the government's repressive ability, which could become much nastier if necessary. Later it did become much nastier. Imprisonment, killings, and documented reports of horrible torture became commonplace, some of them apparently perpetrated by a secret police beyond the control of its formal political superiors.

Economically, after 1964 Brazil entered a period that has been described as "dependent development" because of its rapid but very uneven growth, with modernized high-technology agriculture as well as industry linked closely to the world market and still heavily dependent upon foreign technology and capital. Brazil experienced massive industrialization during the period and emerged as a large-scale exporter of manufactured goods. Exporting became as important to Brazil as manufacture for the home market.

Brazil also emerged as an exporter of capital and technical expertise regionally, with Brazilian government enterprises and Brazilian-based MNCs undertaking large-scale activities in Bolivia, Paraguay, and Uruguay. Politically, Brazilian "expertise" was employed in Chile after the 1973 military coup in that country—torture victims in Chile reported that their Chilean tormentors were tutored by Portuguese-speaking (that is, Brazilian) instructors. Brazil's size and relative economic advancement fitted it for this role, one not available to most LDCs. In the words of one observer,

> Dependent development is not a phase that all peripheral countries will be able to reach. Only a few are chosen. International stratification is accentuated rather than leveled as those countries in which the local bourgeoisie and international capital can arrive at an alliance become increasingly differentiated from the majority of the third world.[13]

The Brazilian economic miracle began to sputter after 1973, when the cost of oil imports began to shoot up, amounting to two thirds of Brazil's total import bill in 1979. The growth rate of GNP dropped and then actually turned negative in 1980. Still, the achievements of the earlier period were impressive. Middle-class and upper-class Brazilians lived very much better, and it might be argued that the industrial and

---

13. Peter Evans, *Dependent Development: The Alliance of Multinational, State, and Local Capital in Brazil* (Princeton, N.J.: Princeton University Press, 1979), p. 33. For other works on Brazil, see the works of O'Donnell cited previously; Alfred Stepan (ed.), *Authoritarian Brazil* (New Haven, Conn.: Yale University Press, 1973); Alfred Stepan, *The Military in Politics: Changing Patterns in Brazil* (Princeton, N.J.: Princeton University Press, 1974).

governmental base for further development, ultimately to benefit the Brazilian masses, had been laid.

Yet the political cost was severe, and it is not at all clear in the 1980s how far Brazil can move toward being a more democratic, less coercive regime. Its congress has little power; the president can recess it at any time. Elections for Congress were held in 1978, and freer ones held in 1983. Full popular election of the president is scheduled to be restored in 1991. Repression has been relaxed considerably, torture has been eliminated as a common coercive measure, and there are few restrictions on the press. Labor organizations and some strikes have been tolerated by the ruling regime, but many middle-class people, who had become accustomed to the good "discipline" of labor during the repressive years, have begun to worry about the effects of new wage demands and work stoppages. As economic stagnation and the foreign debt crisis impose austerity, some Brazilians long for the good old days of imposed order. It is uncertain whether the ruling interests will tolerate full restoration of democratic liberties or, if they do, whether liberalization will turn loose a torrent of pent-up discontent that will engulf society in a new round of terrorism and government counterterrorism.

17

SOME POSSIBLE
ALTERNATIVES TO DEPENDENCE

In Chapter 16 we identified some of the difficulties in achieving growth, equity, and democratic government in third world countries. We examined dependence theory as one explanation of these difficulties, a theory that traces the problem to third world countries' position at the periphery of the world economy. We also looked in detail at the recent experience of Brazil. Nevertheless, it is important to be aware that the processes identified by dependence theory have not yet been adequately established as either general or necessary. For many third world countries, the description seems accurate, but others are exceptions. In this chapter we shall look at several development strategies that seek to avoid the worst features of dependence.

A BASIC-NEEDS STRATEGY

Some countries have successfully industrialized, at times in a quite egalitarian manner (as in South Korea and Taiwan). Why egalitarian growth occurs is not fully understood; it is partly because the growth period begins at a time when the power of established interests is broken. Taiwan and South Korea both implemented vast land reform programs immediately after World War II—Korea under the American occupation and Taiwan when Chiang Kai-shek, after losing all of mainland China to the Communists, fled with his army to Taiwan. To preserve one bastion of his power, Chiang was prepared to do on Taiwan what he had failed to do on the mainland: redistribute land to the peasants. (It was easier on Taiwan, because he arrived with his army and bureaucracy and could impose the program.) South Korea also had the "advantage" of being devastated by the war against Communist North Korea; most established bases of wealth had been destroyed, leaving the country in a condition of forced equality.

Korea and Taiwan, of course, are not democracies, although South Korea has had brief episodes of somewhat democratic government. Other countries, like Turkey and Malaysia, have been able to have moderate equality, decent growth, and partially democratic governments. A very few others—Sri Lanka is the clearest case—have had equality, democracy, and moderate growth. The choice in Sri Lanka was fairly deliberate—to maintain a welfare state as much as possible (given that Sri Lanka is basically a poor country) with subsidized rice, health care, education, and transportation for the masses. Economists sometimes refer to this as a *basic-needs strategy* of development.

A basic-needs strategy is directed toward raising the living standards of the poorest parts of the population. It is not generally concerned with providing consumer goods for immediate use, which might divert scarce resources from investment and leave everyone no better off when the immediate input of consumer goods had been exhausted. Rather, it tries to build human capital that will eventually provide the basis for economic growth. One aspect of a basic-needs strategy is to expand primary education with the expectation that a literate population will be able to acquire the skills needed to operate modern industrial equipment and to employ modern agricultural methods. A second aspect is in trying to improve health conditions—bringing doctors or nurses to rural villages rather than allowing medical specialists to concentrate on ministering to the rich in the cities, helping villages obtain clean drinking water and build sanitation systems to dispose of waste, and programs of mass inoculation and insect control so that major killer diseases can be nearly eliminated at very low per capita cost.

Although Sri Lanka has pursued a basic-needs strategy with only moderate economic growth, Taiwan and South Korea have experienced rapid growth. Economists' studies have now established that countries with basic-needs policies do not necessarily have lower growth rates at first, and they do usually show faster growth rates later on, when education and better health begins to have positive effects on productivity. People who are healthy work better than people who are sick. Children who are well fed do not have their brain development stunted by malnutrition. Moreover, as adults see their own living conditions improve, they become more confident in the future. They become more willing to have their children educated (even at the cost of losing them as productive hands on the farm), and they become more willing to save, such as they are able, for the future.[1]

Basic Needs and Population Growth

One very important and not fully expected consequence of a basic-needs policy seems to be a greater readiness to adopt contraceptive methods and to limit the size of families. Some observers of the third world had feared that improving poor people's health would worsen the world population problem—that by prolonging people's lives and especially by reducing infant mortality, the result would simply be more mouths to feed. In the short run, it is of course true that lowering death rates means increasing the number of people alive. But the effect of longer lives and the better chance that children will live to adulthood make a difference in how people behave. Where children are likely to die before reaching adulthood, a prudent couple who want to be reasonably sure of having heirs or offspring to care for them in their old age will give birth to many children. If, on the other hand, most children can be expected to survive, the need for large families is decreased. Instead, it makes better sense to have fewer children and to invest in those few children by seeing that they are well educated.

Experience in the third world has now shown quite conclusively that giving people access to information and materials for birth control is, by itself, not enough to affect reproductive habits markedly. To make a major impact, the information and material must be supplemented either by coercion—forcing people to accept contraception or sterilization (a policy that led to Indira Gandhi's stunning electoral defeat in the Indian elections of 1977)—or by providing incentives. For a non-coercive policy of limiting population growth, people must be given

---

1. For evidence, see Hollis Chenery et al., *Redistribution with Growth* (London: Oxford University Press, 1974); Norman L. Hicks, "Growth vs. Basic Needs: Is There a Trade-off?" *World Development* 7 (1979), nos. 11–12, pp. 985–994; see also other work by economists at the World Bank.

reasons—principally better health and educational conditions for their offspring. All of the countries identified in Table 16.1 as having relatively equal distributions of income (and which have a strong basic-needs component in their development strategy)—China, Cuba, South Korea, Sri Lanka, and Taiwan—also show birth rates (below 30 per 1,000) and population increase rates (2 percent or less) substantially more favorable than most other countries at low-income levels. Filling basic needs thus seems to offer the incentive as well as the means for controlling population.[2]

Few other countries have pursued a basic-needs strategy intensively. A basic-needs strategy is not easily compatible with a development program that emphasizes urban development and heavy industry, low wage rates to ensure cheap labor, and foreign investment geared to capital-intensive technology and the production of consumer goods. Industrialists and the owners of mining or plantation agricultural facilities usually prefer that a country's scarce public resources be devoted to building *infrastructure:* highways and railroads, communications networks, and electric power plants. The physical means of production and of transporting goods to market take precedence. Although these powerful economic interests may not object to serving basic needs in principle, it is not a high priority to them. Some of them—for example, large landowners—will strongly object to any element of a basic-needs strategy that seems to imply redistribution of land to landless peasants.

A revolutionary Communist government, as in Cuba or China, may be able to follow a basic-needs strategy because it has expropriated the assets of large landowners and private industrialists. With power concentrated in the party and government bureaucracy rather than in private foreign or domestic interests, major obstacles are removed. Such countries nevertheless pay a heavy price in terms of bureaucratization and suppression of political liberties. South Korea and Taiwan policy was aided, as we noted, by wars that greatly weakened the power bases of previous ruling groups. Of the democratically ruled countries, Sri Lanka's experience is the most favorable. Nevertheless, Sri Lanka has had to accept a slow growth rate and remains a poor country. Perhaps its very poverty—the fact that it was not very attractive to foreign interests other than tea companies, whose basic needs for infrastruc-

---

2. See the statement by the then president of the World Bank, Robert S. McNamara, "Population and International Security," *International Security* 2 (1977), no. 2, pp. 25–55.

ture had already been met—meant that there was less opposition to implementing a basic-needs strategy. In recent years the World Bank and some private international development-oriented organizations have encouraged the adoption of basic-needs strategies. It is too early yet to know enough about what conditions are most likely to bring success. Aid-giving institutions have shifted from promoting industrial development to improving agricultural productivity, especially for small and medium-sized farms. This somewhat improves equity within less-developed countries and slows the growth of large numbers of unemployed or underemployed people living meager existences in the big cities.

A NEW INTERNATIONAL ECONOMIC ORDER

The less-developed countries of the world have attempted to create a program of collective international action to lessen their dependence. Demands for restructuring world trade and industry in favor of the LDCs have become identified with demands for a New International Economic Order (NIEO). These demands include: (1) change in the marketing conditions of the world trade in primary commodities, (2) promotion of industrialization in the third world, and (3) increased developmental assistance to and perhaps debt relief for the third world.

Reform of Commodity Markets

Most less-developed countries specialize in exporting agricultural products and minerals, and they import most of their manufactured goods. Although some world commodity export markets (wheat, corn, and some other grains, meat, wool, and wood products) are dominated by the developed countries, the earnings from commodity exports are much more important to poor countries than to rich ones. Widely fluctuating prices for these commodities, and in many cases declining terms of trade, hit less-developed countries very hard. At meetings of the UN Commission on Trade and Development (UNCTAD), the LDCs have pushed for adoption of an Integrated Program for Commodities.[3]

---

3. A good review of the negotiations can be found in Robert Rothstein, *Global Bargaining: UNCTAD and the Quest for a New International Order* (Princeton, N.J.: Princeton University Press, 1979).

This program is advocated by a diverse and sometimes very shaky co-alition of LDCs known as the Group of 77 (which by 1984 had in fact grown to include nearly 130 members). It calls for a variety of measures, such as price and production agreements among producers, the creation of international buffer stocks of commodities financed by a common fund, multilateral long-term supply contracts, and other measures to reduce fluctuations in the price of commodity exports.

Some members also have called for indexing the price of certain commodities so their price will automatically rise with any increase in the price of manufactured goods (much as wages are often tied to the consumer price index in the United States). This last proposal has been opposed by many poor countries who are also major commodity importers and by developed countries (who are obviously reluctant to pay higher prices). The argument against the proposal is that price changes are necessary for conveying information about changes in market supply and demand. Although the developed countries have been more open-minded about schemes for stabilizing prices, they have vigorously resisted anything that hinted of indexing. It is probably true that indexing would be grossly inefficient. It would encourage surplus production (as it has for many agricultural commodities like grain and dairy products in the European Community). It would be very damaging to the producers of natural rubber, jute, cotton, leather, and even some metals, where synthetics could easily satisfy the existing market for natural products if prices for the natural products became too inflated.

Nevertheless, to argue for maintaining current market conditions purely in the name of free competition is very misleading. Most international markets are, in one degree or another, already far removed from the economist's model of perfect competition. In the words of a well-known international trade theorist:

> Market rules of the game, and the determination of which markets are allowed to operate, are essentially political decisions. Power, whether military or corporate, abhors an uncontrolled and truly competitive market. It would be an extraordinary world in which asymmetries in military and economic power were not reflected in asymmetries in economic relations.[4]

---

4. Carlos Diaz Alejandro, "North-South Relations," *International Organization* 29 (1975), no. 1, p. 218.

The most obvious example on the world scene today is, of course, the Organization of Petroleum Exporting Countries (OPEC), which for a while took control of the world oil market and changed the terms of trade markedly in favor of the oil exporters. But many industrial products from the developed countries are also sold in markets that are far from competitive. This is especially the case where a developed country receives preferential status for its exports to a former colony. This preferential treatment may be the result of official government agreements or, more likely, the product of informal arrangements that have solidified over the years. This preferential status is especially damaging to relatively small LDCs (which means most of them), because their domestic markets are not large enough to attract many competitors. Also, some of the most important primary commodities exported in world trade originate in the developed countries. Wheat, corn, and some other grains are important examples, and arrangements among national producers and marketers create not a situation of free competition but one where there are only a few sellers (*oligopolists*), who can largely control price and quantity at least in the short run. Finally, many products sold by LDCs are not sold in a market that is either freely competitive or dominated by the sellers. Rather, it often is dominated by a few buyers (*oligopsonists*).

Table 17.1 indicates the importance of MNCs in the world markets for some important mineral products. In most extractive industries, MNCs have the technical expertise for processing the material and the marketing organization to sell it. It would be very difficult for the government of an LDC to take over the industry completely and to process and market the material itself. Given the existing market structure, one of the MNCs must do the job. Since there are so few MNCs in most of these industries, the MNC, as buyer from the LDC and seller on the world market, has a great deal of control over price.

Relations between MNCs and LDC governments are, however, neither the same for all countries and industries nor static. Small and poor countries, as well as being weak in the traditional bases of power, also typically lack negotiating experiences and skills. Hence, when they have to bargain with MNCs or with developed countries over international marketing agreements, they often do not get very favorable agreements. One recent article quoted a standard economic text on the topic and added some further comment:

> "In a typical situation, a company earns more abroad than the minimum it would accept and a country's net social benefits from the company's presence are greater than the minimum it would accept . . . with a wide

Table 17.1

Company concentration in metal production (excluding Eastern European countries and China).

Metal	Percent share of biggest company	Percent share of first 3 companies	Percent share of first 5 companies
Bauxite production, 1976	17.0	35.0	48.2
Alumina capacity, 1974	22.7	46.1	65.2
Aluminum capacity, 1974	15.3	34.4	48.8
Molybdenum mining, 1974	41.9	59.8	71.6
Chromite mining capacity, 1974	16.5	41.0	53.7
Nickel production, 1976	35.4	54.2	62.4
Platinum production, 1974	48.8	91.5	96.5

Source: Interfutures: Facing the Future (Paris: Organization for Economic Cooperation and Development, 1979), p. 52.

gap between the maximum and minimum demands by the two parties." Thus viewed, the outside limits of acceptability could be located by means of economic theory but the precise terms of the investment would be a function of the relative bargaining strengths of the two parties. Equilibrium analysis must give way to power analysis, economics to political science.[5]

In his study of long-term negotiations between the Chilean government and multinational copper corporations, Theodore Moran found that in the early years, when the companies as yet had little invested, the scope of Chilean resources was unknown, and the Chilean government was both very anxious to have the foreign investment and inexperienced in negotiation, the agreements heavily favored the MNCs. But over the years, as the MNCs accumulated huge investments (and thus had quite a lot to lose if the Chilean government nationalized the foreign-owned enterprises) and the Chileans gained experience, the balance of power and hence the distribution of benefits in subsequent

5. Douglas C. Bennett and Kenneth E. Sharpe, "Agenda Setting and Bargaining Power: The Mexican State versus Transnational Automobile Corporations," *World Politics* 32 (October 1979), no. 1, p. 58. Their initial quotation is from Charles Kindleberger and Bruce Herrick, *Economic Development*, 3rd ed. (New York: McGraw-Hill, 1977), p. 320.

agreements shifted in favor of the Chileans.[6] The power of MNCs has thus led state powers in LDCs to attempt to control those MNCs. LDC governments have frequently taken over, or nationalized, MNCs, especially in the economically stronger LDCs where the government has some sophisticated administrative capacity and where the export sector's economic performance has been poor.[7] Nevertheless, many LDC governments are too weak, small, and inexperienced to drive very hard bargains. Even if one LDC does have most of the requisites for negotiating success, its market position is likely to remain weak. Unless it is an unusually big country or has an unusually large share of the world's resources of a particular commodity, it may be dispensable to the MNC involved. The globally based MNC can usually transfer its operations to a country that will offer more favorable terms. This can provide a powerful restraint.

After the success of OPEC in revolutionizing the world oil market, both LDCs and developed countries anticipated that similar OPEC-type arrangements might arise for other commodities, as the sellers followed OPEC's example to band together in international commodity cartels. In fact, that has not happened, chiefly because the conditions that favored OPEC largely applied to petroleum products alone:

• Previous cultural and political ties among the Arab members of OPEC (however, this factor should not be exaggerated).

• The lack of ready substitutes for oil, making it very difficult for buyers to refuse to pay higher prices.

• Temporary market conditions of high demand and little excess supply.

• The dominant position of Saudi Arabia, and for a while Iran, among oil exporters. If these two could agree on price and quantity, they could bring along the rest of the suppliers; even if one or two small exporters did offer cheaper terms, it did not fundamentally upset the imposed price structure.

As events have transpired, no other major commodity cartel has emerged with anything like OPEC's initial success. Some effort was

---

6. Theodore H. Moran, *Multinational Corporations and the Politics of Dependence* (Princeton, N.J.: Princeton University Press, 1975).

7. David Jodice, "Sources of Change in Third World Regimes for Foreign Direct Investment, 1968–76," *International Organization* 34 (Spring 1980), no. 2, pp. 177–206.

made in the bauxite industry (bauxite is the principal ore from which aluminum is refined), but all of the above conditions were lacking. Most important, other aluminum-bearing ores exist in many of the developed countries and would be brought into production if the price of bauxite were raised too high. Another complication for many commodities is the existence of stockpiles in the developed countries. The United States maintains a "strategic stockpile" of metals, such as tungsten (a stockpile equivalent to eight years of supply), and tin and chromium (about three years' supply of each). In 1962 the United States held 349,000 tons of tin and announced plans to sell 164,000 tons out of the stockpile. Since the entire production of the non-Communist world in 1961 was 136,000 tons, imagine what that did to world markets.[8] It is not enough for an LDC to have a large share of a commodity's production; to control the world price, it must control the market. That is, it must be able to control the MNCs and to control the market in substitutes for its commodity.

Industrialization in the Third World

Even if LDCs could create many new OPEC-like cartels, it is not at all clear that it would be fully in their interests. It would still leave them specializing in primary commodities and deny them the potential benefits of stimulating development that could come from a shift to manufacturing. At the least, most LDCs want to move into a stage of refining and processing the raw materials that they produce. Otherwise, when a nonrenewable resource like a mineral has been extracted, the country is left with little more than a hole in the ground (and perhaps roads and pipelines leading to the hole). However, if the country takes a share in processing or in further manufactures from the raw material, it can benefit from "spin-offs" like technical expertise, an infrastructure of communications and transportation, and physical plants and equipment that can be adapted to many uses. Although a few modern countries have maintained long-term prosperity from agriculture and mineral extraction (Australia is the best example), the persistent wealth of most developed countries today is based on industry. Processing and diversification seem essential to balanced development,

---

8. See the excellent discussion on these matters in L. N. Rangarajan, *Commodity Conflict* (Ithaca, N.Y.: Cornell University Press, 1978).

especially in a world where so many natural materials are giving way to synthetics.

Exports of technologically advanced manufactured products from industrialized countries are typically subjected to low tariffs by other industrialized countries. This is a result of many years of negotiation and the mutual exchange of preferences, chiefly under the General Agreement on Tariffs and Trade (GATT). By the "most-favored-nation" clause, once preferences are given to any country, they must be applied equally to all other countries with whom a state has such an agreement. Most-favored-nation principles apply throughout the non-Communist world and in trade with some Communist countries by industrialized Western countries. But a general reduction of tariffs on imports of, say, automobiles is helpful only to exporters of automobiles. Most LDCs produce simpler manufactures and thus do not benefit. Many LDCs, by contrast, export refined or processed raw materials or relatively simple and labor-intensive manufactures like textiles. On such goods, tariffs and other restrictions on imports into the industrialized countries are often very high. LDCs can thus be effectively shut out of the world market for those exports. Therefore, they lose the revenue from value added by manufacturing and lose the spin-offs for stimulating development.

In negotiations with the developed countries, LDCs have consistently sought to restructure preferences to permit them to export more simple manufactures to industrial countries. Some improvements have been made. Members of the European Community in 1975 signed the Lomé Convention with most of their ex-colonies. Still, the ability of LDCs to export remained restricted because the United States and Japan did not agree to the concessions (meaning that the LDC Lomé signatories still depended on a limited set of markets). However, the United States did institute a Generalized Scheme of Preferences favoring some simple manufactures from LDCs. Despite these concessions by the industrialized countries, exports by LDCs remain a very small drop in the international trade bucket. In 1980, imports from developing countries represented only 4.6 percent of the manufactured goods consumed in the European Community and even less (2.9 and 2.4 percent, respectively) in the United States and Japan.

Many potential LDC exports are in industries that are declining in developed countries, usually because they are low-technology goods requiring labor-intensive production (and labor costs are high in the developed countries). The apparel industry, for instance, is endangered in most European countries, as well as in the United States and Japan.

Clothing manufacturers, their union employees, and regional government agencies—in what are often generally depressed parts of developed countries—understandably, and often with powerful political effect, resist granting preferences to foreigners that will put the domestic
manufacturers out of business. Nontariff barriers to trade, such as imposing "voluntary" quotas on the exporters, are often very restrictive.[9]
In times of recession, when unemployment and the number of business bankruptcies are high, resistance to granting preferences to exports from LDCs is especially great. For this reason, many economists
say that an essential requirement for rising prosperity in LDCs is
continued prosperity in the developed countries that serve as their
markets.

The situation is slowly improving. Some countries have had considerable success in export-led development. World markets have been
able to absorb the new industrial exports of countries like South Korea,
Taiwan, and Singapore, whose governments and businesspeople have
devised some very clever strategies to get around developed countries'
nontariff barriers to their trade. The East Asian NICs were able to
maintain growth rates above 5 percent a year even during the global
recession of the early 1980s, but there may not be room for many more
countries to follow in their path. Could world markets absorb enough
manufactures from such vast countries as China and India to make
much difference in those countries' level of poverty? At the Lima,
Peru, meeting of UNIDO (UN Industrial Development Organization)
in 1975, the Group of 77 set themselves a target of accounting for 25
percent of world industrial output by the year 2000. At that time their
share was 7 percent. In 1980 it had become 9 percent, but there is
virtually no prospect of reaching the group's ambitious target. Table
17.2 shows the progress that was made in opening up markets in the
developed countries.

As an alternative or supplement to export-led development, many
countries are still pursuing policies of import substitution industrialization, substituting domestic manufactures for imported ones. For
some of the larger LDCs—like Brazil, Mexico, India, and Nigeria—this
has some promise. Their governments have instituted various requirements for *indigenization* by MNCs—for instance, that products must be

---

9. See Susan Strange, "The Management of Surplus Capacity; or How Does Theory
Stand Up to Protectionism 1970s Style?" *International Organization* 33 (Summer 1979),
no. 3, pp. 303–334.

Table 17.2

Percentage of manufactured goods consumed in industrial countries that were imported from LDCs, 1970–1980.

Manufactured goods	Percent share	
	1970	1980
Food	3.5	3.7
Clothing	4.0	16.3
Textiles	2.3	5.4
Footwear	2.6	16.3
Leather products	6.2	17.3
Wood products	1.9	3.6
Paper	0.2	0.5
Chemicals	2.0	3.8
Nonmetallic minerals	0.3	1.1
Base metals	3.5	4.1
Machinery	0.4	2.1
Cutlery and hand tools	0.8	3.3
Metal furniture	0.6	1.6
Electronics	1.1	6.7
Other	4.0	8.0
Total	1.7	3.4

Source: Data from World Bank, *World Development Report, 1983* (New York: Oxford University Press, 1983), p. 14.

composed of a certain percentage of locally manufactured components or the firms must have a certain percentage of local ownership or management. These arrangements may be important, though they do not fundamentally address questions of whether Western high-technology goods and production processes are appropriate to LDCs. These arrangements are less helpful in small or poor countries that cannot afford large markets for import-substituting manufactures. (Some efforts at regional economic integration to create larger markets—for instance, the Latin American Free Trade Area—have been made but without much success.) MNCs have found ingenious ways to evade indigenization regulations or to persuade LDC governments to admit more manufacturers than would be optimal for their small markets. For example, when the Mexican government was making plans to license a small number of automobile manufacturers to operate in Mexico, some American and Japanese MNCs feared they would be shut out. They persuaded their governments to pressure the Mexican government to permit them to be included. In the end, ten automobile manufacturers were permitted—far too many for the relatively small Mexican market.[10]

The LDCs also have called for sharing and transferring technology as part of the NIEO. When they attempt to manufacture industrial products in their own countries, they typically have to pay large sums to the MNCs for patents, licenses, and trademarks (which we discussed much earlier as part of technological penetration). Most technological innovation is done in laboratories in the developed world and to developed-world standards. LDCs would like to have more of it done in their countries and generally to have a "code of conduct" for more liberal terms for technology transfer. It is not easy to do this, however, without discouraging MNCs from transferring technology at all.

Another problem is that industrialization, though it may ultimately be desirable or essential for LDCs, usually increases income inequality, at least in the short run. The structural economic distortions are usually not so serious in development plans that stress agriculture. Industrialization is also extremely import intensive, giving rise to severe short-run shortages of foreign exchange.

Finally, developed countries are increasingly happy to see one kind of industry transferred or exported to the LDCs: highly polluting industries. In developed countries, some industries have come under severe governmental regulations to limit their damage to the environment or to workers' health. A good example is the asbestos-processing industry; in the OECD states, it has come under such severe regulation to control its cancer-inducing potential that its costs have almost become prohibitively high. As a result, asbestos-processing MNCs have moved their operations to LDCs, which are glad to have the new industry. Labor unions are weak in most LDCs and unable to protect their workers' health effectively. Even the workers may be very glad to have good industrial jobs. A job now may mean not starving now; cancer is many years in the future.

For these reasons, industrialization as a strategy of integration in the world market has its drawbacks as well as its attractions. It probably must be pursued, but not to the point of ignoring precautions against its abuse or expecting it to solve all of the LDCs' problems.

---

10. Douglas C. Bennett and Kenneth E. Sharpe, "Agenda Setting and Bargaining Power: The Mexican State versus Transnational Automobile Corporations," *World Politics* 32 (October 1979), no. 1, pp. 57–59.

Debt Relief and Developmental Assistance

Some LDCs have called for relief from or rescheduling of their foreign debts. For countries facing international bankruptcy, relief is essential. There are sharp divisions among LDCs on this issue, however; many do not favor it, fearing that the creditworthiness of all LDCs will suffer if some insist on rescheduling debt payments. There is more agreement on demands for more developmental assistance from the industrialized states. Whereas foreign economic aid amounted to 0.51 percent of the OECD countries' GNP in 1960, it fell to about 0.3 percent in the 1980s. This was despite an earlier agreement by the developed countries to accept a target of *raising* economic assistance to 0.7 percent of their GNP. In a world of periodic "stagflation" in most industrialized countries, a major increase in voluntary developmental assistance seems unlikely. At the 1980 UNIDO conferences in New Delhi, the Group of 77 called on the Western developed countries to create a global development fund of $300 billion by the year 2000. The demand was rejected.[11] In 1983 the Reagan administration, preferring bilateral aid programs closely tied to American security policy, cut its contribution to the International Development Association (IDA), a branch of the World Bank, by 25 percent. Since all the industrial countries have agreed to contribute set shares of the budget, this meant a reduction in their contributions as well. As a result, there was a 25 percent cut in IDA lending to poor nations.

SELF-RELIANCE AS AN ALTERNATIVE TO DEPENDENCE

The sometimes extreme and angry words of many LDC representatives, demanding help and concessions from the rich, frequently offend most developed-country residents. People in developed countries often respond that they first must take care of poor citizens within their own countries before they make giveaways to foreigners. (They could possibly do both, but may in fact do neither.) Yet it is important to be aware that the content of these LDC demands is usually not radical but "reformist." That is, they still take for granted the existence of an inte-

---

11. For several different perspectives, see Albert Fishlow, Carlos Diaz Alejandro, Richard Fagen, and Roger Hansen, *Rich and Poor Nations in the World Economy* (New York: McGraw-Hill, 1978).

grated world economy and do not challenge its most fundamental hier-archical characteristics. They wish to reduce their dependence some-what and to obtain better terms of trade for their products. But they are not seeking any basic overthrow of the existing system of international trade and finance, nor are they seeking to withdraw from that system.

By contrast, principles of self-reliance have attracted attention from theorists both in LDCs and developed countries and have to some de-gree been adopted by a few LDCs. Self-reliance is usually meant to operate both internationally and within LDCs. At the local level, it implies self-reliance for groups and villages—restructuring domestic relations to emphasize rural development, a reduction in income inequality, and a decentralization of administration. Village manage-ment in China and the *ujamaa* movement in Tanzanian villages are the best examples. At the international level, self-reliance implies shifting economic ties away from core countries, the MNCs, and Western aid-giving agencies—cutting the ties of foreign penetration and depen-dence. This may indicate some degree of self-reliance as the country seeks to reduce foreign ties generally. Or it may mean a shift in foreign ties toward other peripheral countries (collective self-reliance with other LDCs) and perhaps toward socialist countries. Substantial efforts have been devoted to promote trade and technical exchange among less-developed countries, especially where domestic markets are too small for economies of scale and where simple labor-intensive technol-ogies seem appropriate for export to other LDCs. Perhaps in a later stage, self-reliant countries will try to reassociate with industrial core countries but on a more equal basis, with their own economies and technologies more suited to their needs.

Within these meanings, self-reliance is still a rather vague term that means different things to different advocates. To some it implies a near-total withdrawal from the world market and a reduction of ex-ports and imports (both goods and services) to a bare minimum. Exam-ples of this extreme form are few. Albania, which cut its ties both to the West and to the Soviet Union and Eastern Europe, embarked very nearly on a strategy of economic autarky (self-sufficiency). The govern-ment of Burma has for the past two or three decades cut most of its ties with the world economy; it even sharply reduced tourism in Burma, accepting almost complete economic stagnation as the consequence. China, from its break with the Soviet Union in the late 1950s until its new openings to the West in the mid-1970s, also cut foreign economic and cultural contacts to a minimum. China, however, had some eco-nomic disadvantages—its vast population and the diversity of its natural resources. If self-sufficiency was to work anywhere and to allow economic growth to continue, China had to be the place.

Other countries have pursued much less extreme versions of self-reliance, attempting to reduce, restructure, and control their contacts with the industrial world rather than to cut them sharply or entirely. Tanzania under Dr. Julius Nyerere, a major interpreter of self-reliance, is perhaps the best-known example. Algeria is another—and is an example of the diversity of "self-reliant" countries, since Algeria has remained a major exporter of natural gas and petroleum to the world market. After the overthrow of the shah in 1979, Iran began to follow many aspects of a policy of self-reliance. It sharply cut back oil production and exports, laid plans to favor agriculture and so return to self-sufficiency in food, cracked down on the importation of Western popular culture, and canceled billions of dollars of contracts for high-technology Western investment. Most interestingly, the revolutionary government canceled $8 billion in arms purchases from abroad, in one stroke achieving the world's largest act of disarmament in more than thirty years. Yet the political system was in turmoil, the economy went into stagnation, and the country's future was unclear.

Restructuring Economy and Society

What all these countries' experiences do have in common, however, is a desire not to emulate the development of the industrial West or the development patterns of that large majority of third world countries closely linked with the world capitalist economy. Self-reliance is typically a policy that is instituted as a "revolution from above." That is, it requires a substantial restructuring of the domestic social structure and political system as well as of the economy and international linkages. The more radical dependence theorists see it occurring literally as the result of political revolution, whereby, as in Cuba, the power of domestic and foreign capitalists is smashed and replaced by socialism. Such theorists, however, are usually much clearer about the need to replace the old order than about what is to replace it. They do emphasize the necessity of breaking the power of those domestic capitalists who collaborated with foreign capitalist interests and of replacing private ownership of the means of production with state ownership or (perhaps in the case of agriculture) at least firm state control. They also frequently speak of the need to replace foreign capital and technology with domestic technology appropriate to local needs.

Efforts at self-reliance have been carried out with very different in-
tensities and with varying success. Burma has stagnated. As a total
economy, Algeria has prospered—but much of that prosperity is due
simply to the rise in world oil prices. Tanzania has experienced moderate economic growth, although the *ujamaa* movement is widely considered a failure. Both Algeria and Tanzania have pursued developmental
strategies that emphasize heavy capital-intensive industry ("heavy" at
least in the Tanzanian context, though what looks like heavy industry
there would not seem so in Europe). Incomes of workers and peasants
have been kept low to provide a "surplus" that the government can
invest in industry. By keeping earnings low, the government has fore-
closed the possibility of developing a mass market for consumer goods
(the same problem that arises in other LDCs where income inequality
is great). Consumer goods might be produced by light, labor-intensive
industry, but lacking the mass consumer market, production tends to
go into investment goods and products of heavy industry for export.
Heavy, capital-intensive industry means reliance on advanced foreign
technology. In periods of bad harvests or politically necessary concessions to the peasants, when industrial development cannot be adequately financed from surplus, foreign loans are necessary. As a result,
Algeria has taken loans from private foreign banks, Tanzania is heavily
indebted to international aid-giving agencies and socialist countries,
and even Burma has depended to some degree on war reparations from
Japan. Self-reliance in practice, then, has been limited, and important
elements of dependence remain—perhaps in different forms than before—even among the more successful self-reliant states.[12]

China's experience is in some ways the most disappointing for self-
reliance advocates. After running its economy with a minimum of ties
to the world market, China now is opening up rapidly, inviting foreign
trade and investment. In China's case, however, the causes may be as
much political as economic. Partly the new policy reflects failures and
barriers to self-reliant economic development. Almost as important,
however, has been the Chinese leaders' sense of external political
threats to their security. Ties to the United States seem dictated by a

12. David Sylvan, "State-Based Accumulation and Economic Dependence: Toward an
Optimal Policy," *Journal of Peace Research* 20 (1983), no. 1, pp. 27–48; Thomas Biersteker,
"Self-Reliance in Theory and Practice in Tanzanian Trade Relations," *International Organi-
zation* 34 (Spring 1980), no. 2, pp. 229–264; John G. Ruggie, ed., *Antimonies of Interdepen-
dence* (New York: Columbia University Press, 1983); M. von Freyhold, *Ujamaa Villages in
Tanzania: Analysis of a Social Experiment* (London: Methuen, 1982).

need for the heavy industry necessary for a modern military machine and the Chinese desire for American support against their Soviet neighbor. The degree to which Chinese self-reliance was an economic failure will not be known until much better data on the Chinese economy are available.

The third world is enormously diverse in many ways—in culture, in degree and kind of ties to the rest of the world, in political systems, in resources, and in levels of economic activity. Theories of development and of dependence are important tools for trying to understand what is happening and to set forth some general statements about the economies and political systems of poor countries. The phenomena are so complex, however, that they defy easy generalization. Any theory has to address the effects of different developmental contexts and experiences. World resources and social conditions are changing rapidly. The menu of choice presented to leaders of less-developed countries is constrained by the hierarchical nature of the international political and economic system, by numerous transnational linkages—political, financial, commercial, and cultural—and by the relative strength of various groups and social classes within those countries.

Although some people may think they have easy answers to the third world's dilemmas, the body of tested theory to support reliable policy recommendations is very small. The lives of billions of people—their hopes for relief from the physical misery of poverty and for the implementation of political liberties—are at stake. A responsible analyst, therefore, must tread a treacherous line between irresponsibly ignoring the desperate problems of these people and irresponsibly offering ill-conceived "solutions" that others (not the analysts) will have to live with. A responsible social scientist in a rich industrialized country cannot become, in the words of the West Indian novelist V. S. Naipaul, one of

> those who continue to simplify the world and reduce other men to a cause, the people who substitute doctrine for knowledge and irritation for concern, the revolutionaries who visit centres of revolution with return air tickets . . . the people who wish themselves on societies more fragile than their own, all those people who in the end do no more than celebrate their own security.[13]

13. "The Killings in Trinidad: Part Two," *Sunday Times* (London), May 19, 1974, p. 41.

18

ACHIEVING ORDER
AND COLLABORATION
IN THE WORLD SYSTEM

ORDER AND ANARCHY

In Part II we have presented several central problems that have developed since the end of World War II and that characterize international relations today. These problems are related to the nature of the international system, states, sovereignty, and the quest for security within the changing international environment. The changing menu and states' attempts to adapt to that menu have generated the political, economic, and military conflicts that shape the problems noted above.

But as states and other international actors have come into being and as new technologies and ideologies have altered the international environment, the practices of states and other international actors have adapted to these changes so as to maintain order within the formal anarchy of the international system. As noted earlier, while there is formal anarchy (the absence of a central authority with coercive power), there is indeed much order, cooperation, and collaboration in

494

international relations. There is, as Hedley Bull calls it, an "anarchical society." Bull argues that such a society exists because there are *patterns* of behavior that are more or less predictable and that both produce and conform to the expectations of the actors in the international system.[1]

For those of us interested in international politics, this is crucial, because it means that order can exist without formal rules or with only a primitive system of rules. In this chapter we wish to outline the ways in which order is achieved in the contemporary system: the institutions, mechanisms, and practices that help provide the order, stability, and cooperation that characterize most of the behavior between international actors. The ability to create order and the frequency and virulence of conflict largely depend on the relationships among international actors. One feature of systems and the relationships among the components of those systems is *interdependence*. It is necessary to understand how interdependence both contributes to the problems of creating order and creates the conditions necessary for attaining order.

INTERDEPENDENCE AND THE WORLD SYSTEM

Interdependence is a quality of all systems. As we have seen, we can think of world politics in terms of a *system*. Instead of looking at one state and the foreign policy processes that go on within it, we look at the system of states and other international actors and the various networks of relationships among them. This includes the various distributions or hierarchies of attributes (e.g., how is wealth or military capability distributed among all the states?). Systemic thinking emphasizes wholeness—looking at the larger picture—so looking at the international system means looking at the patterns of interactions among the actors. Interdependence emphasizes the links or interconnectedness among the units of a system. Such links may affect the opportunities of states and the willingness to act. We shall see that interdependence is one form of constraint that the system places on the nation-state. What is on a state's menu very much depends on how that menu is connected to the menus of other states.

How might interdependence constrain the menu? A very simple definition of interdependence is that changes or events in any one part

1. See Hedley Bull, *The Anarchical Society* (New York: Columbia University Press, 1977), chap. 1.

of a system will produce some reaction or have some significant consequence in other parts of the system. For example, an infected finger in
the system of a human organism will affect the entire blood system and
its white cell defenses; it can cause a fever and speed up the heartbeat.
Or, by increasing the air in the carburetor of a car, we affect the explosion in the piston and the speed and smoothness of the ride of the auto.
In world politics, we can think of the effects within the system of a
guerrilla war in a small country in Southeast Asia; of a war involving
three countries in the Middle East in 1973; or a worker in Poland winning the Nobel Peace Prize. These all had major effects on many other
parts of the global system.

Interdependence is a quality of a system. One student of systems
theory reminds us that in systems "things ramify"—there are always
more effects than we imagine or expect, which ripple through the system due to the interdependencies of the system.[2] For example, a
weapon produced by a superpower in order to please one of its armed
services is seen as a major threat by the other superpower, which
matches this development and then builds more, perhaps leading to an
arms race, which then raises tensions that might then get out of hand
in a crisis. Similarly, there are "surprise effects"—when there is a
change in the system, be prepared for surprising consequences; for
example, the French Revolution of 1789, the Russian Revolution of
1917, or the October 1973 war between Israel, Egypt, and Syria, which
led to the Arab use of oil as a weapon.

The images of the "global village," "spaceship earth," or the "shrinking planet" are also based on the idea of interdependence—that the
various states on earth are being linked together in more and more
ways and are being affected by activities going on in other states,
whether they like it or not. One view of interdependence is very positive and optimistic. This view sees interdependence as leading toward
more and more cooperation among states as they are brought together;
according to this view, some sort of world community or world state
will eventually emerge from this process.

---

2. See Jay Forrester, "Counter-Intuitive Behavior of Social Systems," *Technology Review*
73 (1971), 53–68. Systems thinking emphasizes that everything is related to everything
else. By making us think of interdependence, systems thinking makes us aware that the
world is much more complex than we might have thought. This complexity includes the
interconnectedness of our problems, our collective well-being, and survival. Looking at
social systems (such as the international system), Forrester has said: "It is my basic theme
that the human mind is not adapted to interpreting how social systems behave. Our
social systems belong to the class called multiloop nonlinear feedback systems."

There is another view that quite correctly points to interdependence as a possible, very important source of conflict. Interdependencies (especially if they are lopsided, making one party much more dependent than the other) can also generate frustration and anger, as states hopelessly wish for past times when they were not inextricably linked with others and when they had greater freedom of action. It is important to remember that interdependence means only that what goes on within one state or the actions of that state will have important consequences for the other international actors in that system. This can occur with or without increased cooperation. International interdependence has two different dimensions. In the first place, we say that nations are sensitive to developments in other nations. The degree of sensitivity depends on how quickly changes in one country bring about changes in another and how great the effects are. Second, we say that states may be vulnerable to the effects of those changes, with vulnerability measured as the costs imposed on a state by external events, even if the state tries to avoid those costs.[3]

A state is sensitive to environmental interdependence if it has to clean beaches blackened by an oil spill that occurred in another state's territorial waters or if a downstream state like the Netherlands must suffer from the river pollution produced by states further upstream on the Rhine. A state is vulnerable because even after the cleanup, its environment may remain damaged and the effects of that damage may be great; for example, its tourist and fishing industries, which are important to its economy, may be damaged. In discussing economic interdependence, we may say that if Japan's trade with the United States drops as a result of a recession in America, that trade is sensitive; if Japan also goes into a recession because of the trade drop, it is vulnerable. Here we use the term *vulnerability* in much the same way as when we discussed influence and capabilities in Chapter 6. The United States is certainly not vulnerable to a recession in, say, Guatemala, as Guatemala is to a U.S. recession. Guatemala may be dependent on the United States, but the two are not *inter*dependent as we have defined the term.

Interdependence can cause conflict if a sensitive state does not wish to be sensitive; for example, many trading countries were greatly af-

3. For this distinction, see Robert Keohane and Joseph Nye, *Power and Interdependence: World Politics in Transition* (Boston: Little, Brown, 1977), especially chap. 1. Also see Robert Keohane and Joseph Nye, "International Interdependence and Integration," in Fred Greenstein and Nelson Polsby (eds.), *Handbook of Political Science: Vol. 8, International Relations* (Reading, Mass.: Addison-Wesley, 1975), pp. 363–414.

fected in 1971, when the United States surprised them and the world by devaluating the dollar. A sensitive state need not be a vulnerable one. For example, even though the United States was affected as rapidly and almost as severely as were the Europeans by the 1973 oil embargo (sensitivity), the United States was not as vulnerable because it could substitute more of its oil needs from other oil and energy sources than could the European states. Vulnerability can cause military conflict if a state finds it impossible to prevent others from imposing costs on it. Periodic reports of American contingency plans for the military seizure of the Persian Gulf oil fields are an example of a possible negative consequence of interdependence. Population growth in one part of the world or greater demand in another can also affect others by the consumption of nonrenewable resources. The consumption of food that others need or the production of pollution that fouls air or kills fish in the waters of other states will affect vulnerable states whether they want to be affected or not.

The following excerpt from the report to the Club of Rome, *Mankind at the Turning Point,* illustrates the ecological, political, economic, and social interdependencies that exist in the present world system:

The winter 1971–72, with its prolonged low temperatures and strong icy winds all over Eastern Europe, effectively destroyed one third of the Russian winter wheat crop. Surprisingly, the government bureaucracy ignored the situation, and the spring wheat acreage allocation remained unchanged. Since the direct per-capita consumption of wheat in that region is rather high (three times higher than in North America), it was urgent that the deficit be eliminated. In July 1972 the U.S. government extended a $750 million credit to the Soviet Union for the purchase of grain over a three-year period. Actually, the value of the purchase increased significantly before the delivery got underway since food prices soared all over the world. The price of wheat doubled in North America—hitherto a bastion of cheap food supply. Public resentment arose because people felt that in effect they were being made to pay for a transaction that did not involve the ordinary citizen. More important, and much more unfortunately, that same year's late monsoon heavily damaged the crops on the Indian subcontinent, resulting in a disastrous loss in food supply, which came in the aftermath of a tragic war. Nowhere was wheat to be found, for most of the world's surplus had been sold. Then a drought hit China and Africa and while China was acquiring whatever foodstuffs were on the market, hundreds of thousands of Africans faced starvation. In a similar situation several years earlier, millions of tons of wheat had been rushed from North America to avert disaster; but this time only two hundred thousand tons could be made available.

The most outstanding lesson which can be drawn from these events is a realization of how strong the bonds among nations have become. A bureaucratic decision in one region, perhaps the action of just one individual—not to increase the spring wheat acreage—resulted in a housewives' strike against soaring food prices in another part of the world and in tragic suffering in yet another part of the world. If the world is already interdependent to that extent, and interdependence is certain to increase, should regional or national decisions still be made in isolation, in total ignorance of their effects on other parts of the world system?[4]

Some people talk about the extensive "new" webs of interdependence that exist, creating a truly global system for the first time. However, much of what is being seen as interdependence is not new but is just being recognized for the first time. We can talk about both *conditions* of interdependence (the existence of linkages that hold the system together) and the *cognitions* of interdependence (people seeing or perceiving that interdependence exists). Many of today's conditions are indeed quite new, especially in that some states are much more sensitive and vulnerable than ever before. In Chapter 3 we discussed states that are small and poor and have only a token degree of sovereignty. Many of these states are buffeted at will by systemic economic, monetary, and political forces and are far more sensitive and vulnerable than most states in the past have been. But some of the technological developments in the postwar world, especially the development of nuclear weapons and their delivery systems, have made even the superpowers interdependent (militarily vulnerable) to a degree never before experienced by great powers. The alliances of the superpowers have expanded the web of military/strategic interdependence to those states formally allied and supposedly protected by the superpowers as well. Technology—not only in weapons but in communications and transportation as well—has expanded the physical capabilities of people to interact with each other and to know about that interaction. The new interdependence is based to a large degree on new patterns of human attention. Individuals can see things that are happening in faraway places. Today we can perceive and be aware of what is happening in the whole world. If interdependence means that something happening in one part of the system affects what happens in other parts, then not only is there a greater awareness of interdependence, but also another whole dimension to interdependence: psychology.

---

4. Mihajlo Mesarovic and Eduard Pestel, *Mankind at the Turning Point* (New York: New American Library, 1974), pp. 19–20, (emphasis in original).

This psychological aspect means that people are aware not only that activities are taking place elsewhere but that they are aware that they are aware! They understand that they belong to some sort of "global village," to use Marshall McLuhan's famous term—that they exist in some larger world system. Television and radio have brought foreign events—"live and in color"—into homes all around the world.

The amount and degree of interdependence in the international system thus depends on a number of factors, such as the technology of communications and transportation that affect how much and what types of interaction occur between and among states, how resources and capabilities are distributed within the system, and how vulnerable single states and groups of states are. Interdependence grows and increases as states become more vulnerable to penetration of various kinds. Interdependence can only occur when the hard shell of the state—sovereignty—becomes full of holes.

Because of both increased interdependence and increased awareness of interdependence, governmental decision makers have to think about and take into account the effects that their internal policies have on foreign relations with other states (for example, American economic choices affecting the exchange rate of the dollar, South African treatment of its black population, or Soviet treatment of Jewish citizens). There is no doubt, however, that whether actions or events were meant to cross state boundaries or to affect the peoples and governments of other states, they do. This, in a nutshell, is interdependence. These examples of interdependence are also constraints. Being sensitive and vulnerable to the actions of other international actors places limits on what any state is able and willing to do. These constraints can be either negative or positive. They can lead to struggle, conflict, and war or to even greater cooperation and stable areas of peace.

TRANSNATIONAL RELATIONS AND INTERDEPENDENCE

In the contemporary era of increasing interdependences, as Richard Falk has put it, "national boundaries have been less relevant." A number of scholars, writers, and even statesmen feel that continuing to view the world in terms of the traditional Westphalian logic is not very useful and may be downright harmful given the nature of contemporary interdependences. These observers feel that if governments continue to look at the world in terms of these old images (including sovereign nation-states concerned with independent behavior and military power), such views will lead to wrong and inappropriate policies—possibly disastrous for humankind. This view has been most extensively expressed by political scientists who see the world in terms of *transnational relations* rather than *international relations*.

Although there have been a number of different and complex definitions and views of transnational relations, we can start with the following description of transnationalism: the movement of goods, information, and ideas across national boundaries without significant, direct participation or control by governmental actors.[5] A transnational view such as this clearly reduces the importance of the ideas of sovereignty, national boundaries, and the interaction of governments in the world system. Because each state has become so permeable, so open to outside influences, the distinction between domestic and international politics has become indistinguishable. These new patterns of penetration and linkage also involve a heavy participation by various kinds of nonstate actors, particularly international nongovernmental organizations (NGOs). These transnational patterns can be seen more clearly in Figure 18.1, which contrasts the state-centered view of international politics and the transnational (or "cobweb") view of world politics.

Using the definition above, the main point to note is the multiplicity of interactions that bypass the governments of states and act directly on their domestic environments. In the transnational view, nonstate actors (NGOs in particular) are much more important actors than previously thought, as are the interest groups or subnational actors that exist within states. We have previously discussed various tribal, ethnic, or separatist groups within states, as well as various economic interests, multinational corporations, and parts of the governmental bureaucracy. Often parts of the governmental bureaucracy, acting in accordance with the organizational process model, interact directly with comparable parts of other states' bureaucracies, often without the knowledge of the top decision makers of the states involved.[6] Both NGOs and the subnational actors are distinct from state actors and have some independence of behavior from the state actors. Some even argue that there is no neat hierarchical pattern of influence and authority—in other words, that states are not the most powerful or that sub-

5. Richard A. Falk, *A Study of Future Worlds* (New York: Free Press, 1975), p. 74.

6. See Samuel Huntington, "Transnational Organizations and World Politics," *World Politics* 25 (1973), 333–368.

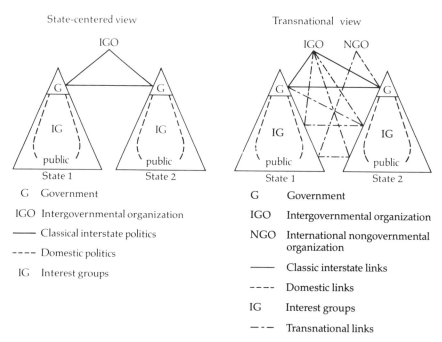

State-centered view   Transnational view

G   Government
IGO Intergovernmental organization
——— Classical interstate politics
———— Domestic politics
IG   Interest groups

G   Government
IGO Intergovernmental organization
NGO International nongovernmental
     organization
——— Classic interstate links
———— Domestic links
IG   Interest groups
—·— Transnational links

Figure 18.1
Comparing the old (state-centered) and new (transnational) views of world politics. [*Source:* Raymond Hopkins and Richard Mansbach, *Structure and Process in International Politics* (New York: Harper & Row, 1973), p. 134. Adapted from Robert O. Keohane and Joseph S. Nye, Jr., "Transnational Relations and World Politics: An Introduction," *International Organization*, Summer 1971, pp. 332–334.]

national actors are the least. It is impossible to rank states above multinational corporations or other groups all the time in all circumstances.

The transnational view holds that these various nonstate actors can affect world politics directly—and not just as they affect nation-states. It is even more important to note, as we did in Chapter 6, that the power of any international actor depends on the issue or situation at hand. Power and influence are a result of the relations between actors. The different needs and vulnerabilities of states, IGOs, and NGOs provide all actors with some levers of influence. This is especially important to the transnational view, because it holds that the issues that have been central to international interaction are changing.

Thus, another feature of transnationalism is the assertion that the issues generated by the various actors are not primarily military security issues. The Westphalian, state-centered view focuses on power and security (best illustrated by the realist view of international politics), but in a transnational view, such matters are no longer central but are replaced by economic concerns. Much of this view is based on the increasing sensitivity and vulnerability of states and nonstate actors to economic interdependence. International economic relationships are becoming more and more sensitive to domestic economics such as taxation and inflation. The reverse is also true. America's relations with its European allies, the strength of the dollar on world money markets, and thus the economic standing of the United States—as well as its trade policies regarding arms, technology, and food—are all related to domestic policies on fuel conservation, such as increased taxes on gasoline. The advocates of the transnational view want to highlight the relationships between international politics and international economics. This is illustrated in Figure 18.2. What is new in this diagram are the diagonal dashed lines. They indicate that domestic politics can influence international economics; for example, the British desire not to devalue the pound in the mid-1960s for internal political reasons had consequences on European trade, British entry into the EEC, and other economic issues. Clearly, domestic economics can influence international politics and vice versa. This aspect of interdependence is also highlighted by those who study "regimes" in world politics. As noted below, this involves the interaction of states *and* nonstate actors, especially in dealing with economic issues.

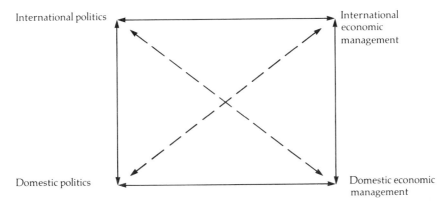

Figure 18.2
Transnational linkages—politics and economics. [*Source:* Susan Strange, "The Dollar Crisis 1971," *International Affairs* 48 (April 1972), 197.]

Rivals of the Nation-State

One of the main instruments by which economic interdependences have increased is the MNC. As noted in Chapter 3, MNCs are just one of the postwar challenges to the nation-state—just one part of the diffusion of power within the world system. In Chapter 3 we discussed several ways in which MNCs rivaled states. This picture of the multinational as rival has been developed and stressed by Richard Barnet and Ronald Muller in their book, *Global Reach*. "The global corporation is transforming the world political economy through its increasing control over three fundamental resources of economic life: the technology of production, finance capital, and marketing." They note that industry is no longer constrained by geography as production makes national boundaries irrelevant. They also argue that production makes the idea of loyalty to any one state irrelevant. Although loyalty is the basis of nationalism, MNCs, they posit, are careful not to favor any country in which they do business over any other such country:

> "For business purposes," says the president of the IBM World Trade Corporation, "the boundaries that separate one nation from another are no more real than the equator. They are merely convenient demarcations of ethnic, linguistic, and cultural entities. They do not define business requirements or consumer trends. Once management understands and accepts this world economy, its view of the marketplace—and its planning—necessarily expand. The world outside the home country is no longer viewed as series of disconnected customers and prospects for its products, but as an extension of a single market."[7]

For all the challenges that MNCs pose, remember that the rise of the multinational corporation also stimulated states to increase and use their own power to try to control the MNCs. This point was made in Chapter 17. In addition to contributing to the economic capability of a state, an MNC is often a focus for discontent in the host country. By directing societal discontent at the MNC, a government can increase the support it needs to nationalize an MNC's property.

Although economically oriented, transnationalism does include nonstate transnational actors that are concerned with military activity. Earlier in this book we mentioned a variety of nonstate actors, as well as forms of military activity that were being used more frequently in the

---

7. Richard J. Barnet and Ronald E. Muller, *Global Reach* (New York: Simon and Schuster, 1974), pp. 14–15, 26.

postwar period. Both guerrilla movements and terrorist groups may be seen as transnational actors, penetrating the state's hard shell. They are revolutionary nongovernmental groups that move across national boundaries for sanctuary and aid in order to make violent attacks on people in power who they identify as enemies. Terrorist groups may take a variety of forms. They may be factions of nationalist or separatist groups—such as those found in Spain, Canada, or Ireland—where groups like the Basques, the Quebeçois, and the IRA have ethnic appeals and support. In addition, there may be ideological sects, such as the German Red Army Faction or the Japanese Red Army; or transnational gangs that recruit from many countries, such as the Carlos gang (responsible for the December 1975 attack on the OPEC ministers).

These groups produce several forms of interdependence. First, using modern communications techniques, they often emulate or copy the tactics of other terrorist groups. Thus, it is not uncommon to find a rash of kidnappings or airplane hijackings occurring around the world after the first use (or a major successful use) of the technique. This illustrates how communications establish a global interdependence—actions in one part of the system affect other parts of the system. Communications, indeed, are crucial to the whole concept of terrorism. The aim of a terrorist group is psychological, to create fear and intimidation. Without the communications technology that broadcasts their acts to a national and world audience, terrorists would have no purpose. As Brian Jenkins has observed, "terrorism is theater"—it needs and is aimed at an audience. The contemporary terrorist has a global audience that can be affected in many ways by a lone act that is geographically distant in the system but psychologically near because of communications technology.[8]

Communications also make individuals and groups aware that there are other people in other parts of the world who are fighting for the same causes. This leads to a major form of transnational activity, the active cooperation of terrorist groups from different countries, of different nationalities, in all parts of the world.

In addition to showing the various transnational links, the easy penetration of the state's boundaries, and the global rippling of conse-

---

8. See, for example, Brian Jenkins, "International Terrorism: A Balance Sheet," *Survival* (July–August 1975), 158–164. Because of the vast literature on terrorism, let us suggest as an introductory treatment and bibliography Timothy Garrigan and George Lopez, *Terrorism*, Learning Packages in International Studies (New York: Learning Resources in International Studies, 1980).

quences, this also indicates the roles that states may play in the interdependences. In Chapter 7 we noted that there could be a situation of "international civil war," where state governments supported each other's rebels or opponents. Here we see the use of Libyan aid to help support an anti-Israeli terrorist action, just as Amin's Uganda was involved in the Entebbe air hijacking. Terrorist and guerrilla activity may also lead to governmental interactions (and thus more interdependence in the system). As noted, governments have begun to act together to train antiguerrilla and terrorist units. Governments have also acted through IGOs to outlaw or provide for cooperation against certain offenses (an antiterrorism "regime"). Members of both the Organization of American States and the United Nations have passed treaties prohibiting offenses against diplomats. On a transnational level, national police forces have been coordinated through Interpol to combat terrorism. Transnational terrorist activities have even prompted countermeasures from purely transnational NGOs, such as the international airline pilots unions, which have brought direct pressure against governments and IGOs to institute measures against hijackings.

Earlier we noted that some see the old view of state-centered, security-oriented politics not only as wrong but as potentially disastrous. In part this is because the old view ignores the interdependences in the system. This is partly because many of these interdependences have a special quality—the activities involved produce consequences called collective goods. If these consequences create problems that are approached without understanding interdependence, then they will not only go unsolved but can be made much worse. The special problems created or worsened by collective goods require people to set up arrangements to help provide order and to settle conflicts. Before we turn to those mechanisms, let us investigate the important concept of *collective goods*.

COLLECTIVE GOODS AND INTERDEPENDENCE

States act to achieve their goals and interests both singly and in groups. As the world has become more tightly linked through various interdependences—including transnational linkages as well as traditional intergovernmental interaction—states have found themselves grouped together in various international organizations and various regional groupings that are economic, political, and military in nature. States also belong to a world system. We may think of each state (as well as the other international actors) as a member of a group that includes the entire globe. Being a member of a group complicates what any individual member can achieve and how the member achieves it. Because of how individual interests relate to group interests, sometimes leaders of states think they are acting in their own interests when they are not. This is yet another argument for transnationalism; it points out that the traditional notion of individual states seeking their own special or national interests is now counterproductive in a world where states are enmeshed in many different kinds of groups. (This includes the overall group of humankind that must together inhabit spaceship earth as it moves through the universe.)

How can we not act in our own best interest? The important point is *how individual interests relate to group interests*. The situation is clearly illustrated by a situation in Joseph Heller's novel about World War II, *Catch-22*.[9] In it, Yossarian, a bombardier in the U.S. Army Air Force in Italy, refuses to fly any more missions. Major Major, a superior officer, in trying to persuade Yossarian to fly, asks, "Would you like to see our country lose?" Yossarian replies, "We won't lose. We've got more men, more money and more material. There are ten million men in uniform getting killed and a lot more are making money and having fun. Let somebody else get killed." Major Major replies, "But suppose everybody on our side felt that way." Yossarian's answer is devastatingly to the point: "Then I'd certainly be a damn fool to feel any other way. Wouldn't I?"

This passage raises the basic dilemma of the individual and the group. If all the other fliers are willing to fly their missions, then Yossarian would be a fool to go along, because with ten million men in the war, his individual presence won't make a difference. On the other hand, if none of the others wished to fly either, then his response, "I'd be a damned fool to feel any other way," is a *rational* answer. His presence would again make no difference if no one else flew. However, if all the other fliers were to take the same position, then the following dilemma develops: Despite the fact that missions have to be flown, it is not rational for any single individual to participate. As a collective—a group of individuals—the goal of winning the war can be achieved only through group action. Yet such group action consists of the activi-

---

9. Joseph Heller, *Catch-22* (New York: Dell, 1961), p. 107. Much of the following section is based on material in Harvey Starr and Charles W. Ostrom, *A Collective Goods Approach to Understanding Transnational Action*, Learning Package no. 18, (New York: Learning Resources in International Studies, 1976).

ties of individuals, and Yossarian makes it clear that it does not seem rational for any single individual to perform the actions needed to achieve the group's goal. Applying this example to individuals and groups in general, how do groups of supposedly rational actors ever accomplish group or collective goals? (For example, why should any single state stop hunting whales, stop polluting the oceans or the air, stop increasing population, stop increasing their use of oil, obey international law, or participate in arms control?)

The reason for this dilemma rests in large part in the nature of the goods being provided—collective goods. In this sense, the word *good* means simply the consequence of an activity. We use it in the same way when we say "goods and services." Such outcomes, consequences, or payoffs may be very tangible things that can be possessed as property by a single person. These are the things that economists call private goods. A steak one person eats cannot be eaten by another; a haircut is a good given to one individual; a pair of shoes one person wears cannot be worn by another at the same time. Land that a person owns cannot be owned by another person. Most analyses in economics are based on the study of private goods. Economists study how supply and demand, influenced by the market mechanism, determine the prices of things and their distribution. Under ideal conditions, private goods and the market solve the individual/group problem illustrated by Yossarian: Each individual, seeking to maximize his or her own interests, buys and sells as desired, affected only by supply and demand. If each individual seeks to do this in an economic system where only private goods exist, the whole group will benefit if each person follows individual interests.

Suppose people were only interested in private goods—that they were not interested in winning a war or preserving democracy. Then they would only fly if they could receive something that they could possess as a private good, like money. Pilots would fly if someone paid them enough, and the market mechanism would work to get some people to fly. If an insufficient number of pilots came forward, the pay for flying would go up and more people would be willing to fly. But as the supply of fliers increased, the pay would go down and fewer people would come forward; eventually there is a fairly stable number of pilots willing to fly bombers.

We all know that the world doesn't work exactly this way. The market mechanism based on supply and demand does *not*, in fact, work perfectly; it does not work very well for many goods, and not at all for some. For many goods a person's choices—costs and benefits—derive from things other than supply and demand; these other things include the nature of collective goods.

Characteristics of Collective Goods

Collective goods possess two special characteristics (a third important aspect will also be discussed). The first characteristic is a prerequisite for the second. More importantly, these two characteristics describe a "pure" collective good, something rarely found in the real world. For that reason we should think of goods being more or less characterized by collective good properties.[10]

The first special characteristic is *jointness of supply*. If a good is supplied to any member of a group, then it is supplied to *all* members of that group. In addition, jointness of supply means that if new members are added to the group the other members who also consume the good, *will not receive a diminished amount*. If a lighthouse is built to guide ships and shines its light to guide one ship, then all other ships in that area (the group) can also use the lighthouse. Also, additional ships will not diminish the amount of the good provided (as long as one ship does not physically impede another). When a government provides deterrence for its population, it is also jointly supplied. When Washington threatens Moscow with retaliation for an attack on the United States, it provides deterrence for every individual in the United States. Once one person is protected by the deterrent threat, all are protected; once California is protected, so are Montana and Delaware. An increase in population does not reduce the deterrence provided to all the rest. The addition of Alaska and Hawaii in 1959 did not diminish the deterrence already being provided to the other forty-eight states.

Remember that goods are the consequences of activities and are not necessarily positive. A factory that produces pollution in an area is producing a jointly supplied good. The pollution that any one individual breathes can be "consumed" by all other individuals in an area. Again, more people in the area will not take away from the pollution available to the others. Any form of air or water pollution, then, is a jointly supplied good. Similarly, clean air—provided by pollution con-

10. For a useful investigation into and elaboration of the concept of a collective good, see Duncan Snidal, "Public Goods, Property Rights, and Political Organizations," *International Studies Quarterly* 23 (1979), 532–566. See also Joe Oppenheimer, "Collective Goods and Alliances," *Journal of Conflict Resolution* 23 (1979), 387–407.

trols and government programs—is also a jointly supplied good. Thus, jointly supplied goods may have either negative or positive consequences.

The second characteristic of an ideal collective good is called *nonexclusiveness*. A jointly supplied good may be either excludable or nonexcludable—that is, even though it is jointly supplied, it can be withheld from nonmembers. Cable television is a good example of a jointly supplied good that is excludable. Once the cable signal is supplied to any one cable subscriber, the addition of new subscribers does not reduce the supply of the good. However, it is excludable. Those who do not pay for the service are not hooked up to the cable and thus cannot receive the service. Jointly supplied goods, then, can be perfectly excludable, such as with cable TV. A lighthouse, on the other hand, is a nonexcludable, jointly supplied good. However, if that lighthouse is altered to use a radar signal rather than a light, then the use of the lighthouse can be regulated. All those who don't buy the equipment to receive radar signals would then be excluded. The pure collective good, then, is jointly supplied and cannot be controlled for exclusion. For example, if the United States is deterring a nuclear attack on its territory, it cannot control the exclusion of any specific group of persons—Soviet diplomats, foreign tourists, or citizens who do not pay taxes. Any people on the territory of the United States are part of the group in nuclear deterrence and cannot be excluded from it.

A third important aspect of collective goods is not whether the group providing the good can exclude others but whether some individual is able to choose whether or not to consume or be affected by the good. Although someone can choose whether to use a toll road (a jointly supplied good for the most part) or subscribe to cable TV, he or she cannot choose whether to be affected by pollution or an epidemic, or even the military draft or taxes (which are both somewhat imperfect means of providing collective goods).

The "Free Rider" Dilemma

These properties of collective goods have important implications for how individuals behave regarding groups. Winning a war may be seen as a good that has some collective properties. If the war is won, all citizens of the country involved will have won—some of the benefits, in terms of political freedom and ideological victory, will go to all if they go to one. It is also difficult to exclude citizens from this good of winning. (It is hard to say, "If you didn't participate, you can't be on the winning side.") Because of this, individuals are faced with the "free rider" decision—to help in achieving the good or to be a free rider on the efforts of others. This is exactly the logic that Yossarian used and the dilemma posed by that logic: If everyone wants to be a free rider, the collective good may never be achieved.

Let us briefly summarize our discussion. We noted that in the ideal case, where only private goods exist, an economic mechanism—the free market—can allocate goods within a group or society. This mechanism does not work well for collective goods. If individuals are strictly rational in the economic sense of desiring to maximize benefits and minimize costs, a collective good may never be provided, even if all members of a group desire that good. This dilemma arises from the clash between individual interests and benefits and group interests and benefits. If the good is a collective good (and thus jointly supplied), the group member will receive its benefits whether that member pays for it or not. The rational individual will not have to pay (incur costs) for a benefit that he or she will gain anyway if others pay. The rational individual thus will not pay and will wait for someone else to pay. In addition, one doesn't want to be the "sucker" or "patsy" and buy the good that others will enjoy while the sucker bears the cost. This is why Yossarian did not want to be one of those getting killed while others were "making money and having fun"—not when there were ten million other men in uniform.

One reason this dilemma is interesting is that it shows the extreme interdependence of group members involved with collective goods. If everyone takes a free ride, an important good may not be produced; for example, there can be no arms stability if everyone decides to cheat on arms control. If many decide to take a free ride, then some good will be only partially provided—for example, when some states refuse to pay dues to international organizations that for various reasons do not wish to throw nonpayers out of the organization. (This has happened with the Soviet Union and France in the United Nations.) If member states refuse to contribute to the military capabilities of their alliance, alliance security will be underprovided. If a river that flows through many countries requires cleaning up, it may never be cleaned if all the countries wait for the others to do it (so they might reap the benefits without paying). Because the condition of the river is jointly supplied and nonexcludable, anyone on the river will benefit from clean water (just as all will be harmed by polluted water due to the action of one or more countries). Here, free riding will either stop the good of clean water from being achieved, cause it to take much longer to achieve, or cause it to be only partially achieved.

The Tragedy of the Commons

We must also remember that in the contemporary world system, more and more objectives of states require group action *because of* interdependence—monetary interdependence, trade, alliances, or other aspects of security (such as nonproliferation of nuclear weapons). The desire to develop economically requires group action, such as aid or special trade policies. The desire to clean up international bodies of water and the air also require group action. Although a free rider state might appear to be following its own interests, in the long run it is acting against them because the good desired may never be achieved—for example, a clean river. Perhaps the best example of this is a variation of the free rider—what Garrett Hardin has called "the tragedy of the commons." Hardin describes a pasture, "the commons," which belongs to all the members of a group:

> The tragedy of the commons develops in this way. Picture a pasture open to all. It is to be expected that each herdsman will try to keep as many cattle as possible on the commons. Such an arrangement may work reasonably satisfactorily for centuries because tribal wars, poaching, and disease keep the numbers of both man and beast well below the carrying capacity of the land. Finally, however, comes the day of reckoning, that is, the day when the long-desired goal of social stability becomes a reality. At this point, the inherent logic of the commons remorselessly generates tragedy.
> As a rational being, each herdsman seeks to maximize his gain. Explicitly or implicitly, more or less consciously, he asks, "What is the utility to me of adding one more animal to my herd?" This utility has one negative and one positive component.
> 1. The positive component is a function of the increment of one animal. Since the herdsman receives all the proceeds from the sale of the additional animal, the positive utility is nearly +1.
> 2. The negative component is a function of the additional overgrazing created by one more animal. Since, however, the effects of overgrazing are shared by all the herdsmen, the negative utility for any particular decision-making herdsman is only a fraction of −1.
> Adding together the component partial utilities, the rational herdsman concludes that the only sensible course for him to pursue is to add another animal to his herd. And another; and another.... But this is the conclusion reached by each and every rational herdsman sharing a commons. Therein is the tragedy. Each man is locked into a system that com-

pels him to increase his herd without limit—in a world that is limited. Ruin is the destination toward which all men rush, each pursuing his own best interest in a society that believes in the freedom of the commons. Freedom in a commons brings ruin to all.[11]

By Hardin's definition, the commons is a jointly supplied and nonexcludable collective good. The tragedy of the commons is the other side of the free rider problem. When there are free riders, some collective good is not provided. In the tragedy of the commons, individuals follow the logic of rational self-interest—but the result is the destruction of a collective good that already exists. These types of goods are called *common pool resources*. There are many examples of such common pool resources, including all of the nonrenewable energy resources like oil, natural gas, and coal. All the world's resources are finite—they can be used up. This includes our air and our water. All of the limits-to-growth issues discussed in the next chapter are related to the tragedy of the commons. The world can and should be seen as a *global commons*. All states on it are similar to the individuals Hardin describes, who can through self-interest destroy a commons that already exists. This is another side to the metaphor of spaceship earth—a single, finite environment whose supplies can be consumed.

As we have seen earlier, development is a major issue between the rich and the poor. The powerful states must continue to industrialize and produce to stay powerful. Similarly, leaders in the less-developed countries must often put economic development and industrialization at the top of their list of objectives. Thus, most countries of the world desire resources—a desire that becomes greater, not smaller. These resources, however, have to come from the global commons. One of the major issues to be discussed in Chapter 19 is the consumption of finite resources (at exponential growth rates), which will eventually leave the resource cupboard bare. These processes are in full swing in the destruction of some fish stocks in the oceans, especially by Japan and the Soviet Union. In the 1940s the global fish catch was 20 million tons; in the 1970s it had risen to 70 million tons.[12] During this period, the world's fishing fleets quadrupled in size. But many species of fish have

---

11. Garrett Hardin, "The Tragedy of the Commons," *Science* 162 (1968), 1244. (Copyright © 1968 by the American Association for the Advancement of Science.) See also Garrett Hardin and John Baden (eds.), *Managing the Commons* (San Francisco: W. H. Freeman and Company, 1977).

12. Robert Keohane and Joseph Nye, *Power and Interdependence* (Boston: Little, Brown, 1977), p. 87.

become scarce due to overfishing, many parts of the ocean have become so polluted that fish can no longer exist, and fish and seafood are threatened by local pollution disasters (such as spills from oil tankers).

The fishing problem is a striking example of the tragedy-of-the-commons process at work. A look at the whaling industry shows what can happen to the sea, the atmosphere, and all overexploited resources. As two observers have noted,

> The results of lack of control over the international commons are apparent in the whaling industry. Since World War II, in spite of repeated warnings and accurate predictions of the biologists hired by the International Whaling Commission, the nations engaged in whaling have systematically hunted many of the largest species of whale until they are now on the verge of extinction. The recent history of the whaling industry might lead to the conclusion that the owners of the fleets have been incredibly stupid, since they seem willing to jeopardize the entire future of their industry for quick profits. The decisions that have led to wide-open hunting of whales are nevertheless rational to those who made them.... This is merely another example of how unfortunate long-run consequences of present behavior are ignored by profiteers who exploit the commons.[13]

Collective Goods and the Prisoners' Dilemma

Again, we have the long-term interest of the group (and the individual as well) in opposition to the short-term interests of individuals.[14] Why are problems such as the free rider and the tragedy of the commons so prevalent in the international arena? One answer is simply the nature of that arena: the Westphalian system of states, each with sovereignty and no higher authority to tell them what to do. In this anarchic system, lack of trust is built into the relations among the international actors. Lack of trust puts each individual actor in the dilemma of choosing between individual and collective welfare, creating the possibility of trusting others and then being taken advantage of by them. Looking carefully, we see just another version of the prisoners' dilemma, which was discussed in Chapter 13, as applied to deterrence and arms control.

---

13. Dennis Pirages and Paul Ehrlich, *Ark II* (San Francisco: W. H. Freeman and Company, 1974), pp. 237–238.

14. The following discussion is based on Harvey Starr, "Collective Goods Approaches to Alternative World Structures," Workshop in Political Theory and Policy Analysis, W78–3, Indiana University, 1978.

The prisoners' dilemma occurs when actors pursue individual gain and benefit over collective interest—just like the free rider and the tragedy of the commons. Without a basis for trust, an actor in a prisoners' dilemma pursues individual benefits so as not to be caught as the "sucker." In the prisoners' dilemma, the sucker is sent to jail for a long period of time, while the other prisoner serves a very short sentence. In an arms race, the sucker does not acquire more arms, while his opponent surges ahead.

One real-world example involves the situation in Europe immediately before World War I. Foreign policy leaders thought any country that had just a few days head start in mobilizing its armies would have a decisive advantage in a war. In this case the sucker would sit by and not mobilize troops, while the opponent mobilized. It was this fear that sent each country headlong into mobilization and ultimately war.[15] In a common-pool resource situation, the sucker similarly, stops hunting whales (in order to give them time to repopulate), but the Japanese or the Russians continue hunting at such a pace that the whales will be hunted into extinction anyway (while the sucker fails to receive any of the profits in the process).

We again have a complex interaction of different levels of analysis. Japan, for instance, is not a single-minded, monolithic actor. A process of bureaucratic politics goes on within Japan that makes it very difficult for the Japanese government to change its whaling policies. We have been talking about rational state behavior in the short term versus rational behavior in the long term and about individual interest versus a global interest. We must remember, however, that certain policies, such as killing whales, may be very rational in terms of domestic political games and the domestic political stakes involved. The perceptions of the issues may then differ from a global perspective. Although outsiders see these issues as middle-range economic objectives (as discussed in Chapter 8), some Japanese interests, such as the whaling companies, see them as core, or survival, issues. Japanese government officials must try to satisfy or compensate those interests. Such differing preceptions make difficult problems more difficult.

---

15. For an elaboration of this example and other examples of the prisoners' dilemma, see Glenn H. Snyder, " 'Prisoner's Dilemma' and 'Chicken' Models in International Politics," *International Studies Quarterly* 15 (1971), 66–103.

Strategies for Achieving Collective Goods

In international organizations, being a sucker might mean, for example, paying one's fair share for defense in an alliance such as NATO, while other allies take a free ride. Some observers suggest that the lack of a strong, centralized authority in the anarchic international system makes the provision of collective goods a very difficult task. Yet we have referred to the order in anarchy. There are some ways in which states in the current system have overcome the prisoners' dilemma pressures "to defect" and have cooperated with each other. There must be strategies to promote the international cooperation required to solve the problems posed by free riders and exploiters of the commons. Collective goods present situations where the strictly economic forces of the marketplace cannot bring about solutions and where *political and social* action must be taken either to achieve desired collective outcomes or to prevent the destruction of common pools. Some strategies for achieving collective goods include the following:[16]

1. An individual's preferences, or calculations of costs and benefits, can be changed, as pointed out in Chapter 6, through punishment or reward. One way to get individuals to cooperate is through *coercion*. Yossarian, for example, was in the army because it was against the law to refuse to be drafted. While he was in the army, the army could threaten imprisonment (even execution) if he refused to fight. Within states, tax systems are backed up by threats of punishment for nonpayment (the member of society who does not pay taxes but enjoys national defense, education, police protection, health benefits, and welfare services of the state is a free rider). When a union institutes a union shop, it forces all workers to join the union; this eliminates the free rider who does not join the union but enjoys most of the benefits obtained by the union from management.

This type of coercion is difficult in international relations. The power to tax is not readily given to IGOs because it is a threat to sovereignty. Sometimes individual states, such as the United States, try to use coercion to get allies to pay their share in an alliance like NATO by threatening to pull U.S. troops out of Europe. It has been argued that if

16. See Bruce M. Russett and John D. Sullivan, "Collective Goods and International Organization," *International Organization* 25 (1971), 845–865.

a group is small, then a free-riding member is more clearly seen and identified; in this case "social pressure" can be applied to encourage the member's cooperation. There may be a loss in prestige of a government and its leaders if other governments feel that that government is not pulling its weight or cooperating. NATO thus has an annual review to identify and spotlight slackers.

2. Positive strategies based on rewards of some kind seem to be more useful in the international sphere. Members of a group will be more likely to act to obtain a collective good if they can receive private goods as side payments.[17] States may join alliances and provide a share of the defense burden if they receive new and sophisticated weapons in return. States might refrain from exploiting a common-pool resource if offered other goods, profits, or a technology that can substitute for the resource. Garrett Hardin argues that the commons brings about irresponsible behavior in those who use it. People have a right to the commons but rarely exercise responsibility in its use because it is large and impersonal—it belongs to everyone.[18]

One way to foster responsibility is to convert parts of the commons into enclosed areas for which individual members are responsible. They must treat these enclosures with care, or else they will destroy their own property. It may be possible to save a common-pool resource by converting at least part of it into private goods by assigning property rights. For example, one outcome of the UN Law of the Sea Conference was the general acceptance of 200-mile-limit economic zones— the extension to 200 miles of coastal jurisdiction for economic purposes. The aim was to evade the collective or prisoners' dilemma by firmly assigning responsibility. In this way, a large part of the seabed has been put under regulation and restriction.

3. In a similar manner, sometimes the collective good is provided as a by-product of policies aimed at private goods. For example, a state might create a large army for internal control or solely for its individual deterrence or defense. If it then joins an alliance, the alliance is provided with some forces that contribute to the collective good of a strong deterrent, even though that was not the first state's intention.

---

17. See, for example, Philip Burgess and James A. Robinson, "Alliances and the Theory of Collective Action: A Simulation of Coalition Processes," *Midwest Journal of Political Science* 13 (1969), 194–218.

18. Garrett Hardin, "An Operational Analysis of 'Responsibility'," in Garrett Hardin and John Baden (eds.), *Managing the Commons* (San Francisco: W. H. Freeman and Company, 1977), pp. 66–75.

4. Another noncoercive strategy is simply an educational approach to increase individual perceptions of self-interest to be gained from group and long-term interests. This task is undertaken mostly by academics interested in "world order studies" or "peace research"; including the World Order Models Project (WOMP) or the Club of Rome. (The latter is a particularly good example. The Club of Rome is a group of academics, scientists, and IGO personnel who were first gathered together in 1968 by the Italian industrialist Aurelio Peccei. The purpose of this group has been to study and educate the world on the nature and consequences of global interdependences.)

International organizations, including many UN agencies, have also worked at this educational task. For example, Malta's representative to the General Assembly, Arvid Pardo, proposed in 1967 that the General Assembly deal with ways to extract the resources of the seabed in the interests of humanity as a whole. This educational strategy is also related to the process of integration that consists of shifting loyalties to new and larger political units with broader interests. But this is a slow process, and a number of our collective goods problems require immediate attention and quick action.

5. A collective good can be provided if one member of the group desires that good so much that it is willing to pay the whole cost (or most of it) by itself and doesn't care that other group members also receive the good. In this case, one member offers to be the sucker. Besides valuing the good highly, this single member is usually richer in resources or wealthier than other members. (Thus, it can provide most of the collective good at much less sacrifice than could another member.) Studies of UN budget assessments and burden sharing in alliances such as NATO and the Warsaw Pact show that the larger members will pay proportionately more to get the things they want, even if others ride free.[19] The evidence for this large-member behavior includes the U.S. desire to provide deterrence for itself and its NATO allies, possibly the American role in stabilizing international trade, and even some tragedy-of-the-commons situations. For example, the maintenance of the upper atmosphere has collective goods properties. A

---

19. See, for example, Mancur Olson and Richard Zeckhauser, "An Economic Theory of Alliances," *Review of Economics and Statistics* 46 (1966), 266–279; Bruce Russett, *What Price Vigilance? The Burdens of National Defense* (New Haven, Conn.: Yale University Press, 1970), chap. 4; Harvey Starr, "A Collective Goods Analysis of the Warsaw Pact after Czechoslovakia," *International Organization* 28 (1974), 521–532.

very large (or what we call a *hegemonic*) state can be very effective in environmental control, both because it is big and rich and can therefore afford to bear the costs and because it can coerce some transnational actors to provide benefits to other countries.

One example of this kind of behavior is the American government decision to ban fluorocarbon propellants in spray cans sold in the American market. That immediately set in motion a 50 percent reduction in the usage of such propellants. Moreover, some MNCs producing for the world market eliminated the propellants from their production, chiefly because it was cheaper not to use fluorocarbons at all than to make one product for sale in the United States and another for sale in countries with less rigorous restrictions. Another example is international airline safety regulations. The American Federal Aviation Administration requires that all aircraft landing in the United States have elaborate safety equipment. Thus, foreign airlines contemplating U.S. flights must install the equipment no matter where their airplanes customarily land. Other countries thus get the free rider's safety benefits without having to make their own safety regulations. These are the kinds of circumstances where it can be very helpful to have a dominant, hegemonic power in the system.

6. Collective goods also make us think about various forms of cooperation, the involvement of international organizations, and the future form of such organizations. One other strategy for achieving collective goods is to create localized or regional organizations from a number of small groups of states and then creating some sort of federal structure to tie together and coordinate these groups. This approach involves alternative world order structures and using IGOs to address collective goods problems.

These general strategies for coping with and resolving collective goods issues involve both formal and informal mechanisms. These mechanisms help states coordinate their activities, collaborate in a positive way, and help to manage and resolve conflict. Possible solutions to collective goods problems include appeals to self-limitation and mechanisms that facilitate both self-restraint and positive cooperation.

We shall take a brief look at formal mechanisms such as international law and IGOs, paying particular attention to the United Nations and the IGOs of the UN system. Following that review, we shall look at how such formal activities combine with informal norms and practices to create "regimes" concerned with order in the world system.

INTERNATIONAL COOPERATION: INTERNATIONAL LAW AND INTERNATIONAL ORGANIZATIONS

To begin solving collective goods problems (or other problems affecting more than one state), states need to cooperate and interact in a smooth, regularized manner. More and more of the transnational issues of the contemporary world—economic and ecological—require action by more than one state. States need each other's aid to solve common problems in an era of interdependence. Much of the order within the formal state of anarchy of the international system derives from these needs. The paradox, of course, is that although states often cooperate on the basis of self-interest, the heart of the collective goods issue is the need to see the connection between individual state interests and the longer-term collective interests of the group. *Order* itself can be thought of as a desired state of affairs with collective goods characteristics. If order is thought of as patterned and predictable sets of interactions that benefit international actors, then once there is order in the system, all the actors benefit; an increase in actors does not detract from that order. States seeking short-term, self-interested advantage can destroy that order not only for themselves but for all.

In earlier chapters (especially Chapter 7), we discussed how states carry on relations with one another. One way in which states attempt to interact in a smooth, regularized manner is through diplomacy. In a previous discussion, we pointed out the limitations of diplomacy as a means of cooperative interaction, for example, when it is used as propaganda or to provide an opponent with false information. Clearly, traditional, bilateral diplomacy must be augmented by other forms and forums of diplomacy. Mechanisms are needed to maintain and increase regular, smooth interactions of states. How can states and other actors collaborate in a noncentralized, anarchic international system to deal effectively with issues involving common and complementary interests?

We must begin by noting that most states usually *do* conform to the rules of international law. In that respect, international law acts in the same way as domestic law—as a set of rules that constrain behavior. However, domestic law is a set of rules typically *legislated* by a *legitimate, centralized* political authority that can *enforce* the law. As we have noted, no legitimate central authority with both legislative and enforcement power exists in the international setting. However, institutions and practices do exist that *make, interpret,* and *execute* rules. One observer notes that, compared with domestic law, international law is "relatively decentralized." Another scholar says simply, "International law should be regarded as true but imperfect law."[20]

Despite the fact that states pay great attention to international law (for example, the legal adviser's staff at the State Department reviews most of the department's work) and that international law is reflected in the constrained behavior of states, many claim that international law cannot be law because there is no authority to enforce sanctions. If the fear of enforcement by armed agents of a central authority is not the cause of states conforming to rules, what is?

As noted many times in these pages, nothing is distributed evenly in the international system. States need all sorts of things possessed by other states and international actors (from petroleum to technology to military equipment to working-age people). The great bulk of world politics and transnational interaction consists of the exchange of goods, services, people, and information. All states benefit from this regular and routine flow of people (including diplomats), goods, and information. Thus, states see it in their own self-interest to constrain their behavior according to the rules of international law, most of which eases and routinizes such interaction. Foreign policy behavior that violates international norms is less probable because of the costs entailed. These costs include fear of chaos and fear of reprisal. In addition, rewards for observing international law are a desire for a good reputation and similar observance by others in return.

Fear of Chaos and Reprisal

States benefit from regular and predictable interactions, especially diplomatic and economic ones. If each state violated international law whenever it wanted, order would soon yield to chaos. Clearly, when the stakes are high and when states are in very conflictual situations, then treaties, agreements, UN resolutions, and all the rest are disregarded. But most of the time such conditions do not prevail. Like Yossarian, why should any single state obey the rules of the game if all the other actors are breaking them? Order seems to be one collective good that states do see in their interest to provide. The cost of chaos, a true

20. See Hedley Bull, *The Anarchical Society* (New York: Columbia University Press, 1977); see also Gerhard von Glahn, *Law Among Nations*, 4th ed. (New York: Macmillan, 1981), p. 4.

"anything goes" system, all the time on all issues would be costly for all states.

One traditional area of international law, for example, concerns the rules of immunity extended to diplomatic personnel. These rules were established so diplomats can help ease and conduct intergovernmental communication without interference. Without them, diplomacy among states would be difficult, if not impossible. The processes of bargaining and negotiation would soon give way either to more violent forms of interaction or to no interaction at all. A good deal of the very strong reaction against the Iranian government's involvement in taking American diplomats hostage in 1979 derived from this fear. If all governments condoned such behavior, based on justifications such as Iranians' grievances against the deposed Shah, then international diplomacy would become impossible.

Related to fear of chaos is the fear of reprisal. By breaking some rule, such as taking hostages or using chemical warfare (as the Soviets were accused of doing in Afghanistan in 1980), a state may be inviting a similar reaction from other states. Although there might be some immediate advantage to such an act—for example, ignoring a UN resolution or a decision by the International Court of Justice—it is often outweighed by the costs imposed by other states ignoring international law. States restrain themselves because they do not want to set a precedent for certain types of behavior. It was left to an unusual and very obstreperous government leader—Ayatollah Khomeini—to set the precedent of supporting actions against diplomats. Such behavior was not on the menu of states even in the most hostile of circumstances. For example, during the world wars and at the height of the Cold War, governments still respected the rights of diplomats.

Finally, the fear of reprisal includes the fear that others will punish a law breaker in some way, not necessarily by similar actions. During the twentieth century, military aggression has been met by economic sanctions, such as those imposed on the Soviet Union by the Carter administration after the Soviet invasion of Afghanistan. Another type of action was the American decision to boycott the 1980 Olympics held in Moscow.

The other side of the international law coin includes a state's desire to appear as a law-abiding citizen in the international community—to be a state that others can depend upon and trust. This sort of reputation enhances a state's influence in many ways. One of these might be called the *golden rule condition:* If a state behaves correctly, then it may expect to receive good behavior from others. Again, this is a collective goods or prisoners' dilemma situation. States do give in to the temptation to break international law during crises or extreme situations. But most states choose to benefit from the good behavior of others.

Sources and Functions of International Law

Scholars of international law cite Article 38 of the Statute of the International Court of Justice in identifying three major sources of international law. These are: (1) international conventions or treaties, (2) custom, and (3) the general principles of law recognized by civilized nations. Two secondary sources are the judicial decisions of international courts and the writings of "qualified publicists," or legal scholars.

The rules resulting primarily from treaties and custom, serve a number of functions in helping states create and preserve order. One basic function of international law is to act as a means or language of communication; a "system of quasi-authoritative communications" as William Coplin says.[21] This communication is needed to educate states and their leaders, to socialize them in the political culture of the international system. In this way, international law also serves management and coordination functions. Finally, international law draws upon these two functions in its better-known conflict-related functions. International law has been used to regulate conflict (including the use of force), to help promote conflict resolution, and to restrain behavior considered undesirable.

These international legal functions apply to all matters involving international politics. International law deals with questions of territory and nationality—what territory and people belong to what state, what states are allowed to do on their own territory and on the territory of others, and what states can do with their own people and to aliens (nationals of other countries). International law specifies which actors are "legal persons" having the capacity to enter legal relations. This is one of the areas in which the state-centric bias of international law is most clearly demonstrated.

Recent activity in regard to human rights represent an expansion of the domain of international law; individuals are considered legal entities separate from their state of national origin. International law also

---

21. See William H. Coplin, *The Functions of International Law* (Chicago: Rand McNally, 1966).

covers the broad range of peaceful interactions between states—including treaties (law on how to make law), diplomacy (law on how to conduct foreign relations), and the creation and work of IGOs. All areas of commerce and economic interaction are also affected by treaties, IGOs, and their activities. As noted, international law is also concerned with the broad issues of war, from the questions of aggression and the legality of war to questions of intervention, terrorism, the conduct of war, the legality of certain weapons, and arms control.

International Law and International Organizations

One major source of international law is the growing number of IGOs in the contemporary system. The charters of these organizations—their rules, agreements, resolutions, and treaties—constitute many of the daily bylaws of international interaction. Other IGOs, such as the UN, have helped to codify, collect, and apply international law derived not only from IGOs but from custom, international courts, or the writings of European jurists since the sixteenth century (such as Hugo Grotius).

IGOs have been useful in applying international law, in helping to coordinate states' compliance, in organizing states around their common interests, and in pointing out the benefits of cooperation. (See Chapter 3 for the various types of IGOs.) Large regional organizations such as the European Community have worked extensively to promote economic cooperation. Others, such as the Organization of American States (OAS) and the Organization for African Unity (OAU), have worked to control and manage conflict in their regions. In general, IGOs provide a place for states to communicate. An IGO is useful as a forum where states can discuss various issues and interact with each other diplomatically at a permanent site. It also helps cooperation by providing a permanent mechanism. States expect the IGO to help in certain problem areas, for example, the World Health Organization in disease control, UNESCO in education, or the United Nations, the OAS, and the OAU in settling conflicts. In addition to being a forum, a permanent mechanism, or an intermediary for problem solving, an IGO often provides a great deal of information on specific problem areas and on its member states. UN publications, for instance, provide voluminous data on a wide variety of economic, demographic, social, cultural, and political matters. Finally, we must note that IGOs also perform regulative and distributive functions. IGOs make and administer rules on how states should behave in certain areas, as does the

International Monetary Fund in monetary policy. IGOs also distribute things, such as loans from the World Bank or court decisions from the International Court of Justice.

It must also be pointed out that IGOs are used as *instruments* for the foreign policy interests of the individual states that comprise them. States use international law and IGOs to legitimize or justify their own behavior (e.g., the use of the OAS to justify U.S. intervention in the Dominican Republic in 1965 or the Soviet use of the Warsaw Pact to justify its 1968 invasion of Czechoslovakia). States use international law and IGOs as ways to pursue diplomacy and to increase their individual influence as well. It should be clear that international law, IGOs, and the United Nations are only as successful as the member states want them to be. They are only as successful as they are perceived to be. As political scientist Stanley Hoffmann has observed, international law is a mirror that "faithfully and cruelly" reflects the essence and logic of international politics. Our view here is positivist; that is, international law is whatever states think it is, not necessarily what it ought to be. Remember that international law is one of the main mechanisms by which the state attained its central place as an international actor. International law legalized the very existence of states. In essence, it created the rules and conditions that permit the individual state, as well as the international system, to survive.

Thus, whatever judgments we make about international law, IGOs, or the United Nations must be tempered by the fact that each reflects the contemporary international system. The United Nations, besides being a major source of international law and the most extensive international organization system in the contemporary world, is also one of the most faithful of the "mirrors" that reflects the nature of international politics.

The United Nations System

In the aftermath of World War II, the United Nations reflected the desire of the victorious states to maintain world peace and to attack the conditions that appeared to foster war: colonialism, poverty, inequality, and ignorance. The charter of the United Nations, drawn up and signed in San Francisco in 1945, was largely the product of American, British, and Soviet negotiations. Much of this bargaining was done at the Dumbarton Oaks Conference, held in Washington, D.C., in 1944.

The founders of the United Nations recognized that the organization was to be comprised of sovereign states and did not see the United Nations as a device to take away or undercut their sovereignty (although some later observers have felt that this should be the UN role). On the other hand, since the international system was comprised of sovereign states and lacked a central authority, one strategy for promoting international cooperation was the creation of a universal IGO. As we saw earlier in this chapter, mechanisms to coordinate behavior and promote cooperation became even more crucial as international interdependences multiplied and as collective goods issues became prominent. Perhaps one reason for the remarkable survival of the United Nations for forty years has been its utility in an era that saw the development of "global ecopolitics." This is Dennis Pirages's term for an era when environmental, economic, and ethical issues have become central in a system with many new international actors and a more sensitive and vulnerable set of international interdependences.[22]

The UN structure reflects the system within which it was created. The Security Council is the primary organ of action, and as such it reflects the unequal distribution of power in the system. The existence of five permanent members—the United States, Britain, France, the Soviet Union, and China—all of whom have vetoes over the actions of the Security Council, gives the major powers control over the issues of political and military security in the United Nations. Each major power can protect its interests. In this way, the charter sought to save the United Nations from a major weakness of its predecessor, the League of Nations: all during the League's existence, at least one of the great powers was a nonmember.

The Security Council reflects the special role that the great powers must play in the world body. The veto permits each power to protect its interests by remaining in the organization. The heavy use of the Soviet veto during the early years of the United Nations reflected American dominance of the General Assembly. Figure 18.3 shows that in 1946 the Americas and Western Europe dominated UN membership with over 60 percent of the membership. Although the General Assembly had been set up as a "world parliament" on the basis of one-state, one-vote "sovereign equality" (Article 2 of the charter), it, too, was dominated by the great powers in the early days of the United Nations. Not only did Cold War or East-West issues dominate the agenda, but

---

22. See Dennis Pirages, *Global Ecopolitics* (North Scituate, Mass.: Duxbury Press, 1978), chap. 1.

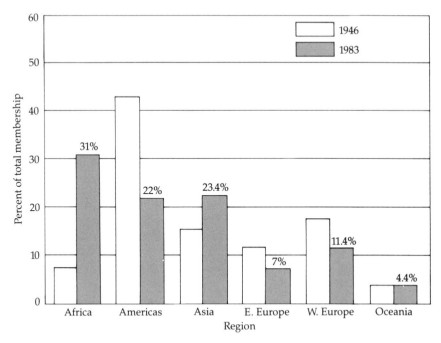

Figure 18.3
UN membership by region, 1946 and 1983. [*Source:* 1946 data from Harold K. Jacobson, *Networks of Interdependence* (New York: Knopf, 1979), pp. 46, 48. © 1979 by Alfred A. Knopf, Inc.]

the United States could and did dominate voting in the General Assembly. For a long period, many small and non-Western countries were dissatisfied with the UN system because of this great-power dominance. (The United Nations was and continues to be financially dependent on the larger states as well, particularly the United States.)

Today the group most dissatisfied with the United Nations is the industrialized "North." The United Nations, by welcoming all "peace loving" states, has grown through the addition of non-Western states created by the process of decolonization. Figure 18.3 shows the dramatic change in African and Asian membership from 1946 to 1983. With this change, which began in earnest in 1960, came a shift in emphasis from East-West to North-South issues of the sort reflected in Chapters 16 and 17. Economic issues, and particularly issues of equity, have come to dominate many areas of the United Nations. The UN membership has powerfully affected the objectives, processes, and success of the organization. The anticolonial stance of the newer members was often joined by the anti-Western Communist states. The United States found itself unable to command a majority in the General Assembly after 1970. The best indicator of this was the admission of the People's Republic of China in 1971 and the rejection of what had been America's "two-China" policy. (Thus, Nationalist China—Taiwan—was expelled from the organization.)

The dominance of the General Assembly and other UN agencies such as UNESCO (UN Educational, Scientific, and Cultural Organization) by the newer non-Western states has made UN dealings with problems of the commons even more difficult, as the industrialized countries become more dissatisfied. The United Nations itself lacks the formal power to solve these problems; it has found itself losing the support of many of the larger, richer countries that have the capabilities to help solve such problems. Robert Rothstein summarizes the criticism that has recently been directed against the United Nations:

> Declining confidence in the UN system is widespread among the industrial countries. A persuasive indictment of what the United Nations has become is well within reach, and it cites as evidence such factors as: the increasing dominance of a Third World Coalition that is occasionally irresponsible and narrowly self-interested; the politicization of even apparently technical issues (that is, differently politicized than when the industrial countries were in effective control of process and outcome); resolutions that patch together everyone's demands, that are masterpieces in the phraseology of ambiguity, and that result in uncertainty about what, if anything, has been decided; the absence of agreed standards by which to evaluate performance; substantial doubts about the competence, the impartiality, the size, and the remuneration of professional staff appointed on increasingly nationalistic grounds; a rigid bureaucratic ethos inevitably accompanied by excessive centralization and documentation; a confusion of responsibility between different institutions and an attempt to legislate or at least declaim on issues that are too complex to be resolved in grand confrontations or open debate; and a pervasive sense that the UN drains increasing amounts of scarce resources from the industrial countries but returns insufficient benefits—to either rich or poor.[23]

Add to these North-South issues the perception of the Reagan administration that Third World countries are anti-American and pro-Soviet, and you can understand why the United States gave its one-year notice for leaving UNESCO in late 1983.

---

23. Robert Rothstein, *Global Bargaining: UNCTAD and the Quest for a New International Order* (Princeton, N.J.: Princeton University Press, 1979), p. 169.

The changing nature of the United Nations has been a function of the nature of its new members. However, many of the newer UN members are independent in part because of the work of the Trusteeship Council, which was established to bring an end to colonialism and to guide the former colonial areas to independence in as peaceful a manner as possible. Most observers agree that the Trusteeship Council has fulfilled its purpose well. The Economic and Social Council is assigned the task of dealing with international economic, social, educational, and health matters. It is supposed to improve the world's living standards by attacking poverty, ignorance, and inequality as causes of war. Many health matters have been successfully dealt with, such as the World Health Organization's program that eradicated smallpox. Many educational and cultural dissemination programs have also had positive results.

The Settlement of Disputes in the United Nations

The various organs of the United Nations, in accordance with the UN Charter, play many roles in promoting international coordination, cooperation, and the settlement of disputes. As noted above, the United Nations acts as a forum for diplomacy and facilitates communication among states. A number of activities directly related to the settlement of disputes are listed in Article 33 of the charter. One not specifically listed is "good offices," where a third party provides a place for negotiations or helps to ease the communication needed for negotiations. This mechanism is built into the structure of the United Nations. Other mechanisms noted are negotiations, inquiry (where a neutral investigating body provides information relevant to the dispute), mediation (where a third party becomes an active participant in negotiations, helping the states in conflict to find acceptable terms), conciliation (where the third party is an IGO, commission, or other body asked to act as a mediator), and arbitration (where the parties involved agree beforehand to be bound by the decision of the group acting as an arbitrator). The last mechanism mentioned in Article 33 is adjudication, or judicial settlement, by which a dispute is brought before an international court.

The International Court of Justice (ICJ) is the judicial organ of the United Nations; it has attempted to settle international disputes through the development of an international legal system. Although the record is quite mixed, the ICJ has proven useful in a number of cases. Between 1947 and 1977, the ICJ issued judgments on twenty-six cases. The issues ranged from fisheries to frontier disputes to nuclear testing. There were also twelve cases that were removed from the ICJ by the parties. Some of these cases were settled out of court. The rest were removed because one party refused to accept the ICJ's jurisdiction in the dispute. Indeed, distrust of the ICJ and unwillingness to let an outside party determine a state's interests are the main reasons why many issues are not brought before the ICJ.[24]

The UN system has also had mixed success in the area of conflict management. Here the Security Council, General Assembly, and the secretary general have all been involved. Many articles of the UN Charter relate to the management of disputes—how they are to be referred to the Security Council or the General Assembly and how the United Nations can be used to help states negotiate instead of fight. Although a number of charter articles (e.g., 43, 45, 46, 47, 48) were directed toward establishing a military force to be used by the Security Council to "enforce peace" (Articles 39–42), the United Nations was involved in peace enforcement only during the Korean War. This was the only occasion when the United Nations assigned guilt for aggression and acted as a collective security body to oppose an aggressor with force. All other UN activities concerning disputes have been called peacekeeping and have involved conflict management or settlement. These activities do not require assigning guilt. They simply recognize that a violent conflict or a "threat to peace" is at hand and assert that the United Nations should act to stop fighting already under way, separate the warring parties, and create conditions for the states to negotiate instead of fight.

Although UN peace-keeping activities have had relatively little success with the two superpowers and Cold War issues, they have been more successful in dealing with minor and medium powers. One study indicates that in 65 conflicts among "smallest," "small," "middle," and "large" powers, (but not "superpowers"), the United Nations had at least "some success" in over half. A follow-up study argues that there has been a slow decay in the management of international conflicts by the United Nations and regional IGOs from 1945 to 1981. Although referrals of conflicts to the United Nations fell to a low point in the mid-1970s, such referrals rose dramatically by 1980–81. However, UN success dropped to its lowest point by 1980–81 to about 10 percent of

---

24. For a fuller treatment of the ICJ, see A. LeRoy Bennett, *International Organizations,* 2nd ed. (Englewood Cliffs, N.J.: Prentice-Hall, 1980), chap. 8.

the cases. A summary of the 123 disputes covered in this follow-up study indicates that disputes arising from decolonization are the most manageable, and Cold War disputes the least. The most intense disputes are also the likeliest to be managed; low-intensity disputes are also influenced, but disputes in the middle range of intensity are most difficult to resolve. Superpower disputes are not successfully managed, but neither are those among the smaller, weaker members. Middle-power disputes are the most successfully managed.[25]

In addition to diplomatic activity of various kinds, the United Nations has dispatched peace-keeping forces to a number of trouble spots to separate warring parties and prevent further outbreaks of violence. These forces have ranged from about 6,000 troops in the Middle East (UNEF) and Cyprus (UNFICYP), to the 20,000 troops sent to the Congo in 1960. There were twelve UN peace-keeping operations before 1970, in areas from the Middle East to Indonesia, to Yemen, to Cyprus. Since then, three others have included UNEF–II, a force dispatched to the Middle East in 1973, to the Golan Heights in 1974, and to Lebanon in 1978.[26]

The United Nations has also attempted to deal with serious environmental, economic, and political problems, which may ultimately be the most crucial the world has faced. The United Nations has held special conferences in all these areas to bring states together to air their differences, to propose various policies, and to try working out agreements. These conferences include the Stockholm Conference on the Human Environment in 1972, the World Food Conference held in Rome in 1974, the Bucharest Conference on Population in 1974, and a series of conferences on the Law of the Sea beginning in 1958. A series of UNCTAD (UN conferences on trade and development) have dealt with problems of trade, development, and the distribution of the world's wealth.

These UN conferences have addressed issues resulting from the interdependence of the world system and world politics. Many issues are complicated by collective goods issues, especially the tragedy-of-the-commons problem. The tragedy of the commons is, in turn, related to the consumption of the world's resources and questions of limits to

---

25. See Ernst B. Haas, Robert L. Butterworth, and Joseph Nye, *Conflict Management by International Organizations* (Morristown, N.J.: General Learning Press, 1972), p. 23; Ernst Haas, "Regime Decay: Conflict Management and International Organizations, 1945–81," *International Organization* 37 (1983), 189–256.

26. See A. LeRoy Bennett, *International Organizations*, 2nd ed. (Englewood Cliffs, N.J.: Prentice-Hall, 1980), p. 157, chap. 7.

growth that will be addressed in the next chapter. As you can see, these issues are transnational in nature, especially given the focus on nonmilitary aspects of security and the roles played by important nonstate actors.

Now that we have introduced a number of economic, ecological, and political issues that are complicated by global interdependence and collective goods, we can turn to a mechanism that includes international law, IGOs, and other nonstate actors. This mechanism, the regime, is used in the quest for coordination, collaboration, and order.

REGIMES AND INTERNATIONAL ORDER

If states and other international actors are to cooperate and deal with the prisoners' dilemma posed by collective goods, how should they organize themselves? We reviewed a number of strategies for achieving collective goods. One method is to "bind the members of the international community to rules of conduct, to which they agree, and which will restrain each member from free riding, and allocate burdens equitably, as a matter of international legal commitment."[27]

International law works in this way, but the rules of conduct that are relevant go beyond those of international law. Scholars have used the idea of *regime* to identify the complete *set* of rules that relate to any specific area of international relations. This concept helps us understand the full array of constraints imposed by international society. Keohane and Nye define a regime as a "network of rules, norms and procedures that regularize behavior and control its effects" and as "sets of governing arrangements."[28] The regularization of behavior means the creation of patterns—patterns of expectations, patterns of procedures, and patterns of compliance to norms and rules.[29] In other words, order.

---

27. See Charles P. Kindleberger, "Dominance and Leadership in the International Economy," *International Studies Quarterly* 25 (1981), 252.

28. Robert Keohane and Joseph Nye, *Power and Interdependence* (Boston: Little, Brown, 1977), p. 19.

29. Expectations are a key element to Stephen Krasner's definition of *regime*. His definition is used as a starting point for the articles in Stephen Krasner, ed., *International Regimes* (Ithaca, N.J.: Cornell University Press, 1983), perhaps the best single treatment of regimes. See especially his article "Structural Causes and Regime Consequences: Regimes as Intervening Variables," (pp. 1–21).

Where do these common understandings come from? The networks consist of national rules (the domestic laws of states), international rules (international law, the charters of IGOs, and the regulations, resolutions, and practices of IGOs), and private rules (the practices of MNCs and other NGOs, the charters of MNCs, and other formal regulations). Thus, we have sets of governing arrangements relating to various issue areas in international relations. Issue areas may be functional and thus be very wide or very narrow, paralleling our earlier discussion of functional IGOs. Regimes may also be geographic, covering the problems that arise within a specific area, such as Antarctica. Just as with IGOs, some regimes have only a few members, such as that overseeing North Pacific fisheries, while some are very large, such as the UN conflict management regime. As Oran Young notes, "We live in a world of international regimes." Their concerns range from monetary issues, to trade issues, to the management of natural resources, to the control of armaments, to the management of power, to the management of outer space and the seabed.[30]

If such issue areas are characterized by interdependence (that is, affected actors are sensitive and vulnerable to each other), sets of governing arrangements will help those actors to collaborate and coordinate their actions. One observer has defined collaboration as agreements designed to avoid the choice of temptation in the prisoners' dilemma (T) and to help the actors choose the second-best strategy, the rewards from mutual cooperation (R). Coordination is defined as the process of developing policy to *avoid* some outcome, such as the rules of the International Civil Aviation Organization, which are designed to prevent air accidents.[31]

We can summarize a large literature on regimes with these observations by Robert Keohane:

> A major function of international regimes is to facilitate the making of specific agreements on matters of substantive significance within the issue-area covered by the regime. International regimes help make governments' expectations consistent with one another. Regimes are developed in part because actors in world politics believe that with such

---

30. See Oran Young, "International Regimes: Problems of Concept Formation," *World Politics* 32 (1980), 331–356.

31. For a fuller treatment, see Arthur A. Stein, "Coordination and Collaboration: Regimes in an Anarchic World," in Krasner, op. cit., 115–140.

arrangements they will be able to make mutually beneficial agreements that would otherwise be difficult or impossible to attain. In other words, regimes are valuable to governments where, in their absence, certain mutually beneficial agreements would be impossible to consummate. In such situations, *ad hoc* joint action would be inferior to results of negotiation within a regime context.[32]

Some of the most extensive analysis of regimes has focused on the post–World War II economic relations of the Western industrialized countries. Returning to our discussion of the relations among the OECD countries presented in Chapter 15, we shall look at some of the economic issues involving these states from the perspective of interdependence, collective goods, and regimes.

REGIMES AND ECONOMIC INTERDEPENDENCE IN THE POSTWAR WORLD

In the post–World War II system, the victorious industrialized countries consciously sought to create an international economic order (or regime) that would tie the states of the world together in order to promote economic growth and peace. The 1920s and 1930s were periods when economic isolationism, protectionism, and conflict helped lead the world into war. After World War II, sets of arrangements were constructed to encourage the coordination, management, and growth of economic interdependences in areas such as international monetary policy and trade. But as we have noted, interdependence involves vulnerability and sensitivity—constraints on a state's behavior and welfare. In the late 1960s and 1970s, when the spectacular economic growth of the postwar era slowed for a number of reasons, economic interdependence began to be increasingly costly as well as beneficial for some of the industrialized states. The story of the 1970s (as it will also be in the 1980s and 1990s) was that of trying to build new arrangements and institutions to solve the problems posed by economic interdependence and to manage the conflict generated by it in a peaceful manner.

---

32. See Robert Keohane, "The Demand for International Regimes," in Stephen Krasner (ed.), *International Regimes* (Ithaca, N.Y.: Cornell University Press, 1983), p. 150.

Hegemony and Regimes

At the end of World War II, the Western powers were agreed in their basic views of the international economy. The cornerstone of their vision was a liberal system, one without the economic barriers that had been set up in the 1930s. This was to be a relatively unhampered economic system based on capitalism, the free market, and minimal barriers to trade. To make the system work, the states had to cooperate. Establishing this system was also seen as a major step toward creating peace and order in the world, particularly within the group of OECD states. Free trade, free movement of capital, and stable monetary relations all depended on an orderly world. Thus, there was also an interdependence between military and economic factors. The area had to be militarily secure from outside threats as well as internally peaceful. The same state that could provide military order—the United States—was also the only state economically strong enough to provide order to the economic system. The United States took the lead in providing and furthering mechanisms for adjusting the balance of payments, establishing a stable reserve standard for free world currencies, and opening access to world trade markets. In this international system based on U.S. military and economic predominance, the United States followed a policy of leadership or, as some observers describe it, *hegemony*. In such a system "one state is able and willing to determine and maintain the essential rules by which relations among states are governed. The hegemonical state not only can abrogate existing rules or prevent the adoption of rules it opposes but can also play the dominant role in constructing new rules."[33] Under U.S. leadership, the major economic features of the postwar period were "rapidly expanding and generally non-discriminatory trade, large-scale and rapid movements of funds from one center to another under fixed exchange rates, and the rapid growth of huge multinational enterprises."[34]

A number of scholars have argued that hegemony is a useful, if not necessary, mechanism for helping a group to achieve collective goods.

---

33. C. Fred Bergsten, Robert Keohane, and Joseph Nye, "International Economics and International Politics: A Framework for Analysis," *International Organization* 29 (1975), no. 1, p. 14. Another good discussion of international trade and finance systems from this perspective is by the economist Charles P. Kindleberger, *International Economics*, 6th ed. (Homewood, Ill.: Irwin, 1978). Our thinking on this issue was sharpened by discussions with Douglas R. Nelson of the University of North Carolina at Chapel Hill.

34. Robert Keohane and Joseph Nye, *Power and Interdependence* (Boston: Little, Brown, 1977), p. 19.

This was the principle discussed earlier in this chapter in the fifth strategy for achieving collective goods. Mancur Olson has said that a large group member can create what he calls a "privileged" group, where this large member provides the collective good for the whole group. Similarly, Charles Kindleberger argues that a stable world economy needs a "stabilizer." Other scholars suggest that a group needs an "entrepreneur" as a leader to help the group achieve the collective goods it desires. In sum, these views argue that whether or not a collective good is supplied, the effectiveness and the stability of the group are affected by the presence or absence of a hegemon. This complements the view that much regime change is related to the appearance or disappearance of a hegemon.[35] The real problem, as pointed out by Kindleberger, is distinguishing between dominance and leadership.

A related perspective on leadership or hegemony was provided by Karl Deutsch. Deutsch suggested that one helpful condition for a security community is a strong "core area" with "the capacity to act—a function of size, power, economic strength, and administrative efficiencies." It is doubtful that the existence of a large core area is essential to the kind of security community that exists among OECD countries, which have an even stabler condition of peace among themselves now, when the United States is much less predominant than just after World War II. Nevertheless, earlier American predominance may have been very important in setting in motion the economic prosperity and interdependence that now underlie that peace. In this sense there is some virtue in having one big power in the international system: If it chooses, it not only can bully others, but it can also make short-term sacrifices that will in the long run benefit all members, not just itself.[36]

Simply put, interdependence has grown and outpaced the ability of states to manage it, especially with the decline of the United States as the protector. Individual states are sensitive to how foreign activity interferes in their ability to control their own economies. Next we shall look at the rise and decline of order in the international monetary system and in international trade.

---

35. See, respectively, Mancur Olson, *The Logic of Collective Action* (Cambridge, Mass.: Harvard University Press, 1971); Charles P. Kindleberger, "Dominance and Leadership in the International Economy," *International Studies Quarterly* 25 (1981), 252; Norman Froelich, Joe Oppenheimer, and Oran Young, *Political Leadership and Collective Goods* (Princeton, N.J.: Princeton University Press, 1971).

36. See Michael W. Doyle, "Imperial Decline and World Order: The World Politics of a Mixed Blessing," *International Interactions* 8 (1981), 123–149.

Monetary Policy and the Bretton Woods System

As a result of agreement in values and outlook, a small number of industrialized states led by the United States created the basis for a liberal international order for the developed, non-Communist states. One aspect of this order had to do with international monetary policy, or "regime." International monetary policy deals basically with the exchange rates between currencies, the nature of the reserve assets used as a common medium of exchange (gold, British pounds, or U.S. dollars, for example), and the degree of control over the movement of international capital.

In July 1944, forty-four states met at Bretton Woods, New Hampshire, intent on creating an international monetary order—one that would promote economic and political stability. This order was to be based on two international organizations (IGOs) that were to manage the system: the International Monetary Fund (IMF) and the International Bank for Reconstruction and Development (or World Bank). The IMF was to keep a watch on exchange rates, which were to be fixed, based on gold, and permitted only slight shifts. Voting in the IMF was weighted to match countries' contributions to the IMF fund. In 1946 the United States contributed one third and thus has 33 percent of the vote. Although its contribution share has declined over the years, the United States has always had a veto over important IMF decisions. The World Bank was established to make loans to help postwar economic development. Despite these agreements, by 1947 it was clear that the Bretton Woods system was not working as designed. The United States, in effect, took over. The world's monetary system went on the dollar standard, managed by the United States.

The dollar became the primary reserve asset in the non-Communist economic system, just as gold had been used in the nineteenth century and the British pound in combination with gold at the end of the nineteenth and beginning of the twentieth centuries. In 1947 only the dollar was strong enough to serve this purpose. It was fixed at $35 per ounce of gold, and with the firm commitment of the U.S. government to convert dollars into gold, this "made the dollar as good as gold. In fact, the dollar was better than gold; it earned interest; it was more flexible than gold; it was needed to buy crucial imports for survival and reconstruction."[37] Indeed, because of the way the dollar was being

---

37. Joan Spero, *The Politics of International Economic Relations*, 2nd ed., (New York: St. Martin's Press, 1981), p. 40. Many of the points made in this section are developed at length by Spero.

used and the need of other countries to have dollars in order to buy from the United States and to back their own currencies, the United States ran a balance-of-payments deficit and so permitted an outflow of dollars from 1947 until 1958.

Some points about monetary interdependence should be made here. Exchange rates, the type of reserve asset, and the degree of control over capital all affect the states being linked in fundamental ways. These items help determine how rich or poor a state may be, what trade advantages it has (cheap or expensive goods), how much and with whom it trades, or how easily it can or cannot expand trade. All of these are significant economic constraints on a state that affect military and security capabilities as well. These relationships expand or reduce a state's menu. In the pre–World War I period, Britain, due to the importance of the pound, could do things both economically and politically that most states could not do—just like the United States in 1947. In 1980, by comparison, with the dollar floating against gold (at a level of $600 per ounce of gold), the rise of gold prices, the decline of the dollar against such strong currencies as the Japanese yen and the West German deutsch mark, the United States had a much more restricted menu. By 1984, this situation had once again changed.

It is commonly agreed that the Bretton Woods system ended in August 1971, when the Nixon administration suspended the convertibility of the dollar to gold at $35 an ounce and added a 10 percent surcharge on import duties (hoping to cut down on imported goods and the outflow of dollars). A number of factors led to this situation. First, there were pressures from outside the OECD system, from the growing number of less-developed countries who were dissatisfied with Bretton Woods and challenged the system. The Communist countries began to have more and more economic interaction with the OECD system, which also had disruptive effects.

More importantly, there were changes within the OECD system itself. The rate of growth in productivity of American workers has lagged behind that of most European and Japanese competitors. The phenomenal economic growth of the Western European countries and the combined strength of the European Community and Japan created new centers of economic power and new challenges to American leadership. With these new centers came changes in monetary interdependence. Multinational corporations from America, Europe, and Japan came to control vast amounts of capital. The amount of "Eurodollars" grew tremendously. [38] In the United States, the Vietnam war and Presi-

---

38. As Spero notes, "Eurodollars are dollars in the form of bank deposits held and traded abroad, primarily in Europe," p. 46.

dent Johnson's Great Society programs to reduce poverty created pressures for inflation.

All of this left the exchange rate of the U.S. dollar fixed at too high a level. For most countries the obvious solution would have been devaluation. But the United States was protector of the system and the provider of the major reserve currency. When nothing else worked and when other countries either couldn't or wouldn't cooperate, the United States finally took the major steps of August 1971. Since that time there have been several international meetings and agreements, but with limited success. At present states continue to devalue their currencies competitively, trying to force each other to pay more. The European Community has attempted a concerted, if regional, response in the European Monetary System (EMS), which set up rules for controlling exchange rates within the EC countries. In 1978–1979, slow movement toward this goal occurred.

International Trade

As with monetary policy, the United States, as the "principal energizer and organizer," has been the primary support behind the postwar system of liberal international trade.[39] The view of a nondiscriminatory, multilateral and market-based system was shared by the industrialized Western powers, in part as a reaction to the protectionism of the 1930s. Cooperation, not protectionism, was the liberal view of trade. Attempts to "beggar-thy-neighbor" only produced losses for all states.

Although the United States was willing to lead in this area also, the issues were much more complex due to the effects of trade on internal political issues. Although discussions on trade policy and arrangements began in 1943, the first element of the international trading order to take hold was the General Agreement on Tariffs and Trade (GATT) in 1947. Reflecting the liberal consensus, GATT was based on free trade and nondiscriminatory policies. All the GATT countries agreed to the "most favored nation" principle. This means that any favorable condition or privilege of trade given to one of the states was to be automatically extended to the others. Furthermore, GATT established rules of trade, commerce, and negotiations for trade in manufac-

---

39. See Raymond Vernon, "International Trade Policy in the 1980s: Prospects and Problems," *International Studies Quarterly* 26 (1982), 483–510 (quote from p. 484). Vernon provides a good overview of the international trade regime, including past history and future prospects.

tured goods; rules aimed at reducing trade barriers and mediating trade disputes.[40] GATT became institutionalized as an IGO, with a secretariat, a director general, and staff to handle the work relating to trade negotiations. Consequently, GATT was the central feature of the non-Communist world trade regime.

As Spero notes, the system worked very well for the developed countries, as quotas and other trade barriers were removed and trade was encouraged. Much of the prosperity discussed earlier derived from this increase in trade. The high point of trade cooperation through GATT came in the tariff reductions during the Kennedy round of negotiations (named after President Kennedy, during whose term the talks began), which was concluded in 1967. However, after this point, all the factors that caused problems in the monetary area also brought trouble to trade.

In addition to inflation, the increased interdependence of trade caused political discontent in economic sectors within countries that were being hurt by the competition of foreign goods. Within each country there were political pressures from segments of the economy seeking protection from foreign competition. The problems in the monetary system also became trade problems, especially as European and Japanese goods came to rival U.S. goods and helped lead to U.S. balance-of-trade deficits. (For example, the United States went from a very small balance-of-payments surplus in 1968 to a deficit of $24 billion in 1971.) The United States no longer was able or willing to protect the system. A number of European actions in particular were highly preferential or protectionist, especially the European Community's Common Agricultural Policy. Japanese restrictions on imports of American agricultural products and American restrictions on imports of Japanese textiles and electronics became major irritants.

Finally, GATT did not cover nontariff barriers (NTBs). These are barriers to trade based on regulations that can be used to discriminate against imports, such as health and safety standards, pollution and environmental standards, technical regulations, and customs valuations

---

40. In addition to the IMF and the World Bank, there was supposed to have been a third institution, the International Trade Organization (ITO), to reduce tariffs and some nontariff barriers and so promote competitive international trade. Because of reservations by the United States, the ITO was never established, but GATT took its place for manufactured goods. No comparable institution, however, was established for trade in raw material commodities, a reflection of the fact that the advanced economies exported chiefly manufactures while at least half of world commodity exports were from less-developed countries.

and procedures. Although GATT helped remove tariff barriers, pressures to protect domestic economic sectors have increasingly led to more NTBs.

From 1967 onward, pressures for trade protection and discrimination increased in the United States, Europe, and Japan. As part of the August 1971 economic "shock," the Nixon administration demanded changes in European and Japanese trade restrictions. By 1973 it was clear that a new international trading order had to be established. In September 1973 representatives of around 100 states met in Tokyo to tackle the complex issues of international trade. The Tokyo Round was basically completed by early 1979. It brought about some reduction of tariff and nontariff barriers, including import licensing codes and customs valuations. It began a new attempt at an international trade order, but one based much more on bargaining among the individual economic interests within and between the various states.

Throughout the decade, the United States attempted to use its willingness to defend Europe militarily as a means to extract economic concessions from West Germany. It repeatedly urged the Germans to buy their military equipment from America and otherwise pay the American costs of stationing troops in Germany. As U.S. military and economic strength diminished, these bargaining sessions between the two allies became increasingly irritating.

We have seen that various economic interdependencies and international cooperative mechanisms were involved in both the economic prosperity of the postwar period and the economic decline of the 1970s. A rather lengthy excerpt from Spero summarizes the main points:

> By the 1970s the agreement on a liberal and limited system, which was the basis of Bretton Woods, had collapsed. States no longer agreed on the ends and the means of management. The most vociferous dissenters from the liberal vision of international management were the less developed countries. In their view the open monetary, trade, and financial system perpetuated their underdevelopment and their subordination to the developed countries. They sought to revise the rules, institutions, and procedures of the system to make possible their development and their economic independence.
>
> For many in the developed countries as well, liberalism was no longer an adequate goal of management. The challenge to liberalism in the developed countries grew out of its very success. The reduction of barriers to trade and capital made possible a vast expansion in international economic interaction among the developed market economies: increased international capital flows, the growth of international trade, and the de-

velopment of international systems of production. As a result, national economies became increasingly interdependent, increasingly sensitive to economic policy and events outside the national economy. Because of the influence of external events, states found it increasingly difficult to manage their national economies.

Interdependence led to two reactions and two different challenges to liberalism. One reaction was to erect new barriers to limit economic interaction and, with it, interdependence. An open international system, in the view of many, no longer maximized economic welfare and most certainly undermined national sovereignty and autonomy. Another reaction was to go beyond liberalism, beyond the idea of a limited management to new forms of international economic cooperation which would manage interdependence. An open system, according to this viewpoint, maximized welfare but required, in turn, new forms of international management which would assume responsibilities and prerogatives formerly assured by the state.[41]

In our earlier discussion of the OECD countries, we reviewed various theories of political integration to understand the peaceful relations among those countries. Integration was seen as both a process and a result of cooperation. Scholars who take a functional view of integration in particular look to the formation of new states as the result of integration. This has not happened in Europe (leading some to decry the failure of integration and to abandon its study). However, the logic of the functionalist approach still leads us to expect the development of *functional* cooperative structures among states. Indeed, one very important way to look at regimes, especially economic regimes that have developed among the OECD countries, is to see them as *informal* structures or results of integrative processes. Rather than the formal creation of new states, the creation of new international organizations, new patterns of interaction among state and nonstate actors, and formal and informal rules and norms that govern behavior may all be seen as the results of integrative processes. In general, the complex set of arrangements found in regimes may be the most promising way to achieve coordination and collaboration in an interdependent world system.

---

41. Joan Spero, *The Politics of International Economic Relations*, 2nd ed. (New York: St. Martin's Press, 1981), p. 27.

19

CONFRONTING
LIMITS TO GROWTH
IN THE WORLD SYSTEM

WORLD ORDER AND WORLD FUTURES

We must now discuss a number of important problems in the global system that constrain all international and transnational actors. We have now come full circle—from Chapters 4 and 5 on the world system to this chapter on the ecological limits of that system. The earlier chapters discussed how the global political structure affects states; this chapter looks specifically at some of the ecological restraints on growth that both link and constrain actors in the contemporary world. These ecological constraints highlight the interdependences in the world system. Many involve common-pool resources, the tragedy of the commons, and other collective goods issues. Thus, we are again confronted by the need for institutions and mechanisms that can handle such issues.

Scholars interested in world order, peace research, international systems, and alternative world futures try to teach us why we should be aware of and interested in the international and transnational problems of interdependence. To appreciate such concern, we need to see where we fit in the global system. Figure 19.1 presents the world system as a set of systems. Individuals tend to give most of their attention to immediate, personal concerns (their families, neighborhoods, and local systems). Our typical area of awareness is really quite limited. However, to become aware of, concerned with, and then to solve the issues discussed in this chapter, we must expand our perspectives both in space (to the world system) and in time (to at least the next 50 to 100 years). Remember the observation of Ervin Laszlo, a futurist and student of world order: "World order reform starts at home: with the ideas and values we entertain, the objectives we pursue, the leaders we elect, and the way we talk with and influence those around us."[1]

Observers of the world scene have always speculated on the possibility and form of alternative structures of world order and world futures. As Barry Hughes notes, "In the decade of the 1970s, there was an explosion of interest in global issues and global futures."[2] This interest has paralleled the use of transnational relations and regimes to study world politics, with a decline in interest in East-West security issues and increasing interest in economic and ecological issues.

The study of global futures ultimately becomes the study of the interconnectedness of systems and issues. The Club of Rome, whose work we shall discuss in detail, has called this interconnectedness the "problematique," or predicament. Other enterprises, such as the World Order Models Project (WOMP), have focused on institutional arrangements, although they still identify a set of interconnected global problems. The transnational scholars of WOMP (from North America, Latin America, Africa, Scandinavia, the Middle East, China, India, the Soviet Union, West Germany, and Japan) have agreed that the world faces five major problems: war, poverty, social injustice, environmental decay, and alienation.[3]

To meet these problems, WOMP scholars have attempted to develop "relevant utopias"—preferred alternative worlds with the necessary

---

1. Ervin Laszlo, *A Strategy for the Future* (New York: Braziller, 1974), p. 79.

2. For a review of futures studies, see Barry B. Hughes, *Alternative World Futures* (forthcoming), chaps. 1 and 2.

3. See Saul H. Mendlovitz, ed., *On the Creation of a Just World Order: Preferred Worlds for the 1990's* (New York: Free Press, 1975), p. xii. See this book and Richard Falk, *A Study of Future Worlds*, for the best overviews of the WOMP perspective. For a review of other world futures approaches, see Louis Rene Beres and Harry Targ, eds., *Planning Alternative World Futures* (New York: Praeger, 1975).

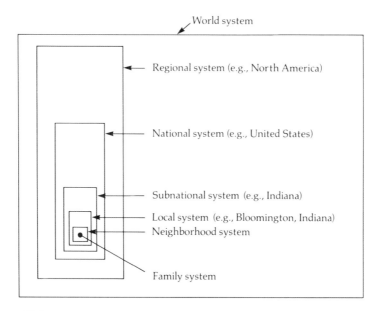

Figure 19.1
A world of systems. [*Source:* Modified from Ervin Laszlo, *A Strategy for the Future* (New York: Braziller, 1974).]

transition steps to reach them. Many of the alternatives consciously go beyond the nation-state system and discuss other configurations of states, regions, IGOs, NGOs, and world institutions. A number of these are based on or derive from the UN system. Such work, though highly speculative, provides a set of future directions that the UN system might take. Such speculation is important because of the need for different forms, or at least different modes of coordination and cooperation, to meet the challenges of ecopolitics. These are the problems of the commons—collective, political, social, and economic problems related to the general phenomenon of limits to growth.

THE IMPACT OF CHANGE

We face serious danger from weapons, pollutants, consumption of the earth's natural resources, and the possibility that the world population will outstrip the world's food supply. These become problems in an era of rapid change—what Alvin Toffler called "future shock." Things have changed so rapidly in so many areas that the consequences of those changes have become challenges to the quality of humanity's existence. Others have observed that we are living in an era of revolutions—rapid changes in communications, transportation, weaponry, and many other areas of technology.

The revolutions in industrial production technology, along with the medical and hygienic advances responsible for much of the increase in population, have also brought about problems in food supply, pollution, and resource depletion. Statistics on the consumption of natural resources (especially nonrenewable resources) and the production of pollution abound. Why have these revolutions brought about world problems today? Why does the Club of Rome, when studying economic development, population growth, resource depletion, and food production, continually come to pessimistic conclusions and predict a marked decline in living standards?

One reason is related to the important phenomenon of *exponential growth*. This form of growth is very much responsible for the "now you don't see it, now you do" nature of these problems. Exponential growth occurs when some quantity continuously increases by a constant *percentage* over a given period of time, for example, when a population grows 2 percent every year. This same principle works when we deposit money in a savings account so that it will grow through compound interest. This is also a very common process in all sorts of natural biological systems. But common as it is, exponential growth can provide very surprising results—we don't think a problem exists until it is there, taking on major proportions.

Two stories are presented in the Club of Rome's important book, *Limits to Growth*, that illustrate these observations. Exponential growth can generate large numbers very quickly.[4] For example, there is the Persian legend of the courtier who presented a beautiful chessboard to the king. In return, the courtier requested one grain of rice for the first square, two grains for the second square, four grains for the third square, eight grains for the fourth square, and so on (a constant percentage of 200 percent). By the fifteenth square, the amount was 16,384 grains; by the twenty-first square, over 1 million grains; and about 18 quintillion grains by the sixty-fourth square. The second example also illustrates the suddenness and surprise of exponential growth. A French riddle supposes that you own a pond. The pond has a water lily that doubles in size every day (again, 200 percent). If left unattended,

---

4. See Donella Meadows et al., *The Limits to Growth*, 2nd ed. (New York: New American Library, 1974), pp. 36–37.

the lily will cover the pond in thirty days. However, the lily seems very small, so you shouldn't worry about cutting it back until it covers one half of the pond. When will that be? The answer, of course, is the twenty-ninth day—you will have one day to save the pond. Statements about the current global plight are similar to this last story; there is only a certain amount of time to save the pond.

These stories also illustrate the value in thinking of exponential growth in terms of doubling time (see Table 19.1). Even low rates of yearly growth, such as 2 percent, can double the size of something in only thirty-five years. When considering population growth, we can understand how it has jumped so relatively suddenly (Figure 19.2). In 1650 the population of the world was half a billion people, and the growth rate was 0.3 percent—a doubling time of 250 years. However, in 1983, the population was 4.7 billion people. Because of advances in medicine, hygiene, and nutrition, the world's population growth rate was 1.8 percent—a doubling time of less than 40 years! If we think we have political, social, and economic problems with the present population, think about the problems with a population twice that size in 40 years or so from now. How long do we have to save the pond?

In Chapters 16 and 17 we discussed dependence, based in good measure on economic and resource differences of the sort described throughout Part I. Given the size of the economic base in such countries as the United States and the differences among countries that already exist in a measure such as GNP per capita, only small differences in exponential growth rates can make large absolute differences in population. Figure 19.3 compares GNP per capita over time for seven countries. Differences in exponential growth rates are widening the economic gap between developed and most developing states.

Table 19.1
Doubling time.

Growth rate (% per year)	Doubling time (years)
0.1	700
0.5	140
1.0	70
2.0	35
4.0	18
5.0	14
7.0	10
10.0	7

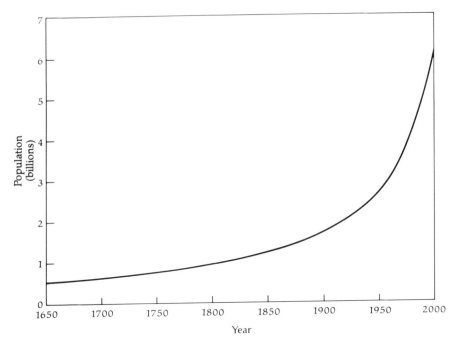

Figure 19.2
The growth in World population. [*Source:* Data from Population Reference
Bureau and World Bank.]

In sum, exponential growth helps us understand why global problems suddenly appear that did not seem to exist before. It also helps to
indicate many of the limits-to-growth problems that we have—growing demand, growing population and growing resource consumption,
and growing pollution. As the economist Kenneth Boulding has observed, "anyone who believes that exponential growth can continue
indefinitely in a finite world is either a madman or an economist."
Exponential growth only complicates the various problems and issues
of interdependence in the system. Furthermore, we are in an era of
rapid change. Another futurist, John McHale, helps us sum up what we
have discussed so far and introduces the sections to follow:

> The last third of the twentieth century has become increasingly charac-
> terized as the age of critical revolution and discontinuity. . . . Our present
> waves of change differ not only in their quantitative aspects from those
> of the recent past, but also in the quality and degree of their
> interrelationships. While previously we might have dealt with relatively
> separate change factors within local and limited contexts, our present
> changes are now global in their spatial and quantitative dimensions.

They are no longer isolatable sequences of events separated in time, in numbers of people affected, and in the social and physical processes which are perturbed.[5]

STEADY STATE AND THE CLUB OF ROME

It is clear that we now face ecological and environmental problems very different from those in the past. The exponential growth of population and economic activity has, for the first time, alerted people to the fact that the earth is finite and that the limits of its carrying capacity can be reached. It is also possible that the earth's carrying capacity is being reduced through the disruption of natural ecosystems, so that they are destroyed or are only slowly regenerating; examples are overfarming in many areas, the southward spread of the Sahara Desert in Africa, and the destruction of the Amazon rain forest. In the past, when a tribe exhausted the productive capability of an area, it simply moved on (or else the tribe died off). Today the threatened ecosystem is not local but global. If our ecosystem is damaged or destroyed, there is nowhere else to go.

Most of the major issues involved in the whole limits-to-growth idea were introduced and discussed by the Club of Rome.[6] While often controversial—criticisms of the Club's work have been directed both at its methods and at the assumptions that lead to its pessimistic outlook—the work of the Club of Rome highlights the current global ecosystem. The first major work, published in 1971, was Jay Forrester's *World Dynamics*. In it Forrester forced the reader to look at the interactions between population, capital investment, and the factors that influence growth, such as food, resources, and pollution. He recognized that his computer model was incomplete, but he emphasized the need to begin to think more of the quality of life rather than sheer quantities, and to think of projecting trends into the future. He suggested that the global quality of life was at a maximum in the mid to late 1960s. He also predicted a collapse of the world system (a dramatic decline in population and quality of life) within the next 50 to 100 years and contended

---

5. John McHale, "World Facts and Trends," *Futures* 3 (1971), 216–301.

6. The Club of Rome has also prompted analyses by other groups and organizations, such as those of the Organization for Economic Cooperation and Development, *Interfutures: Facing the Future* (Paris: OECD, 1979). See also Dennis Pirages, "The Ecological Perspective and the Social Sciences," *International Studies Quarterly* 27 (1983), 243–255, for a review of issues raised by an ecological perspective on world problems.

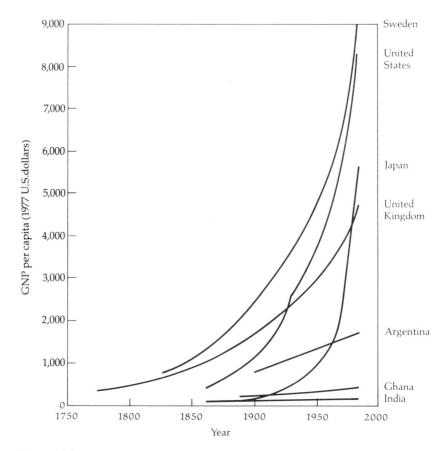

Figure 19.3

Long-term economic growth rates, 1775–1977: the widening gap between rich
and poor countries. [*Source:* Simon Kuznets, *Economic Growth of Nations* (Cambridge, Mass.: Harvard University Press, 1971); World Bank, *World Development
Report, 1979* (Washington, D.C.: World Bank, 1979), pp. 126–127.]

that this trend would not be averted by applying the standard solutions
suggested.

In the Club of Rome's second major publication, *Limits to Growth*, the
nature of exponential growth was more closely examined. One conclusion was that a "steady state" or "equilibrium" situation was an alternative to perpetual growth. The major points made in *Limits to Growth* can
be summarized as follows:

1. The global population system and material capital system grow in
exponential terms.

2. There are physical limits to growth of both population and capital. This conclusion derives from several assumptions—there is only a finite stock of exploitable, nonrenewable resources (such as oil or coal); there is a finite ability for the environment to absorb pollutants; there is a finite amount of arable land; there is a finite yield of food from this land. One important point is that no one really knows what these limits are; they can be expanded by technology or reduced by misuse.

3. There are long delays in the feedback processes. This is a major point of limits—that there is a long time lag between the release of pollutants or other ecological damage and our realization that damage has been done. For example, by the time we discover and are informed about DDT, mercury, or excessive carbon dioxide in the ecological system, the damage has been done (it cannot be prevented and we can only try to stop any further damage), and only time can reverse that damage (if it is reversible).

4. The limits to growth can be addressed in two ways—remove or expand the limits or weaken the forces of growth. The first has been the traditional political and social response. *Limits to Growth* argues that this is no longer a useful solution. The better path is to change attitudes toward growth, from quantitative growth to qualitative improvements.

All of these issues are picked up and developed in the third major work, by Mihajlo Mesarovic and Eduard Pestel, *Mankind at the Turning Point*. Further refining the computer models developed by Forrester and modified in the Meadowses' work, this book supports the view that the world is a system of physical interdependences and that there exists a "simultaneity" of a complex group of problems. The fragile web of the natural ecology is threatened by "undifferentiated" growth. Here, Mesarovic and Pestel develop the quantitative/qualitative distinction by discussing "undifferentiated" and "organic" growth. The first type is sheer growth in numbers (and often likened to the growth of a cancer); the latter means growth in specific areas to meet specific needs.

The authors make several major changes in assumptions for their study from those in the earlier Club books. The previous works looked at the world as one system; here the authors argue that the impacts of global interdependences are different for different regions or groups of states. The global system should be studied in terms of *interacting regions*. This is important, because long before there is a collapse of the world system as such, certain regions may suffer collapse, possibly within the next seventy-five years. Because the world is a system, the collapse of any one region would have profound effects throughout the world. Thus, each region must be interested in all other regions and the world as a whole if collapse is to be averted. Delays in addressing global growth problems will make solving those problems far costlier and more difficult and perhaps even make solutions impossible.

Mesarovic and Pestel summarize their computer analyses in four basic points: (1) the current crises are not temporary, (2) the solution to these crises can only be developed in a global context, (3) the solutions cannot be achieved by traditional means, and (4) it is possible to resolve these crises through cooperation rather than confrontation.

These conclusions also help link the previous chapters with the present one. The systemic and interdependent nature of the world is highlighted by these conclusions, as is the prisoners' dilemma nature of the problems. Points 3 and 4 above recognize that old solutions based on narrow analyses and interests will no longer be sufficient and that the search for individual short-term gains will not work either. The long-term collective viewpoint must be adopted as the basis for cooperation. The analyses of Mesarovic and Pestel also emphasize that the aim should be selective, organic growth concerned with the quality of life. If this is pursued properly within each region, then the collapse predicted by Forrester can be averted.

Both the systems dynamics methods and the basic assumptions of the Club of Rome have been subject to criticism.[7] One book, *Catastrophe or New Society?*, produced by the Bariloche Foundation that worked in Buenos Aires, begins with the assumption that the problems predicted by the Club of Rome have arrived.[8] In the view adopted in this book, the Club of Rome's priorities have to be changed. Before protecting the environment or reducing consumption of the earth's resources (variables omitted from the Bariloche analyses), we should assure every person an "adequate standard of living." To achieve this, the developed states will have to reduce their consumption and give the surplus to the developing countries. Their computer models, in fact, indicate that these steps can be taken and results achieved in just a little more than a generation. However, the developing countries must also guard against

---

7. See, for example, H. Cole et al., *Thinking about the Future* (London: Chatto and Windus, 1973); Guy Poquet, "The Limits to Global Modelling," *International Social Science Journal* 30 (1978), 284–300; Karl Deutsch et al., eds., *Problems of World Modeling* (Cambridge, Mass.: Ballinger, 1977).

8. Amilcar O. Herrera et al., *Catastrophe or New Society? A Latin American World Model* (Ottawa: International Development Research Centre, 1976). After the military coup in Argentina in 1975, all members of this research group fled the country.

making the same mistakes as the developed states, by mindlessly imitating the "undifferentiated growth" of the developed world. *Catastrophe or New Society?* says that the LDCs must attend to satisfying the basic human needs of all citizens and avoid the wasteful consumption and resulting social problems that characterize the industrial states.

To be fair, the Club of Rome has produced more recent books that abandon computer models in addressing some of the above issues. *RIO: Reshaping the International Order* analyzes the problems of creating a more just and equitable world society from the point of view of the world's developing states. In *Goals for Mankind,* the cultures and values of individuals, states, and groups of states are studied in presenting national, regional, international, and transnational goals. The focus of *Goals* "is on the gaps between goals that concentrate on short-term issues and those that manifest a sufficient appreciation of long-term objectives and needs, necessary to tackle global problems."[9] Again, we return to questions of individual versus group interests, short-term versus long-term interests, and private versus collective goods.

POPULATION

Many people feel that at the heart of all the limits-to-growth problems is population. This has been discussed by Richard Falk, who points out three central dimensions of the population problem. The first is the *Malthusian dimension,* which relates population to world food supplies. The problem here is not limited to the possibility of starvation. If population growth strains food resources, then malnutrition will continue to limit the mental and physical development of children and the energies and abilities of adults. This relates directly to the quality of population capabilities discussed in Chapter 6.

The second dimension is what we may call the *deprivation dimension.* This is the political/economic/social dimension of the population problem. It pertains to the discontent produced among people by the lack of food or the inequitable distribution of food—and the political consequences of the development of radical political forces. Discontent from relative deprivation drives various ideological and political movements, especially those seeking revolutionary change.

---

9. Ervin Laszlo et al., *Goals for Mankind* (New York: Dutton, 1977); Jan Tinbergen, ed., *RIO: Reshaping the International Order* (New York: Dutton, 1976).

Third, there is the *ecological dimension*. This is often the most stressed aspect of the population problem: that increases in population inevitably increase the demands on the ecological system for food, natural resources, and goods and services.

At population growth rates of 1.8 percent a year in 1983, world population for the year 2000 will reach 6 billion. It took from 1825 to 1930 to add a billion people to the world's population; the last billion was added in less than fifteen years. The present burst in population growth is due mostly to the drastic reduction in death rates caused by the public health improvements made in the last 200 years (see Figure 19.4). Populations tend to level off after upsurges; eventually birth rates fall, as they have done in the Western industrialized states, where birth and death rates nearly balance each other. (In some European countries, notably West Germany, the population growth rate is now actually negative.) Most of the less-developed countries are experiencing rapid population growth because of greatly reduced death rates. Some, like China and Taiwan, have managed to reduce birth rates sharply, but many others, such as India and Mexico, have yet to do so. Birth rates tend to fall when there is widespread distribution of information about contraception and when people begin to perceive that their basic needs are being met. Social and economic change are thus essential if population growth in LDCs is to be slowed; it is not just a matter of finding a "technological fix."

Even so, the uneven distribution of population will worsen for several decades. It is a mistake to look only at the crude birth and death rates. To get a true picture of population growth, we have to look at the population structure of a country—the numbers of people in different age groups and the fertility rates for those categories. Figure 19.5 shows the different population structures for a developed country (Sweden) and an LDC (Mexico). Mexico will have much greater population growth in the future. Proportionately many more people have yet to reach child-bearing age in Mexico, and a much larger portion of the populace will be reproducing in Mexico—the larger group now at child-bearing age and the young who have yet to reach that age. Even if future parents should merely replace themselves with two children, so that the death rate eventually equals the birth rate, so many people have yet to do this that the population of Mexico will continue to grow for some time.

This is an important aspect of the idea of *deadly delays*. It has been estimated that we need to look at least fifty years ahead. The longer population control is delayed, the more people of child-bearing age

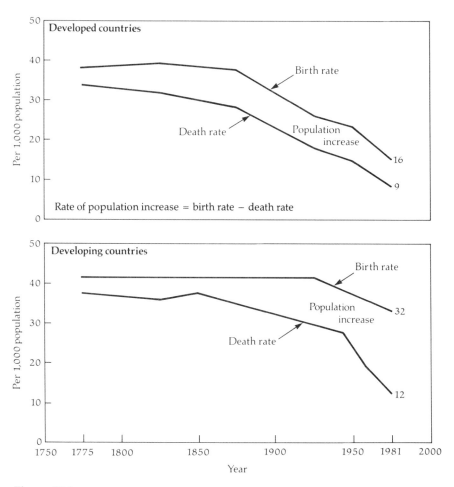

Figure 19.4
Birth and death rates: developed and developing countries, 1775–1981. [Courtesy of the Population Reference Bureau, Inc., Washington, D.C.]

will enter the population. When population growth is indeed level—that is, no growth—the absolute level of population will be much higher. That means that the absolute number of people will continue to grow for decades after a population control policy is initiated. During that time, population will continue to make greater and greater demands on world food production. For example, the uneven rate of population growth is a major factor in the food trade patterns of North America and Latin America. In 1950 both regions had approximately the same population—163 and 168 million, respectively. But the rapid

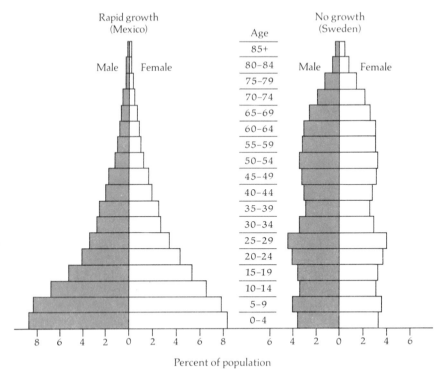

Figure 19.5
Population pyramids for Mexico and Sweden, 1976. [Courtesy of the Population Reference Bureau, Inc., Washington, D.C.]

increase in Latin American population and the stress in commercial agriculture on exports have forced Latin America to become a net importer of basic foodstuffs while North America exports food. Had North America's population since 1960 grown at the same 2.5 percent rate as did Latin America's, then instead of 259 million in 1983, it would have had 352 million people. Those extra people would have absorbed much of the food surplus.[10]

FOOD

What is the food situation in the world today? As many as 40 percent of the world population suffers from some form of undernourishment. The UN Food and Agricultural Organization (FAO) has noted that most

---

10. See Lester Brown et al., "Twenty-two Dimensions of the Population Problem," *Worldwatch Paper* #5 (Washington, D.C.: Worldwatch Institute, 1976).

third world countries suffer calorie intake shortages and that malnour-
ishment due to insufficient protein (which is vital to mental development) is especially serious. The Club of Rome estimates that about half
of the arable land in the world today is being cultivated, but that the
other half would be very costly to prepare for growing food. In fact,
much arable land is lost to cultivation, perhaps permanently, every
year. Cities and highways take up farmland. Farmers leave some
overpopulated countryside to open up new land, which is typically
marginal. Cultivation of that land is precarious, and in heavy rains the
topsoil from the new land, as well as from the longer-cultivated areas
below it, is lost and washed into rivers and the sea. More topsoil is lost
every year than is replaced. In addition, because of enormous increases
in the price of fuel oil, many people in the third world are forced to cut
trees for fuel to cook their food. Rwanda imports its oil through
Uganda. During the Ugandan civil war in 1979, oil imports to Rwanda
were cut off for a while. Desperate people chopped down trees; it was
reported that not a tree was left standing within seventy miles of the
capital. As a result of such practices in some parts of the world, the
desert spreads and agricultural lands as well as forests become barren.
Agricultural scientists try to keep up with population growth and loss
of arable land by introducing new seeds, fertilizers, and pesticides to
raise the productivity of existing land. Nevertheless, it is a hard race,
and the new technologies both consume a great deal of expensive energy and cause new pollution problems. The resources needed for food
production—water, land, fertilizer, and energy—are themselves subject to limits.

How Many People?

Estimates of how many people the world could feed diverge widely
and are part of a major debate. The Club of Rome estimated that if per
capita land requirements and population growth rates remained as
they were in the late 1960s, then by 2000 the amount of agricultural
land needed for the present level of productivity would exceed the
total world supply of arable land. Others argue that there is enough
potential for food production to feed the developing countries as they
move through the period of rapid population growth.

One very optimistic estimate, based on Japanese standards of farm-
ing and nutrition, says the world could support 95 billion people; another estimate, based on Dutch standards, puts the figure at around 30

billion. A projection from the Committee on Resources and Man of the National Academy of Sciences estimates that the earth's "ultimate carrying capacity" is for "about 30 billion people, at a level of chronic near-starvation for the great majority (and with massive immigration to the now less-populated lands)."[11] A much more realistic number, the report adds, is about 10 billion, and the number should be lower for people to be more than merely "adequately nourished."

Part of the problem is in the definition of *adequate nourishment*. Obviously, *adequate* means a certain minimum intake of calories, protein, vitamins, and minerals. It does not, however, require that everyone adopt the dietary habits of people living in the industrial countries, whose diets are heavy on meat and other animal products. By eating meat, people in rich countries indirectly consume much more food than do citizens of poor countries. For instance, a steer must take in six to eight pounds of grain to produce one pound of beef. The more people there are who try to eat a Western diet, the harder it will be to feed everyone at a level necessary to ensure health. Thus we see the virtue of development programs that stress meeting the basic needs of everyone and avoiding a distribution of income and consumption skewed heavily in favor of people in the rich countries or the rich people in poor countries.

Other aspects of development also affect food availability. In many LDCs, food distribution facilities are terribly inadequate. Food may rot on the piers of a port city or be eaten by pests on the farms. International food assistance is sometimes diverted by corrupt officials who sell the food for profit. Development patterns oriented toward the export market—big commercial crops like cotton, coffee, sugar, fruit, and flowers—may bring in foreign exchange, enabling the rich to buy luxuries or giving LDC governments the finances needed for industrial development. But some of that foreign exchange has to be used to import food to feed the agricultural laborers. When subsistence farms are converted into big commercial establishments raising cash crops, an immediate food deficit is created. Laborers who used to raise their own food must now use part of their earnings to buy food.

As a result of these economic changes, most third world countries currently import more grain than they export. Many are dependent for their food supplies on sales from North America, which is now the only major grain-exporting region of the world. Politically and eco-

---

11. Richard Falk, *This Endangered Planet* (New York: Random House, 1971), p. 134.

nomically, third world countries now feel vulnerable in yet another way to actions of the rich countries. Part of this problem could be eased by development programs aimed at strengthening small farmers, who could raise some crops for sale but keep a part of their land for raising their own food.

Land reform and technical assistance to small farmers are receiving increasing attention by international aid-lending organizations like the World Bank. Political and economic resistance to a major reorientation of agricultural development is nevertheless very great. International cooperation has also been channeled through the FAO and other agencies. The World Food Conference, held in Rome in 1974, produced agencies such as the World Food Council to help keep track of and aid in the deliveries of food and the Agricultural Development Fund to help developing countries increase production. Yet such food regime activity only begins to meet the problems—problems requiring a global approach along with investment and food aid, an effective population policy, and balanced economic development within and among the regions of the world.

SCARCITY AND UNMET DEMANDS

A number of other aspects of the scarcity problem have been discussed by students of global ecology. Several are related to what we called the deprivation dimension, because there are political, social, and economic consequences. As politics is the process by which "who gets what, when, and how," anything that creates even more resource scarcities and complicates resource distribution will increase political conflict. Such conflict may be handled peacefully within stable societies, but a struggle for resources will frequently cause instability and political violence within new, poor, and politically underdeveloped states. As population pressures lead to scarcities, there will be deprivation and unmet demands. Such demands may encourage revolutionary movements and terrorism.

Unmet demands range from ideological and philosophical ones to food and social services. More and more government action deals with social problems resulting from overpopulation, many of which accompany urbanization: the move to the cities that has accelerated with population growth in less-developed countries. The crowding of people comes only when the population density is high; this occurs in the large and rapidly growing urban centers of the world (see Table 19.2).

Table 19.2
Growth in populations of the world's largest urban areas.

	1960		1980		2000	
Rank	Urban Area	Population (millions)	Urban Area	Population (millions)	Urban Area	Population (millions)
1	New York–NE New Jersey	14.2	Tokyo–Yokohama	19.7	Mexico City	31.6
2	London	10.8	New York–NE New Jersey	17.9	Tokyo–Yokohama	26.1
3	Tokyo–Yokohama	10.7	Mexico City	13.9	São Paulo	26.0
4	Rhine–Ruhr	8.7	São Paulo	12.5	New York–NE New Jersey	22.0
5	Shanghai	7.4	Shanghai	12.0	Calcutta	19.7
6	Paris	7.4	London	11.0	Rio de Janeiro	19.4
7	Buenos Aires	6.7	Los Angeles–Long Beach	10.7	Shanghai	19.2
8	Los Angeles–Long Beach	6.5	Buenos Aires	10.4	Greater Bombay	19.1
9	Moscow	6.3	Peking	10.2	Peking	19.1
10	Chicago–NW Indiana	6.0	Rio de Janeiro	10.0	Seoul	18.7

Source: United Nations, Department of Economic and Social Affairs, Population Division, *Trends and Prospects in the Population of Urban Agglomerations, 1950–2000, as Assessed in 1973–75*, Working Paper no. 58 (New York, November 21, 1975). p. 61.

Crowding magnifies problems in housing, health care, health services, and educational services. Unemployment can be another major consequence of rapid population growth. Economists estimate that for every 1 percent growth in the labor force, a 3 percent rate of economic growth is needed to create jobs. If so, then countries with 3 percent growth rates in population will need a 9 percent growth rate of the economy just to keep their labor force employed. This will be a very difficult task. (See Figure 19.6 for information on the growth of the labor force in various parts of the world.)

Population growth is, of course, not the only culprit in causing unemployment or other unmet demands. As pointed out in Chapter 16, inappropriate capital-intensive forms of investment in LDCs, whether

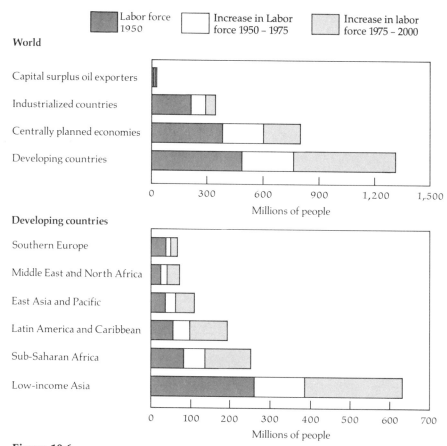

Figure 19.6
Labor force estimates and projections, 1950–2000. [*Source:* World Bank, *World Development Report, 1979* (Washington, D.C.: World Bank, 1979), p. 48.]

by multinational corporations or by their competitors within LDCs, cause much unemployment that could be eased by labor-intensive modes of production. Some critics focus on population pressures. Others focus on distorted development in LDCs. Both views identify important dimensions of the problem.

DEPLETION OF NATURAL RESOURCES

Population growth, plus the demands for maintaining high standards of living in the rich countries and demands for development in the poor ones, has also put great pressures on the world's supply of natural resources. These pressures belong to Falk's ecological dimension of the population problem and are important to our conception of the world as global commons. Many studies indicate that the use of the world's resources is growing exponentially—in many areas and for many resources, at a rate faster than the growth in population.

Every additional human and every new item produced place demands on the earth's mineral and energy resources. The U.S. Bureau of Mines has gathered data on mineral resources. For each resource, we can calculate the number of years of reserves remaining in the earth (1) on the basis of the current rate of usage, (2) on the basis of a projected rate of usage, and (3) on the basis of the projected rate of usage and five times the amount of known reserves. Table 19.3 presents these figures for several resources.

Table 19.3
Estimates for the earth's mineral reserves.

	Years of reserves		
Resource	Current usage rate	Projected rate of increase in usage[a]	Projected rate with five times known reserves
Aluminum	226	48 (5.3%)	78
Copper	62	30 (4.4)	61
Iron	177	65 (2.7)	119
Lead	49	30 (3.1)	69
Natural gas	46	31 (2.5)	76
Nickel	77	41 (2.8)	88
Tin	44	33 (1.6)	94
Petroleum	34	26 (2.0)	74

Source: Based on 1974 data from Bureau of Mines, *Mineral Facts and Problems,* Bulletin no. 667, (U.S. Government Printing Office, 1976); and methods presented in *Limits to Growth,* table 4, pp. 64–68.
[a]Projected rates of increase in usage in parentheses.

Figures on known reserves of minerals and other nonrenewable resources are deceptive. Many parts of the world are not yet fully explored, so new reserves of many minerals will be found. (Geologists sometimes make estimates of these "probable" and "possible" reserves.) Known bodies of resources may be considered too difficult or too expensive to tap into, given current knowledge and prices. New technology may be developed for extracting the materials, and a rise in prices may make it profitable to exploit deposits that previously were too costly to mine. Thus, known reserves can be greatly expanded even without any exploration. This has happened with some petroleum deposits in the United States, where oil fields that were no longer profitable could once again yield valuable supplies. Still, there are limits to this. At some point the world's petroleum really will be exhausted; long before that happens, it will become too expensive to use except for very special purposes where there are no acceptable substitutes. If we expand our reserves of minerals chiefly by making them very expensive, we shall have made a very dubious bargain. Thus, even a much more optimistic view of the world resources than that of Table 19.3 still poses substantial problems.

It is also important to understand that industrialized countries use far more resources than does the overpopulated third world. Thus, a cutback in resource consumption by the industrialized countries (much of which may be called *undifferentiated growth*) could reduce the projected usage rates in Table 19.3 and increase the years of remaining reserves. To illustrate this point, American energy use until recently doubled every decade. The United States—with approximately 6 percent of the world's population—accounts for over 60 percent of the world's consumption of natural gas; over 40 percent of the world's consumption of coal and aluminum; and over 30 percent of nickel, copper, petroleum, and total energy consumption.

Another resource—often neglected because it is not strictly nonrenewable—is water. Only 5 percent of the world's water is fresh water, and most of that is in the icecaps. Only 1 percent of the world's water is fresh water we can work with in the ecosphere: rivers, lakes, water in soil and plants, and vapor in the atmosphere. Though it is a scarce resource, water usage is rapidly increasing—to meet human consumption and food production demands. Water must not only be available but also be of high enough quality for human needs such as drinking, washing, and growing food. Vast quantities of water are needed for opening up new farmland, reclaiming old land, maintaining the land in use, and maintaining the ongoing "green revolution" in overpopulated areas. It is estimated that one pound of grain requires 60 to 225 gallons of water and that the production of one pound of beef requires 2,500 to 6,000 gallons. Industrial activities also require great quantities of water—one ton of steel requires 65,000 gallons, and one automobile requires 100,000 gallons. Water usage grows faster than population. The estimated ratio is that water usage triples as population doubles, and the world demand is expected to double by the year 2000. Demand will rise especially quickly in the more industrialized areas.

This situation is even more pronounced for energy consumption as a whole. We started with a study of population growth, but many people begin with and stress energy consumption. With enough energy, other resources can be mined or otherwise acquired, processed, substituted for, or recycled. In other words, the limits to these resources can be relaxed. Increasing food production or cleaning up polluted air and water also require spending large amounts of energy. Economic development and growth in national wealth correlate with the use of energy; consequently, poor countries will require more energy to develop. A vicious circle emerges here: Birth rates tend to drop and stabilize as countries develop economically, but for this to happen, more energy is needed. Meanwhile, the added population creates demands that devour additional energy and wealth just to stay where they are. This means that very large amounts of energy must be devoted to the less-developed areas.

It is no wonder that energy usage has grown exponentially. For most of the last century, energy consumption increased approximately 4 percent each year (a doubling time of 18 years). This is faster than population growth. This picture is made sharper by looking at the energy consumption of major powers. Though there are some problems of data comparability, the comparisons between energy consumption (measured in million-metric-ton coal equivalents) for 1870 and 1976 indicate the enormous increase in the demand for energy. There has been a 1,000-fold increase for the Soviet Union and a 75-fold increase for the United States. Energy use by the superpowers has grown at a breathtaking rate, but even France has increased consumption 12 times and Germany (East and West) 16 times.

Note also that energy consumption dropped slightly in the early 1980s, in part because of effective conservation (especially in Europe and Japan) and in part because of the worldwide recession. Declines in worldwide economic activity ease the immediate pressures of all limits-to-growth problems. But if recession helps to postpone the dangers of growth, we must not deceive ourselves. With the return of economic prosperity, which most of us hope for, the problems of growth will also return and still demand urgent attention.

There are many other ways to indicate world energy consumption. One measure of the rate of energy consumption is that of kilocalories. For example, the average human burns food at a rate of about 2,000 kcal (kilocalories) per day. (This is also, incidentally, the same as the energy spent by a 100-watt lightbulb.) The per capita use of energy in the United States is approximately 230,000 kcal per person per day. The magnitude of this is indicated by its equivalent—300 persons working strenuously for eight hours. The difference in energy consumption across countries is indicated by the fact that most of the world's population consumes less than 15,000 kcal in energy use per person per day. More than seven times the present energy level would have to be produced for the rest of the world to reach the U.S. level!

The drain on the global commons is highly uneven; by far the greatest drain is made by the developed states. Mesarovic and Pestel have argued that because the world is an interdependent system, even in self-interest we cannot permit any region of it to "drown." We have shown here that usage in fact produces much greater demand than is suggested merely by the worldwide distribution of population. Strategies should therefore include changes in life-styles, as well as changes in the structure of the manufacturing economy—eliminating planned obsolescence, designing longer-lasting and more easily repaired products, recycling, and ceasing to produce disposable products. The current pattern of production and distribution in the industrialized countries probably cannot be maintained even there; an attempt to imitate it worldwide would cause ecological disaster.

In Chapter 18 we noted that individual actions and attitudes can be important. We begin to see the truth of this as people within the developed countries slowly change their habits to reduce consumption and to conserve energy. Yet the problem of collective goods—the tragedy of the commons—continues to hamper these efforts when people (as most people do most of the time) emphasize their own self-interest and do not see how it can be served by making sacrifices. ("Why should I drive at 55 miles per hour if no one else does? Why should I turn off the lights to save electricity—it's priced cheaply enough and it's such a tiny contribution?") Altruism alone cannot produce the necessary sacrifices; we still need a combination of raised costs (money and otherwise) and a heightened awareness of the effects of our actions.

Other strategies for grappling with the problem of resource shortages involve substituting for the resources in question. This may mean changing to other natural resources. For example, in the short run a switch from oil to coal would help solve one aspect of American energy problems (though intensifying pollution) and provide some time needed to develop energy alternatives (such as nuclear fusion and solar energy). Short- and medium-term strategies can allow the development not only of new life-styles but also of whole processes, technologies, and synthetic materials. Short- and medium-term strategies must therefore bring the world through a difficult period of transition to a longer run, where very basic changes must be made in resource usage, population, and substitutes for exhausted resources.

POLLUTION

The increasing use of nonrenewable fuels, as well as the manufacture of chemicals and other industrial products, are producing rising levels of pollution worldwide. For example, burning fossil fuels produces carbon dioxide, carbon monoxide, sulfur oxides, nitrogen oxides, hydrocarbons, and solid particles. These are emitted into the air and water of our planet. They settle into or are washed into the soil and into the plants and animals that exist in polluted areas. Water is also damaged by *thermal pollution*—heat from industrial processes and nuclear energy that disrupts the ecological balance of rivers, streams, and lakes. In addition, nuclear power produces radioactive wastes, which could become the most dangerous pollutants of all. Some of the most difficult, controversial, and critical issues involved with nuclear power concern accidents that produce radiation leaks into the ecosystem around the nuclear power plant. Equally difficult is how to dispose of the highly radioactive wastes that nuclear power plants produce. Many countries simply have no safe disposal site. Hence, it becomes a problem demanding international cooperation.

The spread of pollutants throughout the ecosystem is one of the major indications of global interdependence. For example, lead emitted into the air by the industrial countries has been found in the Greenland icecap. Large DDT deposits have been found in the bodies of whales who have lived almost entirely in the Antarctic region. Large bodies of water such as Lake Erie (which is in the process of being reclaimed), the Baltic Sea, and much of the Mediterranean are becoming unable to support fish life; in fact, the Mediterranean has been called the "world's largest sewer." Increases in the carbon dioxide content of the atmosphere (resulting from burning fossil fuels) threaten to trap heat inside the atmosphere, raise world temperatures, melt part of the polar icecaps, and thus raise the level of the oceans; consequent global changes in climate may drown the world's coastal areas.

Pollution can be anything from a bother or inconvenience to an immediate danger to animal, plant, and human life. It can destroy precious food and water resources and make many of the limited resources of earth unusable. *Limits to Growth* makes four main points about pollution:

1. The few kinds of pollution that have been measured over time seem to be increasing exponentially and even faster than population growth.

2. We have almost no knowledge about what the upper limits to these pollution growth curves are.

3. The presence of natural delays in ecological processes increases the probability of underestimating the control measures necessary and therefore of inadvertently reaching those upper limits.

4. Many pollutants are globally distributed; their harmful effects appear long distances from their point of generation.[12]

Pollution, then, is a clear example of a *collective bad*—a jointly supplied externality generated by interdependence, where individual states have no choice about consumption. Individual action cannot provide the collective good of a clean environment. Collective action is required.

INTERDEPENDENCE AND EQUITY

The problems with pollution apply to all aspects of the limits to growth and all the interdependences involved. People in sovereign states must stop thinking solely in terms of short-term, domestic policy when dealing with resource consumption, population, and pollution. Long-term, collective ways must be devised to cooperate in protecting the global commons and achieving various collective goods. One of the major problems, however, remains the division of the world into haves and have nots. The developed and the developing countries tend to approach these issues from very different perspectives, which makes cooperation even more difficult and complex. This was indicated in our

---

12. Donella Meadows et al., *The Limits to Growth*, 2nd ed. (New York: New American Library, 1974), p. 78.

earlier discussion of the New International Economic Order. A specific example is the negotiation of the UN Law of the Sea Convention.

The Third UN Law of the Sea Conference (UNCLOS III) began meeting in 1973 to settle unresolved issues caused by technology and collective goods problems. Two major strategies for resolving collective goods problems were used. First, coastal states were given, with certain limitations, exclusive use of 200-mile economic zones off their coasts. In these zones (including the continental shelf), states would have the rights of exploration and exploitation of mineral and animal resources. This action, in effect, takes about 40 percent of the seas out of the commons and gives responsibility for its care to specific states. This part of the oceans regime is an international equivalent of the English enclosure movement of the early nineteenth century, which similarly eliminated the remaining commons pastureland.

A second matter addressed by UNCLOS III was the attempt to create some sort of International Seabed Authority to manage the resources beyond the 200-mile limit in the interests of the "common heritage of mankind" (to use the 1967 phrase of Arvid Pardo, the UN representative from Malta). Here was a second mechanism: developing supranational institutions for the oceans regime that were centralized to manage jointly seabed resources for all states. However, the LDCs and the developed states have expressed two different views on how the seabed commons should be regulated. LDCs wanted the International Seabed Authority (and its operational arm, the Enterprise) to control *all* exploitation of the seabed—meaning the nodules of nickel, cobalt, copper, manganese, and other metals that rest on the deep seabed. Developed states, with the Reagan administration in the forefront, desired state control. With their own sophisticated mining industries, the United States, Britain, West Germany, and others wanted free access and less control by the Authority. Because of the Authority, the United States did not sign the draft treaty in April 1982, although it was signed by 130 other states.

The Law of the Sea process illustrates a number of previously discussed topics. As noted in Chapters 16 and 17, such differences in wealth and development, past colonial relationships, and dominance or dependence complicate the uneven distribution of resources and the use of those resources around the world. The LDCs want to become developed, industrialized states. To do this they need vast amounts of resources, energy, capital, and aid. In the process, they will also generate a great deal of pollution. Their view is commonly that the developed states are trying to keep them in an underdeveloped, neocolonial, and subordinate position, especially when ecologically minded people tell them that they should not aim for similar levels of development as the rich countries. They recognize that the gap between the rich and the poor continues to grow wider instead of narrower. The LDCs argue that it is unfair for all states to have to lower their development goals; that would simply put the poor ones at a further disadvantage. So we have a "tragedy of the commons" situation worsened and complicated by a history of colonialism and exploitation.

Many analysts, especially the early Club of Rome writers, have emphasized the need to stabilize the demand for resources—to keep the demand from growing and even to reduce demand in some cases. As we have noted, this is important and can happen. For example, as a result of conservation efforts (partly impelled by higher prices), energy usage in the United States actually declined between 1978 and 1979— before the 1980 recession forced a decline in economic activity. Yet it is also important to remember that demand, especially for undifferentiated growth in the use of resources, depends on great differences in usage.

Garrett Hardin is the best example of analysts who blame the pressures on the world's natural and food resources on population growth in the developing countries. Others have rejected Hardin's metaphor of the "lifeboat," or at least the implication that some people will have to be thrown overboard if the rest want to survive.[13] Instead, we might think of the lifeboat as filled with many people, including quite a few first-class passengers with all their luggage. The need may be to throw overboard some golf clubs and guns rather than people.

Recall that the analyses of groups like the Bariloche Foundation show that if peoples and states cooperate, all humanity could be provided with an adequate standard of living, which satisfies basic needs for food, shelter, and health care. Development strategies based on more equality within nations and across the entire globe could greatly improve the living conditions of the world's poor. This improvement could be bought at a relatively modest cost. One way to see this is to inspect the graph in Figure 19.7, which shows the relation between GNP per capita and life expectancy in all countries of the world. The 1973 GNP per capita is shown on the horizontal axis, and the average life expectancy at birth on the vertical axis.

---

13. See Garrett Hardin, "Lifeboat Ethics: The Case against Helping the Poor," *Psychology Today* 8 (September 1974), 38–43, 124–126. For a response and critique, see Marvin Soroos, "The Commons and Lifeboat as Guides for International Ecological Policy," *International Studies Quarterly* 21 (1977), no. 4, pp. 647–674.

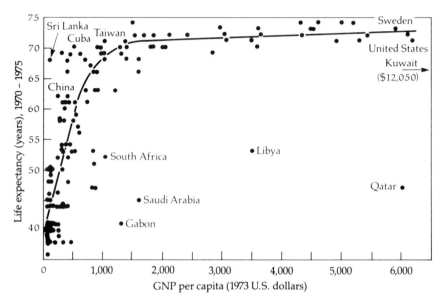

Figure 19.7
GNP per capita and life expectancy across nations. [*Source:* Bruce Russett, "The Marginal Utility of Income Transfers to the Third World," *International Organization* 32 (Autumn 1978), no. 4, p. 916.]

There is a fair amount of scatter among points; nonetheless, it is clear that at GNP levels under $600 per capita—typical of most of Africa, Asia, and much of Latin America—life expectancy varies between under forty to about sixty years. The line that best fits the relationship among countries at this end of the graph indicates that life expectancy goes up about one year for every $28 improvement in GNP per capita. Toward the right side of the graph, from about $1,800 upward, the scatter around the line is more noticeable than the slope itself. Nevertheless, a line can be calculated, showing an average additional year of life per each additional $2,700 in annual GNP per capita. Between these two ends of the graph (between $600 and $1,800), the relationship can best be described by a curve with a gradually flattening slope.

This pattern implies that major improvements in health and living conditions for the poor could be bought at a price not requiring major sacrifices by people in the rich countries. A transfer of income from the rich countries to the poor need not hurt very much and would have an enormous impact. For a transfer of resources to one person in a poor country, the benefits would be almost 100 times greater than the cost (in life expectancy) to the person in a rich country from whom the transfer came. By giving up increased luxuries, in fact, the cost could become nearly painless. This makes sense if you think of what money can buy in basic health care in the two kinds of societies. In a poor country, $1 may cover the cost of an inoculation against some killer disease; in an industrialized country, $1 might buy you one minute with a psychiatrist.

It is also worthwhile to notice the implications of great inequalities within countries. The countries found on the lower right portion of the graph below the line—South Africa and some newly rich OPEC states—all have notoriously unequal internal distributions of income. Shifts to greater equality within those states would also markedly improve the living conditions of their many poor citizens.

Of course, the calculation of costs and benefits for transferring income or wealth from rich to poor is really much more complicated than this simple illustration suggests. Nonetheless, a goal of having a life expectancy of about sixty-five years for people in the poor countries could be achieved by the year 2000 A.D. Its cost would not much exceed a doubling of current international development assistance (nonmilitary foreign aid). It would require some sacrifices, and it would have to be carefully targeted to meet the basic needs for public health, sanitation, and nutrition of poor people. But it could be done.

This issue raises old and ever-present ethical questions about what responsibility each of us owes others. We typically feel the greatest responsibility for those in our immediate systems (see Figure 19.1). Our families and close friends get the highest priority; our fellow nationals may occupy some sort of middle ground; and inhabitants further away, about whom we know little, receive the lowest priority. Yet, given such enormous differences in well-being, to what degree is it just to ignore what could be done?

In a major report to the United Nations, the economist Wassily Leontieff closely examined world demands and resources. His predictions differed significantly from those of the early Club of Rome studies, at least for the next few decades. Leontieff found most mineral resources adequate for maintaining significant growth in the world economy through the year 2000 or beyond. (Some particular resources, like petroleum, would become scarce and require substitutes.) He also found substantial opportunity for expanding agricultural output in poor countries, both by bringing currently unused land into use and by raising the productivity of existing land. Pollution abatement would cost about 1.5 percent of GNP in the industrial countries and at least 0.5 percent of GNP in the LDCs. But with that level of expenditure, pollution could be kept within "manageable limits." He judged greater equality within LDCs to be essential to improving living conditions—as we just suggested here. According to Leontieff, many of the elements called for in the New International Economic Order are essential—especially stabilization of commodity markets and relief of trade restrictions to stimulate industrialization in LDCs and exports of manufactured goods from LDCs to developed countries. All of this would require massive new investment, amounting to 30 to 40 percent of the GNP in the LDCs. Poor countries could not be expected to provide all this new investment by themselves.

Efforts to promote growth in the LDCs, while essential, should not be pursued to the exclusion of some growth in the industrialized world. On the contrary, some continued growth in the industrialized countries seems necessary to provide markets for LDC exports and an increased supply of financial resource transfers—private investment and foreign aid—from rich to poor countries. Leontieff concluded, "The principal limits to sustained economic growth and accelerated development are political, social, and institutional in character rather than physical. No insurmountable physical barriers exist within the twentieth century to the accelerated development of the developing regions."[14]

LIMITING CONFLICT

Trust, cooperation, and common interest—necessary ingredients for solving prisoners' dilemma problems—will not come easily. How difficult the process will be is a matter of debate. Lester Brown has observed: "The widening gap between the rich countries and poor is more than just a quantitative economic difference. It is increasingly a gap in values, in social organization, in contrasting life styles, in perceptions of the world in which we live and, ominously, a gap over which it may be increasingly difficult to communicate effectively."[15]

On the other hand, in discussing the UN Conference on Human Environment held in Stockholm, the Club of Rome was more optimis-

---

14. Wassily Leontieff et al., *The Future of the World Economy* (New York: Oxford University Press, 1977), pp. 10–11. Also see Council on Environmental Quality and State Department, *The Global 2000 Report to the President* (Washington, D.C.: U.S. Government Printing Office, 1980).

15. Lester Brown, *World without Borders* (New York: Random House, 1972), p. 44.

tic. Stockholm was praised as a conference where people of all states identified the problems facing the world and began to come to some consensus on how to approach those problems:

> The Third World countries understood that, far from being an exclusive problem of the industrialized world, environmental degradation and overtaxing of nature formed very much a part of their predicament. On the other hand, the industrialized countries abandoned their initial narrow technocratic view of environment and ended by admitting that patterns of resource use and maldistribution were an important aspect. . . . Both sides really grasped that they were living on only one earth and that the existence of international commons . . . as well as the finiteness of spaceship earth, were binding them into a pattern of real interdependence.[16]

Coming full circle, we see that the constraints of the world system will have significant effects on the behavior of states. Other actors are now on the stage with very active and important roles. All are now being bound by stronger and stronger ties of interdependence. Order, we have seen in previous chapters, has emerged in specific sections of the world to solve common problems. The recognition of common interests needed for such cooperation and order is now required on an even higher level. There is no assurance that it will come. The United Nations and its various conferences and agencies provide evidence for both optimistic and pessimistic assessments of whether such order will emerge. The ecology of the world system has so changed the nature of international politics that there is now serious question whether the present state system based on sovereignty is still appropriate for humankind. We need to question if it is, and if not how it should be modified or changed; we must look for alternative world orders and see how they can evolve from the present system.

The War Problem Again

Remember, too, that ecological problems interact with the ever-threatening risk of massive nuclear war. With conflicting claims to scarce resources like energy and possible conflicts generated by the vulnerabilities and sensitivities of interdependence, political pressures could lead

---

16. Jan Tinbergen, ed., *RIO: Reshaping the International Order* (New York: Dutton, 1976), p. 284.

to a major war long before the ecological system has a chance to collapse. We discussed the work of Choucri and North analyzing World War I several times in this book. Look again at Figure 13.3. We identified a long chain of war causation from population and economic growth to war. In the years leading up to 1914, population growth and economic development led to competition for natural resources, manifested in competition for colonial areas and spheres of influence. This competition helped cause and was heightened by the expansion of military expenditures by the competing states, that is, by the arms race, itself driven in part by domestic and bureaucratic pressures. The arms race and the intensity of competition for spheres of influence in turn led to an increasingly rigid system of international alliances. Ultimately, the whole system blew up in the most devastating war ever experienced to that time.

Some of the parallels between 1914 and the present are very unsettling. We are again in a period of growing resource shortages and increasing fears of the political and economic effects of those shortages. Modern industrial economies require assured access to vital raw materials like oil; their governments must know that suppliers will want to sell the materials (i.e., there will be no boycotts) and that the supplier governments have sufficient political control over their territories to ensure that the oil fields or mines keep operating and that their railroads or pipelines can get the materials to market. To ensure this, developed countries seek reliable political allies within their spheres of influence. In this respect the Soviet Union is hardly different from the capitalist states. It, too, must maintain a growing economy to protect its security and to satisfy the rising expectations of its populace; it, too, requires more and more vital raw materials from outside its borders (as shown by its imminent entry into the world oil market as a major buyer). Thus, big socialist states and capitalist states behave in similar ways in world politics. Thus, competition for spheres of influence grows more threatening, pressures to strengthen alliances intensify, and the arms race is on the upswing. Large, centralized bureaucracies in the competing states add bureaucratic inertia to the ever-growing demands of industrial economies, making it very hard to reverse these dynamics. Major international crises have become more probable and pose ever-greater difficulties for harassed decision makers who must try to manage those crises.

The parallels to 1914 are not exact, of course, but we can see how war could be produced by a "motor" powered by population and technological expansion; such a war could be devastating due to the achievements of modern technology. We thus run the risk that long before the world goes out with an ecological whimper, it will go out with a military bang. If hundreds of millions of people were killed—with industrial, agricultural, service, and governmental structures shattered and long-term havoc inflicted on the environment (e.g., immediate and long-term radioactive fallout, destruction of the atmospheric ozone shield, and nonrenewable resources ravished)—no advanced industrial society would survive in recognizable form. Reconstruction of civilization might be impossible.

WELL-BEING, LIBERTY, AND PEACE

In Part II we focused on two of the foremost desires of all humanity: political liberty and material well-being. In order for this to be achieved, we must combine some degree of economic growth with some degree of equality in the distribution of material goods. People vary in their relative evaluation of growth and equality. Some prefer great equality of condition ("to each according to his or her needs"); others prefer a distribution that heavily rewards great contributions to society. Compounding the differences in value are different theories about economic reality—different theories about the necessary trade-offs between equality and efficiency. Too great equality of reward might destroy incentives and hence stifle growth. There is no easy resolution of the value differences or easy testing of the theories about how reality works. Most people would not accept a total concentration on either equality or growth; thus, most people, while disagreeing about necessary or desirable trade-offs, want a condition of well-being derived from some degree of equality *and* growth.

Stable peace, as we used the phrase in Chapter 15, means security in the enjoyment of well-being under liberty, that is, order without dominance. We all have varying degrees of preference between well-being and liberty. Some of us would accept political repression in return for a decent material living standard; others say, "Give me liberty or give me death." All of us have some sense of the kind of trade-off we would accept—how much liberty for how much creature comfort. As with economic theories about equality versus growth, we also have varying ideas of how much trade-off is actually necessary. But again, most people think it is possible to achieve a substantial degree of both and reject the total exclusion of either.

Growth can be achieved without much equality. The industrialized countries in the nineteenth century and the present conditions of many LDCs and of the globe as a whole, attest to that. Some material equality can be achieved without political liberty, as is evidenced in some LDCs and possibly some Communist states. But material equality not based on a reasonable equality of political power must be precarious in the modern world, where the state is so powerful. We can conceive of this three-way tension among growth, equality, and liberty in the way pictured in Figure 19.8. Stable peace within a nation-state probably requires a combination of all three. The shaded area toward the top of the pyramid suggests that there is some choice about the precise combination of the three values. Equality is possibly more important than growth—at least in rich countries—and so we have drawn one line for the lower bound of stable peace sloping somewhat toward the right. In a poor country, one might tip the line back toward a horizontal position, like the lower line.

In the world at large, these same trade-offs still apply. Demands for material well-being can be peacefully satisfied only by some concessions to equality, both within and between countries. Attempts to improve well-being solely through growth will surely require severe repression. Similarly (and despite the global problems of resource availability and pollution) it is almost impossible to imagine the imposition of a no-growth policy worldwide. With so much of the third world so desperately poor, some real growth in the world economy, as well as greater equality within and between countries, seems unavoid-

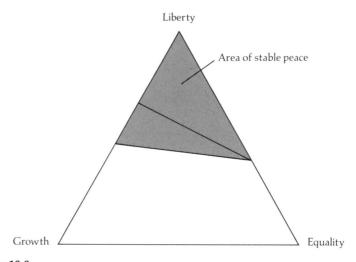

Figure 19.8
Trade-offs among growth, equality, and liberty.

able. If global no growth could be achieved in the near future, it would only be under conditions of catastrophe (ecological collapse or thermonuclear war) or global repression. In the latter case, it could be achieved only if the world's poor were brutally suppressed by elites within their countries and from outside by the rich and powerful states. (In fact, it is possible to imagine circumstances where neither growth nor equality nor liberty was present in the world—in this situation, the area of the triangle in Figure 19.8 could shrink drastically.)

A failure to pursue both equality and some growth at the global level is therefore a sure recipe for repression; if war could be avoided, it would be only by the unstable mechanisms of deterrence or domination. Surely it will not be easy to achieve growth and equality in the global economy, especially given the ecological problems that exist today. Furthermore, there is a threat of increasing conflict as governments try to protect their citizens from the ravages of inflation and recession transmitted through mechanisms of interdependence. There is no guarantee that peace can truly be achieved.

We can see, however, that material well-being, political liberty, and stable peace really are interconnected. The exclusive pursuit of material well-being can end in war and material destruction. The failure to maintain decent living conditions can result in the loss of liberty in industrialized countries (as happened under Hitler during the Great Depression in Germany) as well as in LDCs. Although we may differ about the kind and degree of trade-offs necessary or desirable, it is nevertheless apparent that none can be pursued to the complete exclusion of all others.

In conclusion, we return to questions of levels of analysis raised in the first chapter. Chapters 18 and 19 have dealt with the interactions and interdependences of the world system. We have also spoken about individual states and the consequences of their following narrow self-interests. These interests are derived from the politics of the various governments and societies—bureaucratic politics, the politics of interest groups such as the oil industry and military contractors, and public opinion in general. The outcomes of these political processes help determine whether states will "defect"—exploit the commons or take a free ride on international efforts at cooperation—allowing individual citizens within the individual states to use fluorocarbon spray cans, to hunt whales, to use as much gasoline as they like, to disregard birth control, and so forth. In the domain of military and security affairs, arms races and the search for alliances produce similar effects. The security dilemma may mean that we are "damned if we do and damned if we don't." Weakness can invite attack, but too much strength can threaten others and also invite attack. There is no better way to illustrate how the various levels of analysis can be linked, constraining the menu of choice for everyone.

Although the state system is vast and nation-states continue to play at center stage, the actions of individuals also have an impact on the future. Changes in our own conceptions of our interest (including other people in a larger or long-term way) will make a difference, as will changes in the demands we make on our governments. New social and political structures can be created to channel individual self-interests into collective benefits. We hope you will come away from reading this book with a deeper understanding of what the world looks like and how it works, as well as with a concern to make it work better.

> The creative personality is one that always looks on the world as fit for change and on himself as an instrument for change.... If the world is perfectly all right the way it is, you have no place in it.[17]

---

17. Jacob Bronowski, *The Origins of Knowledge and Imagination* (New Haven, Conn.: Yale University Press, 1978), p. 123.

Appendix A

CHRONOLOGY OF INTERNATIONAL EVENTS

1804	Napoleon becomes emperor of France.
1812	Napoleon invades Russia; disastrous campaign ultimately leads to French defeat.
1814–1815	Congress of Vienna; victorious powers reconstitute European order.
1823	Monroe Doctrine: President James Monroe declares the Western Hemisphere "off limits" to European interference.
1846	Mexican War; the United States defeats Mexico, annexes New Mexico and California (ends February 1848).
1848	*Communist Manifesto* published by Marx and Engels. Antimonarchical liberal revolutions break out in Europe (France, Prussia, Austria-Hungary, and the Italian states).
1852	Napoleon III begins the Second French Empire.
1853	Japan opened to West by American Commodore Perry.
1854–1856	Crimean War; France and Britain ally with Turkey against Russia.

1857–1858	Sepoy Rebellion: Indian soldiers revolt against British rule in India.
1859	Construction begins on Suez Canal (completed in 1869).
1861	Kingdom of Italy established after process of unification led by Sardinia; emancipation of serfs in Russia; U.S. Civil War (1861–1865).
1864	First International organized by Marx in London.
1864–1870	Lopez War; Argentina, Brazil, and Uruguay virtually destroy Paraguay.
1867	British North America Act creates Canada as a confederation; Marx publishes *Capital*.
1867	United States purchases Alaska from Russia.
1870–1871	Franco-Prussian War; Germany invades and defeats France (completing a process of German unification that included the 1864 Second Schleswig-Holstein war against Denmark and the 1866 Seven Weeks War against Austria).
1871	German empire established under Prussia; Wilhelm I becomes kaiser.
1878	Congress of Berlin; European powers meet to thwart Russia and carve up Ottoman Empire.
1882	Triple Alliance is formed by Germany, Austria-Hungary, and Italy.
1894–1895	Sino-Japanese War; Japan defeats China and becomes an imperial power with acquisition of Taiwan.
1898	Spanish-American War; the United States defeats Spain, acquires the Philippines, and becomes a great power.
1899	"Open Door" policy forced on China by the Western powers. Boer War between British and Dutch settlers begins in South Africa (1899–1902).
1900	Boxer Rebellion; forces of the European powers, Japan, and the United States sent to China to put down revolt against foreign penetration.
1904	Entente Cordiale signed between France and England; 1907 Russia joins and forms Triple Entente. Russo-Japanese War; Japan defeats Russia, becomes great power (1904–1905).
1911	Chinese Revolution led by Sun Yat-sen removes emperor and establishes a republic.
1912–1913	First and Second Balkan Wars drive Turkey from Europe.
1914	June: Assassination of Archduke Franz Ferdinand of Austria-Hungary.

August: World War I breaks out between Triple Entente and Central Powers; Panama Canal opens.

1917   April: United States enters World War I on the side of the Allies.

November: Bolshevik Revolution in Russia, led by Lenin.

1918   March: Treaty of Brest-Litovsk; Bolshevik government of Russia signs separate peace with Germany.

November: Armistice signed; World War I ends.

1919   Treaty of Versailles negotiated by victors of World War I (signed by Germans in June).

1920   January: League of Nations, created by Treaty of Versailles, established in Geneva; United States does not join.

1922   October: Mussolini and Fascist party come to power in Italy.

December: Union of Soviet Socialist Republics is officially created, the first Communist state.

1923   October: Ataturk's Westernized Turkish Republic officially proclaimed.

1924   January: Lenin dies; Stalin emerges as Soviet leader.

1929   October: Great Depression begins with the collapse of the stock market.

1931   September: Japan occupies Manchuria.

1933   January: Hitler comes to power in Germany.

1934–1935   Mao Zedong leads the Red Army on the Long March in China.

1936   July: Spanish Civil War begins; clash between Fascists and Communists is a precursor of World War II (ends January 1939 with Fascist Francisco Franco ruler of Spain).

November: Rome-Berlin-Tokyo Axis formed (formalized in 1937 treaty).

1938   September: Munich Agreement: French and British appease Germany over claims to Czechoslovakia.

1939   August: Germany and the Soviet Union sign a nonaggression pact.

September: Germany invades Poland, World War II begins.

1941   December 7: Japan attacks Pearl Harbor; United States enters World War II.

1944   July: Bretton Woods meeting establishes postwar economic system.

1945   February: Yalta Conference; Churchill, Roosevelt, and

Stalin plan postwar Europe.

March: Arab League established.

May 8: V-E (Victory in Europe) Day; Germany surrenders.

June: United Nations charter signed in San Francisco.

August: Hiroshima destroyed by first atomic bomb used in war; V-J (Victory in Japan) Day on August 15—Japan surrenders.

1947   June: Marshall Plan for economic recovery of Europe proposed.

August: British leave Indian subcontinent; India and Pakistan separate and become independent.

1948   February: Communists seize power in Czechoslovakia.

May: Israel established as an independent state; first Arab-Israeli War (ends January 1949); Organization of American States (OAS) established.

June: Berlin blockade; Soviets bar Western access to Berlin (ended May 1949).

1949   April: North Atlantic Treaty Organization (NATO) established.

August: Soviet Union explodes its first atomic weapon.

October: People's Republic of China proclaimed.

1950   June: North Korea invades the South; Korean war begins.

October: Communist China enters Korean war.

1951   March: European Coal and Steel Community formed (forerunner of European Economic Community).

1952   November: United States explodes the first hydrogen (thermonuclear) bomb.

1953   March: Stalin dies.

July: Korean armistice signed.

1954   July: Geneva settlement ends French rule in Indochina; Vietnam divided into North and South.

September: Southeast Asia Treaty Organization (SEATO) formed.

1955   May: West Germany joins NATO; Warsaw Treaty Organization (Warsaw Pact) established.

1956   July: Nasser nationalizes Suez Canal.

October: Hungarian revolt against Communist rule crushed by Soviet troops.

October–November: Britain, France, and Israel invade Egypt (Suez war).

1957   March: European Economic Community (Common Market) established by the Treaty of Rome.

October: Soviet Union launches Sputnik, first man-made satellite.

1958   June: De Gaulle takes over leadership of France (elected president in January 1959).
July: United States sends troops to Lebanon and Britain to Jordan to forestall radical takeovers.

1959   January: Fidel Castro leads the overthrow of Batista in Cuba.

1960   February: France explodes an atomic weapon.
July: The Republic of the Congo becomes independent; civil war begins.

1961   April: United States sponsors ill-fated Bay of Pigs invasion of Cuba.
August: East Germany builds the Berlin Wall.

1962   October: Cuban missile crisis.
October–November: China and India fight border war.

1963   November: President John Kennedy assassinated in Dallas.

1964   October: Khrushchev deposed by Brezhnev and Kosygin; China explodes its first atomic bomb.

1965   April: United States sends troops to Dominican Republic to prevent radical takeover.
July: President Johnson announces major U.S. buildup of 125,000 troops in Vietnam.
September: War between India and Pakistan over Kashmir begins.
November: White-dominated government of Rhodesia unilaterally declares independence from Britain; United Nations imposes economic sanctions.

1966   April: The Mao-inspired Cultural Revolution begins in China.

1967   May: Biafran civil war begins; Nigerian government ultimately defeats attempt at secession (ended January 1970).
June: Six-Day War between Israel and Egypt, Jordan, and Syria.

1968   July: Nonproliferation treaty signed by United States, USSR, and Britain.
September: Soviet and Warsaw Pact troops invade Czechoslovakia.

1969   March: Soviet-Chinese conflict erupts into border fighting at the Ussuri River.
July: American Neil Armstrong becomes first human to

walk on the moon.

1970   August: West Germany and Soviet Union sign treaty of friendship.

September: Marxist Salvadore Allende elected president of Chile (killed during a coup to overthrow his government in September 1973).

1971   October: People's Republic of China admitted to United Nations.

December: Bangladesh established by breakaway of East Pakistan after civil war and India-Pakistan war.

1972   January: Britain, Ireland, and Denmark join European Economic Community.

February: U.S. President Nixon visits People's Republic of China.

May: United States and USSR sign strategic arms limitation treaty (SALT I).

1973   June: East and West Germany establish diplomatic relations.

October: Yom Kippur War between Israel and Egypt and Syria (ends in November).

November: Arab members of OPEC embargo oil to United States, Japan, and Western Europe and begin series of price hikes.

1974   May: Indian explosion of nuclear device.

August: Richard Nixon resigns as president of United States after Watergate affair.

1975   April: Serious fighting begins in civil war in Lebanon; Saigon taken by Communist forces, and Indochina war ends with collapse of U.S.-backed South Vietnam and Cambodia.

June: Indira Gandhi imposes emergency rule in India and arrests opposition.

August: European Agreement on Security and Cooperation signed in Helsinki.

November: Angola becomes independent from Portugal after long guerilla war; struggle between liberation movements supported by different countries (including Cuban troops).

November: Franco dies; Spain holds free elections in 1977.

1976   July: Israeli rescue of hostages from Uganda's Entebbe Airport.

September: Mao Zedong dies.

1977   March: Gandhi allows free elections in India; opposition wins.

     August: United States and Panama sign treaty to cede Panama Canal to Panama (ratified March 1978).

     November: Egyptian president Sadat makes dramatic trip to Israel.

1978   August: China and Japan sign treaty of peace and friendship.

     December: United States and People's Republic of China establish full diplomatic relations.

1979   January: Shah resigns in Iran; Ayatollah Khomeini forms revolutionary government in February.

     February: War breaks out between two Communist states as China invades Vietnam.

     March: Egyptian-Israeli peace treaty signed at Camp David in United States.

     April: Idi Amin, dictator of Uganda, overthrown with aid of troops from Tanzania.

     June: Carter and Brezhnev sign SALT II in Vienna.

     July: Sandinista rebels overthrow dictator Somoza in Nicaragua.

     November: Iranian "students" and government seize U.S. embassy personnel, holding them as hostages.

     December: Soviet troops invade Afghanistan. Agreement reached on independence for Zimbabwe (Rhodesia) under black government; UN-imposed economic sanctions against white government lifted.

1980   January: Indira Gandhi once again becomes prime minister of India.

     September: Iraq attacks Iran.

     October: Strikes by Polish workers' union (Solidarity) force extensive concessions from government.

     November: "Gang of Four" put on trial in China amid criticism of Mao Tse-tung; Ronald Reagan elected president, says United States will observe but not ratify SALT II.

1981   January: Greece becomes tenth member of European Economic Community.

     May: Pope John Paul II shot by Turk perhaps linked to Bulgaria and KGB (Soviet intelligence organization).

     October: Sadat assassinated by Moslem extremists; succeeded by Vice-President Mubarak.

     December: General Jaruzelski declares martial law in

Poland and arrests Solidarity members; United States imposes economic sanctions on Poland and the USSR.

1982   March: Right-wing forces of Roberto d'Aubuisson win El Salvador elections; land reform there halted.
April: Argentina seizes Falkland Islands; British naval and air force retake them by June.
May: Spain becomes sixteenth member of NATO.
November: Brazil holds free congressional elections; Brezhnev dies, succeeded by Yuri Andropov, former KGB chief.
December: Mexico and International Monetary Fund to reschedule payment of Mexico's debts, avoiding economic disaster; Final act of the Law of the Sea Convention signed by 117 states, but not the United States.

1983   August: Menachem Begin resigns as prime minister of Israel, replaced by Yitzhak Shamir.
September: Korean Airlines civilian passenger plane shot down by USSR over Soviet territory.
October: Nearly 300 French and American troops of peacekeeping force killed by terrorist bombs in Lebanon; United States invades Grenada to overthrow Marxist government; Anti-Peronist Raúl Alfonsín elected president of Argentina to replace military government.
November: United States begins missile deployments in Europe; USSR breaks off Intermediate Nuclear Force negotiations and Strategic Arms Reduction Talks.
December: Brazil reaches agreement to reschedule debt; Nigerian army overthrows civilian President Shagari.

1984   February: Soviet leader Andropov dies, succeeded by Konstantin Chernenko.
August: Coalition Labour-Likud government formed in Israel.
October: Prime Minister Indira Gandhi assassinated.
November: Ronald Reagan reelected president.

Appendix B

CHARACTERISTICS OF STATES IN THE CONTEMPORARY INTERNATIONAL SYSTEM

Appendix B lists all of the independent states in the international system as of March 1984. Twelve characteristics or variables are presented for each state. Variables 2 through 11 are taken from Tables II and III in Ruth Leger Sivard, *World Military and Social Expenditures* (1983, © World Priorities, Leesburg, VA 22075). Most of these data are for 1980. States that became independent after 1980 are listed with date of independence and data from *The World Almanac and Book of Facts, 1984* (New York: Newspaper Enterprises Association, 1983) and *Whitaker's Almanack, 1984* (London: Whitaker, 1983). Most of this information is from *The World Almanac*. Information from both works is underlined and comes from various sources dated between 1976 and 1982. However, all underlined population data are 1982 estimates. The last three rows in this appendix show the figures for the developed states, the less-developed states, and the world. Each of the twelve variables are briefly explained below.

1. *Date of independence.* The date of independence is provided for all states that became independent after 1816 (the conclusion of the Napo-

leonic Wars). If no date is provided, then that state was independent prior to 1816. This information came from Bruce Russett, J. David Singer, and Melvin Small, "National Political Units in the Twentieth Century: A Standardized List," *American Political Science Review* 62 (1968), 932–951; and *The World Almanac*.

2. *Population.* The figures provided are in thousands.

3. *Area.* The figures are for thousands of square kilometers. One square kilometer equals 0.386 square mile.

4. *Density.* Number of people per square kilometer of area.

5. *GNP.* The Gross National Product of states is measured in millions of U.S. dollars for 1980.

6. *GNP/pc.* GNP per capita (GNP divided by population). The figure is in U.S. dollars.

7. *Military expenditures.* This figure shows how much a state spends on its military (in millions of U.S. dollars).

8. *Armed forces.* Number of people in the armed forces (in thousands).

9. *Literacy rate.* Percentage of population over age 15 able to read and write.

10. *Infant mortality.* Number of deaths of infants (under 1 year of age) per every 1,000 live births.

11. *Life expectancy.* Expected life span at birth.

12. *Status of freedom.* According to a number of indicators of political rights and civil liberties, states are labeled free (F), partly free (PF), or not free (NF). The data are from *Freedom in the World: Political Rights and Civil Liberties, 1980/1981* (New York: Freedom House, 1980) and apply to 1980.

A dash for an entry in a column other than "Date of independence" means none or negligible value for that item. No entry for an item means that information was unavailable. Note also, as discussed in Chapter 13 (see especially footnote 2), that estimates of Soviet defense spending vary widely. The figure reported here is toward the lower end of the reported range of estimates.

Country	Date of independence	Population (000s)	Area (1,000 km²)	Population density	GNP (Millions of 1980 U.S. $)	GNP/pc	Military expenditures	Armed forces (000s)	Literacy rate	Infant mortality	Life expectancy	Status of freedom
Afghanistan	—	15,245	648	24	3,661	240	80	40	20	205	40	NF
Albania	1912	2,671	29	92	2,400	898	190	41	72	48	70	NF
Algeria	1962	18,828	2,382	8	39,363	2,091	705	101	42	118	56	NF
Angola	1975	6,979	1,247	6	6,299	902		32	15	154	41	NF
Antigua and Barbuda	1981	77	0.4	173								
Argentina	—	28,237	2,767	10	123,138	4,361	1,628	140	93	45	70	NF
Australia	1920	14,616	7,687	2	145,328	9,943	3,645	71	99	11	74	F
Austria	1918	7,553	84	90	79,364	10,508	893	50	99	14	72	F
Bahamas	1973	260	14	19	1,080	4,154			89	32	67	F
Bahrain	1971	346	0.6	577	2,932	8,474	157	2	40	53	66	PF
Bangladesh	1972	88,052	144	611	11,392	129	156	72	41	136	46	PF
Barbados	1966	249	0.4	623	822	3,301	9	1	98	27	70	F
Belgium	1830	9,848	31	318	118,404	12,023	3,959	88	99	11	73	F
Belize	1981	148	23	6	135	1,000			80	28	60	
Benin	1960	3,465	113	31	1,114	322	22	2	28	150	46	NF
Bhutan	1949	1,400	46	30	90				5		41	PF
Bolivia	1825	5,450	1,099	5	5,839	1,071	106	24	63	131	50	NF
Botswana	1966	899	600	1	797	886	33	2	40	83	48	F
Brazil	1822	122,407	8,512	14	245,110	2,002	1,550	273	76	77	63	PF
Brunei	1984	200	6	34								PF

Country	Date of independence	Population (000s)	Area (1,000 km²)	Population density	GNP (Millions of 1980 U.S. $)	GNP/pc	Military expenditures	Armed forces (000s)	Literacy rate	Infant mortality	Life expectancy	Status of freedom
Bulgaria	1908	8,862	111	80	37,390	4,219	1,180	149	94	20	73	NF
Burma	1948	34,433	677	51	5,894	171	204	174	66	101	53	NF
Burundi	1962	4,204	28	150	881	210	35	6	27	122	42	NF
Cambodia	1953	5,692	181	31	—	—	—	30	48	212	40	NF
Cameroon	1960	8,582	475	18	6,373	743	82	7	50	109	46	NF
Canada	1920	24,086	9,976	2	244,683	10,159	4,702	79	98	11	74	F
Cape Verde	1975	340	4	85	57	240	—	—	37	105	58	NF
Central Africa Republic	1960	2,315	623	4	771	333	13	2	33	149	44	NF
Chad	1960	4,416	1,284	3	498	113	22	3	18	149	41	NF
Chile	1818	10,991	757	15	27,548	2,506	1,456	88	92	38	66	PF
China (People's Republic)	—	1,006,712	9,597	105	300,000	298	28,000	4,450	66	56	64	NF
Colombia	1819	26,056	1,139	23	32,600	1,251	306	66	86	64	62	F
Comoros	1975	400	2	200	93	240	—	—	15	52	45	PF
Congo	1960	1,552	342	5	1,574	1,014	61	6	62	130	46	NF
Costa Rica	1820	2,404	51	47	4,623	1,923	—	—	93	24	70	F
Cuba	1902	9,658	115	84	18,000	1,864	1,100	206	95	19	73	NF
Cyprus	1960	629	9	70	2,199	3,496	31	9	85	17	72	PF
Czechoslovakia	1918	15,255	128	119	89,260	5,821	2,750	195	99	17	71	NF
Denmark	—	5,123	43	119	64,059	12,504	1,610	35	99	8	75	F
Djibouti	1977	500	23	22	331	400	—	—	20	50	50	PF

Country	Year											
Dominica	1978	82	0.75	109	40	460	108	19	74	20	61	F
Dominican Republic	1844	5,774	49	118	6,784	1,175	208	39	81	68	61	F
Ecuador	1830	8,021	284	28	10,891	1,358	1,858	367	50	82	55	F
Egypt	1922	42,135	1,001	42	25,273	600	54	7	65	103	62	PF
El Salvador	1821	4,718	21	225	3,420	725	6	5	20	53	46	PF
Equatorial Guinea	1968	250	28	9	152	608	447	230	7	143	40	NF
Ethiopia	—	29,790	1,222	24	4,094	137	10	1	79	147	71	NF
Fiji	1970	634	18	35	1,189	1,874	813	40	99	37	73	F
Finland	1919	4,780	337	14	49,390	10,333	26,466	495	99	8	74	F
France	—	53,811	547	98	654,120	12,156	74	2	60	10	44	F
Gabon	1960	792	268	3	3,389	4,279	—	—	20	117	41	NF
The Gambia	1965	591	11	54	227	384	6,020	162	99	198	72	F
Germany, East	1949	16,737	108	155	120,940	7,226	26,738	495	99	12	73	NF
Germany, West	1949	61,561	249	247	824,886	13,399	50	17	40	13	49	F
Ghana	1957	12,130	239	51	4,359	359	2,279	182	88	103	74	F
Greece	1828	9,642	132	73	42,273	4,384		16	50	18		F
Grenada	1974	108	0.3	360	55	500	20	9	50	24		NF
Guatemala	1839	7,120	215	4	556	1,096	9			72	59	NF
Guinea	1958	5,014	246	20	1,581							NF
Guinea-Bissau	1974											NF
Guyana	1966	817	109	65	7,805	680	101	7	90	44	69	PF
Haiti	—	5,395	28	193	1,436	266	22	8	29	115	51	NF
Honduras	1821	3,816	112	34	2,414	633	45	11	60	90	58	PF
Hungary	1918	10,711	93	115	44,990	4,200	1,100	93	99	23	71	NF
Iceland	1944	228	103	2	2,738	12,009	—	—	99	8	76	F
India	1947	693,578	3,288	211	159,766	230	4,451	1,104	40	123	52	F

Country	Date of independence	Population (000s)	Area (1,000 km²)	Population density	GNP (Millions of 1980 U.S. $)	GNP/pc	Military expenditures	Armed forces (000s)	Literacy rate	Infant mortality	Life expectancy	Status of freedom
Indonesia	1949	151,168	2,027	75	69,467	460	2,337	242	67	93	50	PF
Iran	—	38,752	1,648	24	83,709	2,160	4,899	240	47	108	58	PF
Iraq	1932	13,130	435	30	36,647	2,791	2,709	242	43	78	55	NF
Ireland	1922	3,414	70	49	17,322	5,074	296	15	98	12	73	F
Israel	1948	3,769	21	179	21,237	5,635	6,599	170	88	14	72	F
Italy	1861	56,176	301	187	393,925	7,012	9,598	366	95	14	73	F
Ivory Coast	1960	8,054	322	25	9,950	1,235	125	6	35	127	46	PF
Jamaica	1962	2,243	11	204	2,398	1,069	20	4	89	16	70	F
Japan	—	116,782	372	314	1,048,168	8,975	9,990	241	99	7	76	F
Jordan	1946	3,115	98	32	3,596	1,154	449	67	58	69	60	NF
Kenya	1963	16,431	583	28	6,769	412	300	15	47	87	55	PF
Kiribati	1979	60	0.7	86								F
Korea, North	1948	17,815	121	147	20,500	1,151	1,300	678	85	34	64	NF
Korea, South	1948	39,565	98	404	54,915	1,388	3,603	601	94	34	65	PF
Kuwait	1961	1,372	18	76	33,524	24,434	951	12	63	39	69	PF
Laos	1949	3,458	237	15	300	87		55	44	129	43	NF
Lebanon	1946	2,649	10	265			267	23	76	41	66	PF
Lesotho	1966	1,339	30	45	676	505		—	69	115	50	PF
Liberia	1822	1,898	111	17	977	515	26	5	25	154	50	NF
Libya	1952	3,018	1,760	2	30,540	10,119	503	53	58	100	56	NF

Country	Year											
Luxembourg	—	364	3	121	5,204	14,297	52	1	98	12	71	F
Madagascar	1960	8,665	587	15	3,172	366	94	13	50	71	46	NF
Malawi	1964	6,021	118	51	1,491	248	55	4	33	142	46	NF
Malaysia	1957	14,000	330	42	22,728	1,623	1,362	66	72	31	64	PF
Maldives	1965	155	0.3	517	22	150			36	119		PF
Mali	1960	6,914	1,240	6	1,354	196	39	5	10	154	42	NF
Malta	1964	364	0.3	1,213	1,240	3,406	6	1	85	16	71	F
Mauritania	1960	1,502	1,031	1	622	414	30	8	17	143	42	NF
Mauritius	1968	957	2	479	968	1,011	6		79	33	64	PF
Mexico	1821	70,111	1,973	36	181,611	2,590	756	107	83	60	65	PF
Mongolia	1921	1,662	1,565	1	1,420	854	180	28	95	55	63	NF
Morocco	1956	20,969	447	47	18,283	872	1,120	116	26	107	55	PF
Mozambique	1975	12,103	802	15	4,774	394	160	24	33	115	46	NF
Nauru	1968	8	0.02	400	155	21,400			99	19		F
Nepal	—	14,992	141	106	2,029	135	22	22	19	150	44	PF
Netherlands	—	14,144	41	345	161,227	11,399	5,277	115	99	9	75	F
New Zealand	1920	3,100	269	12	23,954	7,727	440	13	99	13	73	F
Nicaragua	1821	2,497	130	19	2,090	837	70	5	66	90	56	PF
Niger	1960	5,528	1,267	4	1,795	325	17	2	10	146	42	NF
Nigeria	1960	77,082	924	83	79,806	1,035	2,288	146	34	135	48	F
Norway	1905	4,086	324	13	54,578	13,357	1,670	37	99	8	75	F
Oman	1970	891	212	4	4,780	5,365	1,187	14	50	128	47	NF
Pakistan	1947	85,743	804	107	25,043	292	1,271	439	32	126	51	NF
Panama	1903	1,916	76	25	3,193	1,666	18	11	85	34	70	PF
Papua New Guinea	1975	2,991	462	6	2,426	811	39	4	42	104	50	F
Paraguay	—	3,244	407	8	4,367	1,346	69	16	86	47	65	PF

Country	Date of independence	Population (000s)	Area (1,000 km²)	Population density	GNP (Millions of 1980 U.S. $)	GNP/pc	Military expenditures	Armed forces (000s)	Literacy rate	Infant mortality	Life expectancy	Status of freedom
Peru	1824	17,625	1,285	14	18,607	1,056	457	96	80	88	58	F
Philippines	1946	49,253	300	164	35,881	728	633	113	89	55	63	PF
Poland	1919	35,578	313	114	139,780	3,929	4,300	318	99	21	72	PF
Portugal	—	9,884	92	107	23,657	2,393	864	60	80	35	71	F
Qatar	1971	237	11	22	6,644	28,034	602	5	20	53	57	PF
Romania	1878	22,201	238	93	85,500	3,851	1,350	184	98	29	71	NF
Rwanda	1962	5,114	26	197	1,156	226	22	4	50	122	46	NF
St. Kitts-Nevis	1983	44	0.3	170								
St. Lucia	1979	124	0.6	207	100	698			78	22	68	F
St. Vincent and the Grenadines	1979	120	0.4	300	40	250						F
Sao Tome and Principe	1975	100	1	100		270			95	55		NF
Saudi Arabia	1902	9,420	2,150	4	117,595	12,484	17,540	47	25	114	54	NF
Senegal	1960	5,765	196	29	2,717	471	64	9	19	147	42	PF
Seychelles	1976	67	0.4	168	86	1,030			60	26		NF
Sierra Leone	1961	3,429	72	48	1,049	306	14	3	20	180	46	PF
Singapore	1965	2,414	0.6	4,023	10,674	4,422	592	42	92	12	72	PF
Solomon Islands	1978	240	30	8	95	440				52		F
Somalia	1960	5,373	638	8	1,519	283	105	62	6	146	43	NF
South Africa	1920	28,723	1,221	24	68,552	2,387	2,320	86	65	96	60	PF

	Year											Status
Spain	—	37,488	505	74	208,040	5,550	4,004	342	93	11	73	F
Sri Lanka	1948	14,842	66	225	4,138	279	41	15	85	40	66	F
Sudan	1956	18,745	2,506	7	7,844	418	200	68	22	124	46	PF
Suriname	1975	420	163	3	924	2,220	13	1	45	30	68	NF
Swaziland	1968	579	17	34	455	786			99	135	46	PF
Sweden	—	8,310	450	18	116,027	13,962	3,818	66	99	7	75	F
Switzerland	—	6,385	41	156	103,362	16,188	2,113	18	85	9	75	F
Syria	1944	8,795	185	48	13,027		2,255	248	70			NF
Taiwan	1949	17,800	32	556	40,137	2,255	2,659	438	86	24	71	PF
Tanzania	1964	18,618	945	20	4,919	264	250	52	35	103	52	NF
Thailand	—	47,669	514	93	32,928	691	1,240	231	95	55	62	PF
Togo	1960	2,580	57	45	1,001	388	23	4	49	109	46	NF
Tonga	1970	100	0.7	143	430	430			65	21		PF
Trinidad and Tobago	1962	1,159	5	232	6,106	5,268	16	1	52	26	70	F
Tunisia	1956	6,489	164	40	8,440	1,301	337	29	99	100	58	PF
Turkey	—	46,025	781	59	61,078	1,327	2,523	567	56	123	62	PF
Tuvalu	1978	9	0.03	300	9							F
Uganda	1962	12,806	236	54	6,000	468	125	7	52	97	52	PF
USSR	—	265,542	22,402	12	1,212,030	4,564	130,000	3,663	99	36	70	NF
United Arab Emirates	1971	985	84	12	27,555	27,975	1,708	25	56	53	62	PF
United Kingdom	—	56,010	244	230	516,004	9,213	26,776	329	99	12	73	F
United States	—	227,704	9,363	24	2,583,700	11,347	143,974	2,050	99	13	74	F
Upper Volta	1960	6,138	274	22	1,358	221	35	4	9	211	41	PF
Uruguay	1825	2,887	176	16	9,811	3,398	260	30	94	40	71	PF
Vanuatu	1980	126	12	11								F
Venezuela	1821	16,302	912	18	60,743	3,726	755	40	82	42	67	F

Country	Date of independence	Population (000s)	Area (1,000 km²)	Population density	GNP (Millions of 1980 U.S. $)	GNP/pc	Military expenditures	Armed forces (000s)	Literacy rate	Infant mortality	Life expectancy	Status of freedom
Vietnam	1954	53,511	330	162	8,600	161	900	1,029	87	90	63	NF
Western Samoa	1962	158	3	53	50	320				10		PF
Yemen, North	1918	5,331	195	27	3,084	578	386	32	9	170	42	NF
Yemen, South	1967	1,916	333	6	810	423	124	24	27	146	45	NF
Yugoslavia	1878	22,304	256	87	59,132	2,651	2,517	264	87	33	70	NF
Zaire	1960	28,624	2,345	12	5,756	201	200	20	54	112	46	NF
Zambia	1964	5,771	753	8	3,514	609	516	14	60	106	48	PF
Zimbabwe	1980	7,556	391	19	5,424	718	478	14	69	74	54	PF
Developed countries		1,056,736	53,949	20	8,957,570	8,477	426,039	9,538	99	20	73	
Less-developed countries		3,411,376	79,334	43	2,711,941	795	116,872	15,104	59	96	58	
World		4,468,112	133,283	34	11,669,511	2,612	542,911	24,642	70	87	61	

INDEX

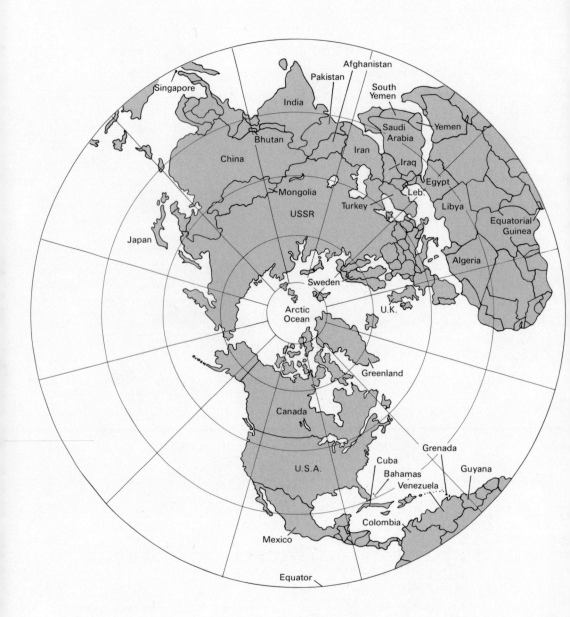